POPULATION TRENDS IN THE UNITED STATES

DEMOGRAPHIC MONOGRAPHS
A series of demographic economics reprints

Additional volumes in preparation

POPULATION TRENDS
IN
THE UNITED STATES

By
WARREN S. THOMPSON

and

P. K. WHELPTON

*Scripps Foundation for Research in Population
Problems, Miami University*

Demographic Monographs
Volume 9

GORDON AND BREACH SCIENCE PUBLISHERS

NEW YORK   LONDON   PARIS

This edition published 1969 by Gordon and Breach, Science Publishers, Inc., 150 Fifth Avenue, New York, N.Y. 10011

Library of Congress catalog card number: 70 $\frac{N}{}$ 83734

Editorial office for the United Kingdom:

Gordon and Breach, Science Publishers Ltd.
12 Bloomsbury Way
London W.C.1

Editorial office for France:

Gordon & Breach
7–9 rue Emile Dubois
Paris 14e

Distributed in Canada by:

The Ryerson Press
299 Queen Street West
Toronto 2B, Ontario

First published by the McGraw-Hill Book Company Inc, New York and London in 1933

PREFACE
Demographic Monographs

Demography has reached the point at which it is now claiming to be considered as a distinct discipline, not merely a field of specialization for sociologists, economists and others. To give perspective to current contributions, the sponsors of the present series of publications are bringing back into print some of the historically oriented monographs of the not-too-distant past in the belief that they will also aid in providing an empirical foundation upon which ongoing and future research can build. Each of the monographs in the series provides a wide range of systematically organized statistical data and emphasizes ways in which primarily demographic data can be organized, empirically, to indicate the nature and direction of interrelations with economic phenomena.

R. A. Easterlin
M. Perlman
D. S. Thomas

FOREWORD BY THE COMMITTEE

POPULATION TRENDS IN THE UNITED STATES by Warren S. Thompson and P. K. Whelpton is one of a series of monographs published under the direction of the President's Research Committee on Social Trends, embodying scientific information assembled for the use of the Committee in the preparation of its report entitled *Recent Social Trends in the United States.*

The Committee was named by President Herbert Hoover in December, 1929, to survey social changes in this country in order to throw light on the emerging problems which now confront or which may be expected later to confront the people of the United States. The undertaking is unique in our history. For the first time the head of the Nation has called upon a group of social scientists to sponsor and direct a broad scientific study of the factors of change in modern society.

Funds for the researches were granted by the Rockefeller Foundation, an expert staff was recruited from universities and other scientific institutions, and a series of investigations was begun early in 1930 and concluded in 1932. The complete report contains the findings of the President's Research Committee on Social Trends together with twenty-nine chapters prepared by experts in the various fields.

Modern social life is so closely integrated as a whole that no change can occur in any of its phases without affecting other phases in some measure. Social problems arise largely from such unplanned reactions of the rapidly changing phases of social life upon the more stable phases. To give a few examples: changes in industrial technique react upon employment, changes in the character of adult work affect educational needs, changes in international relations affect domestic politics, changes in immigration policy affect the growth of population and the demand for farm products, changes in consumption habits affect the demand for leisure and facilities for enjoying it, changes in demands for social service by governmental agencies affect taxes and public debts, changes in methods of communication tend to standardize the mode of life in country and city. The effects noted in this list of illustrations in their turn cause other changes, and so on without assignable limits.

The usual practice of concentrating attention upon one social problem at a time often betrays us into overlooking these intricate relations. Even when we find what appears to be a satisfactory solution of a single problem, we are likely to produce new problems by putting that solution into practice. Hence the need of making a comprehensive survey of the many social changes which are proceeding simultaneously, with an eye to their reactions upon one another. That task is attempted in the Committee's report. Of course the list of changes there considered is not exhaustive. Nor can all the subtle interactions among social changes be traced.

To safeguard the conclusions against bias, the researches were restricted to the analysis of objective data. Since the available data do not cover all phases of the many subjects studied, it was often impossible to answer questions of keen interest. But what is set forth has been made as trustworthy as the staff could make it by careful checking with factual records. Discussions which are not limited by the severe requirements of scientific method have their uses, which the Committee rates highly. Yet an investigation initiated by the President in the hope that the findings may be of service in dealing with the national problems of today and tomorrow, should be kept as free as possible from emotional coloring and unverifiable conjectures. Accuracy and reliability are more important in such an undertaking than liveliness or zeal to do good. If men and women of all shades of opinion from extreme conservatism to extreme radicalism can find a common basis of secure knowledge to build upon, the social changes of the future may be brought in larger measure under the control of social intelligence.

The Committee's researches were not confined to preparing a general report laid out with proper regard for balance. Intensive investigations of considerable length were carried out in several directions where the importance of the subjects warranted and adequate data were available. Some investigators were rewarded by especially valuable developments of their programs on a scale which made it impossible to condense the results into a single chapter without serious loss. In these cases separate monographs are necessary to provide adequate presentation of the evidence and the findings. However, at least a part of the subject matter of each monograph is dealt with in the Committee's general report, which should be read by all who wish to see a rounded picture of social trends.

PREFACE

In the course of gathering the information on population for the President's Research Committee on Social Trends it became evident that many of the trends were of long standing. Extensive compilations were accumulated some of which it was believed would be useful to other students of the subject. This monograph makes available some of the longer tables which could not be included in the report of the Committee and discusses their significance in greater detail. It attempts to give a more complete picture of population in the United States than has been available hitherto and to project past trends into the future in such manner that the probable changes can be evaluated by those who are interested in doing so.

Because the researchs under the auspices of the President's Research Committee were restricted to the analysis of objective data, this monograph deals chiefly with quantitative problems and their significance. Census volumes contain a vast amount of factual material on the size, distribution, and makeup of the population from 1790 to 1930; in comparison, only a small beginning has been made in building up a body of statistical material dealing with the highly important qualitative problems of population.

The authors wish to take this occasion to express their very great indebtedness to Dr. Leon E. Truesdell of the Bureau of the Census for furnishing 1930 census data in advance of publication. They also want to acknowledge the assistance rendered by Mr. J. H. Shera, Mrs. Celia Dorn, Mrs. Evangelyn Minnis, Miss Nelle Jackson, and Miss Mary Logan of the Scripps Foundation staff. Without their very conscientious interest in this work it would contain many more errors than it actually does.

WARREN S. THOMPSON.
P. K. WHELPTON.

Oxford, Ohio,
March, 1933.

CONTENTS

CONTENTS

Chapter I

THE GROWTH OF POPULATION IN THE UNITED STATES

1. GROWTH SINCE COLONIAL DAYS

THE growth of population in this country during the last three centuries has been one of the outstanding phenomena in world history. Its like has never been known elsewhere. In 1650 the total population (excluding Indians) was 52,000, the size of a single small city of today. A century later there were 1,207,000 persons, hardly as many as in Los Angeles in 1930 (Table 1). Even when the Declaration of Independence was signed there were fewer persons than are now in Los Angeles and Detroit. In the century and a half that has elapsed since then, the popula-

TABLE 1.—POPULATION, AND AMOUNT AND RATE OF INCREASE, 1610–1980[a]

Year	Population (thousands)	Increase during decade ending in year indicated		Year	Population (thousands)	Increase during decade ending in year indicated	
		Number (thousands)	Per cent			Number (thousands)	Per cent
1610......	(b)	....	....	1800......	5,308	1,379	35.1
1620......	2	2	1,090.0	1810......	7,240	1,931	36.4
1630......	6	3	128.1	1820......	9,638	2,399	33.1
1640......	28	22	390.3	1830......	12,866	3,228	33.5
1650......	52	24	85.0	1840......	17,069	4,203	32.7
1660......	85	33	64.0	1850......	23,192	6,122	35.9
1670......	114	30	35.0	1860......	31,443	8,251	35.6
1680......	156	41	35.9	1870[c].....	39,818	8,375	26.6
1690......	214	58	37.2	1880[c].....	50,156	10,337	26.0
1700......	275	62	28.8	1890......	62,948	12,792	25.5
1710......	358	82	30.0	1900......	75,995	13,047	20.7
1720......	474	117	32.7	1910......	91,972	15,978	21.0
1730......	655	181	38.1	1920......	105,711	13,738	14.9
1740......	889	234	35.7	1930......	122,775	17,064	16.1
1750......	1,207	318	35.8	1940......	133,100	10,300	8.4
1760......	1,610	403	33.4	1950......	142,900	9,800	7.3
1770......	2,205	595	37.0	1960......	149,800	6,900	4.9
1780......	2,781	576	26.1	1970......	153,800	4,000	2.6
1790......	3,929	1,148	41.3	1980......	155,200	1,400	0.9

[a] For 1610–1780, estimated population as given in Table I, p. 9, from *A Century of Population Growth;* 1790–1930 from *Fifteenth Census of the United States: 1930,* Vol. I, p. 6 except 1870 and 1880 (see Note c); 1940–1980 from authors' estimates (see Chap. X).

[b] Less than 500 population (210 in Virginia).

[c] Data as revised by the Bureau of the Census (see *Fourteenth Census of the United States: 1920,* Vol. II, pp. 15, 29).

tion has increased from 2,500,000 to over 125,000,000; it is now more than fifty times as large as in 1776.

The picture of population growth in Figure 1 shows a slow rise in numbers prior to 1800, then a gradual acceleration. From 1880 to 1930 the population line rises steeply, but after 1930 the estimates indicate that growth will fall off rapidly. A somewhat similar course is followed by the amount of increase. This is smallest during the first decades of colonization, but by 1710–1720 reaches the 100,000 mark, and by 1780–1790 the 1,000,000 mark. Subsequent rises are large and almost unin-

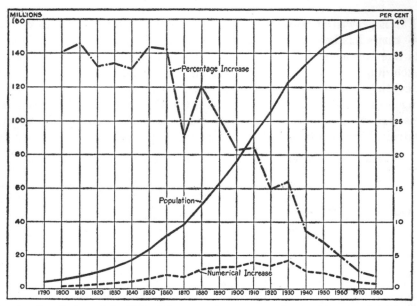

Fig. 1.—Population of the United States, and amount and rate of increase by decades, 1790–1980.[a] (Based on Table 1.)

[a] Estimated for 1940–1980 according to assumptions shown in Table 88, Column H, p. 316.

terrupted until the intercensal gain amounts to 15,978,000 from 1900 to 1910 and 17,064,000 from 1920 to 1930.

The rate of population growth was much larger in the early days of colonial settlement than later on, being nearly tenfold during 1610–1620. After 1660, however, growth only occasionally exceeded 35 per cent in a decade and on the whole was remarkably uniform for the two centuries 1660 to 1860, progressing at about this rate (Figure 1). Thus during these two centuries the population doubled, on the average, in about 23.5 years. After 1860 the rate of growth slowed up and remained at about 25 per cent a decade during the next 30 years, so that the population only doubled from 1860 to 1890. In each of the next two decades, the rate of increase was about 20 per cent, and in the last two decades (1910 to 1930) only slightly in excess of 15 per cent.[1] Consequently the population did not quite double in the 40 years from 1890 to 1930.

Although the largest intercensal increase in numbers occurred between 1920 and 1930, the trend in annual growth was distinctly and strongly downward during the decade (Figure 2 and Table 2). Before the World War, the year of largest increase was 1913, when about 2,111,000 persons were added to the population. An abrupt decline from this high mark

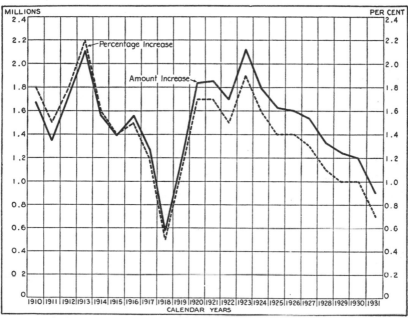

FIG. 2.—Amount and rate of annual population increase, 1910–1931. (Based on Table 2.)

reached a bottom in 1918 when the influenza pandemic and war-time conditions restricted population growth to about 572,000. An equally rapid rise during the first few post-war years reached a peak in 1923, when the population increased about 2,119,000, slightly more than in the highest pre-war year. Since 1923 there has been another marked decline, each year showing a smaller gain than the preceding, until in 1931 only about 872,000 persons were added to the population. Barring the influenza–war-time year of 1918, this number is well below the gain during any other year since 1910 and is less than the average yearly increase at any time since 1870 as shown by the decennial censuses.

[1] Considering the population on the census dates, the rate of increase was 14.9 from April 15, 1910, to January 1, 1920, and 16.1 per cent from the latter date to April 1, 1930. Adjusting both intervals to exactly 10 years raises the 1910–1920 rate to 15.4 per cent and lowers the 1920–1930 rate to 15.7 per cent.

POPULATION TRENDS IN THE UNITED STATES

TABLE 2.—AMOUNT AND RATE OF ANNUAL INCREASE, BY RACE AND NATIVITY, 1910–1931[a]

(Numbers in thousands)

Year	Increase of total population		Increase of whites[b]		Increase of native whites[b]		Increase of foreign-born whites[b]		Increase of Negroes	
	Number	Per thousand	Number	Per thousand	Number	Per thousand	Number	Per thousand	Number	Per thousand
1910	1,676	18.3	1,616	19.9	.....	....	.....	......	...	....
1911	1,351	14.5	1,277	15.4	.....	....	.....	......	...	....
1912	1,739	18.4	1,651	19.6	.....	....	.....	......	...	....
1913	2,111	21.9	2,014	23.5	.....	....	.....	......	...	....
1914	1,564	15.9	1,462	16.7	.....	....	.....	......	...	....
1915	1,398	14.0	1,298	14.6	.....	....	.....	......	...	....
1916	1,563	15.4	1,425	15.7	.....	....	.....	......	...	....
1917	1,274	12.4	1,175	12.8	.....	....	.....	......	...	....
1918	572	5.5	647	7.0	.....	....	.....	......	...	....
1919	1,196	11.4	1,036	11.0	.....	....	.....	......	...	....
1920	1,834	17.3	1,689	17.8	1,485	18.3	204	14.9	128	12.1
1921	1,854	17.2	1,680	17.4	1,651	20.0	29	2.1	156	14.5
1922	1,698	15.5	1,536	15.6	1,531	18.2	5	0.4	139	12.8
1923	2,119	19.0	1,958	19.6	1,567	18.3	391	28.1	135	12.2
1924	1,794	15.8	1,628	16.0	1,614	18.5	14	1.0	141	12.6
1925	1,625	14.1	1,480	14.3	1,500	16.8	− 20	− 1.4	131	11.6
1926	1,602	13.7	1,459	13.9	1,443	15.9	16	1.1	127	11.1
1927	1,536	13.0	1,403	13.2	1,425	15.5	− 22	− 1.5	122	10.6
1928	1,326	11.0	1,223	11.4	1,303	14.0	− 80	− 5.6	93	8.0
1929	1,245	10.3	1,147	10.5	1,221	12.9	− 74	− 5.2	86	7.3
1930	1,204	9.8	1,087	9.9	1,267	13.2	−184	−13.0	99	8.3
1931	872	7.1	780	7.0	1,128	11.6	−356	−25.5	87	7.2
1932	828	6.6	....	....	.....	....	.....	......	...	....

[a] Based on Table 84, p. 301. The sum of the increases for the calendar years 1910 to 1919, inclusive, or for 1920 to 1929, inclusive, is not equal to the intercensal increase shown in Table 1, since the 1910 census was taken on April 15 and the 1930 census on April 1.

[b] Mexicans are classified as whites since births and deaths are so classified by the Division of Vital Statistics.

Looking into the future, it appears probable that the growth of population will continue to slow up. Postponing to Chapter X the more detailed discussion of the future, it can be said here that the population probably will be between 132,000,000 and 135,000,000 in 1940, between 137,000,000 and 151,000,000 in 1950, and between 129,000,000 and 202,000,000 in 1980 (Table 3). This will mean an increase of about 9,000,000 to 12,000,-000 from 1930 to 1940, and about 5,000,000 to 16,000,000 from 1940 to 1950, compared with an actual increase of 17,064,426 from 1920 to 1930 (Table 4). These figures represent the population that would result according to different trends assumed for birth rates, death rates, and immigration discussed in Chapters VII, VIII, and IX. As will be brought out in Chapter X, the authors believe the actual population will be much closer to the lower limit than to the upper (Figure 33, p. 293).

The growth of population from the first census in 1790 up to the year 2,000 may thus fall naturally into three periods of 70 years each. The first period (1790–1860) was one of high percentage increase steadily maintained from decade to decade. In 1860 the population was eight times as large as in 1790, having doubled about every 23.5 years. In the second period (1860–1930) the rate of increase declined, but the absolute numbers added to the population between censuses continued to rise. In 1930 the population was about four times as large as in 1860; 35 years were required for doubling. During the coming 70 year period (1930–2000) there is little doubt that both the amount and rate of increase will decrease. There is no probability of doubling in this period; the population is more likely to be stationary or declining by the end of the period than still to be growing.

TABLE 3.—POPULATION AND PERCENTAGE DISTRIBUTION, BY RACE AND NATIVITY, 1790–1980[a]

Year	Total	White	Native white	Foreign-born white	Negro	Mexican	Indian	Chinese	Japanese	Filipino
POPULATION (THOUSANDS)										
1790	3,929	3,172			757		....	....	...	..
1800	5,308	4,306			1,002		....	....	...	..
1810	7,240	5,862			1,378		....	....	...	..
1820	9,638	7,867			1,772		....	....	...	..
1830	12,866	10,537			2,329		....	....	...	..
1840	17,069	14,196			2,874		....	....	...	..
1850	23,192	19,553	17,313	2,241	3,639		....	....	...	..
1860	31,443	26,923	22,826	4,097	4,442		44[b]	35	...	..
1870	39,818[c]	34,337[c]	28,096[d]	5,494[d]	5,392[c]		26[b]	63[e]	...	..
1880	50,156	43,403	36,843	6,560	6,581		66[b]	105	...	..
1890	62,948	55,101	45,979	9,122	7,489		248	107	2	..
1900	75,995	66,639[e]	56,523[e]	10,116[e]	8,834	171[f]	237	90	24	..
1910	91,972	81,366[e]	68,230[e]	13,136[e]	9,828	366[f]	266	72	72	..
1920	105,711	94,120	80,865	13,255	10,463	701	244	62	111	6
1930	122,775	108,864	95,498	13,366	11,891	1,423	332	75	139	45
Future as calculated:[g]										
"Medium":										
1940	133,100	118,000	106,500	11,500	13,000		....	....	...	..
1950	142,900	126,800	116,300	10,400	13,700		....	....	...	..
1960	149,800	133,200	123,900	9,200	14,200		....	....	...	..
1970	153,800	136,900	128,800	8,100	14,400		....	....	...	..
1980	155,200	138,400	131,100	7,300	14,200		....	....	...	..
"Low":										
1940	131,900	116,900	105,800	11,000	12,900		....	....	...	..
1950	137,100	121,400	113,000	8,400	13,500		....	....	...	..
1960	137,900	122,000	116,200	5,700	13,600		....	....	...	..
1970	134,900	119,300	116,000	3,300	13,400		....	....	...	..
1980	129,200	114,300	112,800	1,500	12,800		....	....	...	..
"High":										
1940	135,100	119,400	107,200	12,100	13,000		....	....	...	..
1950	150,800	132,900	120,300	12,600	14,200		....	....	...	..
1960	167,300	147,100	134,000	13,100	15,400		....	....	...	..
1970	184,200	161,400	147,800	13,600	16,600		....	....	...	..
1980	202,000	176,300	162,000	14,300	17,900		....	....	...	..

TABLE 3.—POPULATION AND PERCENTAGE DISTRIBUTION, BY RACE AND NATIVITY, 1790–1980.[a]—(Continued)

Year	Total	White	Native white	Foreign-born white	Negro	Mexican	Indian	Chinese	Japanese	Filipino

PERCENTAGE DISTRIBUTION

Year	Total	White	Native white	Foreign-born white	Negro	Mexican	Indian	Chinese	Japanese	Filipino
1790	100.0	80.7	.....	.....	19.3	....	....	....	....	.
1800	100.0	81.1	.....	.....	18.9	....	....	....	....	.
1810	100.0	81.0	.....	.....	19.0	....	....	....	....	.
1820	100.0	81.6	.....	.....	18.4	....	....	....	....	.
1830	100.0	81.9	.....	.....	18.1	....	....	....	....	.
1840	100.0	83.2	.....	.....	16.8	....	....	....	....	..
1850	100.0	84.3	74.6	9.7	15.7	....	....	....	..	..
1860	100.0	85.6	72.6	13.0	14.1	....	0.1[b]	0.1	..	..
1870	100.0	86.2[c]	70.6[d]	13.8[d]	13.5[c]	....	0.1[b]	0.2[c]	...	..
1880	100.0	86.5	73.5	13.1	13.1	....	0.1[b]	0.2	...	..
1890	100.0	87.5	73.0	14.5	11.9	....	0.4	0.2	(h)	..
1900	100.0	87.7[e]	74.4[e]	13.3[e]	11.6	0.2[f]	0.3	0.1	(h)	..
1910	100.0	88.5[e]	74.2[e]	14.3[e]	10.7	0.4[f]	0.3	0.1	0.1	..
1920	100.0	89.0	76.5	12.5	9.9	0.7	0.2	0.1	0.1	(h)
1930	100.0	88.7	77.8	10.9	9.7	1.2	0.3	0.1	0.1	(h)
Future as calculated:[g]										
"Medium":										
1940	100.0	88.6	80.0	8.6	9.7	....	....	....	...	..
1950	100.0	88.7	81.4	7.3	9.6	....	....	....	...	..
1960	100.0	88.9	82.7	6.2	9.5	....	....	....	...	..
1970	100.0	89.0	83.8	5.3	9.3	....	....	....	...	..
1980	100.0	89.2	84.4	4.7	9.2	....	....	....	...	..
"Low":										
1940	100.0	88.6	80.2	8.4	9.8	....	....	....	...	..
1950	100.0	88.5	82.4	6.2	9.8	....	....	....	...	..
1960	100.0	88.5	84.3	4.2	9.9	....	....	....	...	..
1970	100.0	88.5	86.0	2.4	9.9	....	....	....	...	..
1980	100.0	88.5	87.3	1.1	9.9	....	....	....	...	..
"High":										
1940	100.0	88.4	79.4	9.0	9.7	....	....	....	...	..
1950	100.0	88.1	79.8	8.4	9.4	....	....	....	...	..
1960	100.0	87.9	80.1	7.8	9.2	....	....	....	...	..
1970	100.0	87.6	80.2	7.4	9.0	....	....	....	...	..
1980	100.0	87.3	80.2	7.1	8.9	....	....	....	...	..

[a] From *Fourteenth Census of the United States: 1920*, Vol. II, pp. 29, 30; and *Fifteenth Census of the United States: 1930*, Vol. III, Pt. 1, p. 12.

[b] Exclusive of Indians in Indian Territory and on Indian reservations, not enumerated at censuses prior to 1890.

[c] Estimated corrected figures. See explanation in *Fourteenth Census of the United States: 1920*, Vol. II, p. 15.

[d] Enumeration in 1870 incomplete.

[e] Estimated number of Mexicans deducted. See Note f.

[f] Estimated by the authors from foreign born of Mexican birth and natives of Mexican parentage. See *Fourteenth Census of the United States: 1920*, Vol. II, pp. 695, 897.

[g] Prepared by the Scripps Foundation for Research in Population Problems. For the assumptions on which these figures are based see Table 88, p. 316, Column H for "medium," Column A for "low," and Column J for "high."

[h] Less than one-tenth of 1 per cent.

2. GROWTH BY RACE

Whites and Negroes have been distinguished in census enumerations since the beginning (1790). The Indians and Chinese were first enumerated separately in 1860, and other races at a still later date; hence comparisons of their rates of growth can be made only for more recent decades.

Negroes decreased from 19.3 per cent of the total population in 1790 to 9.7 per cent in 1930 (Table 3). This decline in proportion of Negroes resulted from the fact that, with the exception of one decade (1800–1810), the rate of increase among Negroes has always been lower than among whites (Table 4). In 1910–1920 the recorded rate of growth of the Negro population was less than half that of the white population, and indeed

TABLE 4.—AMOUNT AND RATE OF DECENNIAL INCREASE, BY RACE AND NATIVITY, 1790–1980ᵃ

Decade ending in	Total	White	Native white	Foreign-born white	Negro	Mexican	Indian	Chinese	Japanese	Filipino
			AMOUNT OF INCREASE (THOUSANDS)							
1800..........	1,379	1,134	....	....	245	...	....	....	..	..
1810..........	1,931	1,556	....	....	376	...	....	....	..	..
1820..........	2,399	2,005	....	....	394	...	....	....	..	..
1830..........	3,228	2,671	....	....	557	...	....	....	..	..
1840..........	4,203	3,658	....	....	545	...	....	....	..	..
1850..........	6,122	5,357	....	....	765	...	....	....	..	..
1860..........	8,251	7,369	5,513	1,856	803	...	....	....	..	..
1870..........	8,375	7,415	5,270	1,397	950	...	−18	28	..	..
1880.;........	10,337	9,066	8,478	1,066	1,189	...	41	42	..	..
1890ᵇ..........	12,466	11,581	9,019	2,562	889ᶜ	...	− 8	2	..	..
1900..........	13,047	11,538	10,544	994	1,345ᶜ	...	−11	−18	22	..
1910..........	15,978	14,727	11,708	3,020	994	195	28	−18	48	..
1920..........	13,738	12,754	12,635	120	635	335	−21	−10	39	..
1930..........	17,064	14,744	14,633	111	1,428	722	88	13	28	40
Future as calculated:										
"Medium":										
1940.......	10,300	9,100	11,000	−1,900	1,100	...	....	....	..	..
1950.......	9,800	8,800	9,800	−1,100	700	...	....	....	..	..
1960.......	6,900	6,400	7,600	−1,200	500	...	....	....	..	..
1970.......	4,000	3,700	4,900	−1,100	200	...	....	....	..	..
1980.......	1,400	1,500	2,300	− 800	−200	...	....	....	..	..
"Low":										
1940.......	9,100	8,000	10,300	−2,400	1,000	...	....	....	..	..
1950.......	5,200	4,500	7,200	−2,600	600	...	....	....	..	..
1960.......	800	600	3,200	−2,700	100	...	....	....	..	..
1970.......	−3,000	−2,700	− 200	−2,400	−200	...	....	....	..	..
1980.......	−5,700	−5,000	−3,200	−1,800	−600	...	....	....	..	..
"High":										
1940.......	12,300	10,500	11,700	−1,300	1,100	...	....	....	..	..
1950.......	15,700	13,500	13,100	500	1,200	...	....	....	..	..
1960.......	16,500	14,200	ᵛ13,700	500	1,200	...	....	....	..	..
1970.......	16,900	14,300	13, 00	500	1,200	...	....	....	..	..
1980.......	17,800	14,900	14,200	700	1,300	...	....	....	..	..

TABLE 4.—AMOUNT AND RATE OF DECENNIAL INCREASE, BY RACE AND NATIVITY, 1790–1980.ᵃ—(*Continued*)

Decade ending in	Total	White	Native white	Foreign-born white	Negro	Mexican	Indian	Chinese	Japanese	Filipino
1800...........	35.1	35.8	.....	......	32.3	.....	......	......	....	.....
1810...........	36.4	36.1	.....	......	37.5	.....	......	......	....	.....
1820...........	33.1	34.2	.....	......	28.6	.....	......	......	....	.....
1830...........	33.5	33.9	.....	......	31.4	.....	......	......	....	.....
1840...........	32.7	34.7	.....	......	23.4	.....	......	......	....	.....
1850...........	35.9	37.7	....	......	26.6	.....	......	......	....	.....
1860...........	35.6	37.7	31.8	82.8	22.1	.....	......	......	....	.....
1870...........	26.6	27.5	23.1	34.1	21.4	.....	−41.5	80.9	....	.....
1880...........	26.0	26.4	31.1	19.4	22.0	.....	158.1	66.9	....	.....
1890ᵇ..........	24.9	26.7	24.5	39.1	13.5ᶜ	.....	−11.4	1.9	1,277.7	.....
1900...........	20.7	20.9	22.9	10.9	18.0ᶜ	.....	− 4.5	−16.4	1,093.0	.....
1910........... :	21.0	22.1	20.7	29.9	11.2	114.5	12.0	−20.4	196.6	.....
1920...........	14.9	15.7	18.5	0.9	6.5	91.5	− 8.0	−13.8	53.8	.....
1930...........	16.1	15.7	18.1	0.8	13.6	103.1	36.0	21.6	25.1	706.9

Future as calculated:
"Medium":

1940......	8.4	8.4	11.5	−14.2	8.9	.....	......	......	....	.....
1950......	7.3	7.5	9.2	− 9.0	6.1	.....	......	......	....	.....
1960......	4.9	5.0	6.5	−11.5	3.4	.....	......	......	....	.....
1970......	2.6	2.8	3.9	−12.6	1.1	.....	......	......	....	.....
1980......	0.9	1.1	1.8	− 9.0	−0.7	.....	......	......	....	.....

"Low":

1940......	7.4	7.3	10.8	−17.6	8.3	.....	......	......	....	.....
1950......	3.9	3.9	6.7	−23.4	4.6	.....	......	......	....	.....
1960......	0.5	0.5	2.9	−31.9	1.1	.....	......	......	....	.....
1970......	−2.2	−2.2	−0.2	−42.9	−1.9	.....	......	......	....	.....
1980......	−4.2	−4.2	−2.8	−55.2	−4.2	.....	......	......	....	.....

"High":

1940......	10.0	9.7	12.3	− 9.2	9.7	.....	......	......	....	.....
1950......	11.7	11.4	12.2	3.9	8.8	.....	......	......	....	.....
1960......	10.9	10.6	11.4	3.8	8.2	.....	......	......	....	.....
1970......	10.1	9.8	10.3	4.1	7.9	.....	......	......	....	.....
1980......	9.7	9.2	9.6	5.1	8.1	.....	......	......	....	.....

ᵃ Based on Table 3.

ᵇ Exclusive of 325,464 persons (117,368 whites, 18,636 Negroes, 189,447 Indians, and 13 Chinese) specially enumerated in 1890 in Indian Territory and on Indian reservations.

ᶜ T. J. Woofter believes Negroes were underenumerated in 1890. For his corrections see Table VIII and accompanying discussion (*Races and Ethnic Groups in American Life*, Monograph in Social Trends Series, New York, McGraw-Hill Book Company, Inc., 1933).

since 1900 the Negro population increased by only about one-third, while the white population increased by almost two-thirds. Unfortunately the comparison of white and Negro growth by decades is occasionally somewhat upset by the less accurate count of Negroes at one time than at another. Thus the census states that the underenumeration of Negroes in 1920 as compared with 1910 and 1930 may have been as large as 150,-000.[1] However, several careful students of the Negro consider this figure

[1] *Fifteenth Census of the United States: 1930*, Vol. III, Pt. 1, p. 7.

too low; Woofter, for example, believes the 1920 census count too low by 150,000 to 450,000.[1] But whatever this error may be, it is clear that since 1900 the Negro population has increased only a little over one-half as fast as the white population. In actual numbers (Figure 3 and Table 4) the white gain during the last 30 years was 42,225,000, while that of the Negroes was only 3,057,000; and in the last 10 years the increases were 14,744,000 and 1,278,000, respectively (adding 150,000 to the number of Negroes in 1920 to allow for underenumeration as estimated by the census).

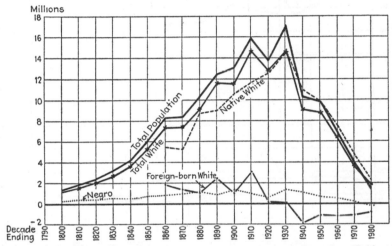

Fig. 3.—Decennial increase, by race and nativity, 1790–1980. (Based on Table 4.)

The white gain from 1920 to 1930 was slightly greater than that from 1900 to 1910, and the Negro gain was second only to that from 1890 to 1900. Both whites and Negroes, however, had a downward trend in annual growth during the last decade, the rate for whites falling the more rapidly (Table 2). The largest annual increase of the white population amounted to about 1,958,000 persons in 1923[2] (Figure 4). Since then there has been an unbroken decline in annual increase to about 780,000 in 1931. The largest Negro growth was about 156,000 in 1921, with a fairly steady decrease during the following years to about 87,000 in 1931. These declines amount to 60 per cent in 8 years for whites and 44 per cent in 10 years for Negroes.

[1] T. J. Woofter, "What Is the Negro Rate of Increase?" *Journal of the American Statistical Association*, Vol. 26, n. s., No. 176 (December, 1931), pp. 461–462.

[2] In the *Fifteenth Census of the United States: 1930* most Mexicans were classed in the Mexican race instead of the white as previously; hence in this chapter the figures for the decennial growth of whites from 1900 to 1930 (both native and foreign born) exclude colored Mexicans. In the annual reports of birth statistics and of mortality statistics the Bureau of the Census does not separate Mexican births and deaths from white; hence the figures for annual growth of whites include all Mexicans.

In the future the proportions of the whites and Negroes probably will change but little as compared with the changes in the past (Table 3). In the "medium" population of 1980 the whites will comprise 89.2 per cent of the total as compared with 88.7 per cent in 1930, and the Negroes 9.2 per cent as compared with 9.7 per cent in 1930. However, it

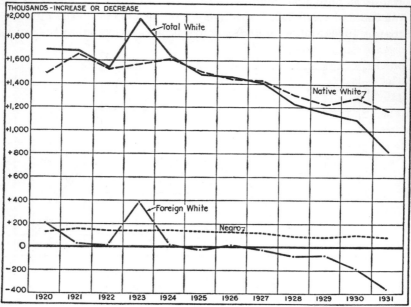

FIG. 4.—Amount of annual population increase, by race and nativity, 1920–1931.[a] (Based on Table 2.)

[a] Mexicans are included with whites because births to white women and to Mexican women are not separated in birth statistics.

should be noted that by 1970 the Negro population will probably begin to decline in numbers, although the white population may still increase, *albeit* very slowly (Table 4). In other words, the present trends seem to the authors to indicate that the ratio of whites to Negroes will increase but little during the next half century.

Data on Indians are available since 1860 but are not of much value until 1890. Even since that time certain changes in methods of enumeration have been made so that figures for Indian growth and rate of increase have fluctuated erratically from decade to decade (Tables 3 and 4). In 1930, for example, enumerators were instructed to return as Indians "all persons of mixed white and Indian blood, except where the percentage of Indian blood was very small, or where the person was regarded as white in the community where he lived." Because no special instructions on this point were given to enumerators in 1920, it seems likely that an appreciable part of the large increase (36.0 per cent) of the Indians between 1920 and 1930 was due to this different basis of enumeration. It is not possible, therefore, to say just what the growth in the Indian population has been in recent decades, nor what the trend is at the present time. But since the first complete count of Indians in 1890, their numbers have risen by only one-third, while whites have almost doubled. As to their future growth, it is impossible to give a rational estimate. It seems reasonably certain that they have a high birth rate and a high death rate. It is probable that the death rate will decline faster than the birth rate, thus leaving a larger natural increase. In any event, the Indians are such a small proportion of the total population and will remain such a small part of it for the next half century that any changes in their numbers will be of little significance in the growth of the total population.

The number of Chinese grew quite rapidly from 1860 (when they were first enumerated separately) until some time after 1880, presumably until the passage of the first Chinese Exclusion Act in 1882, for there was a slight increase between 1880 and 1890 (Tables 3 and 4). For 30 years following 1890 the number declined steadily, largely as a consequence of the return to China of those who had entered before the exclusion acts. Between 1920 and 1930, however, there was a substantial increase in Chinese, which will probably continue for several decades, because the proportion of females in the Chinese population is rapidly increasing and an excess of births over deaths and departures is to be expected in the future. It seems unlikely, however, that the Chinese will ever again amount to as much as 0.1 per cent of the total population.

It was not until the decade 1890–1900 that the Japanese began to come in any appreciable numbers (Tables 3 and 4). Once started, however, they increased rapidly; by 1910 they numbered over 72,000, of whom only slightly over 9,000 were females. During the decade 1910–1920 the females increased far more rapidly than the males. In 1924 Japanese immigration practically ceased, but their numbers increased by 25.1 per cent during the last decade, largely by excess of births over deaths. It seems only reasonable to look for a rather large natural increase among the Japanese for the next two or three decades. Even if they increase much faster than the total population, it will be several decades before they constitute 0.2 per cent of the population.

By far the largest group among the "other colored" are the Mexicans. They were first classified separately in 1930, but the census prepared an estimate for 1920 in order to show their growth during the decade. Estimates for 1900 and 1910 were made by the authors. The Mexicans more than doubled in numbers during the last decade and now constitute about 70 per cent of all the "other colored" in the population (Tables 3 and 4). The reason for their very rapid increase is found in the slowing up of the stream of European immigration, first as a consequence of the

World War and later by the application of the quota system. Neither of these checks applied to Mexicans; on the contrary, Mexican immigration was stimulated by these checks to the movement from Europe. Since the Mexicans also have a high birth rate, it is but reasonable to expect that they will continue to increase for some years, unless the number returning to Mexico should be considerably larger than at present.[1] The present net outflow of Mexicans seems more likely to decrease than to increase, however, especially if the "public charge" restriction on immigration is modified as economic conditions improve.

The latest of the colored races to migrate hither in significant numbers is the Filipino. There were fewer than 200 Filipinos enumerated in 1910, but in 1920 there were about 5,600 and in 1930 over 45,000 (Tables 3 and 4). The Filipinos as nationals of an unincorporated territory are not prevented from entering the United States as are most other Orientals. In fact, the stopping of Japanese immigration undoubtedly stimulated Filipino immigration. As yet the proportion of women among the Filipinos is very small, there being about 14 males to each female. How their numbers will increase in the future will probably depend chiefly upon the political status of the Philippine Islands and economic conditions in the United States. Favorable economic conditions here, with no bars to entrance, will undoubtedly lead to a fairly rapid increase in their numbers. The opposite conditions, political independence (which would probably mean barring them as is now done with other Orientals) and hard times here, will probably greatly restrict their entrance. There will be no significant natural increase of Filipinos for several decades because of the scarcity of women among them.

All other races combined have a total of less than 6,000, hence can scarcely be called a significant element in the population. Hindus and Koreans constitute almost seven-eighths of this group. They are not likely to increase much in the near future, as the numbers allowed to enter are very narrowly restricted and there are but few women here.

To sum up the whole matter of racial growth in the United States, the white race has been growing at a somewhat more rapid rate than the total population and the Negroes at a slower rate. The "other colored" as a whole have been insignificant in numbers and have shown no particular tendency in growth until recently. But from 1920 to 1930 the "other colored" increased 79.2 per cent, or about five times as fast as the whites. If the "other colored" and Negroes are combined, the colored population of the country grew faster than the white population from 1920 to 1930, as it did only once before, from 1800 to 1810. This is one result of the

[1] According to the immigration reports, departures of Mexicans exceeded arrivals by 11,800 in the fiscal year 1931 and by 35,500 in the fiscal year 1932. But much unrecorded movement also takes place.

GROWTH OF POPULATION

immigration policy which applied quota limits on the entrance of Europeans but did not restrict the entrance of Mexicans. This policy was modified in the summer of 1930 by the "public charge" regulation, which affects immigrants from every country. What the future policy will be, only time will tell. Aside from immigration, however, it is possible that in the next few decades, growth by excess of births over deaths may be more rapid in the colored population than in the white population. The benefits of a fair public health service may so reduce the death rate of the colored population that even with some decline in its present birth rate, its rate of natural increase will still exceed that of whites.

3. GROWTH OF WHITES BY NATIVITY AND PARENTAGE

Since there always have been considerable numbers of foreign born in the population of the United States, the growth of the different nativity groups of the white population has long been of interest. It was not until 1850, however, that the foreign born were enumerated separately and not until 20 years later that the natives of foreign and mixed parentage were so enumerated (Tables 3 and 5). From 1860 to 1910 the foreign born remained almost a constant proportion of the whites, varying only between 15.1 per cent and 16.6 per cent. Since 1910, however, they have declined from 16.3 per cent to 12.3 per cent in 1930. This is the inevitable consequence of the war and of the new quota system which has operated in some form or other since June, 1921.

In absolute numbers the foreign born have shown no appreciable gain since 1910 (Tables 3 and 4). Indeed in striking a yearly balance since then (Table 2), it is found that there have been only two years since 1913 (1920 and 1923) when net immigration was sufficiently large to offset the deaths of foreign-born whites and leave much of a surplus for increase. During the other years, from the close of the World War up to 1926, this group remained practically stationary, net immigration balancing deaths. In 1927 an excess of deaths over net immigrants began, which rose to over 356,000 in 1931. If this condition continues, it will reduce rapidly the number of foreign-born whites in the population.[1]

Naturally as the proportion of the foreign born in the white population declined, the proportion of natives increased, since these two groups make up the white population. Simultaneously the composition of the native white population has been changed by fluctuations in the proportion of native whites of native parentage, of foreign parentage, and of mixed parentage. In 1870, the first census year for which parentage information is available, 81.0 per cent of the native white population was of native

[1] The changes in the composition of the foreign-born whites produced by the quota system will be discussed in some detail in Chap. III.

[13]

TABLE 5.—NUMBER, PERCENTAGE INCREASE, AND PERCENTAGE DISTRIBUTION OF NATIVE
WHITES, BY PARENTAGE, 1870–1930[a]

Year	Population (thousands)			Percentage distribution			Percentage increase over preceding census		
	Native parentage	Foreign parentage	Mixed parentage	Native parentage	Foreign parentage	Mixed parentage	Native parentage	Foreign parentage	Mixed parentage
1870[b]	22,771	4,167	1,157	81.0	14.8	4.1	....	....	....
1880	28,568	6,364	1,911	77.5	17.3	5.2	25.5	52.7	65.2
1890	34,476	8,085	3,419	75.0	17.6	7.4	20.3[c]	27.0	78.9
1900	40,949	10,632	5,014	72.4	18.8	8.9	18.8	31.5	46.7
1910	49,489	12,916	5,982	72.4	18.9	8.7	20.9	21.5	19.3
1920[d]	58,422	15,522	6,921	72.2	19.2	8.6	18.1[e]	21.5[e]	16.9[e]
1930	70,137	16,999	8,362	73.4	17.8	8.8	20.1	9.5	20.8

[a] From *Fourteenth Census of the United States: 1920*, Vol. II, pp. 29, 30 and from *Fifteenth Census of the United States: 1930*, Vol. III, Pt. 1, p. 8.
[b] Enumeration in 1870 incomplete.
[c] Exclusive of population specially enumerated in 1890 in Indian Territory and on Indian reservations.
[d] Excludes persons who would have been counted as Mexican in 1930.
[e] Includes Mexicans.

parentage. The proportion declined to 72.4 per cent in 1910 but rose again
to 73.4 per cent in 1930. During this period the native whites of foreign
parentage rose from 14.8 per cent to 19.2 per cent in 1920 and then
declined to 17.8 per cent in 1930. The natives of mixed parentage rose
fairly steadily from 4.1 per cent in 1870 to 8.8 per cent in 1930. A continuation of present immigration restrictions for two or three decades
will cause a marked growth in the proportion of native whites of native
parentage and a corresponding decline in that of native whites of foreign
or mixed parentage.

4. GROWTH OF POPULATION BY REGIONS

Throughout most of our history, population has grown with greatest
rapidity in the newer regions that were in process of settlement.[1] This has
meant that the fastest growing regions were, until recently, usually on or
near the western limits of settlement. It is easy to understand why new
regions offering opportunity to secure good land attracted numerous
settlers. In the days when most men expected to make their living directly
from the land it was agricultural opportunity which exercised the greatest
pull. It is not surprising, therefore, that the higher rates of increase moved
west as the country was settled (Table 6). When the two divisions ranking
first and second in rate of growth are considered, no divisions east of the

[1] High rates of growth should not be confused with large absolute increases, for frequently, if not generally, the two did not coincide.

TABLE 6.—POPULATION AND PERCENTAGE INCREASE, BY DIVISIONS, 1790–1930[a]

Year	New England	Middle Atlantic	East North Central	West North Central	South Atlantic	East South Central	West South Central	Mountain	Pacific
POPULATION (THOUSANDS)									
1790......	1,009	959	......	......	1,852	109	......	.....	.....
1800......	1,233	1,403	51	......	2,286	335	......	.....	.....
1810......	1,472	2,015	272	20	2,675	709	78	.....	.....
1820......	1,660	2,700	793	67	3,061	1,190	168	.....	.....
1830......	1,955	3,588	1,470	140	3,646	1,816	246	.....	.....
1840......	2,235	4,526	2,925	427	3,925	2,575	450	.....	.....
1850......	2,728	5,899	4,523	880	4,679	3,363	940	73	106
1860......	3,135	7,459	6,927	2,170	5,365	4,021	1,748	175	444
1870[b]......	3,488	8,811	9,125	3,857	5,854	4,404	2,030	315	675
1880......	4,011	10,497	11,207	6,157	7,597	5,585	3,334	653	1,115
1890......	4,701	12,706	13,478	8,932	8,858	6,429	4,741	1.214	1,888
1900......	5,592	15,455	15,986	10,347	10,443	7,548	6,532	1,675	2,417
1910......	6,553	19,316	18,251	11,638	12,195	8,410	8,785	2,634	4,192
1920......	7,401	22,261	21,476	12,544	13,990	8,893	10,242	3,336	5,567
1930......	8,166	26,261	25,297	13,297	15,794	9,887	12,177	3,702	8,194
PERCENTAGE INCREASE OVER PRECEDING CENSUS									
1800......	22.2	46.3	.....	.....	23.5	206.7	.....	.....	.....
1810......	19.4	43.6	433.9	.....	17.0	111.3	.....	.....	.....
1820......	12.8	34.0	191.1	236.6	14.4	68.0	116.0	.....	.....
1830......	17.7	32.9	85.4	110.9	19.1	52.5	46.8	.....	.....
1840......	14.3	26.2	99.0	203.9	7.7	41.8	82.8	.....	.....
1850......	22.1	30.3	54.7	106.3	19.2	30.6	109.0	.....	.....
1860......	14.9	26.5	53.1	146.5	14.7	19.6	85.9	139.9	319.3
1870[b]......	11.2	18.1	31.7	77.7	9.1	9.5	16.2	80.3	52.0
1880[b]......	15.0	19.1	22.8	59.7	29.8	26.8	64.3	107.1	65.1
1890......	17.2	21.0	20.3	45.1	16.6	15.1	42.2	85.9	69.4
1900......	19.0	21.0	18.6	15.8	17.0	17.4	37.8	38.0	28.0
1910......	17.2	25.0	14.2	12.5	16.8	11.4	34.5	57.3	73.5
1920......	12.9	15.2	17.7	7.8	14.7	5.7	16.6	26.7	32.8
1930......	10.3	18.0	17.8	6.0	12.9	11.2	18.9	11.0	47.2

[a] From *Fourteenth Census of the United States: 1920*, Vol. I, p. 23 and from *Fifteenth Census of the United States: 1930*, Vol. I, pp. 10–12.

[b] Enumerated population understates population, particularly in the South (see *Fourteenth Census of the United States: 1920*, Vol. I, p. 14); hence understates increase for 1860–1870 and exaggerates it for 1870–1880.

Alleghenies are included since 1800–1810. It should be noted, however, that since 1890 the distinctly agricultural divisions in the Middle West and South (except the West South Central states) have had lower rates of increase than some of the more industrialized regions in the East. Clearly the forces determining the rate of growth of the different regions have changed. Agriculture is rapidly becoming of an almost negligible importance as a positive factor in determining regional, state, and community growth in population. Furthermore, the recent changes in agricultural practice have so increased per capita production that there has been a growing surplus of agricultural products. Under these conditions agriculture normally repels rather than attracts population. Today industry, trade, mineral resources, and climate are the magnets that attract population to particular communities. Rarely are there agricultural communities needing more workers.

It is not surprising then that the Middle Atlantic states, which have many advantages in the pursuit of industry and commerce, have had a relatively high rate of increase ever since 1890 and ranked third in 1920–1930; or that they had the largest absolute increase of any division during this decade, indeed the largest absolute increase any division ever had. Close behind them, both in rate and in absolute amount of increase, were the East North Central states, these two divisions together absorbing 45.8 per cent of the total increase of population during the decade although they contained but 41.4 per cent of the total population in 1920. This is a reversal of the westward movement of population, in spite of the fact that the Pacific states had the highest rate of increase during the last decade. Even in these coast states, it is no longer their agricultural frontier that makes them attractive. This fact will be made clear when the growth of population by states is examined in some detail.

During the last decade the two states which showed the most rapid growth in population were California (65.7 per cent) and Florida (51.6 per cent) (Figure 5). At the other extreme are Montana, which lost in population (−2.1 per cent) during the decade, and Georgia, which was practically stationary (0.4 per cent). Georgia and Florida are contiguous; and Montana would certainly be classed with California as one of the newer states. These facts are cited to show that the conventional geographic regions are no longer units in the attraction of population and that mere newness has ceased to guarantee growth. The factors at work in any locality are more or less peculiar to it and each community should be studied individually to understand why it did or did not grow. Generalizations which quite satisfactorily explained population growth in the past will not do so today.

There can be little doubt that the two fastest growing states (California and Florida) owe a large part of their increase to the attractiveness of their climates, for they grew most rapidly in those parts which were the most attractive climatically. Of the other seven states which had a fairly rapid rate of increase, four (Michigan, New Jersey, North Carolina, and New York) are states which had a large industrial or commercial development. One (Texas) seems to owe its growth in part to agricultural development, as there was a marked expansion of cotton farming into former ranch country; but at the same time the oil industry expanded rapidly and the larger cities grew in commercial importance. In the other two states (Arizona and Oregon) there was very little growth of farm

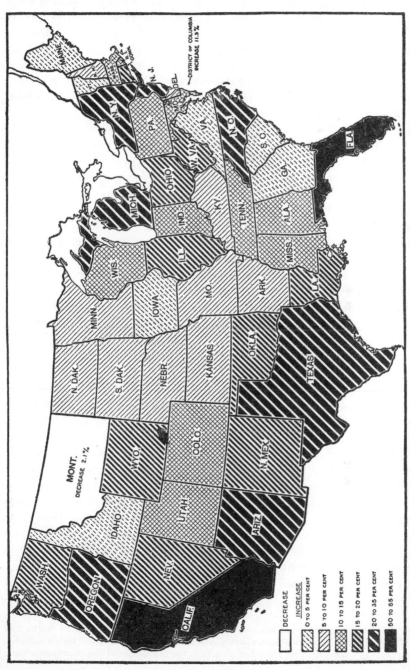

FIG. 5.—Rate of increase of the total population, by states, 1920–1930. (Based on *Fifteenth Census of the United States: 1930*, Vol. I, Table 6, p. 12.)

population (although the area in crops grew considerably); hence it would seem that climate must have been an important factor here, as in California and Florida, although its influence was not nearly so great.

In contrast to these nine rapidly growing states, there were eighteen states whose rate of growth between 1920 and 1930 was less than 10 per cent. For the most part these are states in which agriculture is the important occupation, Maine, New Hampshire, Vermont, and Delaware being the only semi-industrialized states in the group (Figure 5).

The slow upward trend of population in most agricultural states since 1920 is quite different from the rapid growth which occurred in many of them from 1900 to 1920. In the earlier period land settlement was perhaps the most important cause of a high rate of increase, North Dakota, South Dakota, Oklahoma, Texas, the Mountain and the Pacific states all gaining at a very rapid rate. In the rest of the country, only Florida with its warm winters, Michigan with its growing automobile industry, New Jersey and Connecticut with their New York City overflow, and West Virginia with its coal mining, gained with a rapidity comparable with the newer agricultural states. On the other hand, older agricultural states and those lacking a rapid industrial development have had little increase since 1900. In this group are Maine, New Hampshire, Vermont, Indiana, Iowa, Missouri, Nebraska, Kansas, Delaware, Virginia, South Carolina, Georgia, Kentucky, and Tennessee.

5. GROWTH OF RURAL AND URBAN POPULATION[1]

When attention is turned to rural and urban growth, the full effects of the present industrial and commercial development on population growth in different localities are seen. In 1790 there were but six places in the United States having 8,000 or more people; they contained but 3.3 per cent of the total population. Thirty years later there were 13 such places, with 4.9 per cent of the population. At that time (1820), according to a special compilation, only 7.0 per cent of the people lived in places having 2,500 population or more. Since then there has been a steady and rapid growth of urban population on both size bases, decidedly faster since 1880 than prior to that time. In the last half century the people in places of 8,000 and over have grown from 22.7 to 49.1 per cent of the total, and in places of 2,500 and over from 28.5 to 56.2 per cent (Table 7 and Figures 6 and 7).[2]

---

[1] All villages and cities of 2,500 and over and certain densely populated towns and townships in the northeastern states where political organization does not follow the plan of incorporating small cities are classified as urban, the remainder of the population being rural.

[2] For data relating to the different regions, see Appendix Table 1.

The growth of the urban population on both of these bases is even more striking if absolute numbers are considered. Thus the population in places of 8,000 and over grew from 11,366,000 in 1880 to 60,333,000 in 1930 or 431 per cent, and that in places of 2,500 and over from 14,311,000 to 68,955,000 or 382 per cent. During this same period the population in places of less than 8,000 grew from 38,790,000 to only 62,442,000, or 61

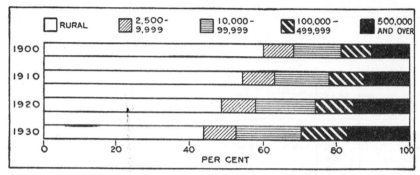

FIG. 6.—Percentage distribution of the total population, by size of city, 1900–1930. (Based on Table 8; 1900 based on special compilation.)

per cent, while that in places of less than 2,500 grew even more slowly, from 35,845,000 to 53,820,000, or only 50 per cent. It is evident, therefore, that the rural population has been growing slowly as compared with the urban population and that the relative rates have become more divergent in recent years.

Since 1920 the increase in population can be classified as urban, rural-nonfarm, and rural-farm. It is interesting, therefore, to note that although there was an increase of almost 2,500,000 in the rural population as a whole, the rural-farm population was actually smaller by about 1,200,000 in 1930 than in 1920, while the rural-nonfarm population was larger by almost 3,700,000 (Table 8).[1] Since the entire rural population has increased only about 4,000,000 in the last 20 years, it appears highly probable that the rural-farm population was smaller in 1930 than in 1910. While this group has been declining, the urban population has been growing rapidly. It increased by 12,260,000 from 1910 to 1920 and by 14,600,-000 from 1920 to 1930.

The decrease in the rural-farm population from 1920 to 1930 is due to the farm-to-city migration that took place, for rural birth rates have long been higher than urban birth rates and rural death rates lower than urban

---

[1] It is probable that the decline in the rural-farm population was even greater than indicated here by some 700,000 since the census of 1930 was taken as of April 1 while that of 1920 was taken as of January 1. The farm population is always larger on April 1 than on January 1 because of the larger number of hired hands on farms after spring work commences.

death rates,[1] giving the rural population a rate of natural increase much higher than that of the cities. The net movement of persons off farms was great enough to absorb not only all the excess of births over deaths on farms, but also 1,200,000 of the 1920 farm population.

TABLE 7.—POPULATION AND PERCENTAGE DISTRIBUTION BY RURAL AND URBAN
COMMUNITIES, 1790–1930
(Population in thousands)

Year	Places of over 8,000[a]		Places of less than 8,000[a]		Places of over 2,500[b]		Places of less than 2,500[b]	
	Population	Per cent of total population	Population	Per cent of total population	Population	Per cent of total population	Population	Per cent of total population
1790	131	3.3	3,798	96.7				
1800	211	4.0	5,097	96.0				
1810	357	4.9	6,883	95.1				
1820	475	4.9	9,163	95.1	677	7.0	8,961	93.0
1830	865	6.7	12,001	93.3	1,085	8.4	11,781	91.6
1840	1,454	8.5	15,615	91.5	1,973	11.6	15,096	88.4
1850	2,898	12.5	20,294	87.5	3,901	16.8	19,291	83.2
1860	5,072	16.1	26,371	83.9	6,531	20.8	24,912	79.2
1870	8,072	20.9	30,486	79.1	10,095	26.2	28,464	73.8
1880	11,366	22.7	38,790	77.3	14,311	28.5	35,845	71.5
1890	18,244	29.0	44,704	71.0	22,230	35.3	40,718	64.7
1900	25,018	32.9	50,977	67.1	30,296	39.9	45,698	60.1
1910	35,570	38.7	56,402	61.3	42,099	45.8	49,873	54.2
1920	46,308	43.8	59,403	56.2	54,356	51.4	51,354	48.6
1930	60,333	49.1	62,442	50.9	68,955	56.2	53,820	43.8

[a] From *Fifteenth Census of the United States: 1930*, Vol. I, p. 9.

[b] For 1930, from *Fifteenth Census of the United States: 1930*, Vol. I, p. 14. For 1820–1920 from special compilations made for this study. For further details see Note a, Table 9.

The chief reason for the large farm-to-city migration during the 1920–1930 decade was the improvement that took place in farm implements and practices. This brought about technological unemployment on farms just as analogous improvement in manufacturing did in cities. The resulting maladjustment of the labor force on farms is more difficult to correct than in cities. In the first place, it is easier to increase the per capita consumption of most factory products than to increase the consumption of the foods which make up the bulk of farm products. Therefore, relatively more of the cities' technologically unemployed can be put to work increasing the output of the same products than is the case in the country. Secondly, many of the workers released by one urban industry may find employment in a new and rapidly growing industry (radio being an excellent example), a process that has almost no counterpart on farms.

[1] See Chaps. VII and VIII.

With little opportunity for an increased demand for farm products to issue in agricultural expansion, or for alternative occupations in the country to absorb labor, most of the farm workers set free by improved machinery and technique migrated to the city. If this trend of the years preceding 1930 continues, machinery may in the future exert an even greater pressure in forcing workers off farms. A satisfactory mechanical cotton picker is said to be ready for the market and the corn husker is being further perfected. Besides, any considerable increase in farm profits is certain to see the more general use of tractors, small combine-harvesters, and the new and more efficient tillage implements already on the market.

During 1930 and 1931, however, the trend has been changing. The number of persons leaving farms in 1930 was the smallest in several years and the number moving to farms the largest. This tendency appears to have been further accentuated in 1931 to such an extent that the farm population not only held its entire excess of births over deaths, but gained about 200,000 from the farm-city interchange. The explanation of the changing trend no doubt is the difficulty of finding employment in cities during 1930 and 1931, and the fact that in cities (especially large cities) all food must be bought at stores, while in the country it is possible to raise much of the family living. Usually those persons going back to the country are accepting a lower standard of living than they previously enjoyed in the city, partly because prices of the products farmers sell have been depressed more than prices of most other classes of products and partly because so many of these migrants are moving to submarginal land. Nevertheless, the farm has been and still is the proverbial place for having enough to eat in hard times. If prosperity again permits a resumption of the movement of the surplus farm population to city jobs, the present urban exodus may do little permanent harm. If this should not occur, there is danger of developing a large poverty-stricken population on the millions of acres of land which is submarginal for business farming, but which will permit self-sustaining farming on a low standard of living.

6. GROWTH OF RURAL-FARM POPULATION BY STATES

Increases in the rural-farm population during the last decade occurred in 16 states.[1] The numerical gains were above 50,000 in only four (California, 85,837; North Carolina, 97,274; Mississippi, 91,957; and Texas, 76,819); in four others they were between 15,000 and 50,000 (Louisiana, 42,427; South Dakota, 27,545; Washington, 20,121; and Col-

---

[1] These exclude Massachusetts and Rhode Island, in which the increases of rural-farm population from 1920 to 1930 shown by the census were due to the change in the basis of rural-urban classification. See *Fifteenth Census of the United States: 1930*, Vol. I, p. 7.

orado, 15,757); and in the other eight they were less than 10,000.[1] In North Carolina and California much of the increase in rural-farm population was more apparent than real, due to persons not employed in agriculture seeking homes in the country and having a few acres of land which they reported as a "farm." In South Dakota, Texas, and the western states there was some of this development no doubt, but in addition there was real growth of rural-farm population owing to the expansion of the farming area into regions previously idle or devoted to ranching. This expansion arose largely from improvements in farming methods and from the introduction of newer types of implements especially applicable to large-scale, dry-land farming, which increased human efficiency and lowered production costs. In parts of Texas the movement of cotton farming, with its higher labor requirements per acre, into former grain or grazing areas was also responsible for considerable growth.

Although the rural-farm population increased in 16 states, it declined in 32 states, these being well distributed outside the West and Southwest. Declines of over 50,000 occurred in New York, Pennsylvania, Ohio, Indiana, Illinois, Michigan, Missouri, Virginia, South Carolina, Georgia, Kentucky, and Tennessee. Except Missouri, these are all states east of the Mississippi River, in the older agricultural region of the country. Part of this region does not have the level land and large fields that are common in states to the west, while the more favored areas have lagged in the use of labor-saving farm machinery. Competition from the more efficient areas elsewhere is here forcing out of use thousands of acres of land not sufficiently level for the latest machinery and is causing the consolidation into larger farms of the land in level regions adapted to such machinery. In both cases, the result has been a decrease in the number of farms and in the farm population. The New England, Middle Atlantic, and East North Central states were especially affected from 1920 to 1930, the number of farms decreasing 13.0 per cent and the rural-farm population decreasing 9.2 per cent.[2] In the South Atlantic and East South Central states the decrease of 5.3 per cent in the rural-farm population was slightly larger than that of 4.1 per cent in the number of farms. It is in this section that the greatest increase in human efficiency and in size of farm, with a large decrease in rural-farm population, may occur in the near future if the mechanical cotton picker comes up to expectations, for this implement will be to cotton farming what the binder and combine harvester are to wheat farming.

[1] Rural-farm gain was less than 10,000 in North Dakota, Nebraska, Alabama, Oklahoma, Wyoming, Arizona, Nevada, and Oregon.

[2] In calculating this percentage, the total farm population for Massachusetts and Rhode Island was used because of changes in rural-urban classification mentioned previously.

The increase of 2,400,000 in the rural population, compared with a gain of over 14,600,000 in the urban population, has interesting implications in the field of politics. Considering only the population eligible to vote, there were 100 persons in rural areas to 86 in urban areas in 1910, 100 to 114 in 1920, and 100 to 142 in 1930. Even this marked change in the relative voting strength of cities and rural areas understates the situation. The rural population now contains some millions of nonfarm people whose interests and outlook are distinctly urban and probably will contain a larger proportion of such persons in the future. Thus the cities are likely to continue to exercise an increasing political influence, the consequences of which may be large.

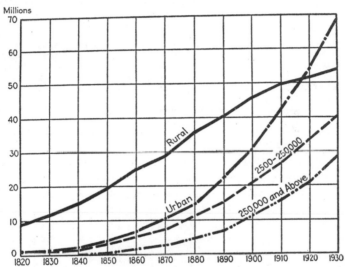

FIG. 7.—Rural population, and urban population by size of city, 1820–1930. (Based on Tables 7 and 8.)

7. URBAN GROWTH BY SIZE OF CITY

A compilation from earlier censuses (Table 8 and Figure 7) shows that there has been a steady increase since 1820, and perhaps earlier, in the proportion of the population living in urban communities. In 1820 there was but one city of over 100,000, and all cities of over 25,000 contained only about 322,000 persons, or 3.4 per cent of the total population. In 1850 New York City had barely passed the 500,000 mark and contained but 2.2 per cent of the total population. There were no cities of 250,000 to 500,000 at that time, and those of between 100,000 and 250,000 held but an additional 2.8 per cent of the population; hence all cities of over 100,000 had just 5 per cent of the total population, or about 1,175,000 out of a total of 23,192,000. Forty years later (1890) such cities had 15.4 per cent of the people compared with 29.6 per cent in 1930. If this entire period (1820–1930) is considered, all sizes of places of over 2,500 have shown a fairly steady and rapid increase in their proportion of the population. However, in the last 20 years there has been no increase in the pro-

TABLE 8.—POPULATION AND PERCENTAGE DISTRIBUTION, BY SIZE OF COMMUNITY, 1820–1930[a]

Size of community	1820	1840	1850	1870	1890	1910	1920	1930
POPULATION (THOUSANDS)								
Total.....................	9,638	17,063[b]	23,192	38,558[c]	62,948	91,972	105,711	122,775
1,000,000+.................	.....	......	......	......	3,662	8,501	10,146	15,065
500,000–1,000,000..........	.....	......	516	1,616	806	3,011	6,224	5,764
250,000– 500,000..........	.....	313	......	1,225	2,448	3,950	4,541	7,956
100,000– 250,000..........	124	205	659	1,289	2,782	4,840	6,519	7,541
25,000– 100,000..........	198	422	897	1,698	4,292	8,206	10,340	12,917
10,000– 25,000..........	120	416	642	1,741	3,439	5,591	7,092	9,097
2,500– 10,000..........	235	617	1,188	2,525	4,801	8,000	9,495	10,615
Rural.....................	8,961	15,091	19,291	28,464	40,718	49,873	51,354	53,820
Farm.....................	.....	......	......	......	......	......	31,359	30,158
Nonfarm..................	.....	......	......	......	......	......	19,995	23,663
PERCENTAGE DISTRIBUTION								
Total.....................	100.0	100.0	100.0	100.0	100.0	100.0	100.0	100.0
1,000,000+.................	.....	.....	.....	.....	5.8	9.2	9.6	12.3
500,000–1,000,000..........	.....	.....	2.2	4.2	1.3	3.3	5.9	4.7
250,000– 500,000...........	.....	1.8	.....	3.2	3.9	4.3	4.3	6.5
100,000– 250,000..........	1.3	1.2	2.8	3.3	4.4	5.3	6.2	6.1
25,000– 100,000..........	2.1	2.5	3.9	4.4	6.8	8.9	9.8	10.5
10,000– 25,000..........	1.2	2.4	2.8	4.5	5.5	6.1	6.7	7.4
2,500– 10,000..........	2.4	3.6	5.1	6.5	7.6	8.7	9.0	8.6
Rural.....................	93.0	88.4	83.2	73.8	64.7	54.2	48.6	43.8
Farm.....................	.....	.....	.....	.....	.....	.....	29.7	24.6
Nonfarm..................	.....	.....	.....	.....	.....	.....	18.9	19.3

[a] From a special compilation by size of community made for this study. Does not agree (1890–1920) at all points with *Fifteenth Census of the United States: 1930*, Vol. I, p. 14, because of changes in classification. For explanation of method, see Table 9. The rural-nonfarm population is secured by subtracting the rural-farm population shown in the census from the rural population compiled for this study.

[b] Excludes 6,100 persons on public ships in the service of the United States, not credited to any division or state.

[c] Enumerated population. Revised figures for 1870 as given in Table 3 are available for total population only.

portion of the population living in the smaller cities (2,500 to 10,000) (Figure 6) and during the last decade the proportion in the cities of 500,-000 to 1,000,000 showed a decrease arising from the passage of Detroit and Los Angeles into the 1,000,000-and-over size group.

During the period 1820–1930 the rural population (places of less than 2,500) declined from 93.0 per cent of the total in 1820 to 64.7 per cent in 1890 and to 43.8 per cent in 1930 (Table 8). No simple set of figures shows better the basic changes in economic life during the last century; from being a people almost wholly concerned with agriculture, we have become so highly industrialized and commercialized that at the present time only 24.6 per cent of the population is classified as rural-farm.

Generally such changes as those just cited are referred to as growth; they are the only facts showing growth directly available from the census. However, what they show is not the growth of an identical group of cities or areas, but how many people are living in communities of certain sizes at each census. This is the distribution of population among cities of different sizes. Although the census shows that of the 14,600,000 urban increase during 1920–1930, the cities of over 1,000,000 absorbed nearly 5,000,000, the fact that Detroit and Los Angeles passed from the next smaller size group into this group accounts for over half of these five millions. The decline of 500,000 in the population of cities having 500,000 to 1,000,000 inhabitants is also due to this movement, for although every city in the group gained in population, the loss of Detroit and Los Angeles was far from compensated for by the accession of Milwaukee. On the other hand, the next smaller group (250,000 to 500,000) showed a very great increase (about 3,500,000), a large part of which was due to the fact that it lost but one city (Milwaukee) to the next higher group, while it gained twelve from the 100,000 to 250,000 group. The three largest size groups thus claimed 8,000,000, or 55 per cent of the total urban increase of 14,600,000.

It is both interesting and important to know that in the 40 years between 1890 and 1930 the proportion of the population living in cities of 500,000 to 1,000,000 increased from 1.3 per cent to 4.7 per cent and that the proportion living in cities of 100,000 to 250,000 increased from 4.4 per cent to 6.1 per cent; also that there were somewhat similar increases in most of the other size groups (Table 8). In order to determine growth more accurately, it is necessary to see what happens to each group of cities from one census to the next, not allowing any changes from group to group during the decade (Table 9 and Figure 8).

The rate of growth of the cities that, with their annexations during the decade, had more than 1,000,000 people in 1920 was not so great proportionally as that of the cities under 100,000 and was but little greater than that of the 500,000 to 1,000,000 group. In the 1910–1920 decade the largest cities grew more slowly than all but one other group when their growth is measured in this way. Further examination of Table 9 also shows that in one decade only (1890–1900) did the largest size group of cities grow faster than any of the smaller size groups. In gen-

TABLE 9.—POPULATION AND RATE OF INCREASE, BY SIZE OF COMMUNITY, 1820–1930[a]

Year	1,000,000 or over	500,000–1,000,000	250,000–500,000	100,000–250,000	25,000–100,000	10,000–25,000	2,500–10,000	Rural[b]	Total

NUMBER OF CITIES

Year	1,000,000 or over	500,000–1,000,000	250,000–500,000	100,000–250,000	25,000–100,000	10,000–25,000	2,500–10,000	Rural[b]	Total
1820	..	..	..	1	4	8	41	......	......
1830	..	..	..	1	6	16	58	......	......
1840	..	..	1	2	9	27	123	......	......
1850	..	1	1	5	15	41	239	......	......
1860	..	2	1	6	25	63	357	......	......
1870	..	2	5	8	36	117	532	......	......
1880	1	3	4	12	58	147	747	......	......
1890	3	..	7	17	99	226	1,004	......	......
1900	3	3	9	22	122	284	1,300	......	......
1910	3	5	11	31	179	375	1,647	......	......
1920	4	8	13	43	219	473	1,948	......	......

POPULATION (THOUSANDS)

Year	1,000,000 or over	500,000–1,000,000	250,000–500,000	100,000–250,000	25,000–100,000	10,000–25,000	2,500–10,000	Rural[b]	Total
1820	......	.....	.....	124	198	120	219	8,978	9,638
1830	......	.....	.....	203	331	244	301	11,782	12,861[c]
1840	......	.....	313	205	422	427	601	15,095	17,063[c]
1850	......	516	409	683	622	623	1,141	19,198	23,192
1860	......	1,371	267	1,043	1,136	958	1,769	24,899	31,443
1870	......	1,645	1,566	1,131	1,597	1,770	2,505	28,343	38,558
1880	1,206	1,976	1,301	1,820	2,442	2,225	3,430	35,755	50,156
1890	4,680	.....	2,462	2,811	4,404	3,394	4,681	40,516	62,948
1900	6,429	1,645	3,011	3,148	5,597	4,403	6,122	45,638	75,995
1910	8,505	3,092	3,972	4,883	8,278	5,614	7,871	49,757	91,972
1920	11,147	5,275	4,546	6,572	10,448	7,158	9,300	51,265	105,711

PERCENTAGE INCREASE[d]

Year	1,000,000 or over	500,000–1,000,000	250,000–500,000	100,000–250,000	25,000–100,000	10,000–25,000	2,500–10,000	Rural[b]	Total
1820–30	....	....	....	63.8	27.6	41.0	46.3	32.3	33.1[e]
1830–40	....	....	....	54.4	37.4	57.6	44.3	31.0	32.3[f]
1840–50	....	....	64.9	39.6	119.6	82.2	57.8	30.7	33.6[g]
1850–60	....	56.3	38.4	44.4	56.9	50.1	39.0	32.6	34.4[h]
1860–70	....	17.9	48.5	47.2	51.5	44.9	40.3	18.1	22.6
1870–80	....	24.8	35.1	28.6	36.2	32.4	29.0	29.8	30.1
1880–90	25.6	49.4	25.4	41.5	57.3	44.4	45.2	17.6	25.1[i]
1890–1900	37.4	....	23.8	25.2	29.8	25.6	25.5	16.4	20.7
1900–10	32.2	16.5	26.5	36.2	40.6	29.9	30.0	13.7	21.0
1910–20	19.3	17.7	34.9	22.3	28.8	26.5	22.1	7.0	14.9
1920–30	24.0	21.8	15.4	20.2	24.6	24.9	26.0	8.7	16.1

[a] Special compilation made for this study. The populations for the different size groups given here will not agree with those in Table 8 because these are for a group of identical cities, having identical areas at the beginning and end of the decade; while those in Table 8 are for the cities having the specified population at each census. For example, during 1920–1930 Detroit annexed certain areas. Since the 1930 populations of these annexed areas were not available, they could not be subtracted from the enlarged Detroit. In order, therefore to be able to compare identical areas for Detroit between 1920 and 1930, it was necessary to add the 1920 populations of these annexed territories to Detroit in 1920, which made its population over 1,000,000. Thus for purposes of securing the growth of cities of over 1,000,000 between 1920 and 1930, Detroit, with its intercensal annexations, was added to the group shown by the census in 1920 and the growth of the four cities was ascertained (*infra*, Note d). This growth was much less than that shown in the census because Los Angeles also came into the census group during the decade. At all censuses and in most size groups similar adjustments were neces-

eral the growth of the smaller cities has considerably exceeded that of the two or three largest size groups during any given decade. The growing concentration of population in large cities does not, therefore, arise from the more rapid growth of large cities than of small cities during

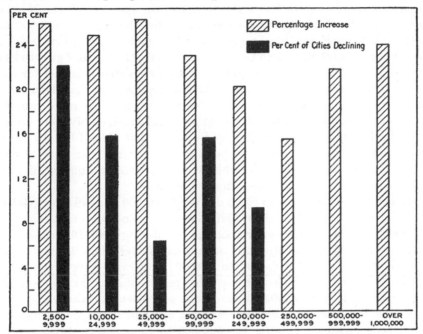

FIG. 8.—Population increase, by size of city, 1920–1930. (Based on Table 9 and Appendix Table 3.)

any given decade, but rather from the cumulative effects of city growth by which the number of cities in the large-city class is steadily increased; for once a city passes into any one of the larger size classes, it remains there and adds its numbers to this group unless it declines or again passes into a still larger size class. Only cities of over 1,000,000 do not lose population by passage to a larger size group.

sary; hence the population for any size group is likely to be different from that given in Table 8. This procedure also explains why there are no data for 1930 in the first two sections of the table.

b The attempt was to apply the 1930 definitions to preceding years, which changes the rural-urban status of a number of towns and townships in the northeastern states from that which they held in earlier censuses (see *Fifteenth Census of the United States: 1930*, Vol. I, p. 7). These rules were followed in cases where data published in the census made it possible: (1) Towns and townships classified as rural in 1930 were considered rural in preceding decades. (2) In cases where a town or township incorporated as a unit, the entire town or township is classified as urban in preceding years if its population exceeds 2,500; or if the incorporating part of a town or township contained 75 per cent or more of the total population at time of incorporation, the entire town or township is classified as urban in preceding years if its population exceeds 5,000. (3) Towns and townships not covered by the above rules but containing 2,500 or more persons in 1820, 1830, and 1840 are classified as urban if more than two-thirds of the employed population was engaged in nonagricultural pursuits. These towns and townships are also classified as urban in subsequent years if their population exceeds 2,500. (4) All other townships for which the census showed no city or village of 2,500 and over in earlier years are classified as rural. A

In comparing the growth of cities by regions,[1] certain interesting differences appear. In general it may be said that the cities of the North Center have grown faster than those of the Northeast. In only one decade (1900–1910) since the North Center had a city of over 1,000,000 did such city or cities fail to grow faster than cities of the same size in the Northeast (Appendix Table 2). The same is true for the cities of 500,000 to 1,000,000. There is not the same uniformity of more rapid growth among the smaller cities of the North Center, but even so, their rate of growth has generally been higher and since 1900 has been consistently higher for the groups between 25,000 and 500,000. Thus it is quite clear that the urbanization of population in the North Center is proceeding more rapidly than in the Northeast, although the latter is still considerably more urban than the former. In passing, it may be noted that since 1900 the rural population of the Northeast has been growing faster than that of the North Center, probably owing chiefly to the greater number of city workers who have sought homes in the country.

In the South there are no cities of over 1,000,000 and only one (Baltimore) of over 500,000; and in 1920 there were only two of 250,000 to 500,000. These three cities grew about as fast during 1920–1930 as similar cities in the North Center and somewhat faster than those in the Northeast. The cities of 25,000 to 250,000, however, have grown considerably faster than those in these other regions during the last decade; and those of 25,000 to 100,000 have done so for several decades.

In the West the growth of Los Angeles and San Francisco during the last decade raises the rate for the 500,000 to 1,000,000 group to a very high point. In other size groups also the rate of increase is in general

---

few of the more populous townships outside of New England probably contained such places, which leads to a slight exaggeration of the rural population in those years.

c Excludes persons on public ships (5,318 in 1830 and 6,100 in 1840) in the service of the United States, not credited to any state or division.

d In calculating growth for each size group, the same places are taken at the beginning and end of each decade and a place is classified according to its size at the beginning of the decade, including the population of areas annexed during the decade. Percentage increase is obtained by dividing growth as thus calculated by the population at the beginning of the decade.

e Excludes Florida (34,730) in 1830 because it was not enumerated in 1820.

f Excludes Iowa Territory (43,112) in 1840, as data are not given in 1830; persons on public ships are also excluded (5,318 in 1830 and 6,100 in 1840).

g Persons on public ships (6,100) are excluded in 1840. In 1850, California, Texas, New Mexico, and Utah (378,116) are excluded since they belonged to Mexico in 1840; Oregon (13,294) is excluded in 1850 due to boundary dispute until 1846.

h Excludes Kansas, Nebraska, and the Dakotas (140,884) in 1860 since these areas were not enumerated in 1850.

i Excludes Indian Territory (180,182) in 1890 since it was not enumerated in 1880.

[1] In many places in this monograph the nine geographic divisions used by the Bureau of the Census have been combined, for the sake of brevity, into four regions as follows: Northeast includes the New England and Middle Atlantic divisions; North Center includes the East North Central and West North Central divisions; South includes the South Atlantic, East South Central, and West South Central divisions; West includes the Mountain and Pacific divisions.

above that of other regions. This is about what would be expected from the rapid growth of the whole Pacific region.

Within the several regions the growth of cities of different sizes shows considerable variation. In the Northeast the cities of over 1,000,000 have in general grown faster since 1890 than most smaller size groups, although there are several exceptions, the most notable of which is the growth of cities of 2,500 to 10,000 during the last decade. The cities of 250,000 to 1,000,000, on the other hand, have generally grown more slowly than the still smaller cities since about 1900. Before that time their growth was more spotted, probably owing to the small number of cities in the larger size groups. In the North Center, on the other hand, only in the decades 1890–1900 and 1920–1930 have the cities of over 1,000,000 grown faster than the smaller cities. Nor is there the same uniformity of more rapid growth in the 25,000 to 250,000 group compared with the 250,000 to 1,000,000 group here as in the Northeast. In the South where there have been few cities of over 100,000, the smaller cities have generally been in the lead. In the West the largest cities have usually increased more rapidly than the smaller ones. When people move west they seem to prefer the larger cities.

Turning to a closer examination of the last decade, it will be noted that although the growth of small cities was more rapid than that of larger cities, it was far more variable. No city of over 250,000 failed to gain in population during the decade, whereas one-eighth of those between 10,000 and 250,000 and over one-fifth of those smaller than 10,000 lost in population (Figure 8 and Appendix Table 3). Furthermore, among cities gaining in population, there was a greater variation in the rate of gain for the smaller cities than for the larger.

8. GROWTH OF SATELLITE AND NON-SATELLITE CITIES

A study of the location of the smaller cities throws much light upon the factors affecting the growth of population in different localities. Most of the smaller cities having an unusually rapid rate of growth during the last decade were within a comparatively short distance of large cities and may properly be called satellites.[1] There can be little doubt that the coming of the automobile and good roads have been the most important factors in diverting some of the growth of the larger central cities to near-by smaller places. To the effects of the automobile must also be added the improvement in communication and commutation facilities around large cities and the extension of central-power-station service.[2]

[1] Satellite cities are here defined as all those cities within metropolitan districts which are not classified as "central cities" in 1930. Non-satellite cities are all cities outside of metropolitan districts.

[2] Malcolm M. Willey and Stuart A. Rice, *Communication Agencies and Social Life,* Monograph in Social Trends Series, New York, McGraw-Hill Book Company, Inc., 1933.

As a consequence, these smaller places around large cities have had a very marked growth during the last decade. This is seen clearly in Table 10 and Figure 9.

TABLE 10.—POPULATION AND RATE OF INCREASE IN METROPOLITAN DISTRICTS, CONTIGUOUS AREAS, AND NON-SATELLITE CITIES, 1920–1930[a]

Area	Population (thousands)		Increase, 1920–30		Cities declining in population, 1920–30	
	1920	1930	Number (thousands)	Per cent	Number	Per cent
Total for 96 metropolitan districts[b]	42,670	54,753	12,083	28.3	...	....
In central cities	30,907	37,815	6,908	22.3	9	7.5
Outside central cities	11,763	16,939	5,176	44.0	...	....
Satellite rural areas	4,961	7,678	2,717	54.8	...	....
Satellite cities[c]	6,802	9,261	2,459	36.2	57	10.2
100,000–250,000	326	367	41	12.5	...	....
50,000–100,000	1,038	1,251	213	20.5	5	31.2
25,000– 50,000	1,692	2,248	556	32.8	3	6.4
15,000– 25,000	1,218	1,542	324	26.6	8	12.3
10,000– 15,000	703	981	278	39.6	9	15.3
5,000– 10,000	1,018	1,504	486	47.7	14	9.6
2,500– 5,000	806	1,368	562	69.8	18	8.0
Non-satellite rural areas	46,304	48,032	1,728	3.7	...	....
Non-satellite cities[c]	16,737	19,990	3,253	19.4	466	23.0
50,000–100,000	951	1,055	104	11.0	3	20.0
25,000– 50,000	3,103	3,746	643	20.7	5	5.7
15,000– 25,000	2,766	3,402	636	23.0	23	16.0
10,000– 15,000	2,442	2,942	500	20.5	35	17.2
5,000– 10,000	3,964	4,741	777	19.6	131	23.1
2,500– 5,000	3,512	4,104	592	16.9	269	26.6
Contiguous areas[d]	1,225	1,472	247	20.2	...	....
Urban	151	174	23	15.0	...	....
Rural	1,074	1,298	224	20.9	...	....

[a] The metropolitan districts used are those of 1930 (see *Fifteenth Census of the United States: 1930*, "Metropolitan Districts"), but the cities and rural areas are classified according to their population in 1920. Territory rural in 1920 is counted rural in 1930, although it may have contained one or more incorporated places in 1930.

[b] Data for 1920 comparable with those for 1930 are available for only 85 of these districts. It was therefore necessary to estimate the 1920 populations for the areas outside 11 central cities. It is believed that only in the case of Los Angeles is there likelihood of an appreciable error.

[c] For definition of satellite and non-satellite cities, see Note 1, p. 29.

[d] The contiguous areas include all territory within a given radius from the center of the central city and not included within the metropolitan district. The radii used were as follows: central cities under 200,000, 10 miles; central cities 200,000 to 500,000, 15 miles; central cities 500,000 to 1,000,000, 20 miles; Chicago, Philadelphia, Detroit, and Los Angeles, 30 miles; New York City, 40 miles. For the rural population, the township was the unit used, so that where half or more of a township fell within the radius, the entire township population was included.

Taken as a group the satellite cities increased 36.2 per cent between 1920 and 1930, while all non-satellite cities increased by only 19.4 per cent. There is a fairly close inverse relation between the size of satellite cities and their rates of growth—the smaller the size class the higher the rate of increase. For non-satellite cities, on the other hand, the relation between size and growth tends to be direct up to 25,000—the larger the city the larger the rate of growth; after that it is inverse, as with satellite cities.

It is of further interest to note that the satellite rural areas (rural areas within metropolitan districts) grew even faster than the satellite cities as a whole. They increased by 54.8 per cent during the decade, their absolute increase being over 250,000 more than that of the satellite

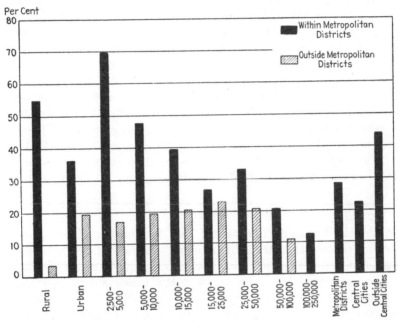

Fig. 9.—Decennial increase, by size of community within and outside of metropolitan districts, 1920–1930. (Based on Table 10.)

cities.[1] In contiguous areas also the rural population grew faster than the urban and, since it was much larger in numbers to begin with, its absolute growth was nearly ten times as great as that of the urban areas.[2] In and around metropolitan districts, therefore, the order of growth of communities of different sizes is as follows: the smallest satellite cities (2,500 to 5,000) have grown most rapidly (69.8 per cent); next in order come the satellite rural areas (54.8 per cent), then the group of satellite cities up to 50,000, followed by the central cities (22.3 per cent), and finally the satel-

[1] It should be noted in this connection that a considerable number of the people classified here as satellite-rural were, in 1930, living in cities since many rural communities of 1920 became urban during the decade.

[2] A study of the urban and rural growth of rapidly growing townships around the metropolitan districts, but beyond the radii noted in Table 10, shows that here, too, rural population grew faster than urban, the rates being 43.7 and 37.3 per cent, respectively.

lite cities of over 50,000 (18.6 per cent). When, however, absolute numbers are considered, it is found that the central cities still contain a far larger population (37,815,000) than the outside areas (16,939,000). During the decade, however, the absolute increase in the central cities was 6,908,000, while that in the metropolitan districts, but outside these cities, was 5,176,000. Clearly the outside areas are gaining on the central cities.

The basic reason for the uneven rates of growth of population in small cities seems to lie in the changing economic and social functions of many of them. Those supported in large part by agriculture are increasing little, if at all, except in a few regions where agriculture is still developing rapidly. Others fortunate in location or climate (as in Florida and California) or favored in securing new industries owing to inherent advantages in access to labor, raw materials, power, and markets (as in the piedmont of North Carolina) are growing rapidly. But as just shown, the most rapid growth of small cities and of the rural population took place within the zones of influence of the larger centers where the economic and social life of small communities is closely integrated with that of the larger community.[1] Clearly, a study of the growth of population in and around metropolitan communities is essential to an understanding of the population movements in the United States today.

9. PLACES OF MOST RAPID GROWTH

While the foregoing analysis of the distribution of the growth of population shows the large differences between certain states and size groups of cities, it does not give a wholly adequate picture of the concentration of growth from 1920 to 1930. It is important to emphasize the fact that almost three-fifths of the total population increase during this decade occurred in five well-defined groups of cities which had but 26.2 per cent of the nation's population in 1920. These five groups may be described as follows:

Group I.—The metropolitan districts of the Middle Atlantic seaboard from New York City to Baltimore by way of Philadelphia.

Group II.—The metropolitan districts of the Great Lakes region from Buffalo to Milwaukee. This includes the Akron, Canton, and Youngstown metropolitan districts in Ohio, the Flint district in Michigan, and the Fort Wayne and South Bend districts in Indiana, as well as those directly on the Lakes.

Group III.—The metropolitan districts in Tennessee, Alabama, Florida, and northern Georgia, together with the cities of 25,000 to 100,-000 in North Carolina and Florida.

[1] Robert D. McKenzie, *The Metropolitan Community*, Monograph in Social Trends Series, New York, McGraw-Hill Book Company, Inc., 1933.

Group IV.—The metropolitan districts from Kansas City to Houston, and cities in Texas of 25,000 to 100,000.

Group V.—The metropolitan districts in the Pacific states, except Spokane.

The metropolitan districts and the smaller cities in these five groups of cities increased 36.1 per cent between 1920 and 1930 compared with a 7.0 per cent increase for the remainder of the United States and 16.9 per cent for the metropolitan districts not included in these five groups (Table 11). They added a total of 10,010,000 to their populations, which is 58.7 per cent of the increase of population in the entire United States during the decade. Furthermore, over three-fifths of the increase in these five groups of cities is found in the first two which are composed entirely of metropolitan districts and which now have about 27,500,000 people concentrated in 11,962 square miles.

Since it is not possible here to go into any detail regarding the causes of this increasing concentration of population within these groups, only a few of the more important factors in each region will be mentioned. In Group I—the Middle Atlantic seaboard—the coast location and a growing sea-borne commerce are of substantial importance. If to these is added the

TABLE 11.—POPULATION AND INCREASE IN AREAS OF RAPID GROWTH, 1920–1930[a]
(Thousands)

Group	Population		Increase, 1920–30	
	1920	1930	Number	Per cent
I. Middle Atlantic seaboard......................	12,580	15,646	3,066	24.4
II. Great Lakes.	8,697	11,845	3,148	36.2
III. Southeast............................	1,627	2,499	872	53.6
IV. Southwest.............................	1,832	2,791	959	52.4
V. Pacific coast............................	3,001	4,966	1,965	65.5
Total in five groups........................	27,737	37,747	10,010	36.1
Metropolitan districts (45) not included in above groups..	15,750	18,419	2,669	16.9
Remainder of the United States................	62,224	66,609	4,385	7.0

[a] For further definition of areas, see pp. 32, 33. See also Note *b*, Table 10.

centripetal pull which New York City (its metropolitan district alone accounts for about four-fifths of the total increase in this group) is exercising upon all large-scale national and international business organization, the most potent of the factors making for growth in these metropolitan districts are accounted for. The future growth of this group, therefore, would seem to be tied up closely with the development of sea-borne commerce, both foreign and domestic, and with the trend in the organization of business. If commerce between these North Atlantic ports and the Gulf and Pacific ports, as well as with foreign countries, should continue to increase, continued growth in these coastal metropolitan districts should be expected. Likewise if business keeps on centralizing control in New York City offices and if the financial control of the world becomes centered in New York City, there can be little doubt that its metropolitan district will continue to grow more rapidly than most other parts of the country.

No one can tell what will happen in these matters, for there are conflicting tendencies which are difficult, if not impossible, to evaluate at the present time. There is no doubt that many types of manufacturing are moving their plants from cities into industrial areas either near the edges of such cities or into adjoining suburbs. But the movement of manufacturing plants into less congested areas does not generally involve a like movement for their office work. Indeed, in many cases, when the plant is moved out, the office work is moved into some downtown location, thus increasing the congestion already existing in that area. Furthermore, in the case of large concerns with several plants in different localities, there appears to be an increasing tendency to centralize the office work for all plants in some large city, and particularly New York City. Every large city shows an increasing proportion of office workers among its gainfully employed. If one can judge from their figures of growth, this centralizing movement of office workers is going on at a faster pace than the decentralizing of manufacturing plants. Thus, up to the present, the data on the growth of New York City and its adjacent territory show beyond doubt that the centripetal pull of office workers into the city has, on the whole, been much stronger than the centrifugal outthrow of employees of manufacturing establishments. The more rapid growth in population of the territory adjacent to New York City (37.6 per cent) than of the city itself (23.3 per cent) during the decade 1920–1930 is only proof that more people who work in New York City are keeping their residence outside the city itself, not that there is any substantial decentralizing force at work in this region. The general trend in business organization will have to change considerably before the growth of the New York City district will cease to claim a lion's share of the national population increase.

On the other hand, there are some indications that such great aggregations of population as that about New York City not only render living less comfortable for most of the people in them but also are inefficient in their economic activities. If proof accumulates that mere size is an economic handicap because of the expense involved in congested transportation of both persons and goods, and because of the growing difficulty of supplying services such as water, gas, electricity, telephones, and sewage disposal to densely settled areas of vast extent, and that the economic efficiency of the worker is lowered, as is frequently averred, by living under crowded conditions, then it seems not unlikely that the large Middle Atlantic cities will be the first of the metropolitan districts to feel the effects of any real centrifugal movement of population. At present, although the authors believe that there are many good economic reasons, as well as many good social reasons, why New York City should not continue to absorb the same proportion of national growth as in the past, they can find no indication in the figures of population growth that decentralization of a fundamental sort is under way. Furthermore, it is too soon to tell whether the present depression will hasten the operation of the more basic social and economic factors making for decentralization or whether it will issue in a greater concentration of industrial and commercial control in a few of the larger cities, which, with the return of more prosperous times, will result in a still more rapid growth of the populations in the great metropolitan districts.

In Group II—Great Lakes—the relatively cheap transportation of heavy raw materials afforded by the lakes (the iron and coal deposits needed for steel-making are located at opposite ends of the lakes) is probably of prime importance in the development of the steel and allied industries in these cities. It should also be noted that their central location favors the relatively cheap and expeditious delivery of the finished products of their heavy industries to a large part of the total population. Future growth here would seem to be bound up more closely with the increased use of iron and steel products than with any other one factor. Concentration of business control and of population has not yet proceeded so far in this area as in the East; hence decentralization would probably not involve so great a redistribution of population. However, the effects of any fundamental decentralizing tendency in industry and commerce would be felt here as well as on the eastern seaboard.

Within Group III—Southeast—climate is undoubtedly the most important factor in Florida; elsewhere, the combination of cheap power, cheap labor, nearness to natural resources, and improving markets is issuing in increased industry and commerce. Although these metropolitan districts and many of the smaller cities, particularly those of the piedmont, are growing rapidly, only a beginning in industrial development has been made as yet. Consequently only a small part of the total national growth (5.1 per cent) was absorbed by these cities. Any general movement towards decentralization of the great northern cities is almost certain to increase relatively the growth of population in the cities in this group.

In Group IV—Southwest—manufacturing plays but a small rôle. These cities are largely commercial centers having only a small proportion of their populations engaged in manufacturing. The expansion of the markets they serve is, therefore, the chief factor in their growth. Important elements in this expansion are the development of the cotton area in western Texas and Oklahoma, the increased oil production and refining in these states, and the increase in transportation and secondary manufacturing which naturally go with an increase in amount of goods distributed. For the future it appears unlikely that these cities will continue to grow at the recent rapid rate. Cotton is already overproduced, as is oil also. Furthermore, there is no reason to anticipate for some time the rapid development of new manufacturing industries, such as textiles or steel, since they are now overbuilt and this region does not possess any unusual natural advantages that would lead to expansion here at the expense of the areas in which these industries are already developed.

In Group V—Pacific—the factor of greatest importance is the climate which is not only pleasant to live in, but which also favors such occupations as the raising of vegetables and citrus fruits and the making of motion pictures. The growing trade with the Far East has no doubt played a part, as have also the distance from the industrial centers of the East and the discovery of large oil fields. However, the predominating influence of climate seems to be shown by the population growth of 120 per cent in southern California (excluding Imperial County) from 1920 to 1930 as compared with 29 per cent in central California (San Francisco district—four counties) and the northern Pacific port districts (Portland and Seattle—one county each). The future growth of population on the Pacific coast would seem to depend in large measure upon the extent to which the lure of climate can be made effective through the increase of a leisure or semi-leisure class which can afford to give up self-supporting work to live in the climate of its choice and through the growth of tourism, also upon the increase of commerce with the Far East. It is not a region with large natural advantages for the development of manufacturing.

The preceding description of the growth of population in the United States and its various parts raises, among others, two questions of prime importance needing further discussion. The first is: What will be the social and economic consequences of such a slackening of population growth as seems reasonably certain to take place in the near future? This will be discussed at some length in Chapter X following the presentation of detailed reasons for believing that such a slackening is probable. The second question is: What are the factors determining the growth of particular communities and is it possible to exercise control over them? This matter will be discussed briefly at this point.

10. FACTORS AFFECTING THE GROWTH OF PARTICULAR LOCALITIES

As has been intimated above, the growth of any particular region or city depends upon such a complicated interaction of economic and social factors that it is quite impossible to foretell its future population growth for any great length of time. The discovery of new and readily exploitable resources of fuel or metals would undoubtedly exert a marked influence upon the growth of the region in which such new resources were located. Perhaps the best example in the United States of such a pull of population into new fields is found in the development of the oil industry in Texas, Oklahoma, and California. But the effects of new discoveries of resources on population growth are not confined to the nation in which the resources lie. Thus the development of copper mines in South America and Rhodesia has been one of the important factors in the decline of population in some of the mining communities in Arizona and Montana. It seems not improbable that similar discoveries and developments in all parts of the world will exert an increasing influence upon the population growth of different areas in the future.

Another factor that may be of importance in this connection is the substitution of one material for another. Oil replaces coal as fuel for ships; hence Texas gains in population and prosperity while Welsh miners are displaced and fall into distress from which there is no relief in sight. Just now there is talk of steel replacing lumber in the building of houses. Should this happen, it is not difficult to imagine a decline of the lumber industry in the Northwest and a growth of the steel industry around the Great Lakes with marked effects upon population growth in both of these regions. Or it may be that in agricultural areas the family house of the future will be made of pressed fiber for which corn stalks and wheat straw will be the basic raw materials, thus reducing the consumption of all other types of building materials. These and a thousand and one other substitutions may be looked for; they will all tend to shift somewhat the locus of industry and as a consequence will affect the growth of population in different areas.

The location of trade routes has always been one of the most important, if not the most important, factor in determining the location of cities and hence of much manufacture. It follows, therefore, that any change in trade routes, either within a country or between countries, affects the growth of population in particular areas, shifting it from one place to another in accordance with the needs of commerce. Perhaps one of the best examples of modern times is the opening of the Panama Canal. The establishment of this route not only was the cause of a considerable growth of population in and near the Canal Zone but undoubtedly affected the growth of the cities on the west coast because they became thereby more economical distributing points for goods brought by water from the east coast. By the same token it made the Atlantic seaboard a more favorable location for certain industries shipping to the West than formerly when they had to depend solely on rail transportation.

It is also possible that the relatively slow growth of an inland city like Spokane as compared with Seattle is partly to be explained by the opening of this new trade route.

New methods and processes affecting the use of already known resources will also affect population growth in different countries and in different regions within a country. Thus it can scarcely be doubted that more efficient processes for the use of low-grade ores would in time alter the present distribution of steel making within the country, and hence would affect the growth of population in many communities; or that more efficient processes for the reduction of aluminum would have similar effects. New or better processes for the use of the resources of any region result either in new industries or in the expansion of industries already established. Because of the great complexity of factors involved in any new situation, it is impossible to guess what the future holds in store for different communities, but that it will bring forth many surprising changes in industrial development and population growth can scarcely be doubted.

Then, too, there is the future of world trade to consider, since it unquestionably plays an important rôle in the growth of population in many regions. There are such violently conflicting tendencies in this field that it is hazardous to assume that any of them will be determinative of the future. Certainly the most obvious trend at work today is that making for the economic self-sufficiency of nations. This is represented most clearly in the increase in number and effectiveness of the tariff barriers everywhere being erected under the stimulus of the leadership of the United States. Even when due allowance is made for the effects of the present (1933) depression, the scramble of all nations to develop their own manufacturing behind high tariffs can but tend to reduce the volume of international trade. If this tendency continues until international trade is confined chiefly to goods which can be made at home only at a prohibitive cost, those regions which have been growing because of increased volume of foreign commerce are bound to be affected and some of their people forced to find new jobs in other localities. Counteracting this effort to become self-sufficient is the fact that modern industry demands a constantly increasing variety of products. If the steel industry is to provide the numerous alloys needed by industry, it must scour the world for them and buy them wherever they are found. If men are to enjoy the food resources and other agricultural products of all climates, they must arrange to trade for them something of value to the peoples who raise them. But it is not possible to say what balance will be struck and how changes in foreign commerce will affect population growth in any particular locality at any given future time. To the authors it seems that the forces making for national self-sufficiency are now in the ascendant and that the volume of foreign trade is not likely to increase rapidly over pre-depression levels in the near future; hence the population of most regions depending largely on foreign trade is likely to grow slowly, while that of some regions may even decline during the next few decades.

11. CAN THE GROWTH OF COMMUNITIES BE CONTROLLED?

Finally, attention should be called to what may prove to be the most potent force in the regional growth of population the world has ever known; namely, national planning. One need but watch what is happening in Russia to be convinced of the possibilities of national planning as a determiner of population growth in the different regions of a nation. In general, under the national planning system of Russia, an attempt is being made to locate industries not only with due regard to nearness of raw materials, the market to be served, and the availability of labor, but also with due regard to the opportunity for a desirable manner of life among the workers. The authors have no intention of arguing here the general advantages of a national plan in locating industry and offices. They are interested, however, in calling attention to the fact that under national planning the growth of cities and regions would be organized on the basis of principles and ideals which the community has decided are good, instead of being left to the haphazard play of forces in a *laissez-faire* social order. Naturally the adoption of national planning would so alter the operation of the forces now determining the growth of the several communities that all previous experience would be of little value as a guide in predicting the growth of a particular region or city. Under national planning the size and the type of the community in which people are to live would always be a consideration in laying out new industrial and commercial projects. No region would be favored as compared with another by discriminatory freight rates and personal preferences as so often happens under the present system. There would be no such thing as a city growing beyond its ability to assure decent living conditions to its people, or of one region levying toll upon the industry of another because of the vested interests of the former. If, under the spur of economic urgency, national planning is introduced into our economic system, the growth of population in the various communities of the country will become a matter of deliberate determination leading to quite different patterns of population growth than those of the past.

In what has just been said, it is not implied that a more rational control of population growth in different communities and regions cannot be attained except under a system of national planning similar to that of Russia. Indeed, it is not difficult to conceive of an economic organization in which production and distribution are carried on in units consistent with living in garden cities, for example, if this is deemed preferable to the present crowding together in large centralized cities.

Electric communication and power, coupled with the automobile and airplane, make such an organization not only possible but entirely feasible. Closely knit businesses of enormous size can now be made up of relatively small units, these units so grouped that people need not live in the huge compact cities of today. That this has not yet been done is probably due as much to inertia as to any other one factor; but to this must be added our obsession with the virtues of bigness and the fact that directors of large enterprises have given little thought to the way in which the prevailing type of business organization affects the living conditions of the workers. Once it is realized that the growth of cities is controllable and that *living* is the aim of life, there would seem to be no insuperable obstacle to directing the growth of population into types of cities where the opportunities of the workers to live decently and comfortably are superior to those they now have.

As for the population growth of different regions, this, too, would seem quite amenable to control without waiting for national planning. According to disinterested experts, the present freight-rate structure favors the eastern seaboard as compared with the Mississippi Valley, and frequently favors certain cities and areas as compared with other cities and areas.[1] The point here is not that such rates are uneconomic, for this is self-evident, but that they have been of influence in determining the population growth of regions and communities. Many such adventitious factors in population growth can undoubtedly be largely removed without any basic change in the economic structure; their removal certainly would lead to changes in the present pattern of growth.

In closing this discussion, it is suggested that there is need to study more carefully than has been done the factors actually determining the growth of population in different localities and the effects of living in different types of communities upon economic and social life with a view to controlling the population growth of different localities in the interest of the common welfare.

---

[1] Malcolm Keir, "Economic Factors in the Location of Manufacturing Industries," *Annals of the American Academy*, Vol. 97 (September, 1921), pp. 83–92. *Cf.* pp. 90, 91. Logan G. McPherson, *Railroad Freight Rates in Relation to the Industry and Commerce of the United States*, New York, Henry Holt and Company, 1909, 441 pp. *Cf.* pp. 69, 70, and *passim*. William Z. Ripley, *Railroads: Rates and Regulation*, New York, Longmans, Green & Co., 1912, 659 pp. *Cf.* particularly Chaps. IV, V, and VII.

CHAPTER II

THE DISTRIBUTION OF THE POPULATION

1. THE DISTRIBUTION OF NATIVE WHITE STOCK

a. By Divisions.—Native whites of native parentage constitute by far the largest and most important group in the population. In every division of the nation, except in the New England and the Middle Atlantic states, the native whites of native parentage (henceforth in this chapter, the native white stock) are a clear majority of the total population; their

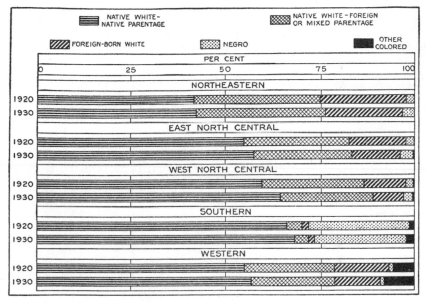

FIG. 10.—Percentage distribution of the population of certain sections, by race, nativity, and parentage, 1920–1930. (Based on *Fourteenth Census of the United States*, 1920, Vol. II, Table 12, pp. 38–39; and *Fifteenth Census of the United States;* 1930, Vol. III, Pt. 1, pp. 25–28. See also Table 12.)

proportion is everywhere increasing at the present time (Table 12 and Figure 10). From 1890, when such information first became available, until the present, the South has had the highest proportion of native white stock of any part of the country, in spite of its large percentage of Negroes. This is due to the following facts: (*a*) most European immigrants since colonial days have settled in the North and West with the conse-

POPULATION TRENDS IN THE UNITED STATES

TABLE 12.—PERCENTAGE DISTRIBUTION OF THE POPULATION, BY RACE, NATIVITY, AND PARENTAGE, UNITED STATES AND DIVISIONS, 1850–1930[a]

	1850	1870	1890	1900	1910	1920	1930
United States......................	100.0	100.0	100.0	100.0	100.0	100.0	100.0
Native white of native parentage.	74.6	72.9	54.8	53.9	53.8	55.3	57.1
Native white of foreign or mixed parentage			18.3	20.6	20.5	21.4	20.7
Foreign-born white.........................	9.7	14.2	14.5	13.4	14.5	13.0	10.9
Negro......................	15.7	12.7	11.9	11.6	10.7	9.9	9.7
Other colored......................	(b)	0.2	0.6	0.5	0.4	0.4	1.6
New England......................	100.0	100.0	100.0	100.0	100.0	100.0	100.0
Native white of native parentage	87.9	80.5	51.8	44.9	39.9	37.9	38.8
Native white of foreign or mixed parentage			23.0	28.3	31.3	35.7	37.5
Foreign-born white.........................	11.2	18.7	24.2	25.7	27.7	25.3	22.5
Negro......................	0.8	0.9	0.9	1.1	1.0	1.1	1.2
Other colored......................	(b)	(e)	0.1	0.1	0.1	0.1	(e)
Middle Atlantic......................	100.0	100.0	100.0	100.0	100.0	100.0	100.0
Native white of native parentage	80.6	77.1	50.8	47.9	43.8	43.3	43.6
Native white of foreign or mixed parentage			25.8	28.4	29.0	31.8	32.2
Foreign-born white.........................	17.3	21.2	21.5	21.4	25.0	22.1	20.1
Negro......................	2.1	1.7	1.8	2.1	2.2	2.7	4.0
Other colored......................	(b)	(e)	0.1	0.1	0.1	0.1	0.1
East North Central......................	100.0	100.0	100.0	100.0	100.0	100.0	100.0
Native white of native parentage	86.8	80.3	53.9	53.1	53.4	54.9	57.3
Native white of foreign or mixed parentage			25.8	28.8	28.0	27.6	25.9
Foreign-born white.........................	12.2	18.2	18.6	16.4	16.8	15.0	12.7
Negro......................	1.0	1.4	1.5	1.6	1.6	2.4	3.7
Other colored......................	(b)	0.1	0.1	0.1	0.1	0.1	0.3
West North Central......................	100.0	100.0	100.0	100.0	100.0	100.0	100.0
Native white of native parentage	78.4	78.8	55.8	54.7	56.1	59.6	64.3
Native white of foreign or mixed parentage			23.8	27.8	27.7	26.9	24.6
Foreign-born white...:.........................	11.3	17.4	17.3	14.8	13.9	10.9	8.0
Negro......................	10.3	3.7	2.5	2.3	2.1	2.2	2.5
Other colored......................	(b)	0.1	0.5	0.4	0.4	0.3	0.7
South Atlantic......................	100.0	100.0	100.0	100.0	100.0	100.0	100.0
Native white of native parentage	58.0	59.3	57.2	58.5	60.2	62.8	65.9
Native white of foreign or mixed parentage			3.6	3.7	3.7	3.9	4.0
Foreign-born white.........................	2.2	2.9	2.3	2.0	2.4	2.3	1.9
Negro......................	39.8	37.9	36.8	35.7	33.7	30.9	28.0
Other colored......................	(b)	(e)	(e)	0.1	0.1	0.1	0.1

TABLE 12.—PERCENTAGE DISTRIBUTION OF THE POPULATION, BY RACE, NATIVITY, AND PARENTAGE, UNITED STATES AND DIVISIONS, 1850–1930.[a]—(Continued)

	1850	1870	1890	1900	1910	1920	1930
East South Central.....................	100.0	100.0	100.0	100.0	100.0	100.0	100.0
Native white of native parentage }	65.1	64.4	62.3	62.6	64.8	68.5	70.5
Native white of foreign or mixed parentage }			3.1	3.0	2.6	2.3	2.0
Foreign-born white.....................	1.5	2.3	1.6	1.2	1.0	0.8	0.6
Negro..................................	33.4	33.2	33.0	33.1	31.5	28.4	26.9
Other colored.........................	(b)	(c)	0.1	(c)	(c)	(c)	(c)
West South Central....................	100.0	100.0	100.0	100.0	100.0	100.0	100.0
Native white of native parentage }	51.6	57.2	58.4	61.7	65.7	68.0	68.6
Native white of foreign or mixed parentage }			6.5	7.3	6.8	6.8	4.7
Foreign-born white.....................	9.2	6.3	4.6	4.0	4.0	4.5	1.4
Negro..................................	39.2	36.4	29.1	25.9	22.6	20.1	18.7
Other colored.........................	(b)	0.1	1.4	1.0	0.9	0.6	6.5
Mountain..............................	100.0	100.0	100.0	100.0	100.0	100.0	100.0
Native white of native parentage }	94.1	71.3	49.6	51.1	55.7	60.0	62.1
Native white of foreign or mixed parentage }			22.3	26.1	23.4	22.7	19.3
Foreign-born white.....................	5.8	24.4	20.2	17.2	16.6	13.6	7.8
Negro..................................	0.1	0.5	1.1	0.9	0.8	0.9	0.8
Other colored.........................	(b)	3.8	6.9	4.7	3.5	2.8	10.0
Pacific...............................	100.0	100.0	100.0	100.0	100.0	100.0	100.0
Native white of native parentage }	77.5	64.5	47.0	48.2	50.3	51.9	54.1
Native white of foreign or mixed parentage }			23.3	27.1	25.1	25.7	23.2
Foreign-born white.....................	21.4	25.6	22.6	19.6	20.5	18.6	14.2
Negro..................................	1.1	0.7	0.7	0.6	0.7	0.9	1.1
Other colored.........................	(b)	9.1	6.3	4.5	3.3	3.0	7.4

[a] For 1850 from *Seventh Census of the United States: 1850*, pp. xxxviii, xliv; 1870 from *Ninth Census of the United States: 1870*, Vol. I, pp. 6–8, 328, 336; 1890 from *Thirteenth Census of the United States: 1910*, Vol. I, pp. 146–147; 1900–1920 from *Fourteenth Census of the United States: 1920*, Vol. II, pp. 38–39; 1930 from *Fifteenth Census of the United States: 1930*, Vol. III, Pt. 1, p. 28. All Mexicans are classified as whites prior to 1930. Percentages for 1930 comparable with those for earlier years are as follows: West South Central—foreign-born white, 3.6; other colored, 0.8. Mountain—foreign-born white, 10.1; other colored, 3.2. Pacific—foreign-born white, 16.5; other colored, 2.9. Changes in other divisions are insignificant.

[b] Not enumerated.

[c] Less than one-tenth of 1 per cent.

quence that the proportion of foreign white stock[1] in the South is very small (about 5 per cent); (b) there has been little immigration of Negroes since the importation of slaves was prohibited in 1808, hence practically the entire increase in Negroes has come from the excess of births over deaths; (c) the natural increase (the excess of births over deaths) of the

[1] Foreign white stock as defined by the census and as used here includes foreign-born whites, native whites of foreign parentage, and native whites of mixed parentage.

southern whites has been higher than that of Negroes ever since the census data permit of comparison; (*d*) finally, the rapid migration of Negroes from the South since 1910[1] tends to increase the proportion of whites in its population.

Native white stock has long constituted a smaller proportion of the population in the New England and Middle Atlantic states than elsewhere; not since 1890 has this group been in the majority in either division. Since 1920, however, the downward trend in these divisions has been reversed so that by 1930 this group had regained about one-half of what it lost from 1910 to 1920.

In the East and West North Central states the upward turn in the proportion of native white stock dates from 1900; and although the movement was quite slow at first, it has become much more rapid in the last two decades. Indeed, in the West North Central states, the upward movement is now so rapid that by 1940 native white stock probably will make up a higher proportion of the total population in these states than in any other part of the country. The reasons for this rapid increase in the West North Central states are: (*a*) this region has had very little immigration for two or three decades, hence the immigrant women in these states are mostly beyond the age of childbearing and their grandchildren, who are native whites of native parentage, are becoming increasingly numerous; (*b*) the surviving immigrants and their older children are both arriving at the ages where they die in relatively large numbers, consequently the foreign stock is being steadily depleted; (*c*) the Negro population in this region is small, in spite of a 19 per cent increase in numbers from 1920 to 1930, and is not likely to increase with sufficient rapidity to offset decreases in foreign white stock. It is quite probable, therefore, that in two or three decades native white stock will constitute 90 per cent or more of the population of this division. This is of particular interest because what is happening in the West North Central states is clearly indicative of what will follow in divisions to the east if the present immigration policy is continued.[2]

b. By States.—In general, it may be said that the native white stock constitutes the largest proportion of the population in those states into which there has been the least migration in recent decades and in which

---

[1] *Infra*, p. 79.

[2] This increase in native white stock as compared with other whites should not be confused with the changes in national origins discussed in Chap. III. The proportions of the population composed of persons tracing their origin to a given country might remain unchanged although persons born in that country and their children entirely disappeared, as they will for all practical purposes in the course of the next five or six decades if present immigration policies are continued. Any change in the national origins of the population, on the other hand, depends upon changes in sources and relative numbers and upon differentials in the increase of the descendants of the people already here. The probabilities of such differentials in increase will be discussed at appropriate points below.

Negroes are relatively few. The highest percentages in 1930 were in Kentucky (86.8 per cent) and West Virginia (84.5 per cent) and are readily accounted for by this explanation. Oklahoma, which ranked third in proportion of native white stock, is, however, a marked exception to these others in that it had a very large population which moved there from the outside. Its high percentage of native white stock arises from the fact that it was settled largely by native whites from neighboring states and from the South. Next in order in 1930 came Indiana, Tennessee, Kansas, and Missouri, followed by other states, chiefly agricultural, which have received but few migrants in recent years and which have relatively few Negroes. Migrants, whether native or foreign born, are generally in search of better economic opportunities. It is quite understandable, therefore, that the population of relatively unsettled regions should contain a high proportion of foreign born and that regions of relative stability in economic opportunity should remain largely native or should become increasingly native once their attractiveness to migrants has begun to wane.

c. **By Size of Community.**—It follows naturally from what has just been said that native white stock has always been and still is preponderantly a rural and small-town population. In 1820 the white population was not subdivided by nativity, but most of it undoubtedly was native born, and nearly all of it (92.7 per cent) was rural. As recently as 1890,[1] 74.7 per cent of the native white stock lived in rural areas, but by 1930 the proportion was only 52.2 per cent, a decline of nearly one-third. For over a century, therefore, it is reasonably certain that native white stock has been becoming less rural, with the rate of change much accelerated since 1890. It will be noted, however, in comparing Tables 13 and 8 that the decline in the proportion of native white stock in the rural population has been considerably slower than the decline in the proportion of the total population in rural communities, particularly since 1870. The smaller cities, like the rural communities, contain a higher proportion of the native white stock than of the total population, but in cities of over 25,000 the opposite is the case and has been as far back as the data go.

When the percentages of native white stock in different communities are compared with those of the foreign white stock in the same communities, the fact that the former is rural is made still clearer (Figure 11). Whereas in 1890 over 82 per cent of the native white stock lived in rural communities or in cities of less than 10,000 (Table 13), only about 48 per cent of the foreign white stock lived in the same communities (Table 14); in 1930 the percentages were 62.0 and 26.1, respectively. Not only is the proportion of the native white stock in small communities much greater

[1] Native whites were not subdivided by parentage for states or subdivisions prior to the census of 1890.

than that of the foreign white stock, but it has been declining more slowly. The rural white population is, therefore, largely native of native parentage. This is an important fact and should be borne in mind. Its significance will be discussed later.

It would be a mistake, however, to assume that the native white stock has not been attracted to the cities. In 1890 cities of 250,000 persons or over contained 1,833,000 native whites of native parentage, whereas in 1930 cities of this size contained nearly six times as many, or 10,806,000.

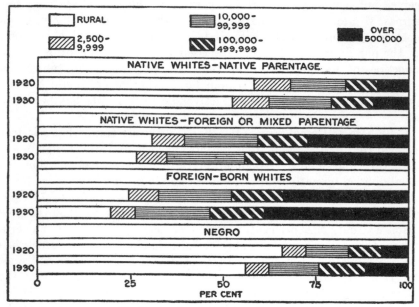

Fig. 11.—Percentage distribution by size of city of native whites of native parentage, native whites of foreign or mixed parentage, foreign-born whites, and Negroes, 1920–1930. (Based on Tables 13, 14, 21, and 25.)

The total population of these cities was barely four times as large in 1930 as in 1890; hence the growth of the native white stock in them was well above that of other groups as a whole. No doubt a considerable part of this increase is made up of the grandchildren of immigrants who settled there; but a large part of it comes from the movement to the cities of the children of natives living in the country and small towns. This is shown by the large amount of migration from the more native rural states to the more urban states[1] and by the country-to-city movement which must include many native whites of native parentage, considering their predominance in the farm population. Drs. C. J. Galpin and T. B. Manny of the Division

[1] *Fifteenth Census of the United States: 1930*, Vol. II, pp. 154–157.

TABLE 13.—NATIVE WHITE POPULATION OF NATIVE PARENTAGE AND PERCENTAGE DISTRIBUTION, BY SIZE OF COMMUNITY, 1820–1930[a]

Size of community	Total white			Native white		Native white of native parentage			
	1820	1840	1870	1870	1890	1890	1910	1920	1930
POPULATION (THOUSANDS)									
Total	7,862	14,189	33,589	28,096	45,979	34,476	49,489	58,422	70,137
1,000,000+	.....	......	......	.....	2,226	908	1,950	2,506	4,345
500,000–1,000,000	.....	......	1,581	979	535	223	998	2,289	2,247
250,000– 500,000	.....	296	1,155	753	1,602	702	1,334	2,062	4,214
100,000– 250,000	113	141	1,162	701	1,820	941	2,088	2,994	3,794
25,000– 100,000	159	385	1,565	1,060	2,926	1,792	3,767	5,102	6,848
10,000– 25,000	93	362	1,610	1,170	2,435	1,574	2,793	3,756	5,205
2,500– 10,000	206	570	2,342	1,815	3,605	2,593	4,691	5,846	6,844
Rural	7,291	12,435	24,174	21,618	30,831	25,743	31,867	33,865	36,639
Farm	.....	......	......	.....	......	......	......	20,906	20,495
Nonfarm	.....	......	......	.....	......	......	......	12,959	16,144
PERCENTAGE DISTRIBUTION									
Total	100.0	100.0	100.0	100.0	100.0	100.0	100.0	100.0	100.0
1,000,000+	.....	.....	.....	.....	4.8	2.6	3.9	4.3	6.2
500,000–1,000,000	.....	.....	4.7	3.5	1.2	0.6	2.0	3.9	3.2
250,000– 500,000	.....	2.1	3.4	2.7	3.5	2.0	2.7	3.5	6.0
100,000– 250,000	1.4	1.0	3.5	2.5	4.0	2.7	4.2	5.1	5.4
25,000– 100,000	2.0	2.7	4.7	3.8	6.4	5.2	7.6	8.7	9.8
10,000– 25,000	1.2	2.6	4.8	4.2	5.3	4.0	5.6	6.4	7.4
2,500– 10,000	2.6	4.0	7.0	6.5	7.8	7.5	9.5	10.0	9.8
Rural	92.7	87.6	72.0	76.9	67.1	74.7	64.4	58.0	52.2
Farm	.....	.....	.....	.....	.....	.....	.....	35.8	29.2
Nonfarm	.....	.....	.....	.....	.....	.....	.....	22.2	23.0

[a] From a special compilation made for this study and from *Fourteenth Census of the United States: 1920*, Vol. II, p. 90. Since native whites of native parentage were not listed separately prior to 1890, in order to have some basis of comparison with earlier dates, the percentage distribution of the native white population is given for 1870 and 1890 and of the total white population 1820–1870. In 1820 the result is probably but little different from what that for native whites of native parentage alone would have been; by 1840, however, enough foreign born were here to affect the rural-urban distribution to some extent. In 1870 native whites can be separated from all whites, but enough of these were the children of immigrants to reduce the proportion rural appreciably below what it would have been if only native whites of native parentage were considered. The decline of the proportion of rural native whites of native parentage between 1820 and 1890 is, therefore, slightly exaggerated by the above figures.

of Farm Population and Rural Life in the Department of Agriculture estimate that there was a net migration from the farms of 6,296,000 in the 10 years 1920–1929.[1] But in spite of this vast cityward movement, a large

[1] C. J. Galpin and T. B. Manny, "Farm Population Now Increasing," *The Agricultural Situation*, Vol. 16, No. 11 (November 1, 1932), pp. 2–5. See also Edmund deS. Brunner and J. H. Kolb, *Rural Social Trends*, Monograph in Social Trends Series, New York, McGraw-Hill Book Company, Inc., 1933 particularly Chap. I.

TABLE 14.—FOREIGN-BORN WHITE POPULATION AND PERCENTAGE DISTRIBUTION BY SIZE OF COMMUNITY, 1870–1930[a]

Size of community	1870	1890	1910	1920	1930
POPULATION (THOUSANDS)					
Total..................................	5,494	9,122	13,346	13,713	13,366
1,000,000+...............................	.....	1,355	3,091	3,195	4,085
500,000–1,000,000......................	602	261	780	1,449	1,104
250,000– 500,000......................	400	699	961	763	897
100,000– 250,000......................	460	732	983	1,138	1,053
25,000– 100,000......................	504	983	1,653	1,747	1,706
10,000– 25,000......................	439	725	956	985	1,021
2,500– 10,000......................	527	781	1,108	1,080	861
Rural.................................	2,558	3,587	3,813	3,356	2,640
Farm..................................	.....	.....	......	1,433	1,084
Nonfarm...............................	.....	.....	......	1,922	1,555
PERCENTAGE DISTRIBUTION					
Total..................................	100.0	100.0	100.0	100.0	100.0
1,000,000+...............................	.....	14.9	23.2	23.3	30.6
500,000–1,000,000......................	11.0	2.9	5.8	10.6	8.3
250,000– 500,000......................	7.3	7.7	7.2	5.6	6.7
100,000– 250,000......................	8.4	8.0	7.4	8.3	7.9
25,000– 100,000......................	9.2	10.8	12.4	12.7	12.8
10,000– 25,000......................	8.0	7.9	7.2	7.2	7.6
2,500– 10,000......................	9.6	8.6	8.3	7.9	6.4
Rural.................................	46.6	39.3	28.6	24.5	19.7
Farm..................................	.....	.....	.....	10.4	8.1
Nonfarm...............................	.....	.....	.....	14.0	11.6

[a] From special compilation made for this study and from Fourteenth Census of the United States: 1920, Vol. II, p. 90. All Mexicans were classified as whites prior to 1930.

part of which undoubtedly consists of native white stock, this group is vastly predominant in rural areas and small towns, comprising 68.1 per cent of the total rural population. It is almost four times as numerous as the foreign born and their children combined, and more than twice as numerous as all other rural dwellers (Table 15).

In this connection it is also of interest to note how the proportions of the native white stock in the populations of different sizes of communities are changing. All sizes of communities have become steadily more native since 1890, with the exception of the three cities of 1,000,000 and over between 1890 and 1910 (New York, Chicago, and Philadelphia). This exception is probably due to the vast influx of "new" immigrants into these cities from about 1900 to 1914 and to the high birth rates of these newcomers. Although, with the foregoing exceptions, all the larger cities have grown more native, their rates of progress in this direction are

TABLE 15.—PERCENTAGE DISTRIBUTION OF THE POPULATION IN COMMUNITIES OF DIFFERENT SIZES, BY RACE AND NATIVITY, 1870–1930[a]

Size of community	Year	Native whites of native parentage	Native whites of foreign or mixed parentage	Foreign-born whites	Negroes
1,000,000+	1890	24.8	36.0	37.0	2.1
	1910	22.9	37.9	36.4	2.6
	1920	24.7	39.7	31.5	3.9
	1930	28.8	36.6	27.1	6.2
500,000–1,000,000	1870	60.5		37.3	2.2
	1890	27.6	38.7	32.3	1.3
	1910	33.1	35.0	25.9	5.9
	1920	36.8	34.1	23.3	5.3
	1930	39.0	34.1	19.1	7.1
250,000– 500,000	1870	61.5		32.8	5.7
	1890	28.7	36.8	28.5	4.9
	1910	33.8	35.3	24.3	6.1
	1920	45.4	29.7	16.8	7.7
	1930	53.0	22.8	11.3	11.7
100,000– 250,000	1870	54.4		35.8	8.9
	1890	33.8	31.5	26.3	8.2
	1910	43.1	28.1	20.3	8.0
	1920	45.9	27.1	17.5	9.3
	1930	50.3	25.9	14.0	8.0
25,000– 100,000	1870	62.4		29.7	7.8
	1890	41.8	20.4	22.9	8.6
	1910	45.9	26.5	20.1	7.3
	1920	49.3	26.6	16.9	7.0
	1930	53.0	25.0	13.2	7.4
10,000– 25,000	1870	67.2		25.2	7.4
	1890	45.8	25.0	21.1	7.9
	1910	50.6	24.5	17.3	7.4
	1920	54.1	24.6	14.2	6.9
	1930	57.2	23.7	11.2	6.9
2,500– 10,000	1870	71.9		20.9	7.1
	1890	54.0	21.1	16.3	8.4
	1910	57.7	20.5	13.6	8.0
	1920	60.9	20.6	11.3	7.0
	1930	64.5	18.7	8.1	6.8
Rural	1870	75.9		9.0	14.8
	1890	63.2	12.5	8.8	14.8
	1910	64.0	13.4	7.7	14.3
	1920	65.9	13.5	6.5	13.4
	1930	68.1	12.5	4.9	12.4
Rural-farm	1920	66.7	11.9	4.6	16.3
	1930	68.0	11.0	3.6	15.5
Rural-nonfarm	1920	64.6	16.2	9.6	9.0
	1930	68.2	14.6	6.6	8.5

[a] From a special compilation made for this study and from *Fourteenth Census of the United States: 1920*, Vol. II, p. 90. All Mexicans were classified as whites prior to 1930. The percentages do not add to 100 because "other colored" are not included.

by no means the same. During the last 40 years, the proportion of the population which the native white stock constitutes in cities of 1,000,000 and over has increased only 4 points, or about one-sixth; in cities of 500,000 to 1,000,000 the increase was 11.4 points, or over two-fifths; while in cities of 250,000 to 500,000 the proportion increased 24.3 points, almost doubling. One important reason for the very high rate of increase of native white stock in this class of cities is the movement of a number of southern cities into it during the last decade. These southern cities have very few foreign born; hence their inclusion increases the native white stock of the group they enter more than would a similar movement among northern cities. The high proportional increase of native white stock in this class of cities between 1910 and 1920 is attributable to the addition of a number of cities in the North Central and Western states whose foreign born were rapidly dying out and to the loss of three cities with relatively high proportions of foreign born in 1910.

It is also of interest that whereas in 1890 only rural communities and cities of less than 10,000 were more than half of native white stock, in 1910 the cities of 10,000 to 25,000 joined them. Between 1910 and 1920 no new group became more than half native white stock, but between 1920 and 1930 all groups of less than 500,000 entered this class. The smallest proportional increase of native white stock during this period was in the rural communities which were already largely composed of this group.

This general increase of native white stock will be much accelerated during the next three or four decades if the present restrictions on immigration are continued and will be most marked in just those communities which heretofore have had a high proportion of foreign-born whites and their children; namely, the larger cities. As the foreign-born whites and their children die out, the proportion of native whites of native parentage automatically rises, provided, of course, the number of Negroes does not increase so rapidly as to replace the former.[1]

By Regions.—The proportion of the native white stock living in rural and urban areas varies considerably from one part of the country to another. In the Northeast, where there are many large cities and where industry and commerce are the most important sources of livelihood, one-third of this nativity group lived in rural communities in 1930 (Appendix Table 4). About 45.0 per cent lived in rural areas and cities of less than 10,000 compared with 54.6 per cent in 1910 and 67.5 per cent in 1890. In the North Center, however, the percentages were 59.2, 74.1, and 84.7, respectively, for these years. In the South they were still higher, being 76.0 per cent, 86.5 per cent, and 91.3 per cent, respectively. In the West they were 54.6 per cent, 66.8 per cent, and 77.3 per cent.

---

[1] See p. 74 for a discussion of the distribution of Negroes.

Conversely, the proportion of the native white stock in the larger cities (over 250,000) in 1930 was low in the South (7.6 per cent), more than twice as high in the North Center (17.4 per cent), about three times as high in the West (22.2 per cent), and still higher (22.9 per cent) in the Northeast. The type of work a region offers largely determines the distribution of its population in different sizes of communities. It should be noted, however, that a population settled on the land, as is the native white stock of the United States, is slower to take advantage of new opportunities in the cities than an immigrant population that has already broken its home ties and set forth in search of new economic-opportunity. When the nature of the opportunity offered changes, as from agricultural to industrial and commercial, the immigrant newly arrived responds almost immediately to the new conditions, while the second or later generation native weighs the relative advantages of his present situation against an unknown and uncertain new situation and frequently ends by remaining where he is. Besides, the American farmer and small-town resident on the whole have had less to gain by going to the city than the peasant immigrant has.

There are also significant differences between regions in the proportion which native white stock constitutes of the population of cities of different sizes (Appendix Table 5). In the Northeast there is no clearly marked trend in the proportion of native white stock in the population of cities of over 1,000,000, the proportion having declined from 26.7 per cent in 1890 to 23.8 per cent in 1910 and then risen to 25.0 per cent in 1920. There was almost no change between 1920 and 1930 (0.3 per cent). In the North Center, on the other hand, the proportion of the population composed of native white stock increased almost one-half in the cities of this size during this same period, most of the increase taking place during the last decade. In Los Angeles, the only city of 1,000,000 and over not in these two regions, the proportion of native white stock in the population is almost twice as great as in the big cities of the Northeast and two-thirds greater than in those of the North Center.

In the smaller cities there are also interesting differences in the proportions of native white stock in the populations of the several regions. The effects of the vast "new" immigration are clearly marked in the smaller cities in the Northeast where these immigrants concentrated. Thus the proportion of the population composed of native white stock in these cities showed practically no increase between 1890 and 1920 and in some groups showed even a decrease; for example, in the cities of 25,000 to 100,000 it declined from 39.9 per cent in 1890 to 38.7 per cent in 1920. In all the other regions there was a steady increase in all sizes of cities, except the 100,000 to 250,000 group in the West.

In the rural population also there is a distinct difference between the Northeast and the other regions. In the former, native white stock constitutes a steadily decreasing proportion of the population, while elsewhere there has been a steady increase of about the same relative size.

Naturally as the proportions of the native white stock in the populations of these several communities and regions change, the proportions of the other nativity and racial groups change. These shifts will be discussed in the appropriate places.

For the future it would seem that the movement of native stock to the cities will be determined, as in the past, by the relative advantages of country and city as seen by members of the group. It seems not improbable, however, that the stoppage of immigration will tend to hasten the cityward movement of native stock, both white and Negro, provided, of course, that the general industrial and commercial expansion of cities interrupted by the depression is resumed; and provided further that the present structure of the processes of production and distribution of goods is not essentially altered.

The larger measure of rural and small-town dwellers among the natives is significant in a number of respects. For one thing it affects the relative rates of growth of groups having different national origins because, as is shown on pages 280 to 282, the rate of natural increase is considerably higher in the more rural states than in the more urban states and the larger cities. In the course of time this greater rural concentration of native stock might well alter the national origins of the white population if immigration should cease and if differentials in birth rates persist, since immigrants from the countries of northern and western Europe settled on farms to a much greater extent than those from southern and eastern Europe.

A second matter of some importance is that a high rurality of native white stock tends to emphasize the inevitable rural-urban conflict, by adding to rural-urban differences the differences of nativity and accompanying outlook on life. An illustration is that whites of native parentage in rural districts and small towns are largely Evangelical Protestant while many cities have a large amount, if not a preponderance, of foreign stock of Catholic or Jewish faith. All such differences tend to make rural-urban understanding more difficult.

In the political field, the unwillingness of the rural group in many legislatures and in Congress to reapportion representation on the basis of the present distribution of population is undoubtedly intensified by the fact that generally the political power of the foreign-stock groups would be enhanced by such a reapportionment. If, however, the present immigration policy is continued for three or four decades, the foreign-born whites will have largely died out; hence this aspect of the rural-urban conflict will no longer be of the same importance. It seems likely, however, that a certain amount of native-alien antagonism will embitter the rural-urban conflict for some time after the foreign-born whites cease to constitute such a large part of the population of the larger cities (about 21 per cent in cities of over 250,000). It can hardly be hoped that these attitudes grounded in nationality and religion will change abruptly with the passing of the foreign-born whites instead of being carried on in lessening degree to their children.

Still another factor of some significance connected with the preponderant rurality of the native whites of native parentage is that they rather unconsciously sense the fact that leadership in many lines is passing from them to people who are in large measure alien. It is easy to understand their resentment against being relegated to a less important place in the community. Perhaps this may be thought of as another phase of the rural-urban conflict referred to above; but even so, it serves to show how this native-alien segregation tends to complicate all aspects of economic and political life. There seems little reason to doubt that a more uniform distribution of both native and foreign-born white stock throughout all types of communities would foster mutual understanding and would make it more difficult for demagogues to play on the traditional prejudices of the different groups.

d. **Interdivisional Migration.**—As far back as the data are available, the older divisions of the country have exported a large number of persons of native white stock to the newer divisions. Since 1890 all of the divisions east of the Mississippi River have shown net losses of native white stock through interdivisional migration (Table 16). In 1920 the West North Central states also showed a net loss for the first time, and in 1930 their net loss was greater than the combined loss of the three northern divisions east of the Mississippi River and was second only to that of the East South Central states. This latter division was the heaviest loser in absolute numbers both in 1930 and 1920 (1,345,000 and 1,130,000, respectively) through the interchange of natives. In 1910, however, the East North Central division was the largest loser (1,067,000), while in 1900 and in 1890 the Middle Atlantic states had the largest net losses. The Pacific division has shown the largest gains in the last two censuses (2,292,000 in 1930 and 1,452,000 in 1920). In both of these censuses the West South Central division was second in its gains. In 1910 and 1900 this division ranked first, with the Pacific division in second place in 1910, and the West North Central division in second in 1900. In 1890 the West North Central division gained more than all other divisions together.

The east-west nature of this interdivisional movement is clearly seen in the fact that for every person of native white stock born west of the Mississippi River and living east of it in 1930 about three and one-half moved in the opposite direction.[1] In 1920 the ratio was 1:5.6. It should be noted in this connection, however, that about two and one-half times as much of the native white stock was born east of the Mississippi River as west of it.[2] Although all the divisions east of the Mississippi River have been losing native white stock for several decades through interdivisional migration, New Jersey, Michigan, and Florida are conspicuous as having large net gains since 1910, each gaining in excess of 275,000 persons in 1930 and 150,000 in 1920.[2] The District of Columbia also had a net gain of about 100,000 in 1930.

TABLE 16.—NATIVE WHITE POPULATION OF NATIVE PARENTAGE, BY DIVISION OF RESIDENCE, BY DIVISION OF BIRTH, AND NET GAIN OR LOSS BY INTERDIVISIONAL MIGRATION, 1890–1930[a]

Division	Net gain or loss (thousands)					1930		
	1890	1900	1910	1920	1930	Persons living in (thousands)	Persons born in (thousands)	Percentage gain or loss
New England.........	− 323	−214	− 180	− 142	− 183	3,152	3,335	− 5.5
Middle Atlantic.......	−1,065	−865	− 741	− 648	− 412	11,365	11,777	− 3.5
East North Central...	− 534	−661	−1,067	− 835	− 319	14,453	14,773	− 2.2
West North Central...	1,563	934	282	− 300	−1,069	8,518	9,587	−11.2
South Atlantic.......	− 582	−520	− 486	− 321	− 334	10,395	10,780	− 3.1
East South Central....	− 606	−749	− 955	−1,130	−1,345	6,964	8,309	−16.2
West South Central...	780	1,094	1,344	1,170	796	8,332	7,536	10.6
Mountain............	311	383	671	755	575	2,287	1,712	33.6
Pacific..............	464	544	1,133	1,452	2,292	4,376	2,083	110.0

[a] For 1890 from *Eleventh Census of the United States: 1890*, Vol. I, Pt. 1, pp. 568–571; 1900 from *Twelfth Census of the United States: 1900*, Vol. I, Pt. 1, pp. 694–697; 1910–1930 from *Fifteenth Census of the United States: 1930*, Vol. II, p. 143. Persons born in outlying possessions, at sea or abroad, and those for whom state of birth was not reported are omitted.

This statement of the interdivisional and trans-Mississippi movements may possibly give an exaggerated impression of the length of the average journey of internal migrants. An examination of the 1930 distribution of the native white population will correct this impression.[2] Of 23.5 per cent of this group not living in the state of birth, almost one-half (11.3 per cent) lives in adjacent states, while a little over half (12.2 per cent) lives in other states. It is also of interest that a state to the west as a rule claims more than one to the east, and a state to the north more than one to the south.[3] Some examples will illustrate the general nature of the interstate movement of native white stock. Of about 290,000 native

[1] *Fifteenth Census of the United States: 1930*, Vol. II, p. 139.

[2] *Loc. cit.*

[3] The Kansas-Oklahoma, Georgia-Florida movements are conspicuous exceptions. In states along the Canadian border, northward movement cannot be taken into account.

whites of native parentage born in Massachusetts who do not live there, about 190,000 live in other New England states and in the Middle Atlantic states; of the more than 1,149,000 persons born in Illinois who do not live there, over one-third are living in adjacent states and an additional 250,000 in the East North Central and the West North Central divisions. The opposite tendency—namely, to move long distances—is well illustrated by California, which stands out conspicuously as drawing heavily from the entire nation. It is a claimant to a high place as the domicile of migrants from all states, even attracting as many as 6–10 per cent of all the migrants of native white stock from New York and each of the East North Central states. The fact remains, however, that almost half of the native white interstate migrants choose new homes in states that are adjacent to their old homes.

Although the automobile has probably caused some changes in the distribution of internal migrants, its chief influence has probably been to render the flow more sensitive to pull exerted by the different areas and the different kinds of jobs available. In the future, as in the past, the movement will be in the direction of economic opportunities. These are no longer in farming, but rather in industry and trade, so that there will be a building up of towns and cities in regions having advantages for such activities. On this account internal migration is quite certain to show less westward movement; but whether it will be more or less northward is difficult to judge. Tending to maintain the northward movement is the fact that the rate of natural increase of population is much larger in the South than in the North and West.[1] The South can supply the people for a considerable industrial and commercial development of its own and still have many left over to move elsewhere. Thus the 1930 census shows that the net loss of the South Atlantic and East South Central states through interdivisional migration of native white stock alone was about 1,680,000 in spite of fairly rapid gains in the population of this nativity group during the last three or four decades.

The division showing the greatest mobility of its native white stock in 1930 is the Mountain, with 26.4 per cent of those born there living elsewhere. Next come the West North Central states with 25.4 per cent, and then the East South Central and East North Central states, with 22.6 per cent and 16.0 per cent, respectively; at the foot of the list is the Pacific division with 7.9 per cent.[2] The high rate of the movement of native white stock from the Mountain, the West North Central, and the East South Central states is probably in part due to their relatively high birth rates during the last three or four decades, and in part due to the fact that they are not so favorably situated for the development of

[1] See Table 79, p. 281.
[2] Loc. cit.

industry as are many other parts of the country. It is not surprising, therefore, that they have had large surpluses of young people to send elsewhere. Furthermore, in the West North Central states the mechanization of agriculture has gone far and as a consequence much technological unemployment on the farms has resulted. Naturally the displaced workers have sought new jobs in more industrialized regions.

2. THE DISTRIBUTION OF THE FOREIGN-BORN WHITES[1]

a. By Divisions.—The most noticeable fact about the distribution of the foreign-born whites is their concentration in the Northeast and the Great Lakes states. In 1850, when such information first became available, New England had 13.6 per cent of the foreign born, the Middle Atlantic states 45.4 per cent, and the East North Central states 24.6 per cent (Table 17). These three divisions together had 83.6 per cent of the foreign born, a larger proportion than they have ever had since, although they are again approximating this proportion with 77.3 per cent in 1930 after falling to a low point of 70.0 per cent in 1890. The Middle Atlantic states in particular have had rather violent fluctuations in their percentage of the foreign-born white, the proportion dropping from 45.4 per cent in 1850 to 30.0 per cent in 1890, and then rising again to 39.4 per cent in 1930. Furthermore, most of this variation took place in New York, which had 29.2 per cent of the foreign born in 1850 but only 17.2 per cent in 1890. It has been gaining rather rapidly since 1890 and now has 23.9 per cent. The proportion of foreign born in New Jersey has grown steadily from 2.7 per cent in 1850 to 6.3 per cent in 1930. In Pennsylvania there has been comparatively little variation since 1870, the percentage today (9.2) being just what it was in 1890. Both the New England states and the East North Central states have maintained a fairly regular porportion of the foreign-born whites, although during the 1850's, 1860's, and 1870's, while there was still much good land to be had cheaply in the latter division, it attracted a somewhat larger proportion than it has since. During the time that the states west of the Mississippi were being settled, chiefly from 1870 to 1890, the proportion of the foreign born in other parts of the country declined, but recently the divisions east of the Mississippi and north of the Ohio have claimed an increasing proportion of the foreign-born whites, while the West North Central states have lost both in proportion and in actual numbers. The result is that in 1930 this division had but 7.9 per cent of the foreign born, or less than one-half as many proportionally as it had in 1890. This is no doubt the direct con-

[1] For more details regarding the distribution of the foreign born, see Chap. III of Niles Carpenter, *Immigrants and Their Children: 1920*, (Census Monograph VII) Washington, Government Printing Office, 1927, 431 pp.
    This monograph goes into considerable detail on almost all phases of the composition of the foreign stock.

sequence of the fact that there has been only a small amount of new land available for settlement in these states since the decade 1890–1900. Because there was also little industrial development in this region, the more recent immigrants were not attracted thither.

TABLE 17.—FOREIGN-BORN WHITE POPULATION AND PERCENTAGE DISTRIBUTION BY DIVISIONS, 1850–1930[a]

Area	1850	1870	1890	1900	1910	1920	1930
POPULATION (THOUSANDS)							
United States	2,241	5,494	9,122	10,214	13,346	13,713	13,366
New England	305	647	1,138	1,437	1,814	1,871	1,834
Middle Atlantic	1,018	1,871	2,737	3,302	4,826	4,913	5,269
East North Central	551	1 659	2,506	2,620	3,067	3,223	3,224
West North Central	100	672	1,547	1,531	1,613	1,372	1,059
South Atlantic	104	166	202	209	291	316	304
East South Central	49	103	101	90	87	72	58
West South Central	86	127	217	264	349	459	170
Mountain	4	78	245	288	437	453	288
Pacific	23	173	428	472	861	1,034	1,160
PERCENTAGE DISTRIBUTION							
United States	100.0	100.0	100.0	100.0	100.0	100.0	100.0
New England	13.6	11.8	12.6	14.1	13.6	13.6	13.8
Middle Atlantic	45.4	34.1	30.0	32.3	36.1	35.8	39.4
East North Central	24.6	30.2	27.4	25.7	23.0	23.5	24.1
West North Central	4.5	12.2	17.0	15.0	12.1	10.0	7.9
South Atlantic	4.6	3.0	2.1	2.0	2.2	2.3	2.2
East South Central	2.2	1.9	1.1	0.9	0.6	0.5	0.5
West South Central	3.9	2.3	2.4	2.6	2.6	3.3	1.3
Mountain	0.2	1.4	2.7	2.8	3.3	3.3	2.0
Pacific	1.0	3.1	4.6	4.6	6.5	7.5	8.7

[a] For 1850 from *Seventh Census of the United States: 1850*, p. xxxviii; 1870 from *Ninth Census of the United States: 1870*, Vol. I, p. 336; 1890, 1900, and 1910 from *Thirteenth Census of the United States: 1910*, Vol. I, pp. 146–147; 1920 from *Fourteenth Census of the United States: 1920*, Vol. II, pp. 38–39; 1930 from *Fifteenth Census of the United States: 1930*, Vol. III, Pt. 1, p. 26. All Mexicans are classified as whites prior to 1930.

The southern states have never had many foreign-born whites. The three southern divisions together had 10.7 per cent in 1850, but the proportion has been declining ever since, with the result that they have but 4 per cent at the present time.[1] It seems highly probable that the necessity of competing with the Negroes was the most important factor in keeping the foreign-born whites who wished to farm or become wage earners from

[1] The proportion found in Texas prior to 1930 is not quite comparable with the latest count because foreign-born Mexicans are included with foreign-born whites at earlier dates, while they are excluded in 1930. However, even when allowance is made for this fact, the trend is as described.

settling in the South, although the fact that the industrial development of this region lagged behind that of the North was also a matter of importance.

In the period following the settlement of the western Mississippi Valley, the Mountain states had a rather large increase in foreign-born whites, attaining a maximum of 3.3 per cent in 1910. Since then there has been a decline and they have but 2.0 per cent now. On the west coast, on the other hand, the increase of the foreign-born whites has been very rapid and has exceeded that of the total population. This division now contains about one-twelfth of all the foreign-born whites as compared with about one-fifteenth of the total population.

The importance of the foreign-born whites during the last decades in the populations of the several divisions is a reflection of their distribution, as noted above. In 1850 the foreign born were considerably more important in the population of the Pacific states (21.4 per cent) than in the Middle Atlantic states (17.3 per cent) and almost twice as important as in the New England and North Central states (Table 12). Then, as in later years, the foreign born were a small part of the population in the South, with the exception of Texas, where there have always been many Mexican immigrants. Between 1850 and 1870 there were marked increases in all the northern and western divisions, the largest being from 5.8 per cent to 24.4 per cent in the Mountain states. By 1890 New England had the highest proportion of foreign born in its population (24.2 per cent), closely followed by the Pacific (22.6 per cent), Middle Atlantic (21.5 per cent), Mountain (20.2 per cent), East North Central (18.6 per cent), and West North Central (17.3 per cent) states. In the 40 years that followed there were only slight changes in the New England and Middle Atlantic states, but decreases of about one-third in the East North Central and Pacific states and of over one-half in the West North Central and Mountain states. In 1930 foreign-born whites constituted about one-fifth of the population in the New England and Middle Atlantic divisions, one-seventh in the Pacific division, one-eighth in the East North Central division, one-thirteenth in the Mountain division, one-twelfth in the West North Central division, and one-seventieth in the South.[1]

In general, it may be said that during the period of rapid land settlement following the Civil War a relatively large proportion of the foreign-born whites moved westward, at first into the western Mississippi Valley, then on to the Mountain and west coast states. Since 1890–1900, however, they have shown a marked preference for the industrial centers of the Northeast (including the Great Lakes area) and the west coast.

[1] See Table 12. If Mexicans are classified in 1930 as in prior censuses, these fractions would be increased somewhat for the Pacific, Mountain, and southern divisions (see Note a, Table 12).

By Country of Birth.—Table 18 showing the three leading nationalities in the United States and its geographic divisions since 1850 will assist the reader in visualizing the distribution of the foreign born. In New England the Irish ranked first in 1850, having 65.7 per cent of all the foreign-born whites; first in 1890 with 36.2 per cent; second in 1910 with 18.6 per cent; and below third in 1930. The Canadians were second in 1850 with 16.4 per cent; also second in 1890 with 33.4 per cent. Since then they have ranked first. British have been third during this entire period with 13.7 per cent in 1850 and 12.3 per cent in 1930. Only in 1930 has one of the "new" immigrant groups, the Italians, taken one of the first three places; they were second then with 13.8 per cent.

This grouping of foreign-born whites in New England is not difficult to understand. Canada, as a rural neighbor against whom no barrier was raised naturally, furnished numerous workers for all of New England's industries. Then, too, the seaboard location made it relatively easy to secure such European immigrants as might be needed by New England's industry and commerce. The British in particular were attracted by the abundant opportunities for skilled laborers in textiles, brass, and tools; while the demand for unskilled labor was met first by the Irish and later by French Canadians and Italians.

In the Middle Atlantic states also the Irish were in the lead in 1850, constituting 52.3 per cent of all the foreign born. They lost this place to the Germans by 1890 (30.5 per cent), who in turn yielded to the Russians in 1910 (18.5 per cent), while the latter were superseded by the Italians in 1930 (19.8 per cent). These four nationalities occupy second place, with the Germans interchanging places with the Irish and the Russians with the Italians. British stock occupied third place in 1850 (18.3 per cent) and 1890 (16.1 per cent) but yielded to the Germans in 1910 (15.6 per cent), who in turn were displaced by the Poles in 1930 (11.7 per cent). The rather rapid shifting in the importance of the different nationalities in these states is correlated with the fact that New York has long been the chief port of entry for immigrants and has retained those who could readily find jobs. Hence each new group of large proportions has soon taken high rank in this division. There can be little doubt that much of the industrial activity of the New York-New Jersey area and even of Pennsylvania has been based upon the abundance of cheap immigrant labor entering the port of New York. Pennsylvania, for all its great industries and large population, has never had so high a proportion of the foreign born as might have been expected. It has generally had only about half as many as New York.

In the East North Central states the Germans have held first place ever since 1850, the percentage varying from 42.0 in 1890 to 16.1 per cent in 1930. Second place was held by the Irish in 1850 (23.2 per cent) and

TABLE 18.—FOREIGN-BORN WHITE POPULATION RANKED BY LEADING COUNTRY OF BIRTH, UNITED STATES AND DIVISIONS, 1850, 1890, 1910, AND 1930ᵃ

Area and year	First — Country of birth	First — Per cent of total foreign-born white population	Second — Country of birth	Second — Per cent of total foreign-born white population	Third — Country of birth	Third — Per cent of total foreign-born white population	Per cent from three leading countries
United States:							
1850	Ireland	43.5	Germany	25.9	Great Britain	17.2	86.6
1890	Germany	30.5	Ireland	20.5	Great Britain	13.7	64.7
1910	Germany	18.8	Russia	12.0	Ireland	10.1	40.9
1930	Italy	12.8	Germany	11.5	Great Britain and Northern Ireland	10.0	34.3
New England:							
1850	Ireland	65.7	Canada	16.4	Great Britain	13.7	95.8
1890	Ireland	36.2	Canada	33.4	Great Britain	15.4	85.0
1910	Canada	29.2	Ireland	18.6	Great Britain	11.5	59.3
1930	Canada	28.2	Italy	13.8	Great Britain and Northern Ireland	12.3	54.3
Middle Atlantic:							
1850	Ireland	52.3	Germany	20.7	Great Britain	18.3	91.3
1890	Germany	30.5	Ireland	30.2	Great Britain	16.1	76.8
1910	Russia	18.5	Italy	16.2	Germany	15.6	50.3
1930	Italy	19.8	Russia	12.5	Poland	11.7	44.0
East North Central:							
1850	Germany	40.8	Ireland	23.2	Great Britain	19.7	83.7
1890	Germany	42.0	Ireland	11.5	Great Britain	11.4	64.9
1910	Germany	30.1	Norway, Denmark, and Sweden	10.5	Austria	10.4	51.0
1930	Germany	16.1	Poland	12.8	Canada	9.0	37.9
West North Central:							
1850	Germany	53.9	Ireland	20.8	Great Britain	12.1	86.8
1890	Germany	33.3	Norway, Denmark, and Sweden	27.7	Ireland	9.4	70.4
1910	Norway, Denmark, and Sweden	29.6	Germany	26.5	Russia	7.4	63.5
1930	Norway, Denmark, and Sweden	30.5	Germany	21.2	Russia	7.7	59.4
South Atlantic:							
1850	Ireland	43.4	Germany	36.0	Great Britain	14.6	94.0
1890	Germany	39.2	Ireland	23.1	Great Britain	14.7	77.0
1910	Germany	21.4	Russia	16.6	Italy	13.0	50.9
1930	Great Britain and Northern Ireland	13.1	Italy	13.0	Germany	12.5	38.6

TABLE 18.—FOREIGN-BORN WHITE POPULATION RANKED BY LEADING COUNTRY OF BIRTH, UNITED STATES AND DIVISIONS, 1850, 1890, 1910, AND 1930.ᵃ—(Continued)

Area and year	First		Second		Third		Per cent from three leading countries
	Country of birth	Per cent of total foreign-born white population	Country of birth	Per cent of total foreign-born white population	Country of birth	Per cent of total foreign-born white population	
East South Central:							
1850	Ireland	57.2	Germany	25.6	Great Britain	15.2	88.0
1890	Germany	43.5	Ireland	23.0	Great Britain	15.3	81.8
1910	Germany	33.2	Great Britain	12.8	Ireland	11.8	57.8
1930	Germany	20.9	Great Britain and Northern Ireland	13.6	Italy	12.5	47.0
West South Central:							
1850	Germany	31.0	Ireland	30.9	France	14.5	76.4
1890	Germany	32.3	Mexico	23.8	Ireland	9.1	65.2
1910	Mexico	37.0	Germany	20.0	Italy	9.1	66.1
1930	Mexico	61.1	Germany	8.8	Italy	5.1	75.0
Mountain:							
1850	Great Britain	36.7	Mexico	33.9	Ireland	9.8	80.4
1890	Great Britain	29.4	Norway, Denmark, and Sweden	17.4	Germany	12.6	59.4
1910	Great Britain	17.3	Norway, Denmark, and Sweden	15.5	Mexico	10.5	43.3
1930	Mexico	23.1	Norway, Denmark, and Sweden	14.5	Great Britain and Northern Ireland	13.5	51.1
Pacific:							
1850	Mexico	28.5	Great Britain	19.6	Germany	13.6	61.7
1890	Germany	20.9	Ireland	17.7	Great Britain	16.4	55.0
1910	Norway, Denmark, and Sweden	16.2	Germany	14.4	Great Britain	12.3	42.9
1930	Mexico	14.3	Norway, Denmark, and Sweden	13.1	Great Britain and Northern Ireland	12.8	40.2

ᵃ For 1850 from *Seventh Census of the United States: 1850*, p. xxxvii. Colored persons born in foreign countries outside Asia and Africa are included with whites. For 1890 and 1910 from *Thirteenth Census of the United States: 1910*, Vol. I, pp. 884-885. Colored persons born in foreign countries outside Asia are included with whites; in 1910 these colored persons constituted about one-third of 1 per cent of all foreign born. In 1880 the Bureau of the Census included persons reported born in Poland under "other Europe"; and in 1910 distributed (in so far as possible) such persons under Germany, Austria, and Russia. For 1930 from *Fifteenth Census of the United States: 1930*, Vol. III, Pt. 1, p. 58. Foreign-born Mexicans are included with whites.

1890 (11.5 per cent), by the Scandinavians in 1910 (10.5 per cent), and by the Poles in 1930 (12.8 per cent). The British held third place in 1850 (19.7 per cent) and 1890 (11.4 per cent); in 1910 the Austrians (10.4 per cent) took it, to yield to the Canadians in 1930 (9.0 per cent). The newer nationalities have been slower coming here than to the Northeast, in spite of the intense industrial and commercial development along the Great Lakes.

This slow penetration of the newer immigrant is even more marked in the West North Central states, where Germans and Scandinavians have long monopolized first and second places because there has been no important industrial development.

In the South there is little of interest to note. The Irish, Germans, and British were predominant at practically all dates, with Italians and Russians occasionally in second and third places in recent years. In the West South Central division Mexicans appear in second place in 1890 (23.8 per cent) and in first place in 1910 (37.0 per cent) and in 1930 (61.1 per cent).

In the Mountain states the British and Scandinavians were greatly predominant most of the time, although Mexicans were second in 1850 (33.9 per cent) and first in 1930 (23.1 per cent).

On the west coast Mexicans were in first place in 1850 (28.5 per cent). In 1890 Germans (20.9 per cent) were most numerous, and in 1910 the Scandinavians, who in turn yielded to the Mexicans in 1930. The British have always been important here, holding second place in 1850 (19.6 per cent) and third place ever since. The Germans, after rising to first place in 1890 (20.9 per cent), were second in 1910 (14.4 per cent) and then lost rank.

This brief survey of the leading foreign-born white groups in different parts of the country is of even more significance if studied in connection with Table 19 and Figure 12 showing the distribution of the leading nationalities by divisions.

The distribution of the different national groups is approximately what would be expected in view of the preceding discussion. More than one-half of three of the newer nationalities, Italians, Russians, and Austro-Hungarians, are found in the Middle Atlantic states, and almost one-half of the Poles. Of the older immigrants, only the Irish are almost as heavily concentrated, 48.5 per cent being in the Middle Atlantic states. With the exception of the Austro-Hungarians, these same groups are also well represented in New England. Consequently from two-thirds to three-fourths of these four groups of foreign born live in the northeastern part of the country, which contains only about 28 per cent of the total population. Why the Irish should have been the only group among the older immigrants to concentrate so heavily in the Northeast, it is impossible to say with any assurance. It may have been due to the greater initial pov-

TABLE 19.—PERCENTAGE DISTRIBUTION OF THE FOREIGN BORN FROM CERTAIN COUNTRIES, BY DIVISIONS, 1870–1930[a]

Country and year	New England	Middle Atlantic	East North Central	West North Central	South Atlantic	East South Central	West South Central	Mountain	Pacific
Italy:									
1870............	4.1	27.0	9.5	6.6	4.6	6.3	12.3	2.2	27.5
1880............	7.8	44.0	8.7	3.7	3.1	2.7	7.2	5.3	17.6
1890............	9.2	55.8	9.1	2.9	2.7	1.2	5.5	4.1	9.6
1900............	12.7	60.1	9.2	2.2	2.2	0.7	4.7	3.0	5.4
1910............	13.4	58.4	10.9	2.8	2.9	0.6	2.4	2.6	6.1
1920............	14.8	57.5	12.6	2.1	2.5	0.5	1.7	1.7	6.5
1930............	14.1	58.4	13.7	1.8	2.2	0.4	1.2	1.3	6.8
Germany:[b]									
1870............	1.7	31.4	40.9	14.5	4.2	2.4	2.6	0.4	1.9
1880............	1.8	30.0	39.8	16.6	3.6	2.0	2.9	0.8	2.5
1890............	2.3	30.0	37.9	18.5	2.9	1.6	2.5	1.1	3.2
1900............	2.6	30.1	38.2	17.6	2.6	1.3	2.6	1.2	3.7
1910............	2.8	30.2	36.8	17.1	2.5	1.1	2.8	1.7	4.9
1920............	3.0	30.1	35.1	17.4	2.4	1.0	2.8	2.0	6.1
1930............	3.1	35.6	32.6	14.2	2.4	0.8	2.4	1.8	7.2
England, Scotland and Wales:									
1870............	10.9	38.1	29.8	8.7	2.8	1.5	0.9	3.7	3.5
1880............	12.0	35.1	26.8	11.0	2.7	1.2	1.4	5.4	4.3
1890............	14.1	35.3	22.9	11.4	2.4	1.2	1.4	5.8	5.6
1900............	15.9	35.8	21.5	9.7	2.4	1.1	1.5	6.0	6.1
1910............	17.0	35.5	19.4	8.1	2.6	0.9	1.6	6.2	8.6
1920............	17.4	34.0	20.3	6.7	3.0	0.8	1.6	5.5	10.7
1930[c]............	16.1	38.0	20.9	4.4	2.9	0.6	1.2	3.6	12.4
Russia:[b]									
1870[d]............	4.8	38.6	18.2	9.3	4.4	3.4	5.4	2.4	13.5
1880[d]............	1.7	19.0	11.4	58.7	1.3	0.7	1.4	1.3	4.5
1890[d]............	6.5	44.4	15.2	23.1	3.2	0.7	0.8	1.9	4.3
1900............	11.0	56.2	13.6	11.3	3.5	0.7	1.3	0.8	1.5
1910............	12.0	55.7	17.2	7.4	3.1	0.5	0.9	1.2	2.1
1920............	11.9	52.9	18.3	7.4	3.4	0.5	1.0	1.8	3.0
1930[e]............	10.8	54.1	18.0	6.5	3.1	0.4	0.8	1.6	4.6
Canada:									
1870............	32.3	18.6	33.6	10.5	0.5	0.5	0.3	1.2	2.6
1880............	33.9	14.0	32.6	12.7	0.5	0.3	0.6	2.0	3.5
1890............	38.8	11.2	28.1	12.9	0.6	0.3	0.5	2.6	5.1
1900............	43.3	11.8	25.2	10.6	0.6	0.3	0.6	2.7	4.9
1910............	43.7	12.3	22.7	8.5	0.7	0.3	0.7	3.0	8.0
1920............	42.3	12.3	22.6	7.2	1.2	0.3	0.8	3.0	10.4
1930............	40.4	14.1	23.0	4.9	1.4	0.2	0.7	2.1	13.1
Poland:[b]									
1920............	11.5	45.2	35.3	3.4	2.2	0.2	0.6	0.4	1.1
1930............	10.8	48.8	32.8	2.7	2.1	0.2	0.5	0.4	1.6
Norway, Denmark, and Sweden:									
1870............	1.3	5.1	42.3	43.4	0.3	0.9	0.8	3.7	2.3
1880............	2.6	6.6	35.0	47.1	0.4	0.3	0.8	4.4	3.0
1890............	4.7	8.1	30.0	46.0	0.3	0.2	0.7	4.6	5.5
1900............	6.6	9.9	29.1	42.2	0.4	0.2	0.9	4.9	6.0
1910............	6.9	11.3	25.6	38.1	0.5	0.2	0.9	5.4	11.1
1920............	7.2	12.0	24.7	35.3	0.7	0.2	1.0	5.7	13.3
1930............	7.3	15.5	25.2	29.4	0.9	0.2	0.9	4.8	15.8

TABLE 19.—PERCENTAGE DISTRIBUTION OF THE FOREIGN BORN FROM CERTAIN COUNTRIES, BY DIVISIONS, 1870–1930.ª—(Continued)

Country and year	New England	Middle Atlantic	East North Central	West North Central	South Atlantic	East South Central	West South Central	Mountain	Pacific
Ireland:									
1870............	19.4	45.9	17.4	7.2	3.2	2.0	1.2	0.6	3.1
1880............	20.0	44.7	16.6	8.0	3.0	1.6	1.3	1.2	3.7
1890............	22.1	44.3	15.4	7.8	2.6	1.3	1.1	1.6	4.1
1900............	24.0	45.0	14.8	6.9	2.3	1.0	0.9	1.7	3.5
1910............	24.7	45.5	13.3	5.8	2.0	0.7	0.9	2.0	5.0
1920............	25.8	45.5	13.0	4.8	1.9	0.6	0.8	1.9	5.6
1930ʄ...........	25.9	48.5	12.6	3.2	1.6	0.4	0.7	1.4	5.7
Austria-Hungary:ᵇ ᵍ									
1870............	1.0	13.4	44.6	31.2	2.0	1.1	4.2	0.6	1.9
1880............	1.0	19.1	36.1	33.4	1.8	0.6	5.0	0.8	2.2
1890............	1.7	37.6	27.8	22.4	1.7	0.5	4.4	1.8	2.2
1900............	4.8	48.4	24.8	13.0	1.5	0.4	3.3	2.2	1.7
1910............	5.2	49.2	28.7	8.4	1.8	0.3	1.8	2.2	2.4
1920............	3.9	51.5	30.3	5.7	2.3	0.4	1.1	1.7	3.1
1930............	3.6	54.7	28.4	4.7	2.2	0.4	0.9	1.2	4.0
Czechoslovakia:									
1920............	2.7	34.2	39.7	14.0	1.8	0.2	4.3	1.5	1.7
1930............	3.3	40.6	38.8	9.4	1.7	0.2	3.0	1.0	2.1
Yugoslavia:ᵍ									
1920............	1.4	28.4	42.7	10.7	2.1	0.5	0.7	6.4	7.1
1930............	0.6	25.9	48.5	8.1	1.4	0.3	0.5	5.7	9.0
Greece:									
1870............	9.0	22.1	6.4	2.8	4.9	7.4	18.2	4.1	25.1
1880............	6.7	17.7	14.4	3.4	7.5	3.2	10.2	2.8	34.1
1890............	4.4	27.6	19.0	2.4	8.9	4.0	10.1	3.2	20.3
1900............	24.7	25.3	24.2	2.4	7.9	2.5	3.1	3.7	6.2
1910............	16.6	15.7	17.7	13.8	4.6	1.4	1.7	13.1	15.5
1920............	18.3	25.3	25.6	6.4	6.5	1.1	2.0	5.5	9.4
1930............	14.6	29.3	28.1	4.6	6.6	1.3	1.9	3.8	9.8

ª In 1930 includes foreign-born whites only. Percentages for 1870 to 1910 calculated from *Thirteenth Census of the United States: 1910*, Vol. I, pp. 800, 834–835; for 1920 from *Fourteenth Census of the United States: 1920*, Vol. II, pp. 697–699; and for 1930 from *Fifteenth Census of the United States: 1930*, Vol. III, Pt. 1, p. 53.

ᵇ Prior to 1900 persons reported as born in Poland are included under "other Europe"; for the censuses of 1900 and 1910 they are distributed under Austria-Hungary, Germany, and Russia, respectively.

ᶜ Includes Northern Ireland.

ᵈ Includes Finland.

ᵉ Includes Lithuania.

ʄ Irish Free State.

ᵍ Prior to 1920 Czechoslovakia and Yugoslavia included with Austria-Hungary.

erty of the Irish, which made land settlement more difficult for them, to the difference in religion (most American farmers being Protestant), or to a more complex group of social and economic factors not readily apparent. In any event, the Irish more nearly resemble the "new" immigrants in their distribution than they do the other "old" immigrants who came in at the same time.

In the early days of Italian and Russian immigration, the west coast attracted a relatively large proportion; as late as 1890 Italians were more numerous in the Pacific states than in New England. Why Italians should have turned from the west coast to the Northeast is not clear, although the shift probably is causally related to the change in the source of Italian immigrants from northern to southern Italy and to Sicily. This change in source may in turn be the consequence of the direction of our national development, which was such as to demand cheap unskilled industrial laborers rather than farmers and skilled artisans.

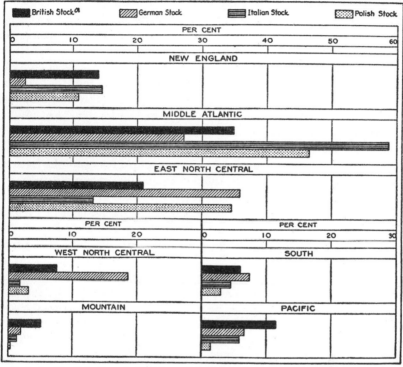

a Includes English, Scotch, Welsh, and North Irish.

FIG. 12.—Percentage distribution of British, German, Italian, and Polish stock in the United States, by divisions, 1930. (Based on Table 19.)

b. By Size of Community.—The first point of importance to notice here is that the foreign-born whites have always concentrated rather heavily in the larger cities. In 1870, when only 10.7 per cent of the total population lived in cities of over 100,000 (Table 8, p. 24), 26.7 per cent of the foreign born lived in such cities (Table 14, p. 48, and Figure 11, p. 46). By 1890 the percentages were 15.4 and 33.5, respectively; by 1910 they were 22.1 and 43.6; and by 1930 they had become 29.6 and 53.5. Thus these larger cities have long contained a higher proportion of the foreign born than of the native born, a situation that has grown steadily more marked since

1870. The increasing concentration has been especially noticeable in the largest cities; those of over 500,000 contained 38.9 per cent of all foreign-born whites in 1930 as compared with 17.8 per cent in 1890 and 11.0 per cent in 1870. The converse of the situation just described is the marked decline in the proportion of the foreign born living in rural communities and small cities. In 1870, 46.6 per cent of the foreign-born whites lived in rural communities and an additional 9.6 per cent in cities of less than 10,000. Subsequent declines lowered these percentages to 39.3 and 8.6, respectively, in 1890; to 28.6 and 8.3 in 1910; and to 19.7 and 6.4 in 1931.

Although an increasing proportion of the foreign-born whites have been going to the larger cities, they constitute a decreasing proportion of the total population in these cities as well as in all other sizes of communities (Table 15). This situation results chiefly from the fact that in recent years the rate of increase of foreign-born whites has been well below that of the total population (Table 4, p. 7). Thus the foreign born made up 37.3 per cent of the total population of cities of over 500,000 in 1870, but only 24.9 per cent in 1930. The declines during the last 60 years have been even more marked in some of the other size groups; for example, from 34.6 per cent to 12.6 per cent in the 100,000 to 500,000 group. In rural communities the foreign-born whites never constituted a very large part of the whole: 9.0 per cent in 1870, 8.8 per cent in 1890, 7.7 per cent in 1910, and 4.9 per cent in 1930 (Table 15, p. 49). With the rapid dying off of the older rural immigrants, the foreign born will soon be a negligible proportion of the rural population.

By Regions.—The distribution of the foreign-born whites between communities of different sizes varies considerably from one section of the country to another, as would be expected. In the Northeast, where considerably more than half of the foreign born live, they are, and always have been, more highly concentrated in the large cities—33.1 per cent in cities of over 250,000 in 1870, 36.4 per cent in 1890, 45.1 per cent in 1910, and 48.5 per cent in 1930—than in the North Center, where the percentages were 4.8, 18.1, 32.4, and 45.3 at the dates given (Appendix Table 6). In the latter region, as these figures show, there have been an even more rapid concentration of the foreign-born whites in large cities than in the Northeast and a correspondingly greater decline in the proportion in rural areas. In the North Center 63.2 per cent of the foreign born lived in rural communities in 1870, 53.0 per cent in 1890, 39.7 per cent in 1910, and only 26.0 per cent in 1930.

In the South the percentage of foreign-born whites in the cities of over 100,000 has always been relatively high. In 1870, 36.5 per cent lived in these larger southern cities, but the percentage declined to 27.8 in 1890 and to 23.5 in 1910, with a rise to 44.8 in 1930. On the other hand, the rural foreign-born white population in the South was always relatively small; 40.7 per cent of the foreign born lived in rural communities in 1870, 43.4 per cent in 1890, 46.8 per cent in 1910, but only 31.8 per cent in 1930. The percentages of rural native white stock were generally about twice as great, as has been shown above (p. 50). Comparatively few of the foreign-born whites in the rural communities of the South went into the Negro belt, most of them being found in the parts of Texas, Maryland, Florida, and West Virginia which have few Negroes. But, as was said, the South attracted relatively few foreign-born white at any time. The number in 1930 was about the same as in 1890.

In the West the general distribution of the foreign-born whites by size of community is much the same as elsewhere. The foreign born have been concentrating rapidly in the larger cities and declining in the rural areas, both relatively and absolutely; 42.9 per cent of them now live in cities of over 100,000, compared with 26.9 per cent in 1870, 18.7 per cent in 1890, and 30.2 per cent in 1910. However, this concentration in large cities is not confined to the foreign born. There has been an equally rapid increase in the proportion of the total population living in such cities, from 15.1 per cent in 1870 to 24.2 per cent in 1910 and to 31.6 per cent in 1930. Here, as elsewhere, the significant point is that the concentration of the foreign-born population in the larger cities is, and always has been, considerably in excess of that of the total population. In 1890 the proportion of the foreign born living in the cities of over 100,000 was less than in 1870. It will be recalled that a similar decline occurred in the South. In the South, however, this was not the case for the total population as it was in the West. The explanation of the situation in the West is found in the peculiar conditions of settlement in California connected with the gold rush and subsequent mining operations.

The entire study of the distribution of the foreign-born whites emphasizes the predominant importance of economic opportunity in their settlement here. In the period between 1850 and 1890, when land settlement offered a real opportunity for economic improvement, vast numbers of immigrants, particularly the British, the Germans, the Scandinavians, and the Canadians, went to the land directly or within a few years after their arrival. Even in 1930 goodly proportions of them were found in the northern Mississippi Valley, although their numbers have been declining in the agricultural areas of this region since about 1890. Sometimes the corresponding increase was found in the West and sometimes in the Northeast. But since 1900 settlement on the land has held few attractions for the immigrant. This was an important reason for the slackening of immigration from northwestern Europe and the coming of poorer peoples who had not the means of settling on land no matter how much they may have preferred to do so. Because these poorer peoples had to work for wages, they stayed in cities where wage jobs could be found, the capital being supplied by the "boss." Whatever immigration may be in the future, it is practically certain that it will go where industry and commerce are located, for they are capable of an expansion of which agriculture is not.

3. THE DISTRIBUTION OF THE NATIVE WHITES OF FOREIGN OR MIXED PARENTAGE[1]

a. By Divisions.—There is much similarity in the distribution of this group (Table 20) and that of the foreign-born whites (Table 17). Children

TABLE 20.—NATIVE WHITE POPULATION OF FOREIGN OR MIXED PARENTAGE AND PERCENTAGE DISTRIBUTION, BY DIVISIONS, 1890–1930[a]

Area	1890	1900	1910	1920	1930
POPULATION (THOUSANDS)					
United States..................................	11,504	15,646	18,898	22,686	25,361
New England...................................	1,080	1,579	2,053	2,642	3,064
Middle Atlantic...............................	3,276	4,402	5,591	7,098	8,453
East North Central...........................	3,480	4,602	5,108	5,925	6,553
West North Central..........................	2,129	2,874	3,215	3,378	3,267
South Atlantic................................	322	390	440	554	633
East South Central..........................	197	229	215	203	195
West South Central..........................	310	478	605	697	576
Mountain.......................................	271	436	617	757	715
Pacific..	439	656	1,054	1,432	1,905
PERCENTAGE DISTRIBUTION					
United States..................................	100.0	100.0	100.0	100.0	100.0
New England...................................	9.4	10.1	10.9	11.6	12.1
Middle Atlantic...............................	28.5	28.1	29.6	31.3	33.3
East North Central...........................	30.2	29.4	27.0	26.1	25.8
West North Central..........................	18.5	18.4	17.0	14.9	12.9
South Atlantic................................	2.8	2.5	2.3	2.4	2.5
East South Central..........................	1.7	1.5	1.1	0.9	0.8
West South Central..........................	2.7	3.1	3.2	3.1	2.3
Mountain.......................................	2.3	2.8	3.3	3.3	2.8
Pacific..	3.8	4.2	5.6	6.3	7.5

[a] For 1890, 1900, and 1910 from *Thirteenth Census of the United States: 1910*, Vol. I, pp. 146–147; 1920 from *Fourteenth Census of the United States: 1920*, Vol. II, pp. 38–39; 1930 from *Fifteenth Census of the United States: 1930*, Vol. III, Pt. 1, p. 25. All Mexicans are classified as whites prior to 1930.

of the foreign-born whites naturally would tend to show concentration in the same areas as their parents, although being a younger generation their present distribution reflects the distribution of the foreign born during the preceding three to six decades as well as their present distribution. Thus

[1] For more details regarding the distribution of native whites of foreign or mixed parentage, see Niles Carpenter, *op. cit.*, Chap. III.

it will be noted that there were but 33.3 per cent of the natives of foreign or mixed parentage in the Middle Atlantic states in 1930, while there were 39.4 per cent of the foreign born in these states. In the West North Central states, on the other hand, the proportion of the natives of foreign or mixed parentage was 12.9 per cent, while the proportion of the foreign born was only 7.9 per cent. Since about 1900 the Middle Atlantic states have been getting a larger and larger share of the foreign born, while the West North Central states have attracted but few; hence the higher proportion of natives of foreign or mixed parentage than of foreign born in the latter division. During the next few decades, assuming the continuance of the quota restrictions on immigration, there will be a rapid increase in the proportion of natives of foreign or mixed parentage in the total whites of foreign stock. This change will be particularly large in the Northeast where such a high proportion (53.2 per cent) of the foreign born now live, although it will also be considerable in the North Center.

In the South, as would be expected, there are comparatively few natives of foreign or mixed parentage. The three southern divisions combined contained but 5.6 per cent of this group in 1930. The proportion has been declining slowly and will probably continue to do so.

It will be recalled that in recent years every division has shown a decline in the proportion of the total population composed of foreign-born whites (Table 12, p. 42). Among the natives of foreign or mixed parentage there is a distinct difference in trend in their proportion of the total population between the New England and Middle Atlantic states and the other divisions. In these two northeastern divisions the proportion of the population composed of native whites of foreign or mixed parentage has been increasing steadily ever since the records became available, while in the rest of the divisions there has been either a decline for the last two or three decades, or practically no change. Thus in New England this group composed only 23.0 per cent of the total population in 1890 but increased to 37.5 per cent in 1930; in the Middle Atlantic states the percentages were 25.8 and 32.2, respectively. In the East and West North Central states a decline commenced in 1900 and has continued since. This is also true for the Mountain and Pacific states, except that in the latter there was a slight increase between 1910 and 1920. In the southern divisions the trends are a little mixed; but since the proportion of native whites of foreign or mixed parentage in the population is so small (4 per cent), they scarcely merit detailed discussion.

The most significant fact in the distribution of this part of the native whites is, therefore, their increasing importance in the Northeast. It seems highly probable that they will continue to form a higher proportion of the total population in this region for the next two or three decades, since (a) as the foreign-born whites decline, the proportion in other groups automatically rises; (b) this group is younger in this region than in the agricultural states and will, therefore, suffer slower diminution by death; and (c) it is still being recruited by births to a greater extent than in other regions. However, many shifts in population might take place in this region which would alter this trend; for example, the migration of great numbers of Negroes into the cities, the relaxation of present immigration restrictions, or a shifting of population from large to small cities which would affect the various nativity groups differently. Two or three decades of restricted immigration, however, will automatically lower the proportion of native whites of foreign or mixed parentage in the population and increase the proportion of native whites of native parentage.

b. By Size of Community.—The native whites of foreign or mixed parentage, like the foreign born, show a tendency to concentrate in the larger cities although to a lesser extent. Thus in 1890, when 25.5 per cent of the foreign-born whites lived in cities of 250,000 or over (Table 14, p. 48), only 22.0 per cent of the natives of foreign or mixed parentage lived in

TABLE 21.—NATIVE WHITE POPULATION OF FOREIGN OR MIXED PARENTAGE AND PERCENTAGE DISTRIBUTION, BY SIZE OF COMMUNITY, 1890–1930[a]

Size of community	1890	1910	1920	1930
POPULATION (THOUSANDS)				
Total	11,504	18,898	22,686	25,361
1,000,000+	1,318	3,230	4,035	5,517
500,000–1,000,000	312	1,054	2,123	1,961
250,000– 500,000	900	1,392	1,350	1,810
100,000– 250,000	879	1,359	1,766	1,952
25,000– 100,000	1,134	2,171	2,745	3,228
10,000– 25,000	861	1,353	1,709	2,158
2,500– 10,000	1,012	1,666	1,977	1,987
Rural	5,088	6,673	6,980	6,749
Farm	......	......	3,733	3,305
Nonfarm	......	......	3,247	3,443
PERCENTAGE DISTRIBUTION				
Total	100.0	100.0	100.0	100.0
1,000,000+	11.5	17.1	17.8	21.8
500,000–1,000,000	2.7	5.6	9.4	7.7
250,000– 500,000	7.8	7.4	5.9	7.1
100,000– 250,000	7.6	7.2	7.8	7.7
25,000– 100,000	9.9	11.5	12.1	12.7
10,000– 25,000	7.5	7.2	7.5	8.5
2,500– 10,000	8.8	8.8	8.7	7.8
Rural	44.2	35.3	30.8	26.6
Farm	.....	.....	16.5	13.0
Nonfarm	.....	.....	14.3	13.6

[a] From special compilation made for this study and from *Fourteenth Census of the United States: 1920*, Vol. II, p. 90.

these cities (Table 21). In 1930 the percentages were 45.6 and 36.6, respectively. In the smaller cities the proportions for the two groups are much the same. In the rural communities the natives of foreign or mixed parentage have long exceeded the foreign-born whites by a substantial proportion, the respective percentages being 44.2 and 39.3 in 1890, 35.3 and 28.6 in 1910, and 26.6 and 19.7 in 1930. This wider or more general distribution of the natives of foreign or mixed parentage among the different sizes of communities is undoubtedly due in large measure to the more rural distribution of the foreign born a generation ago. From 1840 to about 1900 a relatively large proportion of the natives of foreign or mixed parentage were born and brought up in rural communities. Naturally, therefore, the proportion of them still living in rural communities exceeds that of the foreign born, for more of the latter have gone directly to the larger cities since 1900. The size of communities in which the foreign born lived prior to 1870 cannot be obtained, but at that time almost half of them lived in rural communities, and an additional 9.6 per cent lived in cities of 2,500 to 10,000 (Table 14, p. 48). This fact is quite sufficient to explain the greater rurality of the natives of foreign or mixed parentage (since 1890) as compared with the foreign born.

By Regions.—The proportions of the native whites of foreign or mixed parentage in the several sizes of communities differ considerably between regions. These variations are most marked in the two regions, the Northeast and the North Center, where the numbers are not greatly different. In the Northeast the proportion in the large cities has been high ever since 1890. At that time it was 20.8 per cent in cities of over 1,000,000 and 42.0 per cent in cities of over 100,000; by 1930 the percentages were 29.6 and 51.3, respectively (Appendix Table 7). The corresponding percentages in the North Center in 1890 were 7.3 and 21.2, and in 1930, 18.7 and 38.7. Since the natives of foreign or mixed parentage were also more concentrated in the smaller cities of the Northeast than in those of the North Center, there is, of course, a very marked difference between these regions in the proportions in the rural districts. In the Northeast only about one-fourth (24.5 per cent) were in the rural districts in 1890 and the proportion fell to less than one-sixth (15.1 per cent) in 1930. In the North Center, on the other hand, 58.4 per cent lived in the rural districts in 1890 and 36.2 per cent in 1930. Without doubt these differences are largely the consequence of the fact that many of the immigrants who came into the North Center during the last 80 years settled on the land, while but few of those in the Northeast went to the farm.

The distribution of the native whites of foreign or mixed parentage in the South is so much like that in the North Center that it needs no special attention beyond noting that it is preponderantly urban in a region which is still largely rural. In the West the similarity of their distribution to that in the North Center is even greater, so that little need be said about it except that Los Angeles and San Francisco, the only cities of over 500,000, are not industrial cities and hence have not drawn so large a proportion of immigrants and their children as some of the eastern cities have.

There is also a considerable difference between the distribution by size of community of the native whites of foreign parentage and those of mixed parentage. Whereas in 1930, 24.7 per cent of the former lived in cities of over 1,000,000, only 15.7 per cent of the latter lived in such cities; in 1910 the percentages were 19.4 and 12.0, respectively (Table 22). If all cities of over 250,000 are considered, the percentages in 1930 are 40.0 for the native whites of foreign parentage and 29.8 for those of mixed parentage. Conversely, a larger proportion of persons of mixed parentage than of foreign

TABLE 22.—POPULATION AND PERCENTAGE DISTRIBUTION OF NATIVE WHITES OF FOREIGN PARENTAGE AND NATIVE WHITES OF MIXED PARENTAGE, BY SIZE OF COMMUNITY, 1910–1930[a]

Size of community	Native whites of foreign parentage			Native whites of mixed parentage		
	1910	1920	1930	1910	1920	1930
POPULATION (THOUSANDS)						
Total........................	12,916	15,695	16,999	5,982	6,992	8,362
1,000,000+......................	2,512	3,209	4,201	718	827	1,316
500,000–1,000,000.....................	765	1,531	1,404	289	592	558
250,000– 500,000.....................	983	931	1,191	409	419	619
100,000– 250,000.....................	947	1,257	1,335	412	509	616
25,000– 100,000.....................	1,508	1,913	2,172	663	833	1,056
10,000– 25,000.....................	914	1,168	1,413	439	541	745
2,500– 10,000.....................	1,082	1,297	1,243	585	680	744
Rural.........................	4,206	4,390	4,040	2,467	2,590	2,708
Farm.........................	.....	2,282	1,954	.....	1,450	1,352
Nonfarm.........................	.....	2,107	2,087	.....	1,140	1,357
PERCENTAGE DISTRIBUTION						
Total........................	100.0	100.0	100.0	100.0	100.0	100.0
1,000,000+......................	19.4	20.4	24.7	12.0	11.8	15.7
500,000–1,000,000.....................	5.9	9.8	8.3	4.8	8.5	6.7
250,000– 500,000.....................	7.6	5.9	7.0	6.8	6.0	7.4
100,000– 250,000.....................	7.3	8.0	7.9	6.9	7.3	7.4
25,000– 100,000.....................	11.7	12.2	12.8	11.1	11.9	12.6
10,000– 25 000.....................	7.1	7.4	8.3	7.3	7.7	8.9
2,500– 10,000.....................	8.4	8.3	7.3	9.8	9.7	8.9
Rural.........................	32.6	28.0	23.8	41.2	37.0	32.4
Farm.........................	.....	14.5	11.5	.....	20.7	16.2
Nonfarm.........................	.....	13.4	12.3	.....	16.3	16.2

[a] From special compilation made for this study and from *Fourteenth Census of the United States: 1920*, Vol. II, p. 90.

parentage are found in rural communities. In 1910 the percentages were 41.2 and 32.6, respectively, but in 1930 they had fallen to 32.4 and 23.8. Whites of mixed parentage are also relatively more numerous in cities of less than 25,000 than are whites of foreign parentage.

This same difference in the distribution of the native whites of foreign parentage and mixed parentage is found in the Northeast and North Center, the two regions where they are relatively numerous (Appendix Table 8). The native whites of foreign parentage are considerably more numerous in the larger cities than are the native whites of mixed parentage; conversely, they are less numerous in the small towns, and particularly in the rural districts. In the South and West, on the other hand, the differences are not very great.

A probable explanation of these facts is that mixed marriages are more numerous where there is no language barrier (British and Irish) and also tend to increase somewhat as the length of residence of immigrants increases (Germans and Scandinavians also). Hence it would be reasonable to expect that mixed marriages would be more numerous among the older immigrants who settled more largely in rural communities and small cities than among the more recent immigrants who are to be found chiefly in the large cities.

The concentration of the natives of foreign or mixed parentage in the larger cities has been rapid in recent decades, though less rapid than that of the population as a whole (Tables 8 and 21, pp. 24 and 70). This is readily understandable in view of the concentration of the foreign born in such places during the last several decades (a subject which has been discussed in the preceding section of this chapter) and of the decline in the amount of immigration. In sum, the distribution of the native whites of foreign or mixed parentage, both by regions and by size of community, is about what would be expected from a study of the distribution of the foreign born during several decades past, and of the economic and social factors that appear to be determining the distribution of the population as a whole.

c. **Interdivisional Migration.**—Interdivisional migration among the native whites of foreign or mixed parentage has much the same general pattern as migration among native whites of native parentage, but on a somewhat smaller scale. All the divisions east of the Mississippi River, except the South Atlantic in 1900, 1920, and 1930, have been losing through this interchange since 1890, while those to the west have been gaining until 1930, when the West North Central also lost (Table 23). However, the South is little involved in the internal movements of this group, as there have never been many persons of foreign or mixed parentage born there; nor have many moved there. The total net movement of this nativity group into and out of three southern divisions has never exceeded 145,000

TABLE 23.—NATIVE WHITE POPULATION OF FOREIGN OR MIXED PARENTAGE BY DIVISION OF RESIDENCE AND BY DIVISION OF BIRTH, AND NET GAIN OR LOSS BY INTERDIVISIONAL MIGRATION, 1890–1930[a]

Division	Net gain or loss (thousands)					1930		
	1890	1900	1910	1920	1930	Persons living in (thousands)	Persons born in (thousands)	Percentage gain or loss
New England.........	− 47	35	− 46	− 50	−149	3,052	3,200	− 4.6
Middle Atlantic.......	−341	−387	−379	−455	−418	8,415	8,834	− 4.7
East North Central...	−246	−312	−429	−360	−218	6,537	6,750	− 3.2
West North Central...	406	347	191	20	−266	3,261	3,527	− 7.5
South Atlantic........	− 31	29	− 22	27	40	630	590	6.8
East South Central....	− 2	− 7	− 19	− 29	− 28	194	223	−12.7
West South Central...	27	67	90	87	71	574	503	14.2
Mountain............	94	133	186	191	108	713	605	17.8
Pacific..............	141	197	428	568	855	1,880	1,025	83.4

[a] For 1890 from *Eleventh Census of the United States: 1890*, Vol. I, Pt. 1, pp. 572–575; 1900 from *Twelfth Census of the United States: 1900*, Vol. I, Pt. 1, pp. 698–701; 1910–1930 from *Fifteenth Census of the United States: 1930*, Vol. II, p. 143. Persons born in outlying possessions, at sea or abroad, and those for whom state of birth was not reported are omitted.

(1920). This is what would be expected from the distribution of the group as already shown. It is of interest, however, to note that though there are few natives of foreign or mixed parentage in the South, they are extremely mobile compared with those in other divisions, the proportion living outside of the division of birth reaching 39.7 per cent in the East South Central states, whereas it is only 10.6 per cent and 9.8 per cent in the New England and Middle Atlantic states, respectively.[1]

The only division gaining largely from this interchange of natives of foreign or mixed parentage at the present time is the Pacific. It has gained about eight times as many as its nearest competitor, the Mountain division, and almost four times as many as all the other divisions which gained. The Middle Atlantic states have shown the largest loss in each census, except in 1910, when the East North Central states lost more. Considering the very large number of natives of foreign or mixed parentage in the Middle Atlantic states, it is not surprising that this division should export considerable numbers of this group, as well as of native whites of native parentage.

4. THE DISTRIBUTION OF NEGROES

a. By Divisions.—It is among Negroes that the most important changes in distribution have taken place in recent years. Prior to 1910 barely 10 per cent of all Negroes lived outside the South (Table 24). Then, as in former years, they were heavily concentrated in a relatively narrow

[1] *Fifteenth Census of the United States: 1930*, Vol. II, p. 143.

boomerang-shaped belt of counties reaching from Virginia around to eastern Texas. In the South as a whole they comprised nearly one-third of the total population, and in the counties where they were concentrated they frequently outnumbered the whites by as much as two or three to one and occasionally amounted to 70 or 80 per cent of the total population.

There was a slow but steady decrease in the proportion of the Negroes living in the Middle Atlantic states from 1830, and probably earlier, until 1870 and 1890; but since 1890 there has been an increase, much accelerated since 1910 (Table 24 and Figure 13). On the other hand, the East

TABLE 24.—NEGRO POPULATION AND PERCENTAGE DISTRIBUTION, BY DIVISIONS, 1830–1930[a]

Area	1830	1850	1870	1890	1900	1910	1920	1930
POPULATION (THOUSANDS)								
United States........................	2,329	3,639	4,880	7,489	8,834	9,828	10,463	11,891
New England........................	21	23	32	45	59	66	79	94
Middle Atlantic.....................	104	127	148	225	326	418	600	1,053
East North Central..................	16	45	130	207	258	301	515	930
West North Central.................	26	90	143	224	238	243	279	332
South Atlantic......................	1,529	1,861	2,217	3,263	3,729	4,112	4,325	4,421
East South Central.................	502	1,123	1,464	2,120	2,500	2,653	2,524	2,658
West South Central.................	131	369	740	1,378	1,694	1,984	2,064	2,282
Mountain...........................	....	(b)	2	13	16	21	31	30
Pacific.............................	....	1	5	14	15	29	48	00
PERCENTAGE DISTRIBUTION								
United States........................	100.0	100.0	100.0	100.0	100.0	100.0	100.0	100.0
New England........................	0.9	0.6	0.6	0.6	0.7	0.7	0.8	0.8
Middle Atlantic.....................	4.5	3.5	3.0	3.0	3.7	4.3	5.7	8.9
East North Central..................	0.7	1.2	2.7	2.8	2.9	3.1	4.9	7.8
West North Central.................	1.1	2.5	2.9	3.0	2.7	2.5	2.7	2.8
South Atlantic......................	65.7	51.1	45.4	43.6	42.2	41.8	41.3	37.2
East South Central.................	21.5	30.9	30.0	28.3	28.3	27.0	24.1	22.4
West South Central.................	5.6	10.1	15.2	18.4	19.2	20.2	19.7	19.2
Mountain...........................	....	(c)	(c)	0.2	0.2	0.2	0.3	0.3
Pacific.............................	....	(c)	0.1	0.2	0.2	0.3	0.5	0.8

[a] For 1830, 1850, and 1870 from *Ninth Census of the United States: 1870*, Vol. I, p. 5; 1890, 1900, and 1910 from *Thirteenth Census of the United States: 1910*, Vol. I, pp. 146–147; 1920 and 1930 from *Fifteenth Census of the United States: 1930*, Vol. III, Pt. 1, p. 24.

[b] Less than 500.

[c] Less than one-tenth of 1 per cent.

North Central states have had a steady increase ever since 1830, although likewise much accelerated after 1910. The West North Central states had a rather rapid increase from 1830 to 1870, most of which was in Missouri; since that time there has been little Negro migration to these states. As a consequence of the recent northward migration one-seventh of all

Negroes lived outside the South in 1920 and over one-fifth by 1930. Although this movement of Negroes from the South commenced about the time the "new" immigrants began to flock to the United States, it did not attain any considerable proportions until about 1914. It was greatly stimulated by the low price of cotton in 1914 and by the stoppage of immigration during the war. Post-war immigration restrictions and boom years in industry helped to maintain the movement at a relatively high level during the decade 1920–1930. The number of Negroes in the Northeast increased from 484,000 in 1910 to 1,147,000 in 1930, most of the increase being in the Middle Atlantic states. In the North Center during the same

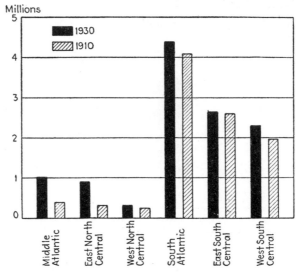

Fig. 13.—Negro population, by divisions, 1910 and 1930.   (Based on Table 24.)

period they increased from 544,000 to 1,262,000, by far the greater part being in the East North Central states. It appears that as immigration fell off, the Negro found increasing opportunity in the great cities in the industrialized North.

It is not possible to tell what the effect of the depression has been on Negro movements, but it seems not unlikely that there is now a return movement to the rural South, just as there is a return movement to the rural districts, both North and South, of whites who had found work in cities during boom times. Since the Negroes moved north because they found there wider opportunities to make a living, it seems highly probable that once the depression is over, most of those who left the northern cities because of it will return, bringing additional recruits with them. If it is correct to attribute the northward migration of Negroes in large part to the restriction of immigration, then future increases of Negroes in these regions will be closely related to the immigration policy which may be followed. The attractiveness of the North to the Negro is enhanced by the absence of unskilled foreign laborers, but the extent of the total movement is also affected by the expulsive forces at work in the South. As will be shown later, there is good reason to believe that the power of these expulsive forces will considerably increase during the next decade or two. Thus it appears highly probable that the northward movement of Negroes will continue for some time.

b. By Size of Community.—The recent movement of Negroes into the North is largely into the big cities (Table 25). In 1890 there were only 2.7 per cent of all Negroes in cities of over 250,000. By 1930 the percentage

TABLE 25.—NEGRO POPULATION AND PERCENTAGE DISTRIBUTION, BY SIZE OF COMMUNITY, 1820–1930[a]

Size of community	1820	1830	1840	1850	1870	1890	1910	1920	1930
POPULATION (THOUSANDS)									
Total	1,772	2,329	2,874	3,639	4,880	7,489	9,828	10,463	11,891
1,000,000+	.....	.....	.....	.....	.....	77	220	396	940
500,000–1,000,000	.....	.....	.....	14	35	10	176	330	408
250,000– 500,000	.....	.....	16	.....	70	120	239	350	933
100,000– 250,000	11	14	64	71	114	227	388	609	601
25,000– 100,000	38	78	38	74	133	371	601	726	958
10,000– 25,000	27	26	54	50	198	272	408	481	628
2,500– 10,000	29	40	47	74	180	403	652	668	727
Rural	1,667	2,172	2,655	3,355	4,219	6,009	7,143	6,904	6,697
Farm	.....	.....	.....	.....	.....	.....	.....	5,100	4,681
Nonfarm	.....	.....	.....	.....	.....	.....	.....	1,804	2,017
PERCENTAGE DISTRIBUTION									
Total	100.0	100.0	100.0	100.0	100.0	100.0	100.0	100.0	100.0
1,000,000+	.....	.....	.....	.....	.....	1.0	2.2	3.8	7.9
500,000–1,000,000	.....	.....	.....	0.4	0.7	0.1	1.8	3.2	3.4
250,000– 500,000	.....	.....	0.6	.....	1.4	1.6	2.4	3.3	7.8
100,000– 250,000	0.6	0.6	2.2	2.0	2.3	3.0	3.9	5.8	5.1
25,000– 100,000	2.1	3.3	1.3	2.0	2.7	5.0	6.1	6.9	8.1
10,000– 25,000	1.5	1.1	1.9	1.4	2.6	3.6	4.1	4.6	5.3
2,500– 10,000	1.6	1.7	1.6	2.0	3.7	5.4	6.6	6.4	6.1
Rural	94.1	93.2	92.4	92.2	86.4	80.2	72.7	66.0	56.3
Farm	.....	.....	.....	.....	.....	.....	.....	48.7	39.4
Nonfarm	.....	.....	.....	.....	.....	.....	.....	17.2	17.0

[a] From special compilation made for this study and from Fourteenth Census of the United States: 1920, Vol. II, p. 90.

had grown to 19.1. This is a larger proportional increase than in any other important group in the population. That this increase occurred chiefly in the North is clear when the numbers of Negroes in the large cities of these regions are considered. In 1890 there were but 82,502 Negroes in the cities of the Northeast having a population of over 250,000; in 1930 their number was 696,032, more than an eightfold increase. In the North Center their increase in such cities was even more rapid, from 55,780 in 1890 to 722,599 in 1930, almost a thirteenfold increase. Even in the South a similar movement was going on with an increase from 67,104 in 1890 to 800,199 in 1930, almost a twelvefold growth (Appendix Table 9). These increases are several times as large as those of the total population in the northern cities, but only about one-half greater than the increase of the total in the southern cities. The net result of this movement of Negroes to cities is, as indicated above, a very rapid increase in the proportion of them found in the larger cities and, conversely, a decrease, not only in the proportion, but, since 1910, in the absolute numbers of those living in rural communities.

The proportion of Negroes living in rural communities in 1890 was 80.2 per cent, but in 1930 was only 56.3 per cent. The decrease in the proportion of Negroes in rural communities is no new thing, however, as 94.1 per cent of them lived in such communities in 1820, 92.2 per cent in 1850, and 86.4 per cent in 1870. Thus while it is clear that Negroes have always shared to some extent in the urban growth of the country, yet until about 1890 or 1900 they were not moving to the cities in very considerable numbers. Since then, however, they are becoming urbanized more rapidly than their white neighbors; the number of rural Negroes even declined 446,000 from 1910 to 1930. Like the foreign born, the migrant Negroes find their opportunities, both economic and cultural, larger in the industrial and commercial centers of the North. On the farms they are being displaced by the use of more and better machinery. This displacement is likely to be accelerated during the next decade or two if a mechanical cotton picker of a satisfactory type, which is said to be ready for the market, should come into general use. Such an implement would probably be of revolutionary significance as regards the distribution of the Negro population. It would in all probability render superfluous somewhere between 2,000,000 and 3,000,000 of the almost 6,400,000 Negroes in the rural South who are now engaged chiefly in cotton growing. Such a change in farming methods will not come in a year or in a decade, but the shifting to industry in the course of even two decades of a large part of the rural Negro population now employed in growing cotton will prove a task of no mean proportions. That it will have to be performed seems probable.

It is also of importance to note that the recent shifts in the Negro population have resulted in its becoming a decreasing proportion of the total population in all sizes of communities in the South since 1910, except in Baltimore, the one city of over 500,000. The decline is particularly large in cities of 2,500 to 5,000 and 100,000 to 250,000. Counterbalancing this is the fact that Negroes constitute an increasing proportion of the population in most northern communities of all sizes, although a few exceptions are found among the smaller sizes of cities and in the rural areas of the North Center (Appendix Table 5). The shifting of the Negro population from the South to the North resulted in an unusually slow growth of this group in the former region during the last decade (5 per cent) but an exceedingly rapid growth in the rest of the country (63.1 per cent). The Negro movement is another evidence that agriculture, because of the relatively inelastic demand for its products, needs a smaller and smaller proportion of the population as methods of production improve.

c. Interdivisional Migration.—The internal migration of Negroes has not followed the same pattern as that of whites. It will be recalled that almost half of the native whites moving from any given state are generally to be found in adjacent states.[1] While this is true of the Negroes for certain states, it is not so generally the case.[2] Kentucky, with over

TABLE 26.—NATIVE NEGRO POPULATION BY DIVISION OF RESIDENCE AND BY DIVISION OF BIRTH, AND NET GAIN OR LOSS BY INTERDIVISIONAL MIGRATION, 1890–1930[a]

Division	Net gain or loss (thousands)					1930		
	1890[b]	1900	1910	1920	1930	Persons living in (thousands)	Persons born in (thousands)	Percentage gain or loss
New England.........	13	22	20	21	24	82	58	41.8
Middle Atlantic.......	69	141	186	297	572	966	394	145.3
East North Central...	74	97	120	296	595	919	323	184.2
West North Central...	47	41	40	68	99	329	280	43.1
South Atlantic........	−378	−412	−393	−455	−794	4,401	5,195	−15.3
East South Central....	− 78	−132	−201	−406	−541	2,652	3,193	−16.9
West South Central...	240	219	195	127	− 36	2,275	2,311	− 1.6
Mountain...........	9	11	13	20	17	30	12	141.0
Pacific..............	6	8	19	31	63	87	23	273.0

[a] For 1890 from *Eleventh Census of the United States: 1890*, Vol. I, Pt. 1, pp. 576–579; 1900 from *Twelfth Census of the United States: 1900*, Vol. I, Pt. 1, pp. 702–705; 1910–1930 from *Fifteenth Census of the United States: 1930*, Vol. II, p. 142. Persons born in outlying possessions, at sea or abroad, and those for whom state of birth was not reported are omitted.

[b] Persons of Negro descent, Chinese, Japanese, and civilized Indians.

one-third of the Negroes born there living elsewhere, closely follows the white pattern, for almost two-thirds of its migrating Negroes live in Ohio, Indiana, and Illinois, the three adjoining states north of the Ohio River. On the other hand, the situation is somewhat different in Georgia. Of almost 410,000 Negroes born there but not living there in 1930, Florida,

[1] *Supra*, p. 54.
[2] *Fifteenth Census of the United States: 1930*, Vol. II, pp. 164–167.

Alabama, North Carolina, South Carolina, and Tennessee have only about 41 per cent. The majority have gone farther afield, the Middle Atlantic division having about 21 per cent, and the East North Central division about 27 per cent. Likewise, more Negroes have gone from Virginia to the Middle Atlantic states than to all other states together. On the whole, it would appear that the concentration of the Negroes in the far South has made it necessary for them to go farther to find work when they left their native state than was the case with the native whites.

Thus it happens that the two southern divisions east of the Mississippi River had been the only losers through the interdivisional migration of Negroes up to 1920, all other divisions having gained (Table 26). By 1930 the West South Central division had sustained a net loss from such migration. Again, unlike the interdivisional migration of whites, the movement of Negroes is not primarily from east to west; it is rather from south to north, the Middle Atlantic and East North Central divisions having gained nearly 1,170,000 by 1930 out of a total loss by the southern divisions of about 1,370,000.

5. THE DISTRIBUTION OF THE OTHER COLORED

a. **Mexicans.**—As has been shown in Chapter I, the Mexicans constitute the largest group of "other colored" according to the 1930 census classification. In the past they have been highly concentrated in the Southwest, the five states Texas, New Mexico, Arizona, Colorado, and California containing over 92 per cent of all of them in 1920. Like most recent immigrants, they first settled near the point of entry among their friends; but as they have become familiar with the opportunities offered by more distant communities, they have begun to take advantage of them, as witnessed by the fact that, in spite of a very rapid increase in numbers, the proportion in these five states declined to 90 per cent by 1930.[1] The East North Central and West North Central states together had almost 100,000 Mexicans in 1930 compared with about 33,000 in 1920, these numbers also indicating that the movement from the rural Southwest towards the industrial opportunities of the North is under way. At present, slightly more than half the Mexicans live in urban communities— a rather surprising distribution considering the part of the country in which they live. This is another piece of evidence that agriculture, even in a relatively new region, cannot absorb many new workers.

Since 1929 it is probable that both the numbers of Mexicans and their distribution have been affected by the depression. The return movement to Mexico has been large because of hard times in industry; it is likely that a number of the incipient Mexican colonies in northern cities have lost a goodly portion of their people. In normal times, however,

[1] *Fifteenth Census of the United States: 1930*, Vol. III, Pt. 1, p. 27.

there is reason to expect a rather rapid increase of Mexicans, unless the quota restrictions are extended to them. Together with the southern Negro, Mexicans will probably supply much of the cheap unskilled labor for which industry has been accustomed to look to southern and eastern Europe, thus hastening their diffusion throughout the nation.

b. Indians.—The Indians, who constitute the next largest group of "other colored," are widely scattered among the states. No division has any great preponderance, although they are more numerous in the Southwest than elsewhere. Their rather wide geographic distribution does not, however, indicate that they are adjusting themselves to the economic and social life of the country, as is the case with immigrants. It merely means that most of them are living in the same general region as during their free tribal days. As a rule, they are a people apart, living on definitely circumscribed reservations, and seem likely to remain so unless they grow in numbers to the point where their reservations will no longer hold them. When this time comes, a new Indian policy will have to be developed. It is quite impossible even to hazard a guess as to how a different policy might affect their distribution, since its character will probably be determined by the political expediencies of the moment.

c. Japanese.—The Japanese are only a small group (138,834), highly concentrated on the Pacific Coast (120,251), with California alone having 97,456. Furthermore, California is the only state in which there has been any significant increase in numbers during the last decade. In 1920 it had 64.8 per cent of all the Japanese in the country and in 1930 it had 70.2 per cent. The Japanese, then, do not yet show any tendency to spread out over the country.

Since almost three-fourths of all Japanese females live in California, it is inevitable that most of the natural increase will occur in that state. Although a significant redistribution is not impossible, it is difficult to see any factors now at work likely to effect it.

In 1920 the Japanese were almost equally divided between urban (48.5 per cent) and rural (51.5 per cent) communities. By 1930 the percentages had changed to 53.8 and 46.2, respectively, indicating a slight movement towards the cities. There was a difference, however, between California and the Mountain states, on the one hand, and the rest of the country, on the other. In the former, the rural population has predominated in the past and is still the more important; in the latter the urban is more important.

d. Chinese.—The Chinese are considerably more widely distributed than the Japanese, although just about half of them live in California, and the proportion there is increasing. The most notable rate of increase in the last 10 years, however, is in the Middle Atlantic states, particularly in New York, where they have increased by about two-thirds between 1920 and 1930. There has also been a marked movement of the Chinese into the larger industrial and commercial cities of the East. But with the Chinese, as with the Japanese, it seems probable that a larger and larger proportion will concentrate in California, since almost two-thirds of the Chinese females live there. The Chinese population, like the Japanese, increases almost entirely by an excess of births over deaths, immigration not being allowed and illegal entries probably being relatively few.

More than any other racial or nativity group, the Chinese are an urban people, 81.1 per cent of them living in cities in 1920 and 87.7 per cent in 1930. In this respect they are quite different from the other colored groups in the population.

e. Filipinos.—The Filipinos numbered over 45,000 in 1930 and constituted almost nine-tenths of the remainder of the "other colored." They are quite recent arrivals and, like the Chinese and Japanese, they are concentrated in California, about two-thirds of them living in this one state. Data are not available on their distribution by size of community, but about 54 per cent live in cities, a rural-urban distribution quite similar to that of the Japanese. There is no basis for hazarding a guess as to whether or how rapidly they will move from California to other parts of the country.

The numbers of the other races included in the remaining "other colored" are too small to render their distribution of any general interest.

CHAPTER III

THE NATIONAL ORIGINS OF THE WHITE POPULATION[1]

1. INTEREST IN NATIONAL ORIGINS AND METHODS OF DETERMINING THEM

THE national origins of the white population would be a matter of interest in any event, but it is doubtful whether the subject would have attracted as much attention or would have been investigated nearly as carefully as has been done, had it not been for the fact that it was desired to base immigration quotas on the proportions of the white population deriving from the several national stocks already here. Since no accurate account of immigration was kept before 1820, since there were no very reliable birth and death statistics in any of the states before 1850 (and in comparatively few prior to 1910), since intermixture of stocks by marriage has gone on from the very beginning of the settlement of the land by different national stocks, and, finally, since there has been for some decades an unknown but considerable difference in the birth rates of the various national groups, it is quite impossible to tell exactly the proportions of the white population which have come from different national stocks. However, national origins have been estimated as accurately as the data permit by a committee representing the Departments of State, Commerce, and Labor under the chairmanship of Dr. Joseph A. Hill of the Bureau of the Census.

The information which it was desired that the Committee obtain may be described by quoting certain paragraphs of the law.[2]

b. The annual quota of any nationality for the fiscal year beginning July 1, 1927, and for each fiscal year thereafter, shall be a number which bears the same ratio to 150,000 as the number of inhabitants in continental United States in 1920 having that national origin (ascertained as hereinafter provided in this

---

[1] For a detailed treatment of the origin of the foreign stock, see Niles Carpenter, *op. cit.*, Chap. V.

[2] U. S. President, 1923–1929 (Coolidge), "Immigration quotas on the basis of National Origin. Message from the President of the United States Transmitting In Response to Senate Resolution 156, a Copy of the Joint Communication of the Secretary of State, the Secretary of Commerce, and the Secretary of Labor to the President," Washington, Government Printing Office, 1928, 12 pp. (70th Congress, 1st Session, Senate Document 65). See pp. 1–2.

section) bears to the number of inhabitants in continental United States in 1920, but the minimum quota of any nationality shall be 100.

c. For the purpose of subdivision (*b*) national origin shall be ascertained by determining as nearly as may be, in respect of each geographical area which under section 12 is to be treated as a separate country (except the geographical areas specified in subdivision (*c*) of section 4) the number of inhabitants in continental United States in 1920 whose origin by birth or ancestry is attributable to such geographical area. Such determination shall not be made by tracing the ancestors or descendants of particular individuals, but shall be based upon statistics of immigration and emigration, together with rates of increase of population as shown by successive decennial United States censuses, and such other data as may be found to be reliable.

d. For the purpose of subdivisions (*b*) and (*c*) the term "inhabitants in continental United States in 1920" does not include (1) immigrants from the geographical areas specified in subdivision (*c*) of section 4 or their descendants, (2) aliens ineligible to citizenship or their descendants, (3) the descendants of slave immigrants, or (4) the descendants of American aborigines.

e. The determination provided for in subdivision (*c*) of this section shall be made by the Secretary of State, the Secretary of Commerce, and the Secretary of Labor jointly. In making such determination such officials may call for information and expert assistance from the Bureau of the Census. Such officials shall jointly report to the President the quota of each nationality, determined as provided in subdivision (*b*), and the President shall proclaim and make known the quotas so reported. Such proclamation shall be made on or before April 1, 1927. If the proclamation is not made on or before such date, quotas proclaimed therein shall not be in effect for any fiscal year beginning before the expiration of 90 days after the date of the proclamation. After the making of a proclamation under this subdivision the quotas proclaimed therein shall continue with the same effect as if specifically stated herein and shall be final and conclusive for every purpose except (1) in so far as it is made to appear to the satisfaction of such officials and proclaimed by the President that an error of fact has occurred in such determination or in such proclamation, or (2) in the case provided for in subdivision (*c*) of section 12. If for any reason quotas proclaimed under this subdivision are not in effect for any fiscal year, quotas for such year shall be determined under subdivision (*a*) of this section.

The explanation of the method followed by the committee in arriving at its estimates of the national origins of the white population of 1920 is also best given in the words of Dr. Joseph A. Hill.[1]

The determination of the immigration quotas on the basis of national origin in accordance with the provision of paragraph (*b*), (*c*), and (*d*) of section 11 of the immigration act of 1924, involves the following processes:

1. From the total population of continental United States as returned in the 1920 census (105,710,620) deductions, as provided in section 11, paragraph (*d*) of the act, must be made for (1) aliens ineligible to citizenship and their descendants, (2) descendants of slave immigrants, and (3) descendants of American aborigines. The deductions total 10,889,705, leaving a balance of 94,820,915.

---

[1] *Op. cit.* pp. 5–11.

2. The remainder of the population must then be attributed to countries of birth or ancestry, as required by section 11, paragraph (c), of the immigration act.

3. The population which is thus attributed to nonquota countries—namely, Canada, Newfoundland, the 20 Latin-American Republics, and the Canal Zone—must then be deducted from the total population of the United States, less the deductions previously made as described above, leaving a remainder of 89,332,158. This comprises the number of "inhabitants in continental United States in 1920" in the sense of section 11, paragraph (d), of the immigration act.

4. The annual quota for each nationality must then be computed by multiplying the number of inhabitants in continental United States attributed to that nationality by the quotient obtained by dividing 150,000 by 89,332,158 (the total number of "inhabitants in continental United States in 1920"), as required by the provisions of section 11, paragraph (b), of the immigration act. In cases where the quota thus computed is less than 100, the minimum quota of 100 must be assigned, as provided by law. The quota totals, therefore, exceed 150,000 by as much as the quotas of the countries with a minimum quota of 100 each exceed the quotas computed by the simple formula indicated above.

In carrying out the above processes the principal and most responsible task which devolved upon the quota committee was, in the language of the immigration act, that of "determining as nearly as may be, in respect of each geographical area which under section 12 is to be treated as a separate country . . . the number of inhabitants in continental United States in 1920 whose origin by birth or ancestry is attributable to such geographical area."

On account of the intermixture of the various national stocks resulting from intermarriage, it is obviously impossible to divide the population of the United States into distinct classes, such that each class shall consist exclusively of persons whose ancestors were all born in the same country. That being the case, it was assumed that the "number of inhabitants" was meant to be used as a measure of the relative size or amount of the various national stocks composing the white population of the United States. So the problem was to determine what proportion or percentage of the white blood in the population of the United States was derived from each country of origin and express the result in terms of an equivalent number of inhabitants. In other words, the "inhabitant" was a unit of measure in which to express the amount or proportion of English blood, Irish blood, etc., in the composition of the American people. That seemed to be a necessary interpretation of the law and is consistent with the provision that the determination of national origin "shall not be made by tracing the ancestors or descendants of particular individuals."

The immigration act provides that the determination of national origin shall "be based upon statistics of immigration and emigration, together with rates of increase of population as shown by successive decennial United States censuses, and such other data as may be found to be reliable."

The act, it may be noted, does not contemplate or require exact figures, but provides that the national origin shall be determined "as nearly as may be." And since there is approximately one unit in the immigration quotas to each 600 inhabitants of the United States, a considerable numerical deviation from exactness in determining the national origin of the population may exist without materially affecting the quotas. Thus a deviation of 6,000 from exactness in the figures for any nationality would make a difference of only 10 in the quota; a deviation of 60,000 would result in a difference of 100; and it would take a deviation of approximately 600,000 to make a difference of 1,000 in any immigration quota.

The principal sources of data available for determining national origin are as follows:

(1) The reports of the decennial censuses, which have classified the foreign-born population by country of birth at each census from that of 1850 to that of 1920, inclusive; the native white population of foreign or mixed parentage by country of birth of parents at each census from that of 1890 to that of 1920, inclusive; and both the foreign-born white population and the native white population of foreign or mixed parentage by mother tongue at the censuses of 1910 and 1920.

(2) A classification by racial stocks of the white population enumerated at the census of 1790 as published by the Bureau of the Census in the volume entitled "A Century of Population Growth," supplemented and modified by recent studies which are referred to in the statement which follows.

(3) The records of immigration giving the number of immigrants arriving in the United States annually from each foreign country from 1820 to 1920.

(4) Emigration statistics of foreign countries showing emigration by counties or provinces.

(5) Local records and histories in regard to the settlement of different sections of the United States.

(6) Standard reference works or census reports giving the population of foreign countries at different periods, by provinces and other small political divisions, and by linguistic and racial groups.

In order to make the best use of the available data it was necessary to determine first of all what proportion of the white population of the United States in 1920 was derived from the population enumerated at the census of 1790, which is termed the original native stock, in distinction from the immigrant stock consisting of immigrants and descendants of immigrants who came to this country after 1790. That proportion was determined by a calculation based upon the classification of the native white population by age and nativity of parents (distinguishing native parents from foreign) as given in the censuses of 1890, 1900, 1910, and 1920. As the age classification is by five-year groups, one can readily compute what percentage of the white children born in the United States in each quinquennial period from 1790 to 1920 were the children of native parents. Then by a series of computations it is possible to determine what percentage of the children, having native parents had also native grandparents, what percentage of those having native grandparents had also native great grandparents, and, finally, what percentage of the native white population in each age group was descended from the population enumerated in 1790.

The rest of the native white population plus the foreign-born white constitutes, of course, the immigrant stock. The results of the division are as follows:

WHITE POPULATION

Census year	Total	Original native stock	Immigrant stock
1890	55,101,258	30,432,466	24,668,792
1900	66,809,196	34,272,951	32,536,245
1910	81,731,957	38,101,175	42,630,782
1920	94,820,915	41,288,570	53,532,345

NATIONAL ORIGINS OF WHITE POPULATION

The national origin of the original native stock in 1920 is assumed to be the same as that of the white population enumerated in 1790 from which the original native stock is descended. The volume entitled "A Century of Population Growth," published by the Bureau of the Census in 1909, contains a classification by nationality of the 1790 white population, which the quota committee in the report submitted on December 15, 1926, accepted without revision as the basis for determining the national origin of the original native stock. But in doing so it was recognized that there was "a considerable element of uncertainty" in a classification based, as that was, upon the names of heads of families. The action of Congress (March 4, 1927) in postponing the operation of the national-origin clause for one year afforded an opportunity to check and revise this classification by a study of other sources of information. It was to be expected that the net result of any errors in the original classification would be in the direction of an overstatement of the English stock, since in 1790 that was the predominant element in most parts of the United States; and consequently there would in all probability be many instances in which a name of non-English origin had been anglicized either deliberately by its possessor or by common usage in the community. The reverse case in which an English name is converted into a name of non-English origin would probably be relatively infrequent. Moreover, where a name is common to two or more countries of origin it would be natural in case of doubt, and justifiable in absence of any evidence to the contrary, for the classifier to assign it to the dominant element.

In the present revision of the 1790 classification valuable assistance was received from experts employed by the American Council of Learned Societies. The data which they compiled, supplemented by information obtained from other sources, indicated that the original native stock previously credited to Great Britain and Northern Ireland on the basis of the unrevised figures of the "Century of Population Growth" should be reduced by 10.4 per cent. That reduction was accordingly made and the amount deducted was distributed among the other nationalities represented in the white population of the original thirteen states in 1790. After this revision had been made, revised figures relating to the small white population in territory which was not covered by the census of 1790 but was subsequently acquired were included. That gave the basis for determining the national origin of the original stock in 1920.

The national origin of the immigrant stock was determined as follows: The immigrant stock was first subdivided into three component parts, namely, (1) the immigrants themselves, (2) the children of immigrants, and (3) the rest of the immigrant stock, consisting of the grandchildren of immigrants and later generations. The division is as follows:

IMMIGRANT STOCK

Census year	Total	Immigrants	Children of immigrants	Grandchildren and later generations
1890	24,668,792	9,121,867	9,794,347	5,752,578
1900	32,536,245	10,213,817	13,139,149	9,183,279
1910	43,630,782	13,345,545	15,907,074	14,378,163
1920	53,532,345	13,712,754	19,190,372	20,629,219

For "immigrants" and the "children of immigrants" the classification by country of origin was directly supplied in the reports of the census, classifying the foreign-born white by country of birth and the native white of foreign-born parents by country of birth of parents. It remained to determine the national origin of the grandchildren and later generations.

In order that census data might be used as far as possible, the census of 1890 was taken as the starting point in this computation, that being the first census to give a complete classification of the native white of foreign or mixed parentage (children of immigrants) by country of birth of parents, as well as a classification of the foreign born by country of birth.

The grandchildren and later generations in 1890 were practically all descendants of immigrants who came to this country prior to 1870, because the immigrants who came to this country after 1870 could hardly have had many grandchildren by 1890. It was assumed, therefore, that the distribution of the grandchildren and later generations in 1890 by country of origin would conform to that of the immigration from 1790 to 1870. The immigration records give the number of immigrants arriving annually from each foreign country from 1820 to 1870. For the period 1790 to 1820 an estimate was made based upon a comparison of studies that have been made by different authorities. This estimate would be a factor of much greater importance if the immigration statistics had been used as a basis for determining the total number of grandchildren and later generations of immigrants included in the census of 1890. But that number having been determined by the process above described, the immigration statistics from 1790 to 1870 were used only for determining the proportions derived from each foreign country.

It is obvious, however, that the immigrants arriving in any given early period would have proportionately more descendants in 1890 and therefore more influence in determining the composition of the grandchildren class than those immigrants who came in a later period. Therefore for the purpose of determining the national origin of grandchildren and later generations in 1890 the immigration figures by decades were weighted, giving each earlier decade a greater weight than the succeeding decade.

Having thus determined the national origin of the grandchildren and later generations in 1890 on the assumption that the percentage derived from each country would correspond to the percentage of immigrants coming from that country prior to 1870, the next step was to determine the national origin of the grandchildren class at the next census, taken 10 years later in 1900.

The grandchildren and later generations enumerated in 1900 consisted in part of (1) the survivors of those who were enumerated in 1890, and in part of (2) grandchildren, etc., who were born between 1890 and 1900.

To determine (1) the number of survivors, the number of grandchildren and later generations living in 1890 was reduced by a certain percentage to allow for the deaths that occurred between 1890 and 1900. The percentage was arrived at by a study of census age figures, death rates, and life tables, and is believed to be a close approximation to the true decennial death rate for that portion of the population. The survivors in 1900 as thus determined were then distributed by country of origin to correspond to the distribution previously ascertained of the grandchildren and later generations in 1890.

The distribution of (2) grandchildren and later generations born between 1890 and 1900 by country of origin would naturally correspond closely to that of the parent class as it existed in 1890, comprising the second and later generations of the immigrant stock. In other words, the parents of those grandchildren and later generations of immigrant stock born between 1890 and 1900 consisted of children of immigrants, grandchildren, and later generations living in 1890. The grandchildren, etc., born between 1890 and 1900 were therefore distributed by country of origin in the same proportions as the parent class.

Having thus determined the classification by country of origin of the grandchildren in 1900 on the basis of the 1890 classification as previously determined, the same process was followed in determining their classification in 1910 and finally in détermining their classification in 1920.

In the process of determining national origin as above described it was necessary to make readjustments in the figures on account of changes in the political geography of Europe. Similar readjustments, it may be noted, were necessary in determining the immigration quotas which are now in effect on the basis of the 1890 foreign-born population, the immigration act providing that where there have been changes in political boundaries through the creation of new countries, or the transfer of territory from one country to another, an estimate should be made of the number of individuals resident in the United States in 1890 born within the area included in such new countries or in such territory so transferred. It was necessary to use similar estimates in determining the immigration quotas on the basis of national origin.

In making these necessary allocations for geographical changes it was possible in some cases to utilize United States census statistics regarding the country of birth or mother tongue of the foreign white stock, and also United States immigration statistics. In some cases the quota committee obtained from foreign publications statistics of emigration by counties or Provinces.

This was the case as regards emigration from Ireland, making it possible to make the division between North Ireland and the Irish Free State on a very satisfactory basis and with a greater degree of accuracy than was attained in the committee's earlier report. Similar statistics exist in the case of Germany, showing emigration by Provinces. In a few cases, in the absence of other data, the division was made on the basis of the relative population of the areas affected.

The results of the determination of national origin of the white population of the United States in 1920 arrived at in the manner above described are given in the appended Table A,[1] which distinguishes the original native stock from the immigrant stock, and subdivides the immigrant stock into (1) immigrants, (2) children of immigrants, and (3) grandchildren and later generations; while Table B shows what part of the quotas for the several countries is derived from each of these classes.

JOSEPH A. HILL,
Chairman of the subcommittee appointed by the Secretary of State, the Secretary of Commerce, and the Secretary of Labor to report regarding the determination of national origin in accordance with the provisions of the immigration act of 1924.

2. RESULTS OF DETERMINATION OF NATIONAL ORIGINS

According to the estimates of this committee, 41.4 per cent of the 1920 white population was of British and North Irish origin (Table 27 and

[1] Table 27, p. 91, is the latest official revision of Table A referred to above. Table B shows quotas now in effect and is not given here.—AUTHORS.

Figure 14).[1] The Germans constituted 16.3 per cent and were the second largest group, while the Irish (Irish Free State) were the third in numbers, comprising 11.2 per cent. These three groups together accounted for the origins of over two-thirds of the entire white population of the United States in 1920. In addition the Scandinavians supplied 4.3 per cent, other

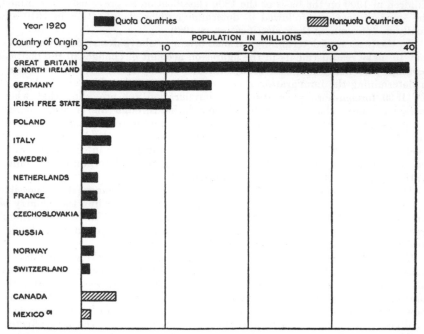

[a] Mexicans are included with whites in accordance with the classification of the 1920 census. Their number here appears large in comparison with the estimated number of persons of the Mexican race in 1920 published in the 1930 census since this latter estimate does not include such persons born in the United States of native-born parents of whom there were large numbers in the Southwest.

FIG. 14.—White population, by country of origin, 1920. (Based on Table 27.)

countries of northwestern Europe 5.8 per cent, and Canada 4.3 per cent. Hence about 83.3 per cent of the total white population in 1920 had its origin in northwestern Europe or Canada. Of the remaining 16.7 per cent, 4.1 per cent came from Poland, 3.6 per cent from Italy, and the remaining 9 per cent chiefly from Russia, Mexico,[2] and pre-war Austria-Hungary.

[1] Since this chapter was written, the report of the Committee of the American Council of Learned Societies "on linguistic and national stocks in the United States" has come to hand (January, 1933). Although there are some differences between Table 27 and analogous tables in this report, due chiefly to the greater detail required of the former as the basis of the new immigration quotas, the two estimates are in substantial agreement where they can be directly compared. It is the authors' understanding that the work of this Committee of the American Council of Learned Societies was utilized in the preparation of the report just quoted. For the full report of the Committee of the American Council of Learned Societies, see *Annual Report of the American Historical Association, 1931*, Washington, Government Printing Office, 1932, particularly pp. 105–441.

[2] Mexicans were classified as whites in the 1920 census.

3. DIFFERENCE IN ORIGINS OF 1790 AND 1920 POPULATIONS

It is interesting to compare the proportions of the different national stocks in 1790 and 1920 (Table 27). Column 7 represents the estimates of the committee of the proportions of the several national stocks actually present in the white population in 1920. Column 8 shows the estimated proportions of the different national stocks present in 1790 which presumably would have continued to the present time if there had been no immigration after 1790. The chief differences are the decline of British

TABLE 27.—APPORTIONMENT OF THE WHITE POPULATION OF THE UNITED STATES, BY COUNTRY OF ORIGIN, 1920[a]

(Thousands)

| Country of origin | Total | Colonial stock | Postcolonial stock | | | | Percentage distribution | |
| | | | Total | Immigrants | Children of immigrants | Grandchildren and later generations | Total | Colonial stock |
	1	2	3	4	5	6	7	8
Total..................	94,821	41,289	53,532	13,713	19,190	20,629	100.0	100.0
Quota countries.........	89,507	40,324	49,182	12,071	17,621	19,400	94.4	97.7
Austria..............	843	14	829	306	415	108	0.9	(b)
Belgium..............	778	602	176	63	62	51	0.8	1.5
Czechoslovakia........	1,715	55	1,660	560	904	197	1.8	0.1
Denmark..............	705	93	612	190	277	144	0.7	0.2
Estonia..............	69	.....	69	34	28	7	0.1	.....
Finland..............	339	4	335	150	147	39	0.4	(b)
France...............	1,842	767	1,075	155	325	594	1.9	1.9
Germany..............	15,489	3,037	12,452	1,672	4,051	6,728	16.3	7.4
Great Britain and Northern Ireland..............	39,216	31,804	7,412	1,365	2,308	3,739	41.4	77.0
Greece...............	183	.....	183	135	47	1	0.2	.....
Hungary..............	519	.....	519	319	184	16	0.6	.....
Irish Free State........	10,653	1,822	8,832	821	2,098	5,913	11.2	4.4
Italy................	3,462	.....	3,462	1,612	1,671	178	3.6	.....
Latvia...............	141	.....	141	69	56	16	0.2	.....
Lithuania............	230	.....	230	117	89	25	0.2	.....
Netherlands..........	1,881	1,367	515	133	205	176	2.0	3.3
Norway..............	1,419	75	1,343	364	597	382	1.5	0.2
Poland..............	3,893	9	3,884	1,814	1,780	290	4.1	(b)
Portugal.............	263	24	239	104	105	30	0.3	0.1
Rumania.............	176	.....	176	89	84	3	0.2	.....
Russia, European and Asiatic	1,661	4	1,657	767	762	127	1.8	(b)
Spain...............	150	38	112	50	25	37	0.2	0.1
Sweden..............	1,977	217	1,760	626	775	360	2.1	0.5
Switzerland..........	1,019	389	630	119	204	308	1.1	0.9
Syria and the Lebanon......	73	.....	73	42	31	.....	0.1	.....
Turkey..............	135	.....	135	103	31	1	0.1	.....
Yugoslavia...........	504	.....	504	221	266	18	0.5	.....
All other............	171	4	167	72	94	2	0.2	(b)
Nonquota countries[c].........	5,314	964	4,350	1,641	1,570	1,139	5.6	2.3
Canada..............	4,037	646	3,391	1,118	1,320	954	4.3	1.6
Newfoundland.........	48	8	40	13	16	11	0.1	(b)
Mexico..............	1,126	294	832	478	218	136	1.2	0.7
West Indies..........	66	10	56	13	10	33	0.1	(b)
Central and South America	37	6	31	19	7	6	(b)	(b)

[a] 70th Congress, 2d Session, Senate Document 259. *Immigration Quotas on the Basis of National Origin*, p. 5. "In this table the proportion of the total white population derived from each country of origin is expressed in terms of the equivalent number of inhabitants. Columns 4 and 5 are census figures, with such adjustments as are necessary on account of changes in political boundaries. Columns 2 and 6 were derived from census and immigration data. The totals in Column 1, arrived at by adding Columns 2 and 3, indicate the national origin of the white population determined 'as nearly as may be' upon the basis of the available data, as required by the provisions of section 11 (c) of the immigration act of 1924."

[b] Less than one-tenth of 1 per cent.

[c] Data contained in a letter from Dr. Joseph A. Hill to the authors, September 20, 1932.

stock from 77.0 per cent to 41.4 per cent, the increase of the German from 7.4 per cent to 16.3 per cent, the increase of the Irish (Irish Free State) from 4.4 per cent to 11.2 per cent, the increase of the Scandinavians from 0.9 per cent to 4.3 per cent, and the emergence of the Italians, Poles, and other peoples from southern and eastern Europe as important groups in the population.[1] A population descended from the 1790 population would consist largely of British (exclusive of Irish) and Baltic peoples, with a few French, chiefly of Huguenot descent, and a scattering of other north-western Europeans. In land of origin such a population would, perhaps, not be greatly different from the English population of about 1200 A. D.— a century and a half after the Norman Conquest.

The chief change in stock arising from immigration during the past 40 years has been the increase in the proportion of central, southern, and eastern Europeans—Germans of Alpine stock, Italians, various nationalities of predominantly Slavic blood, and a relatively large block of people of Jewish descent. The extent of the changes thus under way could not have been known with even approximate accuracy prior to the researches of the committee referred to above. However, it was the realization that such changes were in process and that the increasing immigration from southern and eastern Europe made them steadily greater which led to the enactment of the quota laws. The quota laws establish the *status quo* of national origins in 1920 as far as it is possible for immigration laws to do so.

The factor over which these laws have no control is the differential rates of increase that exist between the various national stocks. That such differentials are of importance is clearly shown by the average number of children ever born to immigrant women from various countries.[2] Thus, among the women who bore children in 1929 those from Poland had, on the average, born 4.9 and those from Italy 4.5, whereas those from Norway, Sweden, and Denmark had born only 3.1 and those from England, Scotland, and Wales 2.7.[3]

Indeed, with the rapid decline in the birth rates of the foreign-born whites just pointed out, it seems quite probable that the rate of increase of the recent immigrant stocks from Europe will not long be much in excess of that of the native whites. This is rendered still more probable by

[1] The attention of the reader is called to the discussion of the effects of immigration on population growth in Chap. IX. The proportions in Column 8 might very well hold good, even though the total population of colonial stock were considerably greater than that given here.

[2] U. S. Bureau of the Census, *Birth, Stillbirth, and Infant Mortality Statistics for the Birth Registration Area of the United States:* 1929, Washington, Government Printing Office, 1932, p. 9. See also comparable tables in earlier reports.

[3] Birth rates for women of various national stocks will be found in a monograph on Fertility in the United States being prepared by the authors for the Bureau of the Census.

the fact that nearly all of the recent European immigrants live in cities, while the native whites live more largely in the rural districts where birth rates are higher. Such European immigrants as are eligible for admission into this country under the present quota system are largely of north-western European origin. This makes it highly probable that the status of 1920 as regards the relative importance of the different European stocks would not be materially altered in the next few decades. The present policy, which allows practically no immigration, is not so favorable to the relative increase of northwestern European stock. Future changes in immigration policy, depending upon their extent and nature, may or may not vary the proportions of different national stocks.

What importance is to be attached to the question of the national origins of our population has been and still is a matter of animated, sometimes bitter, dispute among men. There have not been lacking those who maintained that the British stock together with the nationalities bordering the North and Baltic Seas were a distinctly superior group in their hereditary make-up and that to dilute their blood with Alpine stock from central Europe, and with Italian, Slavic, and Jewish stock from southern and eastern Europe, was bound to have harmful effects upon the national character.

Superior and inferior seem out of place as terms describing the quality of the various national stocks of European origin. However, there are cultural differences, such as language, religion, family customs, legal habits, and perhaps even a part of that rather vague quality called temperament, which make it more difficult for some national groups than for others to adjust themselves to our manner of life. The decision that British and German immigrants are preferred to Italian and Jewish is quite defensible on this ground, whereas to base such a decision upon supposed inherent differences in national stocks seems to be quite without scientific justification. Always and everywhere men determine their personal relations with their neighbors and fellow workers on the basis of congeniality and the ease of making the personal adjustments necessary to get along pleasantly. Does it not seem quite reasonable that the same general rule should apply to immigrants with whom natives must work and live? Surely it is not strange that people prefer others as much like themselves as possible when selecting new neighbors. Basing immigration on national origins is merely saying that immigrants are preferred who will find it relatively easy to adjust themselves to native ways of living and will therefore be more readily understood by their neighbors. It is not a question of the inherent superiority of one set of manners to another, or of the better inheritance of one group than another, or even of the possible contributions the different stocks might make to national life at some future time: it is simply a question of personal preferences based upon such likenesses as can readily be understood and appreciated by the average man.

It would be a great mistake, therefore, to suppose that the present basis of selecting immigrants assures the nation superior ability among its foreign born and their descendants. To secure really superior stock, individual selection would be necessary, since differences in mental ability and in physical constitution are individual. If superior immigrants are to be secured, they must be chosen as individuals because of the qualities they possess. In order to do this well, reliable tests of individual quality must be developed and these tests must be impartially applied to all applicants for entry, somewhat after the manner of civil service examinations. Certainly from the standpoint of probable contribution to a better manner of life, an Italian or Yugoslav of superior ability is greatly to be preferred to a German or an Englishman of inferior capacity.

4. THE COUNTRY OF BIRTH OF THE FOREIGN BORN

It will help in understanding the changes in the national origins of the population discussed above if the country of birth of the foreign born is studied in some detail. Unfortunately, the foreign born were not enumerated separately by country of birth prior to 1850, but from the immigration data beginning in 1820 it is clear that there was comparatively little immigration during the first third of the nineteenth century. In the latter 1830's the number of immigrants increased rapidly, and the 1840's saw a rather large movement (Table 81, p. 294). Most of the immigrants who came during the 1830's and 1840's were still living in 1850, so that it is possible to get a fairly adequate idea of how the changes in national origins between 1790 and 1920 took place. The reasons for immigration during the nineteenth century need not be detailed here. They were essentially what they always had been: hard conditions at home (primarily economic), and the promise of larger opportunity in America (again primarily economic). The relative strength of expulsive and attractive forces varied from country to country and from time to time, but it is hard to see any fundamental change in the motives to migration as between the colonial and post-colonial immigrants. Without going farther into this aspect of the nineteenth century immigration, attention will now be turned to the country of birth of those who came as it is shown in the census data.

In 1850 the Irish (including all Ireland) constituted 42.8 per cent of all the foreign born, the Germans were second with 26.0 per cent, the British (England, Scotland, and Wales) third with 16.9 per cent, and the Canadians fourth with 6.6 per cent (see Table 28 and Figure 15). At that time the Irish were as numerous as the Germans and British combined. Furthermore, it will be seen that the Irish, although declining in proportion, held first place as the most numerous foreign-born group until 1880, when

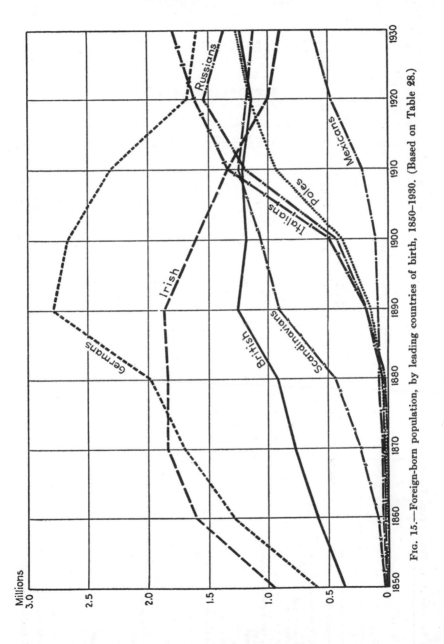

FIG. 15.—Foreign-born population, by leading countries of birth, 1850–1930. (Based on Table 28.)

TABLE 28.—Number, Percentage Distribution, and Percentage Increase of the Foreign Born, by Country of Birth, 1850–1930[a]

NUMBER (THOUSANDS)

Country of birth	1850	1860	1870	1880	1890	1900	1910	1920[b] A	1920[b] B	1930[c]
Total foreign-born	2,245	4,189	5,567	6,680	9,250	10,341	13,516	13,921	13,255	13,366
England, Scotland, and Wales	379	588	770	918	1,251	1,168	1,221	1,135	1,184	1,223
Ireland	962	1,611	1,856	1,855	1,872	1,615	1,352	1,037	1,037	924
Northern Ireland	.....	.....	.....	.....	.....	.....	.....	.....	.....	179
Irish Free State	.....	.....	.....	.....	.....	.....	.....	.....	.....	745
Germany	584	1,276	1,691	1,967	2,785	2,663	2,311	1,686	1,686	1,609
Iceland	.....	.....	.....	.....	.....	.....	.....	.....	.....	3
Norway, Sweden, and Denmark	18	73	242	440	933	1,072	1,251	1,179	1,179	1,123
Netherlands	10	28	47	58	82	95	120	132	132	133
Switzerland	13	53	75	89	104	116	125	119	119	113
France	54	110	116	107	113	104	117	153	153	135
Canada[d]	148	250	493	717	981	1,180	1,210	1,138	1,131	1,302
French	.....	.....	.....	.....	302	395	385	308	308	371
Other	.....	.....	.....	.....	678	785	820	817	810	908
Newfoundland	.....	.....	.....	.....	.....	.....	5	13	13	24
Poland	.....	7	14	49	147	383	938	1,140	1,140	1,269
Czechoslovakia	.....	.....	.....	.....	.....	.....	.....	362	362	492
Austria	1	25	71	124	241	433	846	576	576	371
Hungary	.....	.....	4	12	62	146	496	397	397	274
Yugoslavia	.....	.....	.....	.....	.....	.....	.....	169	169	211
Italy	4	12	17	44	183	484	1,343	1,610	1,610	1,790
Russia	1	3	5	36	183	424	1,184	1,400	1,400	1,154
Latvia and Estonia[e]	.....	.....	.....	.....	.....	.....	.....	.....	.....	24
Lithuania[f]	.....	.....	.....	.....	.....	.....	.....	135	135	194
Finland[g]	.....	.....	.....	.....	.....	63	130	150	150	142
Rumania	.....	.....	.....	.....	.....	15	66	103	103	146
Greece	(h)	(h)	(h)	1	2	9	101	176	176	175
Mexico	13	27	42	68	78	103	222	486	21	24
West Indies	6	7	12	16	23	25	48	79	26	81
All other	52	67	112	180	209	243	435	557	418	504

PERCENTAGE DISTRIBUTION

Country of birth	1850	1860	1870	1880	1890	1900	1910	1920[b] A	1920[b] B	1930[c]
Total foreign-born	100.0	100.0	100.0	100.0	100.0	100.0	100.0	100.0	100.0	100.0
England, Scotland, and Wales	16.9	14.2	13.8	13.7	13.5	11.3	9.0	8.2	8.6	9.2

Ireland	42.8	38.9	33.3	27.8	20.2	15.6	10.0	7.5	7.8	6.9
Northern Ireland	......	......	......	......	......	......	......	......	......	1.3
Irish Free State	......	......	......	......	......	......	......	......	......	5.6
Germany	26.0	30.8	30.4	29.4	30.1	25.8	17.1	12.1	12.7	12.0
Iceland	......	......	......	......	......	......	......	......	......	[i]
Norway, Sweden, and Denmark	0.9	1.8	4.3	6.6	10.1	10.4	9.2	8.5	8.9	8.4
Netherlands	0.4	0.7	0.8	0.9	0.9	0.9	0.9	0.9	1.0	1.0
Switzerland	0.6	1.3	1.3	1.3	1.1	1.1	0.9	0.9	0.9	0.8
France	2.4	2.7	2.1	1.6	1.2	1.0	0.9	1.1	1.2	1.0
Canada[d]	6.6	6.0	8.9	10.7	10.6	11.4	9.0	8.2	8.5	9.7
French	......	......	......	......	3.3	3.8	2.8	2.2	2.3	2.8
Other	......	......	......	......	7.3	7.6	6.1	5.9	6.1	6.8
Newfoundland	......	......	......	......	......	......	[i]	0.1	0.1	0.2
Poland	......	0.2	0.3	0.7	1.6	3.7	6.9	8.2	8.6	9.5
Czechoslovakia	......	......	......	......	......	......	......	2.6	2.7	3.7
Austria	(i)	0.6	1.3	1.9	2.6	4.2	6.3	4.1	4.3	2.8
Hungary	......	......	0.1	0.2	0.7	1.4	3.7	2.9	3.0	2.1
Yugoslavia	......	......	......	......	......	......	......	1.2	1.3	1.6
Italy	0.2	0.3	0.3	0.7	2.0	4.7	9.9	11.6	12.1	13.4
Russia	0.1	0.1	0.1	0.5	2.0	4.1	8.8	10.1	10.6	8.6
Latvia and Estonia[e]	......	......	......	......				......	......	0.2
Lithuania[f]	......	......	......	......	......	......	......	1.0	1.0	1.4
Finland[g]	......	......	......	......	......	0.6	1.0	1.1	1.1	1.1
Rumania	......	......	......	......	......	0.1	0.5	0.7	0.8	1.1
Greece	(i)	(i)	(i)	(i)	(i)	0.1	0.7	1.3	1.3	1.3
Mexico	0.6	0.7	0.8	1.0	0.8	1.0	1.6	3.5	0.2	0.2
West Indies	0.3	0.2	0.2	0.2	0.3	0.2	0.3	0.6	0.2	0.2
All other	2.3	1.6	2.0	2.7	2.3	2.4	3.2	4.0	3.2	3.8
	1850–60	1860–70	1870–80	1880–90	1890–1900	1900–10	1910–20[j]	1920–30[k]		
PERCENTAGE INCREASE										
Total foreign born	84.4	34.5	20.0	38.5	11.8	30.7	3.0	0.8		
England, Scotland, and Wales	55.0	31.1	19.1	36.4	− 6.7	4.6	− 7.0	7.8		
Ireland	67.5	15.2	−0.1	0.9	−13.7	−16.3	−23.3	−11.0		
Northern Ireland	......	......	......	......	......	......	......	......		
Irish Free State	......	......	......	......	......	......	......	......		
Germany	118.6	32.5	16.3	41.6	− 4.4	−13.2	−27.0	− 4.6		
Iceland	......	......	......	......	......	......	......	......		
Norway, Sweden, and Denmark	301.6	233.0	82.2	112.0	14.9	16.7	− 5.8	− 4.8		
Netherlands	187.2	65.5	24.1	40.9	16.0	26.5	9.7	1.0		
Switzerland	299.2	40.9	17.9	17.4	11.1	8.0	− 5.0	− 4.8		
France	103.2	5.9	−8.1	5.8	− 7.9	12.7	30.4	−11.5		
Canada[d]	69.2	97.4	45.3	36.8	20.3	2.5	− 5.9	15.1		
French	......	......	......	......	30.6	− 2.5	−20.1	20.5		
Other	......	......	......	......	15.7	4.4	− 0.3	12.0		
Newfoundland	......	......	......	......	......	......	160.8	81.0		

TABLE 28.—NUMBER, PERCENTAGE DISTRIBUTION, AND PERCENTAGE INCREASE OF THE FOREIGN BORN, BY COUNTRY OF BIRTH, 1850–1930.ª—(Continued)

Country of birth	PERCENTAGE INCREASE							
	1850–60	1860–70	1870–80	1880–90	1890–1900	1900–10	1910–20ʲ	1920–30ᵏ
Poland		97.8	236.4	203.6	160.0	144.6	21.5	11.3
Czechoslovakia								85.6
Austria	2,549.2	182.5	75.2	94.6	79.3	95.4	−31.9ⁱ	−35.6
Hungary			208.4	441.7	138.4	240.1	−19.8ⁱ	−30.9
Yugoslavia								24.8
Italy	217.4	46.9	157.8	312.8	165.1	177.5	19.9	11.2
Russiaᵉ	123.5	47.0	669.2	411.3	166.3	179.5	29.6	−15.9
Latvia and Estoniaᶠ								43.3
Lithuaniaᶠ							15.5	−4.9
Finlandᵉ						107.0	56.0	42.4
Rumania					351.2	338.6	73.7	−0.8
Greece	106.2	18.9	99.0	148.2	32.8	1,089.5	119.2	12.9
Mexico	27.4	54.5	61.2	18.8	9.4	114.6	65.2	19.2
West Indies	29.8	57.4	41.8	41.8		87.3	65.0	28.0
All other		66.4	61.3	15.9	23.6ᵐ	78.9	28.0	20.6

ª For 1850–1920 from *Fourteenth Census of the United States: 1920*, Vol. II, pp. 695–696; 1930 from *Fifteenth Census of the United States: 1930*, Vol. III, Pt. 1, p. 20.

ᵇ Column A is comparable with previous years at all points. Column B excludes foreign-born colored persons in order to render 1930 comparable with 1930 since the foreign born colored by country of birth are not yet available for the latter year.

ᶜ Includes foreign-born whites only.

ᵈ Newfoundland included with Canada prior to 1910, and in calculating percentage increase for 1900–1910.

ᵉ Included with Russia prior to 1930, and in calculating percentage increase for 1920–1930.

ᶠ Included with Russia prior to 1920, and in calculating percentage increase for 1910–1920.

ᵍ Included with Russia prior to 1900, and in calculating percentage increase for 1890–1900.

ʰ Less than 500 population.

ⁱ Less than one-tenth of 1 per cent.

ʲ Calculated by using 1920 (A).

ᵏ Calculated by using 1920 (B).

ˡ Decrease due in part to loss of territory following World War.

ᵐ In calculating this percentage Rumania is included with "all other" in 1900.

the Germans surpassed them. The Irish reached their maximum number in 1890 and have declined in numbers and proportion ever since. In 1930 they barely exceeded 900,000 and constituted but 6.9 per cent of the foreign-born whites. In view of the large immigration movement of Irish to the United States, it is not in the least surprising that Irish of Free State origin increased from 4.4 per cent of the white population in 1790 to 11.2 per cent in 1920 (see Table 27, Columns 7 and 8).

The Germans were relatively more numerous in the colonial population than the Irish, 7.4 per cent compared with 4.4 per cent. But after colonial days they did not begin to come again in considerable numbers until about 1840. In 1850 there were somewhat fewer than 600,000 here, but during the ensuing decade 1850–1860 the number more than doubled. Even during the decade of the Civil War Germans increased by more than 400,000. From 1880 to 1920, inclusive, it was the largest group among the foreign born, but by 1930 it yielded first place to the Italians. This vast movement of Germans explains the increase of persons of German origin from 7.4 per cent of the white population in 1790 to 16.3 per cent in 1920. This group is now second in importance, as it was in 1790. There are now only about 2½ persons of British origin to 1 of German, whereas in 1790 there were 10 of British origin to 1 of German.   *143550*

This change in the proportions of persons of British and German origin in the white population is not due to the falling off of British immigration in absolute amount but rather to the vast increase in German immigration. In fact, persons of British birth grew rather rapidly in numbers until 1890. Since then their numbers have remained nearly stationary.

The Scandinavians did not begin to come in considerable numbers until the decade of the Civil War. They increased rather rapidly and steadily until 1910, when there were 1,251,000 here, comprising 9.2 per cent of the foreign born. This sufficiently explains the increase of persons of Scandinavian origin from 0.9 per cent of the population in 1790 to 4.3 per cent in 1920.

The Canadians also have come in considerable numbers from an early date and have been increasing in numbers steadily ever since 1850 except for the decade 1910–1920 (World War). Persons of Canadian origin were about twice as important an element of the population in 1920 as in 1790. They are predominantly and increasingly of British origin.

The groups discussed above include most of the older immigrants and are those which the quota system was designed to favor as compared with the newer immigrants. These latter did not begin to come in very great numbers until about 1900, after the practical exhaustion of the good land which was available to settlers on easy terms. It is not surprising that when land was no longer the magnet drawing immigrants there should be a change in their national origins. With most of the desirable land in cultivation and with industry expanding rapidly, the need was no longer for agriculturalists but rather for miners, steel-mill hands, and unskilled industrial laborers. The European countries that had formerly supplied farmers were, moreover, increasingly in a position to offer their own peasants jobs in their new mines and factories. In addition, by 1900 the birth rate was declining faster than the death rate in most of the countries of northwestern Europe, so that altogether there was less cause to emigrate from these countries than there had been during the latter half of the nineteenth century.

Thus the changing character of economic life led to a marked change in the sources of immigration at about the turn of the century. In 1890 only about 9 per cent of the foreign born had come from Italy, Poland, Russia (principally Jews), the former Austrian Empire, and other southeastern European countries. By 1930 these same areas supplied about 47 per cent of the foreign-born whites. This is truly a remarkable change and is reflected in the fact that while in 1790 persons of these national origins constituted only 0.2 per cent of the white population, in 1920 they constituted 14.6 per cent.

The fact that the immigration act did not limit by the quota system the entrance of citizens from countries in the Western Hemisphere has no doubt been responsible for the large increase in foreign-born Mexicans during the last decade. This group now constitutes 4.5 per cent of the entire foreign-born population. Among Oriental peoples only the Filipinos are increasing in numbers by immigration. Their entrance is not restricted because they are nationals of an unincorporated territory.

The foreign-born Negro population in the country has never been large enough to be of importance since the slave-importing days. In 1900 there were about 20,000 foreign-born Negroes; by 1920 the number had increased to 74,000, and by 1930 to 99,000. Practically all come from the West Indies, to which the quota system does not apply.

5. ORIGIN OF NATIVE WHITES OF FOREIGN OR MIXED PARENTAGE

At any given time, the proportion of native whites of foreign or mixed parentage having its origin in any specific country is not the same as the proportion of the foreign born from that country. In the first place, the age and sex composition of the foreign born of different nationalities varies considerably, so that, even with the same specific birth and death rates, one group will have more children proportionally than another. In the second place, there are almost certainly differentials in specific birth and death rates among natives of varying national origins.[1] These will

---

[1] This matter will be discussed in detail in a census monograph by the authors dealing with fertility in the United States.

issue in differential rates of increase for the various groups and thus cause the proportion of native whites of foreign or mixed parentage to vary from group to group. It will be of some interest to compare these proportions as given in Table 29 and Figure 16 with the proportion of foreign born from the same country as given in Table 28. Unfortunately, the

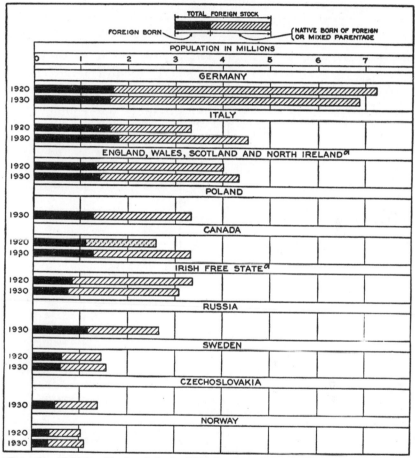

a Proportion of Irish from Northern Ireland and Irish Free State estimated for 1920.

FIG. 16.—Foreign white stock from leading countries, 1920–1930. (Based on Tables 28 and 29.)

data for the native whites of foreign or mixed parentage by country of origin are not available prior to 1890.

The first point worthy of notice is that the proportion of native whites of foreign or mixed parentage from any given country, being cumulative, surpasses that of the foreign born after two or three decades of considerable immigration and remains above it unless a large increase in immigra-

TABLE 29.—NUMBER, PERCENTAGE DISTRIBUTION, AND PERCENTAGE INCREASE OF NATIVE WHITES OF FOREIGN OR MIXED PARENTAGE, BY COUNTRY OF ORIGIN, 1890–1930[a]

Country of origin	1890	1900	1910	1920	1930
NUMBER (THOUSANDS)					
Total[b].....................................	11,504	15,646	18,736	22,434	25,319
England, Scotland, and Wales................	1,471	1,854	2,011	2,068	2,435
Ireland.....................................	2,924	3,212	3,152	2,972	2,859
Northern Ireland...........................	......	......	......	......	517
Irish Free State.........................	......	......	......	......	2,342
Germany.....................................	4,072	5,298	5,781	5,344	5,264
Iceland.....................................	......	......	......	......	5
Norway, Sweden, and Denmark	621	1,109	1,493	1,762	2,069
Netherlands.................................	......	......	174	228	281
Switzerland.................................	......	142	177	211	261
France......................................	146	164	175	209	336
Canada......................................	807	1,295	1,559	1,742	2,059
French.....................................	224	436	547	546	735
Other......................................	583	859	1,011	1,197	1,324
Poland......................................	......	......	......	......	2,074
Czechoslovakia..............................	......	......	......	......	890
Austria.....................................	100	404	827	1,685	584
Hungary.....................................	15	73	205.	513	316
Yugoslavia..................................	......	......	......	......	258
Italy.......................................	67	244	755	1,722	2,756
Russia......................................	76	378	939	1,850	1,516
Latvia and Estonia[c].......................	......	......	......	......	19
Lithuania[c]................................	......	......	......	......	246
Finland[c]..................................	......	......	81	146	178
Rumania.....................................	......	......	22	49	147
Greece......................................	......	......	8	46	129
West Indies.................................	......	......	19	24	32
All other[b]................................	1,205[d]	1,473[d]	1,358[d]	1,866[d]	603

Country of origin	1890	1900	1910	1920	1930	1890–1900	1900–1910	1910–1920	1920–1930
	PERCENTAGE DISTRIBUTION					PERCENTAGE INCREASE			
Total[b].....................	100.0	100.0	100.0	100.0	100.0	36.0	20.8	19.7	12.9
England, Scotland, and Wales..................	12.8	11.8	10.7	9.2	9.7	26.0	8.5	2.8	17.8
Ireland......................	25.4	20.5	16.8	13.2	11.2	9.8	−1.9	−5.7	− 3.8
Northern Ireland........	.....	.....	.....	.....	2.0	.....	.....	.....	......
Irish Free State.........	.....	.....	.....	.....	9.2	.....	.....	.....	......
Germany.....................	35.4	33.9	30.9	23.8	20.8	30.1	9.1	−7.6	− 1.5[e]
Iceland......................	.....	.....	.....	.....	(f)	.....	.....	.....	......
Norway, Sweden, and Denmark...................	5.4	7.1	8.0	7.8	8.2	78.7	34.6	18.0	17.4
Netherlands..................	.....	.....	0.9	1.0	1.1	.....	.....	31.4	23.1
Switzerland..................	.....	0.9	0.9	0.9	1.0	.....	24.7	19.1	24.0
France.......................	1.3	1.0	0.9	0.9	1.3	12.7	6.6	19.3	61.0

TABLE 29.—NUMBER, PERCENTAGE, DISTRIBUTION AND PERCENTAGE INCREASE OF NATIVE WHITES OF FOREIGN OR MIXED PARENTAGE, BY COUNTRY OF ORIGIN, 1890–1930.ª—(*Continued*)

Country of origin	1890	1900	1910	1920	1930	1890–1900	1900–1910	1910–1920	1920–1930
	PERCENTAGE DISTRIBUTION					PERCENTAGE INCREASE			
Canada....................	7.1	8.3	8.3	7.7	8.1	60.5	20.3	11.8	18.2
French.................	2.0	2.8	2.9	2.4	2.9	94.2	25.5	−0.3	34.8
Other..................	5.1	5.5	5.4	5.3	5.2	47.5	17.7	18.3	10.6
Poland...................	....	...	...	...	8.2	.....	......	......	......
Czechoslovakia............	....	...	...	...	3.5	.....	......	......	......
Austria..................	0.9	2.6	4.4	7.5	2.3	303.5	104.5	103.8	−65.3ⁱ
Hungary..................	0.1	0.5	1.1	2.3	1.2	395.3	181.3	150.6	−38.3ⁱ
Yugoslavia...............	....	...	...	...	1.0	.....	......	......	......
Italy....................	0.6	1.6	4.0	7.7	10.9	264.2	209.7	128.0	60.1
Russia...................	0.7	2.4	5.0	8.2	6.0	397.6	170.0ᵍ	97.1	− 3.8ᵉ·ᵍ
Latvia and Estoniaᶜ.......	....	...	...	...	0.1	.....	......	......	......
Lithuaniaᶜ...............	....	...	...	...	1.0	.....	......	......	......
Finlandᶜ.................	....	...	0.4	0.6	0.7	.....	.....	78.8	22.4
Rumania.................	....	...	0.1	0.2	0.6	.....	.....	125.0	199.7
Greece...................	....	...	(ᶠ)	0.2	0.5	.....	.....	442.3	183.7
West Indies..............	....	...	0.1	0.1	0.1	.....	.....	26.3	36.6
All otherᵇ...............	10.5ᵈ	9.4ᵈ	7.3ᵈ	8.3ᵈ	2.4	34.0ʰ	18.3ʰ	37.3	−67.7ⁱ

ª From *Fourteenth Census of the United States: 1920*, Vol. II, p. 897 and from *Fifteenth Census of the United States: 1930*, Vol. III, Pt. 1, p. 20.

ᵇ Excluding Mexicans in 1910, 1920, and 1930 and in percentage increase 1910–1920 and 1920–1930.

ᶜ Probably included with Russia in years for which no data are shown.

ᵈ Includes children of mixed foreign parentage.

ᵉ Of little value owing to changes in boundaries resulting from the World War.

ᶠ Less than one-tenth of 1 per cent.

ᵍ In calculating these percentages, Finland was included with Russia in 1910, and Lithuania, Latvia, and Estonia in 1930.

ʰ In calculating these percentages, Switzerland was included in "all other" in 1900 and Netherlands, Rumania, Greece, and West Indies in 1910.

ⁱ Decrease due mainly to change in classification, children of mixed foreign parentage being included in "all other" in 1920 but distributed by country of birth of father in 1930. This exaggerates the percentages shown in this column for the specified countries.

tion occurs suddenly. Thus the proportion of native born of Irish parents in this group was 25.4 per cent in 1890, whereas the proportion of Irish among the foreign born was 20.2 per cent; for succeeding decades the percentages were 20.5 and 15.6, 16.8 and 10.0, 13.2 and 7.8, and 11.2 and 6.9, respectively. Here the cumulative effect of births upon the proportion of natives of a given nationality is clearly visible.

Among the Germans a similar condition prevailed; beginning in 1890 the percentages for the native whites of foreign or mixed parentage and for the foreign born, respectively, were 35.4 and 30.1, 33.9 and 25.8, 30.9 and 17.1, 23.8 and 12.7, and 20.8 and 12.0. The proportion of the children of German parentage does not fall off so fast as in the case of the Irish, because the Germans came in greatest numbers somewhat later and probably had more children. In this country rural birth and survival rates have generally been higher than urban rates, which would increase German children relatively to Irish because of the greater rurality of the former group. That the Germans actually have contributed more children proportionally to the native whites of foreign or mixed parentage than the Irish is also indicated by the fact that at each age German mothers in the registration area have borne more children than Irish mothers in almost every year for which data are available.[1] Furthermore, in so far as any superior fecundity of the Germans is the result of their greater rurality in the United States, it will be a continuing and compounding factor among their descendants as long as they remain rural and the rural-urban differential persists. In several generations even small differences in rates of growth would materially affect the proportions of the different national stocks in the population.

It is a very general belief that such differentials have long existed as between the older natives and the immigrants, and there is no doubt that this is true for certain regions and groups.[2] It is also believed that at present there are large differentials between newer immigrants and the older groups. This belief, too, probably has some truth in it in recent decades, but it is not now possible to say how great this differential is nor how long it will persist. In Chapter VIII it is shown that there has been a very rapid decline in the specific birth rates among foreign-born white women during the last decade. The differentials in birth rates of foreign and native women about which there has been so much concern lately are rapidly vanishing; hence they are of less importance in changing national origins than is commonly supposed. Besides, under the quota system white immigrants will come very largely from northwestern European countries where birth rates are about the same as in this country. There is very little likelihood, therefore, that the present proportions of the several national stocks in the white population will be greatly changed in the next two or three generations. Over a longer period of time, assuming the quota system but little modified, it seems probable that the predominantly northwestern European origin of the rural population will be a factor of considerable, perhaps decisive, importance in gradually raising the proportion of these stocks in the white population because of higher rural birth and survival rates. Any such tendency might, of course, be readily counteracted by basic alterations in the character of agriculture, and by a variety of other factors tending to equalize the birth and survival rates of the rural and urban populations.

[1] U. S. Bureau of the Census, *Birth, Stillbirth, and Infant Mortality Statistics for the Birth Registration Area of the United States: 1918*, Washington, Government Printing Office, 1920, p. 11. See also comparable tables in later reports.

[2] That it is not so generally true as has commonly been assumed is shown in a census monograph. Warren S. Thompson, *Ratio of Children to Women: 1920*, Census Monograph XI, Washington, Government Printing Office, 1931, 242 pp.

In sum, then, it seems probable that the aim of the present quota laws will be achieved. Not only will the proportion of the population of southern and eastern European origin fail to increase in the future; but (even if their quotas are not filled) the proportion of the population having its origin in northwestern Europe will increase by reason of the fact that these peoples are more rural than those from southern and eastern Europe. Finally, although the authors cannot see any eugenic basis for the present quotas, it does seem probable that keeping the population fairly homogeneous in backgrounds and traditions may make it easier to develop a civilization in which justice and public welfare are the common aim. However, the possibility that the presence of different national stocks with widely different backgrounds and traditions may be an important factor in developing a more humane social system should not be overlooked. It may well be that in the future it will be found wise to modify the present immigration policy deliberately to encourage a moderate number of superior persons having the background of other cultures to migrate hither, to the end that our social order may keep itself fluid and adaptable. That the present laws have procured a breathing spell and are resulting in a less hysterical attitude toward peoples quite different from ourselves is all to the good and would be sufficient to justify them, but they should not be regarded as the last word to be said on migration of foreigners to this country.

CHAPTER IV

THE AGE COMPOSITION OF THE POPULATION

1. THE AGE COMPOSITION OF THE TOTAL POPULATION

AMONG the most important changes in a population with a declining rate of growth, such as the United States has had for some time, are those in age composition. Differences in age composition between regions and communities are also of considerable importance in a nation undergoing a rapid transformation from an agricultural and rural life to an industrial and urban life. It will be the object of this chapter to trace age changes from 1820 to 1930 and indicate possible trends from 1930 to 1980; to contrast the age composition between the several regions; to study the age make-up of communities of different sizes; to take account of the age differences of the various race and nativity groups wherever they appear sufficiently large to be significant; and finally, after presenting and explaining the facts, to endeavor to interpret them so that their significance in the social process will be readily understood.

a. Causes of Age Changes.—Before entering upon the description of age changes, however, it will be well to pause for a moment to note briefly the factors that bring about these changes.

The effects of a declining birth rate upon the age composition of a population need little explanation. Quite obviously the first effect is to reduce the proportion of children, which automatically raises the proportions of persons at other ages. In the course of time all ages are affected in greater or lesser degree, the extent of the changes being dependent upon the extent and the rapidity of the decline in the birth rate. As long as the birth rate continues to decline, the proportion of children, youths, and young adults will decrease and the proportion of older people will increase.

A declining death rate accompanying a declining birth rate will in due time hasten the decrease in the proportion of young persons and the increase in the proportion of elders because it means that a larger proportion of all persons born will live to middle life or later. Temporarily, however, it may mask the declining birth rate because of the saving of lives of infants. It is clear, then, that over a period of several decades a declining birth rate and death rate will lead to a decline in the proportion of the population in the younger ages and an increase in the proportion above middle age. This, as will be seen later, is what has been happening in the United States.

Immigration is another factor that has affected the age composition of the population owing to the fact that a large proportion of those entering are young adults.[1] Thus there were actually almost 700,000 more persons aged 20 to 29 in the country in 1890 than there were persons aged 10 to 19 in 1880 (Table 30). In 1910 the excess of persons aged 20 to 29 over those aged 10 to 19 in 1900 was more than twice as great. Even the 30-to-39 age group shows but little falling off from the 20-to-29 age group of 10 years earlier in several cases.[2] Since there were successive waves of immigrants up to the outbreak of the World War, all age groups above 20 have, in the course of time, come to contain large numbers of persons who did not pass their childhood in the United States. During the last few decades the older age groups have grown faster than they would have grown if the aging process was due merely to the decline in birth and death rates.

TABLE 30.—POPULATION OF KNOWN AGES, BY 10-YEAR AGE PERIODS, 1850–1980[a]

(Thousands)

Year	0–9	10–19	20–29	30–39	40–49	50–59	60–69	70–79	80+	Total
1850...............	6,739	5,420	4,277	2,826	1,847	1,110	610	257	92	23,178
1860...............	9,014	7,082	5,726	4,021	2,614	1,586	889	349	110	31,392
1870...............	10,329	8,827	6,823	4,878	3,519	2,245	1,263	520	149	38,553
1880...............	13,394	10,727	9,168	6,369	4,558	3,111	1,830	777	221	50,156
1890...............	15,209	13,591	11,424	8,445	5,917	3,999	2,468	1,095	312	62,460
1900...............	18,045	15,636	13,864	10,521	7,702	5,154	3,094	1,404	374	75,794
1910...............	20,392	18,171	17,237	13,368	9,731	6,688	3,947	1,781	489	91,803
1920...............	22,971	20,072	18,364	15,846	12,109	8,284	5,051	2,252	613	105,562
1930...............	24,052	23,557	20,704	18,329	15,032	10,621	6,522	3,056	807	122,681
Future as calculated: "Medium":										
1940...........	22,200	23,800	23,000	19,600	17,200	13,600	8,700	4,100	1,100	133,100
1950...........	22,300	22,400	23,800	22,300	18,600	15,600	11,000	5,400	1,400	142,900
1960...........	21,500	22,600	22,600	23,300	21,400	17,100	12,700	6,800	1,900	149,800
1970...........	20,700	21,800	22,700	22,100	22,400	19,700	14,000	7,900	2,400	153,800
1980...........	20,400	21,100	22,000	22,300	21,300	20,600	16,200	8,800	2,800	155,200

[a] 1850 to 1930 from current census reports. 1940 to 1980 calculated according to assumptions in Table 88, Column H, p. 316.

b. **Age Changes among the Youth.**—The first important change to attract attention is the declining proportion of young children in the population. In 1820 almost one-fifth (18.5 per cent) of the white population and probably a slightly higher proportion of the total population was under five years of age (Table 31 and Figure 17). This proportion has been declining ever since that time with the exception of the decade 1850–1860,

[1] Table 32, p. 115.
[2] The increases that frequently occur from the 0-to-9 age period in one census to the 10-to-19 period in the following census, while due in some degree to immigration, result primarily from the underenumeration of young children.

during which there was a slight increase. For the 60 years 1820–1880 the
decline was 4.7 points. This is but little greater than that of the last 50
years (1880–1930), which was 4.5 points. The proportional decline was,
therefore, about one-fourth in the earlier period but almost one-third in
the later period, which was, moreover, 10 years shorter. Today less than
one-tenth (9.3 per cent) of the entire population is under five and children
of this age are now only one-half as numerous relatively as they were in
1820. Furthermore, the end of the decline in percentage of children is not
yet in sight, as will be seen from the estimates in Table 31. In 1940 the

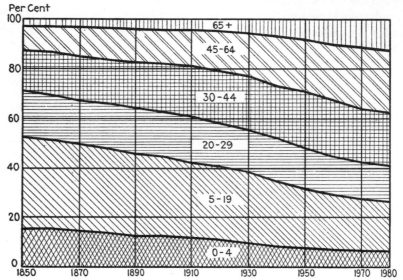

Fig. 17.—Percentage distribution of the population, by selected age periods, 1850–1980.
(Based on Table 31.)

children 0 to 4 will constitute only 8.2 per cent of the "medium" population, in 1960 only 7.0 per cent, and in 1980 only 6.4 per cent. Relatively
they will be only about two-thirds as numerous in 1980 as at the present
time and only about one-third as numerous as they were in 1820.

Those who believe that the authors' "medium" population is less
probable than the "low" or "high" populations[1] will be interested in the
proportions of children in these populations. As would be expected, the
proportion of children in the "low" population declines even faster than
that in the "medium," and in 1980 is only 5.8 per cent. In the "high"
population the proportion of children 0 to 4 also declines steadily from the
present but more slowly than in the "medium" and falls to only 7.6 per
cent in 1980.

[1] For definitions and assumptions, see Chap. X.

TABLE 31.—POPULATION OF KNOWN AGES, PERCENTAGE DISTRIBUTION, AND AMOUNT AND RATE OF INCREASE, BY AGE FOR TOTAL POPULATION, 1820–1980[a]

Year	0–4	5–19	20–29	30–44	45–64	65+	Total
POPULATION (THOUSANDS)							
1850........................	3,498	8,662	4,277	3,850[b]	2,285[b]	606[b]	23,178
1860........................	4,842	11,253	5,726	5,470[b]	3,267[b]	833[b]	31,392
1870........................	5,515	13,641	6,823	6,818	4,602	1,154	38,553
1880........................	6,915	17,206	9,168	8,888	6,305	1,723	50,156
1890[c].......................	7,635	21,165	11,424	11,630	8,188	2,417	62,460
1900........................	9,171	24,510	13,864	14,768	10,400	3,080	75,794
1910........................	10,631	27,931	17,237	18,630	13,424	3,950	91,803
1920........................	11,573	31,470	18,364	22,192	17,030	4,933	105,562
1930........................	11,444	36,165	20,704	26,319	21,415	6,634	122,681
Future as calculated:[d]							
"Medium":							
1940......................	10,900	35,100	23,000	28,200	27,200	8,800	133,100
1950......................	10,900	33,800	23,800	32,100	30,600	11,600	142,900
1960......................	10,400	33,600	22,600	34,400	34,100	14,700	149,800
1970......................	10,100	32,400	22,700	33,100	38,900	16,500	153,800
1980......................	10,000	31,400	22,000	33,100	40,000	18,800	155,200
"Low":							
1940......................	10,500	34,800	22,700	28,000	27,100	8,800	131,900
1950......................	9,900	32,000	22,800	30,900	29,900	11,600	137,100
1960......................	8,900	29,900	20,700	31,700	32,300	14,400	137,900
1970......................	8,100	27,100	19,500	29,300	35,200	15,700	134,900
1980......................	7,500	24,800	17,700	27,400	34,700	17,200	129,200
"High":							
1940......................	11,600	35,600	23,300	28,400	27,300	8,800	135,100
1950......................	12,900	36,600	25,000	33,200	31,200	11,800	150,800
1960......................	13,400	40,300	24,800	36,800	35,700	16,100	167,300
1970......................	14,300	42,500	27,700	37,000	42,500	20,300	184,200
1980......................	15,300	45,100	29,200	40,400	45,900	26,100	202,000
PERCENTAGE DISTRIBUTION							
1820[e].......................	18.5[f]	39.4[f]	30.0[f]		12.2		100.0
1840[e].......................	17.4	37.2	18.2	15.7[b]	9.0[b]	2.5[b]	100.0
1850........................	15.1	37.4	18.5	16.6[b]	9.9[b]	2.6[b]	100.0
1860........................	15.4	35.8	18.2	17.4[b]	10.4[b]	2.7[b]	100.0
1870........................	14.3	35.4	17.7	17.7	11.9	3.0	100.0
1880........................	13.8	34.3	18.3	17.6	12.6	3.4	100.0
1890[c].......................	12.2	33.9	18.3	18.6	13.1	3.9	100.0
1900........................	12.1	32.3	18.3	19.5	13.7	4.1	100.0
1910........................	11.6	30.4	18.8	20.3	14.6	4.3	100.0
1920........................	11.0	29.8	17.4	21.0	16.1	4.7	100.0
1930........................	9.3	29.5	16.9	21.5	17.5	5.4	100.0
Future as calculated:[d]							
"Medium":							
1940......................	8.2	26.4	17.2	21.2	20.4	6.6	100.0
1950......................	7.7	23.6	16.7	22.5	21.4	8.1	100.0
1960......................	7.0	22.4	15.1	22.9	22.8	9.8	100.0
1970......................	6.6	21.0	14.8	21.5	25.3	10.7	100.0
1980......................	6.4	20.3	14.2	21.3	25.8	12.1	100.0

TABLE 31.—POPULATION OF KNOWN AGES, PERCENTAGE DISTRIBUTION, AND AMOUNT AND RATE OF INCREASE, BY AGE FOR TOTAL POPULATION, 1820–1930.[a]—(*Continued*)

Year	0–4	5–19	20–29	30–44	45–64	65+	Total
"Low":							
1040	8.0	26.4	17.2	21.2	20.6	6.6	100.0
1950	7.2	23.3	16.6	22.6	21.8	8.5	100.0
1960	6.4	21.7	15.0	23.0	23.4	10.5	100.0
1970	6.0	20.1	14.4	21.7	26.1	11.6	100.0
1980	5.8	19.2	13.7	21.2	26.8	13.3	100.0
"High":							
1940	8.6	26.4	17.3	21.0	20.2	6.5	100.0
1950	8.6	24.3	16.6	22.0	20.7	7.8	100.0
1960	8.0	24.1	14.9	22.0	21.4	9.7	100.0
1970	7.7	23.0	15.0	20.1	23.1	11.0	100.0
1980	7.6	22.3	14.5	20.0	22.7	12.9	100.0

INCREASE (THOUSANDS)

Year	0–4	5–19	20–29	30–44	45–64	65+	Total
1850–60	1,345	2,592	1,449	1,621[b]	982[b]	226[b]	8,214
1860–70	672	2,388	1,097	1,347[b]	1,336[b]	321[b]	7,161
1870–80	1,400	3,565	2,345	2,021	1,703	570	11,603
1880–90[c]	720	3,959	2,256	2,792	1,883	694	12,304
1890–1900[c]	1,536	3,345	2,440	3,138	2,212	663	13,334
1900–10	1,461	3,421	3,373	3,862	3,024	869	16,009
1910–20	942	3,538	1,127	3,562	3,606	984	13,759
1920–30	− 129	4,695	2,340	4,127	4,385	1,701	17,119
Future as calculated:[d]							
"Medium":							
1930–40	− 500	−1,100	2,200	1,800	5,800	2,100	10,300
1940–50	20	−1,300	900	4,000	3,400	2,800	9,800
1950–60	− 500	− 200	−1,300	2,200	3,600	3,100	7,000
1960–70	− 300	−1,200	200	−1,300	4,800	1,800	3,900
1970–80	− 200	− 900	− 800	− 20	1,100	2,300	1,500
"Low":							
1930–40	− 900	−1,400	2,000	1,600	5,700	2,100	9,100
1940–50	− 700	−2,800	100	2,900	2,800	2,800	5,200
1950–60	−1,000	−2,100	−2,100	800	2,400	2,800	800
1960–70	− 700	−2,800	−1,200	−2,500	2,900	1,200	−3,000
1970–80	− 700	−2,300	−1,800	−1,800	− 600	1,500	−5,700
"High":							
1930–40	100	− 600	2,600	2,100	5,900	2,200	12,300
1940–50	1,400	1,000	1,700	4,800	3,900	3,000	15,700
1950–60	500	3,700	− 200	3,600	4,600	4,400	16,500
1960–70	800	2,100	2,800	200	6,800	4,200	16,900
1970–80	1,100	2,600	1,500	3,400	3,400	5,800	17,800

PERCENTAGE INCREASE

Year	0–4	5–19	20–29	30–44	45–64	65+	Total
1850–60	38.4	29.9	33.9	42.1[b]	43.0[b]	37.3[b]	35.4
1860–70	13.9	21.2	19.2	24.6[b]	40.9[b]	38.6[b]	22.8
1870–80	25.4	26.1	34.4	29.6	37.0	49.4	30.1
1880–90[c]	10.4	23.0	24.6	31.6	29.9	40.3	24.5
1890–1900[c]	20.1	15.8	21.4	27.0	27.0	27.4	21.3
1900–10	15.9	14.0	24.3	26.2	29.1	28.2	21.1
1910–20	8.9	12.7	6.5	19.1	26.9	24.9	15.0
1920–30	− 1.1	14.9	12.7	18.6	25.7	34.5	16.2

TABLE 31.—POPULATION OF KNOWN AGES, PERCENTAGE DISTRIBUTION, AND AMOUNT AND RATE OF INCREASE, BY AGE FOR TOTAL POPULATION, 1820–1930.[a]—(*Continued*)

Year	0–4	5–19	20–29	30–44	45–64	65+	Total
Future as calculated:[d]							
"Medium":							
1930–40..................	− 4.7	−3.0	10.8	6.9	26.9	32.1	8.4
1940–50..................	0.2	−3.8	3.8	14.1	12.4	32.4	7.3
1950–60..................	− 4.7	−0.5	−5.3	7.0	11.7	26.7	4.9
1960–70..................	− 2.7	−3.7	0.8	−3.7	14.0	12.1	2.6
1970–80..................	− 1.8	−2.8	−3.4	−0.1	2.8	13.8	0.9
"Low":							
1930–40..................	− 8.1	−3.8	9.5	6.3	26.5	32.1	7.4
1940–50..................	− 6.3	−8.1	0.5	10.5	10.3	32.2	3.9
1950–60..................	−10.1	−6.7	−9.2	2.6	7.9	24.4	0.5
1960–70..................	− 8.4	−9.3	−5.8	−7.8	9.1	8.6	−2.2
1970–80..................	− 8.2	−8.6	−9.2	−6.3	−1.6	9.6	−4.2
"High":							
1930–40..................	1.2	−1.6	12.6	7.8	27.5	32.5	10.0
1940–50..................	11.7	2.9	7.3	17.0	14.1	33.9	11.7
1950–60..................	3.8	10.2	−0.8	10.7	14.6	37.0	10.9
1960–70..................	6.2	5.2	11.4	0.6	18.9	25.7	10.1
1970–80..................	7.5	6.1	5.5	9.2	7.9	28.8	9.7

[a] For 1820 from *Fourth Census of the United States: 1820*, p. 1; 1840 from *Sixth Census of the United States: 1840*, p. 474; 1850 to 1920 from *Fourteenth Census of the United States: 1920*, Vol. II, p. 154; 1930 from *Fifteenth Census of the United States: 1930*, Vol. III, Pt. 1, p. 14.

[b] Number of persons 40 to 44 and 60 to 64 is estimated from those 40 to 49 and 60 to 69.

[c] Excluding 325,464 persons specially enumerated in 1890 in Indian Territory and on Indian reservations, for whom statistics of age are not available.

[d] Prepared by the Scripps Foundation for Research in Population Problems. For the assumptions on which these figures are based, see Table 88, p. 316, Column *H* for "medium," Column *A* for "low," and Column *J* for "high." Unknown ages are distributed in these calculations.

[e] Free whites only. Since they constituted over four-fifths of the total population, their percentages have been used here. The effect of this procedure is undoubtedly to understate the proportion in the younger ages in these years since the Negroes were a younger group than the whites. However, the percentage difference cannot be large so that no significant error is involved in using them for the total population. For numbers used in calculating these percentages, see Table 38, p. 141.

[f] Estimated from the age groups shown by the census.

Numbers of Children 0 to 4.—It will perhaps assist in understanding what has happened and what is likely to happen to the age composition of the population if increases in numbers of children 0 to 4 during the last 80 years are studied in some detail. It is of particular interest to note that in 1860, when the total population of the country was 31,443,000, the increase during the preceding decade in number of children 0 to 4 was 1,345,000 while in 1880, when the population was 50,156,000, or about 60 per cent larger than in 1860, the increase in number of children 0 to 4 in the preceding decade was only 1,400,000, or only 4 per cent greater than in the decade 1850–1860 (Table 31). Even the increase between 1890 and 1900, which was the largest increase ever recorded, was only 1,536,000, or less than 200,000 in excess of that between 1850 and 1860 although the total population in 1900 was more than three times as large as in 1850.

Since 1900 the absolute increase has declined steadily, rather slowly during the decade 1900–1910 but since then with startling rapidity. The consequence of this is that there was not only no increase in number of children 0 to 4 between 1920 and 1930 but instead a decline of about 129,000. This is approximately the number of children in Los Angeles, San Francisco, and Seattle, or in the entire state of Connecticut. It may also be noted that in 1930 a population of almost 123,000,000 had only about 800,000 more children 0 to 4 than a population of 92,000,000 in 1910. In the "medium" population of the future the decline in the number of young children continues for the next 50 years with only one small increase in 1940–1950 when the large number of persons born in 1920–1923 come into childbearing. In 1980 the total number of children 0 to 4 will be just about what it was in 1905, although the population will then be about 72,000,000 greater. In 1980 the total number of children of this age in the "low" and "high" populations will be smaller and larger, respectively, than the number in 1930 by about 4,000,000; in the "high" population the children will be somewhat more than twice as numerous as in the "low." The greater part of these differences is the inevitable consequence of the different birth rates used in calculating the two populations. There are also differences in death rates and in amount of immigration, but they are of less significance in determining the number and proportion of children.[1] Even in the "high" population the increase in number of children 0 to 4 between 1930 and 1980 is not quite so large as that which actually took place between 1890 and 1920. Only changes in the birth rate so great that they will necessarily be described as revolutionary will prevent a steady decline in the proportion of children (0 to 4) in the future population.

There is still another point of importance in this connection. The 1930 census shows for the first time that the 0-to-4 group was smaller than an older five-year group; in fact it was outnumbered by the next three older groups (Appendix Table 10). But after allowance is made for under-enumeration in the 0-to-4 age group (probably about 550,000, or 4.8 per cent) only the 5-to-9 age group outnumbered it and that by only about 600,000 instead of over 1,150,000, as shown in the census. This means that the number of children born during 1925–1929 was less than the number born during 1920–1924 by about 600,000 plus the deaths that would have occurred in the five years' longer exposure of the children in the older group, a not insignificant difference. Furthermore the 0-to-4 age group (corrected for underenumeration) was almost exactly the same size as the 10-to-14 age group—the children born during 1915–1919. After making

[1] *Infra*, pp. 312–320.

allowance for the deaths that would be expected in this older age group this leaves an excess of births in 1915–1919 of about 500,000 over those during 1925–1929 in spite of an increase of 17,000,000 in the population from 1920 to 1930. In the light of these facts, it would seem that there can be no reasonable doubt of the future trend in the proportion of children shown in Table 31.

The decline in number of children under five is shown graphically in Figure 18, the 1930 pyramid being narrower at the base than higher up. Such a contraction in the base foreshadows the changes shown by the "medium" population during 1930–1980. These are in sharp contrast to those which occurred during 1880–1930.

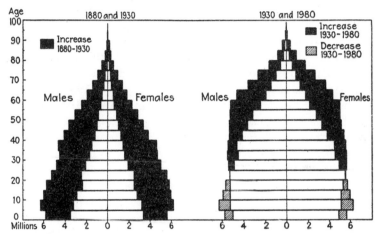

Fig. 18.—Distribution of the population, by five-year age periods, 1880–1930 and 1930–1980. (Based on Appendix Table 10.)

The 5-to-19 Group.—The proportion of the population in the 5-to-19 age group has also been declining almost steadily. In 1820, 39.4 per cent of the white population belonged in this group, but in 1930 only 29.5 per cent of the total population, a decline of just one-fourth as compared with a decline of one-half in the 0-to-4 age group. In the "medium" population of the future the decline in proportion will be considerably accelerated during the next two decades but will proceed more slowly from 1950 to 1980. In 1980 this group will constitute only 20.3 per cent of the total population. According to the "medium" assumptions the relative decline of this 5-to-19 age group during the next 50 years will be considerably greater than during the last 110 years.

At any given moment this 5-to-19 age group is made up of the survivors from persons born 5 to 19 years before, plus the balance between immigrants and emigrants in those ages. Since there are comparatively few foreign born of these ages, it is obvious that the slower growth in numbers

[113]

of children 0 to 4 must soon show its effects on the numbers 5 to 19. It happens, however, that this effect is considerably less in 1930 than might be expected by reason of the large number of post-war births during 1920–1923; nevertheless this group increased only 14.9 per cent during the decade 1920–1930 compared with 16.2 per cent for the total population. The decline of numbers in the 5-to-19 age group, because it can follow that of the 0-to-4 age group only after a proper interval, does not appear until the decade 1930–1940 ("medium" population, Table 31 and Figure 17). Thereafter, except during 1950–1960, when the children of the persons born 1920–1923 are numerous in this group, the decline is rather large; hence by 1980 the group will be about the same size as in 1920. Again, as in the case of children 0 to 4, the numbers 5 to 19 in the "low" population decline rapidly, while those in the "high" population increase fairly rapidly after a drop of about 600,000 during 1930–1940, a drop arising from the decline in births since 1923 and still continuing. In the "low" population this 5-to-19 age group will be about one-third smaller in 1980 than it was in 1930, or just about what it was in 1900; in the "high" population it will be about one-fourth greater than in 1930.

It is of greater significance, as will be shown later, that whereas about 58 per cent of the white population of 1820 was under 20, only 38.8 per cent of the total population was of this age in 1930, and of the "medium" population of 1980 only 26.7 per cent will be in this group—truly a remarkable decline in the proportion of young dependents in the population.

c. The Middle Groups.—In the 20-to-29 age group there was little change in proportion from 1840 until 1910, but since then there has been a decline (Table 31, p. 109). Such variations as there are in the proportion in this group would seem to be caused largely by the variations in immigration, because a very considerable proportion of all immigrants are of these ages (Table 32). However, it seems highly probable that the relatively stable proportion at these ages in the face of a steadily decreasing proportion 0 to 19 is to be attributed to the increasing number of immigrants culminating in the avalanche of 1900–1913. The effects of immigration on this group are still more apparent when numbers are examined. Between 1900 and 1910, a period of very great immigration, this group increased by almost 3,400,000. In the decade of the World War and the influenza epidemic (1910–1920) the increase was only about 1,100,000. In the last decade (1920–1930) the increase was about 2,300,000 with quota restrictions in effect much of the time.

In view of the decline in the proportion of persons under 20 since 1880, and the slowing up of immigration since 1914, it is not surprising that there was a marked decline in the proportion of persons 20 to 29 following 1910. This decline seems quite likely to continue, with the group reaching the low point of 14.2 per cent in 1980. The proportion in this group in the "low" and "high" populations varies but little from that of the "medium," but the numbers are quite different. In the "low" population as in the "medium," there is a decline in numbers after 1950, but at a much faster rate, while in the "high" population there is an increase after 1960.

As a result of the long-continued decreases in the proportion of the population under 20 and the recent decreases in the proportion 20 to 29

TABLE 32.—PERCENTAGE DISTRIBUTION OF IMMIGRANTS ARRIVING, BY AGE, 1820–1931[a]

Years[b]	Under 15	15–40		40+
1820–29.............................	16.4	71.9		11.7
1830–39.............................	23.9	65.9		10.1
1840–49.............................	23.4	66.8		9.8
1850–59.............................	21.6	67.9		10.5
1860–69.............................	19.1	60.3		11.6
1870–79.............................	20.9	65.9		13.1
1880–84.............................	22.4	67.4		10.2
1885–89.............................	20.0	69.5		10.5
1890–94.............................	15.1	77.0		7.9
1895–98.............................	15.0	75.5		9.4
	Under 14	14–44		45+
1899–1904...........................	12.5	82.0		5.5
1905–09.............................	11.9	83.4		4.7
1910–14.............................	12.7	81.7		5.6
1915–17.............................	16.0	73.8		10.2
	Under 16	16–44		
1918–19.............................	19.0	68.9		12.2
1920–24.............................	18.6	72.2		9.2
		16–29	30–44	
1925–29.............................	16.3	54.2	20.5	9.0
1930–31.............................	17.1	52.1	20.0	10.8

[a] For 1820–1924 from *International Migrations* (edited by Walter F. Willcox), New York, National Bureau of Economic Research, Inc., 1929, Vol. I, pp. 397–398; 1925–1931 from *Annual Reports of the Commissioner General of Immigration, 1925–1931*, Washington, Government Printing Office.
[b] From 1820 to 1866 there were several changes in date at which the official year ended so that the periods included in the first five decades are not of equal length. This probably makes no difference in percentages. For details of change, see source of data. Since 1870 the official fiscal year ends June 30 of year designated.

there have been corresponding increases in the proportions of the population in the older age groups. In the 30-to-44 age group there has been a steady proportional increase since 1840 and probably since 1820 (Table 31, p. 109). It is now about one-third greater than in 1840. In the "medium" population of the future there is but little change from the present proportion of 21.5 per cent. It declines slightly from 1930 to 1940 and then rises slowly to 22.9 per cent in 1960, after which it again declines and in 1980 is practically the same as it is today. In the "low" population the proportion remains almost the same as in the "medium" throughout the ensuing half century, but in the "high" is somewhat lower.

Numbers in this 30-to-44 group increased very rapidly in the past. In 1850 it was smaller by about 425,000 than the 20-to-29 age group, but by 1870 the two groups were practically equal in numbers. The 30-to-44 group fell slightly behind again in 1880, no doubt as a consequence of the Civil War, only to overtake the 20-to-29 group in 1890. Since then it has been steadily increasing its lead until now the 30-to-44 age group outnumbers the 20-to-29 age group by almost 6,000,000. Like the 20-to-29 age group, its growth has been greatly affected by immigration, although not to the same extent (Table 32). Its increasing numbers in recent years come chiefly from the rapidly increasing number of births prior to 1900.

In the "medium" population of the future, immigration plays a less important rôle than in the past. By 1940 most of the immigrants of the great influx of 1900–1913 will have passed into the older age groups; hence the growth of the 30-to-44 age group between 1930 and 1940 will not be so large as during the last four or five decades. By 1950, however, the large number of births between 1905 and 1920 will swell this group rapidly; hence it will continue to increase until 1960, after which it will decline rather slowly. In the "low" population the growth will be slower and the decline will begin after 1960 also; while in the "high" population there will be no decline in numbers because this is a population growing fairly rapidly and steadily, also having a moderate number of immigrants. There is, however, a decline in its proportion of the total population, attributable largely to the greater number of youths.

d. The Older Groups.—It is in the age groups over 45, however, that the most important increases in proportion are taking place. The percentages in the 45-to-64 age group almost reverse those in the 0-to-4 group. About 9 per cent of the total population belonged to this group in 1840, whereas 17.5 per cent belonged there in 1930. The proportion almost doubled in about a century and will keep on increasing in the "medium" population of the future, reaching 25.8 per cent in 1980. The numerical increase of this age group has been very rapid throughout the eight decades for which data are available, growing from 2,285,000 in 1850 to 21,415,000 in 1930—an increase of 837 per cent, while the increase of the 0-to-4 age group was 227 per cent. It is of particular importance to note that during the last 30 years, while the 45-to-64 age group has more than doubled, having added approximately 11,000,000 to its numbers, the 0-to-4 age group increased only about one-fourth, 2,273,000 being added to it. This 45-to-64 group is gaining steadily on all younger age groups and within about 30 years will undoubtedly surpass in numbers the 30-to-44 age group.

Unlike all the younger age groups in the "medium" future population, the population aged 45 to 64 does not begin to decline either in proportion or numbers by 1980, although its rate of growth slows up appreciably after 1970. By that time all those born before 1925 will have entered this age group and because the number of births has fallen off rapidly since then, it is not surprising that the gain from 1970 to 1980 will be small. In the "low" population the proportional increase of this group is even faster than in the "medium," but its numbers begin to decline after 1970. In the "high" population also the proportion increases steadily, although more slowly, until 1970, after which it begins to fall, while the numbers continue to increase. Although the "high" population in 1980 is almost one-third greater than the "medium," yet the 45-to-64 age group is only between one-seventh and one-sixth greater. The difference is chiefly attributable to the effects of a higher birth rate on the composition of the "high" population.

It is in the oldest age group (65 and over) that the greatest proportional changes have occurred and will continue to occur. This group, which was about 2.5 per cent of the total population of 1840, more than doubled by 1930 (5.4 per cent) and was then just beginning to increase rapidly, as its proportion in all three calculations of the future population shows. It more than doubles in the "medium" population between 1930 and 1980 and grows even faster in both the "low" and "high" populations. In numbers the increase is in some respects even more striking. Elders were more than ten times as numerous in 1930 as in 1850, although the total population was only a little over five times as large. In the "medium" population of the next 50 years this group will grow to almost three times its present size, although the increase of the total population will be but little over one-fourth. In 1980 about one-eighth of the total population will be over 65 years of age and this group will be almost twice as large as the 0-to-4 age group. This is a great change from the situation in 1840 when the 0-to-4 age group in the white population was about seven times as numerous as the 65-and-over age group. Even today there are almost twice as many children 0 to 4 as elders over 65. Thus it seems likely that the positions of these two groups will be practically reversed in the next 50 years if the "medium" population is actualized. In the "low" population of 1980 the elders (persons 65 and over) will outnumber the children aged 0 to 4 by considerably more than 2:1, and even in the "high" population they will outnumber the children 5:3.

The changes in the age composition of the population which have taken place in the past and those which are probable in the future may be likened to the movement of a seesaw. In the past the board has been heavily loaded with children and young people under 30, this group constituting about three-fourths of the total population in 1820. Gradually the load has been shifting to the opposite end of the board. By 1930 almost one-fifth of the total population had thus shifted its position and only 55.7 per cent remained on the young end. Some time between 1940 and 1950 the proportions under 30 and over 30 will so shift that what has, theretofore, been the heavy (young) end will begin to rise and the older people will henceforth hold the balance of numbers, those over 30 amounting to about 59 per cent of the total in 1980.

The comparison of age changes with the movement of a seesaw is also à propos in that the changes are greatest at the extremes and diminish as the mid-point is approached. Henceforth, the population will become steadily more weighted with old people, even much more so than that of France today. This is a very different situation from anything that has existed in this country in the past. It will demand manifold social and economic adjustments of an entirely new and unfamiliar character. These matters will be discussed at some length after a description of the age changes in the chief locality, racial, and nativity groups has been completed.

e. By Regions.—*The 0-to-4 Group.*—There have long been significant differences in the proportion of children 0 to 4 in the several geographic regions of the United States. As early as 1820 the Northeast had an appreciably lower proportion of children 0 to 4 in the white population than the other regions had (Table 33). The highest proportion at that time (21.6 per cent) was found in the most recently occupied region—the North Center. The proportion in the South was 19.8 per cent and in the Northeast 16.9 per cent. Thus the North Center had relatively over one-fourth more children 0 to 4 in its population at that time than the older states in the Northeast and almost one-tenth more than the South. By 1840 there was practically no difference between the North Center and the South in the proportion of children 0 to 4, but they both had almost one-fourth more than the Northeast. In 1870 the North Center and the South still had like, though smaller, proportions and were still about one-fourth in excess of the Northeast as in 1840.

In 1850 data for the West first become available and, strangely enough, instead of the high proportion of children that would be expected in a new region, this proportion was only about one-half that of the North Center and the South and about two-thirds that of the Northeast. This was probably due to the very small proportion of females 15 to 44 in the population at that time (12.7 per cent).[1] By 1870 the proportion of the

---

[1] This can be compared with 24.0 per cent in the Northeast, 21.3 per cent in the North Center, and 21.7 per cent in the South.

population 0 to 4 in the West had risen to 13.0 per cent as compared with 15.6 per cent in the South, 15.1 per cent in the North Center, and 12.2 per cent in the Northeast. Since the proportion of females 15 to 44 in the population of the West was still low (18.2 per cent), the specific birth rates must have been quite high at that time. In 1890 the proportion of children 0 to 4 in the West was still well below that of the North Center and the South; since then it has been below that of any other region. By 1890 also the South was well in the lead of the other regions in its proportion of children and has remained there.

Why the West should always have been low in its proportion of children is a puzzle. Perhaps the manner of its early settlement, by miners and cattlemen rather than by farmers, had much to do with it, for in the West, until quite recently, the ratio of males to females was very high and is still well above that of other regions.[1] This means comparatively few women to bear children. The scarcity of women may also have given the wife a larger share in determining the size of her family than in regions where women were more plentiful. But whatever the explanation, the West has never had a very prolific population and at present has only about three-fourths as high a proportion of children 0 to 4 as the South (Figure 19).

Although there have been and still are considerable differences in the proportions of children 0 to 4 in the several regions, the same steady downward trend is clearly discernible in all of them except in the Northeast where there was a very slight upward movement from 1890 to 1920. This is probably attributable to the large influx of young immigrants during this period, among whom birth rates were high. The slackening of the downward course of the proportion of children 0 to 4 in the North Center between 1910 and 1920 may also be credited to this cause. The renewed downward plunge in these regions since 1920 would then be explained in part by the slackening of the current of immigration since 1914 and the aging of those who came in before that time. In the South the decline in the birth rate among the native whites and Negroes is responsible for practically the entire decline. In the West the decline in the native white birth rate is by far the most important factor, although the decline in immigration is also of some significance.[2]

The 5-to-19 Group.—In the 5-to-19 age group, in the white population, there were practically no differences between regions in 1820. By 1840, however, there was a significant difference between the Northeast, and the North Center and the South. The proportion in the Northeast declined almost one-tenth during these two decades, while it declined but little in

[1] Chap. V. That this is not the sole explanation is shown very clearly by the comparison of birth rates on pp. 272–278.
[2] *Infra,* p. 297.

the other regions. In 1850, when the West first came into the picture, the differences were great. The South had the highest proportion (39.4 per cent), followed closely by the North Center (39.2 per cent). In the Northeast the proportion aged 5 to 19 had fallen to 34.4 per cent, almost one-seventh behind the South, while in the West the proportion was extremely low, being only 23.0 per cent. Since that time, the relative positions of the regions have not changed. The proportion of persons aged 5 to 19 in the South now exceeds that in the West by one-fourth, that in the Northeast by one-fifth, and that in the North Center by one-sixth.

TABLE 33.—POPULATION OF KNOWN AGES AND PERCENTAGE DISTRIBUTION BY AGE, BY REGIONS, 1820–1930[a]

Region and year	0–4	5–19	20–29	30–44	45–64	65+	Total
POPULATION (THOUSANDS)							
Northeast:							
1850......................	1,136	2,966	1,667	1,559[b]	998[b]	295[b]	8,621
1870......................	1,506	3,973	2,192	2,373	1,741	512	12,296
1890......................	1,781	5,122	3,374	3,542	2,662	881	17,361
1910......................	2,691	7,071	4,960	5,778	4,101	1,235	25,836
1920......................	3,107	8,043	5,186	6,643	5,200	1,453	29,633
1930......................	2,905	9,518	5,755	7,885	6,416	1,926	34,404
PERCENTAGE DISTRIBUTION							
1820[c]......................	16.9	39.1	30.7		13.3		100.0
1840[c]......................	15.4	35.7	18.6	16.9	10.2	3.3	100.0
1850......................	13.2	34.4	19.3	18.1[b]	11.6[b]	3.4[b]	100.0
1870......................	12.2	32.3	17.8	19.3	14.2	4.2	100.0
1890......................	10.3	29.5	19.4	20.4	15.3	5.1	100.0
1910......................	10.4	27.4	19.2	22.4	15.9	4.8	100.0
1920......................	10.5	27.1	17.5	22.4	17.5	4.9	100.0
1930......................	8.4	27.7	16.7	22.9	18.6	5.6	100.0
POPULATION (THOUSANDS)							
North Center:							
1850......................	883	2,117	959	869[b]	474[b]	98[b]	5,401
1870......................	1,960	4,739	2,266	2,258	1,445	313	12,981
1890......................	2,744	7,494	4,128	4,169	2,929	855	22,319
1910......................	3,219	8,826	5,571	6,101	4,654	1,462	29,833
1920......................	3,561	9,589	5,953	7,307	5,781	1,787	33,978
1930......................	3,414	10,832	6,371	8,526	7,035	2,391	38,570
PERCENTAGE DISTRIBUTION							
1820[c]......................	21.6	40.0	29.2		9.2		100.0
1840[c]......................	19.3	38.7	18.2	14.7	7.5	1.6	100.0
1850......................	16.3	39.2	17.8	16.1[b]	8.8[b]	1.8[b]	100.0
1870......................	15.1	36.5	17.5	17.4	11.1	2.4	100.0
1890......................	12.3	33.6	18.5	18.7	13.1	3.8	100.0
1910......................	10.8	29.6	18.7	20.5	15.6	4.9	100.0
1920......................	10.5	28.2	17.5	21.5	17.0	5.3	100.0
1930......................	8.9	28.1	16.5	22.1	18.2	6.2	100.0

TABLE 33.—POPULATION OF KNOWN AGES AND PERCENTAGE DISTRIBUTION BY AGE, BY REGIONS, 1820–1930.[a]—(*Continued*)

Region and year	0–4	5–19	20–29	30–44	45–64	65+	Total
POPULATION (THOUSANDS)							
South:							
1850......................	1,464	3,538	1,586	1,379[b]	799[b]	211[b]	8,977
1870......................	1,920	4,646	2,170	1,920	1,315	317	12,288
1890......................	2,791	7,699	3,274	3,219	2,184	603	19,770
1910......................	4,053	10,274	5,300	5,133	3,591	983	29,335
1920......................	4,034	11,502	5,711	6,110	4,447	1,271	33,076
1930......................	4,153	12,693	6,606	7,148	5,628	1,603	37,830
PERCENTAGE DISTRIBUTION							
1820[c]......................	19.8	39.9	29.0		11.3		100.0
1840[c]......................	19.2	38.4	17.5	14.6	8.3	2.2	100.0
1850......................	16.3	39.4	17.7	15.4[b]	8.9[b]	2.4[b]	100.0
1870......................	15.6	37.8	17.7	15.6	10.7	2.6	100.0
1890......................	14.1	38.9	16.6	16.3	11.0	3.1	100.0
1910......................	13.8	35.0	18.1	17.5	12.2	3.4	100.0
1920......................	12.2	34.8	17.3	18.5	13.4	3.8	100.0
1930......................	11.0	33.6	17.5	18.9	14.9	4.2	100.0
POPULATION (THOUSANDS)							
West:							
1850......................	15	41	65	42[b]	13[b]	2[b]	178
1870......................	128	284	196	267	101	12	989
1890......................	318	850	649	700	414	78	3,010
1910......................	668	1,760	1,406	1,618	1,078	269	6,799
1920......................	870	2,336	1,514	2,131	1,602	422	8,875
1930......................	973	3,122	1,972	2,760	2,336	715	11,878
PERCENTAGE DISTRIBUTION							
1850......................	8.4	23.0	36.4	23.4[b]	7.5[b]	1.2[b]	100.0
1870......................	13.0	28.7	19.8	27.0	10.3	1.2	100.0
1890......................	10.6	28.2	21.5	23.3	13.8	2.6	100.0
1910......................	9.8	25.9	20.7	23.8	15.9	3.9	100.0
1920......................	9.8	26.3	17.1	24.0	18.1	4.8	100.0
1930......................	8.2	26.3	16.6	23.2	19.7	6.0	100.0

[a] For 1820 from *Fourth Census of the United States: 1820*, p. 1; 1840 from *Sixth Census of the United States: 1840*, p. 474; 1850 and 1870 from *Ninth Census of the United States: 1870*, Vol. II, pp. 560–577; 1890 from *Eleventh Census of the United States: 1890*, Vol. I, Pt. 2, pp. 104–105; 1910 and 1920 from *Fourteenth Census of the United States: 1920*, Vol. II, pp. 170–186; 1930 from *Fifteenth Census of the United States: 1930*, Vol. III, Pt. 1, pp. 38, 39.

[b] Number of persons 40 to 44 and 60 to 64 is estimated from those 40 to 49 and 60 to 69.

[c] Free whites only. Since they constituted over four-fifths of the total population, their percentages have been used here. The effect of this procedure is undoubtedly to understate the proportion in the younger ages in these years since the Negroes were a younger group than the whites. However, the percentage difference cannot be large so that no significant error is involved in using them for the total population, except possibly in the South. For numbers used in calculating these percentages, see Appendix Table 14, p. 364.

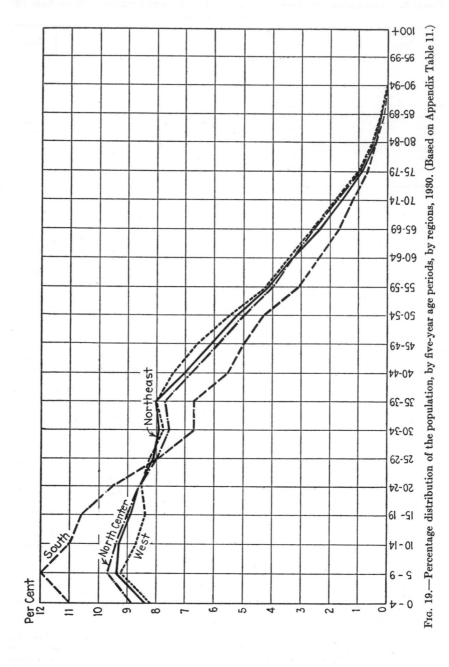

Fig. 19.—Percentage distribution of the population, by five-year age periods, by regions, 1930. (Based on Appendix Table 11.)

Here, as in the 0-to-4 age group, the trend is steadily downward in all regions, with only two insignificant exceptions. This is just what would be expected from the general trend described above and from the trend in the 0-to-4 age group.

The net effect of the regional differentials in the youth groups is that the South now has 44.6 per cent of its total population in the groups under 20 as compared with 34.5 per cent in the West, 36.1 per cent in the Northeast, and 37.0 per cent in the North Center. Hence there is the same proportion of persons under 20 in the South today as there was in the entire United States in 1900, while in the West the proportion under 20 is what is to be expected in the entire country in about 1940 (Table 31, p. 109).

About all that can be said, with reasonable assurance, of the future growth of the 5-to-19 age group by regions is that the downward trend will be somewhat less precipitous in the South during the next two or three decades than in other divisions because the proportion of children aged 0 to 4 has been declining somewhat more slowly there than elsewhere.

The Middle Groups.—In the 20-to-29 age group the differences between regions are not large. The downward trend of this group in the entire population noted above is clearly marked in all regions except in the South. Here the proportion in the total population in 1930 is the same as in the white population in 1840 and the variations during these 90 years have not been large except in 1890 and 1910. It seems highly probable that the downward trend already noted for the younger ages will soon pull down the proportion in this age group in the South and bring it into closer conformity with the other regions.

In the 30-to-44 age group the trend has long been upward in all regions, except the West, which had a very high proportion in 1870 (27.0 per cent). There the proportion dropped to 23.3 per cent in 1890 and has changed but little since. Thus the West has always had a higher proportion of persons in the 30-to-44 age group than any other region. The Northeast and the North Center are rapidly approaching the high proportion found in the West. The South is still as it has been for at least 90 years—well below the other regions, with the result that it has an appreciably smaller proportion of its population in this age group than has any other portion of the country. Taking the 20-to-29 and 30-to-44 age groups together as the most productive ages, in 1930 the South had 36.4 per cent of its total population in these ages, while the North Center had 38.6 per cent, the Northeast 39.6 per cent, and the West 39.8 per cent. These are appreciable differences and their significance merits attention, particularly when studied in connection with the proportions of dependent young persons (0 to 19) in the several regions.

In the West for each 100 persons in the most productive ages (20 to 44), there were 87 persons under 20. In the Northeast the ratio was 100:91; in the North Center, 100:96; and in the South 100:122. Clearly such differences in the proportion of young dependents create problems of child care and education that are different in the several geographic regions. The productive workers in the South carry a burden of about two-fifths more young dependents than the workers in the West and about one-third more than those in the Northeast and North Center. Is it surprising that educational facilities are less adequate in the South than elsewhere, or that child labor laws are less stringent, or that standards of child welfare are generally lower there than in other regions? Suppose New York City and Chicago had more than half again as many young dependents as they do have; would they provide as good schools and look after the general welfare of their children as well as they do? This question cannot be answered, No! categorically, but it seems to the authors that it is not probable. Standards of education and child welfare are correlated with the proportion of children in the population and particularly with their ratio to persons in the most productive ages who must provide for their care.

Older Groups.—This difference in the proportion of young dependents is in small part counterbalanced by the differences in the proportion of older people in the populations of the several regions, the proportions aged 45 to 64 and 65 and over being higher in the other regions than in the South. As would be expected, in 1820, the Northeast had a considerably larger proportion of its population in these older age groups (13.3 per cent) than the South (11.3 per cent) or the North Center (9.2 per cent). There has been a steady increase in the proportions in both the 45-to-64 and 65-and-over age groups since that time, but there have also been significant differentials in rates of increase which have led to a considerable shift in the relative positions of the several regions. In 1930, the South had the lowest proportion of persons over 45 years of age (19.1 per cent) and the ratio of persons aged 20 to 44 to those 45 and over was 100:53; then came the Northeast with a ratio of 100:61, followed by the North Center with 100:63, and lastly the West with 100:64. If only the persons 65 years of age and over, where dependency again becomes important, are considered, the ratios are much smaller: South, 100:12; Northeast, 100:14; North Center, 100:16; and West, 100:15. Beyond question then the South has a considerably larger proportion of naturally dependent persons (under 20 and over 65) than any other section of the country, while the West has a much smaller proportion. If the two groups of dependents (0 to 19 and 65 and over) are taken together, the South has a ratio of 100 persons aged 20 to 44 to 134 in these groups; in the North Center, the ratio is 100:112; the Northeast,

100:105; and in the West 100:102. Clearly the care of those who are naturally dependent is a much greater problem in some parts of the country than in others.

Effects of Migration on Age.—In 1920 there were 1,427,000 persons aged 15 to 24 in the West; at the next census (1930) when these persons were 25 to 34 years of age, they numbered 1,898,000. Thus it is clear that the gain from migration was about 471,000 plus an additional number equal to the deaths occurring in this group. It is much the same in other age groups also: the 25-to-34 age group of 1920 numbered 1,550,000 and the 35-to-44 age group of 1930 contained 1,831,000 persons, a net gain of about 281,000 over and above deaths during the 10 years. In the older age groups also there is a movement into the West, although the absolute numbers are not so large. Thus the 55-to-64 age group of 1920 was 620,000 and the 65-to-74 age group of 1930 was only about 100,000 less (517,000), in spite of a normal death loss in this age group which according to 1920 life tables would amount to about 180,000. There must have been, therefore, during this decade, a net movement into the West of approximately 80,000 older people who were 65 to 74 in 1930. Expressing these movements in terms of the 1930 population, the age group 25 to 34 had gained about 25 per cent by migration, the 35-to-44 group about 15 per cent, and the 65-to-74 group about 15 per cent. Clearly such movements as these affect in pronounced manner the age composition of a region, and, in view of them, there is no difficulty in understanding the rather peculiar age make-up of the West. The West has drawn much of its population from other parts of the country and probably will continue to do so as long as any considerable number of people are attracted by its climate and have the means to indulge their preference. It should not be forgotten, however, that the West has a very low birth rate which, of course, reduces the proportion of youths (persons 0 to 19 years of age) and thus automatically raises the proportion in the older age groups.

The effects of emigration on the age composition of a region are the reverse of the effects just noted. They can be seen to best advantage in certain parts of the South. In 1920 there were 4,409,000 persons aged 15 to 24 in the East South Central and South Atlantic states but only 3,663,000 aged 25 to 34 in 1930. Since the natural loss through deaths with no migration would have been about 330,000, there should have been about 4,080,000 in this group in 1930. Obviously nearly 420,000 persons who were aged 25 to 34 in 1930 must have moved from these southern states to other areas during the decade, thus reducing the age group by about one-tenth. Clearly emigration has been a factor of considerable importance in determining the age composition of these two southern divisions.

There has also been a considerable migration westward from the Northeast and North Center, but it has not affected the age composition here in the same manner as in the South because of the large inward movement of foreign born and of persons from other parts of the United States. In the Northeast the age group 25 to 34 in 1930 gained about one-sixth by migration during 1920–1930, whereas the 65-to-74 age group lost slightly. In the North Center the 25-to-34 age group gained about one-fourteenth, while in the 65-to-74 group the inward and outward movements practically balanced. It is clear then that emigration and immigration have been important factors in causing differences in the age composition of the various regions.

f. **By Size of Community.**—*The 0-to-4 and 5-to-19 Groups.*—From the earliest time for which data are available there were considerable variations between communities of different sizes in the proportion of children

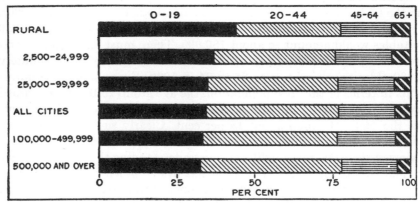

Fig. 20.—Percentage distribution by age of the rural population and of the urban population by size of city, 1930. (Based on Table 34.)

aged 0 to 4 in their populations. Thus in 1820 New York City (the only city in the 100,000 to 500,000 size group) had 15.9 per cent of its white population in the 0-to-4 age group, while the rural areas had 18.7 per cent, a difference of almost one-fifth (Table 34). In the cities of 25,000 to 100,-000, which were perhaps more characteristic of the urban population of that day, the proportion of children aged 0 to 4 was even smaller (14.7 per cent) than in New York City. Although the cities of 2,500 to 25,000 had a higher proportion of children aged 0 to 4 than the cities of 25,000 to 100,000, they had a slightly lower proportion than New York City. This same general pattern of the proportions of children aged 0 to 4 in the several sizes of communities persisted until 1930; that is, the largest cities had a higher proportion of children than the smaller cities (except those of 2,500 to 25,000 in 1910 and 1920). In 1930, however, there is a steady increase in the proportion of children aged 0 to 4 as the size of the community decreases. The proportion in the smallest cities (2,500 to

25,000) is about one-eighth higher than that in the largest cities (500,000 and over) and the proportion in rural communities over one-third higher than that in the latter cities (Figure 20). The proportion in the rural-farm population is also substantially higher than in the rural-nonfarm population in both 1920 and 1930, the only years for which these facts are available. Thus there can be little doubt that the more distinctly agricultural a community the larger the proportion of young children (0 to 4) in its population. The explanation of the relatively high proportion of children in the populations of the largest cities until 1930 is probably to be found in their high proportions of immigrants with high birth rates. Until quite recently many of these cities had more immigrant women than native white women of native parentage.[1]

In the 5-to-19 age group there has generally been an increase in proportion as the size of the community decreased, the exceptions being both few and unimportant. In 1910 and 1920 the higher proportion in the very large cities than in the next smaller places is to be attributed to the high proportion of immigrant women in them. In addition, the decline in the proportion aged 5 to 19 has been greater in all sizes of cities than in the rural districts, thus increasing the spread between the large cities and the rural districts, from over one-seventh in 1820 to over one-third in 1930. Here, too, there is a substantial spread between the farm and nonfarm populations. The proportion of the nonfarm population 5 to 19 is but little different from that of the smaller cities and only one-sixth to one-fifth higher than that of the largest cities, while the proportion of the farm population of this age is almost one-half higher than that of these cities. Taking the 0-to-4 and 5-to-19 age groups together, their proportion of the population in the largest cities has declined from 50.3 per cent in 1820 to 32.7 per cent in 1930, while in the rural districts the percentages are 58.4 per cent and 44.1 per cent, respectively. In the former size of community, the decline amounts to over one-third, in the latter to a little less than one-fourth. The fact that in 1930 the proportion aged 0 to 19 in the rural-farm population was 47.3 per cent while it was only 40.1 per cent in the rural-nonfarm population also emphasizes the more rapid urban decline in the proportion of children.

These data show very clearly that the decline in the birth rate has been greater in the cities than in the country, also that there has been such a differential for more than a century. This is of special interest in view of the fact that the cities of over 500,000 in each census have been made up chiefly of immigrants and their children, while the rural areas have been peopled chiefly by the descendants of old native stock—the

[1] In 1890 there were over two-fifths more foreign-born women in cities of over 500,000 than women of native white parentage; in 1910 there were almost one-third more, but by 1920 the native white women of native parentage in such cities were more numerous than the foreign-born women by about one-thirtieth, and in 1930 by over one-fourth.

TABLE 34.—POPULATION OF KNOWN AGES AND PERCENTAGE DISTRIBUTION BY AGE, BY SIZE OF COMMUNITY, 1820–1930[a]

Size of community	0–4	5–19	20–29	30–44	45–64	65+	Total
POPULATION (THOUSANDS)[b]							
1890:							
500,000 and over.............	500	1,258	994	988	591	126	4,458
100,000–500,000.............	560	1,527	1,150	1,126	689	159	5,211
25,000–100,000.............	436	1,269	932	914	583	138	4,273
2,500– 25,000[c] }	6,139	17,111	8,348	8,602	6,324	1,993	48,517
Rural[c]							
1910:							
500,000 and over.............	1,180	3,104	2,462	2,707	1,659	366	11,478
100,000–500,000.............	792	2,224	1,907	2,112	1,358	328	8,721
25,000–100,000.............	798	2,183	1,748	1,913	1,246	324	8,211
2,500– 25,000.............	1,426	3,882	2,765	3,067	2,202	674	14,015
Rural......................	6,390	16,432	8,273	8,739	6,893	2,243	48,969
1920:							
500,000 and over.............	1,592	4,121	3,257	4,034	2,719	579	16,301
100,000–500,000.............	1,006	2,738	2,226	2,694	1,896	449	11,009
25,000–100,000.............	1,003	2,672	1,994	2,419	1,768	446	10,303
2,500– 25,000.............	1,662	4,609	2,918	3,596	2,821	862	16,468
Rural......................	6,254	17,217	7,896	9,349	7,760	2,580	51,056
Farm......................	3,952	11,291	4,587	5,350	4,596	1,378	31,155
Nonfarm...................	2,303	5,925	3,309	3,999	3,163	1,202	19,901
1930:							
500,000 and over.............	1,578	5,154	3,964	5,298	3,693	892	20,580
100,000–500,000.............	1,189	3,874	2,846	3,725	2,824	778	15,236
25,000–100,000.............	1,049	3,385	2,310	2,997	2,335	676	12,752
2,500– 25,000.............	1,686	5,474	3,281	4,266	3,533	1,159	19,399
Rural......................	5,656	17,598	7,913	9,649	8,803	3,079	52,697
Farm......................	3,254	10,718	4,154	5,008	4,888	1,535	29,557
Nonfarm...................	2,402	6,880	3,759	4,641	3,914	1,544	23,140
PERCENTAGE DISTRIBUTION[b]							
1820:[d]							
100,000–500,000.............	15.9	34.4	38.4		11.4		100.0
25,000–100,000.............	14.7	35.4	38.9		11.0		100.0
2,500– 25,000.............	15.5	37.1	34.5		12.9		100.0
Rural......................	18.7	39.7	29.4		12.2		100.0
1840:[d]							
100,000–500,000.............	15.3	29.6	25.1	20.4	8.0	1.6	100.0
25,000–100,000.............	14.5	30.2	25.3	19.7	8.4	1.9	100.0
2,500– 25,000.............	14.7	32.8	22.9	18.3	9.0	2.3	100.0
Rural......................	17.8	38.0	17.3	15.2	9.1	2.6	100.0
1890:							
500,000 and over.............	11.2	28.2	22.3	22.2	13.3	2.8	100.0
100,000–500,000.............	10.7	29.3	22.1	21.6	13.2	3.1	100.0
25,000–100,000.............	10.2	29.7	21.8	21.4	13.7	3.2	100.0
2,500– 25,000[c] }	12.7	35.3	17.2	17.7	13.0	4.1	100.0
Rural[c]							

THE AGE COMPOSITION OF THE POPULATION

TABLE 34.—POPULATION OF KNOWN AGES AND PERCENTAGE DISTRIBUTION BY AGE, BY SIZE OF COMMUNITY, 1820–1930.[a]—(Continued)

Size of community	0–4	5–19	20–29	30–44	45–64	65+	Total
1910:							
500,000 and over............	10.3	27.0	21.4	23.6	14.5	3.2	100.0
100,000–500,000............	9.1	25.5	21.9	24.2	15.6	3.8	100.0
25,000–100,000............	9.7	26.6	21.3	23.3	15.2	3.9	100.0
2,500– 25,000............	10.2	27.7	19.7	21.9	15.7	4.8	100.0
Rural......................	13.0	33.6	16.9	17.8	14.1	4.6	100.0
1920:							
500,000 and over............	9.8	25.3	20.0	24.7	16.7	3.6	100.0
100,000–500,000............	9.1	24.9	20.2	24.5	17.2	4.1	100.0
25,000–100,000............	9.7	25.9	19.4	23.5	17.2	4.3	100.0
2,500– 25,000............	10.1	28.0	17.7	21.8	17.1	5.2	100.0
Rural......................	12.2	33.7	15.5	18.3	15.2	5.1	100.0
Farm......................	12.7	36.2	14.7	17.2	14.8	4.4	100.0
Nonfarm..................	11.6	29.8	16.6	20.1	15.9	6.0	100.0
1930:							
500,000 and over............	7.7	25.0	19.3	25.7	17.9	4.3	100.0
100,000–500,000............	7.8	25.4	18.7	24.4	18.5	5.1	100.0
25,000–100,000............	8.2	26.5	18.1	23.5	18.3	5.3	100.0
2,500– 25,000............	8.7	28.2	16.9	22.0	18.2	6.0	100.0
Rural......................	10.7	33.4	15.0	18.3	16.7	5.8	100.0
Farm......................	11.0	36.3	14.1	16.9	16.5	5.2	100.0
Nonfarm..................	10.4	29.7	16.2	20.1	16.9	6.7	100.0

[a] From special compilation made for this study. No age data by size of community are available for 1850 to 1880.

[b] Excludes "other colored," data for whom were not available by size of community, except in 1890 when they were included with those for Negroes.

[c] In 1890 it was impossible to separate the rural population by age from the population of cities of 2,500 to 25,000. At that time the total rural population (under 2,500) was 40,649,000 while the number of persons in cities of 2,500 to 25,000 was only 8,309,000, or but little over one-fifth as great. It may safely be said, therefore, that the age characteristics of the under-25,000 size group would be predominantly rural.

[d] Whites only, as available age data for Negroes are for broad age groups. It seemed worth while, however, to use percentages for the white population for these years to assist in indicating the trends. This undoubtedly involves some error; but since whites constituted over four-fifths of the total population, the percentage error cannot be large in the country as a whole. For numbers used in calculating these percentages, see Table 35, p. 130.

foreign born and their children being only about one-fifth of the total until 1930, when they were only 17.4 per cent.[1]

Considering for a moment the total number of persons under 20 years of age in communities of different sizes, as would be expected, it is found that the numbers aged 0 to 4 have increased rapidly until quite recently.[2] Since 1910, there has been a decrease in the number of children 0 to 4 in rural communities. This decrease was less than 150,000 between 1910 and 1920 but amounted to almost 600,000 between 1920 and 1930, most of which occurred in the rural-farm population (Table 34). As a consequence there are now about three-fourths of a million fewer children 0 to 4 in the rural population than there were in 1910 although the total rural population is almost four millions greater. It will

[1] Table 15, p. 49.

[2] Table 35. This table deals only with the white population, but there is no good reason to doubt that the same has been true for the Negroes. See Table 34 for data since 1890.

be recalled, however, that during this decade (1920–1930) the rural-farm population has declined by about 1,200,000 (Table 8, p. 24) and, as will be noted in a moment, the emigration of young adults from the farm has been very rapid. Since 1920 there has also been a slight decline (14,000) in the number of children in cities of over 500,000 in spite of over a four million increase in the population of these cities. In the cities of 100,000 to 500,000 the increase in population has also been over four

TABLE 35.—WHITE POPULATION OF KNOWN AGES AND PERCENTAGE DISTRIBUTION BY AGE, BY SIZE OF COMMUNITY, 1820–1930[a]

Size of community	0–4	5–19	20–29	30–44	45–64	65+	Total
POPULATION (THOUSANDS)							
1820:							
100,000–500,000.............	18	39	43			13	113
25,000–100,000.............	23	56	62			18	159
2,500– 25,000.............	46	111	103			39	299
Rural......................	1,365	2,891	2,146			889	7,291
1840:							
100,000–500,000.............	67	129	110	89	35	7	437
25,000–100,000.............	56	116	97	76	32	7	385
2,500– 25,000.............	137	306	213	170	84	22	932
Rural......................	2,214	4,724	2,156	1,888	1,128	325	12,435
1890:							
500,000 and over............	493	1,238	969	962	581	124	4,367
100,000–500,000.............	528	1,424	1,062	1,034	642	149	4,838
25,000–100,000.............	400	1,153	844	830	538	129	3,895
2,500– 25,000 } .... Rural	5,158	14,326	7,220	7,624	5,635	1,800	41,762
1910:							
500,000 and over............	1,151	3,026	2,357	2,586	1,606	357	11,083
100,000–500,000.............	744	2,073	1,749	1,948	1,272	311	8,097
25,000–100,000.............	750	2,027	1,597	1,762	1.169	308	7,613
2,500– 25,000.............	1,322	3,559	2,529	2,842	2,066	639	12,958
Rural......................	5,356	13,677	7,011	7,642	6,136	2,026	41,848
1920:							
500,000 and over............	1,542	3,981	3,069	3,805	2,615	565	15,577
100,000–500,000.............	938	2,510	2,000	2,432	1,751	423	10,054
25,000–100,000.............	948	2,487	1,819	2,233	1,666	427	9,580
2,500– 25,000.............	1,568	4,269	2,676	3,341	2,650	821	15,325
Rural......................	5 379	14,524	6,763	8,248	6,900	2,348	,44,162
Farm..................	3,270	9,178	3,826	4,598	3,972	1,215	26,060
Nonfarm..................	2,108	5,345	2,937	3,650	2,928	1,133	18,102
1930:							
500,000 and over............	1,468	4,866	3,641	4,886	3,506	868	19,235
100,000–500,000.............	1,066	3,493	2,506	3,313	2,589	739	13,705
25,000–100,000.............	968	3,121	2,089	2,751	2,193	650	11,771
2,500– 25.000.............	1,573	5,083	3,010	3,971	3,325	1,110	18,071
Rural......................	4,853	15,051	6,795	8,570	7,890	2,846	46,004
Farm..................	2,665	8,805	3,438	4,329	4,261	1,380	24,878
Nonfarm..................	2,188	6,246	3,356	4,241	3,629	1,466	21,126

TABLE 35.—WHITE POPULATION OF KNOWN AGES AND PERCENTAGE DISTRIBUTION BY
AGE, BY SIZE OF COMMUNITY, 1820–1930[a].—(*Continued*)

Size of community	0–4	5–19	20–29	30–44	45–64	65+	Total
			PERCENTAGE DISTRIBUTION				
1820:							
100,000–500,000............	15.9	34.4	38.4		11.4		100.0
25,000–100,000............	14.7	35.4	38.9		11.0		100.0
2,500– 25,000............	15.5	37.1	34.5		12.9		100.0
Rural.....................	18.7	39.7	29.4		12.2		100.0
1840:							
100,000–500,000............	15.3	29.6	25.1	20.4	8.0	1.6	100.0
25,000–100,000............	14.5	30.2	25.3	19.7	8.4	1.9	100.0
2,500– 25,000............	14.7	32.8	22.9	18.3	9.0	2.3	100.0
Rural.....................	17.8	38.0	17.3	15.2	9.1	2.6	100.0
1890:							
500,000 and over............	11.3	28.3	22.2	22.0	13.3	2.8	100.0
100,000–500,000............	10.9	29.4	21.9	21.4	13.3	3.1	100.0
25,000–100,000............	10.3	29.6	21.7	21.3	13.8	3.3	100.0
2,500– 25,000 ⎱............ Rural ⎰	12.4	34.3	17.3	18.3	13.5	4.3	100.0
1910:							
500,000 and over............	10.4	27.3	21.3	23.3	14.5	3.2	100.0
100,000–500,000............	9.2	25.6	21.6	24.1	15.7	3.8	100.0
25,000–100,000............	9.8	26.6	21.0	23.1	15.4	4.0	100.0
2,500– 25,000............	10.2	27.5	19.5	21.9	15.9	4.9	100.0
Rural.....................	12.8	32.7	16.8	18.3	14.7	4.8	100.0
1920:							
500,000 and over............	9.9	25.6	19.7	24.4	16.8	3.6	100.0
100,000–500,000............	9.3	25.0	19.9	24.2	17.4	4.2	100.0
25,000–100,000............	9.9	26.0	19.0	23.3	17.4	4.5	100.0
2,500– 25,000............	10.2	27.9	17.5	21.8	17.3	5.4	100.0
Rural.....................	12.2	32.9	15.3	18.7	15.6	5.3	100.0
Farm..................	12.5	35.2	14.7	17.6	15.2	4.7	100.0
Nonfarm..............	11.6	29.5	16.2	20.2	16.2	6.3	100.0
1930:							
500,000 and over............	7.6	25.3	18.9	25.4	18.2	4.5	100.0
100,000–500,000............	7.8	25.5	18.3	24.2	18.9	5.4	100.0
25,000–100,000............	8.2	26.5	17.7	23.4	18.6	5.5	100.0
2,500– 25,000............	8.7	28.1	16.7	22.0	18.4	6.1	100.0
Rural.....................	10.5	32.7	14.8	18.6	17.2	6.2	100.0
Farm..................	10.7	35.4	13.8	17.4	17.1	5.5	100.0
Nonfarm..............	10.4	29.6	15.9	20.1	17.2	6.9	100.0

[a] From special compilation made for this study. No age data by size of community are available from 1850 to 1880.

millions, or over one-third in a decade, yet the increase in children is only a little over one-sixth. In the cities of less than 100,000 the increase of children was only 70,000, or about 3 per cent, while the increase of population was over five millions, or about 20 per cent.

In the 5-to-19 age group only the rural-farm population shows a decline in numbers between 1920 and 1930. This is because of the large amount of emigration of young adults from the farm before 1930. Had they remained on the farms they would have contributed large numbers of children to this age group. The urban population, because it is still growing rapidly, will not begin to lose numbers in this 5-to-19 group for another decade or two unless the present depression should cut off immigration to the cities for several years. It is also of interest to note that the 5-to-19 groups in the country and the city are now about equal in numbers although the urban population is over one-fourth greater than the rural population.

The Middle Groups.—In the 20-to-29 age group the relative positions of the city and country are just the reverse of those in the 5-to-19 age group, although the time trend is the same—downward—for all sizes of communities. The largest cities have the highest percentages of persons aged 20 to 29, and the proportion gradually diminishes as the size of place decreases, being lowest of all in the rural-farm population. The proportion in the rural-nonfarm population is only slightly lower than in the smallest cities (2,500 to 25,000 and only about one-sixth below that in the largest cities, while the proportion in the rural-farm population is over one-fourth lower than in the largest cities (Table 34). There are several exceptions to this relationship, however, which are probably to be explained, as are the differences between the cities and the country, by the numbers of migrants, both native and foreign-born, received by communities of different sizes. Thus the larger cities, which have always drawn heavily from the surrounding rural populations and from foreign lands, have had from one-fourth to one-third higher proportion in the 20-to-29 age group than have the rural districts. There has not been much change in this spread since 1840, when it was over two-fifths. How long such differences between city and country will endure cannot be told, but it seems fairly safe to assume that as long as the city draws population into it, it will draw a preponderance of young adults and consequently will have a higher proportion in the 20-to-29 age group than will the rural districts and small towns. The city offers most opportunity to men and women workers who are in the prime of life.

By 1910 the cities surpassed the rural districts in numbers in the 20-to-29 age group and had 51.8 per cent of all persons in these ages, although only 46.4 of the total population was then urban (Tables 34 and 36). Since 1920 the number of persons aged 20 to 29 in the rural-farm population has declined almost 10 per cent, while in the cities and rural-nonfarm population the increase has been steady and rapid. In 1930 the cities contained 61.1 per cent of this age group as compared with 56.4 per cent of the total population.

It will be recalled that in the 30-to-44 age group the general trend was upward, an increasing part of the total population being found in

TABLE 36.—PERCENTAGE DISTRIBUTION OF POPULATION OF SPECIFIED AGES, BY SIZE OF COMMUNITY, 1820–1930[a]

Year and size of community	0–4	5–19	20–29	30–44	45–64	65+	Total
1820:[b]	100.0	100.0	100.0	100.0	100.0	100.0	100.0
100,000–500,000............	1.2	1.3	1.8		1.3		1.4
25,000–100,000............	1.6	1.8	2.6		1.8		2.0
2,500– 25,000............	3.2	3.6	4.4		4.0		3.8
Rural......................	94.0	93.4	91.1		92.8		92.7
1840:[b]	100.0	100.0	100.0	100.0	100.0	100.0	100.0
100,000–500,000............	2.7	2.5	4.3	4.0	2.7	1.9	3.1
25,000–100,000............	2.3	2.2	3.8	3.4	2.5	2.0	2.7
2,500– 25,000............	5.5	5.8	8.3	7.7	6.6	6.0	6.6
Rural......................	89.5	89 6	83.7	84.9	88.2	90.1	87.6
1890:	100.0	100.0	100.0	100.0	100.0	100.0	100.0
500,000 and over............	6.6	5.9	8.7	8.5	7.2	5.2	7.1
100,000–500,000............	7.3	7.2	10.1	9.7	8.4	6.6	8.3
25,000–100,000............	5.7	6.0	8.2	7.9	7.1	5.7	6 8
2,500– 25,000 } Rural	80.4	80.8	73.1	74.0	77.2	82.5	77.7
1910:	100.0	100.0	100.0	100.0	100.0	100.0	100.0
500,000 and over............	11.1	11.2	14.4	14.6	12.4	9.3	12.6
100,000–500,000............	7.5	8.0	11.1	11.4	10.2	8.3	9.5
25,000–100,000............	7.5	7.8	10.2	10.3	9.3	8.2	9.0
2,500– 25,000............	13.5	14.0	16.1	16.5	16.5	17.1	15.3
Rural......................	60.4	59.1	48.2	47.1	51.6	57.0	53.6
1920:	100.0	100.0	100.0	100.0	100.0	100.0	100.0
500 000 and over............	13.8	13.1	17.8	18.3	16.0	11.8	15.5
100,000–500,000............	8.7	8.7	12.2	12.2	11.2	9.1	10.5
25,000–100,000............	8.7	8.5	10.9	11.0	10.4	9.1	9.8
2,500– 25,000............	14.4	14.7	16.0	16.3	16.6	17.5	15.7
Rural......................	54.3	54.9	43.2	42.3	45.7	52.5	48.6
Farm....................	34.3	36.0	25.1	24.2	27.1	28.0	29.6
Nonfarm.................	20.0	18.9	18.1	18.1	18.6	24.5	18.9
1930:	100.0	100.0	100.0	100.0	100.0	100.0	100.0
500,000 and over............	14.1	14.5	19.5	20.4	17.4	13.6	17.1
100,000–500,000............	10.7	10.9	14.0	14.4	13.3	11.8	12.6
25,000–100,000............	9.4	9.5	11.4	11.6	11.0	10.3	10.6
2,500– 25,000............	15.1	15.4	16.2	16.4	16.7	17.6	16.1
Rural......................	50.7	49.6	39.0	37.2	41.5	46.8	43.7
Farm.....................	29.2	30.2	20.4	19.3	23.1	23.3	24.5
Nonfarm.................	21.5	19.4	18.5	17.9	18.5	23.5	19.2

[a] Based on Tables 34 and 35, pp. 128 and 130.
[b] White population only

this group. This is true for all different sizes of communities, except the rural-farm group, where there was a slight decline between 1920 and 1930. The proportional increases are much the same in all sizes of cities. There is, however, a large difference in the proportion in this group in communities of various sizes. In 1820 the proportions in the rural communities and the largest cities are not known exactly but were probably about 13 or 14 per cent and 17 or 18 per cent, respectively; in 1840 they were 15.2

per cent and 20.4 per cent, the cities having slightly over one-third more in this age group than the rural districts had (Table 34). In 1930 the proportion in the rural-farm population was 16.9 per cent, in the rural-nonfarm population 20.1 per cent, in cities of 100,000 to 500,000, 24.4 per cent, and 25.7 per cent in cities of over 500,000. Thus the largest cities have over one-half more in this age group than the farm population has. The rate of increase has been about the same in all sizes of communities. In this age group also the differences between city and country are largely to be explained by the movement from the country to the city and the coming of the foreign born to the cities, particularly to the larger cities.

In numbers of persons aged 30 to 44 the cities have had a considerable lead over the rural districts since about 1900. In 1910 there were over 1,000,000 more persons of these ages in the cities than in the country, and they constituted 52.9 per cent of all such persons in spite of the fact that the urban population was only 46.4 per cent of the total (Table 36). Between 1920 and 1930 the rural-farm population of these ages declined by about 350,000, or a little over 6 per cent. It was the only group having a decline.

The situation as between city and country is much the same as between the South and the other regions (pp. 123 and 124). The number of persons in these most productive ages (20 to 44) is relatively small in the rural districts (especially in the rural-farm population), and relatively high in the cities (particularly in the larger cities). Even as early as 1820 there were far more persons under 20 to each 100 persons 20 to 44 in the rural districts than in the cities; 198:100 in the rural districts against 131:100 in New York City (only city over 100,000) and 128:100 in all cities of 25,000 to 100,000 (Table 37). Although the ratios of persons under 20 to those 20 to 44 in all sizes of communities have declined greatly since 1820 and the differential in ratios between the largest cities and the rural districts was less absolutely in 1930 than in 1820 (59 as compared with 67), yet this difference in ratios is greater proportionally now than it was 110 years ago. At no time within the period covered by these data has the rural population had less than a 50 per cent (1820) higher ratio of persons under 20 to those aged 20 to 44 than the largest cities and in 1930 the excess in the rural districts was 80 per cent. Even when compared with the smallest cities, the rural excess has always been above 30 per cent.

Clearly the rural communities, especially the rural-farm communities, have a much heavier burden of young dependents to provide for than the cities and particularly the largest cities. Furthermore, this burden is growing relatively heavier, as the data just cited abundantly prove. It is not an idle question then to ask whether these age differences between

TABLE 37.—NUMBER OF PERSONS UNDER 20 AND OVER 65, PER 100 PERSONS 20 TO 44, BY SIZE OF COMMUNITY, 1820–1930[a]

Year and size of community	Number per 100 persons 20–44		Year	Number per 100 persons 20–44	
	Under 20	Over 65		Under 20	Over 65
1820:[b]			1910:		
500,000 and over	...	..		83	7
100,000–500,000	131	5		75	8
25,000–100,000	128	5		81	9
2,500– 25,000	152	8		91	12
Rural	198	9		134	13
1840:[b]			1920:		
500,000 and over	...	..		78	8
100,000–500,000	99	3		76	9
25,000–100,000	99	4		83	10
2,500– 25,000	115	6		96	13
Rural	172	8		136	15
Farm	...	..		153	14
Nonfarm	...	..		113	16
1890:			1930:		
500,000 and over	89	6		73	10
100,000–500,000	92	7		77	12
25,000–100,000	92	8		84	13
2,500– 25,000 }	137	12		95	15
Rural				132	18
Farm	...	..		152	17
Nonfarm	...	..		110	18

[a] Based on Tables 34 and 35, pp. 128 and 130.
[b] White population only.

rural and urban communities are not of some importance in determining the quality of the educational facilities and of the standards of welfare that prevail in different sizes of places. Assuming for the moment that a high school education or its equivalent is desirable for all children and that on the average this will require school attendance through the eighteenth year, 100 persons in the most productive ages (20 to 44) would have to provide facilities for 80 per cent more children in the country than in the cities of over 500,000. This would also be true for all other types of care which are needed by the children of a community. The fact is, of course, that rural children, as a whole, do not have so good school facilities as urban children and that in many other respects, particularly in certain health matters, they are not getting the care bestowed on city children. The question raised here is: How far is this the result of the fact that there are so many more of them, particularly on the farms, in relation to that part of the population which has to produce the wherewithal to provide these facilities?

The Older Groups.—In the 45-to-64 age group there is a marked upward trend in the proportion in all sizes of communities, as would be expected from the general trend noted above. In the first half of the nineteenth century or even until the last quarter it seems rather probable that this group was relatively largest in the rural communities, decreasing slightly as the communities increased in size. By 1890, however, there was a slightly higher proportion of persons aged 45 to 64 in the cities than in the country. The difference was not great, but the highest proportion was found in the smaller cities. This pattern still persists with the modification that the highest proportions are not now found in the smaller cities but in the 100,000-to-500,000 size group. With the steadily increasing proportion in these ages, the percentage is almost twice as high in the cities today as it was in the white population of 1840. The increase in the rural population has not been so rapid, and in 1930 there was very little difference between the farm and nonfarm populations in the proportion in this group. The net result is that, although there were more persons of these ages in the rural districts than in the cities as late as 1910, the cities now have over one-third more. Again it appears that the cities strongly attract those in the productive ages.

It is of some interest to note that of all the age groups dealt with here, the 45 to 64 is more nearly normal than any other in spite of the rural-urban differences just noted (Table 36, p. 133). The proportion of persons aged 45 to 64 is generally more like that of the total population in the same size of community than in the case of any other age groups, and this has apparently been the case ever since 1840.

The increase in the proportion of elders (persons over 65 years of age) in the population during the last century has been very large in every size of community, more than doubling in all of them and more than trebling in the cities of 100,000 to 500,000 (Table 34, p. 128). In general, the proportion of older people increases as the size of community decreases, but beginning with 1910 the small cities (2,500 to 25,000) have had a higher proportion than the rural districts, although not so high as the nonfarm population. This is undoubtedly attributable chiefly to the large number of old people who retire from the farms to the neighboring village or small city. It is interesting that these small cities and villages should have such high proportions of old people when for the last 40 years and more the foreign born have gone so largely to the big cities. The foreign born, as will be pointed out below, have a high proportion in the older ages and thus raise the proportion of the total population in these ages above what it would be but for their presence. That they do not raise the proportion in the larger cities above that of the rural districts is due to several factors.

For one thing, the death rate is lower in the rural districts than in the cities, so that a larger proportion of persons survive to old age in the country.[1] A second factor is that before 1890 the movement of immigrants into rural communities was much greater than it has been since; hence the rural population today contains a larger proportion of earlier immigrants grown old. By 1940 the cities will be more heavily weighted with elderly immigrants than they now are. Another factor, of course, is the relatively large movement of young adults from the country to city. For the time being this not only raises the proportion of young adults in the cities, but also lowers the proportion of elders and youths. In the course of time, however, this movement may work to reverse this situation as regards the elders since there are more persons in the middle groups in the cities to become old.

Whether the cities will have more old people than the rural districts within 20 or 30 years or whether the differences in death rates and the pull of villages on older people will keep the proportion larger in these latter cannot be told with any assurance. However, since the proportion of elders in the cities of over 500,000 is increasing more rapidly than in the rural districts, it may be that the preponderance of persons in the middle groups in the cities 30 to 40 years ago is beginning to manifest itself and that in the future the cities will come to have a larger proportion of elders than the rural districts.

There are exceedingly wide variations between cities in their age composition. Thus the two large cities which made the most rapid growth during the last decade are about as different from one another as they can be. Clearly they attract population for quite different reasons as is shown beyond question in their age composition. Los Angeles has more than twice as high a proportion in the 65-and-over age group (6.3 per cent) as Detroit (2.7 per cent) (Appendix Table 12). There is much the same difference between them in the 45-to-64 age group, Los Angeles having 21.6 per cent and Detroit 13.8 per cent. In the younger ages, as would be anticipated, the situation is reversed; Los Angeles has only 6.4 per cent of children 0 to 4 while Detroit has 9.4 per cent. In the 5-to-19 age group the percentages are 20.1 and 25.8, respectively. The difference in middle groups is not so large, Detroit having 48.3 per cent in the 20-to-44 groups and Los Angeles having 45.7 per cent.

This comparison shows very clearly how a manufacturing city like Detroit differs from a city like Los Angeles which depends largely on climate for its attraction.

Much the same kind of difference exists between many smaller cities, for example, San Diego, California, and Birmingham, Alabama; Portland,

[1] Table 67, p. 242.

Oregon, and Dallas, Texas. Even within the same state, Cincinnati and Cleveland have quite dissimilar proportions of older and younger people. All these differences are to be explained by the nature of the attraction and the rapidity of growth. A place growing rapidly necessarily draws much of its population from other areas, either here or abroad. On the other hand, cities which have not grown rapidly, for example, Boston, St. Louis, and Cincinnati, naturally have an older population because they receive fewer migrants in the young adult ages. In general, they will also have fewer children just because of having fewer young adults, although variations in birth rates are probably the most important causes of the differences in proportions of children.

Probable Future Trend.—But even if the proportion of old people in the cities increases rapidly, it will be some time before the ratio of elders (ages over 65) to persons in the most productive ages (20 to 44) is as large in the cities as in the country (Table 37). At present there are but 10 elders in the cities of over 500,000 to 100 persons in the most productive ages, while there are 18 in the rural districts, an excess of 80 per cent. Hence the most productive age group (20 to 44) of the rural districts is carrying a much heavier burden of old people than the same group in the cities. For the future, only the most general predictions can be made regarding the proportions which will be found in the several age groups in different sizes of communities. In so far as the raising of a family remains an easier and simpler task in the country than in the city, it seems probable that the birth rate will remain higher in the country and that the proportion of youths in the rural population will remain relatively high. As regards the other extreme of life, it is impossible to say whether old people will always prefer the simpler and cheaper life of the country or small town, or whether, if means permit, they will prefer homes for the aged and small apartments in the cities.

As for those in the more productive ages, it seems probable that the cities will continue to attract many young adults from the rural areas although loading the 20-to-44 groups less heavily and depleting those of the country less rapidly than in the past. Consequently the main change in the present pattern of the age distribution between communities of different sizes will be a gradual narrowing of the present extremes between cities and the country. But it should be recognized that any profound changes in the general distribution of the population, for example the decentralization of industry, will almost inevitably work large changes in the age composition of the communities most affected. There is no way of telling whether there will be any such changes, or how much they will affect existing proportions.

By Regions.—In the several regions, the general trends by size of community are much the same as in the country as a whole (Appendix

Table 13, p. 362). There is a decrease in the younger ages (0 to 4 and 5 to 19) in all regions and in all sizes of communities although it is not equally steady in all of them. There is also a general downward trend in the 20-to-29 age group and the familiar upward trend in all the older groups. However, there are variations between regions which merit brief notice. There is comparatively little difference between the proportions in the several age groups in the Northeast and North Center. The most noticeable is the somewhat higher proportions 45 to 64 and 65 and over in the rural population of the Northeast. Here the proportions in these ages reach the high points of 19.4 per cent and 7.6 per cent, respectively, in 1930. Within their rural populations, however, there are significant differences. In the Northeast the proportions at these ages are decidedly higher in the farm population, while in the North Center the high proportions are found in the nonfarm population. The proportion 65 and over reaches the high point of 9.3 per cent in the nonfarm population of the North Center. As between the cities and the rural districts of these regions there are the same differences that were noted for the United States, the rural population having more young and old people and fewer in the productive ages, particularly in the most productive ages, than the cities.

It is the South and West which are most distinctive in their age composition. Even in these regions in recent years the differences between their cities and those of other regions are not striking, except in the low proportion of persons 0 to 19 in the West. There are also proportionally more persons 20 to 29 and fewer 45 to 64 and 65 and over in the South than elsewhere. It is in the rural districts of the South, however, that the most significant differences occur. Thus 48.7 per cent of the rural population (51.1 per cent in the rural-farm population) of the South is under 20 as compared with about 34 per cent in the cities of over 100,000. When compared with rural areas in other regions, the South still stands well in the lead with its 48.7 per cent; the percentages elsewhere are: Northeast, 39.4; North Center, 40.8; and West, 39.1. The South has a lead of about one-fifth over any other region. When compared with the proportion of the same age in the cities of over 100,000, the rural South is far in the lead. In the Northeast the percentage of the population 0 to 19 in cities of over 100,000 is about 35, in the North Center about 33, and in the West about 27. Thus the rural South has over one-third more young persons (0 to 19) than the larger cities of any region and about four-fifths more than such cities in the West. Age causes of differences in educational and child welfare standards, previously noted for the several regions and size groups of communities in the entire United States, become still more significant when the rural South is compared with the cities in the West.

It is quite impossible to do more than guess at future changes in age groups in different sizes of communities by regions. The rapid industrialization of the South, by keeping the young adults at home, would undoubtedly increase the proportion at the most productive ages in this region. Such industrialization would also tend to reduce the birth rate and the proportions of youths and in time would raise the proportions of older people. If such development should take place and present immigration restrictions should be continued, the Northeast and the North Center, particularly the former, would show a rapid decline in the proportion aged 20 to 44 and an almost equally rapid increase in the older age groups. These changes would undoubtedly affect different sizes of communities unequally, probably raising the proportion of elders in the rural districts faster than in the cities. But obviously future developments are extremely uncertain. Everywhere the rural areas appear to be more hospitable to the young and the old than the cities do, and there is no good reason to anticipate any fundamental change in this respect in the near future.

2. THE AGE COMPOSITION OF WHITES BY NATIVITY

Thus far the discussion of age composition has dealt chiefly with the total population. Since 1890, however, the data for the more important nativity and racial groups are available, so that they can be compared both with the total population and with one another.

a. **Total White Population.**—Little need be said about the total white population since it is such a large part of the total population that its characteristics dominate the total and differ in only a few significant respects from it. Perhaps the most significant difference between the two is in the larger decline in number of children aged 0 to 4 among the whites than in the total population during the last decade. It will be recalled that the decline in number of children (0 to 4) in the total population was about 129,000. In the white population it was 447,000 (Table 38). Unfortunately this comparison is of no value as it stands because in 1930 the Mexicans were classed by the census as colored whereas in previous censuses they were treated as part of the white population. When the Mexican children aged 0 to 4 in 1930 are added to the white population aged 0 to 4 as given by the census, the decline from 1920 to 1930 is not 447,000 but only 232,000. Since this is about 100,000 more than the total decline, there must have been an increase of about this number in the colored population, aside from the Mexicans. It is known that Mexicans increased rapidly during this decade, although the increase by age is not available. Hence it is probably not far wrong to say that the decline in number of children 0 to 4 in the white population between 1920 and 1930 was about 300,000. In no other age group are the differences between

TABLE 38.—WHITE POPULATION OF KNOWN AGES AND PERCENTAGE DISTRIBUTION, BY AGE, 1820-1980[a]

Year	0-4	5-19	20-29	30-44	45-64	65+	Total[b]
			POPULATION (THOUSANDS)				
1820	1,451	3,097	2,356		958		7,862
1830	1,896	4,013	1,876	1,550	929	268	10,531
1840	2,474	5,275	2,576	2,224	1,279	361	14,189
1850	2,896	7,235	3,628	3,297	1,968	519	19,543
1860	4,117	9,494	4,917	4,767	2,850	751	26,897
1870	4,720	11,799	5,917	6,028	4,092	1,031	33,586
1880	5,800	14,675	7,944	7,818	5,622	1,544	43,403
1890	6,580	18,140	10,095	10,450	7,395	2,202	54,863
1900	7,920	21,141	12,098	13,317	9,382	2,807	66,664
1910	9,323	24,362	15,244	16,770	12,250	3,640	81,598
1920	10,374	27,771	16,327	20,060	15,582	4,583	94,697
1930	9,927	31,614	18,040	23,492	19,502	6,212	108,787
Future as calculated:[c]							
"Medium":							
1940	9,500	30,600	20,200	24,900	24,500	8,100	118,000
1950	9,600	29,400	21,000	28,600	27,600	10,700	126,800
1960	9,100	29,300	19,800	30,600	30,800	13,500	133,200
1970	8,900	28,300	20,000	29,400	35,200	15,100	136,900
1980	8,800	27,500	19,300	29,400	36,200	17,200	138,400
"Low":							
1940	9,200	30,400	20,000	24,800	24,400	8,100	116,900
1950	8,600	27,800	20,000	27,500	26,900	10,600	121,400
1960	7,700	25,900	18,100	28,200	29,000	13,200	122,000
1970	7,100	23,400	17,000	25,800	31,700	14,300	119,300
1980	6,500	21,400	15,400	24,100	31,200	15,600	114,300
"High":							
1940	10,100	30,900	20,500	25,100	24,600	8,100	119,400
1950	11,300	31,700	21,900	29,300	27,900	10,700	132,000
1960	11,700	34,900	21,600	32,400	31,700	14,700	147,100
1970	12,400	36,600	24,100	32,300	37,700	18,400	161,400
1980	13,200	38,700	25,300	35,200	40,400	23,500	176,300
			PERCENTAGE DISTRIBUTION				
1820	18.5	39.4	30.0		12.2		100.0
1830	18.0	38.1	17.8	14.7	8.8	2.5	100.0
1840	17.4	37.2	18.2	15.7	9.0	2.5	100.0
1850	14.8	37.0	18.6	16.9	10.1	2.7	100.0
1860	15.3	35.3	18.3	17.7	10.6	2.8	100.0
1870	14.1	35.1	17.6	17.9	12.2	3.1	100.0
1880	13.4	33.8	18.3	18.0	13.0	3.6	100.0
1890	12.0	33.1	18.4	19.0	13.5	4.0	100.0
1900	11.9	31.7	18.1	20.0	14.1	4.2	100.0
1910	11.4	29.9	18.7	20.6	15.0	4.5	100.0
1920	11.0	29.3	17.2	21.2	16.5	4.8	100.0
1930	9.1	29.1	16.6	21.6	17.9	5.7	100.0

TABLE 38.—WHITE POPULATION OF KNOWN AGES AND PERCENTAGE DISTRIBUTION, BY AGE, 1820–1980.[a]—(*Continued*)

Year	0–4	5–19	20–29	30–44	45–64	65+	Total[b]
Future as calculated:[c]							
"Medium":							
1940...............	8.1	25.9	17.2	21.1	20.8	6.9	100.0
1950...............	7.6	23.2	16.6	22.5	21.8	8.4	100.0
1960...............	6.9	22.0	14.9	23.0	23.1	10.1	100.0
1970...............	6.5	20.6	14.6	21.5	25.7	11.0	100.0
1980...............	6.3	19.9	14.0	21.2	26.1	12.4	100.0
"Low":							
1940...............	7.8	26.0	17.1	21.2	20.9	7.0	100.0
1950...............	7.1	22.9	16.5	22.6	22.2	8.8	100.0
1960...............	6.3	21.2	14.8	23.1	23.8	10.8	100.0
1970...............	5.9	19.6	14.2	21.7	26.6	12.0	100.0
1980...............	5.7	18.7	13.5	21.1	27.3	13.7	100.0
"High":							
1940...............	8.5	25.9	17.2	21.0	20.6	6.8	100.0
1950...............	8.5	23.9	16.5	22.1	21.0	8.1	100.0
1960...............	7.9	23.8	14.7	22.0	21.6	10.0	100.0
1970...............	7.7	22.7	14.9	20.0	23.3	11.4	100.0
1980...............	7.5	21.9	14.3	20.0	22.9	13.4	100.0

[a] For 1820 from *Fourth Census of the United States: 1820*, p. 1; 1830 from *Fifth Census of the United States: 1830*, p. 162; 1840 from *Sixth Census of the United States: 1840*, p. 474; 1850–1870 from *Ninth Census of the United States: 1870*, Vol. II, pp. 602–621; 1880–1890 from *Thirteenth Census of the United States: 1900*, Vol. I, p. 322; 1900–1910 from *Fourteenth Census of the United States: 1920*, Vol. II, pp. 158–160; 1920–1930 from *Fifteenth Census of the United States: 1930*, Vol. III, Pt. 1, p. 14. For method of compilation, see Table 31, p. 109.

[b] These totals do not agree with those in Table 3 for the following reasons: (a) Except in 1880 when no persons of unknown ages were reported, the total here is lower than the total of Table 3 when like populations are considered. (b) In 1900, 1910, and 1920 it was possbile to estimate with reasonable accuracy the total number of Mexicans and deduct them from the white population in conformity with census usage in 1930. The results are given in Table 3. It was not possible, however, to deduct Mexicans by age; hence the figure for total whites of known ages in this table are higher than those for total whites for these years given in Table 3.

[c] For the assumptions on which these calculations are based, see Table 88, p. 316, Column *H* for "medium," Column *A* for "low," and Column *J* for "high." Unknown ages are distributed in these calculations.

the total white population and the total population sufficient to merit more than passing mention.

In all age groups under 30 the white population has a slightly smaller proportion than the total population in 1930 and generally for several decades past. In the age groups over 30, on the other hand, the proportions are generally greater in the white population. This would be the natural consequence of immigration of whites and of somewhat higher birth rates and death rates among the Negroes. It may also be noted that the trends in the several age groups already indicated are generally slightly less pronounced in the white population than in the total at ages under 30, except at ages 0 to 4 as just indicated, and slightly more pronounced at ages over 30.

In all the regions, except the South, the total population and total white population have been and still are so nearly identical that no attention need be given to possible regional differences between them. Even in the South the differences are much less than might be expected. (Compare Table 33, p. 119, and Appendix Table 14, p. 364.)

In communities of different sizes in the country as a whole the total population and the white population are very much alike (Table 34, p. 128 and Table 5, p. 14). The chief point of interest is that the proportion over 65 is appreciably larger in the white population than in the total in practically all sizes of communities. In the geographic regions no differences would be expected in different sizes of communities except in the South. Examination shows that even here they are so small that they merit but little attention (Appendix Table 13, p. 362, and Appendix Table 15, p. 366). The proportion of people over 30 in the white population of the South is slightly higher than in the total population of the same region but not so much higher as might be anticipated, and conversely the proportion of younger persons is somewhat lower than in the total but not significantly lower.

b. Native Whites.—Among the native whites the proportion in the different ages is so affected by the fact that the children of immigrants are natives while the immigrants themselves are not that the age composition of the native whites is of little scientific value. This results in higher proportions of young persons in the native white population than in the total population or total white population and in lower proportions in the older age groups (Table 39 and Figure 21).

The differences in the age composition of the native whites and all whites within the various regions arise from the uneven regional distribution of the foreign born and do not deserve further discussion[1] (Appendix Table 14, p. 364, and Appendix Table 16, p. 369).

c. Foreign-born Whites.—The age composition of the foreign-born whites has always been notably different from that of the total population (Figure 1, p. 2, Table 31, p. 109, and Table 40, p. 146). In 1870, when this nativity class can first be distinguished, only 1.5 per cent of the foreign-born whites were aged 0 to 4 as compared with 14.3 per cent of the total population. By 1930 these percentages had fallen to 0.2 and 9.3, respectively. The same kind of difference exists in the 5-to-19 age group. Among the foreign-born whites only 12.8 per cent were in this age group in 1870 compared with 35.4 per cent in the total population. Here, too, there has been a marked decline and the percentages in 1930 were 4.4 and 29.5, respectively. It is not difficult to understand the reasons for these great differences. Immigrants are chiefly young adults. Many of them are married and bring some dependents (both young and old) with them, but most of their children are born here and are classified with the native population. This results in a small proportion of children in the foreign-

---

[1] *Supra*, pp. 56–58, for regional distribution of foreign-born whites.

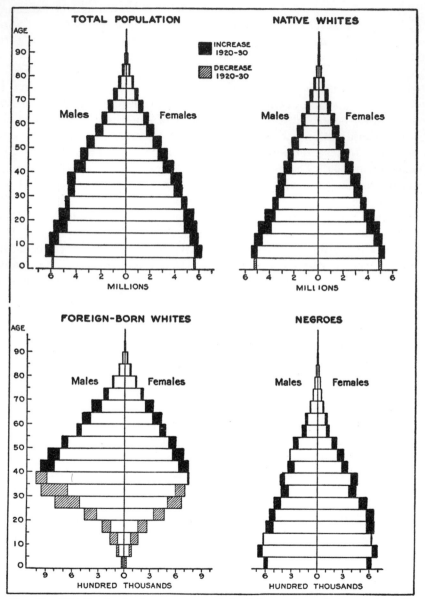

Fig. 21.—Distribution by five-year age periods of the total population, native whites, foreign-born whites, and Negroes, 1920–1930. (Based on *Fifteenth Census of the United States; 1930*, Vol. II, pp. 576, 578, 580.)

TABLE 39.—NATIVE WHITE POPULATION OF KNOWN AGES AND PERCENTAGE DISTRIBUTION, BY AGE, 1870–1980[a]

Year	0–4	5–19	20–29	30–44	45–64	65+	Total[b]
POPULATION (THOUSANDS)							
1870	4,636	11,094	4,599	4,069	2,885	811	28,094
1880	5,738	13,935	6,745	5,554	3,730	1,142	36,843
1890	6,493	16,974	8,106	7,778	4,895	1,520	45,765
1900	7,868	20,120	10,081	10,000	6,550	1,856	56,475
1910	9,220	23,031	12,150	12,562	8,857	2,457	68,278
1920	10,329	26,742	13,946	15,243	11,491	3,255	81,005
1930	9,900	31,020	16,357	18,919	14,680	4,554	95,430
Future as calculated:[c]							
"Medium":							
1940	9,500	30,300	19,600	22,100	18,900	6,100	106,500
1950	9,600	29,000	20,100	27,000	22,700	8,000	116,300
1960	9,100	28,900	18,800	29,000	27,700	10,400	123,900
1970	8,900	27,800	19,000	27,500	33,000	12,600	128,800
1980	8,800	27,100	18,300	27,500	33,900	15,600	131,100
"Low":							
1940	9,200	30,200	19,500	22,000	18,900	6,100	105,800
1950	8,600	27,800	19,900	26,400	22,300	8,000	113,000
1960	7,700	25,900	18,100	27,900	26,500	10,200	116,200
1970	7,100	23,400	17,000	25,800	30,800	12,000	116,000
1980	6,500	21,400	15,400	24,100	31,000	14,400	112,800
"High":							
1940	10,100	30,500	19,600	22,100	18,900	6,100	107,200
1950	11,300	30,900	20,200	27,100	22,800	8,100	120,300
1960	11,600	34,100	19,600	29,300	28,100	11,300	134,000
1970	12,300	35,700	22,000	28,600	34,200	15,000	147,800
1980	13,200	37,800	23,200	31,200	35,900	20,700	162,000
PERCENTAGE DISTRIBUTION							
1870	16.5	39.5	16.4	14.5	10.3	2.9	100.0
1880	15.6	37.8	18.3	15.0	10.1	3.1	100.0
1890	14.2	37.1	17.7	17.0	10.7	3.3	100.0
1900	13.9	35.6	17.8	17.7	11.6	3.3	100.0
1910	13.5	33.7	17.8	18.4	13.0	3.6	100.0
1920	12.8	33.0	17.2	18.8	14.2	4.0	100.0
1930	10.4	32.5	17.1	19.8	15.4	4.8	100.0
Future as calculated:[c]							
"Medium":							
1940	9.0	28.5	18.4	20.7	17.8	5.7	100.0
1950	8.2	24.9	17.2	23.2	19.5	6.9	100.0
1960	7.4	23.3	15.2	23.4	22.3	8.4	100.0
1970	6.9	21.6	14.7	21.4	25.6	9.7	100.0
1980	6.7	20.7	14.0	21.0	25.9	11.9	100.0
"Low":							
1940	8.7	28.6	18.5	20.8	17.8	5.7	100.0
1950	7.6	24.6	17.6	23.4	19.7	7.1	100.0
1960	6.6	22.2	15.5	24.0	22.8	8.8	100.0
1970	6.1	20.2	14.6	22.2	26.6	10.3	100.0
1980	5.8	19.0	13.6	21.4	27.5	12.8	100.0
"High":							
1940	9.4	28.4	18.3	20.6	17.6	5.6	100.0
1950	9.4	25.7	16.8	22.5	19.0	6.7	100.0
1960	8.7	25.4	14.6	21.8	21.0	8.4	100.0
1970	8.3	24.2	14.9	19.3	23.1	10.2	100.0
1980	8.1	23.3	14.3	19.3	22.1	12.8	100.0

[a] For 1870 from *Ninth Census of the United States: 1870*, Vol. II, pp. 624–634; 1880 to 1910 from *Thirteenth Census of the United States: 1910*, Vol. I, pp. 322–325; 1920 and 1930 from *Fifteenth Census of the United States: 1930*, Vol. III, Pt. 1, p. 14.

[b] For explanation of differences in "Total" in this table and native white population in Table 3, see Note b, Table 38.

[c] For the assumptions on which these calculations are based, see Table 88, p. 316, Column H for "medium," Column A for "low," and Column J for "high." Unknown ages are distributed in these calculations.

TABLE 40.—FOREIGN-BORN WHITE POPULATION OF KNOWN AGES AND PERCENTAGE DISTRIBUTION, BY AGE, 1870–1980[a]

Year	0–4	5–19	20–29	30–44	45–64	65+	Total[b]
POPULATION (THOUSANDS)							
1870	84	705	1,318	1,958	1,207	220	5,492
1880	62	740	1,199	2,265	1,892	402	6,560
1890	87	1,166	1,990	2,673	2,500	682	9,097
1900	52	1,021	2,017	3,317	2,832	950	10,189
1910	103	1,331	3,093	4,217	3,393	1,183	13,319
1920	45	1,029	2,381	4,817	4,092	1,328	13,692
1930	28	594	1,683	4,573	4,822	1,657	13,357
Future as calculated:[c]							
"Medium":							
1940	10	300	600	2,900	5,600	2,100	11,500
1950	20	400	900	1,600	4,900	2,600	10,400
1960	20	400	1,000	1,600	3,100	3,000	9,200
1970	20	400	1,000	1,900	2,200	2,600	8,100
1980	20	400	1,000	2,000	2,300	1,600	7,300
"Low":							
1940	...	100	500	2,800	5,600	2,100	11,000
1950	...	.....	100	1,000	4,600	2,600	8,400
1960	...	.....	.....	300	2,500	3,000	5,700
1970	...	.....	.....	30	900	2,300	3,300
1980	...	.....	.....	.....	200	1,300	1,500
"High":							
1940	30	500	900	3,000	5,700	2,100	12,100
1950	50	800	1,800	2,200	5,100	2,700	12,600
1960	50	900	2,000	3,200	3,600	3,400	13,100
1970	50	900	2,100	3,800	3,500	3,300	13,600
1980	50	900	2,100	3,900	4,600	2,800	14,300
PERCENTAGE DISTRIBUTION							
1870	1.5	12.8	24.0	35.7	22.0	4.0	100.0
1880	1.0	11.3	18.3	34.5	28.8	6.0	100.0
1890	1.0	12.8	21.9	29.4	27.5	7.5	100.0
1900	0.5	10.0	19.8	32.6	27.8	9.3	100.0
1910	0.8	10.0	23.2	31.7	25.5	8.9	100.0
1920	0.3	7.5	17.4	35.2	29.9	9.7	100.0
1930	0.2	4.4	12.6	34.2	36.1	12.4	100.0
Future as calculated:[c]							
"Medium":							
1940	0.1	2.4	5.6	24.9	49.0	18.0	100.0
1950	0.2	3.6	8.8	15.4	46.8	25.3	100.0
1960	0.3	4.6	10.6	17.8	33.6	33.0	100.0
1970	0.3	5.3	12.8	23.0	27.0	31.6	100.0
1980	0.3	5.8	14.1	26.5	30.9	22.4	100.0
"Low":							
1940	...	1.3	4.1	25.2	50.7	18.7	100.0
1950	...	.....	1.7	12.1	55.0	31.2	100.0
1960	...	.....	.....	4.6	44.0	51.4	100.0
1970	...	.....	.....	0.8	28.1	71.1	100.0
1980	...	.....	.....	.....	14.5	85.5	100.0
"High":							
1940	0.3	3.9	7.7	24.5	46.6	17.0	100.0
1950	0.4	6.3	14.1	17.8	40.4	21.1	100.0
1960	0.4	6.7	15.5	24.1	27.5	25.9	100.0
1970	0.3	6.4	15.5	27.6	25.8	24.5	100.0
1980	0.3	6.1	14.8	27.5	31.8	19.5	100.0

[a] For 1870 from *Ninth Census of the United States: 1870*, Vol. II, pp. 636–645; 1880–1910 from *Thirteenth Census of the United States: 1910*, Vol. I, pp. 322–324; 1920–1930 from *Fifteenth Census of the United States: 1930*, Vol. III, Pt. 1, p. 14.
[b] For explanation of differences in "Total" in this table and foreign-born white population in Table 3, see Note b, Table 38.
[c] For the assumptions on which these calculations are based see Table 88, p. 316, Column H for "medium," Column A for "low," and Column J for "high." Unknown ages are distributed in these calculations.

born population and a high proportion in the native population, as noted above. The steady decline in the proportion of children in the foreign-born white population is undoubtedly attributable chiefly to the change in the character of immigration in recent decades when land settlement has ceased to be an attractive force. Families are not the advantage to the wage worker that they were to the prospective farmer.

With the coming of many young adults, it would be expected that the 20-to-29 and 30-to-44 age groups among the foreign born would constitute a much higher proportion than in the total population. This is generally the case, although in 1880 and in 1920 there was no significant difference in the proportion aged 20 to 29 in the foreign born and total population. Since 1910 there has been a marked decline in the proportion in this age group in the foreign-born population, and since 1920 it has fallen almost one-fourth below the corresponding proportion in the total population. The decline in the proportion of foreign born aged 20 to 29 arises chiefly from the falling off of immigration since 1914. The young-adult age group is not being recruited by new arrivals as in earlier days (Table 83, p. 298). In the past the proportion in this age group has fluctuated with the amount of immigration.[1] A second factor but one of far less importance than the volume of immigration is the aging of the foreign born; the larger the proportion in the older age groups the smaller the proportion in this group. Most of the survivors of the great immigration of the 1870's and 1880's were in the 65-and-over age group by 1920. A third factor of some importance is the changing age composition of the immigrants themselves. Since the World War there has been a marked increase in the proportion of immigrants over 45 years of age. What will happen to the 20-to-29 age group in the future on the different assumptions regarding the amount of future immigration is indicated in Table 40. In the "medium" future population the proportion in this age group will decline rapidly until 1940, after which it will begin to rise. In 1980 it will be relatively somewhat above its present level. With no immigration, as in the "low" population, this group will practically disappear by 1950. In the "high" population this age group will constitute about the same proportion of the foreign born that it does in the total population.

It is in the 30-to-44 age group, however, that the adult character of immigration is most apparent. In 1870 the proportion of persons in this age group was twice as great among the foreign born as in the total population. This age group, too, fluctuates with immigration, but the cutting down of numbers has not yet affected it so seriously as the 20-to-29 age group. During the next two decades, however, it seems

[1] For the ages of immigrants entering the United States, see Table 32, p. 115. The age groups as given are not satisfactory, but they show the great preponderance of young adults.

almost certain to drop to about one-half or less of its present proportion. Its future growth beyond 1950 depends almost entirely upon immigration policy.

In the 45-to-64 age group the difference between the foreign born and the total population is pronounced and has been increasing during the last 20 years. There is now more than twice as high a proportion of persons aged 45 to 64 among the foreign born as in the total population, and this proportion will increase rapidly during the next decade on all of the assumptions underlying the calculations in Table 40. If there should be no immigration in the future, over one-half of all the foreign born will be in this age group in 1940 and 1950, after which it will decline rather rapidly. With about present quotas, it will begin to decline after 1940 but will remain well above that of the total population, as would be expected.

In the 65-and-over age group the differences between the foreign-born whites and the total population are even greater than those already noted in other age groups (except children aged 0 to 4) and the rate of change is faster. Whereas the proportion of persons over age 65 in the total population has increased only from 2.6 per cent to 5.4 per cent in 80 years, in the foreign-born white population the increase has been from 4.0 per cent to 12.4 per cent in 60 years. The growth of the 65-and-over age group among the foreign-born whites almost exactly reverses the decline in the 5-to-19 age group. In the future there will be a marked increase in this age group; it will remain from two to three times as large relatively as in the total population.

By Regions.—There are very considerable differences between the regions in the age distribution of the foreign-born whites (Appendix Table 18, p. 372). In the Northeast where, as has been shown elsewhere,[1] recent arrivals are relatively more numerous than in other regions, the proportions in the 20-to-44 age groups are larger than in other regions and the proportion in the 65-and-over age group correspondingly smaller. This affects the age make-up of the total population in the different regions. The fluctuations within practically all the age groups of the foreign-born white are more violent in the South than in other regions, owing to the relatively small number in this region. The fact that foreign-born whites in the South have a slightly higher proportion in the age group 45 and over than the foreign-born whites in any other region may be due in part to the fact that a large proportion of the former are merchants, who probably are older on the average than the foreign-born whites in other regions where there is a wider occupational distribution.

By Size of Community.—The age distribution of the foreign-born whites in communities of various sizes follows the general pattern of their

[1] *Supra*, p. 56.

age distribution already noted. Disregarding the 0-to-4 age group because it is so small, the tendency of the foreign-born whites to go into the large cities in recent years is reflected in the higher proportion of persons aged 5 to 44 in these cities than in the smaller cities and rural districts (especially in the farm population) (Table 41). In 1930 the proportion 20 to 29 in the rural districts was only half as high as in the largest cities. In the age groups over 45, however, this relation is reversed, and very strongly so, the largest communities having the smallest proportions of older people and the smallest communities and the open country having the highest proportions. This difference is particularly marked in the 65-and-over age group because it has been about 40 years since many immigrants went to the rural districts. In 1930 over 60 per cent of the rural foreign-born whites were 45 years of age or over (farm population 66.4 per cent). These age differences represent the response of a particular nativity class to the relative economic opportunities in the city and the country at different periods. Consequently they are of interest in connection with the distribution of the population as well as with its age composition. The proportion of foreign-born whites over 65 years of age has been twice, or more, as great in rural communities as in the larger cities during the last 40 years. This is certainly an indication that important social and economic forces have been at work in different communities in selecting and distributing the immigrants. It should also be remembered that there are differential death rates in city and country which aid in raising the proportion of old persons in the latter.[1]

The differences between divisions in the age distribution of the foreign-born whites by size of community are of interest as showing how the stoppage of immigration affects various localities. The communities most affected by the turning of immigration almost exclusively to the cities since about 1890 are the rural communities of the North Center. In these communities over one-fourth of all the foreign-born whites were over 65 years of age in 1930 and this group, together with the 45-to-64 age group, constituted 70 per cent of the total foreign-born whites (Appendix Table 19, p. 373). In the 65-and-over group in this region the nonfarm population has a considerably higher proportion than the farm population—29.4 per cent as compared with 24.1 per cent. This is the opposite of the situation in other regions where the higher proportion in this age group is found in the farm population (South and Northeast) or where it is the same in both types of communities (West). In contrast to the high proportions of persons over 45 among the rural foreign born, those communities which have received most of the recent immigrants, namely, the cities of over 500,000 in the North Center and Northeast, had only 41.7 per cent and 40.6 per cent, respectively, of

[1] *Infra.* p. 242.

TABLE 41.—FOREIGN-BORN WHITE POPULATION OF KNOWN AGES AND PERCENTAGE DISTRIBUTION BY AGE, BY SIZE OF COMMUNITY, 1890–1930[a]

Size of community	0–4	5–19	20–29	30–44	45–64	65+	Total
POPULATION (THOUSANDS)							
1890:							
500,000 and over............	15	210	408	512	388	80	1,613
100,000–500,000.............	13	169	328	439	385	93	1,428
25,000–100,000.............	11	136	233	288	255	58	980
2,500– 25,000 } Rural	47	652	1,021	1,434	1,472	452	5,077
1910:							
500,000 and over............	28	478	1,012	1,260	865	224	3,867
100,000–500,000.............	14	176	450	634	507	159	1,941
25,000–100,000.............	15	178	415	538	392	124	1,661
2,500– 25,000.............	18	204	512	683	535	200	2,151
Rural.....................	27	295	704	1,103	1,093	476	3,699
1920:							
500,000 and over............	10	354	943	1,728	1,288	315	4,637
100,000–500,000.............	6	140	339	674	570	170	1,899
25,000–100,000.............	6	133	325	626	500	144	1,734
2,500– 25,000.............	8	152	340	726	621	225	2,072
Rural.....................	15	250	434	1,064	1,113	474	3,351
Farm..................	6	103	138	405	555	225	1,432
Nonfarm................	10	147	296	658	558	250	1,918
1930:							
500,000 and over............	12	254	827	1,940	1,703	449	5,185
100,000–500,000.............	4	86	235	665	717	237	1,945
25,000–100,000.............	4	81	213	597	614	199	1,707
2,500– 25,000.............	4	82	198	629	703	266	1,881
Rural.....................	4	91	209	741	1,085	507	2,638
Farm..................	1	32	70	261	496	223	1,084
Nonfarm................	3	59	139	480	589	284	1,554
PERCENTAGE DISTRIBUTION							
1890:							
500,000 and over............	0.9	13.0	25.3	31.7	24.1	4.9	100.0
100,000–500,000.............	0.9	11.8	23.0	30.7	27.0	6.5	100.0
25,000–100,000.............	1.1	13.8	23.8	29.4	26.0	5.9	100.0
2,500– 25,000 } Rural	0.9	12.8	20.1	28.2	29.0	8.9	100.0
1910:							
500,000 and over............	0.7	12.4	26.2	32.6	22.4	5.8	100.0
100,000–500,000.............	0.7	9.1	23.2	32.7	26.1	8.2	100.0
25,000–100,000.............	0.9	10.7	25.0	32.4	23.6	7.5	100.0
2,500– 25,000.............	0.8	9.5	23.8	31.7	24.9	9.3	100.0
Rural.....................	0.7	8.0	19.0	29.8	29.6	12.9	100.0
1920:							
500,000 and over............	0.2	7.6	20.3	37.3	27.8	6.8	100.0
100,000–500,000.............	0.3	7.4	17.9	35.5	30.0	8.9	100.0
25,000–100,000.............	0.3	7.7	18.7	36.1	28.8	8.3	100.0
2,500– 25,000.............	0.4	7.3	16.4	35.0	30.0	10.9	100.0
Rural.....................	0.5	7.5	13.0	31.7	33.2	14.2	100.0
Farm..................	0.4	7.2	9.7	28.3	38.8	15.7	100.0
Nonfarm................	0.5	7.7	15.4	34.3	29.1	13.0	100.0
1930:							
500,000 and over............	0.2	4.9	15.9	37.4	32.8	8.7	100.0
100,000–500,000.............	0.2	4.4	12.1	34.2	36.9	12.2	100.0
25,000–100,000.............	0.2	4.7	12.5	35.0	35.9	11.6	100.0
2,500– 25,000.............	0.2	4.3	10.5	33.4	37.4	14.1	100.0
Rural.....................	0.2	3.5	7.9	28.1	41.1	19.2	100.0
Farm..................	0.1	3.0	6.5	24.1	45.8	20.6	100.0
Nonfarm................	0.2	3.8	9.0	30.9	37.9	18.3	100.0

[a] From special compilation made for this study.

their foreign born in these ages in 1930. These are the extreme differences, but in all regions the proportion of older people among the foreign-born whites is much greater in the rural districts than in the cities. The practical stopping of immigration will be followed by an increase in the older groups in all sizes of communities in all divisions. For a decade or two this increase will be most rapid in the rural districts of the North Center followed by those of the South and West. In the Northeast the aging of the foreign-born whites will take place somewhat more slowly because a considerably larger proportion of them are in the young adult ages. Everywhere the foreign-born whites in the large cities will age the most slowly for the reason just cited—these cities contain the largest proportion of recently arrived immigrants.

3. THE AGE COMPOSITION OF THE NEGROES

a. The Younger Ages.—Although the general age trends are much the same in the Negro population as in the white population, there are certain significant differences. In the 0-to-4 and 5-to-19 age groups the trends are practically identical but the proportions are somewhat different. Ever since 1870 there has been a higher proportion in both of these age groups among Negroes than among whites, except in the 0-to-4 age group in 1920, when they were identical (Figure 21, p. 144, and Tables 38 and 42, pp. 141 and 152). In general, the proportions in the 0-to-4 and 5-to-19 age groups among the Negroes have been from 10 to 20 per cent higher than among the whites.[1] In numbers there were about 33,000 fewer Negro children aged 0-to-4 in 1930 than in 1910, although the total Negro population grew by somewhat more than 2,000,000, or over one-fifth, from 1910 to 1930.[2] This indicates a very rapid decline in the Negro birth rates, which is even greater than these figures suggest because there has also been a marked decline in the death rates of Negro children during the last two or three decades. Hence the survivors aged 0 to 4 in 1930 come from a smaller number of births than an equal number of survivors in 1900.[3]

For the future it appears to the authors that the trends in the white and Negro populations aged 0 to 4 and 5 to 19 will be practically identical, although in both age groups the proportion will remain somewhat higher

[1] The comparison of the Negroes aged 0 to 4 with the whites is made precarious by the fact that more Negroes than whites of these ages fail of enumeration by the census. It is also known that certain censuses have omitted more Negroes than other censuses. Whether this would affect the proportions in the several age groups at different times cannot be answered positively, but it is difficult to see why more persons of a particular age should be overlooked at one time than at another even if a greater total remains unenumerated.

[2] The comparison of numbers between 1920 and 1930 is invalidated because of the large underenumeration of 1920.

[3] *Infra*, pp. 270–272, for decline in the birth rate of Negroes.

TABLE 42.—NEGRO POPULATION OF KNOWN AGES AND PERCENTAGE DISTRIBUTION, BY AGE, 1850–1980[a]

Year	0–4	5–19	20–29	30–44	45–64	65+	Total[b]
POPULATION (THOUSANDS)							
1850	601	1,427	650	553	317	87	3,635
1870	791	1,826	878	760	503	122	4,880
1880	1,114	2,532	1,224	1,020	683	180	6,753
1890[c]	1,055	3,025	1,329	1,180	793	215	7,597
1900	1,216	3,277	1,707	1,367	958	261	8,785
1910	1,263	3,462	1,912	1,757	1,108	294	9,797
1920	1,144	3,586	1,965	2,031	1,381	333	10,440
1930	1,230	3,870	2,275	2,443	1,686	373	11,877
Future as calculated:[d]							
"Medium":							
1940	1,200	3,900	2,300	2,800	2,200	500	13,000
1950	1,200	3,800	2,500	3,000	2,500	800	13,700
1960	1,100	3,700	2,400	3,200	2,800	1,000	14,200
1970	1,100	3,600	2,400	3,200	3,100	1,100	14,400
1980	1,000	3,400	2,300	3,100	3,100	1,300	14,200
"Low":							
1940	1,200	3,900	2,300	2,800	2,200	500	12,900
1950	1,100	3,700	2,400	3,000	2,500	800	13,500
1960	1,000	3,500	2,300	3,000	2,800	1,000	13,600
1970	900	3,200	2,200	2,900	2,900	1,100	13,400
1980	800	2,900	2,000	2,800	2,900	1,200	12,800
"High":							
1940	1,200	4,000	2,300	2,800	2,200	500	13,000
1950	1,300	4,000	2,500	3,100	2,500	800	14,200
1960	1,400	4,200	2,500	3,300	3,000	1,000	15,400
1970	1,400	4,400	2,700	3,400	3,400	1,200	16,600
1980	1,500	4,700	2,800	3,700	3,700	1,600	17,900
PERCENTAGE DISTRIBUTION							
1850	16.5	39.3	17.9	15.2	8.7	2.4	100.0
1870	16.2	37.4	18.0	15.6	10.3	2.5	100.0
1880	16.5	37.5	18.1	15.1	10.1	2.7	100.0
1890[c]	13.9	39.8	17.5	15.5	10.4	2.8	100.0
1900	13.8	37.3	19.4	15.6	10.9	3.0	100.0
1910	12.9	35.3	19.5	17.9	11.3	3.0	100.0
1920	11.0	34.4	18.8	19.5	13.2	3.2	100.0
1930	10.4	32.6	19.2	20.6	14.2	3.1	100.0
Future as calculated:[d]							
"Medium":							
1940	9.2	30.3	18.0	21.4	17.2	3.8	100.0
1950	8.5	27.8	17.9	22.2	18.1	5.6	100.0
1960	7.8	26.1	16.9	22.4	19.7	7.0	100.0
1970	7.4	24.8	16.4	22.3	21.3	7.7	100.0
1980	7.2	24.0	15.9	22.1	22.1	8.8	100.0
"Low":							
1940	9.3	30.1	18.0	21.5	17.3	3.9	100.0
1950	8.4	27.6	17.8	22.1	18.4	5.7	100.0
1960	7.6	25.8	16.8	22.2	20.3	7.3	100.0
1970	7.0	24.2	16.4	22.1	22.0	8.3	100.0
1980	6.6	23.0	15.8	22.1	22.8	9.7	100.0
"High":							
1940	9.4	30.4	17.9	21.4	17.0	3.8	100.0
1950	9.2	28.2	17.6	21.8	17.8	5.4	100.0
1960	8.8	27.6	16.3	21.5	19.3	6.5	100.0
1970	8.6	26.7	16.1	20.7	20.5	7.4	100.0
1980	8.4	26.0	15.7	20.4	20.5	8.9	100.0

[a] For 1850 and 1870 from *Ninth Census of the United States: 1870*, Vol. II, pp. 648–660; 1880–1910 from *Thirteenth Census of the United States: 1910*, Vol. I, pp. 319–325; 1920–1930 from *Fifteenth Census of the United States: 1930*, Vol. III, Pt. 1, p. 14. Some colored included in 1880 and 1890.

[b] For explanation of differences in "Total" in this table and Negro population in Table 3, see Note b, Table 38.

[c] All colored but excluding 18,636 Negroes, 189,447 Indians, and 13 Chinese specially enumerated in 1890 in Indian Territory and on Indian Reservations, for whom statistics of age are not available.

[d] For the assumptions on which these calculations are based see Table 88, Column H for "medium," Column A for "low," and Column J for "high." Unknown ages are distributed in these calculations.

among the Negroes than among whites because of birth rate differentials and in spite of infant mortality differentials.

b. The Middle Groups.—In the 20-to-29 age group the movement in the past appears erratic. There has been no definite direction to the trend as in the case of the whites. However, since it seems safe to assume that there will be few Negro immigrants, it is probable that the proportion in this age group for the next two decades will show a decline similar to that among the whites, although still remaining somewhat higher. In the 30-to-44 age group the upward trend has been more marked among Negroes than among whites, particularly since 1910, with the number of white immigrants declining. The proportion of Negroes in this age group is still somewhat below that among the whites and seems likely to remain so for the next three decades, after which it will probably be a little higher.

c. The Older Groups.—In the 45-to-64 age group the proportion of Negroes is significantly lower (15 per cent to 25 per cent) than among the whites, as it has been since 1850, when age data for Negroes first became available. The rate of increase in the 45-to-64 age group has been almost the same in the two races.

In the 65-and-over age group of Negroes there is an upward trend, but it is much less rapid than among whites and the proportion has changed but little since 1900. At all times it has been lower than in the white population and the difference is increasing. In 1850 the percentages of the population 65 and over in the white and Negro populations were 2.7 and 2.4, respectively; by 1930 they were 5.7 and 3.1. In the white population the proportion in this age group is more than twice as great in 1930 as in 1850; in the Negro population it was only about one-third greater.

The explanation of the small proportion of older Negroes is to be found chiefly in their higher death rate, as the following facts clearly show. The number of Negroes 65 years of age and over in 1930, over 80 per cent of whom are survivors from the 5-to-19 age group in 1870, is in the ratio of 1 of the former to 5 of the latter. In the native white population the ratio of the 65-and-over age group of 1930 to the 5-to-19 age group of 1870 is 1:2.4. Thus the number of survivors 60 years later from each 1,000 Negro children aged 5 to 19 in 1870 was slightly less than half as great as in the native white population. This comparison is unsatisfactory in several respects, but even when allowance is made for the large under-enumeration of Negroes in 1870, the emigration of native whites, the immigration of Negroes, and the inaccuracies of age reporting there cannot be any reasonable doubt that the chief reason for the small proportion of older Negroes is the higher death rate of the Negroes.[1] But it is obvious that in a population with declining birth and death rates like

[1] *Infra*, pp. 231, 245, for data in recent years.

that of the Negroes the proportion in the older age groups cannot remain as low as it has been in the past. The natural consequence of these lower rates is seen in the steady and rapid increase in this age group in the calculations of future population. It will be noted, however, that, even with this increase, the 65-and-over age group in 1980 is only about two-thirds as large proportionally among Negroes as in the white population, although the rate of increase is greater because of the low proportion of Negroes in this age group at present.

Turning attention for a moment to the numbers in the future Negro population, it will be noted that in the "medium" population of all ages there is very little increase after 1960 and an actual decline between 1970 and 1980. In the 0-to-4 and 5-to-19 age groups, however, there is a steady decline from present numbers. In the 20-to-29 age group there is but little change, while in the next older age group (30 to 44) there is considerable increase, but even this group begins to decline after 1970. It is in the older age groups that large and steady increases are found, as would be expected; and this is true even in the "high" population. The differences in the assumptions as to declines in birth rates and death rates account for the different behavior of the "low" and "high" future populations.[1]

d. By Regions.—The age composition of the Negroes in the several regions has been much affected by the movement of young adults from the South to the North in recent years. The proportion of Negro children aged 0 to 4 is appreciably higher in the South than in other regions, while in the 5-to-19 age group the difference between the North and the South is so large that at first one is disposed to doubt the figures. In both the Northeast and the North Center the proportion aged 5 to 19 in 1930 was just over 23 per cent, while in the South it was over 35 per cent (Appendix Table 20). Conversely, the proportions in the most productive ages are low in the South and high in the North, that in the 20-to-29 age group being about one-fifth higher in the North than in the South and that in the 30-to-44 age group being over one-half higher. These differences are readily explained by the number and age make-up of the ,northward migrants and by the fact that this movement is very recent; so recent, indeed, that relatively few of the children of these migrants have yet reached the 5-to-19 age group.

In the 45-to-64 age group it might be expected that northward migration would have the effect of raising the proportion in the South and lowering it in the North. This has been the case to some extent. There has been an appreciable increase in this age group in the South during the last two decades but not much greater than in the white population. In the North there was some decline between 1920 and 1930, but it was much

[1] *Infra*, pp. 260, 261, 289–291.

smaller than might have been anticipated. The proportion in this age group has always (since 1850) been less in the South than in the North and, with heavily loaded 20-to-44 groups to draw upon in the North, the present differentials are likely to remain for several decades.

Rather strangely, until the recent northward movement, the proportion of persons aged 65 and over was generally greater in the North than in the South. This must have been the effect of an earlier migration of young adults because Negro death rates have been higher in the North than in the South.[1]

Naturally with these differences in the age composition of Negroes in the several regions, there is little point in comparing Negroes with whites except in the South (Appendix Tables 14 and 20, pp. 364 and 375). Here the proportion of children aged 0 to 4 has been practically the same in both races since 1850. In the 5-to-19 age group the decline has been more rapid among the whites so that the proportion is now higher among Negroes. There is no significant difference in the 20-to-44 age groups. In both the 45-to-64 and 65-and-over age groups the proportion is higher among the whites than among the Negroes. These differences can undoubtedly be attributed largely to the differences in death rates noted above, since both Negro and white populations in the South have sent out large numbers of emigrants to other regions.[2]

e. **By Size of Community.**—The age distribution of the Negroes by size of community, though basically like that of the whites, shows several peculiarities worth studying. However, it is not possible to be so certain of the trends among Negroes as among the whites where a longer series of data is available.

The 0-to-4 Group.—The first point to notice is that there is a considerably greater difference in the proportion of children aged 0 to 4 in large cities and rural communities among Negroes than among whites. In 1890 the proportion of Negro children aged 0 to 4 was practically twice as high in rural communities (14.5 per cent) as in cities of over 500,000 (7.3 per cent) (Table 43). By 1930 this difference had decreased to almost one-half, the proportion of children in large cities having increased in the meantime to 8.2 per cent and that in rural communities having decreased to 12.0 per cent (12.6 per cent in the farm population). Unlike the whites, the proportion of Negroes aged 0 to 4 has always been lowest in the largest cities, except in 1930, when it was slightly higher in cities of over 500,000 than in those of 100,000 to 500,000, and has increased as the size of the community decreased. Also until 1930 the proportion of Negroes of this

[1] *Infra*, pp. 242–245.
[2] Nothing has been said here of Negroes in the West, both because they are few and because in 1890 all "colored" are lumped together. At that time the majority of the colored in that region were Chinese and Indians.

TABLE 43.—NEGRO POPULATION OF KNOWN AGES AND PERCENTAGE DISTRIBUTION BY AGE, BY SIZE OF COMMUNITY, 1890–1930[a]

Year and size of community	0–4	5–19	20–29	30–44	45–64	65+	Total
POPULATION (THOUSANDS)							
1890:[b]							
500,000 and over.............	7	20	25	26	11	2	91
100,000–500,000.............	32	103	88	92	48	10	373
25,000–100,000.............	36	116	88	83	45	10	379
2,500– 25,000 } .... Rural	980	2,785	1,128	978	690	194	6,755
1910:							
500,000 and over.............	29	78	105	121	53	9	395
100,000–500,000.............	48	151	158	164	86	17	624
25,000–100,000.............	49	156	151	150	76	16	599
2,500– 25,000.............	103	323	236	224	136	35	1,057
Rural.....................	1,034	2,755	1,262	1,097	757	217	7,121
1920:							
500,000 and over.............	50	140	188	229	104	14	725
100,000–500,000.............	68	228	227	262	145	26	955
25,000–100,000.............	55	185	175	186	102	19	723
2,500– 25,000.............	94	341	242	254	171	42	1,143
Rural.....................	876	2,693	1,133	1,100	859	232	6,894
Farm....................	681	2,113	761	752	624	164	5,095
Nonfarm.................	194	580	372	349	235	69	1,799
1930:							
500,000 and over.............	110	288	323	412	188	25	1,345
100,000–500,000.............	123	381	341	412	235	39	1,531
25,000–100,000.............	81	264	221	246	143	27	981
2,500– 25,000.............	114	391	272	295	208	49	1,327
Rural.....................	803	2,547	1,118	1,079	912	234	6,693
Farm....................	589	1,913	715	679	627	156	4,679
Nonfarm.................	214	634	403	400	285	78	2,014
PERCENTAGE DISTRIBUTION							
1890:[b]							
500,000 and over.............	7.3	22.0	27.7	28.8	11.8	2.4	100.0
100,000–500,000.............	8.6	27.6	23.7	24.7	12.8	2.6	100.0
25,000–100,000.............	9.6	30.8	23.2	22.0	12.0	2.5	100.0
2,500– 25,000 } .... Rural	14.5	41.2	16.7	14.5	10.2	2.9	100.0
1910:							
500,000 and over.............	7.3	19.7	26.5	30.7	13.5	2.3	100.0
100,000–500,000.............	7.7	24.2	25.3	26.2	13.8	2.8	100.0
25,000–100,000.............	8.2	26.0	25.3	25.1	12.8	2.6	100.0
2,500– 25,000.............	9.8	30.5	22.3	21.2	12.8	3.3	100.0
Rural.....................	14.5	38.7	17.7	15.4	10.6	3.0	100.0
1920:							
500,000 and over.............	6.9	19.3	25.9	31.6	14.3	2.0	100.0
100,000–500,000.............	7.2	23.8	23.7	27.4	15.2	2.7	100.0
25,000–100,000.............	7.7	25.6	24.2	25.7	14.1	2.6	100.0
2,500– 25,000.............	8.2	29.8	21.2	22.3	14.9	3.6	100.0
Rural.....................	12.7	39.1	16.4	16.0	12.5	3.4	100.0
Farm....................	13.4	41.5	14.9	14.8	12.3	3.2	100.0
Nonfarm.................	10.8	32.2	20.7	19.4	13.1	3.8	100.0
1930:							
500,000 and over.............	8.2	21.4	24.0	30.6	13.9	1.8	100.0
100,000–500,000.............	8.0	24.9	22.2	26.9	15.4	2.6	100.0
25,000–100,000.............	8.3	26.9	22.5	25.0	14.6	2.7	100.0
2,500– 25,000.............	8.6	29.5	20.5	22.2	15.7	3.7	100.0
Rural.....................	12.0	38.1	16.7	16.1	13.6	3.5	100.0
Farm....................	12.6	40.9	15.3	14.5	13.4	3.3	100.0
Nonfarm.................	10.6	31.5	20.0	19.8	14.2	3.9	100.0

[a] From special compilation made for this study.
[b] All colored but excluding 18,636 Negroes, 189,447 Indians, and 13 Chinese specially enumerated in 1890 in Indian Territory and on Indian reservations, for whom statistics of age are not available.

age in all sizes of cities has been lower than the proportion of whites in the same cities. On the other hand, the proportion of Negro children 0 to 4 in the rural districts has been higher than among the whites ever since such a comparison could be made.[1] If it were not for the rise in the proportion of Negro children in the cities in 1930 it could be said that there was a general downward trend in all sizes of communities among Negroes as among whites.

Why there should have been an increase in the cities at this time is not altogether clear, since there is no evidence of an increasing birth rate among urban Negroes during the last decade. It is necessary, therefore, to search for other factors. One factor undoubtedly is the very great abnormality of the Negro population in northern cities in 1920. The movement north was very recent and the high proportions in the 20-to-29 and 30-to-44 age groups reduced the proportions in other groups. Furthermore the recent migrants had not yet had time to get settled and raise families. By 1930 life was probably more normal with them; hence children were more numerous. Also there have been considerable improvements in recent years in infant mortality among Negroes, particularly in the cities. This in itself, even in the face of a slowly declining birth rate, might lead to an increase in the proportion of children. Besides, in comparing 1920 with 1930, it may be that the better enumeration of 1930 raised the proportion of children somewhat.

The 5-to-19 Group.—The proportion of Negroes in the 5-to-19 age group in the larger cities has been small but highly variable from decade to decade. Thus it dropped as low as 19.7 per cent and 19.3 per cent in the cities of over 500,000 in 1910 and 1920, compared with 27.3 per cent and 25.6 per cent for the whites in the same years. It rose a little by 1930 (21.4 per cent) but was still well below that of the whites (25.3 per cent). Undoubtedly the rapid northward migration of Negroes also explains this situation in large measure.

In the rural population, on the other hand, the proportion in the 5-to-19 age group has always been very high, higher than in the white population, and has shown but little decline during the past 40 years—from 41.2 per cent in 1890 to 38.1 per cent in 1930. Consequently the proportion of the rural Negro population under 20 was and still is considerably higher than that of the white population, the percentages being 55.7 and 46.7, respectively, in 1890, and 50.1 and 43.2 in 1930. Among rural Negroes, as among rural whites, the proportion under 20 in both 1920 and 1930 is much higher in the farm population than in the nonfarm population; the

[1] It should be noted in making these comparisons between whites and Negroes that the underenumeration of Negro children aged 0 to 4 is generally supposed to be considerably greater than that of white children. It is probable, therefore, that the proportion of Negro children in the cities is not so much lower than that of whites as these figures indicate and that the excess in rural communities is greater.

percentages in 1920 are 54.9 and 43.0, and in 1930 they are 53.5 and 42.1, respectively. Rural Negroes, as a whole, are, therefore, a comparatively young population with farm Negroes constituting the youngest element in the entire population.

The Middle Groups.—The contrast between rural and urban Negroes is fully as marked in the 20-to-44 groups as in the younger ages. The larger cities have exceedingly high proportions in the 20-to-29 and 30-to-44 age groups. In 1890 almost 56.5 per cent of the Negroes in cities of over 500,000 were of these ages, this proportion was even higher in 1910 and 1920, and by 1930 it had fallen only to 54.6 compared with 44.3 per cent for the whites. The proportion of the population in these age groups declines as the size of the city decreases, but even the smallest cities (2,500 to 25,000) have a proportion well above that in rural communities, the 1930 figures being 42.7 and 32.8, respectively (29.8 per cent in the farm population). Thus in 1930 the proportion in the 20-to-44 age groups in the largest cities was two-thirds greater than in the rural districts, and in the smallest cities almost one-third greater. Nothing could show better the abnormal age composition of the urban Negroes than these comparisons. The cities draw heavily from the young adults in the rural districts, and most heavily from the farms. This is an important fact to remember.

The Older Groups.—There is not much difference in the proportion of Negroes in the 45-to-64 age groups in the cities and in the country at the present time; nor is there much difference between the farm and nonfarm populations. However, it is almost certain that in the future the proportion in the cities will increase faster than that in the country because of the larger proportion now in the 30-to-44 age group in the cities. It might happen, of course, that the older Negroes in the cities would tend to move back to their former homes in the country, but this does not seem very probable. At all times the proportion of Negroes in this age group has been much lower in all sizes of communities than in the white population, a fact to be anticipated from the relatively small proportion of all Negroes in these ages.

In the 65-and-over age group the differences between communities of different sizes are very considerable and have been increasing in recent years. Thus in 1890 this age group constituted 2.4 per cent of all Negroes in the largest cities and 2.9 per cent in rural areas. By 1930 these percentages had become 1.8 and 3.5, respectively. Elders were, therefore, but half as numerous relatively in the largest cities in 1930 as in the rural districts. In all sizes of places Negroes over 65 years of age are far less numerous than whites, but there is considerably less difference relatively between communities among whites than among Negroes. Again the recent migrations of the Negroes must be invoked in explanation of the differences between cities and country, and for the differences between whites and Negroes attention must again be called to differences in death rates.[1]

By Regions.—As would be expected, there are some significant differences between regions in the age composition of the Negroes in the several sizes of communities. In the cities of over 500,000 the proportion at the younger and older ages is somewhat higher in Baltimore, the only city of this size in the South, than in the large cities of the North or West. Thus in Baltimore in 1930, 33.2 per cent of the Negroes were under 20, as compared with 29.7 per cent in the Northeast, 28.7 per cent in the North Center, and 25.9 per cent in the West (Appendix Table 21). Among the smaller cities the proportion of youths does not vary so much from region to region but is generally higher in the South than elsewhere. In all sizes of cities the proportion 0 to 19 is lowest in the West.[2]

In the 20-to-29 group the West stands below other regions in most sizes of cities. In the 30-to-44 age group, however, the South has a lower proportion in all sizes of cities than the other regions. This is also the case in the 45-to-64 age group except in cities of over 100,000. The 65-and-over group does not vary significantly from region to region.

f. **Rural and Urban Differences.**—In the rural districts the proportion in the younger ages (under 20) is much higher in the South than elsewhere. In 1930, 50.6 per cent of all rural Negroes in the South were under 20, while in the Northeast 39.0 per cent, in the North Center 37.6 per cent, and in the West only 32.2 per cent were of this age. In all regions there was also a significant difference in 1930 between the farm and nonfarm populations in the proportion under 20. In the South the percentages were 53.6 and 42.9, in the North Center 43.7 and 34.4, in the Northeast 41.8 and 38.7, and in the West 43.0 and 27.7, respectively. The opposite situation prevailed in the middle groups. The proportion in the 20-to-44 age groups was very low among the rural-farm Negroes of the South and very high in the cities of all regions. Contrary to expectation, the South does not have a high proportion of Negroes over 65 in its rural population. The distinction for high proportions of old Negroes goes to the smallest cities and the rural districts of the North Center. This suggests a relatively large movement of Negroes into these places in the two or three decades following the Civil War with but few additions by migration since. Their rather slow increase in numbers supports this view. In the West the proportion of Negroes in the older ages is surprisingly high for a region peopled so largely by migration. This is additional evidence confirming the general attractiveness of the West for older people.[3]

[1] *Infra,* pp. 232, 245.
[2] The number of Negroes in the West is small; hence not much importance is to be attached to proportions there.
[3] *Supra,* pp. 16, 36.

4. THE AGE COMPOSITION OF THE OTHER COLORED

a. **Mexicans.**—Little can be said about the age composition of the other races in the population. The largest group, the Mexican, was separated from the white population for the first time in 1930; hence nothing can be said with certainty of its age composition in earlier decades. A few comparisons between Mexicans and whites in 1930 will bring out the most important differences between them. Among Mexicans 15.1 per cent were aged 0 to 4 compared with 9.1 per cent in the white population (Tables 38 and 44, pp. 141 and 161). As elsewhere, when the proportion aged 0 to 4 is high, the proportion aged 5 to 19 is generally high; so here the proportion of Mexicans of this age is 34.5, while that of whites is 29.1. Mexicans are still well in the lead in the 20-to-29 age group—19.8 per cent against 16.6 per cent, but from this point on, the situation is reversed. Only 18.6 per cent of the Mexicans were in the 30-to-44 age group, while 21.6 per cent of the whites were of these ages. In the 45-to-54 age group the difference is much greater, the whites having almost twice as high a proportion, the percentages being 9.9 and 17.9, respectively. In the 65-and-over age group the proportional differences between Mexicans and whites are still greater, only 2.0 per cent of the former, compared with 5.7 per cent of the latter, being of this age.

The high proportion of persons under age 20 (49.6 per cent) undoubtedly is to be attributed to a high birth rate among Mexican women rather than to the large excess of persons aged 20 to 44 that might be expected in a population recruited so largely from immigrants; since percentages in these age groups among Mexicans (38.4) and whites (38.2) are almost identical. But women under 30 are more fertile than women 30 to 44 and 29.0 per cent of all Mexican women are 15 to 29 compared with 26.4 per cent of all white women. This may in part explain the high proportion of children among the Mexicans, although this advantage is to a certain extent offset by the deficiency of Mexican women of these ages (192,000) compared with Mexican men (227,000). Again the small proportions of older persons in the Mexican population would naturally raise the proportion of young persons; but even so, there must be a high birth rate among Mexican women to result in such a high proportion of young persons in spite of the high infant death rates among them.

If, on the other hand, the present curtailment of Mexican immigration should continue, the 20-to-44 age groups will decline and the older age groups will increase quite rapidly. Whether age groups under 20 will decline more rapidly than those 20-to-44 will depend chiefly upon how fast the birth rate falls.

The regional distribution of the Mexicans has already been discussed.[1] Only in the West and parts of the South (Texas, Arkansas, and Okla-

[1] *Supra,* p. 80.

TABLE 44.—POPULATION OF KNOWN AGES AND PERCENTAGE DISTRIBUTION OF THE PRINCIPAL "OTHER COLORED" RACES, BY AGE, 1900–1930[a]

Race and year	0–4	5–19	20–29	30–44	45–64	65+	Total
POPULATION (THOUSANDS)							
Indian:							
1900......................	34	84	37	37	30	11	233
1910......................	40	96	40	42	33	13	265
1920......................	33	90	37	39	32	13	244
1930......................	47	122	52	52	42	16	332
Chinese:							
1900......................	1	4	11	41	29	2	89
1910......................	1	6	9	21	30	2	70
1920......................	3	7	10	15	22	4	61
1930......................	6	14	14	22	15	4	74
Japanese:							
1900......................	(b)	5	12	6	1	(b)	23
1910......................	3	4	31	29	3	(b)	71
1920......................	19	15	21	43	12	(b)	111
1930......................	18	47	14	33	26	1	139
Mexican:[c]							
1930......................	215	491	282	264	141	28	1,421
Filipino:[c]							
1930......................	1	5	26	11	1	(b)	45
PERCENTAGE DISTRIBUTION							
Indian:							
1900......................	14.5	36.1	15.8	16.0	13.0	4.6	100.0
1910......................	15.3	36.4	15.1	15.9	12.4	4.9	100.0
1920......................	13.7	36.8	15.0	15.9	13.2	5.4	100.0
1930......................	14.1	36.9	15.8	15 8	12.6	4.9	100.0
Chinese:							
1900......................	1.3	4.6	12.7	46.4	33.2	1.8	100.0
1910......................	1.9	9.0	12.9	30.5	42 4	3.3	100.0
1920......................	4.7	11.9	16.5	25.0	35.3	6.6	100.0
1930......................	7.8	19.2	18.3	29.2	20.2	5.3	100.0
Japanese:							
1900	0.7	20.8	51.3	24.7	2.5	(d)	100.0
1910......................	4.8	6.0	43.8	40.8	4.6	0.1	100.0
1920......................	17.2	13.2	18.9	39.2	11.2	0.2	100.0
1930......................	12.8	33.7	10.4	23.8	18.9	0.5	100.0
Mexican:[c]							
1930......................	15.1	34.5	19.8	18.6	9.9	2.0	100.0
Filipino:[c]							
1930......................	3.2	11.4	57.6	25.2	2.5	0.1	100.0

[a] For 1900 from *Twelfth Census of the United States: 1900*, Vol. II, Pt. 2, pp. xl-xli, lv; 1910 from *Thirteenth Census of the United States: 1910*, Vol. I, pp. 303, 306; 1920 from *Fourteenth Census of the United States: 1920*, Vol. II, p. 157; 1930 from special photostat sheets secured from Bureau of the Census.

[b] Less than 500.

[c] Data for Mexicans and Filipinos not available by age before 1930.

[d] Less than one-tenth of 1 per cent.

homa) are they an important element. Data are not available to show the age distribution by size of community, but the urban and rural can be separated. Although the differences are not so marked as among the whites and Negroes, yet the proportion of young persons (0 to 19) is smaller in the urban population (47.7 per cent) than in the rural population (51.6 per cent), whereas the proportion 20 to 44 is larger in the urban population (40.1 per cent) than in the rural (36.6 per cent). In the older age groups the differences are not significant. The majority of the foreign-born Mexicans are comparatively recent arrivals and there are few old people among them.

b. Indians.—The Indians are the only group in Table 44 whose age composition is not affected greatly by immigration. Its age distribution if shown graphically would be a pyramid much like that of the Negro population—the normal shape for a population growing rather rapidly by an excess of births over deaths (Figure 21, p. 144). Indians differ from whites in having a higher proportion of children aged 0 to 4 and youths aged 5 to 19 and a somewhat smaller proportion in the 20-to-44 age groups. The proportion in the older age groups is much the same in both populations. The Indians being very largely rural, there is no need to discuss urban-rural contrasts.

c. Chinese.—The peculiarities in the age structure of the Chinese, Japanese, and Filipinos are almost wholly due to the fact that they are largely immigrants and that they brought comparatively few women with them, particularly the Chinese and Filipinos. Chinese immigration has been quite effectively restricted for many years. Since there were but few women here at the time of restriction, changes in the age composition represent the transition from an immigrant group growing older, because receiving comparatively few recruits, to a native population maintained by natural increase. The 0-to-4 and 5-to-19 age groups are growing larger steadily as the entire population becomes more and more native with the departure of the older immigrants and the gradual increase of females by births. At present the 30-to-44 and 45-to-64 groups and particularly the former are heavily weighted. It is surprising that the proportion of Chinese over 65 is not larger. The chief reason must be that many of the immigrants return to China in their old age, although the increase in young persons and a high death rate might be sufficient to account for the decline in the proportion of elders since 1920.

d. Japanese.—The age composition of the Japanese is quite different from that of the Chinese. In the first place, they are more recent immigrants. In the second place, before restriction shut off new arrivals, a relatively large number of women had come. Consequently the proportion under 20 has grown rapidly, from 10.8 per cent in 1910 to 46.5 per cent in 1930. The proportion in the 20-to-29 age group shows the effects of recent restriction, and the negligible percentage in the 65-and-over age group shows the newness of the entire movement. For both the Chinese and Japanese it takes no prophet to foretell a rather rapid approach to the age composition of a native population.

e. **Filipinos.**—The Filipinos are still more recent immigrants with very few women, hence their extremely abnormal age composition. Almost three-fifths are in the 20-to-29 age group and an additional one-fourth in the 30-to-44 age group. There are, therefore, very few in the younger and older age groups. The future of Filipino immigration is so uncertain that any estimate of future age trends is pure guess work.

5. CONSEQUENCES OF AGE DIFFERENTIALS AND TRENDS

Some of the consequences of recent trends in age composition are already noticeable and will become more pronounced in the future since these age trends are almost certain to continue. Other and perhaps the more important consequences will not be noticeable for some time. An attempt will be made here to point out those already in evidence and also to call attention to others which seem likely to develop within the not distant future. Naturally these latter are problematical, but it is believed that their importance justifies suggestions as to what they may be.

a. **Fewer Children.**—As noted above there were fewer children under five years of age in 1930 than in 1920; hence there will be a smaller number to enter the first grade of school during 1930–1935 than during 1920–1925. By 1940 there will be a smaller number of the age for each grade up to senior high school. This is almost a certainty rather than a mere possibility, for most of the children who will be in these grades in 1940 will have been born during 1924–1933, just as most of the children in these grades in 1930 were born during 1914–1923. The number of births in the later period will be almost 1,900,000 fewer than the number in the earlier period; hence there will be about 1,600,000 fewer children aged 7 to 16 in 1940 than in 1930, making a liberal allowance for falling death rates. Judging from the number of births in past years the number of youths of senior high school, college, and university age will increase up to about 1945 and then decline.[1]

It must be remembered, however, that the number of children will increase rapidly in some localities, will be nearly stationary in other localities, and will decrease in still others, depending on local population growth.

Although the decline of population growth will decrease the number of children of school age, this may be offset by an increase in the proportion attending school. If the highest attendance standards prevailing in 1930

---

[1] Table 75, p. 266. In estimating the number of births 1924–1933 it is assumed that the number in 1932 and 1933 will be the same as in 1931.

in any geographic division had been universal, there would have been about 1,300,000 more children 7 to 16 years of age in school than there actually were.[1] This would offset about four-fifths of the decline in the population of this age that may be expected during the next decade.

There are several reasons for believing that attendance standards may be increased in this manner. The southern states, which for some time have had the lowest rates of attendance, improved rapidly during 1920–1930. Another such decade will bring them almost to the level of the rest of the country. Secondly, most communities in the United States already have the organization and perhaps the plant to care for some increase in these younger pupils; hence the additional expense involved in better attendance will be relatively small since the number of births is declining. Finally, child labor laws and school attendance laws are steadily becoming more stringent and show no signs of being relaxed even at this time of depression. It is quite probable, therefore, that within 20 years the highest requirements of school attendance now prevailing in any state will become general.

With regard to school attendance of persons 17 to 20, an increase may be expected up to about 1945 because of the growth of this age group. But while this increase should not be ignored, it is of small moment compared with the increase that may result from higher attendance standards. Only about one-fourth of those 17 to 20 are now in school; hence there is room for a relatively vast increase; even now in California over 40 per cent of the persons of these ages are in school.

A large increase in attendance in this group will involve great changes not only in the educational system but in society as a whole. High schools and colleges are far more expensive to build and operate than common schools. Those now in use are crowded; hence a large increase in attendance will require greatly increased expenditures chiefly of public money. Furthermore, most college students live away from home; consequently private expenditures would also mount rapidly with much increase in college attendance. But even if the community and the individual could meet these costs, there is the still more difficult matter of finding suitable jobs for two or three times the present number of high school and college graduates. Is the present economic structure prepared to absorb such an increase of persons with a relatively good school training? Is it true that white-collar jobs are already too scarce for those who feel that their education entitles them to such work? It is not within the province of this monograph to discuss these matters, but it is quite proper to suggest that the trends in the growth of the school population and in school attendance will demand careful study if a nice adjustment is to be main-

---

[1] In "The Population of the Nation," *Recent Social Trends*, p. 33, this possible increase in persons attending school was erroneously given as 2,300,000.

tained between the educational system on the one hand and the general social and economic structure on the other.

At the present time the ratio of children aged 0 to 19 to persons in the most productive ages (20 to 44) is about 80 per cent higher in rural areas and 108 per cent higher in the farm population than in cities of over 100,000 (Table 37). With such a difference, there can be no question that the educational task of rural areas is far greater than that of the cities. This difference also helps to explain why rural schools and rural standards of child welfare are often inferior to those in urban communities. When it is further realized that most, if not all, of the large cities depend upon migration from the country, especially from the farms, not merely for growth but even for their very maintenance, it will be seen that the problem of educating and caring for rural children is not merely a rural problem. It affects the future of the country as a whole and should be treated as a national problem. A beginning has been made in this direction by means of grants-in-aid and other types of state assistance to rural schools.

The ratio of children aged 0 to 4 to the most productive adults is also higher in the South than in the other regions of the country; hence the South carries a much heavier load of youth than the rest of the country. It would appear that if the children of this region are to be given opportunities in life approximately equal to those elsewhere, the South will have to be assisted in much the same way as some states are now assisting their rural districts.

b. More Elders.—When the social and economic significance of the increase of elders is considered, many points of interest emerge. For example, the problem of old-age pensions is one thing in 1930 with 5.4 per cent of the population over 65 years of age but will be a different thing in 1980 when the proportion over 65 years of age probably will be more than twice as large (over 12 per cent) (Table 31, p. 109). Furthermore, employment policies which are practicable and work but little hardship when only 22.9 per cent of the population is over 45 years old, as in 1930, may not be equally satisfactory when nearly 38 per cent is over 45, as may be expected in 1980.

The rising proportion of people over 45 years of age in the population may also demand considerable revision in the educational system, particularly if industrial processes continue to change at the rapid rate of the past. The need would seem to be for some type of adult education that will retrain middle-aged people to work efficiently under the new conditions. Additional adult education not strictly vocational may also be demanded if there is a general rise in income levels, for a growing proportion of adults will have leisure to devote to matters not directly concerned with the getting of bread and butter. This may well mean a relatively vast increase in the opportunities for study and training offered to mature people through the public school system. As yet comparatively little has been done in these fields. It seems probable that the general economic condition of the country will be the decisive factor both in creating the demand for adult education and in providing the means for its satisfaction.

The great increase in the aged will certainly result in an increase in the dependent aged, unless employment opportunities for older persons expand, unless accumulations during the working period of life increase greatly, or unless old-age pensions should become general. It should be remembered, however, that the decline in the number of children will decrease the group of young dependents. The net result should be a decrease in the total amount of dependency if savings and employment opportunities continue as in the past, or if older people can keep at suitable work longer or can accumulate more while young.

At present there are some very significant differences between country and city in ratio of elders (persons over 65 years of age) to persons in the most productive ages (20 to 44). In the largest cities there are but 10 persons over 65 to each 100 aged 20 to 44; this number increases steadily as the size of community decreases until in the rural districts the ratio is 18:100 (Table 37). Thus the rural communities of the country are found to be carrying a burden of old people, among whom dependency is very common, about 80 per cent in excess of that of the largest cities and 50 per cent greater than in cities of 100,000 to 500,000. There is no way of knowing whether the proportion of old people who are actually dependent is greater in the city or in the country, although there is some reason to think that dependents are relatively more numerous among persons over 65 years of age in the cities. There is also some reason to think that a considerable number of the aged dependents living in small cities and rural communities are being supported by children who have gone to the cities. Furthermore, in so far as the aged dependents are supported by county funds, many cities are sharing in the support of the rural aged. But even when these facts are taken into consideration, it seems likely that country people, both as individuals and as taxpayers, are carrying a heavier burden on account of the dependent aged than urban dwellers. However, the relative burdens of country and city for the care of the aged cannot be known with any degree of exactness until more detailed and careful studies are made. If as a result of such studies it is found that the relative burdens of different communities are unequal, then the question must inevitably arise whether these burdens should not be equalized by state or national contributions to those communities which are carrying an undue share of the load. As matters now stand, it seems probable that the cities are not carrying their fair share of the costs of caring for the dependent aged.

It is all very well to say that people do not need to raise children unless they want to and that the old people need not stay in the country, but actually these matters are not susceptible of immediate control by the local group. The great economic and social forces at work producing age differences—migration and the differential birth rate in particular—are for the time being overwhelming, as far as groups and localities are concerned. If the nation as a whole derives benefit from the free movement of people from place to place in response to economic demand and from a growing population, then it would seem that the federal government and the states should stand ready to equalize the costs of dependency as affected by these movements of population. It has not been customary to think of age differences between communities as matters of general concern, but when these arise as the natural result of generalized trends or forces then they become of more than local concern and the problems created need to be regarded from the standpoint of the general welfare.

Finally, it is interesting to speculate regarding some general consequences of the aging of the population. Since more of the voters will be older people, will the political parties be more under their control and will they undertake a stronger defense of the *status quo* in both domestic and foreign policies than has been customary hitherto? As the average age of stockholders in corporations increases, will a larger proportion of older men be elected to the boards of directors? If so, will they be increasingly conservative in the conduct of business and defend more stubbornly the rights of property? In the past the nation has been noted for the extent to which its business men would adopt new methods and scrap expensive systems and machines because of improvements which offered a chance to cut costs. It has been a common boast of American business men that they were less bound than men elsewhere by traditions and customs which prevented them from discarding out-of-date and wasteful processes and usages. The progressiveness of American business organization has no doubt been exaggerated, particularly as regards its ready adjustment to the larger social consequences of improved techniques. Nevertheless it has made possible a genuine improvement in living conditions for the masses of the population. The suggestion here is that a part of this progressiveness arose from the youth of the persons in control of business. If this is true, it may well be that in the future the same spirit of progress can be maintained only by deliberate efforts on the part of the older people who are coming into control. There is good reason to believe that such deliberate efforts to search out better methods will always yield high returns to the community, but the point is that improvements in business may not safely be left to spontaneous generation in the minds of business managers and stockholders as their average age increases.

With the slowing up of population growth and the increase in the proportion of elders, it is not improbable that there may also be a greater concern with the personal aspects of cultural life. Youth is more concerned with doing things, forging ahead, and making a place in the world. Age is apt to be more reflective, perhaps because the spur of poverty is less sharp, the inner driving force is weaker, or time and thought have brought about a change of ideas as to the goal of life. The mere shift in age distribution, therefore, may lead to more interest in cultural activities and increased support for the arts. Such developments in turn will influence the outlook and taste of the whole population.

c. The Productive Ages.—Thus far the discussion of the consequences of age changes has dealt chiefly with those flowing from changes in the proportions of youths (ages 0 to 19) and elders (ages over 65) since they are by far the most important changes to be anticipated. Taking persons in the productive ages (20 to 64) as a whole, there has been as already noted a steady increase in their proportion in the population since 1840. In that year they constituted but 42.9 per cent of the total; 50 years later they had grown to 50.0 per cent, and in 1930 they constituted 55.9 per cent. The prospect is that they will continue to increase relatively and will constitute over 60 per cent in 1980.

It was pointed out on page 114, however, that young adults aged 20 to 29 are, and probably will continue to be, a decreasing proportion of the population; that there has not recently been, nor is there likely to be, much change in the 30-to-44 age group; and finally that most of the increase in the productive ages just noted has been in the 45-to-64 group, which had been increasing steadily and will probably continue to do so for the next 50 years. Now it is obvious that such changes within the 20-to-64 age group may offset, from the standpoint of productiveness, the 5 or 6 point increase in the group as a whole which is to be expected by 1980. For this reason an attempt has been made to measure the probable changes in the productive power of the population in relation to its consumption needs by assigning weights for both factors by age and sex (Table 45).

The results of the computations based upon these weights indicate that there has been a rather slow increase in the productive power of the population in relation to its consumption between 1870 and 1930, the ratio being 1 productive unit to 1.81 consumption units in 1870 and 1:1.67 in 1930. In other words, the decline in proportion of persons in the younger productive ages was more than compensated for by the increase in the older age groups with the weights used. By 1950 the ratio will probably decline still farther to 1:1.62; and in 1980 it will be 1:1.63. Thus, provided, that people have opportunity to use the productive power indicated by these weights and that consumption needs remain as as-s'med, the burden of dependency on those in the productive ages should be somewhat lightened during the ensuing half century although not quite so much as in the past 60 years.

The general bearing on employment of this relative increase of productive units would seem to be in the direction of making it more difficult to

TABLE 45.—PRODUCING AND CONSUMING UNITS IN THE POPULATION, 1910, 1930, 1950, AND 1980[a]

	1870	1890	1910	1930	1950[b]	1980[b]
Producing units (thousands)....................	14,565	25,104	39,118	52,958	65,110	70,426
Consuming units (thousands)....................	26,325	43,721	65,464	88,441	105,340	114,829
Ratio of producing units to consuming units......	1:1.81	1:1.74	1:1.67	1:1.67	1:1.62	1:1.63

Age	Productive weight assigned to different ages		Consumption weight assigned to different ages	
	Male	Female	Male	Female
0– 4...	0.00	0.00	0.30	0.30
5– 9...	0.00	0.00	0.40	0.40
10–14...	0.00	0.00	0.60	0.60
15–19...	0.50	0.25	0.85	0.75
20–24...	1.00	0.50	1.00	0.80
25–29...	1.00	0.50	1.00	0.80
30–34...	1.00	0.50	1.00	0.80
35–44...	1.00	0.50	0.95	0.80
45–54...	0.80	0.40	0.90	0.75
55–64...	0.60	0.30	0.85	0.70
65–74...	0.40	0.20	0.70	0.65
75+...	0.10	0.00	0.55	0.55
Unknown...	0.75	0.40	0.80	0.70

[a] This method of measuring changes in producing and consuming units was suggested by Ernst Gunther in an article "Der Geburtenrückgang als Ursäche der Arbeitslosigkeit?" *Jahrbücher für Nationalékonomie und Statistik*, Vol. 134, Pt. 6 (June, 1931), pp. 921–973. The weights assigned to males and females by age are an adaptation of those used in the above study to bring them into closer conformity with the findings of Willford I. King and Edgar Sydenstricker in their study "The Classification of the Population According to Income," *Journal of Political Economy*, Vol. 29 (July, 1921), pp. 571–594. Many faults can be found with any such set of weights. All that is claimed for these is that they are fairly reasonable in the light of such facts as are available and help to measure the economic effects of the age changes during the period covered. Clearly age changes are a minor factor in the total situation.

[b] Based on the "medium" population by age, Table 31, p. 109.

find work unless consumption is so changed as to take up the slack. There should be no difficulty in accomplishing the latter because an improvement in standards of living has come to be regarded as normal. For the next half century, therefore, age changes should be mildly favorable to a higher standard of living because of the relative increase in that portion of the population which is productive.

However, it will be noted that the above conclusion is based on the assumption that people at the several ages will actually be in position to use their productive power. If, as is quite commonly believed, industry and commerce are scrapping men at younger ages than formerly and if they hire older men only at very low wages—lower than will enable them to maintain the consumption standards assumed in the weights used in Table 45—then the shift within the productive ages (20 to 64) noted above may prove to be of far more significance than this relative increase in productive units on a hypothetical basis. The fact that the 45-to-64 age group will probably increase proportionally by almost one-half during the next 50 years need not prevent a steady improvement in living conditions if the productive power of these persons is used to the full. But if industry turns them off and refuses to adapt its processes to their diminished physical vigor, an increasing proportion of them will become dependent or semi-dependent and must be added to the naturally dependent young and old. It would seem then that the increasing proportion of those in the older productive ages may create some very urgent problems in employment and dependency unless the economic organization allows them to produce in accord with their capacity. A marked reduction in the actual productiveness of the one-fourth of the population which will soon be found in the 45-to-64 age group could not but prove a very serious matter. On the other hand, an improvement in their productive capacity through retraining and the maintenance of health, and a more intelligent organization of business and industry to make use of older workers, would furnish the basis for better standards of living not only among these workers but among the entire population.

In conclusion, it would be urged that changes in ages be watched more carefully than in the past and that adjustments in the social and economic organization of the country anticipate these age changes so that their burden may not fall unevenly on individuals and communities. It is difficult to believe that the managers of industry and commerce cannot arrange the work to be done so that there will be places for men and women not in the very prime of life. Surely, too, the engineers can make machines which a healthy man of 50 or 60 can operate nearly as well as a man of 30, and office managers can keep workers who are past their prime even though they do not turn out so much work as formerly. Great parade is made of the resourcefulness of the American business men; surely this resourcefulness will not be allowed to fail when it is a matter of adjusting business to use its share of an aging population instead of throwing an undue portion of this load on agriculture. The quality of management will more and more have to be judged by its ability to adjust work to the human make-up of the community. Low costs alone will not be sufficient to stamp a manager a success if they are achieved at the expense of human beings discarded because no longer in their prime.

Furthermore, if it is believed that the present population is not too large, or that still further increase is needed, then the financial burden of raising the next generation, which is very unevenly distributed at the present time, should be redistributed so that those who raise the children will not be compelled to forego their reasonable share of the material enjoyments of life. If children, in reasonable numbers, are a national asset, the cost of rearing them should not be loaded so heavily on the rural population as is now being done.

Chapter V

SEX COMPOSITION

A S FAR back as figures are available, there have been more males than females in the United States. In 1820, the first census year in which the sex of each person was tabulated, there were 103.3 males per 100 females (Table 46). In prior censuses only the white population was

Table 46.—Sex Ratio, by Race, Nativity, and Parentage, 1790–1930[a]

| Year | Total | White | Native white | | | | Foreign-born white |
			Total	Native parentage	Mixed parentage	Foreign parentage	
1790	.....	103.8	.....	....	....	....	.....
1800	.....	104.0	.....	....	....	....	.....
1810	.....	104.0	.....	....	....	....	.....
1820	103.3	103.2	.....	....	....	....	.....
1830	103.1	103.8	.....	....	....	....	.....
1840	103.7	104.5	.....	....	....	....	.....
1850	104.3	105.2	103.1	....	....	....	123.8
1860	104.7	105.3	103.7	....	....	....	115.1
1870	102.2	102.8	100.6	....	....	....	115.3
1880	103.6	104.0	102.1	....	....	....	115.9
1890	105.0	105.4	102.9	103.5	....	....	118.7
1900	104.4	104.9	102.8	103.7	99.1	101.0	117.4
1910	106.0	106.6	102.7	104.0	98.5	100.0	129.2
1920	104.0	104.4	101.7	103.0	97.7	99.1	121.7
1930	102.5	102.7	101.1	102.3	96.7	98.6	115.1

	Negro	Mexican	Indian	Chinese	Japanese	Filipino	All other
1820	103.4	.....	.....	....	....	....	.....
1830	100.3	.....	.....	....	....	....	.....
1840	99.5	.....	.....	....	....	....	.....
1850	99.1	.....	.....	....	....	....	.....
1860	99.6	.....	119.0	1,858.1	....	....	.....
1870	96.2	.....	95.0	1,284.1	....	....	.....
1880	97.8	.....	104.8	2,106.8	....	....	.....
1890	99.5	.....	102.6	2,678.9	687.3	....	.....
1900	98.6	.....	101.5	1,887.2	2,369.6	....	.....
1910	98.9	.....	103.5	1,430.1	694.1	....	.....
1920	99.2	.....	104.8	695.5	189.8	1,410.2	777.0
1930	97.0	114.3	105.1	394.7	143.3	1,437.7	435.3

[a] Number of males per 100 females. From *Fifteenth Census of the United States: 1930*, Vol. II, pp. 97, 98.

classified by sex, the ratio of males to females being slightly higher, 103.8 in 1790 and 104.0 in 1800 and 1810. From 1820 to 1930 the sex ratio of the total population has been between 103 and 105 in 9 out of 12 census years, the exceptions being a high point of 106 in 1910, and low points of 102.2 in 1870 and 102.5 in 1930. The most marked upward or downward movement is the decline from 106 in 1910 to 102.5 in 1930. With such slight fluctuations from year to year, the trend of sex ratios for the total population is well represented by a horizontal straight line.

1. EXCESS OF MALES AMONG IMMIGRANTS

As would be expected in an immigrant-receiving country, the sex ratio has been closely related to the volume and character of immigration.

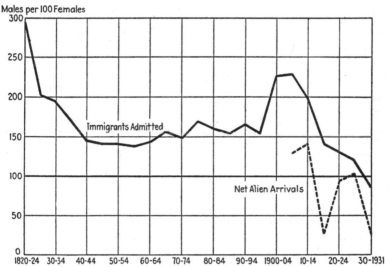

FIG. 22.—Sex ratio of immigrants admitted and of net alien arrivals, 1820–1931. (Based on Table 47.)

With but three exceptions, males have exceeded females among immigrants arriving in every year since records were begun in 1820. The excess of males has been greater during certain periods than others, depending on the extent to which immigration was a family affair or a movement of male workers. From 1820 to 1824 there were 296 male to every 100 female immigrants, but the ratio declined rapidly in following years, the average by five-year periods varying between 138 and 173 from 1840–1844 to 1895–1899 (Figure 22 and Table 47). The rapid development of the so-called "new immigration" commencing about 1900 modified the sex ratio greatly, for at first this movement was heavily masculine. During 1895–1899 there were 152 male per 100 female arrivals, but the proportion rose rapidly to 228 during 1900–1904 and 230 during 1905–1909, the high point for a single year being 262 in 1907.[1] A slight decline during 1910–1914 was followed by a rapid drop due at first to the

TABLE 47.—SEX RATIO AMONG IMMIGRANTS ADMITTED, AND AMONG THE EXCESS OF ALIEN ARRIVALS OVER DEPARTURES, 1820–1931

Year	Males (thousands)	Females (thousands)	Males per 100 females
Immigrants admitted[a]			
1820–24	22	7	296
1825–29	55	27	203
1830–34	141	72	197
1835–39	191	111	172
1840–44	238	162	147
1845–49	600	423	142
1850–54	1,121	792	142
1855–59	520	377	138
1860–64	416	291	143
1865–69	938	599	157
1870–74	1,110	745	149
1875–79	542	314	173
1880–84	1,870	1,168	160
1885–89	1,342	869	154
1890–94	1,447	873	166
1895–99	828	546	152
1900–04	2,264	991	228
1905–09	3,446	1,501	230
1910–14	3,443	1,732	199
1915–19	689	484	142
1920–24	1,578	1,197	132
1925–29	836	685	122
1930–31	158	181	87
Excess of alien arrivals over departures[b]			
1908–09	544	417	130
1910–14	1,944	1,372	142
1915–19	88	344	26
1920–24	965	1,003	96
1925–29	626	613	102
1930–31	34	130	26

[a] For 1820–1870 from *International Migrations*, Vol. I, pp. 395–396; 1871–1931 from *Annual Report of the Commissioner General of Immigration: 1931*, p. 238, fiscal year ending June 30.
[b] From current reports of the Commissioner General of Immigration. Includes immigrant and nonimmigrant aliens arriving and emigrant and nonemigrant aliens departing.

World War and later to the regulations affecting immigration. During 1925–1929 the sex ratio of immigrant arrivals was 122, but during 1930–1931 it was 87. These two years and 1922 are the only ones in which females have been in the majority among entrants.

[1] References to years after 1870 are to fiscal years ending June 30.

The effect on the population of the excess of males among immigrants has not been so marked as these figures would indicate, chiefly because of the still larger excess of males among persons leaving the United States. Data on the sex ratio of emigrants are not available before 1908, but since that time the ratio has averaged 373, the low point being 180 (in 1930) and the high point 657 (in 1908). Considering the excess of arrivals over departures, there was only one year (1908) before the World War in which females were in the majority. From 1915 to 1931, however, net immigration added more females than males in 12 out of the 17 years. Among net arrivals the sex ratio varied from 26 during 1915–1919 and 1930–1931 to 102 during 1925–1929, and averaged 82 for the 1915–1931 period as a whole (Table 47). During the war it was more difficult for men than for women and children to leave Europe for the United States. In the post-war period the total number of entrants has been limited by law and regulation; furthermore, within these limits preference has been given to relatives of immigrants already in the country. Men had come in greater numbers previously; hence women predominated in the movement to unite families.

2. SEX RATIO OF RACE AND NATIVITY GROUPS

With males predominating to such an extent among immigrants, it is natural that they have constituted a majority among the foreign-born white population in census years.[1] From 1860 to 1900 the sex ratio of this group was quite steady at a little above 115 (Table 46). The rapidly increasing excess of males among immigrants after 1900 raised the ratio to the high point of 129.2 in 1910, but since then there has been a decline to 115.1 in 1930. A continuation of recent immigration regulations, which is probably to be expected, will cause this decline to proceed further.

A considerable number of Mexicans and Japanese and a high proportion of Chinese and Filipinos are foreign born; hence their sex ratios are correspondingly high. Among Mexicans there were 114.3 males per 100 females in 1930, about the same as among foreign-born whites, since Mexican immigration has been a movement of families to quite an extent. The sex ratio of Japanese in 1930 was 143.3, an enormous drop from the high point of 2,369.6 in 1900. Immigration from Japan consisted almost entirely of men up to 1910, but since then more women than men have entered, and the birth rate has been high. Because immigration of these people has been at a standstill for some years and is likely to continue so, further declines in the sex ratio may be expected until equality in numbers is approached. Chinese males still greatly outnumber females (394.7 to 100

[1] The sex ratios for immigrants presented above were for all immigrants, but whites outnumbered colored to such an extent that sex ratios for white immigrants are almost identical with those for all immigrants.

in 1930). Nevertheless this is a huge decline from the 1890 ratio of 2,678.9. Chinese women never have immigrated in large numbers, but the exclusion of Chinese males in recent years means that this group is gradually being made up of native-born persons, with a consequent evening up of the sexes. This process undoubtedly will continue. The sex ratio among Filipinos is still high (1,437.7 in 1930), like that of Chinese and Japanese some decades ago. Since immigration from the Philippines is not subject to the same restrictions as that from foreign countries, the sex ratio of this group in future years will depend to a large extent on changes in the political status of the Philippines with respect to the United States.

Among the native-born groups the sexes have been fairly equal in numbers. The highest sex ratio for native whites as a whole was 103.7 in 1860 and the lowest 100.6 in 1870 (Table 46). In recent decades there has been a slight but steady downward movement, from 102.9 in 1890 to 101.1 in 1930. Information regarding sex of the different parentage groups begins in 1890 and 1900 and shows a larger proportion of males among whites of native parentage than among those of foreign or mixed parentage. In fact, females have outnumbered males among the mixed-parentage group since 1890 and among the foreign-parentage groups since 1900, and the sex ratio has declined in every decade in both groups.

Most of the Negroes and Indians are native born, immigration having been negligible among both races. Negro males, unlike whites, have been exceeded by females since 1830, but in only 3 of the 10 census years was the ratio below 98.5. The 1930 ratio of 97 is next to the lowest on record. The sex ratio of Indians, first ascertained in 1860, has shown an excess of males in all census years but one. During recent decades there has been a small but consistent rise, from 101.5 in 1900 to 105.1 in 1930.

3. SEX DIFFERENCES IN BIRTHS AND DEATHS

Although the sex ratio of the foreign born in the United States is determined chiefly by the proportion of males among immigrants, the sex ratio of the native born is determined almost entirely by the excess of male births and the difference in death rates of the two sexes. There is no universal agreement as to the reasons why more boys than girls are born,[1] but there is no disputing the fact that this is generally the case. The sex ratio at birth in Massachusetts since 1851 (the longest state series available) has averaged 105.7, the lowest figure for a five-year period being 104.9 and the highest 106.7 (Table 48). Considering single years, the range is from a low of 103.6 in 1858 and 1889 to a high of 109.8 in 1851. In the United States birth-registration area since its commence-

---

[1] For a discussion of certain causes, see the following: John B. Nichols, "A Study of Sex Ratios," *Memoirs of the American Anthropological Association*, Lancaster, Pennsylvania, Vol. 1, Pt. 4, pp. 245–300. Winston Sanford, "The Influence of Social Factors upon the Sex-ratio at Birth," *American Journal of Sociology*, Vol. 37, No. 1 (July, 1931), pp. 1–21.

SEX COMPOSITION

TABLE 48.—SEX RATIO AT BIRTH, MASSACHUSETTS, 1851–1931, AND UNITED STATES BIRTH-REGISTRATION AREA, BY RACE AND PARENTAGE, 1915–1929

Massachusetts[a]		United States birth-registration area[b]					
			White births				Negro births
Year	All births	Year	All births	To native parents	To mixed parents	To foreign-born parents	
1851–54	106.7	1915	105.5	105.7	104.4	106.0	99.5
1855–59	105.3	1916	105.7	105.7	106.3	105.7	102.0
1860–64	106.7	1917	105.8	105.5	105.0	105.9	102.8
1865–69	105.6	1918	105.8	106.3	106.3	105.4	103.3
1870–74	106.2	1919	105.7	106.0	106.3	105.5	102.4
1875–79	105.5	1920	105.7	106.2	106.1	105.2	102.7
1880–84	105.3	1921	105.9	106.2	106.5	105.7	103.0
1885–89	104.9	1922	105.6	106.2	106.0	104.8	103.0
1890–94	105.4	1923	105.7	105.8	105.4	105.9	104.0
1895–99	105.5	1924	105.8	106.2	105.9	105.0	104.0
1900–04	106.3	1925	106.0	106.5	105.5	105.4	104.0
1905–09	106.2	1926	105.7	106.1	105.3	105.0	103.8
1910–14	105.4	1927	105.8	106.4	105.8	105.0	103.5
1915–19	105.3	1928	105.7	106.4	105.4	105.2	102.6
1920–24	105.6	1929	105.7	106.2	105.4	104.3	103.8
1925–29	105.3	....	.....	.....	.....	.....	.....
1930–31	104.8	....	.....	.....	.....	.....	.....

[a] From current *Annual Report on the Vital Statistics of Massachusetts.*
[b] From current *Birth, Stillbirth, and Infant Mortality Statistics.*

ment in 1915, the sex ratio at birth has also averaged 105.7, the highest figure being 106.0 and the lowest 105.5.

The sex ratios at birth of the different race and parentage groups are similar. The excess of male births has been somewhat larger among whites than among Negroes, the former usually varying between 105 and 106.5 males per 100 females in the birth-registration states and the latter between 102 and 104. Within the white group the differences have been even smaller, the sex ratio of births to native parents averaging 106.1, to mixed parents 105.7, and to foreign-born parents 105.3.

The slight fluctuations in sex ratio at birth from year to year have not constituted a definite trend. If there has been any change in Massachusetts, it has been an insignificant decline. In the birth-registration states, the sex ratio of births to native white and to Negro parents has moved upward very slightly since 1915, that of births to foreign-born white parents has moved slightly downward, and that of births to mixed parents has teetered.

Working against the excess of males at birth is the higher death rate of the masculine group. This may not be judged accurately by comparing the number of male and female deaths, because the former is exaggerated by the excess of males in the population. A comparison of male and female death rates avoids this difficulty, however. These rates are available for Massachusetts in every fifth year beginning with 1860 and show, without exception, the male rate higher than the female. The smallest difference was in 1920, when the male rate was 14.1 per 1,000 and the female rate 13.8; the largest difference in 1865 when the male rate was 21.7 and the female 19.6.[1] In the death registration states a similar differential has existed.

The above comparisons of crude rates may be somewhat inaccurate because the age composition of the sexes is not exactly the same. To overcome this, standardized rates for the registration states of 1920 published by the Division of Vital Statistics may be used.[2] They corroborate the crude rates, the standardized rate for males being higher than that for females in each year. During 1920–1927 the male standardized rate averaged 12.3 per 1,000 and the female rate 11.0.

The effect of differences in age composition may also be eliminated by using data from life tables. This subject will be discussed in more detail in Chapter VII, but it may be pointed out here that life tables computed for large groups of the white population almost invariably show that females of any given age have a longer expectation of life than males of the same age. According to Table 66, page 240, the expectation of life at birth has been from 1.8 to 3.8 years longer for females than for males in Massachusetts. In tables for the original death-registration states,[3] the greater longevity of white females has ranged from 2.4 to 3.6 years and of Negro females from 1.9 to 3.6 years.[4] At older ages the differences are smaller but are still in favor of the feminine sex. But among Negroes in the southern states (which include a large majority of all Negroes) the expectation of life at birth of males was longer than that of females by 0.9 years according to the 1919–1920 life tables.

Considering death rates by age shown in the United States life tables, there were only three years of age (15 to 17) in 1900–1902 and seven years of age (92 to 98) in 1909–1911 in which female rates were not lower than male rates among the white population. In 1919–1920 death rates of white females were somewhat higher than those of white males at ages 20 to

---

[1] *Annual Report on the Vital Statistics of Massachusetts, 1931,* p. 32; ditto *1916,* p. 127.

[2] *Mortality Statistics: 1927,* Pt. II, p. 16. The rates are also referred to as adjusted rates.

[3] These states are the New England states, New York, New Jersey, Michigan, Indiana, and District of Columbia.

[4] James W. Glover, *United States Life Tables: 1890, 1901, 1910, and 1901–1910,* Washington, U. S. Bureau of the Census, 1921, pp. 64–75. Elbertie Foudray, *United States Abridged Life Tables: 1919–1920,* Washington, U. S. Bureau of the Census, 1923, pp. 24–27. *Recent Social Trends,* Chap. 12, "The Vitality of the American People," by Edgar Sydenstricker, New York, McGraw-Hill Book Company, Inc., 1933. See p. 610.

32, but were lower at all other ages.[1] Among Negroes, female rates were lower than male rates at all ages except 2 to 4, 6 to 18, and 66 in 1900–1902, and at all ages except 4 and 10 to 18 in 1909–1911. In the 1919–1920 life tables Negro rates are given for only every fifth year after age 2. In the northern states, Negro female rates were higher at ages 12, 52, 57, 62, and 92 and male rates higher at other ages, the average for females being well below that for males. In the southern states the opposite was true, for Negro female death rates were higher than those of males at the majority of ages.

What sex differences in specific death rates and expectation of life mean in the sex composition of the population is summed up best by the number of survivors. In the white population surviving from an equal number of male and female births in the 1918 registration states, there would be a gradual decrease in sex ratio to 97.5 at age 25, 96.5 at age 50, and 89.1 at age 75 according to the 1919–1920 life tables (Table 49). Life tables for other years show larger declines in sex ratio with advancing age for whites and for Negroes in northern states. For Negroes in southern states the life tables for 1919–1920 show a sex ratio of 99.6 at age 25, but of 106.4 at age 50, increasing to 112.9 at age 75.

4. WHY HAS THE SEX RATIO OF NATIVE WHITES DECLINED?

An examination of the changes in sex ratios of immigrants explains why the variations in the sex ratio of the foreign-born whites have occurred. It is a much more complex matter to account for the decrease in the sex ratio of native whites which Table 46 shows has been going on since 1890. The sex ratio of white births has fluctuated so little (Table 48) that it has not been a factor of consequence.

According to the expectation of life values shown in Table 66, page 240, the mortality status of females in Massachusetts was not so much above that of males from 1850 to 1890 as it has been since 1890. If these sex differentials were typical of those in the United States, the higher relative standing of the males should have meant higher sex ratios in those years than later, as was actually the case in the native white population. In the original death-registration states the mortality of white males improved a little less rapidly than that of white females from 1900–1902 to 1909–1911, considerably more rapidly from 1909–1911 to 1919–1920, but more than lost this gain from 1919–1920 to 1929. This is shown more clearly by the sex ratios of white survivors in life tables for the original death-registration states, the sex ratios at age 50 declining from 93.9 in 1900–1902 to 92.6 in 1909–1911, then rising to 95.9 in 1919–1920,

---

[1] Metropolitan Life Insurance Company, *Statistical Bulletin*, Vol. 9, No. 8 (August, 1928).

TABLE 49.—NUMBER OF SURVIVORS AT SELECTED AGES FROM 100,000 MALE AND 100,000 FEMALE BIRTHS, 1900–1929[a]

Year	Age 25			Age 50			Age 75		
	Male	Female	Sex ratio	Male	Female	Sex ratio	Male	Female	Sex ratio
WHITES IN THE ORIGINAL DEATH-REGISTRATION STATES									
1900–02............	73,907	76,588	96.5	57,274	61,005	93.9	21,387	25,362	84.3
1909–11............	77,047	79,865	96.5	60,741	65,629	92.6	21,585	26,569	81.2
1919–20............	81,004	83,402	97.1	66,025	68,827	95.9	25,793	29,073	88.7
1929..............	85,805	88,101	97.4	71,281	75,934	93.9	25,299	32,190	78.6
WHITES IN THE 1918 DEATH-REGISTRATION STATES[b]									
1919–20............	82,134	84,280	97.5	67,385	69,829	96.5	27,965	31,402	89.1
NEGROES IN THE ORIGINAL DEATH-REGISTRATION STATES									
1900–02............	53,285	55,795	95.5	34,766	37,681	92.3	8,892	11,066	80.4
1909–11............	57,736	61,430	94.0	35,427	40,886	86.6	7,494	10,657	70.3
1919–20............	65,962	68,856	95.8	44,124	46,862	94.2	11,230	12,339	91.0
NEGROES IN SEVEN SOUTHERN STATES[c]									
1919–20............	73,692	73,990	99.6	50,690	47,639	106.4	18,314	16,217	112.9

[a] For 1900–1902 and 1909–1911 from James W. Glover, *United States Life Tables: 1890, 1901, 1910, and 1901–1910;* for 1919–1920 from Elbertie Foudray, *United States Abridged Life Tables: 1919–1920;* for 1929 from unpublished data supplied by Edgar Sydenstricker of the Milbank Memorial Fund.

[b] The 1918 death-registration states, excluding Colorado, Montana, and Louisiana. This is the "aggregate" of the Foudray life tables.

[c] Missouri, Maryland, Virginia, North Carolina, South Carolina, Kentucky, and Tennessee. Missouri is in the West North Central division, but was included by Miss Foudray with southern states instead of northern because Negroes constituted more than 5 per cent of the population in 1920.

but losing most of this gain by 1929[1] (Table 49). At age 75 there were changes in the same direction, but on a somewhat larger scale. The improvement in the relative mortality status of males from 1909–1911 to 1919–1920 might be expected to raise the native white sex ratio from 1910 to 1920, yet this was the decade in which the largest decrease occurred since the Civil War. Moreover, the reverse change in comparative mortality status of males might be expected to lower the sex ratio of native whites from 1900 to 1910 and from 1920 to 1930, decades in which the sex ratio declined only slightly. It is probable, therefore, that these

[1] The values for expectation of life in Table 66 and for the number of survivors at selected ages in Table 49 are for all whites, but the sex differentials shown are approximately true for native whites in 1900–1902 and in 1909–1911, as may be seen by comparing similar life tables for all whites and native whites.

changes did not continue sufficiently long in one direction to yield the expected results.

A third factor bearing on the sex ratio of the population should not be overlooked; namely, its age distribution. From what has been said, it is evident that the sex ratio is high in the younger ages because of the excess of male births and is low among elders because of the higher death rates among males than females.[1] Certain changes in the age composition of the population, therefore, would affect the sex ratio of the population. In Chapter IV it was pointed out that there have been a considerable falling off in the proportion of the native white population in the younger age periods and a corresponding increase in the proportion in the upper age periods. This is the type of change that would do the most to decrease the sex ratio. There is little doubt that it has had an important effect in lowering the sex ratio of native whites.

The future trend of the native white sex ratio will depend on the course of the last two factors discussed, for there seems little probability of any significant change in sex ratio at birth. The proportion of youths in the population is likely to continue to decrease, and the proportion of elders to increase, for reasons given in Chapter IV. This will tend to lower the sex ratio of native whites still further. Whether the mortality status of males will improve in the future more or less rapidly than that of females is not clear. The expectation of life of white females rose considerably more rapidly than that of white males from 1919–1920 to 1929–1930, but this proves nothing for coming years. On the whole, female death rates have been lowered more rapidly than those of males during the last half century when industrialization and urbanization have proceeded rapidly. Apparently these changes have been harder on men than on women, but increased efforts to control diseases that bear more heavily on male industrial workers in urban areas may modify this differential.

5. SEX RATIOS BY REGIONS

The ratio of males to females in certain parts of the United States varies considerably from that in other parts and in the nation as a whole. In the northeastern states, for example, the sex ratio has been from two to five points below that in the entire United States. In fact, females have exceeded males in several census years, whereas in the United States males have always been more numerous. On the other hand, the sex ratio in the western states has always been above the average in the United States; as recently as 1890 there were 142.3 males per 100 females in the West (Figure 23 and Table 50). In the North Central states, like the West, the sex ratio has been higher than in the United States, but the differences have not been so large. In 1820 the excess of males in the southern states

[1] Sex ratios by age will be discussed in more detail in a later section of this chapter.

was larger than in the nation as a whole, but in subsequent years it has been smaller.

Among the more important race and nativity groups much the same differences are found between the sex ratio in the United States and in the various regions as presented above for the entire population. Both native whites and foreign-born whites have had a lower sex ratio in the northeastern states than in the nation as a whole, but Negroes had a higher ratio in 1920 and 1930. Ratios of all three groups were highest in the West. The sex ratio of foreign-born whites has been higher in the South than in

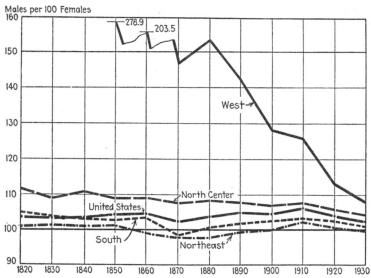

FIG. 23.—Sex ratio of the United States and regions, 1820–1930. (Based on Tables 46 and 50.)

the nation as a whole for many years, and that of the native whites higher since 1890, but the Negro sex ratio has been lower since 1870.

Regional differences in sex ratio are in part the result of regional differentials in the spread between male and female death rates. For the white population, the 1919–1920 life tables show that female death rates in those years were considerably lower than male death rates in the northeastern states and the western states, but were slightly higher in the southern states. Thus among the survivors from an equal number of male and female white births, the sex ratio according to these life tables gradually declined in the northeastern states to 94.7 at age 50 and 85.5 at age 75, and in the Pacific states to 94 and 81.6, respectively (Table 51). In the southern states, on the contrary, the ratio was above 100 at age 50, and only declined to 96.6 at age 75. An intermediate course was followed

TABLE 50.—SEX RATIO OF REGIONS, BY RACE AND NATIVITY, 1820–1930[a]

Region	1820	1850	1870	1890	1910	1920	1930
TOTAL POPULATION							
Northeast.....................	100.8	101.2	97.7	99.4	102.1	100.5	99.9
North Center.................	111.4	108.7	107.1	107.6	107.3	105.8	104.0
South........................	104.4	102.8	98.3	101.9	103.1	102.5	100.8
West.........................	.....	278.9	147.0	142.3	125.7	113.0	107.7
WHITES							
Northeast.....................	100.9	101.4	97.8	99.3	102.2	100.5	99.9
North Center.................	111.4	108.9	107.3	107.6	107.3	105.7	104.0
South........................	104.6	104.9	99.6	103.4	105.2	104.3	102.5
West.........................	.....	277.9	146.9	135.5	125.8	112.8	107.8
NATIVE WHITES							
Northeast.....................	.....	99.4	96.9	98.0	97.7	97.6	98.2
North Center.................	.....	105.7	103.9	104.2	102.9	102.4	101.8
South........................	.....	103.1	98.4	102.4	104.0	103.3	102.0
West.........................	.....	241.7	132.7	124.2	114.9	106.6	104.3
FOREIGN-BORN WHITES							
Northeast.....................	.....	112.0	101.5	104.1	116.2	110.6	106.7
North Center.................	.....	132.9	123.8	123.7	134.4	128.9	122.4
South........................	.....	154.1	125.0	131.6	141.9	135.6	130.2
West.........................	.....	770.1	194.2	182.1	183.7	148.2	133.8
NEGROES							
Northeast.....................	94.9	92.7	93.0	102.1	95.2	101.0	98.0
North Center.................	111.4	100.6	101.6	107.5	107.9	110.7	103.8
South........................	104.0	99.3	96.0	99.0	98.4	97.7	95.9
West.........................	.....	502.4	157.4	426.7	120.6	131.8	103.9

[a] Compiled from current census reports.

in the North Central states, the sex ratio remaining above 97 up to age 50 and above 90 up to age 75.

As mentioned a little earlier, this matter seems to be related to rural-urban distribution. The northeastern states were the most urban in 1920, followed by the Pacific states, the East North Central states, the West North Central states, and last of all the southern states. The same order is followed if these regions are ranked by the amount by which male death rates exceed female rates. The rural-urban comparison can be made more definite by using the 1919–1920 life tables for large cities and rural states. In the large cities, the sex ratio declined to 93.9 at age 50 and to 79.3 at

TABLE 51.—NUMBER OF SURVIVORS AT SELECTED AGES FROM 100,000 MALE and 100,000 FEMALE WHITE BIRTHS, BY REGIONS, 1919–1920[a]

Region	Age 25			Age 50			Age 75		
	Male	Female	Sex ratio	Male	Female	Sex ratio	Male	Female	Sex ratio
Northeast[b].........	80,776	83,286	97.0	65,035	68,688	94.7	24,145	28,240	85.5
East North Central..	82,349	84,335	97.6	68,691	70,272	97.8	29,931	32,946	90.8
West North Central[c].	84,071	86,121	97.6	70,885	72,318	98.0	33,583	36,807	91.2
South[d].............	83,496	84,805	98.5	69,736	69,415	100.5	31,522	32,644	96.6
Pacific.............	83,361	85,741	97.2	67,135	71,418	94.0	28,621	35,090	81.6
14 large cities[e]......	79,801	82,362	96.9	63,039	67,155	93.9	20,367	25,692	79.3
11 rural states[f]......	83,965	85,682	98.0	70,589	71,118	99.3	32,885	35,008	93.9

[a] From Elbertie Foudray, *United States Abridged Life Tables: 1919–1920*. In combining states by regions, the number of survivors for each state was weighted according to the number of white children 0 to 1 in the 1920 census.

[b] Includes only Massachusetts, Connecticut, New York, Pennsylvania, and New Jersey, life tables not being available for other states.

[c] Includes only Minnesota, Missouri, and Kansas.

[d] Includes only Maryland, Virginia, North Carolina, South Carolina, Kentucky, and Tennessee.

[e] Baltimore, Boston, Buffalo, Chicago, Cleveland, Detroit, Los Angeles, New Orleans. New York, Philadelphia, Pittsburgh, St. Louis, San Francisco, and Washington, D. C.

[f] Includes all states in the Foudray life tables having more than 50 per cent of their population living in rural areas in 1920; namely, Wisconsin, Minnesota, Missouri, Kansas, Virginia, North Carolina, South Carolina, Kentucky, Tennessee, Utah, and Oregon.

age 75, whereas in the rural states it was much higher, 99.3 at age 50 and 93.9 at age 75.

One condition may be advanced as by far the most important in explaining why death exacts a heavier toll of males as compared with females in cities and the more urban states than in the more rural states. A large proportion of women still find their major occupation to be keeping house whether they live in the city or the country; hence a change from one environment to the other should have little effect on their mortality rates in so far as they are affected by occupation. With men the case is entirely different. A farmer lives an active out-of-door life, quite in contrast to the sedentary in-door occupations of office workers in cities and without the particular hazards, such as fumes and dust, which affect miners and many types of factory workers. The effect of these differences on death rates is all too plain; the number of survivors at age 50 from 100,000 male white births according to the 1919–1920 life tables varies from a low of 63,039 in large cities and 65,035 in the northeastern industrial states to a high of 70,589 in the 11 most rural states and 70,885 in the West North Central states (Table 51). With females, the large cities are low with 67,155 survivors at age 50, the northeastern states second with 68,688, and the Pacific and West North Central states at the top with 71,418 and 72,318, respectively. The variation from low to high is

7,846 for males but only 5,163 for females. At age 75, the relative standing of the city and state groups is the same, but the differences are larger.

In Chapter VIII it will be pointed out that birth rates are significantly higher in rural states than in cities or urban states. It might be thought that this would mean higher death rates of women in rural states than in the other groups because of the greater exposure to the risks of maternal mortality. Such is not the case, however, for at ages 25, 50, and 75 there are practically as many survivors from 100,000 female births in the rural states where birth rates are highest as in the Pacific states where birth rates are lowest.[1] Female survivors in both of these groups of states and in the West North Central states considerably outnumber those in the 14 large cities and in other states (Table 51). Judging from the ratio of children to native white women, birth rates are by far the lowest in these cities.[2]

Although sex differentials in death rates are important in accounting for regional differences in sex ratios, a still more significant cause is migration. For much the same reasons that there has been a large excess of males among European immigrants to the United States, there has been an excess of males among migrants from one part of the United States to another. Whether a region has been settled by foreign born or by natives from other regions, the sex ratio during the process of settlement has been high. In early colonial days the predominance of males among colonists undoubtedly raised the sex ratio in the Atlantic seaboard states much above the present figure. When the wave of settlement moved west of the Appalachians, the newer region drew not only from Europe but also from the seaboard, lowering the ratio in the latter area.

Sex ratios of regions have also varied with their attractiveness to foreigners. The heavy Irish immigration of 1845–1856 swelled the population of the northeastern states and cities; the Scandinavian movement in later years was directed to the farm land in the North Central states. From 1900 to the World War the large number of immigrants from eastern and southern Europe went to the northeastern and East North Central states in particular, while the more recent immigration of Mexicans has gone to the Southwest. In all cases the tendency was to raise the sex ratio of the immigrant-receiving region.

The preceding outline of the situation regarding internal migration and the sex ratio for the total population applies quite well to the white population because of its predominance numerically. Prior to 1910 the interstate movement of Negroes also was largely from the east to the west, although limited to the southern states. Since then, however,

---

[1] See Table 77, p. 274, for birth rates.
[2] Warren S. Thompson, *Ratio of Children to Women: 1920*, Census Monograph XI, Washington, Government Printing Office, 1931, 242 pp. See pp. 41–42.

the movement from south to north, which formerly was unimportant, has become the outstanding feature. This helps to explain why the sex ratio of Negroes is lower in the South than elsewhere.[1]

Differences in the age composition of the population from one region to another have had some effect in causing regional differences in sex ratio. In Chapter IV it was pointed out that the proportion of elders in the population has been higher in the Northeast than elsewhere, and the proportion of children and youths higher in the South. This would tend to lower the sex ratio in the former region and to raise it in the latter, because of the excess of male births and the usual decline in sex ratio with advancing age. But this factor of age composition has undoubtedly been of minor importance in comparison with migration.

With these ideas in mind regarding the causes of variation in sex ratios by regions, it is easier to see why the differences have become steadily smaller during recent decades. The marked falling off in immigration since the start of the World War has greatly lessened the importance of this factor in raising the sex ratio in immigrant-receiving areas; hence these areas are becoming more nearly like the remainder of the nation. Internal migration is not so important a factor as formerly in contributing to differences in sex ratios between regions. Not that there is less migration; on the contrary, the flow of people has increased considerably. But no longer is it directed so largely to the settlement of new and undeveloped regions; much more than formerly, it has become a movement from country to city. Males greatly outnumbered females in the earlier westward migration, but in recent years the mobility of females has been increasing relatively faster than that of males. In the cityward movement there has even been an excess of females, as will be pointed out later. These changes in direction of migration and in the sex ratio of the migrants have been important in equalizing sex ratios of different regions.

6. SEX RATIOS BY SIZE OF COMMUNITY

Sex ratios vary not only from region to region but also from farming areas to large cities within each region. The latter differences are not so large as the former; nevertheless they are significant. As far back as records go, sex ratios for the total population have averaged higher in rural communities throughout the United States than in cities of any size group (Table 52). In 1820 the sex ratio for all rural persons was 104.4, but the highest for a city group was 93.8 in places of 2,500 to 25,000. In 1930 the difference was about the same, the rural ratio being 108.0 and that of the rural-farm population 111.0, whereas the highest city ratio

---

[1] The extent to which the occupations of various places call for men compared with women is a factor affecting the sex ratio of migrants. *Infra*, p. 192.

TABLE 52.—SEX RATIO IN RURAL AREAS AND IN CITIES GROUPED BY SIZE, BY RACE AND NATIVITY, 1820–1930[a]

Year	Rural[b]		Cities with population of:				
	Farm	Nonfarm	2,500– 25,000	25,000– 100,000	100,000– 250,000	250,000– 500,000	500,000 and over
TOTAL POPULATION[c]							
1820	104.4		93.8	83.3	93.2	.....	.....
1840	104.7		96.9	93.7	96.5	91.8	.....
1860	106.7		97.7	97.2	99.0	91.3	93.2
1890	.....		.....	100.0	101.5	100.7	98.8
1910	109.6		101.6	101.0	101.9	102.4	100.3
1920	109.1	106.5	99.2	100.1	99.9	98.5	101.4
1930	111.0	105.0	97.2	96.3	97.1	95.6	100.5
WHITE POPULATION							
1820	103.9		96.2	97.5	96.2	.....	.....
1840	105.4		98.3	95.8	110.2	92.9	.....
1860	107.8		98.4	97.7	101.3	91.6	93.9
1890	.....		.....	100.6	102.6	99.5	98.9
1910	111.0		102.5	101.9	102.8	103.5	100.7
1920	110.8	106.6	99.7	100.6	100.4	99.1	101.4
1930	112.7	104.7	97.9	97.1	97.4	96.3	100.7
NATIVE WHITE POPULATION							
1890	.....	.....	.....	99.3	100.0	97.3	97.6
1910	107.1		97.3	97.4	98.3	97.1	96.2
1920	109.5	102.7	96.6	97.0	101.3	94.8	97.3
1930	111.6	102.9	96.1	95.0	95.5	94.0	97.5
FOREIGN-BORN WHITE POPULATION							
1890	.....	.....	.....	104.8	109.6	105.0	101.2
1910	160.6		133.4	120.0	120.3	124.0	109.6
1920	136.2	146.2	121.7	118.5	115.5	120.8	111.7
1930	139.4	130.4	114.3	110.0	108.8	113.2	110.1
NEGRO POPULATION[d]							
1820	105.5		81.9	69.4	67.1	.....	.....
1840	101.5		84.2	75.0	71.7	73.4	.....
1860	101.2		87.0	89.1	69.7	77.6	72.5
1910	102.1		90.5	90.5	92.2	87.4	91.7
1920	100.3	103.7	92.9	94.5	95.6	92.5	101.3
1930	101.2	102.8	88.2	87.7	92.8	90.4	97.3

[a] From special compilations made for this study, based on current census reports.

[b] Data are not available for rural areas and cities of 2,500 to 25,000 separately in 1890, or for rural-farm and rural-nonfarm prior to 1920.

[c] Includes whites and Negroes only, except in 1890. See Note d.

[d] Ratios are available for the colored population but not for Negroes in 1890.

was 100.5 in places of over 500,000. This was the only city group which had as many males as females in 1930.

Comparing cities of different sizes, no relation is apparent between size and sex ratio, one size group standing highest in one year, and another group in other years. In 1930 the sex ratio of the total population was considerably higher in cities of over 500,000 than in smaller cities. This appears to be due to the higher proportion of foreign born in these cities, for the sex ratio of native and foreign-born whites was not particularly high in them compared with smaller cities, and the number of Negroes was too small to affect significantly the ratio of all persons.

The situation is similar in the various race and nativity groups. Sex ratios by size of community can be calculated for white persons back to 1820. In only one case has a city group had a higher sex ratio than the rural area; in 1840 there were 110.2 males per 100 females in the two cities of 100,000 to 250,000,[1] compared with 105.4 in rural places (Table 52).

Sex ratios of native and foreign-born whites by size of community cannot be ascertained prior to 1890 but since then have been consistently higher in rural areas than in cities. The margin has been especially large both absolutely and relatively among the foreign born; in 1910 the rural ratio was 160.6 compared with the highest urban ratio of 133.4 (in places of 2,500 to 25,000). Comparing cities grouped by size, there may have been a tendency for the sex ratio of foreign-born whites to decline with an increase of size of city, but it has not been marked. With the change in the character of migration since the beginning of the World War, the sex ratios of the foreign born have fallen decidedly and have become more uniform between cities of various sizes. Differences between the sex ratio of rural areas and of city groups have been much smaller for native whites than for other groups, except Negroes in 1920 and 1930. Furthermore, there has been little variation in sex ratio between one size of city and another, and almost no correlation between size and sex ratio.

Among Negroes, the rural sex ratio formerly was higher relative to those of the city groups than was the case with whites. But since 1900 the larger cities have had high sex ratios, cities of over 500,000 even surpassing the rural-farm group in 1920. This is due in part to the fact that most of the largest cities are in the North and have had relatively small Negro populations in which migrants with an excess of males have been an important element.

a. **Why Rural Sex Ratios Are High.**—Several reasons may be advanced to account for variations in sex ratios by size of community. That the rural sex ratio is so high probably results mainly from farming being distinctly a man's job. Most farms are still family affairs; many farmers do almost all the field work themselves, although others have the help of

[1] Baltimore and New Orleans.

a son or hired man. In former decades the number of hired men was swelled by the immigrants who worked by the month on farms as a stepping stone to tenancy and eventually to ownership. For various reasons there has been a large decrease in this group in the last two decades, while hired girls in farm homes have become almost unheard of. The number of children remaining on the farm is also smaller than formerly; yet of those who do stay, boys are in the majority. The increasing importance of this factor, more than anything else, is believed to account for the rise in the rural-farm sex ratio from 109.1 in 1920 to 111.0 in 1930.

A second explanation of the higher rural sex ratio is the fact that female death rates are not so much below those of males in rural communities as in cities. This situation was discussed above, hence needs no further consideration here.

It is probable that there is a larger movement from farms of middle-aged adult women than of men, which also helps to raise the rural sex ratio. When farm families below the retiring age are broken by death, it is difficult for a farmer's widow to continue on the farm unless she has sons ready to take over its operation. The common occurrence is a sale of the livestock and equipment within a few months of the farmer's death, the rental or sale of the farm, and the removal of the family to a near-by village or town. There the widow can more easily find work to support herself and children if it is necessary to add to the income from the estate left her, as is usually the case. A farmer may find it hard to obtain a housekeeper after his wife dies, a task that is more necessary for him than for a city widower who has rooming houses and restaurants to fall back on. But farming has been his business; hence he is likely to continue at it. In the case of older farm couples, the death of one partner is more likely to mean movement off the farm if the survivor is a woman than if a man. In addition to the foregoing reasons, there is the greater economic help that the farmer can contribute by working on the farm if a married son or daughter lives on it.[1]

Influences that work directly to lower the sex ratio in cities also have an indirect effect in raising the ratio in the country. One of these, the fact that certain types of work in cities are particularly suited to women, is worth considering here. The 1930 census shows that women operatives outnumbered men by nearly two to one in candy, cigar, and tobacco factories, in factory clothing industries, and in knitting mills. Nearly all stenographers, typists, and telephone operators were women, over five-sixths of the teachers, and a vast number of clerks in stores. Many city women also find personal or domestic work outside of the home as

---

[1] The statistical evidence for this discussion is in Table 56, p. 200, and Table 61, p. 220. See also the discussion on pp. 201 and 217.

employees of laundries, restaurants, and hotels. In the country, on the other hand, there is much less opportunity for a woman to find a paying position; she has comparatively few alternative occupations to housework for her own family.

The foregoing arguments applied generally to the entire rural population before the last decade or two, but since then are becoming restricted to the rural-farm group. The rural-nonfarm group has grown with great rapidity of late and to an increasing extent is made up of people who work in cities and are affected by city conditions and social standards rather than by those of the farm.

b. Regional Variations in Rural-farm Sex Ratios.—To quite an extent, rural sex ratios vary from one region to another like the sex ratios of the total population. Certain differences exist, however, which seem worth analyzing. In particular, considering the regional variations shown in Table 50, it would not be expected that the rural-farm sex ratios would be about as high in the northeastern as in the North Central states, or that the rural-farm sex ratios of native whites would be higher in both of these regions than in the South. Yet this was the case in 1930, and approximately so in 1920 (Table 53).

That the sex ratio was so much lower on farms in the South than on those elsewhere in these years probably results from two interrelated factors in addition to those of migration and sex differentials in death rates which affect the total population of the regions, as pointed out previously. The most obvious is that the rural South has a high proportion of Negroes among whom the sex ratio is low; secondly, it has almost no

TABLE 53.—SEX RATIO OF RURAL-FARM POPULATION BY RACE AND NATIVITY, BY DIVISIONS, 1920 AND 1930[a]

Division	Total population		Native white		Foreign-born white		Negro	
	1920	1930	1920	1930	1920	1930	1920	1930
United States........	109.1	111.0	109.5	111.6	136.2	139.4	100.3	101.2
New England........	111.4	115.5	111.5	115.8	110.7	113.1	(b)	(b)
Middle Atlantic......	110.3	115.0	109.5	114.1	122.7	125.3	(b)	(b)
East North Central..	111.5	115.2	110.4	114.1	127.2	132.3	(b)	(b)
West North Central..	114.5	116.1	112.2	114.3	139.0	144.2	(b)	(b)
South Atlantic.......	103.5	104.8	105.7	107.1	(b)	(b)	99.7	100.1
East South Central...	103.8	104.9	105.8	106.8	(b)	(b)	99.0	100.3
West South Central..	107.9	109.0	109.2	110.4	(b)	(b)	101.9	103.1
Mountain..........	119.7	121.2	117.0	119.7	152.1	161.3	(b)	(b)
Pacific.............	127.0	127.9	118.0	119.1	168.6	160.3	(b)	(b)

[a] From *Fifteenth Census of the United States: 1920*, Vol. II, pp. 108, 109.
[b] Sex ratio not given when group made up less than 1 per cent of the rural-farm population of the division.

foreign-born whites among whom the sex ratio is high. The effect that these differences in race and nativity composition would have on the sex ratio of the farm population of the division may be seen by examining Table 53.

But when native whites alone are considered, the same variations between divisions are found, though in smaller degree: western states had the highest sex ratios, and southern states the lowest. Probably the chief reason for this situation is the importance in the South of cotton farming with its large requirements for hand labor. While farming is carried on mostly by power rather than by hand, especially if the implements used are drawn by a tractor or several horses, there is less farm work for women to do outside the home and the excess of males is high. This is the situation in much of the North and West, though in lesser degree in the New England and Middle Atlantic states, which nevertheless have high sex ratios. Where hoe farming is more predominant and much work is done by hand, there more women work in the fields and the sex ratio is lower. Cotton farming more than any other major type of farming requires much hand work, chopping and picking being chiefly hand operations outside the drier cotton areas of Texas and Oklahoma; hence the sex ratio is correspondingly low on southern farms. A century ago agricultural implements were relatively simple in all parts of the country; corn and wheat farming were then carried on by hand about as much as cotton farming is today. It is not surprising, therefore, that in 1840 the sex ratio of the rural white population was 103.0 in the Northeast and 104.9 in the South, or that in 1820 the ratios were 101.9 and 104.5 (Appendix Table 22, p. 379). In those years machinery was not used appreciably more in the North Central states than elsewhere; it was probably their newness and the fact that more pioneering was still going on in them that explain their higher sex ratios of 111.4 in 1820 and 110.4 in 1840.

c. **Range of Sex Ratios between Cities.**—The range in sex ratio in 1930 was wider relatively among cities of 25,000 and over than among the rural population of the states. Heading the list were East Chicago (126.7), Michigan City (124.2), and Hoboken (122.6), while at the foot were Brookline (69.3), Pasadena (79.7), and Newton (81.8). Among cities of over 100,000, Gary was high (119.1) and Nashville low (87.8). To some extent, these differences were due to such factors as the proportion of foreign-born whites and Negroes. But much more important in all probability was the type of work carried on in each city. East Chicago, Michigan City, and Gary specialize in steel;[1] steel requires men; hence

---

[1] The proportion of employed males in 1920 who were furnacemen, smeltermen, heaters, pourers, etc.; rollers and mill hands (metal); and laborers or semi-skilled operatives in iron and steel industries was 42.4 per cent in East Chicago and 44.3 per cent in Gary. Michigan City was then too small for the census to tabulate similarly.

there is a larger than usual excess of males among migrants coming to these and other steel cities in search of work. The same could be said of cities of which mining, the automobile and tire industries, or heavy industries in general are of outstanding importance; for Butte, Flint, Akron, Detroit, and many other places.

The lowest sex ratios in cities are found where occupations for women predominate. In Brookline, Pasadena, and Newton per capita wealth is unusually high; hence there is an exceptionally large number of servants, most of whom are women.[1] The New England textile centers, Lowell, New Bedford, and Fall River, specialize in industries having a high proportion of women among their employees; consequently the sex ratios of these cities are relatively low. Southern cities as a rule also have low sex ratios among the total population. The chief factor in this case seems to be the low ratio among Negroes and the high proportion of Negroes in their populations, for the native white ratios in southern cities do not differ particularly from those of other cities (Appendix Table 22, p. 379). That the Negro sex ratio is lower in southern cities than northern seems to be chiefly the result of migration, for, as previously indicated, males have exceeded females in the movement out of the South. Furthermore, Negro women probably are in greater demand as servants in southern cities than elsewhere.

The sex ratio of native whites varies widely from city to city, but when cities are grouped by regions and then compared, no definite relation is evident. One reason for this situation is that a region may contain some cities having industries employing a high proportion of men and other cities in which the proportion of women is relatively high among employed persons, the two types of cities tending to balance each other. In addition, native whites are distributed more evenly throughout the United States than are foreign-born whites or Negroes. As pointed out previously, the excess of males tends to be unusually high in any racial or nativity group which constitutes a small proportion of the population in any city or region. Furthermore, there may be some tendency for cities in which employment opportunities are rather specialized to use relatively higher proportions of the less skilled workers. This would be true for the steel and textile cities and for the wealthy suburbs employing a large servant class. Since in cities a smaller proportion of native whites than of foreign-born whites and Negroes would be classified as unskilled workers, such a relation would result in smaller variations between cities in the sex ratios of native whites than of foreign-born whites and Negroes.

---

[1] In Brookline in 1920 there was 1 female servant to 4.5 other women over 15 years of age compared with 1 to 22.2 in Boston.

7. SEX RATIO BY AGE PERIODS

At several places in this chapter reference has been made to variations in the sex ratio from one age period to another. The excess of male births, the higher male death rates at most ages, and the variations in the excess of males among immigrants of different ages suggest the type of variations that are to be expected among the age periods of the race and nativity groups.

a. **Foreign-born Whites.**—With foreign-born whites, the sex ratio at ages 0 to 9 has been about the same as that of native whites, because most of the foreign born of this age on a census date came to this country with their parents. In a migration of families, the sex ratio of young children should not differ significantly from that of children of the same age in the nonimmigrating population. Between the ages of 10 and 19 a point is reached above which individuals in increasing numbers begin to immigrate independently of their families, which causes the excess of males to rise sharply among immigrants arriving and hence among the foreign-born population. Thus during 1910–1914 the sex ratio of immigrants arriving at ages 0 to 13 was 104.5, compared with 226.2 at ages 14 to 44[1] (Table 54). As age rises still farther, a point is reached at which the proportion of single males declines, the movement being composed more largely of families and including more dependent women coming to be supported by relatives already here. This is shown in 1910–1914 by the sex ratio of 153.1 at ages 45 and over, scarcely two-thirds of the ratio at ages 14 to 44.

Since 1925 the sex ratio of immigrants and emigrants is available for narrower age periods. The excess of males among alien arrivals during 1925–1929 rose from 102.9 at ages 0 to 15 to a high point of 141.1 at ages 22 to 29, and then declined to 86.0 at ages over 45 (Table 54). These ratios are well below those of 1910–1914 because of the preference given under the quota regulations to women and children having male relatives already in the United States. For several years there has been a very large excess of males at certain ages among aliens leaving the United States. During 1925–1929 the sex ratio rose from 104.0 at ages 0 to 15 to 345.1 at ages 38 to 44 and was 272.0 at ages over 45. Apparently the call to return to the old country was much stronger among single men and widowers, especially among those old enough to have spent some years in the United States and to have had an opportunity to accumulate a competence. When allowance is made for this outward movement, it is found that the sex ratio among net alien arrivals during 1925–1929 rose

---

[1] The only age groups reported by the Bureau of Immigration during 1910–1914 were under 14, 14 to 44, and 45 and over.

from 102.8 at ages 0 to 15 to 128.5 at ages 16 to 21, remained at about this level at ages 22 to 29, but fell rapidly thereafter. At ages 30 to 37 there were 55.4 males to 100 females, but at ages over 45 only 2.1 males to 100 females. Sex ratios of net arrivals over 15 were still lower in 1930–1931; at age 45 and over there was even a net departure of 33.9 males for each 100 females arriving.

TABLE 54.—SEX RATIO AMONG IMMIGRANT ALIEN ARRIVALS, EMIGRANT ALIEN DEPARTURES, AND EXCESS OF ARRIVALS OVER DEPARTURES, BY AGE, 1910–1931[a]

Fiscal year	Age period					
	0–15[b]	16–21[b]	22–29	30–37	38–44	45+
IMMIGRANT ALIEN ARRIVALS						
1910–14	104.5		226.2			153.1
1915–17	105.2		154.8			143.0
1918–19	110.9		145.9			127.8
1920–24	103.0		146.2			97.7
1925–29	102.9	129.6	141.1	124.2	120.7	86.0
1930–31	104.7	90.8	95.4	75.7	69.1	62.5
EMIGRANT ALIEN DEPARTURES						
1918–19	108.1		412.9			550.0
1920–24	106.8		315.9			459.8
1925–29	104.0	152.8	228.5	275.8	345.1	272.0
1930–31	106.7	168.1	199.2	200.0	213.9	194.6
EXCESS OF ARRIVALS OVER DEPARTURES[c]						
1918–19	112.4		−56.3			−321.4
1920–24	102.6		106.9			−58.8
1925–29	102.8	128.5	127.0	55.4	6.2	2.1
1930–31	104.3	84.7	71.0	19.0	−15.0	−33.9

[a] From current reports of the Commissioner General of Immigration. Data on sex by age groups were not published prior to years shown.

[b] From 1910 to 1917, inclusive, the age groups are 0 to 13 and 14 to 44

[c] A minus sign indicates net departure of males and net arrival of females. Thus at age 45 and over in 1918–1919 there was a net departure of 321.4 males for the net arrival of each 100 females.

These differences in sex ratio by age among aliens coming to and departing from the United States are of prime importance in determining the sex ratio by age of the foreign-born white population in the United States. As far back as data are available, there has been only a slight excess of males among foreign-born whites aged 0 to 9, for reasons pointed out above. The sex ratio usually has declined from ages 0 to 9 to ages 10 to 19, then risen to ages 30 to 39 or 40 to 49, and declined throughout the remainder of the life span (Table 55). In 1910, however, the situation was somewhat different. Immigration had been rising rapidly during the preceding decade and had reached an unusually high figure both in the number of net arrivals and in the excess of males among arrivals. This made the sex ratio of the foreign-born population as a whole higher in 1910 than ever before by raising to unusually high marks the excess of males in the age periods containing most of the recent arrivals. These were the 20-to-29 period in particular, and the 10-to-19 and 30-to-39 periods to lesser degree. The sex ratio at ages 20 to 29 was 141.9, over 34 points above that of 1900, while at ages 10 to 19 and 30 to 39 the ratio was nearly 10 points above 1900. At ages over 60, sex ratios of the foreign born were lower on the whole in 1910 than in 1900, the new immigration movement not having added significantly to these older groups by 1910.

In 1930 the foreign-born population was not swelled in numbers by recent immigrants as in 1910; hence the age periods 10 to 19 and 20 to 29 contained a much smaller proportion of new arrivals and a correspondingly larger proportion of persons who had come as children prior to 1915. The result was the lowest sex ratio for years, the ratio of 98.3 at ages 20 to 29 being over 43 points below that of 1910 and almost as low as the native white ratio (Table 55). Even in the 30-to-39 age period foreign-born whites had the lowest sex ratio in more than half a century, partly for the foregoing reason, though the preference granted women under the quota regulations probably was more important. By far the highest sex ratio in 1930 was 130.3 at ages 40 to 49, a carry-over from the remarkably high ratio at ages 20 to 29 in 1910.

In all age periods over 50 there has been a decline in sex ratio among the foreign-born white in every census, and also from a given age period in one census to the period 10 years older in the following census. The decline with increasing age has been due in part to higher death rates among males than females, but probably more to the excess of males among older aliens returning to their native lands. The erratic changes within the same age period between census years would seem to result in large measure from the variations in quantity of immigration and in the sex ratio of immigrants during previous decades, which are only partially smoothed out by sex differentials in death rate and by an excess of males departing.

b. Native Whites.—Sex ratios by age among the native white population should be determined by the excess of male births and by the difference in male and female death rates at various ages, because emigration of native whites has been of negligible importance relative to the size of the group. Accordingly, the high sex ratio should be in the young age period, and decreases in the ratio should accompany increases in age. Actually, the sex ratio of native whites has been fairly high (between

TABLE 55.—SEX RATIO BY AGE PERIODS, BY RACE AND NATIVITY, 1830–1930[a]

Year	Age period								
	0–9	10–19	20–29	30–39	40–49	50–59	60–69	70–79	80+

TOTAL POPULATION

Year	0–9	10–19	20–29	30–39	40–49	50–59	60–69	70–79	80+
1850	102.4	100.0	105.4	111.6	110.1	107.8	103.0	98.2	88.4
1870	102.7	100.5	96.5	101.2	108.3	116.9	108.8	99.5	84.3
1890	103.0	100.8	103.2	112.8	108.0	108.5	108.5	105.8	87.0
1900	102.0	100.4	100.5	110.3	113.5	110.9	105.0	102.7	89.5
1910	102.2	101.0	104.9	110.7	113.1	116.5	108.1	100.5	88.1
1920	102.2	100.1	97.5	107.4	112.2	114.1	111.4	100.1	82.4
1930	102.7	100.8	97.0	101.7	108.1	109.8	106.2	101.5	83.9

WHITE POPULATION

Year	0–9	10–19	20–29	30–39	40–49	50–59	60–69	70–79	80+
1830	104.9	100.6	104.1	106.7	103.3	102.6	102.9	99.0	89.9
1850	103.2	100.1	106.3	114.2	112.2	108.5	103.2	98.9	89.6
1870	103.1	100.6	97.5	102.3	109.7	117.3	108.4	100.1	86.5
1890	103.2	101.0	104.1	113.5	108.6	107.4	107.7	106.0	88.7
1900	102.5	100.8	101.3	111.0	114.0	109.8	103.8	102.9	91.2
1910	102.6	101.6	106.5	111.3	113.4	115.5	106.8	100.1	89.0
1920	102.6	100.8	98.8	108.4	111.4	112.4	110.1	99.4	82.5
1930	103.3	101.5	97.7	102.1	108.2	108.1	105.1	101.2	84.1

NATIVE WHITE POPULATION

Year	0–9	10–19	20–29	30–39	40–49	50–59	60–69	70–79	80+
1870	103.1	100.8	94.4	96.7	102.0	110.3	105.2	97.5	84.3
1890	103.2	101.1	100.8	107.5	102.8	103.5	104.3	103.1	86.3
1900	102.5	101.1	100.1	105.2	108.6	106.0	101.0	99.4	87.4
1910	102.6	101.2	99.1	103.5	106.2	111.6	104.9	98.1	85.5
1920	102.6	100.9	96.9	101.0	105.6	107.9	107.4	97.9	79.8
1930	103.3	101.6	97.6	99.4	102.1	104.7	102.3	98.7	82.4

FOREIGN-BORN WHITE POPULATION

Year	0–9	10–19	20–29	30–39	40–49	50–59	60–69	70–79	80+
1870	102.5	97.2	108.7	115.6	126.7	136.9	118.7	110.1	96.5
1890	103.2	100.0	118.4	135.3	122.9	115.5	114.2	113.4	96.0
1900	101.0	96.6	107.7	131.0	131.4	118.8	109.3	109.9	100.6
1910	102.1	106.8	141.9	140.2	135.1	127.3	111.1	104.2	96.2
1920	102.3	98.5	110.3	136.4	131.1	125.5	117.8	103.2	88.5
1930	102.0	95.6	98.3	115.5	130.3	119.5	113.2	108.9	88.4

NEGRO POPULATION

Year	0–9	10–19	20–29	30–39	40–49	50–59	60–69	70–79	80+
1850	98.7	99.7	100.3	97.1	97.6	103.6	101.9	93.7	83.0
1870	100.8	99.4	86.6	87.5	93.7	112.4	110.8	94.2	73.6
1900	99.3	97.2	92.4	98.4	100.5	116.0	116.0	101.1	79.3
1910	99.0	96.1	89.7	100.6	104.3	122.1	120.0	106.1	80.5
1920	99.2	94.9	86.6	94.5	115.8	131.3	126.5	107.5	80.7
1930	98.7	95.0	86.3	93.3	101.1	124.8	119.3	103.1	80.1

[a] Compiled from current census reports.

102.5 and 103.3) at ages 0 to 9, and has declined to ages 20 to 29 (Table 55). But from ages 20 to 29 there has been a rise to a high figure at ages 50 to 59 as a rule, with a decline thereafter. This rise would not be expected from the sex differentials in the death rates.

To take a specific example, in 1910 there were 99.1 native white males aged 20 to 29 per 100 females of that age. According to the life tables of 1909–1911 the male death rates were higher than the female rates from ages 20 to 40, but according to the 1919–1920 tables male rates were lower at ages 22, 27, and 32, though higher at 37. Considering the size of the differences, it seems safe to conclude that males aged 20 to 29 in 1910 should have suffered a slightly larger relative loss by 1920 than females aged 20 to 29 in 1910. Nevertheless, the sex ratio of native whites aged 30 to 39 in 1920 rose to 101. Death rates of white males aged 30 to 50 were well above those of white females of those ages during 1920–1929; hence the sex ratio of this age period should have declined from 1920 to 1930. Instead there was an increase, the sex ratio of native whites aged 40 to 49 in 1930 being 102.1. Similarly, the sex ratio at ages 40 to 49 in 1920 was 105.6, compared with 100.1 at ages 20 to 29 in 1900, although the death rates would have had the opposite effect.

Why has the sex ratio risen when sex differentials in death rates would cause it to decline? A possible explanation is that some of the foreign born are enumerated as native born, carrying to the native group part of the high sex ratio of the foreign group. This would not seem possible on a large scale, however, except for those born in Canada, Great Britain, or Ireland and speaking English well. A more probable explanation may be that many women do not state their age correctly to the census enumerator. They may believe that their age is nobody's business and report themselves as young as they feel. According to this hypothesis, women between 20 and 30 or thereabouts have little urge to be thought older or younger than they are; hence they report their age correctly. But women between 30 and some upper limit, perhaps 60 or 70, dislike to admit their age and wish to be thought as youthful as possible; hence they understate their age by 5 or 10 years, or perhaps more, when answering the enumerator's question. At still older ages, however, there may be a desire to claim longevity which may not only counteract the above tendency, but even lead to exaggerating age.

If there were comparable discrepancies in the age reports for men, the above argument would have no weight. It is believed, however, that male age data do not have so large a bias. A man in his forties may have good reason to understate his age when applying for a job with a concern that has established a deadline at 45. But as a rule it is the woman rather than the man who has the personal vanity that leads to an attempt to exaggerate youthfulness with an utter stranger, as most urban enumerators are. Furthermore, the majority of the census questions are answered by women and not by men. Thus the personal factor is involved correspondingly more frequently with a woman than with a man, which should make male age data more accurate than female. The fact that men are likely to be absent when the enumerator calls may have an influence, for a woman whose desire for youth might lead her to understate both her own age and that of her husband if he were present, may report the latter correctly if the enumerator does not see him. In addition, the rather widespread feeling that a wife should be younger than her husband probably leads to understatement of age in most cases where a woman is the older.

c. **Negroes.**—Somewhat similar discrepancies exist in the age data of Negroes, judging by the Negro sex ratios in Table 55, the ratios at birth in Table 48, page 177, and among life table survivors in southern states in Table 49, page 180. The proportion of Negroes living in the death-registration states has been much smaller than the proportion of whites; hence data on specific death rates and expectation of life of Negroes by sex do not furnish so adequate a basis for questioning the census figures on age of Negroes as was the case with whites. Furthermore, death registration undoubtedly is less complete among Negroes than whites, and less attention probably is paid to stating age of Negroes correctly on the death certificates and on enumerators' schedules.

Nevertheless, it appears that there is a marked tendency for Negro women over 30 to misstate their age. In each census the sex ratio at ages 20 to 29 is much lower than the ratio of ages 10 to 19 in the preceding census, whereas the available mortality data indicate a rise should occur. At ages 40 to 49 the sex ratio is about as would be expected, perhaps because the number of women actually of this age who report themselves in the thirties is balanced by the number over 50 who say they are in the forties.

If the understatement of age by women in certain age periods actually is as common as it appears to be from the foregoing analysis, it has an appreciable effect on death rates by age. The number of women 20 to 29 appears to be considerably exaggerated; hence the female death rate at that age would be lowered correspondingly. At ages 40 to 49 and 50 to 59 in particular there seems to be a marked undercount of women, which raises female death rates at these ages in similar degree. Such a distortion of female death rates affects the differentials between these and male death rates. At ages 20 to 29 a correction for misstatement of age would raise the female death rate relative to the male rate, whereas at ages 40 to 49 and 50 to 59 the female death rate would be lowered relative to the male rate. But the net effect of these various corrections would not be to lower appreciably the generally favorable differential of female death rates relative to male, because a narrowing of the differential at ages 20 to 29, for example, would be balanced by a widening of it at ages 40 to 49 and 50 to 59.

If there were misstatements of age of women on death certificates comparable with those on enumerators' schedules, the above argument would have no weight. This is not believed to be the case, however, because questions on the death certificate are not answered by the person concerned. Lack of exact knowledge no doubt leads to inaccuracies, but the desire to be youthful, which apparently leads many a woman to understate age to a census enumerator, should not be found to the same extent after her death when a relative or friend gives the information for the death certificate.

d. **By Size of Community.**—In the preceding discussion it has been pointed out that sex ratios by age do not appear to be very exact for the United States as a whole. These inaccuracies undoubtedly carry over into the different parts of the United States and into places of various sizes in much the same degree. Perhaps farm women, living closer to nature, may have less vanity and report their age more accurately than city women. More important, however, the rural census enumerator usually knows personally a much higher proportion of the people he visits than does the city enumerator, hence is not so easily misled regarding the age question. Nevertheless, it seems unlikely that the rural-urban differences in accuracy of sex ratios by age are large. In the discussion which follows it will be assumed that the discrepancies in age are similar in different regions and in communities of different sizes to those discussed above for the United States as a whole. The point stressed will be the variation in sex ratio at a given age from communities of one size to those of other sizes.

At ages 0 to 4, the sex ratio of the various race and nativity groups has been about the same in one size of city as in another or in rural areas (Appendix Table 23, p. 383). This is natural, because the excess of male births should be the governing factor and there is no reason to expect a variation in sex ratio at birth to result from differences in place of residence. By the time the 20-to-29 age period is reached, migration has had a chance to cause differences in sex ratio. Its chief effect has been to raise the rural ratio and lower the urban ratio, a large differential being found in each race and nativity group in 1930 and in prior census years[1] (Table 56). The rural-farm sex ratio was well above the rural-nonfarm for native whites in 1920 and 1930, and for foreign-born whites in 1930. For both of these groups and for Negroes as well the rural-farm sex ratio at ages 20 to 29 rose considerably during the decade in relation to the rural-nonfarm ratio. When cities of different sizes are compared,

[1] Causes of the higher rural ratios were discussed on pp. 188–190.

TABLE 56.—SEX RATIO AT SELECTED AGES, BY SIZE OF COMMUNITY, BY RACE AND NATIVITY, 1890–1930[a]

Size of community	Ages 20–29				Ages 65 and over			
	1890	1910	1920	1930	1890	1910	1920	1930
TOTAL POPULATION[b]								
500,000+...........................	92.7	98.6	94.5	94.6	80.0	80.3	83.0	84.7
250,000–500,000....................	96.5	103.8	90.8	87.9	83.3	84.5	83.0	82.9
100,000–250,000....................	99.0	101.7	95.8	89.8	83.8	84.6	82.6	85.7
25,000–100,000....................	98.0	101.2	94.3	89.7	82.2	83.4	84.7	83.0
2,500– 25,000....................	(c)	101.6	93.8	90.4	(c)	90.6	90.2	89.1
Rural { Nonfarm....................	(c)	108.5	102.3	98.5	(c)	114.4	104.7	104.2
Rural { Farm....................			101.5	111.1			129.8	138.6
NATIVE WHITE POPULATION								
500,000+...........................	92.5	91.9	93.6	95.2	73.4	74.6	76.5	76.1
250,000–500,000....................	92.6	95.2	88.4	88.9	76.9	80.3	78.9	77.7
100,000–250,000....................	97.8	96.1	94.4	90.7	79.5	79.6	78.3	81.2
25,000–100,000....................	98.9	95.4	92.6	91.1	77.4	78.9	81.3	78.5
2,500– 25,000....................	(c)	93.6	92.2	91.5	(c)	86.8	86.4	84.8
Rural { Nonfarm....................	(c)	104.1	98.8	98.0	(c)	109.3	100.4	100.0
Rural { Farm....................			105.0	115.2			127.0	137.1
FOREIGN-BORN WHITE POPULATION								
500,000+...........................	92.9	110.5	97.2	96.2	84.6	84.3	88.9	94.2
250,000–500,000....................	100.0	139.6	112.6	98.4	89.0	88.5	90.5	96.8
100,000–250,000....................	106.9	131.6	110.3	92.8	90.3	91.7	90.6	95.8
25,000–100,000....................	99.8	130.2	108.9	94.2	91.5	90.8	92.1	94.8
2,500– 25,000....................	(c)	156.5	115.3	95.1	(c)	100.1	101.1	105.0
Rural { Nonfarm....................	(c)	210.5	146.4	106.2	(c)	131.0	122.2	124.8
Rural { Farm....................			131.7	151.8			139.9	153.3
NEGRO POPULATION[d]								
500,000+...........................	.....	82.4	91.6	86.2	....	71.0	75.0	73.8
250,000–500,000....................	.....	79.2	82.1	78.1	....	73.2	72.8	77.6
100,000–250,000....................	.....	85.1	85.2	79.4	....	79.9	79.2	84.1
25,000–100,000....................	.....	80.8	84.0	75.0	....	81.2	82.4	79.7
2,500– 25,000....................	.....	81.3	83.3	76.6	....	88.9	90.0	86.5
Rural { Nonfarm....................	.....	94.0	99.1	100.4	....	118.5	101.5	101.2
Rural { Farm....................			82.1	90.7			134.3	130.3

[a] Compiled from current census reports. For similar ratios for other are periods, see Appendix Table 23, p. 383.

[b] Includes whites and Negroes only, except in 1890. See Note d.

[c] Sex ratio by age in 1890 cannot be computed separately for cities of 2,500 to 25,000 and for rural areas, the data not having been published by the Bureau of the Census.

[d] Ratios are available for the colored population but not for Negroes in 1890.

no significant relation is apparent between size and sex ratio. The sex ratio of urban native whites was highest in cities of over 500,000 in 1930 and lowest in these cities in 1890; and was nearly as erratic in cities of smaller size. The same can be said for the sex ratio of foreign-born whites of this age. With Negroes, however, the sex ratio at ages 20 to 29 has tended to be somewhat higher in cities of over 500,000 than in smaller cities. This is due in part to the fact that these cities, with the exception of Baltimore, are all in the North and draw negro migrants from a greater distance, with males predominating. Furthermore, a large majority of the Negroes in cities of less than 500,000 are found in the South; it is in southern cities that the Negro sex ratio at ages 20 to 29 is particularly low.[1] It is doubtful if the mere fact of size has been an important cause of this high Negro sex ratio at ages 20 to 29 in the large cities.

Among older people (over 65), the sex ratio of rural areas is farther above that of urban communities and the rural-farm sex ratio much farther above the rural-nonfarm than is the case at younger ages (Table 56). This bears out the discussion on pages 189 and 217 that older men tend to remain on farms to a greater extent than older women. When cities of different sizes are compared, the sex ratio is found to be considerably higher in places of 2,500 to 25,000 than in larger cities in each year, with a slight tendency among the cities over 25,000 for the ratio of each race and nativity group to vary inversely with size prior to 1930. Evidently more elderly men than elderly women have preferred to live in the smaller cities. This may be because many of them still retain an interest in a farm and wish to be close to it for business reasons; or it may be that they feel there is more opportunity for an active life in a small than in a large community, age being more of a handicap in the whirl of the metropolis. It is true that in the total population the sex ratio at ages over 65 does not increase as size decreases to the same extent as in the race and nativity groups, but this is due almost entirely to the fact that the foreign born, with their high sex ratios, make up a larger proportion of the elders in large than in small cities.

When cities of the different regions are considered separately, certain peculiarities are apparent. Among native whites the sex ratio at 65 and over has not varied inversely with size of city to the same extent in the northeastern states as in other regions (Appendix Table 24, p. 385). This was the case particularly in 1930 and may foreshadow the future trend. As has been mentioned before, however,[2] the variations between cities of different size groups are much smaller than between cities where different types of industries and occupations are important.

[1] See discussion, p. 192.
[2] *Supra*, p. 192.

The 20-to-29 age period and the 65-and-over period have been emphasized because they represent the extremes of the prime and twilight of life. At ages 5 to 19 the situation is intermediate between that at 0 to 4 and 20 to 29, and at ages 30 to 44 and 45 to 64 it is intermediate between the 20-to-29 and 65-and-over age periods. The ratios in Appendix Tables 23 and 24, pages 383 and 385, will permit careful comparison on these points.

CHAPTER VI

MARITAL CONDITION

THERE has been a steady increase during the last 40 years in the proportion of the population that is married. In 1890 only 53.9 per cent of the males over 15 years of age were married, but by 1930 the percentage had increased to 60.0 (Table 57). For females the percentages are 56.8 and 61.1, respectively. These facts standing by themselves give the impression that the proportion of the marriageable population that is married is growing, in spite of the large proportional increase in divorced persons, and in spite of a practically stationary proportion of widowed persons. It will be recalled, however, that there has been a considerable shift of population into the age groups over 30 during recent decades; hence, before concluding that there has been any increase in marriage among the marriageable population as a whole, it will be necessary to examine marital condition by age.

1. BY AGE

During the last 40 years there has been an increase in the proportion of the population married at most of the marriageable ages—at all ages under 45 in the case of males and at all ages under 65 in the case of females (Table 57 and Figure 24). At ages 15 to 19 there was a steady and rather rapid increase in the proportion of males married from 0.5 per cent in 1890 to 2.1 per cent in 1920, after which there was a decline to 1.7 per cent in 1930. Among females there has been a steady increase during this entire period, from 9.5 per cent in 1890 to 12.6 per cent in 1930. In the 20-to-24 age group the proportion of males married increased steadily from 18.9 per cent in 1890 to 28.3 per cent in 1920, after which there was a slight decline to 28.1 per cent in 1930. Among females of this age there was a slight decline from 46.7 per cent in 1890 to 46.5 per cent in 1900 and then a rather rapid rise until 1920 when 52.3 per cent of them were married. Since 1920 there has been a slight decline to 51.6 per cent in 1930.

In the 25-to-29 group of males there was a very slight downward movement from 1890 to 1900; after this there was a steady increase from 52.5 per cent to 61.3 per cent in 1930. Among females of this age there was a rather large decline, from 71.3 per cent in 1890 to 68.9 per cent in 1900. Since then there has been a steady increase to 74.3 per cent in 1930.

TABLE 57.—PERCENTAGE DISTRIBUTION OF THE POPULATION 15 YEARS OF AGE AND OVER, BY MARITAL CONDITION, BY SEX, AND BY AGE, 1890–1930[a]

Year and age	Male					Female				
	Total	Single	Married	Widowed	Divorced	Total	Single	Married	Widowed	Divorced
All ages:										
1890	100.0	41.7	53.9	3.9	0.2	100.0	31.8	56.8	11.0	0.4
1900	100.0	40.2	54.5	4.6	0.3	100.0	31.2	57.0	11.2	0.5
1910	100.0	38.7	55.8	4.5	0.5	100.0	29.7	58.9	10.6	0.6
1920	100.0	35.1	59.2	4.8	0.6	100.0	27.3	60.6	11.1	0.8
1930	100.0	34.1	60.0	4.6	1.1	100.0	26.4	61.1	11.1	1.3
15–19:										
1890	100.0	99.5	0.5	(b)	(b)	100.0	90.3	9.5	0.2	(b)
1900	100.0	98.8	1.0	(b)	(b)	100.0	88.7	10.9	0.2	0.1
1910	100.0	98.3	1.1	(b)	(b)	100.0	87.9	11.3	0.2	0.1
1920	100.0	97.7	2.1	(b)	(b)	100.0	87.0	12.5	0.3	0.1
1930	100.0	98.0	1.7	(b)	(b)	100.0	86.8	12.6	0.2	0.2
20–24:										
1890	100.0	80.7	18.9	0.2	(b)	100.0	51.8	46.7	1.2	0.2
1900	100.0	77.6	21.6	0.4	0.1	100.0	51.6	46.5	1.4	0.4
1910	100.0	74.9	24.0	0.4	0.1	100.0	48.3	49.7	1.2	0.5
1920	100.0	70.7	28.3	0.5	0.2	100.0	45.6	52.3	1.4	0.6
1930	100.0	70.8	28.1	0.3	0.4	100.0	46.0	51.6	1.0	1.1
25–29:										
1890	100.0	46.0	52.7	1.0	0.1	100.0	25.4	71.3	2.8	0.4
1900	100.0	45.8	52.5	1.2	0.2	100.0	27.5	68.9	2.9	0.6
1910	100.0	42.8	55.5	1.1	0.4	100.0	24.9	71.8	2.4	0.7
1920	100.0	39.4	58.7	1.1	0.5	100.0	23.0	73.4	2.6	0.9
1930	100.0	36.7	61.3	0.8	1.0	100.0	21.7	74.3	2.1	1.8
30–34:										
1890	100.0	26.5	71.3	1.8	0.2	100.0	15.2	79.7	4.5	0.5
1900	100.0	27.6	69.8	2.0	0.4	100.0	16.6	78.0	4.6	0.7
1910	100.0	26.0	71.4	1.8	0.5	100.0	16.1	79.0	3.9	0.8
1920	100.0	24.1	73.2	1.8	0.7	100.0	14.9	80.1	3.9	1.0
1930	100.0	21.2	76.0	1.3	1.4	100.0	13.2	81.5	3.3	1.9
35–44:										
1890	100.0	15.3	80.9	3.3	0.3	100.0	9.9	80.6	8.8	0.6
1900	100.0	16.9	78.8	3.6	0.5	100.0	11.1	79.5	8.6	0.7
1910	100.0	16.7	79.2	3.2	0.7	100.0	11.4	80.1	7.5	0.9
1920	100.0	16.1	79.8	3.0	0.9	100.0	11.4	80.3	7.2	1.1
1930	100.0	14.3	81.5	2.5	1.6	100.0	10.0	81.5	6.5	1.9
45–54:										
1890	100.0	9.1	84.3	6.0	0.4	100.0	7.1	73.9	18.4	0.5
1900	100.0	10.3	82.2	6.8	0.6	100.0	7.8	73.9	17.6	0.6
1910	100.0	11.1	81.5	6.4	0.8	100.0	8.5	74.8	15.7	0.8
1920	100.0	12.0	81.0	5.8	1.0	100.0	9.6	74.0	15.3	1.0
1930	100.0	11.4	81.6	5.2	1.6	100.0	9.1	75.2	14.0	1.6
55–64:										
1890	100.0	6.8	82.3	10.2	0.5	100.0	5.8	60.4	33.3	0.4
1900	100.0	7.6	79.7	11.9	0.6	100.0	6.6	60.5	32.3	0.5
1910	100.0	8.3	79.0	11.7	0.8	100.0	7.1	62.2	30.0	0.6
1920	100.0	9.8	77.9	11.2	1.0	100.0	8.4	61.2	29.5	0.8
1930	100.0	10.1	78.0	10.2	1.5	100.0	8.9	62.0	27.8	1.1
65 +:										
1890	100.0	5.6	70.5	23.3	0.4	100.0	5.6	35.3	58.6	0.3
1900	100.0	5.7	67.1	26.4	0.5	100.0	6.0	34.2	59.3	0.3
1910	100.0	6.2	65.6	27.1	0.7	100.0	6.3	35.0	58.1	0.4
1920	100.0	7.3	64.7	26.9	0.7	100.0	7.1	33.9	58.4	0.4
1930	100.0	8.4	63.7	26.6	1.1	100.0	8.1	34.7	56.5	0.5

[a] For 1890–1900 from *Twelfth Census of the United States: 1900*, Vol. II, Pt. 2, pp. lxxxvii–xc; 1910 from *Thirteenth Census of the United States: 1910*, Vol. I, p. 519; 1920 from *Fourteenth Census of the United States: 1920*, Vol. II, p. 390; 1930 from *Fifteenth Census of the United States: 1930*, Vol. II, p. 844. Total includes persons of unknown marital condition.
[b] Less than one-tenth of 1 per cent.

In the 30-to-34 age group the proportion of males married declined from 71.3 per cent in 1890 to 69.8 per cent in 1900. From that time it has been increasing steadily and amounted to 76.0 per cent in 1930. Among females of this age the percentage married also declined from 1890 to 1900 and has risen since, but the rise is much smaller—from 78.0 per cent in 1900 to 81.5 per cent in 1930. At ages above 35 males and females do not follow the same trend. Among males the proportion married at ages 35 to 44 has fluctuated some but has remained practically stationary during the last 40 years, rising only from 80.9 per cent in 1890 to 81.5 per

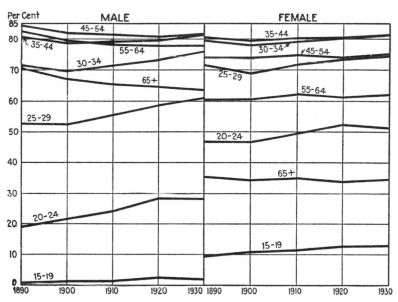

Fig. 24.—Percentage of population 15 years of age and over, married, by sex, 1890–1930. (Based on Table 57.)

cent in 1930. Above 45 years of age there has been a net decline in the proportion of males married at each age although the decline has not been steady in all cases. Among women, on the other hand, the proportion married continued to rise at all ages up to 65 although not always steadily. At ages over 65 there was a slight decline.

From this survey of the proportions married at the different ages it is clear that there has been a real increase in the proportion of the population over 15 years of age which is married and that it affects chiefly those under 35. It is especially marked at ages 20 to 29 when marriages are the most important from the standpoint of fertility. The slight decline during 1920–1930 in proportions married at the younger ages is not sufficient to be of any particular significance. Whether it represents the beginning of a new trend cannot be said. That there has been a fairly steady increase in the proportion of the younger people of marriageable age who are married does not mean that the aging of the population has not affected the proportion of the total population over 15 that is married. It has added materially to this proportion during 40 years but it is probably no more important in bringing about this increase than the tendency to marry somewhat younger.

Widowhood, as would be expected, increases directly as age increases and is generally several times as high among women as among men (Table 57). Two factors will explain the larger proportion of widows than widowers. In the first place, more marriages are broken by the death of the husband than by the death of the wife, because the death rates of men at practically all ages are greater than those of women, and the husband is usually older than his wife.[1] In the second place, but much less important, there appear to be about 10 per cent more widowers than widows among persons marrying again.[2]

The proportion of widowers and widows in the population as a whole shows no very significant trend during the last 40 years, although there is a slight downward trend among males at most ages under 55 and among females at all ages. This might arise from the decline in the death rates, as a result of which fewer marriages are broken by death, or from an increase in the proportion of widowed persons remarrying, or more probably from a combination of both of these factors. The proportion of widowed persons in the total population shows very little change because of the increasing proportions of older men and women in the population, among whom widowhood is relatively common. That there is a decline in the proportion of older widows, while there is practically no decline in the proportion of older widowers, is difficult to explain in view of the fact that female death rates at the older ages have, on the whole, improved faster than male rates during the last three decades.[3] It may also be that relatively more elderly widows than widowers have been remarrying in recent years, but there is no evidence that this is the case. Altogether it seems more probable that prior to about 1900 the proportion of young married persons, particularly women, had been declining so that with fewer married 30 years ago there are fewer elderly widows in recent years. None of these explanations, nor indeed, all of them together, are satisfactory. This situation needs far more detailed study than can be given it here.

[1] *Supra*, pp. 177–179, for death rates by sex.

[2] J. V. DePorte, *Marriage Statistics, New York State, 1921–1924*, Albany, State Department of Public Health, 1924; and *Annual Report of New York State Department of Health* for recent years.

[3] *Recent Social Trends*, Chap. 12, "Vitality of the American People," by Edgar Sydenstricker, New York, McGraw-Hill Book Company, Inc., 1933.

The proportion of divorced persons in the population has increased steadily ever since 1890. At that time 0.2 per cent of the males over 15 were divorced and 0.4 per cent of the females, but by 1930 the percentages had risen to 1.1 and 1.3, respectively. These percentages are far from being a satisfactory measure of the amount of divorce in the nation, however, because such a high proportion of divorced persons remarry.[1] There does not appear to be any significant difference between ages in the increase of divorce, although divorcees have increased a little more at ages under 35 than at those above 35 and particularly at those above 65. This may be surprising to many in view of the large number of younger divorced persons remarrying. Because of remarriage the relative increase in divorces at the several ages is considerably understated by these figures.

It follows from what has been said that the proportion of single persons in the population has been declining steadily since 1890. Single males have declined from 41.7 per cent of all males over 15 in 1890 to 34.1 per cent in 1930 and single females from 31.8 per cent to 26.4 per cent during the same period. Among males this decline was rather large and steady up to about 45 years of age, but beyond that point the proportion of bachelors has increased steadily (Table 57). Among females the movement is much the same although the definite decrease in single women was checked at about 35 years of age, the proportion remaining nearly stationary for 10 years, after which it began to increase. The net effect of these changes is a decided decrease in the proportion of single persons under 45 and an increase in the proportion of them above that age. The increase in the proportion of single persons at the older ages would seem to indicate that the tendency, since 1890, to increased marriage at the younger ages reversed an earlier tendency in the opposite direction, or at least that the smaller proportions of young married persons in 1890 had prevailed for some time.

2. BY RACE AND NATIVITY

With a few minor exceptions, among Negroes and foreign-born whites, there has been a steady and fairly large increase in the proportions of the different race and nativity groups that are married. However, the rates of increase of married persons during the last 40 years are by no means the same in all the groups. Among native whites of native parentage the increase has been comparatively small, from 55.4 per cent of males aged 15 and over in 1890 to 60.0 per cent in 1930 and from 58.2 per cent to 61.6 per cent for females (Table 58). Among Negroes the increases are about the same, but unlike the native whites of native parentage the proportion of Negro women married is slightly smaller than the propor-

[1] DePorte, *op. cit.*, p. xv.

tion of Negro men. These two groups have changed the least in marital condition, probably in part because they have undergone the smallest changes in age composition.[1]

The native whites of foreign or mixed parentage on the other hand have aged rapidly and, since the proportion of a population that is married generally increases up to about 45 years of age, it is but natural that the married portion of this group should have increased greatly. Among males over 15 the increase was from 36.2 per cent in 1890 to 52.4 per cent in 1930—an increase of almost one-half—and among females it was from 44.3 per cent to 55.1 per cent, an increase of almost one-fourth. Among the foreign born the increase was large because they, too, have been aging rapidly during the last two or three decades. Since a very high proportion of them were married to begin with, the propor-

TABLE 58.—PERCENTAGE DISTRIBUTION OF THE POPULATION 15 YEARS OF AGE AND OVER BY MARITAL CONDITION, BY SEX, BY RACE AND NATIVITY, 1890–1930[a]

Year	Male					Female				
	Total	Single	Married	Widowed	Divorced	Total	Single	Married	Widowed	Divorced
Native white of native parentage:										
1890	100.0	40.1	55.4	4.0	0.3	100.0	30.6	58.2	10.6	0.4
1900	100.0	39.7	55.0	4.5	0.4	100.0	31.0	57.7	10.6	0.5
1910	100.0	38.1	56.3	4.5	0.5	100.0	29.9	59.4	9.8	0.6
1920	100.0	35.5	58.9	4.6	0.7	100.0	28.4	60.4	10.2	0.8
1930	100.0	34.5	60.0	4.2	1.2	100.0	27.2	61.6	9.7	1.4
Native white of foreign or mixed parentage:										
1890	100.0	61.9	36.2	1.7	0.1	100.0	51.0	44.3	4.4	0.3
1900	100.0	54.5	42.7	2.4	0.3	100.0	44.4	49.4	5.7	0.4
1910	100.0	50.2	46.3	2.8	0.4	100.0	41.7	51.1	6.5	0.5
1920	100.0	45.1	50.8	3.4	0.6	100.0	37.0	54.0	7.3	0.7
1930	100.0	43.0	52.4	3.5	1.0	100.0	34.9	55.1	8.7	1.1
Foreign-born white:										
1890	100.0	32.1	62.2	5.2	0.2	100.0	20.7	63.9	15.1	0.2
1900	100.0	29.4	63.8	6.2	0.3	100.0	19.5	64.2	15.8	0.3
1910	100.0	31.8	62.1	5.4	0.3	100.0	18.3	66.5	14.7	0.4
1920	100.0	25.6	67.6	6.0	0.4	100.0	14.1	69.7	15.5	0.5
1930[b]	100.0	21.5	70.8	6.6	0.9	100.0	12.7	70.0	16.4	0.9
Negro:										
1890	100.0	39.8	55.5	4.3	0.2	100.0	30.0	54.6	14.7	0.5
1900	100.0	39.2	54.0	5.7	0.4	100.0	29.9	53.7	15.4	0.8
1910	100.0	35.4	57.2	6.2	0.7	100.0	26.6	57.2	14.8	1.1
1920	100.0	32.6	60.4	5.9	0.8	100.0	24.1	59.6	14.8	1.3
1930	100.0	32.2	59.8	6.3	1.4	100.0	23.3	58.5	15.9	2.2

[a] *Fifteenth Census of the United States: 1930*, Vol. II, p. 842. Total includes persons of unknown marital condition.

[b] Does not include Mexicans.

[1] *Supra*, pp. 145, 146, 152. For native whites of foreign or mixed parentage see *Fifteenth Census of the United States: 1930*, Vol. III, Pt. 1, p. 14.

tional increase was by no means so rapid as among the native whites of foreign or mixed parentage. The proportion of married males among the foreign born over 15 increased from 62.2 per cent in 1890 to 70.8 per cent in 1930 and of married females from 63.9 per cent to 70.0 per cent. The proportion of married women among the foreign born is all the more striking when the proportion widowed is considered. This is from one-sixth to one-seventh of the total, slightly higher even than among Negroes, almost one-half higher than among native whites of native parentage, and, except in 1920 and 1930, about twice as high as among native whites of foreign or mixed parentage. With a high and increasing proportion of foreign-born women married or widowed it is not surprising that in 1930 only 12.7 per cent of all foreign-born women over 15 were single, whereas 20.7 per cent belonged in this group in 1890. This change follows naturally the changes in the age composition of the foreign born which were described above (pp. 143 and 146–148).

In proportion of divorced persons in the population the foreign born are considerably below any other group, having only a little over one-half as many as the Negroes, about two-thirds as many as the native whites of native parentage, and about four-fifths as many as the native whites of foreign or mixed parentage. There is no significant difference between race and nativity groups, however, in their rates of increase of divorced persons. In all groups such persons are now several times as numerous, relatively, as they were in 1890.

a. **By Age.**—*Native Whites of Native Parentage.*—Among the native whites of native parentage there is the same general pattern of marital condition by age as in the aggregate population. An increasing proportion of both males and females at the younger ages are marrying now as compared with 40 years ago (Appendix Table 25). For males the increase seems to stop at about age 35. At 35 to 44 years of age there is still a small increase at the end of this period over the proportion at the beginning, but this proportion fluctuates so much from one decade to the next that it is impossible to speak of a definite trend. Above 45, however, there is a distinct downward trend which increases with age. Clearly when the white men of native parentage over 65 in 1930 were in their twenties and thirties the proportion of the population marrying must have been declining rather than increasing as has been the case more recently. Among the white women of native white parentage, on the other hand, there is an increase in proportion married at all ages under 65, although the increase is not regular nor is it large above 25.

The proportion of widowed persons among the native whites of native parentage shows nothing peculiar. There is a tendency for it to decline slightly at all ages and for both sexes, except for men at 65 and over. Divorced persons are an increasing part of the white population of native parentage of both sexes and of all ages, with a somewhat more rapid increase at ages under 55 than above that point.

The proportion of single white persons of native parentage has been decreasing steadily in the younger ages, as would be expected from what has already been said. The decline for both sexes ceases at about 35 years of age, and after 45 there is a definite increase, although it is not very large until after 55.

Native Whites of Foreign or Mixed Parentage.—The differences between the native whites of foreign or mixed parentage and the older native group just discussed are not so much in the trends as in the proportions of given marital status. Natives of foreign or mixed parentage are much less given to marrying than those of native parentage. The difference is particularly noticeable in the younger ages. At ages 15 to 19 the proportion of native whites of foreign or mixed parentage of both sexes who are married is less than one-half as high as among the older natives; and at ages 20 to 24 the difference is still very large although proportionally much less. All through life there is a significant difference between these two groups in proportion married, although as age increases it becomes less. This is true for both sexes.

The reasons for this are no doubt many and complicated. It may be suggested here, however, that the first native generation of immigrant parentage finds satisfactory adjustment to American life very difficult and often impossible and is, therefore, disposed to avoid family life as one of the most difficult of adjustments. Moreover it may be that in this group the gap between the desired standard of living and the income is particularly wide, with the result that many of these people feel they cannot bridge it if they attempt to raise a family. In this group also there is a marked increase of single men and women at the older ages, indicating that the present tendency to marry younger must have reversed an opposite tendency previous to 1900 or 1890.

Foreign-born Whites.—At the opposite extreme from their children are the foreign born, most of whom are married, especially the women. Until 1920 the proportion of women who were married was increasing at all ages up to 65. Among males the increase stopped at about 35. Since 1920 the proportion married has fallen slightly at most ages under 30 but has risen at most older ages. This change since 1920 in the direction of the trend at the younger ages is probably closely related to the change in the country of origin of the foreign born which has taken place since the quota laws came into effect.

The other differences worth noting in marital condition between the foreign born and the groups already discussed are the large proportion of widows among the former at ages over 35 and the small proportion of divorced persons at all ages.

Negroes.—The Negroes are clearly differentiated from the white population in their marital condition. The first and most important difference between Negroes and whites is in the high proportion of the former married at the younger ages. At ages 15 to 19 the proportion of Negro females married is almost one-half greater than that of native whites of native parentage and three to four times that of the native whites of foreign or mixed parentage. Among males the relative differences are about the same, although the proportion married is much smaller than for females. At ages 20 to 24 the proportion of Negroes married is also much above that in any other group, particularly among males, but the relative differences are not so great. After 25 years of age the proportion of Negroes married is generally less than that of native whites of native parentage, the difference increasing with age. For Negro females from about 35 years of age the proportion married is even lower than that of the native whites of foreign or mixed parentage.

Among Negroes divorce reaches its maximum, being particularly high at ages 25 to 34 for women and 30 to 44 for men. The proportion of widows and widowers is also high among Negroes, running almost twice as high at all ages under 55 as among whites. This is closely correlated with differences in racial death rates.[1] Above 55 the relative differences are not so great, but the proportion of Negroes widowed is very much above that of the whites. The Negroes are also clearly differentiated from the whites in that there is no increase in the proportion single at the older ages. Apparently the trend toward earlier marriages is of longer standing among Negroes than among whites.

3. BY REGIONS

There are significant differences between regions in the marital condition of the populations. In general, the proportion of married males (over 15) is low in the Northeast and increases to the west and south, although in the West it is even lower than in the Northeast (Appendix Table 26). Among women the proportions married in the different regions follow the same course as those of males, except that in the West they are higher, instead of lower, than in any other region, although the regional differentials are decreasing.

The differences in the proportion of married women in the several regions are probably directly attributable, in part, to their differences in sex ratios. In the preceding chapter it has been shown that the sex ratio has generally been lower in the Northeast and higher in the West than in the other regions. Thus it appears that a low sex ratio—the Northeast has seldom had much over 100 males to 100 females—is accompanied by a low proportion of women married, while a high sex ratio—the West

[1] *Infra*, p. 245.

has never had fewer than 107.7 males to 100 females—is accompanied by a high proportion of women married (Table 50, p. 183). In the South and the North Center, where the sex ratios are intermediate between the Northeast and the West, the proportions of married women are also intermediate. The greater relative importance of the Negro in the South, contrary to what might be expected, lowers the proportion of women married, for the proportion of southern Negro women who are married is lower than that of white women. Here, too, the sex ratio is very low, so low, indeed, that it appears to be accompanied by a high proportion of married males at certain ages as well as a low proportion of married females. This point will be discussed more fully later.

It would probably be a mistake, however, to look upon sex ratio as a true causal factor in producing a high or a low proportion of married women. It stands to reason that if there are 115 males to 100 females in a population, the proportion of males married will be lower, and of females married will be higher, than if the sex ratio is 95:100. But it is quite likely that both the sex ratio and the proportion married are determined by a common factor which is rather closely related to the economic life of the region. Thus in the Northeast there are many cities with much light industry and office work by which women can become self-supporting. Such jobs naturally attract women and most cities have a relatively low sex ratio, as has been shown in the preceding chapter. In the South, on the other hand, agriculture is still dominant and, since it is chiefly a man's job, the sex ratio is higher than in the Northeast. But it is rather the fact that the South offers relatively little opportunity to women for independent work, than the fairly high sex ratio, that lies at the basis of the high proportion of southern women who are married, particularly in the younger ages. In the West no doubt much the same situation has existed, but where there is such a large excess of adult males as there has been in the West until recently, there can be little doubt that women are at a premium and many men will remain unmarried, and that this does affect the percentages of both sexes that are married.

a. By Age.—The first point to notice here is that the increase in the proportion married at the younger ages in the population of the nation as a whole is also present in each of the regions and to almost equal degree (Appendix Table 26). For at least 40 years, however, the South has had a higher proportion of its young people married than the other regions. Among males the differences between the South and the West are sufficiently large to be significant, but it is among females that the really important differences occur. At ages under 25 the South has a relatively large excess of married women compared with any other region. In 1890 in the South 14.0 per cent of the women 15 to 19 were married, compared with 11.6 per cent in the West, 7.9 per cent in the

North Center, and 5.4 per cent in the Northeast. At ages 20 to 24 the percentages were 55.3, 51.5, 46.6, and 37.4, respectively. By 1930 the percentages in the 15-to-19 group had grown to 18.9, 12.6, 10.4, and 7.0, and in the 20-to-24 group to 59.3, 55.2, 50.8, and 42.0, respectively. The large percentage of Negroes in the South raises the proportion of married women at these younger ages, although lowering the proportion in the aggregate population as already noted. There can be no reasonable doubt, however, that even when allowance is made for the increase in young married women arising from the presence of Negroes, the white women of the South marry somewhat younger than those of other regions.

In contrast to the high proportion of young married women in the South the proportion of older women who are married is lower than in the North Center and the West and about the same as in the Northeast. The proportion of single women over 45 is generally higher in the South than in the North Center and the West, but lower than that in the Northeast, where many types of light industrial and clerical jobs are open to women. In all regions, except the South, the proportion of these older single women is increasing.

In proportions of the population widowed the South generally has a higher proportion of both sexes widowed at all ages than the other regions. This is undoubtedly due in part to the presence of the Negro. Within the several regions there is a slight tendency for the proportions widowed to decline. This is true at most ages and for both sexes, as was the case in the total population. The same differences between widowed males and females, noted above in the United States, are found in each of the regions. The proportion of the population widowed rises rapidly in all regions after 45 years of age and is generally from two to three times as great among women as among men. The higher death rate of males and the higher age of husbands are probably the most important factors in bringing this about.

Divorce is on the increase in all parts of the nation. The proportion of divorced persons is considerably higher in the West at every age and in both sexes than in other regions and apparently has been so ever since records were kept. In 1930 divorced persons of every age were relatively three to four times as numerous in the West as in the Northeast, while the South and the North Center stood about midway between these two extremes. There is less difference in the ratios of divorced males and females in the West than elsewhere. Whereas in 1930 there were 98.1 divorced males to 100 divorced females in the West, there were only 95.0 in the North Center, 78.8 in the Northeast, and 70.1 in the South. In all regions the percentage of persons divorced increases up to about 30 or 35 years of age. It then remains almost stationary for about 20 years, after which there is a decline. The decline at the older ages is generally more marked among women than men. The rather large proportion of men over 65 who are divorced—the proportion in all regions being about twice as high as among women of the same age—is probably to be accounted for chiefly by the fact that men average several years older than their wives. It also suggests the possibility that elderly men who have married young women are particularly likely to find themselves in the divorce courts.

It would be a mistake to conclude from the differences in the proportions of the population divorced in the several regions that the family is in a more unsettled state in one region than in another. Divorce is controlled by state laws, and the differences between regions probably reflect the differences in these laws fully as much as differences in the unity of the family.

4. BY SIZE OF COMMUNITY

The only information on this point available in the census is for married, widowed, or divorced persons 15 years of age and over as a whole by sex and by race and nativity in 1910.[1] In that year the general trend was a decrease in proportion married, widowed, or divorced as the size of the community increased.[2] There are no exceptions to this inverse relation in the case of the native whites of native parentage, although there is very little difference between rural communities and the smallest cities (2,500 to 25,000) for males. Among native whites of foreign or mixed parentage there is a slight increase for males from rural

TABLE 59.—PERCENTAGE OF PERSONS 15 YEARS OF AGE AND OVER MARRIED, WIDOWED, OR DIVORCED, 1910[a]

Class of population	Rural communities		Cities of 2,500–25,000		Cities of 25,000–100,000		Cities of 100,000 and over	
	Male	Female	Male	Female	Male	Female	Male	Female
All classes..................	62.1	73.2	61.5	69.0	60.0	67.4	57.9	65.5
Native white—native parentage......................	62.8	72.6	62.2	68.3	59.9	66.7	54.6	62.0
Native white—foreign or mixed parentage.................	51.5	64.0	51.6	58.0	49.1	55.4	46.5	53.9
Foreign-born white...........	67.4	89.8	67.8	82.8	67.9	78.9	68.0	77.6
Negro.......................	64.8	73.7	62.9	71.8	62.8	73.0	61.5	71.6

ᵃ *Thirteenth Census of the United States: 1910*, Vol. I, p. 536.

[1] The authors are having a special compilation made for 1910 and 1930 by size of community by age, but since the information for 1930 did not become available until November, 1932, there has not yet been time to complete this work.

[2] Table 59 and *Thirteenth Census of the United States: 1910*, Vol. I, Table 29, p. 536.

communities to the smallest cities. Otherwise there is a steady decrease as among the native whites of native parentage.

The only nativity group having a consistent increase from rural communities to the largest cities is the foreign-born white males; but the increase is small, from 67.4 per cent to 68.0 per cent, and is of significance only as reversing the usual order.

Among Negro males there is a consistent decline in the proportion married, widowed, or divorced as the size of the community increases, though it is not very large; but among Negro females the proportion is higher in cities of 25,000 to 100,000 than in the smallest cities but lower than in rural communities.

In general, then, it appears that there is a tendency for the proportion of the population married, widowed, or divorced to decrease as the size of the community increases. Unfortunately this does not tell much that is of real interest because of the differences in age composition between communities and also because of their differences in proportions widowed and divorced. This deficiency is in some slight degree remedied by the details of marital condition in urban and rural communities set forth below.

5. IN URBAN AND RURAL COMMUNITIES

In both urban and rural communities and for both sexes the proportions married have increased steadily, as was the case in the United States as a whole. As between urban and rural communities, however, there are significant differences. In 1910, the first census in which such tabulations were made, the proportion of males married was higher in the country population than in the city population (Table 60). By 1920 there was little difference between them, and by 1930 there were more married males in the city than in the country. In 1930, for the first time, the marital status of the rural-farm and rural-nonfarm populations was tabulated. The results showed that in rural communities it is not the farm but the nonfarm population which has a high proportion of married males. The percentages in 1930 were 57.9 and 61.1, respectively, while that for urban males was 60.5, considerably above that of farm males.

On the other hand, the proportion of females married is now, as it was in 1910, higher in the country than in the city. It was about one-sixth higher in 1910 and remained over one-tenth higher in 1930. Also in contrast to what is found among males it is the farm women, rather than the nonfarm women of the rural communities, who have the higher proportion married; in 1930 the percentages were 66.0 and 63.9, respectively, as compared with 58.5 in urban communities. The explanation of these differences between city and country women in proportions married is to be found largely in differences in opportunity for independent self-

TABLE 60.—PERCENTAGE DISTRIBUTION OF THE URBAN AND RURAL POPULATIONS 15 YEARS OF AGE AND OVER BY MARITAL CONDITION, BY SEX, AND BY RACE AND NATIVITY, 1910–1930[a]

Race and year	Male					Female				
	Total	Single	Married	Widowed	Divorced	Total	Single	Married	Widowed	Divorced
All races:										
Urban:										
1910	100.0	40.0	54.7	4.2	0.5	100.0	32.8	54.6	11.6	0.7
1920	100.0	35.5	58.9	4.6	0.7	100.0	29.0	57.6	12.2	0.9
1930	100.0	33.7	60.5	4.3	1.3	100.0	27.8	58.5	11.8	1.6
Rural:										
1910	100.0	37.5	56.8	4.8	0.5	100.0	26.6	63.3	9.4	0.5
1920	100.0	34.7	59.5	5.0	0.5	100.0	25.2	64.3	9.8	0.6
1930	100.0	34.5	59.3	5.0	0.9	100.0	24.2	65.0	9.8	0.9
Farm	100.0	36.5	57.9	4.8	0.7	100.0	25.2	66.0	8.1	0.6
Nonfarm	100.0	32.1	61.1	5.3	1.2	100.0	23.0	63.9	11.8	1.1
Native white of native parentage:										
Urban:										
1910	100.0	40.2	54.1	4.2	0.7	100.0	34.0	53.5	11.3	0.9
1920	100.0	36.2	58.0	4.4	0.9	100.0	31.1	56.2	11.4	1.2
1930	100.0	33.9	60.5	3.8	1.5	100.0	29.2	58.1	10.5	2.0
Rural:										
1910	100.0	36.8	57.7	4.7	0.5	100.0	27.2	63.3	8.9	0.5
1920	100.0	34.9	59.6	4.8	0.5	100.0	26.2	64.1	9.1	0.5
1930	100.0	35.0	59.5	4.5	0.9	100.0	25.1	65.2	8.8	0.8
Farm	100.0	37.7	57.2	4.4	0.7	100.0	26.4	66.0	7.1	0.5
Nonfarm	100.0	31.5	62.3	4.8	1.2	100.0	23.6	64.4	10.7	1.1
Native white of foreign or mixed parentage:										
Urban:										
1910	100.0	51.5	45.1	2.7	0.4	100.0	44.6	47.5	7.2	0.6
1920	100.0	46.3	49.6	3.3	0.6	100.0	39.6	50.6	8.9	0.8
1930	100.0	44.5	51.2	3.2	1.0	100.0	37.5	52.1	9.0	1.2
Rural:										
1910	100.0	48.2	48.2	2.9	0.4	100.0	35.8	58.5	5.1	0.4
1920	100.0	42.7	53.1	3.5	0.5	100.0	30.8	62.0	6.7	0.4
1930	100.0	39.6	55.3	4.1	0.9	100.0	27.4	63.8	8.0	0.7
Farm	100.0	41.1	54.4	3.8	0.6	100.0	26.5	67.1	5.9	0.4
Nonfarm	100.0	38.0	56.3	4.5	1.1	100.0	28.2	60.9	9.9	0.9
Foreign-born white:										
Urban:										
1910	100.0	31.7	62.7	5.0	0.3	100.0	20.9	63.9	14.6	0.4
1920	100.0	25.3	68.4	5.6	0.4	100.0	15.6	68.3	15.5	0.5
1930	100.0	21.3	71.6	6.0	0.9	100.0	13.7	69.1	16.2	0.9
Rural:										
1910	100.0	32.0	60.7	6.4	0.4	100.0	10.0	74.6	14.9	0.3
1920	100.0	26.4	65.4	7.4	0.5	100.0	9.1	74.8	15.6	0.4
1930	100.0	22.1	67.8	8.9	1.0	100.0	8.2	73.9	17.3	0.6
Farm	100.0	20.1	69.6	9.4	0.8	100.0	5.3	78.3	15.9	0.4
Nonfarm	100.0	23.5	66.5	8.6	1.1	100.0	10.1	70.9	18.2	0.7
Negro:										
Urban:										
1910	100.0	37.0	54.8	6.7	0.8	100.0	27.7	51.4	19.1	1.4
1920	100.0	33.3	59.1	6.2	1.1	100.0	22.8	57.1	18.1	1.7
1930	100.0	31.3	60.4	6.4	1.7	100.0	22.2	56.6	18.4	2.7
Rural:										
1910	100.0	34.7	58.2	6.0	0.6	100.0	26.0	60.2	12.6	0.9
1920	100.0	32.1	61.3	5.7	0.6	100.0	25.0	61.2	12.6	1.0
1930	100.0	33.1	59.3	6.2	1.2	100.0	24.3	60.4	13.5	1.7
Farm	100.0	33.0	60.3	5.7	1.0	100.0	25.6	61.3	11.7	1.4
Nonfarm	100.0	33.4	57.4	7.1	1.6	100.0	21.8	58.7	17.1	2.2

[a] For 1910 from *Thirteenth Census of the United States: 1910*, Vol. I, p. 586; 1920 from *Fourteenth Census of the United States: 1920*, Vol. II, p. 576; 1930 from *Fifteenth Census of the United States: 1930*, Vol. II, pp. 848–850.

support offered women in the country and in the city, a difference that is also coupled with variations in sex ratios as already noted. In this connection it may be of some interest to compare the proportions of married persons in certain cities having widely different sex ratios. In 1930 Michigan City, Indiana, with a sex ratio of 124.2 males to 100 females, 57.2 per cent of the males and 64.3 per cent of the females 15 years of age and over were married. In Brookline, Massachusetts, the sex ratio was only 69.3, and the proportions of males and females married were 58.6 and 38.6 per cent, respectively. Even in large cities where the sex ratios are not so widely different as those just cited the same relation between sex ratio and proportions of females married is clearly marked. Thus in Detroit, with a sex ratio of 110.1 (high for a large city), 60.0 per cent of the males over 15 and 66.1 per cent of the females are married; while in St. Louis, with a sex ratio of 95.6 (low for a large city), the percentages are 60.6 and 57.1. The proportion of women married is almost one-seventh lower in St. Louis than in Detroit.

The rural districts generally have a higher proportion of males widowed than the cities, while among females the situation is the opposite. In neither type of community and in neither sex is there any clear trend; the proportion was about the same in 1930 as it was in 1910. The excess of widows in the cities is probably to be explained chiefly by the higher male death rates there as compared with those of rural communities, although the movement of widows from rural communities to cities should not be overlooked. It may also be that rural widows remarry more frequently than city widows, but on this point no information is available. As between the aggregate rural-farm and rural-nonfarm populations the widowed are relatively more numerous in the latter. This would be expected because a farm family lacking either husband or wife finds it difficult to carry on (particularly when the survivor is past middle life) and is likely to move to the near-by village. This is especially true of widows.[1]

Divorced persons are more common in the cities than in the country among both males and females and appear to be increasing somewhat faster among the city population than among the country population. Here, too, it appears that broken homes are considerably more common in the rural-nonfarm population than in the rural-farm population. The farm is still the stronghold of the family.

a. By Race and Nativity.—In all race and nativity groups, for both sexes and in both urban and rural communities, except foreign born and Negro females in the country, there have been fairly steady increases in the proportions of married persons. Also in the rural communities the proportions married are higher than those in urban communities, with

[1] *Supra*, p. 189.

the exception of the foreign-born males in all years and of the Negro males in 1930.

The differences between the several groups are much the same as those already described for the total population. Among native whites of native parentage the proportion married corresponds rather closely to that in the total population in both urban and rural communities (Table 60). The highest proportions for both sexes and both types of communities are those of the foreign-born whites, and the lowest are among their children, except in 1920 and 1930 among the Negro women in rural communities. Within rural communities (1930) the native whites (both groups) have more married males in the nonfarm population than in the farm population, while the opposite is the case for foreign-born whites and Negroes. Among females, however, the proportion of farm women married is considerably in excess of that of nonfarm women in all race and nativity groups and in all years.

The proportions of the widowed and divorced in urban and rural communities show about the differences that would be expected from what has already been said. Widowed males are more common in rural communities for all race and nativity groups, except for the Negroes, and widowed females are more common in all groups in the cities, except among the foreign born. In the foreign-born group there is very little difference in the proportions in urban and rural communities. Divorced persons, both male and female, are relatively more numerous in the city than in the country, except among foreign-born males. There are, however, considerable differences between the several race and nativity groups in both urban and rural communities. In the cities the Negroes have the highest proportions of both widowed and divorced persons of both sexes, while the native whites of foreign or mixed parentage have the lowest proportion of widowed, and the foreign born the lowest proportion of divorced in both sexes. In the rural districts, on the other hand, the proportion of widowed persons is highest among the foreign born (both sexes) and lowest among the native whites of foreign or mixed parentage, while the Negroes still retain the lead in proportion of divorced persons, and the foreign born have the lowest proportion. The native whites of foreign or mixed parentage stand slightly below the average in proportion of divorced persons of both sexes. In all race and nativity groups the rural-nonfarm population has a higher proportion of both widowed and divorced persons than the farm population, except for widowed males among the foreign born.

b. By Age.—At all ages and for both sexes the proportions of married persons are significantly higher in rural than in urban communities. The differences are particularly large for females at the younger ages. In 1910 only 7.7 per cent of the urban females 15 to 19 years of age were married as compared with 14.3 per cent of the rural females of the same age (Table 61 and Figure 25). In 1930 the percentages were 10.2 and 15.5, respectively—an increase in both types of community but more rapid in the cities. However, the proportion is still over one-half higher in the country. At ages 20 to 24 the differences are greater absolutely (1910 urban, 42.4 per cent; rural, 57.5 per cent; 1930 urban, 47.1 per cent; rural, 58.8 per cent), but the relative excess of the rural communities is much smaller. Among males at these ages the relative excess of rural over urban communities is about the same as among females, but the

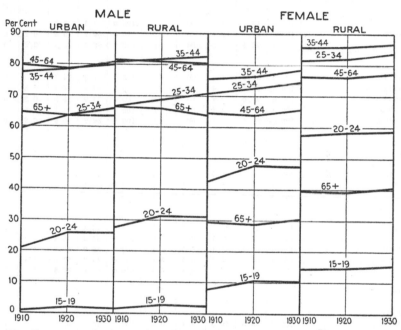

Fig. 25.—Percentage of urban and rural populations 15 years of age and over, married, by sex, 1910–30. (Based on Table 61.)

proportions married are only one-sixth to one-seventh as high at ages 15 to 19 and only about one-half as high at ages 20 to 24.

At ages 25 to 34 the differences between urban and rural communities in proportions married are still large (1910 urban females, 69.6 per cent; rural females, 81.4 per cent; 1930 urban females, 74.6 per cent; rural females, 83.4 per cent), but the relative excesses in rural communities are less. The same is true for males. At the older ages both relative excesses and percentage differences are still less, but always there are relatively more married persons in the country than in the city.

In view of these facts it may appear strange that the excess of married persons in the rural population is not larger than is shown in Table 60.

TABLE 61.—PERCENTAGE DISTRIBUTION OF THE URBAN AND RURAL POPULATIONS 15 YEARS OF AGE AND OVER, BY MARITAL CONDITION, BY SEX, AND BY AGE, 1910–1930[a]

Age, community, and year	Male					Female				
	Total	Single	Mar-ried	Wid-owed	Di-vorced	Total	Single	Mar-ried	Wid-owed	Di-vorced
15–19:										
Urban:										
1910................	100.0	98.7	0.7	(b)	(b)	100.0	91.5	7.7	0.1	0.1
1920................	100.0	98.1	1.7	(b)	(b)	100.0	89.2	10.4	0.2	0.1
1930................	100.0	98.4	1.3	(b)	(b)	100.0	89.3	10.2	0.2	0.2
Rural:										
1910................	100.0	97.9	1.4	(b)	(b)	100.0	84.8	14.3	0.3	0.1
1920................	100.0	97.4	2.4	(b)	(b)	100.0	84.9	14.5	0.3	0.1
1930................	100.0	97.6	2.2	(b)	(b)	100.0	83.9	15.5	0.3	0.2
Farm............	100.0	97.6	2.2	(b)	(b)	100.0	84.7	14.7	0.3	0.2
Nonfarm...........	100.0	97.7	2.1	(b)	(b)	100.0	82.7	16.8	0.3	0.2
20–24:										
Urban:										
1910................	100.0	78.5	20.6	0.3	0.1	100.0	55.8	42.4	1.0	0.5
1920................	100.0	73.3	25.8	0.4	0.2	100.0	50.4	47.6	1.2	0.7
1930................	100.0	73.2	25.8	0.2	0.4	100.0	50.6	47.1	0.9	1.2
Rural:										
1910................	100.0	71.5	27.3	0.5	0.2	100.0	40.3	57.5	1.5	0.4
1920................	100.0	67.7	31.1	0.6	0.2	100.0	39.3	58.4	1.6	0.5
1930................	100.0	67.7	31.1	0.5	0.4	100.0	38.9	58.8	1.3	0.9
Farm............	100.0	69.7	29.2	0.5	0.4	100.0	40.6	57.0	1.4	0.9
Nonfarm...........	100.0	65.2	33.7	0.4	0.4	100.0	36.9	60.8	1.1	1.0
25–34:										
Urban:										
1910................	100.0	38.5	59.5	1.2	0.5	100.0	26.1	69.6	3.3	0.9
1920................	100.0	34.2	63.5	1.4	0.7	100.0	22.8	72.6	3.3	1.2
1930................	100.0	30.7	66.9	0.9	1.3	100.0	20.3	74.6	2.7	2.3
Rural:										
1910................	100.0	31.1	66.5	1.6	0.4	100.0	15.0	81.4	2.9	0.6
1920.:...............	100.0	29.2	68.5	1.6	0.5	100.0	14.3	82.0	3.0	0.7
1930................	100.0	26.7	70.9	1.2	1.0	100.0	12.9	83.4	2.5	1.0
Farm............	100.0	28.7	69.0	1.4	0.8	100.0	12.8	83.9	2.4	0.9
Nonfarm...........	100.0	24.8	72.8	1.1	1.1	100.0	13.1	82.9	2.6	1.4
35–44:										
Urban:										
1910................	100.0	18.3	77.5	3.1	0.8	100.0	14.6	75.4	8.9	1.1
1920................	100.0	17.5	78.3	3.0	1.0	100.0	14.0	76.2	8.3	1.4
1930................	100.0	14.9	80.9	2.4	1.8	100.0	11.9	78.4	7.3	2.4

TABLE 61.—PERCENTAGE DISTRIBUTION OF THE URBAN AND RURAL POPULATIONS 15 YEARS OF AGE AND OVER, BY MARITAL CONDITION, BY SEX, AND BY AGE, 1910–1930.[a]—(*Continued*)

Age, community, and year	Male					Female				
	Total	Single	Married	Widowed	Divorced	Total	Single	Married	Widowed	Divorced
Rural:										
1910	100.0	14.9	81.0	3.3	0.6	100.0	7.8	85.6	5.9	0.7
1920	100.0	14.4	81.7	3.0	0.7	100.0	7.8	85.8	5.7	0.7
1930	100.0	13.4	82.7	2.6	1.2	100.0	6.8	86.8	5.2	1.1
Farm	100.0	12.9	83.6	2.6	0.9	100.0	5.7	89.3	4.3	0.7
Nonfarm	100.0	13.9	81.7	2.6	1.5	100.0	8.2	83.9	6.3	1.6
45–64:										
Urban:										
1910	100.0	10.8	79.7	8.5	0.8	100.0	9.9	64.1	25.1	0.9
1920	100.0	11.7	78.9	8.1	1.1	100.0	11.0	63.7	24.1	1.1
1930	100.0	11.0	80.0	7.1	1.7	100.0	10.8	65.4	22.0	1.7
Rural:										
1910	100.0	9.5	81.3	8.2	0.8	100.0	6.0	76.1	17.1	0.6
1920	100.0	10.5	80.9	7.6	0.9	100.0	6.6	76.0	16.5	0.7
1930	100.0	10.8	80.4	7.2	1.4	100.0	6.4	77.0	15.5	1.0
Farm	100.0	9.6	82.4	6.8	1.1	100.0	4.8	82.0	12.5	0.6
Nonfarm	100.0	12.4	77.8	7.8	1.8	100.0	8.2	71.1	19.1	1.4
65+:										
Urban:										
1910	100.0	6.2	64.2	28.8	0.6	100.0	7.2	29.6	62.7	0.3
1920	100.0	7.4	63.3	28.4	0.7	100.0	7.9	28.7	62.8	0.4
1930	100.0	8.1	63.4	27.1	1.1	100.0	9.4	30.4	59.5	0.6
Rural:										
1910	100.0	6.2	66.6	26.1	0.7	100.0	5.6	39.7	54.1	0.4
1920	100.0	7.3	65.9	25.8	0.8	100.0	6.2	39.4	53.7	0.4
1930	100.0	8.7	63.9	26.0	1.2	100.0	6.4	40.4	52.5	0.5
Farm	100.0	7.5	66.2	25.2	1.0	100.0	5.4	45.0	49.1	0.4
Nonfarm	100.0	10.2	61.2	27.0	1.4	100.0	7.4	36.5	55.3	0.6

[a] For 1910 from *Thirteenth Census of the United States: 1910*, Vol. I, p. 585; 1920 from *Fourteenth Census of the United States: 1920*, Vol. II, p. 576; 1930 from *Fifteenth Census of the United States: 1930*, Vol. II, p. 848.
[b] Less than one-tenth of 1 per cent.

The explanation of this situation is that the cities have higher percentages of persons at those ages where the proportions of married persons are high than the rural communities have (Table 35, p. 130); hence, the proportion of the total marriageable population that is married is higher than might be expected from comparing the married population by age in urban and rural communities.

Within the rural population the proportion married is higher in both sexes in the nonfarm population at ages under 35, except males 15 to 19 and females 25 to 34, than in the farm population. At older ages it is higher in the farm population. Apparently the rural-nonfarm population marries relatively young.

The proportion of widowed males is not significantly different in urban and rural communities at any age. The slightly larger proportion in the rural communities at the younger ages is probably attributable to the larger proportion married in such communities. Among females the proportion widowed is lower in the country than in the city at all ages over 25. As among the males, the larger proportion of widows under 25 in the country is probably attributable to the larger proportion of young rural women who are married. The lower death rate of rural males than of urban males is undoubtedly the prime factor in keeping the proportions of rural widows below those of cities.

Within the rural community there is no significant difference between the farm and nonfarm populations in the proportion of widows under 35. At older ages, however, the proportion of widows in the nonfarm population is much higher than in the farm population. This is additional evidence[1] that farm widows move to neighboring villages in rather large numbers. At ages over 45 it also appears that farm widowers move to the villages rather frequently, since there is generally a slight excess in the nonfarm population as compared with the farm population. What part death rates might play in producing this situation cannot be told because there are no data showing the relative death rates in farm and nonfarm populations.

Among males the proportions divorced at the different ages are generally higher in the urban than in the rural population, but the differences are slight and of little significance. Among women, on the other hand, the differences are much greater. At ages 25 to 44 more than twice as large a proportion of women in the cities as in the country are divorced. At younger and older ages the differences decrease until the proportions are about the same in both types of communities at ages 15 to 19 and 65 and over. Here again there is a difference between farm and nonfarm women. The proportion of divorced women in the nonfarm population is about twice as high as in the farm population at ages 30 to 64, although it is still well below that among urban women of the same ages (Table 61). At younger and older ages the differences in the proportions of divorced women in the rural-farm and nonfarm populations are smaller.

c. **By Race and Nativity, by Age.** *Native Whites of Native Parentage.*— The marital condition of the native whites of native parentage is so much like that of the total population in both urban and rural communities that little need be said about it. This is particularly true of the rural

[1] *Supra*, p. 221.

population which is preponderantly native white of native parentage.[1] In the urban population the proportion of native white males of native parentage who are married is generally slightly above that for the total population. The differences are small, however, at ages above 25 and probably are of no particular significance. This is even more true for women because the differences are smaller. As far as data for so short a period permit of speaking of a time trend, it is generally upward at all ages and for both sexes up to age 65 (Appendix Table 27). There are a few cases, however, in which there was a slight decline in proportion between 1920 and 1930. The differences between the rural and urban communities in proportions widowed and divorced are practically the same as those already pointed out in the total population as are also those between the rural-farm and rural-nonfarm populations. There are more widowed males in the rural population than in the urban population at all ages and more widowed females in the urban population. Divorced persons of both sexes and all ages are relatively more numerous in the urban population.

Native Whites of Foreign or Mixed Parentage.—The native whites of foreign or mixed parentage follow the same pattern as the total population in the differences between urban and rural communities. They have a very low proportion married in practically all age groups. They also have relatively few widowed persons, probably, in part, because of the smaller proportion married. In proportion divorced they stand between the older native whites and their own foreign-born parents. All this applies to both sexes and in the rural districts as well as in the cities.

Foreign-born Whites.—The marital condition of the foreign-born whites is almost as peculiar as their age[2] and sex[3] composition. Indeed, many of their marital peculiarities are to be attributed to their distinctive age and sex composition. In the first place, the proportion of the foreign born married at ages under 35 is not so high as might be expected from the proportion of the total married. Because of the fact that the foreign-born whites are older than any other group, they have very high proportions in the ages where most persons are married, which raises the proportion of the total married. Then, too, it should be noted that the sex ratios among the foreign born are very high. This tends to reduce the proportion of males married, particularly at the younger ages, and to raise the proportion of females married at practically all ages. In general then it may be said that there is a wider divergence in the proportions of the sexes married among the foreign born than in any other group. The rural-urban differences in proportions married, are, however, much the same

[1] *Supra*, p. 48.
[2] *Supra*, pp. 143, 146–148.
[3] *Supra*, pp. 172, 175.

as those found in other groups, although one or two exceptions are conspicuous. Thus the proportion of married males among the foreign born in the cities is higher than in the country at all ages between 20 and 65. This is exactly the opposite of the usual situation. Among females the proportion married is always higher in the rural communities than in the cities. Also it is of some interest that at the younger ages the foreign born in neither country nor city show a steady rise in proportion married. Since 1920 there has been a distinct downward movement that is quite marked at all ages under 35. This is probably rather closely connected with the placing of immigration on the quota basis, which reduced the number of southern and eastern Europeans and increased the proportion coming from northern and western Europe, thus tending to make marriage among the foreign born somewhat more difficult.

The proportion of the foreign born who are widowed is about the same as in the total population and among females is generally higher in the cities than in the country. This is the usual pattern. Divorced persons are relatively scarce among the foreign born in both urban and rural communities at all ages. There are, however, the usual excess in urban communities in the middle groups and the usual approach to parity at the younger and older ages.

Negroes.—The marital condition of Negroes by age in urban and rural communities shows several peculiarities. The first point to attract attention is that there is no steady upward trend in the proportion of Negroes married at the younger ages, as was the case for the native white groups. In certain groups, however, the 20-to-24 and 25-to-34 age groups of urban males and the 15-to-19 group of rural females, the trend is reasonably certain. In most other age groups and in both urban and rural communities the erratic movement of the figures renders it practically impossible to speak of trends for Negroes by age; nor are the usual differences between urban and rural populations so clearly defined among Negroes as among native whites. Thus in the 15-to-19 group of males there was, in 1910, a higher proportion married in the rural communities. Since that time there has been practically no difference between urban and rural communities. Among females of the same ages the proportion married was also higher in the rural communities in 1910 but by 1920 had become greater in the cities, only to yield again to the rural districts in 1930. However, as in the case of males, the difference between country and city is negligible. Hence rural Negroes do not show the large excess of married persons at these ages that is usual among the whites. It should be noted, however, that the proportion of Negro males 15 to 19 who are married is generally several times as high as that of whites and that among females it is about twice as high as that of whites in the cities and from one-fifth to one-third higher in the country. In the 20-to-24 age group the proportion of Negroes married, both male and female, is also well above that of the whites, although the excess is much smaller relatively than in the 15-to-19 group. In this group, however, the usual rural excess makes its appearance and is maintained henceforth.

In the 25-to-34 age group the proportion of Negro males married was slightly less in 1930 than that of the native whites of native parentage in the cities, but somewhat higher in the country. At ages over 35 the proportion of Negro males married is distinctly lower than that of the native whites in the cities, but about the same, or a little higher, in the country. Among Negro females, on the other hand, the proportion married is much lower than among native whites of native parentage at all ages over 25 in both urban and rural communities. As compared with the native whites of foreign or mixed parentage, the Negroes have much higher proportions married in both types of communities and in both sexes at all ages under 35. At ages over 35, however, only rural Negro males have a higher proportion married than the native whites of foreign or mixed parentage; both urban and rural Negro females and urban Negro males have smaller proportions married than are found among the native whites of foreign or mixed parentage.

The proportion of Negroes widowed is much higher at all ages than that of whites, for both sexes and in urban and rural communities. The rural-urban differences are also greater than among the whites, the excess in the urban population amounting to 50 per cent or more at ages 35 to 64 among females. For males the differences are not large until 45 years of age, after which they are from one-fourth to one-third higher. These high proportions of widowed persons are the inevitable result of the high death rates among Negroes, assuming that remarriage is not sufficiently more frequent to offset the effects of these higher death rates. Divorce is also more common among Negroes of all ages than in the rest of the population and is more frequent in the city than in the country. Even the short period for which data are available leaves no doubt that there is an upward trend in the proportion of divorced Negroes in both urban and rural communities. The age incidence of divorce appears to be about the same in the Negro population as in the white population; namely, the proportion of persons divorced increases up to about 35, shows but little change for 10 or 20 years, and then declines. When the Negro farm and nonfarm populations are compared, much the same differences are found as in the native whites of native parentage. Among females the proportions married at ages 15 to 19 and 20 to 24 are higher in the non-farm population. At all older ages the opposite is the case, and the proportional differences between farm and nonfarm people increase as age increases. Among Negroes this difference is greater than among either native whites of native parentage or native whites of foreign or mixed parentage, as is also the difference in the proportions single and widowed. In the farm population the proportion single and widowed is decidedly lower than in the nonfarm population and the difference is relatively greater among males than among females.

On the whole the data on the marital condition of Negroes bear out the common belief that their married life is less regular than that of whites and that it is particularly demoralized in the cities whither so many have recently moved.

6. SUMMARY

Two trends in marital condition stand out clearly. They are (a) the increase in the proportion of the population married at the younger ages, and (b) the increase of divorced persons in all classes of the population and in all regions. A third point of interest, but not a trend, is the difference between urban and rural populations in their proportions married. A full explanation of these points is both beyond the competence of the authors and out of place here. It may be pertinent, however, to suggest one or two points in connection with the trend toward earlier marriage and regarding the differences in proportions married in urban and rural communities, because they have been much less discussed than the increase in divorce.

The trend toward earlier marriage no doubt arises from a complex of social conditions, but the authors wish to call attention to the fact that earlier marriage has been taking place concomitantly with the rapid spread of contraceptive information. It seems reasonable to believe that young people, knowing that marriage does not necessarily involve continence, parenthood, or abortion, are more ready to marry than they would be were they reasonably certain they would have children born at rather regular and frequent intervals if they do not practice continence or abortion.

The relation between early marriage and the spread of contraceptive information seems all the more likely in view of the fact that a growing proportion of the population lives in the cities where the raising of a large family is not to be lightly undertaken. The city worker's difficulties in raising a family multiply more rapidly than the farmer's with each additional child; hence it is hard to understand the greater increase of young married persons there than in the country (Table 61), if they did not possess means of preventing births until they were ready for children and of limiting the number of children as they see fit.

It is also possible that the knowledge that divorce is relatively easy encourages marriage at an earlier age. On this point there is no evidence, and while it cannot be said that it is a factor of no importance, it seems rather unlikely that many young people are influenced by such knowledge at the time they decide to marry.

Again the influence of the improvement in general economic conditions between the latter part of the 1890's and 1930 should not be overlooked as a factor in earlier marriage. But when all these other factors making for earlier marriage are given due weight, it seems highly probable that the spread of contraceptive practices is a factor of considerable importance.

The higher proportion of married persons in the rural districts than in the cities and the fact that this is largely the result of earlier marriage in the country is of importance as having a bearing upon the rates of reproduction of city and country people. Specific birth rates of married women are always higher during the 20-to-29 age period than later; hence a population having a relatively larger proportion of its women of these ages married than another will, under present conditions, produce more children and increase faster. There is clear evidence that the rural population is growing faster by an excess of births over deaths than the city population. There is reason to believe that one factor in causing this difference is the earlier marriage of women in the country. It probably is not the most important factor making for urban-rural differences in the birth rate, but any change in the proportions of younger persons married in city and country would probably presage a change in their relative rates of natural increase.

Chapter VII

DEATHS AND DEATH RATES[1]

THE downward movement of the decennial rate of population growth since 1860 was pointed out in Chapter I of this monograph, but little was said about the part played by changes in immigration, birth rates, and death rates in bringing it about. In this and following chapters each of these factors will be examined as to its past trend and present status, which should throw light on the reasons for fluctuations in population growth during past decades and recent years. There may then be some basis for judging possible future trends of births, deaths, and perhaps even of immigration, and for calculating the population growth that will take place during the next half century.

1. SOURCES OF INFORMATION

Although yearly records of immigration were commenced by the federal government in 1820, 80 years elapsed before statistics on deaths were gathered annually by the Bureau of the Census. Beginning with 1900 there are reports on mortality in those states and cities requiring the registration of deaths and possessing records meeting certain tests for completeness and accuracy. The earlier reports included the New England states, New York, New Jersey, District of Columbia, Indiana, Michigan (the original death-registration states), and 134 cities outside these states but mostly in the Middle Atlantic and East North Central divisions. This area in 1900 contained 40.5 per cent of the nation's population; hence its mortality rates should be representative of the more urbanized and industrialized parts of the United States and should indicate roughly the situation of the white population as a whole. After 1906 the death-registration area was extended rapidly, so that it contained 58.3 per cent of the population by 1910, 82.2 per cent by 1920, and by 1929 the entire population except that of the rural areas and smaller cities of South Dakota and Texas. Prior to 1913 no state with a large number of Negroes had been admitted to the death-registration area, but by 1920 enough southern states had joined so that 69.0 per cent of

---

[1] For additional material regarding many parts of this chapter, see Edgar Sydenstricker, *Health and Environment*, Monograph in Recent Social Trends Series, New York, McGraw-Hill Book Company, Inc., 1933, particularly Chap. VIII, "The Trend of Mortality." See also Warren S. Thompson, *Population Problems*, New York, McGraw-Hill Book Company, Inc., 1930, Chap. IX.

the Negro population was then included, and 94.4 per cent by 1930. The mortality reports of the federal government, therefore, indicate fairly accurately the trend of white death rates from 1900 to date, and of Negro death rates from 1920 to date, and provide a basis for estimating the number of deaths in the entire United States during these years.

For tracing the trend of death rates for the white population prior to 1900, reliance must be placed on state or city reports and on special studies based on them. The registration of deaths was begun at an early date in some localities, but the first state-wide report published is that of Massachusetts for 1841, followed within a few years by reports for Connecticut, Rhode Island, and Vermont. During the first years of death registration the records were not particularly complete as a rule, several years' experience being necessary to insure the reporting of almost all of the deaths. Massachusetts apparently had the most accurate system of death registration, as is indicated by the fact that contemporary statisticians chose its data more often than those of other states for use in the preparation of life tables. Among the nine more important American life tables including the population at all ages and computed before 1900, five are for Massachusetts (based on deaths in 1850, 1855, 1878–1882, 1890, and 1893–1897), one for Massachusetts and New Hampshire (1789), one for New Jersey (1880), one for white males in the United States (1860), and one for Maryland (1850).[1] Only for Massachusetts have life tables been prepared at sufficiently short intervals to give an adequate idea of the trend of mortality rates and of expectation of life for the white population prior to 1900.[2]

While it would be highly desirable to know the expectation of life and specific death rates for the white population of the United States since 1789, it is probable that the Massachusetts data picture the trend fairly accurately. In 1789 Massachusetts had the fourth largest population of the various states and territories, and no doubt was typical of those of the North which had half of the nation's population at that time. In 1900–1902, 1909–1911, 1919–1920, and 1929 life tables are available for Massachusetts and for the original death-registration states. A comparison of these tables shows small differences between Massachusetts and the larger area, specific death rates being a little higher in Massachusetts in 1900–1902 and 1909–1911, about the same in 1919–1920, and a little lower in 1929, with corresponding inverse differences in expectation of life.[3] Because mortality conditions in Massachusetts may have been

---

[1] For bibliographical notes concerning these life tables, see footnotes to Tables 62, 65, and 66.

[2] The Massachusetts life tables are based on the total population, but the proportion of Negroes is insignificant (the maximum being 1.2 per cent in 1930) so that the tables virtually represent whites.

[3] *Infra*, Tables 65 and 66, pp. 236 and 240.

about the same as in the United States in 1789 instead of slightly below the national average as since 1900, a corresponding allowance may be necessary in judging the trend for the United States from data for Massachusetts.

2. THE CRUDE DEATH RATE

The huge reduction in death rate that has been brought about in Massachusetts represents a wonderful achievement. Less than a century

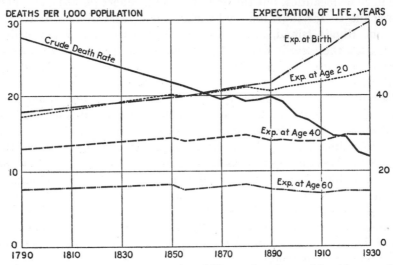

FIG. 26.—Crude death rate and expectation of life at selected ages, Massachusetts, 1789–1931. (Based on Tables 62 and 66.)

and a half have elapsed since the first life table was computed for Massachusetts; yet in that time the crude death rate[1] has been reduced by about 60 per cent; from a high of 27.8 per 1,000 in 1789 there was a falling off to 21.4 in 1855 and to 11.4 in 1931 (Figure 26). Much of this decline is of comparatively recent origin; the reduction in death rate in the last 40 years (1888–1892 to 1928–1931) was about 7.9 per 1,000 as against 8.0 in the preceding 100 years (Table 62). The rate of decline has been still larger during recent years than formerly, averaging 0.8 per 1,000 by decades from 1789 to 1890, and 2.0 per 1,000, or more than twice as much, from 1890 to 1931. That the lower rates of recent years have been reduced more rapidly than the higher rates of former years is a gratifying situation. While several factors have been important in bringing this about, due credit should be given to the public health program which Massachusetts has developed.

[1] The crude death rate is obtained by dividing the total number of deaths by the total population and expressing the result as deaths per 1,000 persons.

DEATHS AND DEATH RATES

To show the year-by-year trend of crude death rates of the white population since 1900, these data for Massachusetts may be supplemented with rates published in current mortality reports for the registration area. From 1900 to 1931 the crude death rate of white persons in the original death-registration states declined 34 per cent, at almost exactly the same pace as in Massachusetts (Table 63). The decline in the current registration area was somewhat more rapid, amounting to 38 per cent.

TABLE 62.—CRUDE DEATH RATE IN MASSACHUSETTS, 1789–1931[a]

Year	Deaths per 1,000 persons	Year	Deaths per 1,000 persons
1789	27.8	1898–1902	17.3
1855	21.4	1903–07	16.7
1868–72	19.5	1908–12	15.6
1873–77	20.0	1913–17	14.7
1878–82	19.2	1918–22	14.6
1883–87	19.4	1923–27	12.5
1888–92	19.8	1928–31	11.9
1893–97	19.2		....

[a] For 1789 from Edward Wigglesworth, *Memoirs of the American Academy of Arts and Sciences*, Vol. 2, old series, Pt. 1 (1793). For 1855 from E. B. Elliott, *Proceedings of the American Association for the Advancement of Science*, eleventh meeting, 1857. For 1868–1872 and subsequent years from state registration reports. The latter are not used prior to 1868 because of the possibility of incomplete death registration. In 1855, for example, the crude death rate based on deaths registered in the entire state was 18.4, while in the 166 towns chosen by Elliott in part because of supposedly more accurate records, the crude death rate was 21.4. However, this difference may have been caused to some extent by the change in area.

In both cases the change from year to year was upward almost as often as downward, yet the drops were greater than the rises and progress was fairly steady. From 1900 to 1909 the crude death rate in the original registration states varied between 17.0 and 14.8, from 1910 to 1919 between 15.4 and 13.3 (excluding 1918 when the influenza pandemic raised the rate to 18.3), and from 1920 to 1931 between 13.6 and 11.2. The more rapid decline in the current registration area resulted from the early addition of states with low rates. The differential between the crude death rate of whites in the original registration states and the current registration area has fluctuated comparatively little since 1909.

The crude death rate of Negroes in the current registration area decreased a little more rapidly than that of whites from 1910 to 1921 and 1922; but since then the Negro rate has increased somewhat, whereas the white rate has fallen slightly. The addition of several southern states to the registration area from 1916 to 1926 exercised an important downward influence on the Negro death rate in this period because Negro death rates have been lower in southern than in northern states.[1] In opposition

[1] *Infra*, p. 243.

TABLE 63.—CRUDE DEATH RATE AND INFANT MORTALITY IN THE REGISTRATION AREA, BY RACE, 1900–1931

Year	Deaths per 1,000 persons[a]			Deaths under 1 per 1,000 births in current birth-registration area[b]	
	Whites[c]		Negroes		
	Original death-registration states[d]	Current death-registration area	Current death-registration area	Whites[c]	Negroes
1900............................	17.0	17.0	.....	....	....
1901............................	16.2	16.1	.....	122	234
1902............................	15.3	15.4	.....	....	....
1903............................	15.4	15.6	.....	....	....
1904............................	16.2	16.0	.....	....	....
1905............................	15.7	15.5	.....	....	....
1906............................	15.7	15.2	.....	....	....
1907............................	16.0	15.5	.....	....	....
1908............................	15.0	14.4	.....	....	....
1909............................	14.8	14.1	.....	....	....
1910............................	15.4	14.6	23.5	113	203
1911............................	14.8	13.8	22.2	....	....
1912............................	14.4	13.5	21.4	....	....
1913............................	14.5	13.7	20.9	....	....
1914............................	14.2	13.2	20.7	....	....
1915............................	14.1	13.1	20.6	99	....
1916............................	14.8	13.6	19.5	99	184
1917............................	14.7	13.7	20.7	91	149
1918............................	18.3	17.4	25.3	97	162
1919............................	13.3	12.4	17.8	83	134
1920............................	13.6	12.6	17.8	82	136
1921............................	12.0	11.2	15.7	72	111
1922............................	12.4	11.4	15.3	73	112
1923............................	12.7	11.8	16.6	74	120
1924............................	12.1	11.2	17.2	67	114
1925............................	12.1	11.2	17.6	68	112
1926............................	12.6	11.6	18.1	70	112
1927............................	11.6	10.8	16.7	61	100
1928............................	12.1	11.6	17.3	64	106
1929............................	12.1	11.4	17.1	63	101
1930............................	11.3	10.8	16.2[e]	60	102
1931............................	11.2	10.6	15.9[e]	57[f]	97[f]

[a] For 1900 to 1929 from current numbers of *Mortality Statistics;* for 1930, and 1931 from multigraphed releases or letters from the Division of Vital Statistics, or preliminary estimates of the authors based on state reports or letters. No allowance made for incomplete registration of deaths in the registration area; cf. Table 64, Note [a].

[b] For 1900–1902 and 1909–1911 from James W. Glover, *United States Life Tables: 1890, 1901, 1910, and 1901–1910,* the rates being for the original death-registration states; for 1915 to 1929 from current numbers of *Birth Statistics;* for 1930 and 1931 from multigraphed releases or letters from the Division of Vital Statistics, or preliminary estimates as in Note [a].

[c] Mexicans are classified as white, since their deaths are so classified by the Division of Vital Statistics.

[d] Includes the New England states, New York, New Jersey, District of Columbia, Indiana, and Michigan.

[e] Estimated on the assumption that the crude death rate of Negroes declined after 1929 at the same rate as that of the whites.

[f] Estimated on the assumption that the white and Negro infant mortality rates each declined 4.6 per cent from 1930 to 1931, as did the total rate.

to this influence, the heavy northward migration of Negroes since 1914[1] has tended to raise the crude rate because the higher death rates of northern states have come to apply to a larger proportion of the Negro population.

3. NUMBER OF DEATHS

Commencing about 1910 the death-registration area became sufficiently large and representative of the total and the white population of

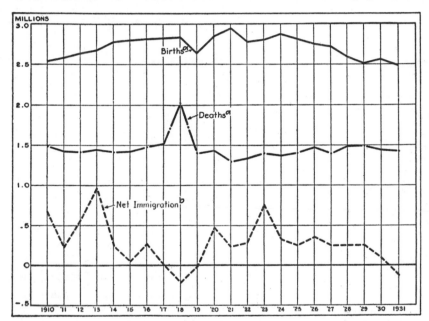

FIG. 27.—Annual births, deaths, and net immigration for the total population, 1910–1931.[c]
(Based on Tables 64, 75, and 84.)

[a] Contains allowance for estimated number of births and deaths not registered.
[b] The excess of aliens and citizens arriving in, over those departing from, continental United States.
[c] Preliminary estimates.

the United States to provide a basis for estimating the approximate number of deaths occuring each year in the entire nation. From 1910 to 1931 the number of deaths showed only a slight upward movement, the decrease in crude death rate having almost offset the growth of population[2] (Figure 27 and Table 64). Barring the influenza year of 1918, total deaths varied between a high of 1,501,000 in 1917 and a low of 1,294,000 in 1921, while in two-thirds of the years the variation was between 1,490,000 and 1,380,000. The holding of deaths so nearly constant while the population increased from under 92,000,000 to over 123,000,000 has

[1] *Supra*, pp. 75, 76.
[2] Excluding 1918, the straight-line secular trend of deaths calculated by the method of least squares moved upward at the rate of slightly less than 3,000 per year.

been a remarkable accomplishment. That it is not likely to continue is indicated by the fact that the average number of deaths per year rose from 1,372,000 during 1920–1925 to 1,453,000 during 1926–1931.[1]

White deaths have followed a course similar to that of total deaths since 1910, as would be expected in view of the great preponderance of

TABLE 64.—ESTIMATED NUMBER OF DEATHS IN THE UNITED STATES, BY RACE AND NATIVITY, 1910–1931[a]

(Thousands)

Year	Total	White[b]	Native white[b]	Foreign-born white[b]	Negro
1910	1,424	1,211	....	....	....
1911	1,369	1,160	....	....	....
1912	1,361	1,154	....	....	....
1913	1,402	1,190	....	....	....
1914	1,378	1,167	....	....	....
1915	1,389	1,171	....	....	....
1916	1,459	1,247	....	....	....
1917	1,501	1,267	....	....	....
1918	1,934	1,615	....	....	....
1919	1,394	1,186	....	....	....
1920	1,433	1,219	969	250	204
1921	1,294	1,103	873	230	183
1922	1,331	1,141	895	246	181
1923	1,403	1,196	936	260	198
1924	1,367	1,151	897	254	208
1925	1,406	1,181	919	262	216
1926	1,476	1,243	969	274	225
1927	1,397	1,179	916	263	210
1928	1,490	1,261	976	285	220
1929	1,494	1,266	983	283	220
1930	1,439	1,219[c]	947[c]	272[c]	212[c]
1931	1,424[c]	1,206[c]	937[c]	269[c]	210[c]
1932	1,361[c]	.....	....	....	....

[a] Prepared by the Scripps Foundation for Research in Population Problems from data in *Mortality Statistics* and the census of population on the assumptions (a) that 3 per cent of total deaths, 2 per cent of white deaths, and 8.6 per cent of Negro deaths occurring in the current registration area are not registered, and (b) that the crude death rate of the entire United States is the same as that of the current registration area with the above adjustment.

[b] Mexicans are classified as white, since their deaths are so classified by the Division of Vital Statistics.

[c] Preliminary estimate.

NOTE: Subtracting white deaths from total deaths during 1910–1919 will not give an equally accurate estimate of colored deaths. Neither will subtracting white and Negro deaths from total deaths during 1920–1931 give an equally accurate estimate of "other colored" deaths.

white persons in the population (Table 64). White deaths by nativity and Negro deaths cannot be estimated closely prior to 1920. Since that year deaths of native whites have fluctuated between 870,000 and 985,000

[1] Monthly reports on number of deaths from January to October, 1932, are available for eight states, mostly in the northeastern one-fourth of the United States, which contained 23.4 per cent of the population in 1930. They show 232,118 deaths, a decrease of 7,878, or 3.3 per cent from 1931.

with perhaps a slight movement upward. Deaths of foreign-born whites have risen more sharply because of the rapid increase in the average age of the foreign-born population. These deaths averaged 250,000 annually during 1920–1925 and 274,000 during 1926–1931. Negro deaths have varied between 180,000 and 225,000, with a small upward trend.[1]

4. SPECIFIC DEATH RATES OF WHITES

Crude death rates do not tell the exact story of mortality trends because they are influenced by changes in age composition as well as by

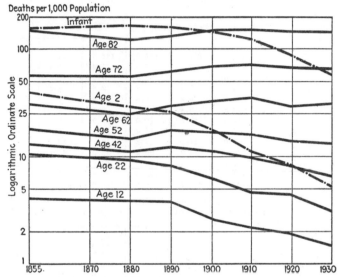

FIG. 27A.—Specific death rates, Massachusetts, 1855–1930. (Based on Table 65.)

changes in death rates at each age of life. Age changes have been large, an increasing proportion of the population being found in older age periods where death rates are high.[2] On this account, a more accurate idea of the trend of mortality can be had by examining specific death rates; that is, the deaths in a given age period divided by the population in that age period. These rates for the white population of Massachusetts show a rapid and consistent decline at most ages from 1855 to 1929 (Table 65 and Figure 27A). The largest absolute decrease took place under one year of age and exceeded 90 points, from 155.1 in 1855 to 61.6 in 1929. Over two-thirds of this reduction was brought about after 1909–1911. The largest relative decline in Table 65 occurred at age 2, the 1929

[1] The straight-line secular trend of deaths from 1920 to 1931 shows an increase per year of over 4,000 for native whites, 3,500 for foreign-born whites, and 2,500 for Negroes.

[2] *Supra*, pp. 140–143.

rate of 5.5 being less than one-seventh of the 1855 rate of 40.0. Here, however, the rapid decrease began as early as 1890. Present rates at most ages below 35 are less than one-third of the 1855 rates, and from 35 to 50 are less than two-thirds of the 1855 rates. Only a small decrease has occurred at ages from 50 to 60, however, while at 60 to 70 a decline since

TABLE 65.—SPECIFIC DEATH RATES OF THE WHITE POPULATION IN MASSACHUSETTS, 1855–1929 AND IN THE ORIGINAL DEATH-REGISTRATION STATES, 1900–1929[a]

Age	Deaths per 1,000 persons[b]						
	1855	1878–82	1890	1900–02	1909–11	1919–20	1929
MASSACHUSETTS							
0	155.1	167.0	157.9	145.3	125.3	88.7	61.8
2	40.0	29.4	26.6	17.2	11.3	8.6	5.5
7	7.2	7.8	6.8	4.3	3.3	3.0	2.1
12	4.1	3.9	3.8	2.6	2.2	1.9	1.5
17	8.9	6.9	6.4	4.3	3.3	3.2	2.3
22	10.8	9.4	8.3	6.1	4.7	4.5	3.2
32	12.0	10.1	10.0	7.9	6.8	6.5	4.4
42	13.3	11.2	12.4	11.1	9.8	8.1	6.8
52	18.0	14.9	17.6	17.1	16.1	14.1	13.5
62	30.6	24.9	29.2	33.0	35.1	29.2	31.0
72	57.5	55.8	61.0	68.8	71.2	68.0	65.8
82	153.1	124.0	133.0	147.2	151.4	146.5	148.5
92	297.2	260.2	314.3	292.0	281.2	267.9	....
ORIGINAL DEATH-REGISTRATION STATES[c]							
0	....	....	....	124.5	114.6	83.3	63.0
2	....	....	....	15.7	12.3	8.6	5.7
7	....	....	....	4.1	3.3	3.1	2.2
12	....	....	....	2.6	2.2	2.1	1.6
17	....	....	....	4.4	3.5	3.7	2.7
22	....	....	....	6.6	5.2	5.2	3.7
32	....	....	....	8.4	7.1	6.9	4.8
42	....	....	....	10.7	10.1	8.4	7.8
52	....	....	....	16.3	16.0	14.1	15.0
62	....	....	....	30.8	33.0	29.0	30.7
72	....	....	....	65.9	69.4	66.6	66.7
82	....	....	....	148.0	153.1	145.1	154.9
92	....	....	....	285.7	279.9	278.0	413.4

[a] From the following life tables:

1855—E. B. Elliott, *Proceedings of the American Association for the Advancement of Science*, eleventh meeting, 1857.

1878–1882—*Tenth Census of the United States: 1880*, Vol. XII.

1890, 1900–1902, and 1909–1911—James W. Glover, *United States Life Tables*.

1919–1920—Elbertie Foudray, *United States Abridged Life Tables*.

1929—From data furnished by Edgar Sydenstricker of the Milbank Memorial Fund.

Rates for 1919–1920 are for the white population only; all others are for the total population, which in these areas is so predominantly white that the rates are virtually white rates.

Weighted averages are used in combining life table data shown by sex.

[b] The rates are based on a life table population.

[c] Includes the New England states, New York, New Jersey, District of Columbia, Indiana, and Michigan.

1910 has not offset the increase that went on during preceding years. Rates at ages above 70 have fluctuated considerably but have shown little definite trend, though averaging somewhat higher in recent life tables than in earlier ones.

Trends of specific rates similar to those for Massachusetts are shown for the white population in the original death-registration states from 1900–1902 to 1929 (Table 65). Infant mortality has been reduced by over 60 points (from 124.5 to 63.0), which is by far the largest absolute decline in rates. The largest relative decrease shown in the table occurred at age 2, the 1929 rate of 5.7 being about one-third of the 1900–1902 rate. Important reductions also occurred up to age 40, becoming smaller with increasing age. Beyond age 40 there was either a slight improvement, or an increase in the death rate, the latter being especially noticeable from 1919–1920 to 1929.

It is plainly evident, therefore, that the large decline in the crude death rates has not come about through equal reductions in rates at all ages. The prevention of infant deaths has proved to be a much easier task than prolonging the life of older persons. In fact, the large gains in the early part of life have been offset to some extent by losses at the upper ages. During the next few decades greater effort probably will be centered on causes responsible for deaths of middle-aged and older adults with the result that these rates may be lowered considerably.[1] Two possible obstacles in this program should be mentioned, however. It may be that the reduction of infant and child mortality has postponed until middle life the deaths of weaklings that formerly would have occurred at an early age; carrying such persons through to a ripe old age may prove impossible. Secondly, it may be that the nerve-wracking pace of modern city life is too strenuous; hence breakdowns of the human machine on reaching the forties and fifties may occur with increasing frequency.[2]

Unless considerable progress is made in lowering death rates at older ages in the United States, a continuation of past trends in age composition with the consequent increase in the average age of the population will

---

[1] Increased attention also may be given children 1 to 4. "It is doubtless a fact that while there has been an increase in public health activities among children of all ages, those in the preschool group are not receiving, relatively, as much care and attention as the infants under one and the children of school age." Elizabeth Parkhurst, "Trends in Childhood Mortality in New York State (exclusive of New York City)" Albany, Division of Vital Statistics, New York State Department of Health. Paper read before the American Public Health Association at Montreal, September 17, 1931.

[2] Cf. R. Broda, "Must We Pay for Modern Living with Shortened Lives?" Social Forces, Vol. 7, No. 3 (March, 1929), pp. 403–406. For a discussion of the effect of mental strain on the death rate from heart disease, see Julien E. Benjamin, "Why the Increase in the Death Rate in Heart Disease in the Fifth and Sixth Decades of Life," Journal of Medicine, Cincinnati, Ohio, April, 1932. See also his "Some Present Day Ideas Concerning Heart Disease from the Public Health Point of View," Ohio State Medical Journal, December, 1932.

bring about a rise in the crude death rate.[1] The extent to which the age composition of the population has become less favorable from a mortality standpoint may be seen by applying the specific death rates of 1925–1929[2] to the 1900 and the 1930 populations. These specific rates give 10.6 deaths per 1,000 persons in 1900 as against 11.7 in 1930, the increase of 1.1, or over 10 per cent, resulting entirely fom the change in age composition that took place during the 30-year interval, chiefly the rise in the proportion of persons in the older ages. Changes in age composition are likely to occur at a more rapid rate in the future than in the past,[3] and specific death rates to decline more slowly;[4] hence it may not be many years before the declines in the latter are no longer sufficient to offset the effect on the crude death rate of changes in the former.

According to the "high" assumptions regarding the future, population growth will be so rapid, the decline in specific death rates so large, and the changes in age composition so small that the past decrease of the crude death rate will continue, although at a declining pace.[5] The crude rate for the total population will be lowered from about 11.5 in 1931[6] to 10.0 in 1960, after which it will be practically stationary. The "high" assumptions are quite optimistic, however. The moderate declines in specific death rates used in the "medium" assumptions, together with other differences, result in less future growth of population and a rising crude death rate after 1940. In this case there will be a decline from about 11.5 in 1931 to 11.3 in 1938, followed by a rise to 11.7 in 1950 and to 14.5 in 1980. If the "low" assumptions are realized, the bottom was reached by the crude death rate in 1931 or 1932, for the 1935 rate will be about 11.5, the 1950 rate 13.1, and the 1980 rate 17.5. It should be remembered that in all cases it is assumed that *specific* death rates will not rise after 1930 but will remain stationary at some ages and decline at others, the size and frequency of the declines being greatest in the "high" and least in the "low." Hence the upward course of the *crude* death rates in the "medium" and "low" populations results from the changes in age composition that will accompany such a slowing up of growth.

[1] *Cf.* Henry P. Fairchild, "The Influence of Population Change on Death Rates," Rome, Istituto Poligrafico dello Stato, 1931. (At head of title: Comitato Italiano per lo Studio dei Problemi della Popolazione.)

[2] These specific death rates are for native whites, foreign-born whites, and Negroes combined, computed from data on which Table 69 is based.

[3] *Supra*, pp. 106–118.

[4] *Infra*, pp. 257–261.

[5] The various assumptions for specific death rates are discussed on p. 260 and, together with those for immigration and specific birth rates, are shown in Table 88, Columns *A*, *H*, and *J*, p. 316.

[6] Based on the sources mentioned in Table 63 with the estimated allowance for non-registered deaths stated in Table 64.

5. EXPECTATION OF LIFE OF WHITES

The combined effect of the varying changes in mortality rates at different ages may be expressed conveniently by the expectation of life, which is the average number of years that persons of a stated age will live under given specific death rates. With the large declines of death rates in Massachusetts, the expectation of life at birth has been lengthened greatly, from 35.5 years in 1789 to 59.7 years[1] in 1929 (Figure 26 and Table 66). As in the case of crude death rates, the movement was much more rapid during the latter part of this interval than earlier, the increase averaging 0.8 years per decade from 1789 to 1890 as against 4.2 years per decade from 1890 to 1929. Since 1900–1902 the upward trend in Massachusetts has been a little sharper than in the original registration states, but since 1919 to 1920 it has been about the same as in the more extensive registration area of 1920 (Table 66).

The discussion of specific death rates brought out the fact that declines in rates at younger ages had been much larger than at older ages. The result of this is seen in comparing the increase in the expectation of life at birth with similar figures for later years of life. In Massachusetts the expectation of life at birth was lengthened by over 68 per cent from 1789 to 1929, at age 20 by 36 per cent, and at age 40 by 14 per cent, but at age 60 there was a decrease of nearly 5 per cent. Similar changes took place from 1900–1902 to 1929 in the original registration states, and after 1920 in the 1920 death-registration states. In the former area the expectation of life at birth increased by 18 per cent, at age 20 by 6 per cent, and at age 40 by 2 per cent, but decreased by 2 per cent at age 60. Changes in the latter area were much the same except for being smaller because of the shorter period for which rates are available.

The huge lengthening of the expectation of life at birth may well be a matter of national pride. But the impression should not be left with the reader that adults of any given age may expect to live many more years than could those of the same age in preceding generations. This is certainly not the case for persons who are much past 50, nor is more than a small increase in longevity probable for those in the thirties and forties.[2] The large gains in expectation of life have been achieved mainly by bringing many more infants safely through the dangerous early months, so

[1] These are averages of the values for males and females in Table 66.
[2] Cf, C. H. Forsyth, "The Decline in the Average Length of Life," *Science*, Vol. 70, No. 1804 (July 26, 1929), pp. 85–88. Dealing with males 10 years and over in the original death-registration states, Forsyth finds the expectation of life rose from 1920 to 1921, declined fairly steadily to 1926, then rose to 1927 (the latest year shown). In 1927 the expectation of life was lower than in 1920 at each age over about 12 to 14 (the exact age cannot be read from his graph). At ages 50 to 80 he finds the expectation of life higher in 1890 and 1900 than in any year from 1922 to 1927.

TABLE 66.—EXPECTATION OF LIFE, BY SEX, OF THE WHITE POPULATION AT SELECTED AGES IN MASSACHUSETTS, CERTAIN REGISTRATION STATES, THE UNITED STATES, AND NEW ZEALAND[a]

| Year | Average years of life remaining at age | | | | | | | |
| | 0 | | 20 | | 40 | | 60 | |
	Males	Females	Males	Females	Males	Females	Males	Females
MASSACHUSETTS[b]								
1789	34.5	36.5	34.2	34.3	25.2	26.9	14.8	16.1
1850	38.3	40.5	40.1	40.2	27.9	29.8	15.6	17.0
1855	38.7	40.9	39.8	39.9	27.0	28.8	14.4	15.6
1878–82	41.7	43.5	42.2	42.8	28.9	30.3	15.6	16.9
1890	42.5	44.5	40.7	42.0	27.4	28.8	14.7	15.7
1893–97	44.1	46.6	41.2	42.8	27.4	29.0	14.4	15.7
1900–02	46.1	49.4	41.8	43.7	27.2	28.8	13.9	15.1
1909–11	49.3	53.1	42.5	44.8	27.0	29.0	13.4	14.8
1919–20	54.1	56.6	44.6	45.5	28.8	30.0	14.4	15.4
1929	58.1	61.4	45.5	47.7	28.6	30.6	14.0	15 4
ORIGINAL DEATH-REGISTRATION STATES[b]								
1900–02	48.2	51.1	42.2	43.8	27.7	29.2	14.4	15.2
1909–11	50.2	53.6	42.7	44.9	27.4	29.3	14.0	14.9
1919–20	54.0	56.4	44.4	45.4	28.8	30.1	14.6	15.5
1929	56.8	60.4	44.4	46.8	27.8	30.1	13.9	15.1
1920 DEATH-REGISTRATION STATES[c]								
1920	52.9	55.1	44.3	44.8	29.1	29.9	14.7	15.4
1921–22	56.9	59.1	45.8	46.7	29.7	30.8	15.2	15.9
1923–26	56.6	59.2	44.7	46.1	28.5	30.0	14.2	15.2
1928–30	58.9		....	....	....	....	....	....
UNITED STATES (ESTIMATED)[d]								
"Medium":								
1940	62.7		48.6		31.8		16.2	
1950	64.7		49.8		32.3		16.3	
1960	65.7		50.5		32.7		16.4	
1970	66.0		50.7		32.8		16.4	
1980	66.0		50.7		32.8		16.4	
"High":								
1940	63.1		48.8		31.9		16.3	
1950	66.2		50.9		33.1		16.7	
1960	69.1		53.3		35.2		18.5	
1970	71.5		55.4		37.2		20.0	
1980	73.0		56.8		38.5		21.1	
"Low":								
1940	61.5		47.4		31.4		16.2	
1950	62.1		47.4		31.4		16.2	
1960	62.4		47.4		31.4		16.2	
1970–80	62.5		47.4		31.4		16.2	
NEW ZEALAND[e]								
1891–95	55.3	58.1	....	....	....	....	....	....
1901–05	58.1	60.5	46.7	48.2	30.3	32.0	15.4	16.6
1911–15	61.0	63.5	47.6	49.1	30.7	32.3	15.5	16.7
1921–22	62.8	65.4	48.7	50.4	31.6	33.2	16.0	17.3

[a] Data for 1919–1920, 1940, and future years are for the white population only; all others are for the total population, which in these cases is so predominantly white that the rates are virtually white rates. The data by sex for 1789 and 1855 are estimated by Edgar Sydenstricker from the life table data for both sexes. See *Recent Social Trends*, p. 605.

[b] From life tables listed in Tables 62 and 65, and the following: Kennedy, quoted in Metropolitan Life Insurance Company, *Statistical Bulletin*, Vol. 9, No. 3 (March, 1928). Samuel W. Abbott, *Thirtieth Annual Report of the State Board of Health for Massachusetts*.

[c] For 1920 to 1926 calculated from tables in Metropolitan Life Insurance Company, *Statistical Bulletin*, Vol. 4, No. 6; Vol. 5, No. 5; Vol. 6, No. 7; Vol. 7, No. 3; and Vol. 9, No. 2. For 1928–1930 furnished by Louis I. Dublin and Alfred J. Lotha "from advance information, drawn from a book prepared in this Bureau [the Statistical Bureau of the Metropolitan Life Insurance Company], the publication of which is planned some time this year [1933]."

[d] Prepared by the Scripps Foundation for Research in Population Problems according to assumptions discussed on p. 260 and shown in Table 88, Columns A, H, and J, p. 316.

[e] From *New Zealand Official Year Book*, 1914, 1927, 1931, and 1932.

that death may occur after the fiftieth birthday instead of before the first. In this event, over 50 years are added to life, which is five times as important in lengthening the expectation of life as postponing until 70 a death that in earlier decades would have occurred at 60. The small decreases in death rates at certain ages past 60 which have occurred in Massachusetts since 1789 have not been sufficient to offset the increases that have occurred at other ages and allow the expectation of life at age 60 to remain above the 1789 figure. But the large decreases in death rates at ages below 20 have been mainly responsible for lengthening the expectation of life at birth from 35.5 to 59.7.

6. REGIONAL DIFFERENTIALS IN MORTALITY OF WHITES

In view of the large differences between states in such matters as climate and country of origin of population, it might be expected that there would be corresponding differences in mortality. This possibility appears to be borne out by the crude death rate of the white population, which was below 8 per 1,000 in North Dakota and Oklahoma during 1930 but above 13 per 1,000 in Maine, New Hampshire, Vermont, Delaware, Arizona, and New Mexico—the lowest rate (7.8 in Oklahoma) being barely half the highest (15.5 in New Mexico). Crude death rates do not permit an accurate comparison, however, for they depend too much on the age composition of the population, which may differ widely from one state to another. An examination of the expectation of life at birth for the white population of various states shows much smaller differences, the shortest expectation of life (54.3 years in New York) being only 10 per cent below the longest (60.4 years in Kansas).[1] When states are grouped by divisions, it is found that the expectation of life is longest in the West North Central states (59.0 years) and shortest in the Middle Atlantic states (54.6 years) (Table 67). On the whole, the more industrialized the division and the higher the proportion of persons in urban centers the shorter the expectation of life; conversely, the more rural the division and the more dependent on agriculture the longer the expectation of life.

The rural-urban differential may be seen more definitely by comparing 14 large cities with 11 rural states, the expectation of life in 1919–1920 being 53.3 years in the former as against 58.6 years in the latter.[2] Still

[1] This discussion is based on *United States Abridged Life Tables: 1919–1920* because later tables have not yet been calculated for states by the Division of Vital Statistics. However, there is no apparent reason why life tables for 1930 would not show approximately the same differentials. It is possible, though not probable, that if states not covered by the 1919–1920 life tables could be included in this comparison, the lowest expectation of life might be 20 per cent below the highest.

[2] Comparisons of other areas would be preferable to show the rural-urban differentials in expectation of life but cannot be made because the necessary life tables are lacking.

TABLE 67.—EXPECTATION OF LIFE OF THE WHITE POPULATION AT SELECTED AGES IN CITIES, RURAL AREAS, AND DIVISIONS, 1900–1920

Year and area	Average years of life remaining at age[a]			
	0	20	40	60
1900–02:[b]				
Cities..	45.9	40.5	26.2	13.4
Rural parts......................................	54.7	46.0	30.9	15.9
1909–11:[b]				
Cities..	49.3	42.0	26.6	13.4
Rural parts......................................	56.2	46.4	30.7	15.6
1919–20:[c]				
14 large cities[d].................................	53.3	43.2	27.8	14.0
11 rural states[e].................................	58.6	46.6	31.4	16.3
Massachusetts and Connecticut...................	55.3	44.9	29.4	14.9
Middle Atlantic states...........................	54.6	44.0	28.8	14.6
East North Central states........................	57.0	46.0	30.6	15.7
Minnesota, Missouri, and Kansas.................	59.0	47.0	31.7	16.6
Maryland, Virginia, North Carolina, and South Carolina..	57.1	45.5	30.5	15.5
Kentucky and Tennessee..........................	58.1	46.2	31.4	16.3
Pacific states....................................	57.3	45.2	30.4	15.9

[a] In combining life table data shown by sex, weighted averages are used where needed.

[b] From James W. Glover, *United States Life Tables: 1890, 1901, 1910, and 1901–1910*, for the original registration states only; namely, New England States, New York, New Jersey, Indiana, Michigan, and District of Columbia.

[c] From Elbertie Foudray, *United States Abridged Life Tables: 1919–1920*. Data for ages 20, 40, and 60 estimated by interpolation.

[d] Baltimore, Boston, Buffalo, Chicago, Cleveland, Detroit, Los Angeles, New Orleans, New York, Philadelphia, Pittsburgh, St. Louis, San Francisco, and Washington, D.C.

[e] Includes all states in the Foudray life tables having more than 50 per cent of their population living in rural areas in 1920; namely, Wisconsin, Minnesota, Missouri, Kansas, Virginia, North Carolina, South Carolina, Kentucky, Tennessee, Utah, and Oregon.

larger rural-urban differentials occurred in the original registration states during earlier years. This is true in spite of the fact that cities of less than 10,000 were then classified as rural in the life tables and undoubtedly lowered the rural expectation of life.[1] During 1900–1902 the expectation of life at birth in the cities was 45.9, but in the "rural" area it was 54.7, or nearly one-fifth higher. During 1909–1911 the corresponding figures were 49.4 and 56.2, the "rural" expectation being one-seventh higher. Similar differentials between "rural" and urban expectation of life are found at older ages, usually being relatively larger at ages over 40 than at birth.

7. NEGRO MORTALITY

Some idea of the trend of mortality can be secured for white persons in the United States since 1789, but there was almost no accurate informa-

---

[1] In the census of population, cities and incorporated places of 2,500 or over and a few northeastern "towns" are classified as urban and the remainder of the population as rural.

tion for Negroes prior to 1900. Even the 1900–1902 life tables for Negroes were based on deaths in the original registration states only; hence were typical of that comparatively small proportion of the Negro population that was located in northeastern cities. It was not till the life tables of 1919–1920 that Negroes of the southern states, with a majority living in rural communities, were adequately represented.

Considering Negroes in the original registration states, the trend since 1900 is similar to that of the white population. The male expectation of life at birth increased rapidly, from 32.5 years in 1900–1902 to 40.4 years in 1919–1920 and the female from 35.0 to 42.4, with most of the improvement occurring after 1910 (Table 68). At ages 20, 40, and 60 no significant gains were made in the average length of life. The figures for 1909–1911 were lower in every case than those for 1900–1902, but those for 1919–1920 were either slightly above or below the 1900–1902 level. The increase in expectation of life at birth results from the rapid lowering of death rates at ages under 5. The Negro infant mortality rate was 132.8 in 1919–1920 compared with 234.1 in 1900–1902, a decline of 43 per cent. Similar progress was made in preventing deaths at ages 1 to 4. Mortality rates at ages 5 to 14 were somewhat lower in 1919–1920 than in 1900–1902; at ages 15 to 59 they were practically unchanged; at ages 60 to 75 they were higher; but again they were lower at older ages. These changes at age 5 and over practically balanced one another; hence little lengthening of life took place. The original registration states have contained only a small proportion of the Negro population, however, so that these trends may not be typical of those of the entire race.

In 1919–1920 the mortality status of Negroes was considerably more favorable in the southern than in the northern states. For males, the expectation of life at birth was 46.4 in the South compared with 40.5 in the North, the differential decreasing gradually up to about age 85, and northern values being larger at 87 and older. For females, the differential in favor of the South was smaller at birth, was reversed in favor of the North from about age 7 to 30 owing chiefly to lower death rates in the North during the childbearing period, but again favored the South from about age 30 to 80. These large regional differences may result in part from climate but are probably due in larger measure to the fact that in those years over 85 per cent of the Negroes in the northern states lived in cities, while in the southern states over 70 per cent lived in rural communities.

No official life tables have been computed for Negroes later than 1919–1920, hence it is impossible to state exactly what has happened since then. The crude death rate in 10 southern states[1] has remained practically

[1] These are Delaware, Maryland, Virginia, North Carolina, South Carolina, Florida, Kentucky, Tennessee, Mississippi, and Louisiana. No other southern states were in the death-registration area in 1920.

TABLE 68.—EXPECTATION OF LIFE OF NEGROES AT SELECTED AGES, BY SEX IN CERTAIN AREAS, 1900–1920[a]

| Year | Average years of life remaining at age | | | | | | | |
| | 0 | | 20 | | 40 | | 60 | |
	Male	Female	Male	Female	Male	Female	Male	Female
ORIGINAL REGISTRATION STATES[b]								
1900–02.....................	32.5	35.0	35.1	36.9	23.1	24.4	12.6	13.6
1909–11.....................	34.0	37.7	33.5	36.1	21.6	23.3	11.7	12.8
1919–20.....................	40.4	42.4	35.7	36.4	23.5	23.7	12.3	12.9
16 NORTHERN STATES[c]								
1919–20.....................	40.5	42.8	35.7	36.5	23.8	24.0	12.9	13.3
7 SOUTHERN STATES[d]								
1919–20.....................	46.4	45.5	38.0	35.9	26.5	25.1	14.8	14.7
12 LARGE CITIES[e]								
1919–20.....................	38.4	40 6	34.3	34.9	22.0	22.4	11.6	12.7

[a] From James W. Glover, *United States Life Tables: 1890, 1901, 1910, and 1901–1910*; and Elbertie Foudray, *United States Abridged Life Tables: 1919–1920*. In 1919–1920 data for ages 20, 40, and 60 estimated by interpolation.

[b] New England states, New York, New Jersey, Indiana, Michigan, and District of Columbia.

[c] Massachusetts, Connecticut, New York, New Jersey, Pennsylvania, Ohio, Indiana, Illinois, Michigan, Wisconsin, Minnesota, Kansas, Utah, Washington, Oregon, and California.

[d] Missouri, Maryland, Virginia, North Carolina, South Carolina, Kentucky, and Tennessee. Missouri is in the West North Central division, but was included by Miss Foudray with southern states instead of northern because Negroes constituted more than 5 per cent of the population in 1920.

[e] Baltimore, Boston, Buffalo, Chicago, Cleveland, Detroit, New Orleans, New York, Philadelphia, Pittsburgh, St. Louis, and Washington, D.C

stationary (16.6 per 1,000 in 1920 and 16.4 in 1930) and in 10 northern states[1] has declined about 15 per cent (from 20.9 in 1920 to 17.7 in 1929[2]). But this may have been due in part to age changes as well as to changes in specific death rates. The infant mortality rate of Negroes declined from 129 to 110 in southern states from 1920 to 1930 and from 161 to 106 in northern states from 1920 to 1929. Evidently the public health movement made much progress during the last decade in reducing Negro infant mortality, particularly in northern cities. The result should be an increase

[1] These are Massachusetts, New York, New Jersey, Pennsylvania, Ohio, Illinois, Indiana, Michigan, Missouri, and Kansas. No other northern state had over 40,000 Negroes in 1920.

[2] Negro death rates for northern states after 1929 and for southern states after 1930 had not been published by the Division of Vital Statistics at time of writing (September, 1932).

in the expectation of life at birth in both regions and a narrowing of the differential between the North and the South. Considering the Negro population as a whole, however, it is doubtful if the expectation of life was as long in 1930 as in 1920. Specific death rates of Negroes in the 1920 death-registration states were lower at most ages in 1920–1924 than in 1925–1929, indicating a decrease in average longevity (Table 69). Part of this change probably resulted from the northward migration of Negroes between 1920 and 1930, the proportion of the Negro population exposed to the higher Negro death rates of northern states being much larger in 1930 than in 1920.[1]

8. RACE AND NATIVITY DIFFERENTIALS

Although differentials between mortality rates of whites and Negroes may be smaller than they were several decades ago, they have been fairly large during recent years. At younger ages the white rates are lower, but at ages above 80 the Negro rates are lower[2] (Table 69). The largest absolute difference is in the infant mortality rate, that of Negroes in 1925–1929 being 106.3, over 40 points above the white rate of 65.2. Relative differences are largest from about 15 to 60, the Negro death rates at these ages being over twice those of whites. Although there may be several reasons for this condition, probably the most important is the superior economic and educational status of the white race. With more money to spend for such things as food, clothing, housing, and medical attention, and greater knowledge about matters of health and sanitation, it is natural that white death rates should be lower. Such a small part of the population is over 80 years of age that the lower Negro rates at these ages do not count for much. Probably selection has been more rigorous at younger ages for Negroes than whites; hence those who survive to a ripe old age have unusual vitality.[3]

The combined effect of differentials in mortality rates at all ages may be shown by the crude death rate, the standardized death rate, or the expectation of life. The crude death rate of Negroes was 16.6 and of

[1] *Supra*, pp. 74–80.

[2] Negro death rates probably are less accurate than white rates because of less accurate age data and less complete death registration.

[3] See also the following: Forrest Clements, "Racial Differences in Mortality and Morbidity," *Human Biology*, Vol. 3, No. 3 (September, 1931), pp. 397–419. Mary Gover, "Mortality among Negroes in the United States," U. S. Public Health Service, Public Health Bulletin 174, Washington, Government Printing Office, 1928. S. J. Holmes, "Differential Mortality in the American.Negro," *Human Biology*, Vol. 3, No. 1 (February, 1931), pp. 71–106; "Differential Mortality in the American Negro," *Human Biology*, Vol. 3, No. 2 (May, 1931), pp. 203–244. Eldridge Sibley, "Differential Mortality in Tennessee," Nashville, Fisk University Press, 1930, 152 pp. Amanda L. Stoughton and Mary Gover, "A Study of Negro Infant Mortality," Washington, Government Printing Office, 1929 (Reprint No. 1331 from *Public Health Reports*, Vol. 44, No. 45 (November 8, 1929), pp. 2705–2731).

TABLE 69.—DEATH RATES IN THE 1920 REGISTRATION STATES, BY AGE, BY RACE AND NATIVITY, 1920–1924 AND 1925–1929[a]

Age period	Annual deaths per 1,000[b]					
	Native white[c]		Foreign-born white[c]		Negro	
	1920–24	1925–29	1920–24	1925–29	1920–24	1925–29
0–4	22.4	18.9	28.0[d]	14.7[d]	37.1	34.4
0–1	73.6	65.2			118.4	106.3
5–9	2.5	2.1	3.3	2.9	3.0	2.8
10–14	1.8	1.6	2.5	2.1	3.1	2.9
15–19	2.9	2.5	3.9	3.4	7.5	7.4
20–24	3.8	3.4	4.6	4.2	10.9	10.8
25–29	4.3	3.7	5.0	4.1	11.3	11.9
30–34	4.9	4.3	5.7	5.1	12.4	13.4
35–39	5.5	5.1	6.6	6.0	13.3	14.6
40–44	6.8	6.6	8.5	9.2	17.1	19.6
45–49	8.5	8.6	10.5	11.2	18.6	22.0
50–54	12.0	12.5	14.3	14.5	25.6	31.5
55–59	16.8	18.4	21.6	21.9	32.4	39.7
60–64	25.2	24.7	31.8	34.9	37.6	43.7
65–69	39.9	41.9	44.6	48.1	50.8	58.8
70–74	61.0	65.4	67.2	63.1	72.8	76.8
75–79	92.3	97.3	102.1	104.5	94.8	107.2
80–84	146.2	152.3	159.2	167.2	144.0	156.9
85–89	205.8	215.9	222.7	235.8	171.1	168.6
90–94	298.3	310.1	322.7	329.1	217.5	181.8
95+	335.8	342.4	344.4	365.8	281.8	275.4
All ages:						
Crude	10.4	10.1	17.2	18.6	16.6	17.7
Standardized[e]	10.7	10.3	12.8	11.3	18.2	19.4

[a] Deaths by age are from current *Mortality Statistics*. The population by age on July 1, 1922, and July 1, 1927, is estimated by straight-line interpolation between the 1920 and 1930 censuses. No allowance is made for underenumeration of children.

[b] One-fifth of the deaths during five years divided by the mid-point population gives the rates shown, except that 0 to 1 is the average of infant mortality rates in current numbers of *Birth Statistics*.

[c] Mexicans are included with whites, their deaths being so classified by the Division of Vital Statistics.

[d] Because of the interval between date of birth and date of arrival in the United States the rate for foreign-born whites in this age period is not comparable with those for native whites and Negroes.

[e] Standardized to the age composition of the United States population in 1920.

foreign-born whites was 17.2 during 1920–1924, or 60 per cent above the native white rate of 10.4. During 1925–1929 the latter rate was slightly lower, but rates for Negroes and foreign-born whites were higher. The effect of an unfavorable age composition is well illustrated here by the foreign-born white group. The standardized death rate of foreign-born whites was about two-thirds that of Negroes in both periods and less than one-fifth above that of native whites, quite different from the relative standing of the crude rates. Owing to the aging of the foreign born from 1920–1924 to 1925–1929, the crude rate rose 1.4; but the standardized

[246]

rate, which is not affected by age changes, declined 1.5 because of decreases in a majority of the specific death rates. Negro age composition varied but little from 1920–1924 to 1925–1929; hence the standardized death rate rose about the same as the crude, increasing the large spread between whites and Negroes. According to the 1919–1920 life tables the expectation of life at birth was 56.4 years for whites in the entire area included, compared with 45.9 for Negroes in the seven southern states, which at that time were typical of the bulk of the Negro population.[1] This was an advantage of 10.5 years, or over 20 per cent in favor of the white race. Practically the same relative differential held at ages 20 and 40, but at age 60 the average years of life remaining were 15.5 for whites and 14.7 for Negroes, only a 5 per cent difference in favor of the former.

Differences between specific death rates of native and of foreign-born whites are small numerically during the first third of the life span. After age 40 the rates of foreign-born whites are above those of native whites, the numerical difference increasing rapidly as age rises, but the relative difference remaining at about 10 per cent in most cases (Table 69). Higher specific death rates of foreign-born whites as compared with native whites are attributable in part to differences in educational and economic status, as in the case of Negroes compared with all whites. In addition, the proportion of foreign-born whites in cities is larger than that of native whites; hence the higher urban death rates bear more heavily on the former.[2]

When the first and last half of the 1920 decade are compared, the trend of specific death rates of native and foreign-born whites are seen to be similar. At ages 5 to 40 there was a small decline for both nativity groups, but at older ages there were increases in most cases.

9. CAUSE OF DEATH

So far the discussion of mortality has dealt with deaths from all causes. To understand better how rates have been lowered in the past and to provide a broader basis for judging what may occur in the future, some of the more important causes of death will be considered separately.

The large decline in the crude mortality rate previously discussed has been accompanied by decreases in rates from many causes of death. A few diseases have been largely controlled, perhaps because of the perfecting of modes of treatment or because of special public health campaigns directed against them. At the other extreme are a few causes where no progress has been made and the mortality rate has risen. Comparing

---

[1] Elbertie Foudray, *United States Abridged Life Tables, 1919–1920*.

[2] Similarly, the percentage of employed persons who are in the occupations having greater health hazards is considerably higher among foreign-born than native whites.

1926–1930 with 1900–1904, the largest decreases (over 80 per 100,000) have been brought about in deaths from diarrhea and enteritis (chiefly of infants and young children) and from tuberculosis (Figure 28 and Table 70). The 1926–1930 rate for diarrhea and enteritis is less than one-fourth of the 1900–1904 rate, while the rate for tuberculosis (all forms) is barely 40 per cent of the former figure. A large absolute decrease (65.1 per 100,000) has been secured in the rate from influenza and pneumonia; nevertheless the 1926–1930 rate is nearly 60 per cent that of 1900–1904. Notable progress has also been made in preventing deaths from typhoid

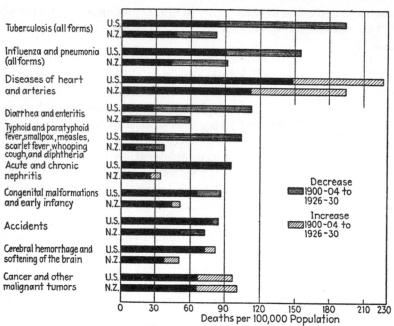

FIG. 28.—Death rates by important causes, United States and New Zealand, 1900–1904 and 1926–1930. (Based on Table 70.)

fever, diphtheria, and meningitis, the mortality for each of these causes having been reduced more than 25 per 100,000, so that in 1926–1930 each rate was less than one-fourth of the 1900–1904 figure. Smaller reductions have been made in death rates from a number of other causes, which together have far more than offset the increases that have occurred, chiefly from cancer, diseases of the heart and arteries, cerebral hemorrhage, and diabetes mellitus. With syphilis and related causes (locomotor ataxia and general paralysis of the insane) there was a marked rise in the death rate from 12.8 during 1900–1904 to 18.2 during 1915–1920, followed by a steady drop to 14.6 during 1926–1930.

TABLE 70.—DEATH RATES BY IMPORTANT CAUSES OF DEATH IN THE CURRENT REGISTRATION AREA, 1900 TO 1930, IN KANSAS AND WISCONSIN, 1926 TO 1930 AND IN NEW ZEALAND, 1900 TO 1904 AND 1926 TO 1930

Cause	Deaths per 100,000 persons								
	Current registration area[a]						Kansas and Wisconsin[a]	New Zealand[b]	
	1900–04	1905–09	1910–14	1915–20 (excl. 1918)	1921–25	1926–30	1926–30	1900–04	1926–30
Typhoid and paratyphoid fever	33.7	26.8	18.9	11.2	7.6	5.2	2.0	8.7	1.1
Malaria	5.6	2.9	2.6	3.2	2.9	2.9	0.2	....	(c)
Smallpox	3.7	0.3	0.3	0.4	0.6	0.2	0.1	0.1	(c)
Measles	10.0	9.8	9.8	8.7	6.0	4.7	3.2	7.5	0.8
Scarlet fever	11.8	9.5	8.5	3.7	3.0	2.2	2.7	5.2	1.8
Whooping cough	11.2	11.4	10.5	9.4	7.9	6.5	4.1	10.5	3.3
Meningitis	33.0	23.9	11.4	7.2	1.1	2.7	2.7	0.7	4.1
Diphtheria	33.6	23.0	19.1	15.4	12.3	6.8	3.7	5.3	5.0
Influenza and pneumonia (excl. bronchopneumonia)	155.2	123.7	99.8	131.9	82.7	90.1	75.4	92.4	43.3
Tuberculosis of the respiratory system and acute disseminated tuberculosis	173.3	153.3	132.8	118.8	82.5	71.2	43.9	73.9	39.6
Other forms of tuberculosis	21.2	22.6	20.0	16.2	10.4	7.8	6.8	23.5	9.2
Syphilis, locomotor ataxia, and general paralysis of the insane	12.8	13.5	16.1	18.2	16.1	14.6	5.0	1.8	....
Cancer and other malignant tumors	66.2	71.3	77.3	81.9	88.9	96.0	104.6	65.8	100.1
Diabetes mellitus	10.9	13.3	15.3	16.5	17.2	18.5	19.8	10.0	13.5
Cerebral hemorrhage and softening of the brain	72.6	73.9	77.2	81.8	84.2	81.9	95.3	37.5	50.0
Diseases of the heart	139.8	152.1	158.2	162.4	171.4	205.4	186.1	103.2	171.7
Diseases of the arteries	8.1	15.6	23.7	23.6	22.6	21.9	19.6	9.1	22.7
Bronchitis and bronchopneumonia	69.8	66.0	66.9	65.6	50.3	43.1	36.4	39.2	37.3
Diarrhea and enteritis[d]	112.7	112.8	92.5	68.1	40.8	27.6	19.0	59.7	6.7
Appendicitis and typhlitis	10.5	11.3	11.8	12.6	14.6	15.2	16.6	....	7.1
Hernia, intestinal obstruction[e]	12.7	13.2	11.9	11.0	10.6	10.6	10.4	10.1	7.6
Cirrhosis of the liver	14.0	14.5	13.6	10.3	7.3	7.3	7.2	5.8	3.3
Acute and chronic nephritis	93.9	98.4	101.1	99.2	89.5	93.7	76.2	25.8	34.5
Puerperal septicemia and other puerperal causes	13.9	15.3	15.7	16.9	15.6	13.6	11.6	3.2	9.5
Early infancy and malformations	86.5	90.3	94.1	88.6	78.1	65.7	64.4	44.2	51.1
Senility	43.9	31.5	22.9	15.9	12.8	11.1	16.1	58.8	45.9
Suicide	13.0	16.0	16.1	13.2	12.0	13.9	14.8	12.3	13.9
Homicide	2.4	5.6	6.7	7.3	8.4	8.8	3.6	0.4	0.9
Automobile accidents[f]	} 83.8 {	0.6	3.0	8.4	14.3	21.2	18.7	} 72.5	51.8
Other accidents[f]		86.4	80.2	70.1	59.3	58.4	54.1		
All causes	1,650.4	1,536.9	1,415.5	1,355.6	1,181.8	1,180.1	1,056.8	994.5	859.8

[a] From *Mortality Statistics, 1910; Mortality Rates, 1910–1920;* current numbers of *Mortality Statistics,* 1921 to 1929; and multigraphed tables of the Division of Vital Statistics, 1930.

[b] From *New Zealand Official Year Book.* Acute disseminated tuberculosis is included with other forms of tuberculosis.

[c] Less than 0.05 per 100,000.

[d] Includes ulcer of the duodenum, from 1900 to 1920.

[e] Includes adhesions of intestines, from 1900 to 1920.

[f] Deaths from collision of automobiles with railroad trains and street cars are included in other accidents.

It should be pointed out that some of the differences between the 1900–1904 and 1926–1930 rates are due to differences in classification as to cause of death. For example, the decrease of 32.8 in the death rate from senility from 1900–1904 to 1926–1930 is almost entirely the result of stating more accurately the real cause of death. This has meant increases in the rate from certain other causes, especially chronic myocarditis. It is unlikely, however, that improvement in classification is of great importance in accounting for the changes in rates for most of the causes above discussed. The fact that 36 states were added to the death-registration area between 1904 and 1930 is also responsible for part of the changes in rates. Fifteen per cent of the reduction in the death rate from all causes in the current registration area from 1900–1904 to 1926–1930 was due to additions to the area (Table 63), but the difference may have been somewhat larger for certain causes, and smaller, or even in the opposite direction, for others. The change in area should not reverse the trends for most causes, however.

A more exact comparison of the progress made in preventing deaths from various causes can be had from rates by cause of death by age periods. As pointed out in Chapter IV there were important changes in age composition from 1900 to 1930, particularly a decrease in the proportion of children and an increase in the proportion of elders. The former has exaggerated the decline in the death rate of the entire population for causes confined chiefly to infants, while the latter has minimized the decline or exaggerated the increase for causes affecting older persons mostly.

An examination of rates by important causes of death for different age periods in the 1900 death-registration states shows that in the majority of cases the trend in each age period from 1900 to 1928 is similar to that for the population as a whole, differences being in degree rather than in direction (Table 71). The death rate from influenza, pneumonia, and tuberculosis decreased most rapidly at the younger and older ages rather than in middle life. With cancer and diabetes mellitus the rate went up at most ages, the relative rise becoming increasingly larger in the older age groups. Few people under 45 died from cerebral hemorrhage and softening of the brain in 1900 or in 1928; but in these years the rate at ages 45 to 54 decreased, while the rate at ages over 75 increased by nearly one-half. Somewhat similar changes took place in death rates from diseases of the heart; the rate for all ages nearly doubled, for ages under 45 there was little change, but for ages over 75 the rate rose to 2.6 times the 1900 figure. Part of the rise in rates at older ages from this cause, however, is due to the ascribing to chronic myocarditis of deaths formerly ascribed to old age. With nephritis there were large relative decreases in the death rate at ages below 55, but an increase of about 50 per cent in the

65-and-over age group as a whole. Accidental deaths have become comparatively less numerous at ages under 45, but at ages above 55 there have been increases of one-third to three-fourths.[1]

TABLE 71.—DEATH RATES PER 100,000 PERSONS BY AGE BY IMPORTANT CAUSES OF DEATH IN THE ORIGINAL DEATH-REGISTRATION STATES, 1900 AND 1928[a]

Cause of death	Year	0–4	5–14	15–24	25–34	35–44	45–54	55–64	65–74	75+	All ages
Influenza and pneumonia (excluding bronchopneumonia)	1900	511	34	47	74	110	171	311	656	1,585	179
	1928	162	19	28	43	70	98	158	289	745	86
Tuberculosis (all forms)	1900	146	36	208	292	257	219	220	259	262	194
	1928	45	13	85	101	92	97	99	96	89	75
Cancer and other malignant tumors	1900	4	2	4	15	55	144	270	429	565	66
	1928	5	2	5	16	62	185	421	782	1,204	117
Diabetes mellitus	1900	2	3	4	5	7	17	39	68	68	11
	1928	1	2	3	3	8	28	95	182	198	24
Cerebral hemorrhage and softening of the brain	1900	35	3	5	11	30	94	240	584	1,356	77
	1928	3	1	2	5	19	80	261	727	1,994	95
Diseases of the heart	1900	43	23	29	44	82	177	417	900	1,800	137
	1928	18	19	28	42	96	262	683	1,767	4,712	260
Diseases of the arteries	1900	.....	...	...	...	3	6	16	42	103	5
	1928	.....	...	...	1	4	13	49	189	1,060	31
Bronchitis and bronchopneumonia	1900	376	8	5	7	11	23	70	204	659	68
	1928	274	7	5	8	13	22	52	143	585	50
Acute and chronic nephritis	1900	29	12	23	45	83	145	274	485	773	89
	1928	6	4	9	17	42	108	259	618	1,626	95
Accidents	1900	87	38	54	63	79	81	92	132	320	72
	1928	72	47	53	53	65	90	122	197	564	79
All causes	1900	4,995	387	587	817	1,037	1,516	2,725	5,672	14,098	1,719
	1928	1,956	204	315	439	679	1,267	2,610	5,632	14,258	1,231

[a] Deaths by age from *Mortality Statistics* for 1900 and 1928, the report for 1929 being received after the table was prepared (September, 1932). Population by age for 1900 from the 1900 census, for 1928 estimated by straight-line interpolation between the census populations of 1920 and 1930.

The frequency with which death rates from these important causes have increased at the older ages helps to explain why death rates from all causes declined so little or even increased during the latter part of life.

[1] For a discussion of death rates by cause of death by age for adult males and females, see Dorothy G. Wiehl, "Some Recent Changes in the Mortality among Adults," *Journal of Preventive Medicine*, Vol. 4, No. 3 (May, 1930), pp. 215–237.

10. INFANT MORTALITY BY CAUSE OF DEATH

In contrast with the increases or small decreases in death rates after middle life are the large decreases that occurred in early life, particularly among infants. These merit special consideration by cause of death. Deaths of infants under one by cause of death per 1,000 births have been published for the birth-registration states since 1917 and can be computed

TABLE 72.—INFANT MORTALITY RATES BY CAUSE OF DEATH IN THE ORIGINAL DEATH-REGISTRATION STATES, 1900 AND 1910, AND IN THE CURRENT BIRTH-REGISTRATION AREA, 1917–1929[a]

Cause of death	Deaths per 1,000 births						
	1900	1910	1917	1920	1923	1926	1929
Measles..	1.3	1.3	1.2	1.0	1.2	1.1	0.3
Scarlet fever..	0.3	0.3	0.1	0.1	0.1	0.1	0.1
Whooping cough......................................	2.8	2.6	2.4	3.0	2.4	2.3	1.9
Diphtheria[b]...	0.8	0.8	0.5	0.5	0.4	0.2	0.2
Influenza and pneumonia.............................	11.5	6.5	5.0	5.9	5.1	5.3	5.9
Meningitis...	5.8	2.0	0.8	0.6	0.1	0.1	0.3
Tuberculosis (all forms).............................	2.7	2.3	1.5	1.0	0.8	0.6	0.4
Syphilis..	0.7	1.2	1.2	0.9	0.8	0.6	0.8
Convulsions..	7.5	2.8	1.1	1.0	0.7	0.6	0.4
Bronchitis and bronchopneumonia....................	10.3	13.3	10.5	9.6	8.8	8.8	7.0
Diseases of the stomach[c]...........................	2.3	2.3	1.2	1.2	0.8	0.5	0.4
Diarrhea and enteritis[c].............................	39.5	37.4	20.0	14.9	11.5	9.7	7.1
Congenital malformations............................	4.5	6.3	6.3	6.2	6.3	6.2	5.5
Congenital debility and other diseases of early infancy[d]..............	16.3	10.9	8.8	7.7	6.5	5.5	4.7
Premature birth......................................	13.2	18.4	19.1	19.4	17.8	17.7	17.5
Injuries at birth.....................................	1.6	3.5	3.8	3.7	4.6	4.9	4.8
Unknown or ill defined..............................	10.3	5.2	2.9	2.5	2.4	2.3	3.8
All other causes.....................................	14.2	11.2	7.4	6.7	6.7	6.9	6.5
All causes...	145.7	128.2	93.8	85.8	77.1	73.3	67.6

[a] For 1900 and 1910 births are estimated from James W. Glover, *United States Life Tables, 1890, 1901, 1910, and 1901–1910*, pp. 428 and 452; deaths are from current *Mortality Statistics*. For 1917 to 1929, rates are from current numbers of *Birth Statistics*.

[b] Includes croup from 1910 to 1920.

[c] Ulcer of the duodenum included with diarrhea and enteritis from 1917 to 1920, but with diseases of the stomach in other years.

[d] For 1917 to 1929 includes causes numbered 160, 162, and 163 in the *Detailed International List*.

for 1900 and 1910 for the states in the Glover life tables. Infant mortality from all causes dropped from 145.7 in 1900 to 93.8 in 1917 and to 67.6 in 1929[1] (Table 72). The greatest improvement occurred in the rate from diarrhea and enteritis, which was lowered steadily from 39.5 in 1900 to 7.1 in 1929. This is a decrease of about 82 per cent, practically the same as the decrease achieved from this cause in the population of all ages. The

[1] Infant deaths by cause for 1930 had not been published by the Division of Vital Statistics at time of writing (December, 1932).

second largest decrease was in the death rate from congenital debility,[1] which fell from 16.3 in 1900 to 4.7 in 1929. Progress in the prevention of infant deaths from influenza and pneumonia was important early in the century, this death rate per 1,000 births having been lowered from 11.5 in 1900 to 5.0 in 1917, with little change since then except for a high point during the epidemic of 1918. Infant deaths from meningitis have been almost eliminated, the rate being 0.3 in 1929 compared with 5.8 in 1900. These four causes account for nearly three-fourths of the total reduction in infant mortality rate.[2] Small declines have occurred in rates for most other causes of death from 1900 to 1929. The chief exceptions are rates for malformations, injuries at birth, and premature birth. The last named rose from 13.2 in 1900 to 19.4 in 1920, since when it has dropped to 17.5 in 1929. During recent years it has been the highest, replacing the rates for diarrhea and enteritis, which formerly stood at the top.

The best chances for decreasing infant mortality still more would seem to be through further control of diarrhea and enteritis, and of bronchitis, bronchopneumonia, influenza, and pneumonia. Losses due to premature birth are nearly as large as from all of these combined but may be less subject to human control except as further spread of modern knowledge regarding birth control may check pregnancies among women subject to premature delivery.[3]

11. URBAN-RURAL DEATH RATES BY CAUSE OF DEATH

Earlier in this chapter it was pointed out that death rates were higher and expectation of life shorter in urban than in rural communities. When particular causes of death are considered, it is found that urban rates are much higher than rural in some cases, but considerably lower in others.[4] Furthermore, with certain causes the differential has been narrowing during this century, while with others it has been widening.

In considering the size and trend of these differentials, allowance needs to be made for several factors. In the first place, deaths by cause of death are tabulated by the Division of Vital Statistics according to the place of occurrence of death, not by place of residence of the decedents. Chiefly because the medical and hospital facilities of cities usually are superior to those of villages and the open country, there are more deaths

[1] Includes *Detailed International List* Nos. 160, 162, and 163 from 1917 to 1929.

[2] The proportion of the total decline due to control of these four causes is really larger, since the rate from "convulsions" and "unknown and ill defined" causes was lowered from 17.8 in 1900 to 4.2 in 1929 chiefly by more accurate classification as to cause of death.

[3] See also Robert Morse Woodbury, *Causal Factors in Infant Mortality*, U. S. Children's Bureau, Publication 142, Washington, Government Printing Office, 1925.

[4] In classifying deaths prior to 1931 the Division of Vital Statistics used two groups: (a) cities of 10,000 and over, and (b) smaller cities and rural areas. This urban-rural classification is followed here.

TABLE 73.—DEATH RATES BY IMPORTANT CAUSES OF DEATH IN CITIES AND RURAL PARTS OF THE CURRENT REGISTRATION STATES, 1900–1929[a]

Cause	Deaths per 100,000 persons											
	1900–04		1905–09		1910–14		1915–20 (excluding 1918)		1921–25		1926–29	
	Cities	Rural parts	Cities	Rural parts	Cities	Rural parts	Cities	Rural parts	Cities	Rural parts	Cities	Rural parts
Typhoid and paratyphoid fever	25.9	27.7	25.8	24.0	17.2	19.8	8.7	13.3	4.9	9.9	3.1	7.0
Malaria	3.8	4.7	1.5	2.3	1.0	3.1	0.8	4.9	0.7	4.8	0.6	4.9
Smallpox	3.4	1.5	0.2	0.2	0.2	0.3	0.2	0.4	0.8	0.4	0.2	0.2
Measles	11.9	7.6	12.3	7.5	10.9	8.9	9.0	8.5	6.3	5.8	5.0	5.1
Scarlet fever	15.6	7.0	12.0	6.3	10.1	5.8	4.1	3.0	4.0	3.4	2.3	2.2
Whooping cough	12.0	9.0	11.5	11.2	9.8	11.4	8.7	10.2	7.0	8.7	5.8	7.8
Diphtheria (including croup)	43.0	20.1	28.5	16.9	21.9	15.0	18.3	12.0	13.7	11.2	8.5	6.1
Influenza and pneumonia (all forms)	214.4	146.7	185.0	132.5	165.8	119.8	202.2	162.2	136.4	115.0	144.6	124.4
Tuberculosis (all forms)	216.1	145.4	198.4	135.8	168.9	128.5	145.3	121.4	94.1	90.9	81.5	78.8
Syphilis, locomotor ataxia, and general paralysis of the insane	13.7[b]	12.1[b]	14.7[b]	11.7[b]	17.7	13.2	20.7	15.0	18.3	14.0	16.9	12.6
Cancer	69.9	64.5	77.3	65.6	85.2	68.7	95.2	69.4	107.6	72.8	118.2	76.4
Diabetes mellitus	12.6	11.7	14.9	12.8	17.3	13.5	19.6	13.8	21.2	13.9	23.4	14.0
Cerebral hemorrhage and apoplexy	74.3	77.0	74.1	78.4	74.4	79.2	80.0	82.7	82.2	85.3	78.4	84.3
Diseases of the heart	147.8	147.0	161.5	152.9	168.9	146.2	180.4	146.0	196.9	151.0	238.3	174.6
Diseases of the arteries	8.6	5.8	17.8	12.6	25.9	21.5	25.1	22.6	24.1	21.4	23.8	20.6
Diarrhea and enteritis (all ages)[c]	141.0	80.0	133.4	88.9	103.7	73.5	74.2	57.5	40.4	40.5	24.4	30.0
Cirrhosis of the liver	16.2	9.4	17.0	10.3	16.1	10.0	12.2	·7.9	8.8	6.0	9.5	5.5
Acute and chronic nephritis and Bright's disease	112.7	69.5	116.0	73.0	115.9	79.4	113.3	83.5	100.4	79.8	105.2	84.6
Puerperal septicemia and other puerperal causes	14.7	12.1	16.7	13.5	16.9	13.8	18.0	15.4	17.4	13.9	15.7	11.8
Early infancy and malformations[d]	103.4	65.6	106.2	74.6	104.4	84.1	96.4	81.8	85.1	72.0	73.3	60.9
Senility	33.8	59.0	23.6	41.1	16.0	30.6	9.2	22.5	6.5	18.5	5.4	15.9
Suicide	12.4	9.0	17.0	12.0	18.7	12.3	15.6	10.5	14.6	9.6	16.6	10.6
Homicide	1.6	0.7	4.6	3.3	6.7	4.5	8.1	5.3	9.7	6.7	10.2	7.0
Automobile accidents[e] }	85.2	71.1 }	1.2[f]	0.4[f]	4.1	1.8	11.5	5.3	19.0	9.9	25.4	15.9
Other accidents[e] }			85.7	85.8	80.7	79.4	72.2	67.2	60.7	58.3	61.4	56.7

[a] From current numbers of *Mortality Statistics*. The registration states include District of Columbia. "Cities" include only cities of 8,000 population or more in 1900; for later years include only cities of 10,000 or more in the last preceding census; "rural part" includes smaller cities, villages, and the open country.

[b] Includes gonorrhea.

[c] Includes ulcer of the duodenum, from 1900 to 1920.

[d] Includes injuries at birth which were classified under accidents during 1900–1909.

[e] Deaths from collision of automobiles with railroad trains and street cars are included with "other accidents."

[f] Four-year average, 1906–1909.

of rural dwellers in cities than of city dwellers in rural areas. If deaths occurring in cities are adjusted to omit deaths of nonresidents and to include deaths of residents that take place outside of cities, the crude death rate of cities is lowered and that of rural areas is raised by about 3 per cent in 1919, with a rise to about 6 per cent in 1929. For those causes of death for which hospitalization occurs with above average frequency

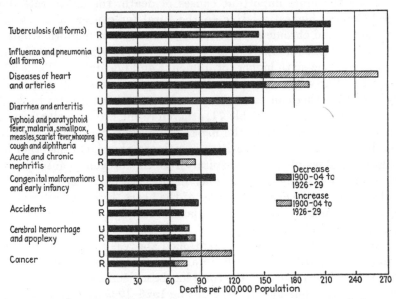

FIG. 29.—Death rates by important causes in cities and rural parts of the current registration states, 1900–1904 and 1926–1929. (Based on Table 73.)

the adjustment would be larger; for others it would be smaller.[1] In the second place, the proportion of children and elders in the population is higher in rural than in urban communities, and the proportion of young adults is lower. Hence the death rate at all ages combined for causes that affect children and elders more than young adults should be higher in the

[1] Harold F. Dorn, "The Effect of Allocation of Non-resident Deaths upon Official Mortality Statistics," *Journal of the American Statistical Association*, Vol. 27, No. 180 (December, 1932), pp. 401–412. In this study, based on all deaths occurring in Ohio during 1930, it was found that adjusting the death rate to place of residence of decedent instead of place of occurrence of death raised the urban death rate for tuberculosis by 7 per cent but lowered the urban rate for the other causes shown in Table 73. The decreases over 10 per cent were for puerperal causes (18 per cent) and automobile accidents (14 per cent), with small decreases (3 per cent or less) for cerebral hemorrhage and apoplexy, diseases of the heart, diseases of the arteries, early infancy and malformations, and syphilis, locomotor ataxia, and general paralysis of the insane. Similarly, this adjustment lowered the rural death rate for tuberculosis by 17 per cent but raised the rural rate for the other causes. The increases over 15 per cent were for puerperal causes (84 per cent) and automobile accidents (24 per cent), with small increases (3 per cent or less) for cerebral hemorrhage and apoplexy, diseases of the heart, and diseases of the arteries.

country than in cities simply because of these age differences. This would tend to offset the error in crude death rates due to nonresident deaths. But the death rate at all ages combined for causes that affect young adults more than children or elders should be higher in the cities than in the country simply because of age, which would augment the error in crude rates due to nonresident deaths.

Among the more important causes of death, the urban rate during 1926–1929 was highest relative to the rural for cancer, diseases of the heart, acute and chronic nephritis, early infancy and malformations, and influenza and pneumonia, the differentials varying from one-half higher for cancer to one-sixth higher for influenza and pneumonia (Table 73 and Figure 29). Early infancy and malformations are causes affecting infants only. For the other causes mentioned above, the death rates by age rise rapidly after middle life (Table 71); therefore the rates for all ages should be higher in the rural than the urban population because of the urban-rural differences in age composition mentioned above. On the other hand, deaths of rural people in city hospitals from the foregoing causes probably vary from a relatively large number in the case of cancer to a relatively small number in the case of diseases of the heart. But even after allowing for these conflicting errors, urban death rates from these causes would seem to be well above rural rates.[1]

For three of the five causes mentioned above—namely, influenza and pneumonia, nephritis, and early infancy and malformations—the excess of the urban death rate over the rural has been decreased since 1900, being only one-third to one-half as large during 1926–1929 as during 1900–1904. With cancer and diseases of the heart, however, the rural and urban rates were practically identical during 1900–1904, but since then the urban rate has risen considerably faster than the rural. A partial explanation of the fact that the urban death rate for cancer and diseases of the heart has become less favorable relative to the rural, while the opposite change has taken place with the other three causes, may be that deaths from cancer and diseases of the heart are less subject to control; hence have been less affected by the superior public health program carried on in the cities.

Cities have far outstripped the country in the control of certain germ diseases. In some cases this has meant that the former unfavorable differential of cities has been reduced or reversed, while in others a favorable margin has been widened. The death rate for typhoid fever was practically identical in urban and rural areas 30 years ago but has since been reduced by nearly 90 per cent in the former so that its recent rate is less than half as large as that of the latter. Malaria has been almost wiped

---

[1] This is true if the change in rates caused by adjusting to place of residence which was found in Ohio is typical of other states. *Cf.* Harold F. Dorn, *op. cit.*

out as a cause of death in cities, but the rural death rate continues much as in earlier years. Death rates for scarlet fever and diphtheria were about twice as high in urban as in rural areas during 1900–1904 but were much lower in both instances during 1926–1929, with a small differential still in favor of the country. In the case of tuberculosis the city rate has been reduced from 216.1 to 81.5, while the rural rate was reduced from 145.4 to 78.8.[1] Similarly, the urban rate for diarrhea and enteritis has been lowered from 141.0 to 24.4, compared with a decrease from 80.0 to 30.0 in the country rate. Public health work has been particularly efficacious in lowering the latter rate in cities, giving them a slightly better standing than rural areas in contrast to one much worse.

Throughout the entire consideration of the trend of death rates by cause of death the large differences between germ diseases and so-called degenerative diseases stand out clearly. Rapid declines in rates have been confined chiefly to the germ diseases and usually have been greater for these diseases in cities than in rural areas because of the more intensive city programs for improving public health. For the degenerative diseases, on the other hand, the trend has usually varied from slightly downward to sharply upward, with the standing of cities becoming less favorable relative to that of rural areas. These diseases cause a much higher proportion of all deaths now than formerly. Past experience shows they are much harder to control than germ diseases, which does not auger well for the future.

12. FUTURE TRENDS

The course that mortality rates and expectation of life at different ages will follow in the United States during future years is a matter of conjecture. In the light of past trends it is reasonable to assume that certain specific death rates will be further lowered and average length of life at birth increased. These assumptions are strengthened by the fact that much of what is now known regarding the prevention and control of disease is not being put into general practice.[2] In 1921 when the expectation of life in the death-registration area was 58.0 years, Dr. Louis I. Dublin estimated that the duration of human life could be extended to 65 years by the application of conservation measures very well known to

---

[1] Judging from the situation in Ohio, adjusting for place of residence would decrease the reduction in the urban rate and increase the reduction in the rural rate. *Cf.* Harold F. Dorn, *op. cit.* The number of persons with tuberculosis who are in sanatoria has increased greatly during the twentieth century, most of the sanatoria being located in rural communities.

[2] According to Grace Abbott, 24,500 infants survived their first years of life who would have died had the conditions of 1921 prevailed, yet probably half the 138,000 deaths which occurred could have been prevented. See "Accomplishments and a Challenge," *Public Health Nurse,* Vol. 20, No. 12 (December, 1928), pp. 616–619.

the medical and public health professions.[1] Part of this gain has already been achieved, the expectation of life having risen to 59.5 years in 1930.[2] At the same time, further additions have been made to the store of knowledge in the fields of medicine and public health, so that if an extension of seven years was possible then, it should be equally possible now.

Perhaps a more concrete idea of the improvement in expectation of life and in specific death rates that may reasonably be expected in the United States during this century can be obtained by a comparison with New Zealand. It should be remembered, however, that certain conditions may be more favorable to a low death rate in New Zealand than in the United States, particularly the milder climate, the absence of Negroes, and the lower proportion of the population affected by intensified industrialization and urbanization. For these reasons, it would be more fair to compare New Zealand with states like Wisconsin and Kansas, which have lower specific death rates and a higher expectation of life than the United States as a whole. Nevertheless, the fact that New Zealand has the most favorable mortality status of any country in the world makes a comparison with the United States of some interest.

With an increase in longevity going on for over a century, the United States reached in 1930 the level attained by New Zealand in 1901–1905. The expectation of life at birth was about 60 years in each case, but the expectation at most ages from 10 to 70 was a year or more longer in New Zealand in 1901–1905 than in the United States in 1930 (Table 66, p. 240). The last official life table for New Zealand (1921–1922) shows that since 1901–1905 the average length of life at birth had increased nearly 10 per cent, and at ages 20 to 60 about 5 per cent. By 1930 the expectation of life at birth in New Zealand had risen to over 65 years,[3] more than five years above the United States figure.

The greater average longevity in New Zealand is due primarily to lower death rates at the younger ages of life. In 1929[4] the death rate at ages under 5 was only about half as much in New Zealand as in the United States. At ages 5 to 24 the New Zealand rate was from one-half to three-fifths that of the United States, at ages 25 to 74 from three-fifths to four-fifths, while at older ages the rates were practically the same in the two countries. The fact that the larger differences were at the younger

---

[1] Metropolitan Life Insurance Company, *Statistical Bulletin*, Vol. 2, No. 12 (December, 1921), p. 3.

[2] The 1930 figure, furnished by Drs. Louis I. Dublin and Alfred J. Lotka, is "from advance information, drawn from a book prepared in this Bureau [the Statistical Bureau of the Metropolitan Life Insurance Company], the publication of which is planned for sometime this year [1933]."

[3] Estimated by the authors from specific death rates.

[4] Deaths by age in the United States for 1930 had not been published by the Division of Vital Statistics at time of writing (December, 1932).

ages where the opportunities for preventing deaths are more favorable emphasizes the possibility of attaining New Zealand longevity in this country.

Comparing the mortality rates of the United States and New Zealand for different causes of death indicates those which seem to offer the best chance for conserving life. In some cases the differentials between rates in the two countries may be due in part to differences in the classification as to cause of death, but this factor is not believed to be important for most of the causes here discussed, particularly because the manual of joint causes of death prepared by the United States Bureau of Vital Statistics has been adopted in New Zealand. Although it would be more exact to have these death rates by cause standardized for age and sex, the age and sex composition of the New Zealand population was so much like that of the United States in 1930 that the use of crude rates by cause of death should be quite accurate.

As may be seen from Table 70, the death rates from nearly every cause are lower in New Zealand than in the United States, and in most cases considerably lower. The rates from typhoid fever and measles in New Zealand are only about one-fifth as high as in the United States, from diarrhea and enteritis (mostly of children) about one-fourth as high, and from nephritis, influenza, cirrhosis of the liver, appendicitis, and whooping cough from one-third to one-half as high. The relative chance to reduce deaths from these causes would seem to be large judging from such differences. Furthermore, most of these causes are quite subject to human control; it is chiefly a matter of putting the best methods of prevention or treatment into general practice.

Large absolute differences between rates for the United States and New Zealand are found in the case of nephritis (difference of 59.2 per 100,000), influenza and pneumonia (46.8), and diarrhea and enteritis (20.9), mentioned above as having large relative differences, and also in the case of tuberculosis of the respiratory system (31.6), cerebral hemorrhage and softening of the brain (31.9), diseases of the heart (33.7), risks of early infancy (14.6), and accidental causes (27.8). Among this latter group it should be possible to secure large reductions in the death rates from tuberculosis, pneumonia, risks of early infancy, and diabetes mellitus in view of what is now known regarding their prevention and treatment. Whether the lower rates of New Zealand can be obtained for cerebral hemorrhage and diseases of the heart may be more doubtful, for at the present time these afflictions seem to be less subject to human control.

One of the highest death rates in both New Zealand and the United States is from cancer. Although knowledge of the control of this disease is quite fragmentary at present, the vast amount of research being

[259]

conducted may result at any time in startling discoveries that will permit a reduction in the cancer death rate equal to that already achieved in the tuberculosis rate.

The rapid rise in expectation of life in the United States during past decades and the fact that New Zealand, Kansas, and Wisconsin have progressed farther than the United States as a whole may presage a fairly large rise in the future. With a gradual diminishing of the past upward trend, the expectation of life for whites in the United States may be about 63 years in 1940, 66 years in 1950, and 73 years in 1980, with little subsequent rise (Figure 35, p. 315, and Table 66, p. 240). At this rate the 1930 figure for New Zealand would be reached between 1945 and 1950, and the entire future gain would be but little larger than that in the original registration states from 1900 to 1930. For Negroes the expectation of life may be as much as 51.7 years in 1940, 54.9 years in 1950, and 62 years in 1980, with little subsequent rise. These values for whites and Negroes seem quite high and unlikely to be exceeded.[1] They are the "high" assumptions shown in Table 66 and used in the calculations of future population growth (Table 88, Columns G, I, and J, p. 316).

A more conservative assumption is that differences in climate, in industrialization, and in concentration in large cities will prevent the average length of life in the United States from ever becoming appreciably longer than it now is in New Zealand. In this event the past upward trend in expectation of life will slow down more rapidly; the figure for whites will rise to about 64.7 in 1950 and will never exceed 66 years, corresponding figures for Negroes being 52.6 and 54 years (Figure 35 and Table 66). The effect on future population growth of this "medium" assumption of expectation of life is shown in Columns C, D, E, F, and H, of Table 88.

While the suggestion may not be popular, it is possible that even the estimates just given will prove to be too high. The expectation of life in the registration states of 1920 was lengthened only from 58.0 in 1921[2] to 59.7 in 1930,[3] which is at the rate of 1.85 years a decade. Nearly all of this small increase was secured by lowering the infant mortality rate from 75.6 in 1921 to 63.2 in 1930 (registration states of 1920), decreases in death rates of children and young adults having been scarcely large enough to balance increases in death rates of those middle aged or older. A continuation of this trend will mean some further drop in infant mortality, a smaller relative drop in specific death rates at ages 1 to 4, and practically

---

[1] To Dr. Irving Fisher, however, it "does not seem unreasonable" that the expectation of life at birth will exceed 80 years by the end of this century. "The Lengthening of Human Life—in Retrospect and in Prospect," *Proceedings of the Third Race Betterment Conference,* January 2–6, 1928, Battle Creek, Michigan.

[2] Metropolitan Life Insurance Company, *Statistical Bulletin,* Vol. 4, No. 6 (June, 1923), p. 5.

[3] Louis I. Dublin and Alfred J. Lotka, *ibid.*

no change in rates at older ages. In case the infant mortality rate of whites should be reduced from 59.6 in 1930 to a minimum of 35.0 by 1965 (practically the rate for New Zealand during 1929–1930) and other rates behave as just stated, the expectation of life will rise to only about 62.3 years, or less than three years above the 1930 figure (Figure 35 and Table 66). Similar changes for Negroes will reduce the infant mortality rate from 102 in 1930 to 60 and increase the expectation of life to about 51.4 years. The "low" assumption may appear to be a pessimistic view of what can be accomplished in extending life, but the behavior of specific death rates and of average length of life at certain ages from 1921 to 1930 indicates that it is possible (Tables 66 and 69). The effect on future population growth is shown in Columns *A* and *B* of Table 88.

CHAPTER VIII

BIRTHS AND BIRTH RATES

1. SOURCES OF DATA

RECORDS of births in the United States are much less adequate than records of deaths, and still less adequate than those of immigration. Although statistics on immigration were compiled by the federal government as early as 1820, and the first annual report on deaths in the registration area was for 1900, the birth-registration area was not organized until 1915. The report on birth statistics for that year covered 10 states and the District of Columbia, an area which contained 31 per cent of the nation's population. Additional states joined the birth-registration area almost every year after its formation so that since 1929 it has included the entire United States except South Dakota and Texas. Prior to 1915 a few states practiced birth registration on their own initiative, the first Massachusetts report on births being for 1841, followed within a few years by reports for Connecticut, Rhode Island, and Vermont. In the earlier years registration was quite inaccurate in these states, but laws passed between 1880 and 1900 placed responsibility for registration upon the attending physician or midwife and raised the proportion of births registered to a high figure.

In tracing the trend of births in the United States, however, it is not necessary to depend entirely on registration data. For the period prior to 1910 a much more adequate source of information is the census enumeration of children, which is available for every tenth year from 1800 to date. White children under 10 were tabulated from 1800 to 1820, and those under 5 from 1830 to 1930. For Negroes, children under 10 were tabulated for 1830 and 1840, and under 5 from 1850 to date. Although there has been a fairly uniform relation between the number of children under 5 enumerated in a census and the number of births during that census year, the former has increased more rapidly than the latter for one important reason, namely, the decline in the death rates of infants and children which has been going on for many years.[1] On this account, it seems desirable to estimate white births for the period before 1910, taking the census of children as a base and using the available specific death rates of children to obtain an approximate allowance for deaths.[2]

---

[1] *Supra*, pp. 235–237.

[2] Lack of information as to mortality rates of Negro children prior to 1919–1920 prevents a similar estimate of Negro births.

2. THE INCREASE IN BIRTHS AND CHILD POPULATION

With the tremendous growth of population in the United States the number of children under 5 enumerated in each census increased rapidly up to 1920. In 1800 there were about 818,000 white children under 5, but in 1920, 10,374,000, or nearly thirteen times as many (Table 74). Because

TABLE 74.—NUMBER OF CHILDREN AND RATIO OF CHILDREN TO WOMEN BY RACE, AND ESTIMATED WHITE BIRTHS AND BIRTH RATE, 1800–1980[a]

Year	Children 0–4[b]		Children 0–4 per 1,000 women 15–44		Estimated white births[c] (thousands)	Estimated white birth rate[d]	
	White (thousands)	Negro (thousands)	White	Negro		Per 1,000 population	Per 1,000 women 15–44
	A	B	C	D	E	F	G
1800	818	....	952	....	239	55.0	278
1810	1,115	....	953	....	321	54.3	274
1820	1,452	290[e]	905	810[e]	418	52.8	260
1830	1,895	421[e]	835	830[e]	545	51.4	240
1840	2,474	505[e]	797	785[e]	690	48.3	222
1850	2,897	601[e]	659	741[e]	852	43.3	194
1860	4,117	719	675	724	1,122	41.4	184
1870	4,720	791	610	692	1,295	38.3	167
1880	5,800	1,114[e]	586	759[e]	1,536	35.2	155
1890	6,580	1,048	517	621	1,741	31.5	137
1900	7,920	1,216	508	582	2,022	30.1	130
1910	9,323	1,263	484	519	2,252	27.4	117
1920	10,374	1,144[f]	471	429	2,497	26.1	113
1930	9,927	1,230	386	393	2,227	20.1	87
Future as calculated:[g]							
"Medium":							
1940	9,543	1,197	340	355	2,091	17.7	74
1950	9,599	1,164	322	328	2,050	16.1	69
1960	9,143	1,115	301	311	1,954	14.6	64
1970	8,915	1,067	300	301	1,912	13.9	64
1980	8,782	1,021	301	297	1,876	13.5	64
"Low":							
1940	9,161	1,193	329	355	1,974	16.8	71
1950	8,578	1,127	300	325	1,809	14.9	63
1960	7,692	1,035	278	303	1,625	13.3	59
1970	7,054	940	276	287	1,492	12.5	58
1980	6,497	843	276	274	1,370	12.0	58
"High":							
1940	10,128	1,231	357	364	2,274	19.1	80
1950	11,313	1,308	366	363	2,455	18.5	79
1960	11,685	1,350	356	360	2,529	17.2	77
1970	12,361	1,421	359	360	2,687	16.6	78
1980	13,234	1,509	360	362	2,859	16.2	78

[a] Mexicans are included with whites from 1800 to 1920, inclusive.

[b] For 1800 to 1930 from census for year indicated. It is estimated that 55.3 per cent of the white children under 10 in 1800, 1810, and 1820 were under 5 (as in 1830) and that 52.8 per cent of the colored children under 10 in 1830 and 1840 were under 5 (as in 1850).

It is probable that the increase in number of children and of estimated births is exaggerated by a greater underenumeration of children in early than in recent censuses. An intensive study of Washington, D. C., by Miss Foudray indicated that 9 per cent of the white children and 25 per cent of the Negro children under one were not enumerated in the 1920 census. She estimated that these percentages would hold true for the 27 states for which life tables were computed. Rough checks by the Scripps Foundation, based on births, deaths, and census data, indicate that about 5 per cent of the white and 14 per cent of the Negro children under 5 in the United States were not enumerated in 1920 or in 1930. A rough estimate of underenumeration at earlier dates may be had by taking native white children under 5 in 1870, deducting deaths in 10 years estimated from Massachusetts

of the downward trend of infant and child mortality, the estimated number of white births increased less rapidly. Nevertheless, births rose to
more than ten times their former level, from about 239,000 during 1800
to 2,497,000 during 1920. In 1930 there were fewer white children and
fewer white births than 10 years earlier, but even so there were over
twelve times as many children and over nine times as many births as in
1800. Negro children under 5 increased from 290,000 in 1820 to 1,230,000
in 1930. This was a slower rise than that of whites, the ratio of 1930 to
1820 for Negro children being 4.2:1, but for whites being 6.8:1. As was
the case with whites, the maximum number of Negro children was reached
prior to 1930; in 1910 there were 1,263,000 Negroes under 5.

Notwithstanding these large increases of births and children, neither
movement kept pace with the growth of population. The white population
was twenty-two times as numerous in 1920 as in 1800, but children under
5 were only about 12.7 times as numerous and births about 10.4 times.
The differentials were still larger in 1930, corresponding figures being
25.3 for population, 12.1 for children, and 9.3 for births. A similar situation exists among Negroes, the 1930 population being 5.1 times as large
as that of 1830, but the number of children under 5 being only 2.9 times
as large. The significance of these differentials will appear in the discussion
of crude birth rates which follows.

Considering the annual figures which commence in 1910, total births
increased steadily from 2,542,000 in 1910 to 2,834,000 in 1918 (Figure
27, p. 233, and Table 75), continuing the trend of earlier decades. In 1919
there was an important break in this upward movement, the first that is
known to have occurred. Owing chiefly to the mobilization of the large
army and probably in minor degree to the influenza epidemic there were

---

specific death rates of 1878–1882, and comparing the survivors with native whites 10 to 14 in 1880. According
to this process the underenumeration of white children under 5 amounted to 12 per cent in 1870 and to 9 per
cent in 1880. Although attention is hereby called to the probability of increasingly accurate counting of children
in the census and to the effect of this in exaggerating the upward trend of numbers of children and of births, it is
not felt that there is sufficient basis for estimates to eliminate this factor. The relative amount of undernumeration in each census prior to 1920 is assumed to be the same as in 1920.

  c For 1800 to 1900, an average of 5 years centering on census date. Children in Column A are increased to
allow for undernumeration (see Note b), and for deaths estimated from rates in Table 65. The result is estimated
births during 5 years ending on census date. Births for 5 years centering on census date are obtained by interpolation, e.g., adding to births during 5 years ending on census of 1810 one-fourth of the increase between these
births and births 10 years later gives estimated births for 5 years centering on 1810 census. For 1910 to 1930
births are for single years, from Table 75. For 1940 to 1980 an average of 10 years centering on census date.
Estimates for some years prior to 1900 may be as much as 5 per cent too high (see Table 85, and discussion,
pp. 302–304).

  d Births in Column E divided by the census population indicated.

  e Include an unknown but probably small and unimportant proportion of other colored; for example in
1860 there were 725,051 colored children 0 to 4 and the colored ratio of children to women was 721, only slightly
different from the figures for Negroes in that year.

  f Probably low compared with other years owing to undernumeration of Negro population mentioned in
Fifteenth Census of the United States: 1930, Vol. III, Pt. 1, p. 7.

  g The assumptions on which these calculations are based are discussed on pp. 288–291 and shown in Table
88, Columns A, H, and J.

about 200,000 fewer births in 1919 than in 1918. With the end of the war and the return of the soldiers there was again an increase in the number of births, the peak of 2,950,000 being reached in 1921. A high level was maintained fairly well up to 1924, but since then there has been a rapid and almost uninterrupted drop. Preliminary reports for 1931 indicate 2,443,000 births, which is 507,000 below the 1921 figure, and even lower than in 1910 when the population was smaller by about 31,000,000 persons.[1]

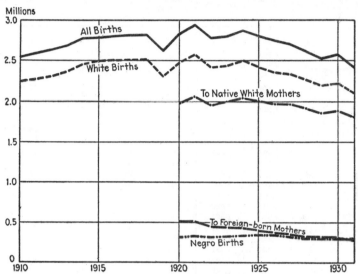

Fig. 30.—Number of births, by race and nativity of mother, 1910–1931. (Based on Table 75.)

It is true that a larger number of births occurred between 1920 and 1930 than during any preceding decade; nevertheless these annual figures show an important reversal of trend. The high decennial total is not due to a consistent increase from 1920 to 1930 such as seems to have occurred in prior decades. Instead, it results from the unusually large number of births during 1920–1925, which no doubt represents in considerable measure the making up, after demobilization of the births postponed because of the World War.

Because white births constitute such a large proportion of all births in the United States, they have followed nearly the same trend as total births (Figure 30 and Table 75). There was a steady rise from 2,252,000 births in 1910 to 2,522,000 in 1918, a drop to 2,336,000 in 1919, followed

[1] Monthly reports on number of births from January to November, 1932, are available for 11 states, mostly in the northeast, which contained 39 per cent of the population in 1930. They show 767,184 births, a decrease of 27,674 or 3.5 per cent from 1931. It is probable, however, that the percentage decrease in the more agricultural states of the South and West will be smaller by at least one-third to one-half.

TABLE 75.—ESTIMATED NUMBER OF BIRTHS AND CRUDE BIRTH RATE IN THE UNITED STATES, BY RACE AND NATIVITY OF MOTHER, 1910–1931[a]

| Year | Births (thousands) | | | | | Crude birth rates (per 1,000) | | |
| | Total | White[b] | | | Negro | Total | White[b] | Negro |
		Total	To native mothers	To foreign-born mothers				
1910........	2,542	2,252	.....	....	....	27.5	27.4	.....
1911........	2,588	2,296	.....	....	....	27.6	27.5	.....
1912........	2,633	2,338	.....	....	....	27.6	27.5	.....
1913........	2,674	2,378	.....	....	....	27.5	27.4	.....
1914........	2,781	2,475	.....	....	....	28.1	28.0	.....
1915........	2,800	2,500	.....	....	....	27.8	27.8	.....
1916........	2,816	2,506	.....	....	....	27.6	27.5	.....
1917........	2,821	2,508	.....	....	....	27.3	27.1	.....
1918........	2,834	2,522	.....	....	....	27.1	26.9	.....
1919........	2,636	2,336	.....	....	....	25.1	24.8	.....
1920........	2,848	2,497	1,989	508	334	26.7	26.1	31.3
1921........	2,950	2,583	2,070	513	348	27.1	26.5	32.2
1922........	2,781	2,435	1,965	470	328	25.2	24.6	29.9
1923........	2,809	2,457	2,000	457	334	25.0	24.4	30.1
1924........	2,875	2,501	2,051	450	357	25.2	24.4	31.7
1925........	2,813	2,435	2,020	415	360	24.3	23.4	31.7
1926........	2,750	2,373	1,987	386	363	23.4	22.5	31.6
1927........	2,715	2,358	1,987	371	343	22.8	22.0	29.5
1928........	2,612	2,278	1,932	346	320	21.7	21.0	27.3
1929........	2,527	2,200	1,871	329	313	20.7	20.1	26.4
1930........	2,569	2,227	1,901[c]	326[c]	318[c]	20.9	20.1	26.7[c]
1931........	2,443[c]	2,125[c]	1,827[c]	298[c]	305[c]	19.7[c]	19.1[c]	25.4[c]
1932........	2,378[c]	....	.....	....	....	19.1[c]	....	.....

[a] Prepared by the Scripps Foundation for Research in Population Problems from births registered in the New England states, New York, Pennsylvania, Michigan, and Minnesota during 1910–1914, and in the current birth registration area 1915 to date. Based on *United States Abridged Life Tables* 1919–1920, pp. 58–60, it is estimated that (a) 95.2 per cent of the white births were registered in the above states during 1910 to 1916 but that the additions to the registration area lowered this to 93.1 per cent during 1917 to 1931; and (b) 81.0 per cent of the Negro births were registered during 1920 to 1931. It is assumed that the ratio of births in the United States to births in the registration area is the same as the ratio shown by the census for children 0 to 1 in the United States to children 0 to 1 in the registration area. It is possible that the percentage of births registered increased from 1920 to 1930, in which case the above figures are too high. *Cf.* P. K. Whelpton, "Trends in Population Increase and Distribution during 1920 to 1930," *American Journal of Sociology*, Vol. 36, No. 6 (May, 1931), pp. 865–879.

[b] Mexicans are classified as white, since their births are so classified by the Division of Vital Statistics.

[c] Preliminary estimate.

NOTE: Subtracting white births from total births during 1910–1919 will not give an equally accurate estimate of colored births. Neither will subtracting white and Negro births from total births during 1920–1931 give an equally accurate estimate of other colored births.

by a rise to 2,583,000 in 1921. This level was fairly well maintained until 1924, after which there was a decline to 2,125,000 in 1931.

From 1920 to 1931 the number of births to native white mothers and to Negro mothers has followed a somewhat similar trend. The former was fairly stable at a high level from 1920 to 1927 (about 2,000,000 annually), then declined about 8 per cent to the low figure of 1,827,000 in 1931. Negro births averaged nearly 7 per cent more numerous during 1924–1926 than during the four preceding years (about 360,000 compared with 336,000), then declined slightly more than 15 per cent to a low point of about 305,000 in 1931. In contrast with native whites and Negroes the trend of births to foreign-born white mothers was much more distinctly downward. These births amounted to 513,000 in 1921 (1 per cent higher than in 1920), then declined almost uninterruptedly to about 300,000 in 1931, the total fall being over 40 per cent (Table 75).

3. THE DECREASE IN BIRTH RATES

Although the number of white births increased rapidly until recent years and is still above the level prior to 1900, the crude birth rate has declined almost uninterruptedly for over a century[1] (Table 74). In 1800 the estimated crude birth rate was 55.0 per 1,000, but by 1930 it had fallen to 20.1, a reduction of 63.5 per cent. Some decrease occurred in each intercensal period, the largest during 1920–1930 and 1840–1850 and the smallest during 1800–1810, 1820–1830, and 1910–1920.

Considering single years since 1910, the increase in the number of births nearly kept pace with the increase in population up to 1918. The crude birth rate of the total population fluctuated little in this period, rising from 27.5 in 1910 to 28.1 in 1914, then declining to 27.1 in 1918 (Table 75). A drop to 25.1 occurred in 1919, apparently owing chiefly to mobilization, which was regained by 1921. Since then there has been a decrease of over one-fourth to about 19.7 in 1931, with the downward trend being broken only by slight rises from 1923 to 1924 and from 1929 to 1930. The crude birth rate of the white population has followed practically the same trend. The crude birth rate of Negroes was 31.3 in 1920 and remained near this level until 1926, when a decline started which carried the rate down nearly one-fifth to about 25.4 in 1931.

Although crude birth rates are useful for certain purposes, they often are misleading because of the extent to which they are determined by the age and sex composition of a population as well as by the number of births. For more exact comparisons it is desirable to have specific birth rates, that is, the number of births per 1,000 women of specified ages. Rates by five-year age periods are desirable, but they may be calculated only for years near the census date when the number of women of each age is known, and for states which register births by age of mother. The latter practice was almost nonexistent before 1910 and has become general only since 1920; hence the nearest approach to a specific birth rate that can be obtained over several decades is births per 1,000 women in the

[1] The crude birth rate is obtained by dividing births by the total population expressed in thousands.

childbearing period, which is approximately from 15 to 44 years of age. Although this rate leaves much to be desired compared with specific rates by five-year age periods, it is a marked improvement over the crude birth rate for measuring the fertility of the population, because it eliminates the effect of changes in the proportion of females under 15 or over 44 and of all males in the total population. Variations in the age composition of women within the 15-to-44 period can affect this rate, but, although not insignificant, these variations have been of less importance than the factors above mentioned.[1]

The birth rate for white women 15 to 44 shows an even more rapid decline from 1800 to 1930 than does the crude birth rate, the 1930 rate of 87 being about 31 per cent of the 1800 figure whereas the 1930 crude rate is about 37 per cent of the 1800 (Table 74). The smaller decline of the crude rate results from the fact that women of the childbearing ages (15 to 44) constituted 23.6 per cent of the white population in 1930 compared with 20.0 per cent in 1800, an increase of almost one-sixth. Much of the drop in the birth rate for women 15 to 44 occurred in the earlier decades, the decline from 1840 to 1850 being 28 points, which is 2 points above the change from 1920 to 1930. The next largest numerical decreases (18 to 20 points) took place between 1820 and 1830, 1830 and 1840, and 1880 and 1890. A rapid absolute decline in the specific birth rate, therefore, is not a new thing in the United States. But considering that births to women 15 to 44 had been declining since 1800 and in 1920 were only 40.6 per cent of the 1800 figure, it is most surprising that such a large absolute drop should have come after 1920. On a relative basis it was a decrease of 23.0 per cent, by far the largest that had occurred, as the slightly greater absolute decline from 1840 to 1850 represented a reduction of only 12.6 per cent.[2]

The calculations of future birth rates in Table 74 indicate that the crude birth rate will decline more rapidly in the future than will births per 1,000 women 15 to 44. This reversal of what has occurred in past years will be caused by the changes in the age make-up of the population that are to be expected. In the past, the proportion of the population consisting of women in the childbearing ages has been increasing; hence

[1] For changes in age and sex composition, see Chaps. IV and V.

[2] For further measurement and discussion of the declining birth rate in the United States, see Allyn A. Young, "The Birth Rate in New Hampshire," *American Statistical Association, Publications*, Vol. 9, n.s., No. 71 (September, 1905), pp. 263–291. Walter F. Willcox, "The Change in the Proportion of Children in the United States and in the Birth Rate in France during the Nineteenth Century," *American Statistical Association, Publications*, Vol. 12, n.s., No. 93 (March, 1911), pp. 490–496. Frederick S. Crum, "The Decadence of the Native American Stock. A Statistical Study of Genealogical Records," *American Statistical Association, Publications*, Vol. 14, n.s., No. 107 (September, 1914), pp. 215–222. Alfred J. Lotka, "The Size of American Families in the Eighteenth Century," *Journal of the American Statistical Association*, Vol. 22, n.s., No. 158 (June, 1927), pp. 154–170.

the decline in birth rate has been more marked per 1,000 women of childbearing age than per 1,000 persons of all ages. But in the future, it is almost certain that women in the childbearing ages will decrease relatively in the population. Under this condition a decline in birth rates will be greater per 1,000 persons of all ages than per 1,000 women 15 to 44.

4. SPECIFIC BIRTH RATES BY RACE AND NATIVITY

Specific birth rates for women by five-year age periods are first available for an important part of the population in years near the 1920 census,

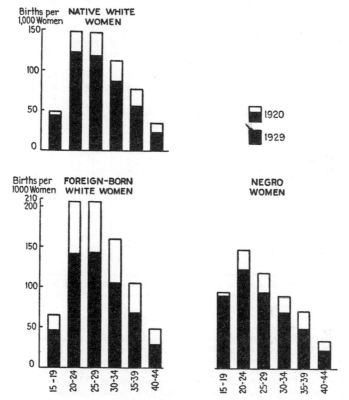

FIG. 31.—Birth rates by age, by race and nativity of women, 1920 and 1929. (Based on Table 76.)

when they may be calculated for birth-registration states. In years near prior censuses the few states which registered births did not tabulate them by age of mother in most cases. The latest year for which such rates may be obtained is 1929, the tabulation of births by age of mother for 1930 not being published by the Division of Vital Statistics at the time of writing (December, 1932). To ascertain the recent trend, 1920 and 1929 will be compared. The crude birth rate of 1920 is practically

TABLE 76.—SPECIFIC BIRTH RATES IN THE 1919 BIRTH-REGISTRATION AREA AND THE UNITED STATES, BY RACE AND NATIVITY OF WOMEN, 1920 AND 1929[a]

Race and nativity	Year	Births per 1,000 women aged						
		15–19	20–24	25–29	30–34	35–39	40–44	15–44[b]
1919 BIRTH REGISTRATION AREA								
Native-born white women[c]....	1920	43	141	141	105	69	30	90
	1929	41	121	118	86	54	22	76
Percentage change..........		−6.0	−14.6	−16.1	−18.3	−22.2	−26.8	−16.0
Foreign-born white women[c]...	1920	66	207	209	161	106	47	136
	1929	46	143	144	107	70	29	92
Percentage change..........		−29.2	−31.0	−31.3	−33.4	−34.3	−37.9	−32.1
Negro women...............	1920	90	155	127	97	72	34	100
	1929	91	136	104	76	53	24	85
Percentage change..........		1.4	−12.4	−18.2	−21.8	−26.0	−30.9	−14.9
UNITED STATES (ESTIMATED)[d]								
Native-born white women[c]....	1920	47	147	146	112	76	34	96
	1929	44	122	117	86	55	23	77
Percentage change..........		− 5.2	−17.0	−20.0	−22.9	−27.8	−32.5	−19.8
Foreign-born white women[c]...	1920	65	207	207	160	106	48	135
	1929	46	142	143	106	68	29	91
Percentage change..........		−30.1	−31.2	−31.1	−33.6	−35.7	−39.3	−32.4
Negro women...............	1920	94	147	118	90	70	34	96
	1929	90	123	94	69	49	22	78
Percentage change..........		− 4.3	−16.3	−19.9	−22.8	−29.9	−35.6	−18.2

[a] Number of births by age of mother from *Birth Statistics* for 1920 and 1929. Number of women by age on July 1, 1920, and July 1, 1929, estimated by straight-line interpolation between census of January 1, 1920, and April 1, 1930. Unknown ages distributed.

[b] A standardized birth rate; that is, specific rates are averaged using as weights the age distribution of all women 15 to 44 in the 1930 census.

[c] Mexicans are classified as white, since their births are so classified by the Division of Vital Statistics.

[d] Calculated on the assumption that specific birth rates of a nonregistration state may be obtained by adjusting the rates of a near-by registration state with similar rates upward or downward to such an extent that multiplying these adjusted rates by the number of women of corresponding age in the nonregistration state and adding the products give a number of births equal to the number estimated for the given nonregistration state from the census enumeration of children under one. Usually the required adjustment is small.

the same as the average of 1917–1921 or 1916–1922, which indicates 1920 is fairly typical with respect to births. Similarly, the crude birth rate of 1929 is practically the same as the average of 1928–1931.

Comparing the specific birth rates for 1929 with those for 1920, a marked downward trend is found in both the 1919 registration area and the United States (Figure 31 and Table 76). Native white, foreign-born white, and Negro women had large declines in specific birth rates, the size of the drop in each group increasing with a rise in age. Among native white women in the 1919 area the birth rate in the 15-to-19 age period was reduced only 6.0 per cent, but at older ages the decreases varied from 14.6 per cent at ages 20 to 24 to 26.8 per cent at ages 40 to 44. If the native white birth rates at each age are weighted according to the number of all women of that age in the 1930 census and averaged, the standardized birth rate for ages 15 to 44 is obtained, which fell 16.0 per cent.[1] Among foreign-born white women in the 1919 area, the specific birth rate at ages 15 to 19 fell nearly 30 per cent, while at older ages the drop increased to nearly 38 per cent. These declines averaged about twice as large as those of native whites. In the 1919 registration area Negro women maintained their specific birth rates much nearer the 1920 level than foreign-born white women and their standardized rate somewhat more so than native white women; there was even an increase in the Negro rate at ages 15 to 19. At ages 20 to 24 the decline of the Negro rate was somewhat smaller than that of native white women, but at older ages it was larger.

Specific birth rates of foreign-born women and the decreases in these rates from 1920 to 1929 were practically identical in the 1919 birth-registration area and the United States, because such a large proportion of these women live in the former area. Among native whites and Negroes, however, declines averaged one-fifth larger in the United States than in the 1919 area. Most of the nonregistration states of 1919 were in the South and West (excluding the Pacific states) and had a higher proportion of rural inhabitants, these facts having a relation to the trend of birth rates as will be indicated shortly.

Declines in specific birth rates were much higher among foreign-born white women than among native whites or Negroes in spite of certain changes that tended to raise the rates for the foreign born. In the first place, there was a slight decrease in the proportion of foreign-born white women from the lower birth rate countries; those from northern and western Europe and Canada[2] constituting 49.1 per cent of the group in 1930 compared with 51.3 per cent in 1920. Furthermore, the foreign-born population from northern and western Europe averaged considerably older in 1930 than that from southern and eastern Europe, owing chiefly to the earlier time at which they arrived in the United States. On this account the former women have been moving out of the childbearing ages faster than the latter; hence the decrease in the proportion of women from northern and western Europe was larger in these ages than is given

---

[1] For earlier changes in the birth rate of native white women, see Xarifa Sallume and Frank W. Notestein, "Trends in the Size of Families Completed Prior to 1910 in Various Social Classes," *American Journal of Sociology*, Vol. 38, No. 3 (November, 1932), pp. 398–408.

[2] The European countries included are Sweden, Germany, Switzerland, France, and all countries to the north and west; French Canadians are excluded.

above for all ages. On the other hand, however, the fact that only 16 per cent of the excess of alien arrivals over departures from 1920 to 1929 was from countries in eastern and southern Europe with young adults predominating would help to decrease the proportion of foreign-born women in the childbearing ages who came from these countries.

The large reduction in specific birth rates to foreign women in the face of the foregoing changes favoring an increase probably was due chiefly to the great importance of the Americanizing of the foreign born, a process that has little counterpart among the native population. Immigration was much larger from 1900 to 1914 than from 1915 to 1930 owing to the effect of the World War and the quota restrictions of post-war years. On this account, the foreign-born women in the 1920 population had spent fewer years in the United States on the average than the foreign-born women in the 1930 population. The latter had thus had more opportunity to shed the ideals and standards of the old country, often of a peasant environment, and to adopt those of native American white women, including their preference for smaller families. Perhaps the emphasis on 100 per cent Americanism since the war helped to accelerate this change.

Although the estimated rates for the United States in Table 76 are the same at ages 15 to 44 for native whites and Negroes in 1920 and one point higher for Negroes in 1929, it is probable that the Negro rates have been relatively larger compared with the white. No allowance for nonregistered births was added in the preparation of these rates; they are for registered births only. The indications are that failure to register births is more common among Negroes than whites, about 19 per cent of Negro births, compared with 6.9 per cent of white births, not being registered in 1920.[1] Such adjustments in the rates of Table 76 raise the standardized rate of native whites to 103 in 1920 and 82 in 1929, and of Negroes to 119 and 96, respectively, making the Negro figure higher than the white by about 15 per cent in 1920 and 17 per cent in 1929.

5. SPECIFIC BIRTH RATES BY REGIONS

So far, only specific birth rates for the 1919 birth-registration area and the United States have been considered. The rates themselves and the degree of change have varied considerably between different parts of the nation, as may be seen from Figure 32 and Table 77, which gives the rates in 1920 and 1929 for urban and rural United States and for groups of states with similar rates. In each case there was a decline in the standardized birth rate for native white and foreign-born white women, and in four out of five cases for Negro women. The specific birth rates for foreign-born white women declined at every age in all areas, and

[1] Based on Elbertie Foudray, *United States Abridged Life Tables*, 1919–1920, pp. 58–60.

for native white women in every case except those 15 to 19 in seven North Central states. Among Negroes, there were increases in the rates for younger women in the groups composed of urban areas and northern states, but decreases elsewhere.

Among native white women, the specific birth rates as a whole, and hence the standardized rate, declined the least in New Hampshire and Vermont, and the most in five southern states.[1] Rates for urban United

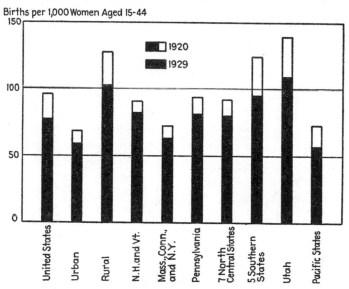

FIG. 32.—Standardized birth rates of native white women, United States and selected states, 1920 and 1929. (Based on Tables 76 and 77.)

States decreased somewhat more than those for the northeastern states, which are so highly urbanized and industrialized, but rates for rural United States did not decrease so much as those for five southern states, where agriculture is more important relatively than in most states.[2]

[1] The decline in specific birth rates of native white women in the New England states from 1920 to 1929 may represent a reversal of the trend in preceding years. From a study covering the period 1870 to 1920, Spengler concludes, "There is no evidence whatsoever tending to show a decrease of the fecundity of native women in the last 50 years." Joseph J. Spengler, *The Fecundity of Native and Foreign-born Women in New England*, The Brookings Institution Pamphlet Series, Vol. II, No. 1, p. 41, Washington, The Brookings Institution, 1930. See also Sallume and Notestein, *op. cit.*

[2] In a rural area of western New York the standardized birth rates per 100 native white wives of farmers was higher in 1929 than in 1910 or 1900. Edgar Sydenstricker, "A Study of the Fertility of Native White Women in a Rural Area of Western New York," *Quarterly Bulletin of The Milbank Memorial Fund*, Vol. 10, No. 1 (January, 1932), pp. 16–32. For trends during 1800 to 1920 in the ratio of children to women for the white population of industrial, semi-industrial, and agricultural states, see P. K. Whelpton, "Industrial Development and Population Growth," *Social Forces*, Vol. 6, Nos. 3 and 4 (March and June, 1928), pp. 458–467 and 629–638.

TABLE 77.—SPECIFIC BIRTH RATES IN URBAN AND RURAL AREAS AND SELECTED STATES, BY RACE AND NATIVITY OF WOMEN, 1920 AND 1929[a]

Race and nativity	Year	Births per 1,000 women aged						
		15–19	20–24	25–29	30–34	35–39	40–44	15–44
UNITED STATES, URBAN (ESTIMATED)[b]								
Native-born white women.....	1920	32	111	111	83	48	20	69
	1929	32	98	94	66	38	14	59
Percentage change.........		− 1.5	−11.4	−15.2	−20.5	−20.1	−29.3	−15.0
Foreign-born white women....	1920	61	193	197	151	98	41	126
	1929	42	133	137	101	64	26	86
Percentage change.........		−31.7	−31.0	−30.8	−33.1	−34.3	−36.0	−32.0
Negro women..............	1920	86	97	67	48	36	15	62
	1929	88	90	60	41	26	11	57
Percentage change.........		2.6	− 7.2	−10.4	−15.1	−28.7	−29.1	− 8.5
UNITED STATES, RURAL (ESTIMATED)[b]								
Native-born white women.....	1920	61	193	192	147	110	51	128
	1929	59	159	153	116	80	36	103
Percentage change.........		− 2.6	−17.6	−20.3	−20.6	−27.2	−30.1	−19.5
Foreign-born white women....	1920	85	288	261	199	139	72	178
	1929	70	211	186	136	91	42	126
Percentage change.........		−18.5	−26.6	−28.7	−31.6	−34.8	−41.8	−28.9
Negro women..............	1920	98	181	161	127	99	49	124
	1929	92	154	137	107	78	34	104
Percentage change.........		− 6.7	−15.0	−14.5	−15.8	−21.0	−30.0	−16.1
NEW HAMPSHIRE AND VERMONT								
Native-born white women.....	1920	44	141	148	109	66	26	91
	1929	43	128	133	96	60	20	82
Percentage change.........		− 2.5	− 8.7	−10.3	−11.9	− 9.4	−22.4	− 9.9
Foreign-born white women....	1920	54	204	217	160	116	55	136
	1929	48	175	176	126	85	35	110
Percentage change.........		−10.6	−14.2	−19.2	−21.6	−26.8	−35.5	−19.4
MASSACHUSETTS, CONNECTICUT, AND NEW YORK								
Native-born white women.....	1920	27	112	124	88	50	19	72
	1929	26	99	108	77	43	14	63
Percentage change.........		− 3.4	−11.6	−13.1	−12.7	−15.1	−23.7	−12.3
Foreign-born white women....	1920	49	191	203	160	100	41	126
	1929	37	130	143	107	65	26	86
Percentage change.........		−24.6	−31.9	−29.3	−32.9	−34.6	−36.8	−31.5
PENNSYLVANIA								
Native-born white women.....	1920	47	150	144	108	71	32	94
	1929	42	130	126	92	58	24	81
Percentage change.........		− 9.8	−13.2	−12.4	−14.5	−18.4	−25.1	−14.2
Foreign-born white women....	1920	95	250	255	201	145	66	172
	1929	30	170	164	135	102	47	109
Percentage change.........		−68.3	−31.9	−35.8	−33.1	−29.4	−29.6	−36.7
NEW YORK AND PENNSYLVANIA								
Negro women..............	1920	94	122	85	58	39	17	74
	1929	107	124	80	54	31	12	73
Percentage change.........		14.6	0.8	− 5.0	− 6.2	−19.9	−27.7	− 0.5

TABLE 77.—SPECIFIC BIRTH RATES IN URBAN AND RURAL AREAS AND SELECTED STATES, BY RACE AND NATIVITY OF WOMEN, 1920 AND 1929.[a]—(Continued)

Race and nativity	Year	Births per 1,000 women aged						
		15–19	20–24	25–29	30–34	35–39	40–44	15–44

NORTH CENTRAL STATES[c]

Race and nativity	Year	15–19	20–24	25–29	30–34	35–39	40–44	15–44
Native-born white women.....	1920	42	145	143	107	71	31	92
	1929	43	128	123	90	58	24	80
Percentage change.........		2.1	−11.5	−14.0	−15.6	−18.4	−22.4	−13.1
Foreign-born white women....	1920	75	224	208	156	108	53	141
	1929	61	167	146	104	68	32	100
Percentage change.........		−18.9	−25.3	−29.6	−33.2	−36.6	−40.2	−29.2
Negro women...............	1920	100	118	80	59	38	15	73
	1929	112	122	80	53	33	15	74
Percentage change.........		11.7	3.0		− 9.0	−14.1	1.3	2.1

SOUTHERN STATES[d]

Race and nativity	Year	15–19	20–24	25–29	30–34	35–39	40–44	15–44
Native-born white women.....	1920	66	181	176	144	110	52	124
	1929	58	142	137	107	77	37	95
Percentage change.........		−11.7	−21.6	−22.5	−25.7	−29.9	−30.0	−23.0
Foreign-born white women....	1920	57	207	210	157	102	44	132
	1929	36	139	132	96	62	26	84
Percentage change.........		−37.8	−33.1	−37.2	−38.6	−38.8	−40.6	−36.6
Negro women...............	1920	89	171	153	122	92	44	115
	1929	85	146	128	100	74	32	98
Percentage change.........		− 4.3	−14.7	−16.1	−18.4	−19.6	−27.4	−15.3

UTAH

Race and nativity	Year	15–19	20–24	25–29	30–34	35–39	40–44	15–44
Native-born white women.....	1920	50	204	209	168	124	75	139
	1929	46	165	168	130	90	45	109
Percentage change.........		− 7.0	−19.3	−19.5	−22.7	−27.6	−39.3	−21.8
Foreign-born white women....	1920	106	255	219	186	140	85	168
	1929	62	229	188	134	107	51	132
Percentage change.........		−41.7	−10.3	−14.0	−27.8	−23.6	−39.2	−21.8

PACIFIC STATES

Race and nativity	Year	15–19	20–24	25–29	30–34	35–39	40–44	15–44
Native-born white women.....	1920	·44	127	112	76	44	17	73
	1929	39	102	86	57	31	11	57
Percentage change.........		−10.3	−19.6	−23.5	−25.5	−28.0	−37.6	−21.8
Foreign-born white women....	1920	91	198	164	114	74	30	117
	1929	48	126	109	72	41	15	72
Percentage change.........		−46.6	−36.0	−33.6	−36.5	−44.6	−50.3	−38.7

[a] See Table 76, Notes a, b, and c for method of computation of state rates and source of data.
[b] See Table 76. Note d for method of estimating. It is assumed that the relative size of specific birth rates at the different age periods is the same (a) in urban United States as in Massachusetts, Connecticut, New York, Pennsylvania, District of Columbia, and the Pacific states combined for whites and as in New York, Pennsylvania, Ohio, Indiana, Michigan, Wisconsin, Maryland, District of Columbia, and Kentucky combined for Negroes, and (b) in rural United States as in Indiana, Wisconsin, Minnesota, Nebraska, Kansas, Virginia, North Carolina, South Carolina, and Kentucky combined for whites and as in Virginia, North Carolina, and South Carolina combined for Negroes. Only birth-registration states of 1920 could be used, of which the above are believed most typical in each case.
[c] Ohio, Indiana, Michigan, Wisconsin, Minnesota, Nebraska, and Kansas for whites. Ohio, Indiana, Michigan, and Kansas for Negroes.
[d] Maryland, Virginia, North Carolina, South Carolina and Kentucky.

The tendency was strong for declines to be larger in areas having higher rates in 1920, and to be smaller in areas having the lower rates. The Pacific states were an outstanding exception to this tendency, however, for their specific birth rates were barely half those of Utah and the five southern states in 1920, yet they declined nearly as much.

Declines in the specific birth rates of foreign-born white women were greater than in those of native white women in every case except Utah, where the standardized rate of each group declined the same. New Hampshire and Vermont again showed the least change, while the largest occurred in the Pacific states, where the 1920 rates were lowest. Contrary to the native white rates, the foreign-born white rates declined more in urban than in rural areas and showed little if any tendency for larger decreases in areas with the higher rates in 1920.

Among Negro women by far the largest decline in the standardized rate took place in the rural group and in five southern states where Negroes are quite rural. However, specific rates at ages 35 to 39 and 40 to 44 went down nearly as much in urban United States and in New York and Pennsylvania as in the rural areas. A rise in the rate at ages 15 to 19 took place in the northern areas, and because northern Negroes are so largely urban, in urban United States as well. The trend in the northern areas may be considered somewhat erratic, however, since the make-up of their Negro population in 1920 probably was quite abnormal owing to the recentness of the large northward migration of Negroes that had taken place.

In spite of the larger decreases of specific rates of foreign-born white women than of native white or Negro women, the former are still much the highest in most areas[1] (Table 77). The single exception is in five southern states, where the Negro rates in 1929 were slightly higher than those of native white women and rates of foreign-born white women lowest of all.[2] The chief explanation of the foreign-born white being in third place here instead of first as elsewhere is the fact that so many of these people in the South are merchants and traders living in villages or cities. Among southern native whites and Negroes, however, the proportion of farmers is large.

Although the variations between areas in declines of birth rates for native whites, foreign-born whites, and Negroes have narrowed the differentials in some cases, rates were far from uniform in all areas during 1929. The native white rates decreased considerably more both relatively and absolutely in rural than in urban communities from 1920 to 1929; nevertheless in 1929 there were 103 births per 1,000 rural native white women aged 15 to 44 compared with only 59 for urban. With the age

[1] For a comparison of the fecundity of native and foreign-born white women in 1900, see United States Immigration Commission: *Fecundity of Immigrant Women*, prepared by Joseph A. Hill, Washington, Government Printing Office, 1911, 61st Congress, 2d Session, Senate Document 282.

[2] The Negro rates would be still higher compared with the native white if an allowance was added for nonregistered births (see p. 272).

composition and specific death rates as they were in 1929 these birth rates were sufficiently large to give an excess of births over deaths in both cases. But if the urban rate continues to decline 15 per cent in nine years (as it did from 1920 to 1929) and if the trend toward a less favorable urban age composition continues,[1] not many years will elapse before deaths of native whites exceed births to native white women in cities. Even the specific birth rates of urban native white women in 1920 when increased to allow for nonregistered births were not sufficiently large to maintain the urban population on a permanent basis.[2] Since 1920 there has been some decline in specific death rates of native whites, but specific birth rates have declined still more. It follows, therefore, that although the 1929 urban birth rates yielded an excess of births over deaths for native whites in that year, they are well below the level needed to maintain the urban population on a permanent basis.

The birth rate of foreign-born white women 15 to 44 in 1929 was 86 per 1,000 in urban areas and 126 in rural areas. The differential widened from 1920 to 1929, the rural rate being barely 41 per cent higher than the urban in 1920 compared with 46.5 per cent higher in 1929. Because the average age of the foreign born is so much higher in the country than in cities,[3] the higher rural birth rate to women 15 to 44 does not mean a larger excess of births over deaths relative to population in rural areas. In fact, deaths of foreign-born white persons were approximately equal to births to foreign-born white women in rural areas in 1929, though well below in cities. With a continuation of present immigration regulations, however, the average age of the foreign born in cities will rise rapidly. This combined with the continued decline in the birth rate that is to be expected will soon bring about a greater number of deaths than births among city as well as rural foreign born.

By far the best showing of urban rates relative to rural in 1929 occurred among Negroes 15 to 19, the urban rate being nearly as large as the rural. At older ages the urban showing was worse among Negroes than among native or foreign-born whites, the urban Negro rates at ages above 25 being only 33 to 45 per cent of the rural rates. More Negro deaths than births were registered in cities during 1929, but in rural areas births registered out-numbered deaths by nearly 3:2. Allowing for nonregistered births would give an excess of births in both cases but would leave the rural excess much larger relative to population than the urban.

The differences in native white birth rates between the groups of states in Table 77 are closely related to the urban-rural variations just discussed.

[1] See Appendix Table 17, p. 370, for age composition of native whites in cities.
[2] From P. K. Whelpton, "Differentials in True Natural Increase," *Journal of the American Statistical Association*, Vol. 24 n.s., No. 167 (September, 1929), pp. 233–249.
[3] *Supra*, pp. 148–150.

Massachusetts, Connecticut, and New York, and the Pacific states are highly urbanized and have relatively low birth rates; the North Central and southern states are much more rural and have relatively high birth rates. Utah has birth rates well above what would be expected from her rural-urban status, but this no doubt results chiefly from the influence of the Mormon Church. The high birth rates of Pennsylvania relative to the degree of urbanization are more difficult to account for, although the fact that large families are so common among miners is important.

Regional differences in birth rates to foreign-born white women are not so closely related to the extent of urbanization. The age distribution of foreign whites varies more from region to region than that of native whites. Furthermore, immigrants from certain foreign countries have tended to settle in one part of the United States but those from other countries elsewhere. Because birth rates vary between the national groups, the uneven distribution causes regional variations.

Most of the Negroes outside the South are found in cities, whereas in the South a high proportion are rural. The rural-urban birth rate differential thus carries over to the regional comparison for Negroes, birth rates to women in each age period in the southern states being well above those in other regions (Table 77).

6. BIRTH RATES BY SIZE OF COMMUNITY

Births are not classified by age of mother for any city except Washington, D. C.; hence only the crude birth rate or else the rate per 1,000 women in the childbearing ages can be calculated. Partly on this account, and also because births were registered in so few cities prior to 1920, the ratio of children under 5 to women 20 to 44 will be used to indicate variations in birth rates in this section.

In every census year for which data are available, the ratio of children to women has been much higher in the rural population than in cities of any size, with the farm ratio well above the rural-nonfarm. This is true for the total population as well as for whites and Negroes. In 1930 the rural ratio for the total population was 660, more than 50 per cent above the highest urban ratio (436 in cities of 2,500 to 25,000) (Table 78). In 1820 the differential was nearly as large among the white population, the rural ratio of 1,286 being 42 per cent above the highest ratio (906 in cities of 2,500 to 25,000). The rural population cannot be divided into farm and nonfarm prior to 1920, but it is probable that the farm ratio formerly was from one-fifth to one-fourth larger than the rural-nonfarm ratio, as was the case in 1920 and 1930.

Among cities of different sizes the ratio of children to women has been consistently higher in places of 2,500 to 25,000 than in larger cities. Considering only cities above 25,000, there is no apparent relation in

TABLE 78.—RATIO OF CHILDREN UNDER 5 TO WOMEN 20 TO 44 BY SIZE OF COMMUNITY, BY RACE AND NATIVITY, 1820–1930[a]

Size of community	1820	1840	1890	1900	1910	1920	1930
	TOTAL POPULATION[b]						
500,000 and over.............	.....	.....	507	493	463	443	343
250,000–500,000.............	.....	.....	490	478	417	381	330
100,000–250,000.............	.....	.....	516	452	396	429	378
25,000–100,000.............	.....	.....	480	457	446	457	386
2,500– 25,000.............	.....	.....	} 757	742 {	500	507	436
Rural......................	.....	.....			794	744	660
Farm......................	.....	.....	...	...	...	806	730
Nonfarm...................	.....	.....	...	...	...	656	584
	WHITES[c]						
500,000 and over.............	.....	.....	513	503	474	455	347
250,000–500,000.............	.....	665	500	492	427	393	335
100,000–250,000.............	827	778	529	460	409	449	384
25,000–100,000.............	786	863	487	470	460	472	393
2,500– 25,000.............	906	739	} 731	722 {	507	521	442
Rural......................	1,286	1,138			782	744	653
Farm......................	.....	.....	...	...	...	802	718
Nonfarm...................	.....	.....	...	...	...	669	589

Size of community	NATIVE WHITES	FOR-EIGN-BORN WHITES	NEGROES				
	1920[d]	1920[d]	1890[e]	1900	1910	1920	1930
500,000 and over.............	334	664	263	268	249	242	295
250,000–500,000.............	328	681	343	332	290	264	298
100,000–250,000.............	381	758	390	310	278	271	322
25,000–100,000.............	390	766	415	336	307	294	317
2,500– 25,000.............	459	868	} 931	875 {	422	356	364
Rural......................	721	998			868	743	707
Farm......................	.....	... .	...	...	...	826	794
Nonfarm...................	.....	.....	...	...	...	548	543

[a] Compiled from current census reports. Data on age by size of community were not published by the census for 1850 to 1880, inclusive.

[b] Includes whites and Negroes in all years, Mexicans prior to 1930, and other colored in 1890. In 1820 and 1840 only whites were classified according to the age periods used herein.

[c] Includes Mexicans prior to 1930 in accordance with current census classification.

[d] From Warren S. Thompson, *Ratio of Children to Women, 1920*, Census Monograph XI, Washington, Government Printing Office, 1931. No classification of white children by nativity of mother was made prior to 1920. That for 1930 will appear shortly in a census monograph by the authors.

[e] Based on data for all colored, 95.4 per cent of whom were Negroes. Age data not published for Negroes separately.

Table 78 between size of city and ratio of children to women for the total population or for whites. In one year a certain size may have had the largest ratio, but in another year the smallest ratio. Among Negroes, however, there has been a marked tendency for the ratio of children to women to vary inversely with size of city. In 1890 there was an uninterrupted rise in the Negro ratio from 263 in cities of 500,000 and over to 415 in cities of 25,000 to 100,000, and in 1920 from 242 to 294. In 1900 and 1910 the relation was less regular, while in 1930 the variation was smaller.

If ratios for native whites and foreign-born whites could be shown separately, the relation between the birth rate and size of city would be more clear. Unfortunately this is now possible only for 1920. In that year the native white ratios in cities of over 250,000 were well below those in cities of 25,000 to 250,000, while the ratio of children to foreign-born white women rose consistently from 664 in the largest cities to 766 in those of 25,000 to 100,000. Within each size group, however, the native white ratio was well below the foreign white. This situation, combined with the higher proportion of foreign-born whites in larger cities than in smaller, completely obscures the relation between size of city and ratio of children to women when the total population is considered. But when native whites, foreign-born whites, or Negroes are examined separately, the lowering of the ratio as size increases becomes apparent.[1]

7. REGIONAL DIFFERENTIALS IN TRUE RATE OF NATURAL INCREASE

The differentials in specific birth rates of various areas which have just been pointed out, together with the differentials in death rates discussed on pages 241 to 245, suggest that there is considerable variation in contributions to natural increase from these areas. Natural increase may be measured in several ways, the most accurate in certain respects being the "true" rate of natural increase. This is the rate which would occur in a population if its actual specific birth and death rates at some given time were to remain in operation indefinitely and no migration were to occur. Under these assumptions, the age and sex composition would become stabilized and have a definite relation to the given specific birth and death rates. It is this condition that makes true rates superior to others for measuring the long-time effect of present differentials in natural increase.[2]

---

[1] For a much more detailed discussion covering states and cities in 1920, see W. S. Thompson, *Ratio of Children to Women, 1920*, Census Monograph XI, Washington, Government Printing Office, 1931. Detailed data for 1930 now being compiled by the Bureau of the Census will be presented in a census monograph to be prepared by the authors.

[2] For further explanation, and for method of computation, see Louis I. Dublin and Alfred J. Lotka, "On the True Rate of Natural Increase," *Journal of the American Statistical Association*, Vol. 20, n.s., No. 151 (September, 1925).

BIRTHS AND BIRTH RATES

TABLE 79.—TRUE RATE OF NATURAL INCREASE OF WHITES AND NEGROES IN SELECTED AREAS, 1920 AND 1928[a]

Race and area	True rate of natural increase per 1,000[b]		
	1920	1928	Change 1920–1928
Whites in			
Massachusetts, Connecticut, New York......................	1.9	− 4.3	−6.2
Pennsylvania...	11.8	4.9	−6.9
Ohio. Indiana, Michigan, Wisconsin........................	8.6	3.3	−5.3
Minnesota, Nebraska, Kansas..............................	10.1	3.1	−7.0
Virginia, North Carolina, South Carolina, Kentucky.............	19.7	12.8	−6.9
Washington, Oregon, California............................	3.2	− 0.3	−3.5
9 large cities[c]...	0.6	− 5.1	−5.7
Negroes in			
5 southern states[d]......................................	13.0	8.9	−4.1
8 northern states[e]......................................	− 4.8	− 1.1	3.7
9 large cities[f]...	−12.7	− 9.9	2.8

[a] From P. K. Whelpton, "Population Trends in Differential of True Increase and Age Composition," *American Journal of Sociology*, Vol. 35, No. 6 (May, 1930), pp. 870–880. Nearly all areas for which the necessary birth data and life tables are available for 1920 are included. Because adequate life tables are not available for whites and Negroes in these areas in 1928, the rates shown for 1928 are only approximately correct, probably being low rather than high. The same method of estimating survival values was followed throughout, so the error in the 1928 rate of one area should be approximately the same as that of other areas, and the relative standing of the areas should not be affected significantly.

[b] In computing these rates an allowance was added for nonregistered births based on Elbertie Foudray, *United States Abridged Life Tables, 1919–1920*, pp. 58–60.

[c] Baltimore, Boston, Cleveland, Detroit, New York, Philadelphia, Pittsburgh, San Francisco, Washington. D. C.

[d] Maryland, Virginia, North Carolina, South Carolina, Kentucky.

[e] Massachusetts, Connecticut, New York; Pennsylvania, Ohio, Indiana, Michigan, Kansas.

[f] Baltimore, Boston, Chicago, Cleveland, Detroit, New York, Philadelphia. Pittsburgh, Washington, D. C.

The outstanding fact shown by the true rates of natural increase in Table 79 is the great shrinkage in population growth caused by the more rapid decline in specific birth rates than in specific death rates from 1920 to 1928. The white population in every area had some true natural increase in 1920, but striking declines occurred in the following years so that 1928 rates were well below the level for a stationary population in two areas and slightly below in one other area. Negroes in northern states and in large cities were not maintaining their numbers on a permanent basis in either 1920 or 1928. Although the true rate of these two Negro groups increased during the interval, the increase was more than offset by the decline in the South, where the majority of Negroes are found. Taking all areas as a whole, the decline in true rates from 1920 to 1928 amounted to about 60 to 65 per cent for whites and 30 to 45 per cent for Negroes.[1] The negative rates do not mean that there was an excess of

[1] The decline for Negroes is larger than would appear at first glance because the proportion of Negroes in northern states increased rapidly from 1920 to 1928.

deaths over births in these areas in 1928, for this was not the case. They simply are the rates at which the populations would eventually decline if specific birth and death rates remained as in 1928 and if there was no migration. Under these conditions the growth that has taken place in recent years would gradually disappear, and a loss set in that would finally reach the rates indicated.

Variations in the true rate of natural increase shown for different areas in Table 79 are much larger relatively than the variations in specific birth rates. In 1920 the highest rate, 19.7 for whites in Virginia, North Carolina, South Carolina, and Kentucky, was ten times the low rate of 1.9 for whites in Massachusetts, Connecticut, and New York. The standardized birth rate of these southern states, however, was over 30 per cent higher than the rate of Massachusetts, Connecticut, and New York (Table 77[1]), while the expectation of life was only 5 per cent higher (Table 67, p. 242). Nevertheless, the 10:1 difference in true rate of natural increase seems reasonable when it is remembered that this rate is based on differences between births and deaths. Subtracting a fairly stable series (death rates) from a fluctuating series (birth rates) gives a still more variable series—natural increase in this case. Changes in specific death rates since 1920 have been of almost insignificant importance compared with decreases in specific birth rates in reducing the true rate of natural increase. The close relation in most areas between the change in specific birth rates (Table 77) and in true natural increase (Table 79) is apparent upon examination of the data. Since the change in true natural increase occurred on a smaller base, it is larger relatively.

8. CAUSES OF DECLINE IN BIRTHS

The discussion of births and birth rates has brought out several facts so far. In the first place, births have been declining in numbers since 1921 in spite of the larger population, one of the causes of this situation being the large drop in specific birth rates. It has also been shown that specific birth rates vary with age of women, with their race and nativity, and with their residence in urban and rural communities. Other chapters of this monograph have brought out these facts: (a) native whites have increased faster than Negroes, while foreign-born whites have remained almost stationary;[2] (b) the proportion of each race and nativity group living in urban communities has increased;[3] and (c) the average age of each group has risen.[4] These four factors are not the only ones that have

[1] The fact that Maryland is included with these southern states in Table 77 but not in Table 79 accounts for a small part of this difference.
[2] *Supra*, pp. 7–14.
[3] *Supra*, pp. 45–48, 66, 77–78.
[4] *Supra*, pp. 140–148, 151–154.

been responsible for the decline in births in the last few years. Nevertheless, they are of apparently outstanding importance among the factors that can be measured. Hence it may be of interest to ascertain approximately the comparative effect of changes in each on the number of births.[1]

TABLE 80.—COMPARATIVE IMPORTANCE IN REDUCING BIRTHS FROM 1920 TO 1929 OF CHANGES IN SPECIFIC BIRTH RATES, URBAN-RURAL DISTRIBUTION, AGE, AND RACE AND NATIVITY

	Total[a]		Native whites		Foreign whites		Negroes	
	Number (thousands)	Per cent	Number (thousands)	Per cent	Number (thousands)	Per cent	Number (thousands)	Per cent
Estimated number of births in 1929 (four conditions as in 1920)[b]...............	3,246	100.0	2,279	100.0	583	100.0	383	100.0
Actual number of births in 1929 (four conditions as in 1929)[c]...................	2,434	75.0	1,833	80.4	288	49.4	313	81.5
Reduction in births due to:								
Four conditions as in 1929.............	811	25.0	446	19.6	295	50.6	71	18.5
Specific birth rates as in 1929[d].........	655	20.2	442	19.4	158	27.1	54	14.0
Urban-rural distribution as in 1929[d]....	82	2.5	58	2.5	5	0.8	19	5.0
Age composition as in 1929[d]..........	61	1.9	33	1.4	27	4.7	1	0.2
Race and nativity composition as in 1929[d].............................	14	0.4	87[e]	3.8[e]	105	17.9	3[e]	0.8[e]

  [a] Total of three groups to right, excluding Mexican and "other colored."
  [b] Computed by dividing the 1929 population (Tables 1 and 2, pp. 1 and 4) into urban-rural, race and nativity, and age groups as of 1920 and applying urban and rural specific birth rates of 1920 (Table 77).
  [c] Births for 1929 in Table 75 minus Mexican and "other colored." The allowance for incomplete birth registration used in Table 75 is used here also.
  [d] Computed by using 1929 values for the specified factor and 1920 values for the other three factors. A slight adjustment is then necessary to make the sum of the declines due to each cause separately equal to the decline due to all four causes working together.
  [e] Increase.

If the population had had the same age, race, and nativity composition, and urban-rural distribution in 1929 as in 1920, and if the 1920 specific birth rates had remained in operation, there would have been about 3,246,000 births in 1929 instead of 2,434,000[2] (Table 80). Changes in these four factors, therefore, caused a decrease of about 811,000 births, or about one-fourth. Of this amount, 655,000 (80.7 per cent) appears as a result of lower specific birth rates, 82,000 (10.1 per cent) as a result of the higher proportion of urban dwellers, 61,000 (7.5 per cent) as a result of an increase in the average age of women, and 14,000 (1.7 per cent) as a

[1] A fifth factor, the proportion of women married in each five-year age period, would have been included if these data had been available at the time the computations were made. Similarly, 1930 instead of 1929 would have been compared with 1920 if data on births by age of mother had been available for 1930.
[2] This discussion includes whites and Negroes (Mexicans being considered as white) but omits other colored.

result of the larger proportion of native white and smaller proportion of foreign-born white women in the population. The drop of the specific birth rates is thus seen to have been four times as important as changes in the three other conditions combined.

If either native whites, foreign-born whites, or Negroes are considered separately, the decline in specific birth rates is seen to be by far the most important factor in each case in accounting for the smaller number of births (Table 80). The higher proportion of urban population stands a low second for native whites and Negroes, with age composition a poor third. Native whites and Negroes made up a larger proportion of the population in 1929 than in 1920, which tended to increase their births but not nearly enough to offset the downward influence of the other factors. The proportion of foreign-born whites in the population was considerably lower in 1929 than in 1920, and births to these women were cut heavily on this account. Changes in age composition and in urban-rural distribution were of minor importance among the foreign born. However, because the average age of the foreign born increased more rapidly than that of the native-born or Negro groups, the factor of age change was correspondingly more important in reducing births to this group.

Although the preceding discussion of the relative importance of specific birth rates, age composition, race and nativity makeup, and urban-rural distribution in decreasing the number of births may help to explain what has happened, it is realized that certain more fundamental causes remain relatively untouched. Have specific birth rates declined because of biological changes affecting fecundity, because birth control is more general, because abortion is practiced to a greater extent, because of disease (particularly venereal), or because of the nervous strain of city life? How important are differences in each of these matters in explaining the differentials in specific birth rates of the race and nativity groups? To what extent do the higher rural specific birth rates reflect differences due to diet, or to an active outdoor life compared with a sedentary occupation?

Unfortunately no body of data exists upon which to base an accurate and conclusive answer to questions such as those just raised. It is natural, therefore, that the social scientist, the physician, and the biologist approaching the problem from different angles should hold opinions that are widely at variance. The authors, belonging to the first of these three groups, can only believe that the practice of contraception is so much simpler and safer than abortion that it would be preferred very generally. They believe such a change in personal habits as is involved in contraception is so much easier to effect than a change in the physiological functioning or the biological constitution of the individual that contraception must be more important than the other factors. However, it should be clearly understood that this is simply an opinion which should be altered as facts warrant.[1]

Reference to certain trends and differentials pointed out earlier may help to explain rationally this belief in the importance of birth control. For one thing, the larger decreases in specific birth rates at the older ages than the younger from 1920 to 1929 are what would be expected to result from voluntary control. Among the great mass of the working classes, older married couples with all the children they could care for would almost certainly make more effort to prevent additional conceptions than younger couples still childless or having only one or two children. This might not be so true during years like 1931 and 1932 when many young married men could not find employment and were supported by their wives or parents, but it should hold true for 1920–1929 and for other long periods.

Considering another factor, the differentials between urban and rural specific birth rates seem explainable to an important extent by differences in the practice of birth control. Children have been less of an economic burden on the farm than in the city, particularly because much of the family food is raised at home instead of being bought for cash at the store, and because there is productive work at which children can help after school hours and during vacations. From the standpoint of personal freedom, farming is an exacting occupation because livestock require

[1] Of the 1,000 married women who replied to Dr. Davis' questionnaire 730 employed contraceptive methods. Katharine B. Davis, *Factors in the Sex Life of Twenty-two Hundred Women*, New York, Harper & Brothers, 1929.

Thirty years ago J. S. Billings wrote regarding causes of the lessening birth rate. "It is probable that the most important factor . . . is the deliberate and voluntary avoidance or prevention of childbearing on the part of a steadily increasing number of married people, who not only prefer to have but few children, but who know how to obtain their wish." John S. Billings, "The Diminishing Birth Rate in the United States," *Forum*, Vol. 15 (June, 1893), p. 475.

In a sample study of hospital cases Pearl finds the pregnancy rate per 100 person-years' exposure to be about 20 per cent lower among white women who have regularly or intermittently used contraceptive methods than among those who report never having used them. This is a small difference; in interpreting it his "second limitation" on p. 385 needs careful consideration. Raymond Pearl, "Contraception and Fertility in 2,000 Women," *Human Biology*, Vol. 4 No. 3 (September, 1932), pp. 363–407.

For a discussion of other causes of the decline in births, see Edward L. Thorndike, "The Decrease in the Size of American Families," *Popular Science Monthly*, Vol. 63 (May, 1903), pp. 64–70. F. A. E. Crew, "The Falling Birth Rate: The Biological Aspect," *British Medical Journal*, September 15, 1928, pp. 477–479. Frank H. Hankins, "Does Advancing Civilization Involve a Decline in Natural Fertility?" *American Journal of Sociology*, Vol. 24, No. 2 (May, 1930), pp. 115–122; "Has the Reproductive Power of Western Peoples Declined?" G. H. L. F. Pitt-Rivers, editor, *Problems of Population*, London, George Allen and Unwin, Ltd., 1932, pp. 181–188 (also published as "Civilization and Fertility," *Eugenics Review*, Vol. 23, No. 2, pp. 145–150). Wagner-Manslau, *Heredity as an Explanation of the Declining Birth Rate*, Cold Spring Harbor, Eugenic Research Association (Monograph Series VI), 1931, 48 pp.

care twice a day or oftener. Farm women usually look after the chickens and often help with other stock; hence if they feel tied down, it may be because of these duties rather than because of children. With city women, on the other hand, the husband's business is usually at some distance from the residence, so that there is only housekeeping to do at home. This is easier than in the country because near-by grocery or delicatessen stores simplify cooking and restaurants may not be far distant. Home duties, in childless families, therefore, are much less confining in the city than in the country. Partly on this account many city women seek full-time occupations outside the home and independent of their husband's business, which gives an additional reason for postponing childbearing temporarily and sometimes permanently. This situation has no counterpart on the farm. Again, social or recreational life in the country has been organized around families to a much greater extent than in cities, the tendency in the latter being to individualize and commercialize it. For these reasons there may be less desire to restrict size of family among farmers than among city dwellers, less use of contraceptive measures, and hence a higher birth rate.

Furthermore, it is probable that the spread of knowledge regarding contraception has been slower in the country than in the city. Where large numbers of people come together in close daily contact, there is more opportunity for this type of information to spread by word of mouth, the method to which its spread has chiefly been restricted, partly by law and partly by social or moral standards. Factories and stores are ideal for this purpose. If the employees are women rather than men contraceptive information probably spreads more rapidly because preventing an excessive number of births may ease a woman's life much more than that of her husband.

All this does not mean that there are no differences in diet, in type of work, in amount of time spent outdoors, and in the practice of abortion which may be partially responsible for higher birth rates in rural than in urban communities, but simply that these factors are less important than differences in birth control. Neither is it implied that the rural-urban birth rate differential may not disappear in time if factory methods are applied to farming or if country-city ties are strengthened in other ways. The movement back to the land that is now going on because of the depression may hasten the disappearance of this differential.[1]

In both city and country it seems reasonable that birth control would be practiced first among the so-called upper classes, made up chiefly of professional and business men in the city and farm owners in the country. Members of this group have usually progressed further in their education;

[1] P. K. Whelpton, "The Extent, Character and Future of the New Landward Movement," *Journal of Farm Economics*, Vol. 15, No. 1 (January, 1933), pp. 57–66.

hence would know more about the various means of preventing conception.[1] Many of them have acquired upper-class standing as a result of their own efforts in business or the professions, their parents having been unskilled workers with little property. Their success in this matter may have been due in part to the deliberate avoidance of many children, lessening family cares and expenses, and allowing the devoting of more energy to economic and social striving. The results of certain studies of the Milbank Memorial Fund are in accord with this hypothesis, for they show a marked relation between fertility and social class in the native white population of 1910. In the urban sample studied, the standardized cumulative birth rate by classes was 129 for professional, 140 for business, 179 for skilled workers, and 223 for unskilled workers. In the rural sample the rate was 247 for farm owners, 275 for farm renters, and 299 for farm laborers.[2] When the age of the wife at marriage was from 14 to 19, the inverse relation between birth rate and social class was even more marked, but when marriage took place from age 25 to 29 the birth rate differed little among the urban classes, although the inverse relation was apparent to some extent in the farm groups.[3] In discussing this matter Notestein states:

The cause of this shift from an inverse to a direct association between fertility and social status as marriage age advances cannot be determined from our data. Probably a number of factors were involved. As pointed out in the English Census Report, "Fertility of Marriage," the fact that the upper-class birth rates were relatively high for women whose late marriages offered slight inducement to family limitation, and relatively low for those whose early and perhaps impecunious marriages made family limitation most desirable, suggests that for early marriages birth is increasingly subject to voluntary control as social status rises.

The decrease in standardized birth rates found in going from unskilled laborers to professional people results from fewer large families rather than from more childless families, for the proportion of urban wives aged 40 to 49 in 1910 who had borne no children varied from 16.3 per cent for unskilled to 19.8 per cent for professional, whereas the proportion who had borne five or more children varied from 28.4 per cent for unskilled

[1] In the Davis study the percentage of women employing contraceptive methods was 76.48 among university and college graduates, 71.29 among college undergraduates and high school and normal school graduates, 64.51 among less than high school, and 63.63 among the private school or tutor groups. Katharine B. Davis, *loc. cit.*, p. 14.

[2] Edgar Sydenstricker and Frank W. Notestein, "Differential Fertility According to Social Class," *Journal of the American Statistical Association*, Vol. 25, n.s., No. 169 (March, 1930), pp. 9–32.

[3] Frank W. Notestein, "The Relation of Social Status to the Fertility of Native-born Married Women in the United States," G. H. L. F. Pitt-Rivers, editor, *Problems of Population*, London, George Allen and Unwin, Ltd., 1932.

to 8.2 per cent for professional.[1] Complete sterility, whether involuntary or otherwise, thus appears of considerable less importance than the factors holding the number of births per wife below five. Class difference in age at marriage probably plays only a minor part in this connection for the modal age at marriage of brides under 40 married between 1900 and 1905 varied only from 18.5 for unskilled laborers to 23.5 for professional.[2] Nevertheless it is probable that a large part of the decrease in the proportion of large families with a rise in social status remains to be accounted for by abortion, by causes of involuntary sterility after one or more births have occurred, or by the practice of contraception to prevent births beyond a certain number or to increase the interval between births thus allowing fewer to occur between marriage and the menopause.

If it is true that the increased practice of contraception has been the means by which much of the decline in the birth rate has been brought about, there still remains the important question as to why contraceptive methods are used to a greater extent now than formerly. A number of hypotheses have been advanced to answer this question, among them the emancipation of women, the lessening influence of the church, the change in the attitude toward sex relations (the abandonment of the double standard), the desire for a higher economic and social standard of living, and the influence of city life. No doubt all of these and others as well have had some influence, but the exact importance of each is undeterminable at the present time.[3]

9. FUTURE TREND OF BIRTH RATES

In view of past trends in births and birth rates and the factors influencing these trends, what may be expected in the future? This question is more difficult to answer than a similar one as to deaths, because births are subject to human control to a much greater extent than deaths. The universal practice of the best methods now known for preventing conception and for causing abortion would reduce the birth rate nearly to zero. Although there is little chance of this extreme being reached, it is

[1] Frank W. Notestein, "The Decrease in Size of Families from 1890 to 1910," *The Quarterly Bulletin of the Milbank Memorial Fund*, Vol. 9, No. 4 (October, 1931), pp. 181–188.

[2] Frank W. Notestein, "The Relation of Social Status to the Fertility of Native-born Married Women in the United States," *op. cit.*

[3] For a discussion of these factors, see the following: Roderich von Ungern-Sternberg, *The Causes of the Decline in Birth-rate within the European Sphere of Civilization*, Cold Spring Harbor, Eugenics Research Association (Monograph Series IV), August, 1931, 202 pp. Ernst Kulka, *The Causes of Declining Birth-Rate*, same series, No. V, 29 pp. Nellie S. Nearing, "Education and Fecundity," *American Statistical Association, Publications*, Vol. 14, n.s., No. 106 (June, 1914), pp. 156–174. George J. Englemann, "Education Not the Cause of Race Decline," *Popular Science Monthly*, Vol. 63 (June, 1903), pp. 172–184. Warren S. Thompson, *Population Problems*, New York, McGraw-Hill Book Company, Inc., 1930, Chap. VIII.

difficult to foretell how rapidly the reduction of the birth rate will proceed and at what point it will cease. As far as deaths are concerned, there is no thought of reducing the death rate to zero—of keeping people alive forever; the goal in the fields of medicine and public health is simply to increase the expectation of life more nearly to the life span of approximately 100 years.

The number of births that will occur in the next few years may perhaps be indicated fairly accurately by prolonging the trend of the recent past. The trend from 1924 to 1931 shown in Figure 30, page 265, is approximately a straight line, the decline per year being about 60,000 for total births, 51,000 for white births, 30,000 for births to native white women, 20,000 for births to foreign-born white women, and 9,000 for Negro births.[1] A continuation of these declines will mean barely 2,260,000 births in 1934, the average for 1930 to 1934 being about 2,400,000, including nearly 2,100,000 white and 300,000 Negro.[2] This assumption is used in Columns *A*, *C*, *D*, *E*, *F*, *G*, and *H* of Table 88, p. 316.

Although the foregoing trend seems probable for the immediate future, it is possible that the decline in births will be checked soon. There may not be such a rise as occurred from 1910 to 1918, but rather a relative stabilization near the 1931 level. According to the "high" assumption, births during 1930–1934 will average about 2,465,000 annually, 2,150,000 being white and 305,000 Negro. Columns *I* and *J* of Table 88 are calculated on this basis.

At the other extreme, there is the possibility that the downward trend of births has been greater than is shown in Figure 30. In Table 75 (on which this figure is based) it is assumed that no improvement in the completeness of birth registration occurred in the registration area from 1920 to 1931, whereas some may have taken place. In the latter case, a more accurate estimate for births for 1931 is 2,375,000, and for 1930 to 1934 an average of nearly 2,300,000 annually, including 2,000,000 white and 275,000 Negro. This assumption is used in Column *B* of Table 88.

To obtain an idea of the number of births that may be expected in the more distant future, it is probably less accurate to extrapolate the past trend of the number of births than to calculate the number of births by extrapolating birth rates and applying them to the population. The latter method makes possible a more adequate allowance for the effect on the number of births of the changes in age and sex distribution that

[1] Calculated by the method of least squares. Judging from the monthly reports of states which are available on March 20, 1933, there were about 65,000 fewer births in 1932 than in 1931, a decline slightly larger than the prior trend.

[2] The trend for total births from 1910 to 1931 is approximately the parabola whose equation is $y = -3.2x^2 + 126.9x + 1,593.9$ with origin 1900, zero. Continuing this parabola indicates 2,210,000 births in 1934, slightly fewer than the straight line.

are to be expected in the future. The trend of birth rates in recent years has been more consistently downward than that of the number of births; hence the future course of the former may be more clearly marked. If the number of births during 1930–1934 averages 2,400,000 as suggested above, there will have been an average decline in specific rates from 1925–1929 to 1930–1934 amounting to about 10 per cent for native whites, 16 per cent for foreign-born whites, and 8 per cent for Negroes. "Low" birth rates for the future may be indicated by a gradual slowing up of these declines and by the reaching in 1970 of an approximately stationary level at rates which would be 67 per cent of the 1925–1929 level in the case of native whites, 65 per cent in the case of foreign-born whites, and 64 per cent in the case of Negroes. This "low" assumption is shown in Table 74 and used in Columns A, C, D, F, and G of Table 88. The effect of about 100,000 fewer births annually during 1930–1934 (2,300,000 a year) with a subsequent decline to the levels just indicated for 1970 is shown in Column B of Table 88, p. 316.

If the number of births during 1930–1934 averages 2,465,000 annually (the "high" estimate given above), the percentage decline of specific rates from 1925–1929 to 1930–1934 will be about 8 per cent for native whites, 14 per cent for foreign-born whites, and 8 per cent for Negroes. "High" specific rates for the future may be indicated by a rapid slowing up of the decline and by the reaching of an approximately stationary level in 1945 or 1950 with native white rates at about 88 per cent of the 1925–1929 level, foreign-born white rates at 82 per cent, and Negro rates at 86 per cent (Table 74 and Table 88, Columns I and J).

These different assumptions regarding birth rate trends have corresponding effects on the trend of number of births. According to the "low" assumptions for birth rates the number of white births will decline rapidly from about 2,227,000 in 1930 to 1,370,000 in 1980, or to about the same number as in 1870 (Table 74, p. 263). If the "medium" assumptions are followed, the decline in number of births will be much more gradual. White births in 1980 will amount to 1,876,000, intermediate between the number in 1890 and 1900. Should the "high" assumptions hold true, however, the decline in number of births that has been going on since 1921 will be checked during this decade, so that births in 1940 will be slightly in excess of those in 1930. By 1980 there will have been a large increase, Table 74 showing 2,859,000 white births, or nearly 30 per cent more than in 1930. Similar trends will be followed in each case by the number of Negro births and total births.

The estimates of future trends of birth rates and births are not reached by any occult process, but are merely an attempt to extrapolate past trends so as to indicate the lowest or the highest birth rates that seem likely to occur during the next 50 years. The authors believe that actual rates will be between these two extremes, perhaps like the "medium," which are considerably nearer the "low" than the "high" (Table 74 and Table 88, Column *H*). It is entirely possible, however, that rates may be either above or below the limits indicated. All that is certain is the great influence which the future course of birth rates will have on the size of the population.

CHAPTER IX

POPULATION GROWTH FROM IMMIGRATION AND NATURAL INCREASE

1. IMMIGRANT ARRIVALS

THE number of immigrants entering the United States has varied much more than the number of births and deaths from year to year and decade to decade. Fortunately, certain records of the movement have been kept by the federal government since 1820, though it is only during recent years that these have been relatively complete. From 1820 to 1867 the alien passengers arriving were counted, of whom it has been estimated that 98 per cent from 1820 to 1855 and 98.5 per cent from 1856 to 1867 were immigrants expecting to remain permanently in the United States.[1] More recently the record is of "immigrants arriving" (1868–1903), "aliens admitted" (1904–1906), and "immigrant aliens admitted" (1907 to date), these different terms being applied to practically identical groups.[2] In addition there has been a count since 1908 of the citizens and nonimmigrant aliens arriving, and of the emigrant and nonemigrant aliens departing, and since 1910 of the citizens departing. These movements became of increasing importance with the great expansion of the so-called new immigration from eastern and southern Europe early in the twentieth century. This immigration was less a family affair than that of previous years from northern and western Europe; single men expecting to work a few months or years and return, with their savings, to the old country constituted a larger proportion of all immigrants.

Although there are several discrepancies in the earlier immigration data, there is little basis for adjustment prior to 1892. A "consistent series" of immigrant arrivals from 1892 to 1927 has been prepared by the National Bureau of Economic Research[2] and will be used here. The chief adjustments made are as follows: (a) the data are restricted to continental United States and Alaska; (b) aliens debarred and tourists have been deducted from total arrivals where necessary; (c) entries through Canada, Canadian and Mexican immigrants, and immigrants arriving as cabin passengers have been included; and (d) aliens resuming domicile in the United States have been omitted. These adjustments make significant

---

[1] National Bureau of Economic Research, *International Migrations*, Vol. II, edited by Walter F. Willcox, New York, Author, 1931, pp. 647–648.

[2] *Ibid.*

differences in certain years before 1908 but are of minor importance subsequently, particularly since 1925. Although the figures for each year may not be absolutely correct, the trend should be clearly indicated from 1892 to 1932 and should be approximated previous to 1892.

The general trend of immigration to the United States has been a long and large upward movement culminating in the years preceding the outbreak of the World War and declining subsequently (Figure 33). Altogether, more than 37,950,000 immigrants have entered since 1820,

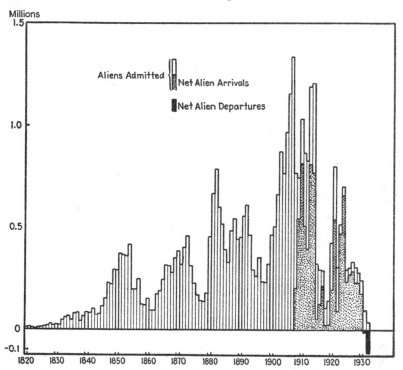

FIG. 33.—Immigrants admitted and net alien arrivals, 1820–1932. (Based on Tables 81 and 82.)

which stamps this as one of the greatest migrations of population in all history. Examining the figures in more detail, an almost uninterrupted increase in immigrants arriving is found, from 8,217 in the fiscal year[1] 1820 to nearly fifty times that number (419,000) in 1854, followed by a reaction that reached the low point of 91,000 in 1861 and 1862 (Table 81). The upward trend was resumed subsequently, with wavelike movements corresponding roughly to economic conditions. High levels were reached in 1872 and 1873, 1881 and 1882, 1891 and 1892, 1906 and 1907, and 1913 and

[1] Fiscal years will be referred to in all cases in this section on immigration (see Table 81, Note *b*).

1914, each of these highs usually above the preceding high, with intervening lows in 1877 and 1878, 1885 and 1886, 1897 and 1898, and 1908 and 1909. The outbreak of the World War and the entrance into it of the United States reduced the number of immigrants arriving by over 90 per

TABLE 81.—IMMIGRANTS ADMITTED TO THE UNITED STATES, 1820–1932[a]
(Thousands)

Fiscal year[b]	Number	Fiscal year[b]	Number	Fiscal year[b]	Number	Fiscal year[b]	Number
1820..........	8	1850..........	290	1880..........	457	1910..........	1,036
1821..........	9	1851..........	372	1881..:......	669	1911..........	878
1822..........	7	1852..........	364	1882..........	789	1912..........	830
1823..........	6	1853....,.....	361	1883..........	603	1913..........	1,191
1824..........	8	1854..........	419	1884..........	519	1914..........	1,212
1825..........	10	1855..........	197	1885..........	395	1915..........	323
1826..........	11	1856..........	197	1886..........	334	1916..........	295
1827..:......	18	1857..........	248	1887..........	490	1917..........	291
1828..........	27	1858..........	121	1888..........	547	1918..........	107
1829..........	22	1859..........	119	1889..........	444	1919..........	138
1830..:......	23	1860..........	151	1890..........	455	1920..........	427
1831..........	22	1861..........	91	1891..........	560	1921..........	802
1832..........	47	1862..........	91	1892..........	613	1922..........	307
1833..........	58	1863..........	174	1893..........	467	1923..........	520
1834..........	64	1864..........	191	1894..........	297	1924..........	704
1835..........	44	1865..........	244	1895..........	266	1925..........	294
1836..........	75	1866..........	314	1896..........	354	1926..........	304
1837..........	78	1867..........	311	1897..........	238	1927..........	335
1838..........	38	1868..........	278	1898..........	236	1928..........	307
1839..........	67	1869..........	353	1899..........	324	1929..........	280
1840..........	82	1870..........	387	1900..........	467	1930..........	242
1841..........	79	1871..........	321	1901..........	506	1931..........	97
1842..........	102	1872..........	405	1902..........	664	1932..........	36
1843..........	69	1873..........	460	1903..........	875	....	.....
1844..........	77	1874..........	313	1904..........	770	....	.....
1845..........	112	1875..........	227	1905..........	970	....	.....
1846..........	151	1876..........	170	1906..........	1,156	....	.....
1847..........	230	1877..........	142	1907..........	1,337	....	.....
1848..........	222	1878..........	138	1908..........	771	....	.....
1849..........	291	1879..........	178	1909..........	749	....	.....

[a] Data for 1892 to 1927 are "consistent series" from *International Migrations*, Vol. II, p. 657. Data for 1820 to 1891 and 1928 to 1932 are from *Annual Report of the Commissioner General of Immigration: 1932*, pp. 186–187, adjustments being made to place 1832, 1843, 1850, and 1868 on a 12-month basis, and a deduction being made for nonimmigrants arriving amounting to 2 per cent from 1820 to 1855 and 1.5 per cent from 1856 to 1867 (cf. *International Migrations*, Vol. II, pp. 647–648).

[b] For 1869 and thereafter the fiscal years end June 30 of year indicated. For definition of fiscal years prior to 1869, see *Annual Report of the Commissioner General of Immigration: 1932*, p. 216.

cent, from 1,212,000 in 1914 to 107,000 in 1918, the smallest amount since the Civil War years of 1861 and 1862. After the signing of the Armistice immigration rose rapidly to 802,000 in 1921 and probably would have exceeded pre-war levels had it not been for the new laws and regulations put into effect. During the fiscal years 1922 to 1924 the maximum number of immigrants admissible according to the quota system varied between 356,995 and 357,803, but the number was reduced to 164,667 on July 1, 1924, and to 153,714 on July 1, 1929. Nonquota immigrants (chiefly from Canada and Mexico) were almost as numerous as quota immigrants in some of these years, total immigrants amounting to 704,000 in 1924 and 335,000 in 1927, nearly double the quota allotment in each case.

Commencing in the summer of 1930, immigration was still further restricted by a regulation denying visas to aliens deemed likely to become public charges. Since the contract labor law of 1885 prohibits the entrance of immigrants with jobs, about the only ones allowed to enter are those with independent means, or the wives, husbands, and minor children of United States citizens. During the fiscal year 1930 there were 242,000 immigrant aliens admitted, but the number was reduced to 97,000 during 1931 and still further to 36,000 during 1932, chiefly owing to the foregoing regulation and the depression which caused its promulgation. Immigration may be expected to remain at this low level until there is considerable recovery from the depression and the "public charge" regulation is modified.[1]

2. NET IMMIGRATION

Although the flood of arrivals has been the outstanding feature of international migration as far as the United States is concerned, other movements should not be overlooked. Many persons coming as immigrants have not remained permanently but have returned to the old country, often to live on savings from earnings here (Table 82). Furthermore, the number of nonimmigrant aliens arriving since 1908[2] has been smaller than the number of nonemigrant aliens departing, particularly during 1908, 1910–1916, and 1931–1932. As a result, the excess of arrivals over departures has been considerably below the number of immigrants entering (Figure 33). Because of the World War, immigration was so decreased and departures of aliens so increased that in 1915 and 1918 the net addition to the population was reduced to less than one-fifth of the immigrants entering. But even before the war the return movement was so large as to amount to at least 20 per cent of the arrivals in every year, and to over 70 per cent in 1908. During the first years under the quota system of immigration, net additions to the population usually amounted to 80 to 90 per cent of immigrants arriving, but the more

[1] In his speech of acceptance on August 11, 1932, President Hoover said, "I favor rigidly restricted immigration. I have by executive direction, in order to relieve us of added unemployment, already reduced the inward movement to less than the outward movement. I shall adhere to that policy."

[2] Data before 1908 are not available as to nonimmigrant aliens arriving and emigrant and nonemigrant aliens departing.

TABLE 82.—ARRIVALS AND DEPARTURES OF ALIENS, AND EXCESS OF ARRIVALS OF ALIENS
AND CITIZENS, 1908–1932[a]

(Thousands)

Fiscal year[b]	Immigrant aliens arriving[c]	Emigrant aliens departing[c]	Nonimmigrant aliens arriving[c]	Nonemigrant aliens departing[c]	Excess of arrivals over departures	
					Aliens[d]	Citizens[e]
1908...................	771	390	140	317	205	......
1909...................	749	223	190	172	545	.....
1910...................	1,036	199	154	175	817	− 97
1911...................	873	294	149	218	512	− 79
1912...................	830	332	176	278	398	− 75
1913...................	1,191	307	226	299	815	− 63
1914...................	1,211	302	181	325	768	− 84
1915...................	322	203	104	175	51	66
1916...................	294	129	64	106	126	12
1917...................	290	65	63	74	217	2
1918...................	107	93	98	93	20	−200
1919...................	138	123	93	88	22	−123
1920...................	427	287	188	133	195	− 30
1921...................	802	246	169	172	554	− 44
1922...................	306	197	119	140	88	− 68
1923...................	520	81	146	114	473	44
1924...................	703	76	168	135	662	32
1925...................	294	92	161	128	234	21
1926...................	304	77	188	145	271	15
1927...................	335	73	198	174	287	30
1928...................	307	77	188	191	228	15
1929...................	279	69	193	177	228	35
1930...................	241	50	198	215	175	31
1931...................	97	61	178	224	− 10	− 3
1932...................	35	103	135	180	−112	− 42

[a] From Table 1 of *Annual Report of the Commissioner General of Immigration* for years indicated, except as noted below.

[b] For the 12 months ending June 30 of year indicated.

[c] Includes movement between United States and elsewhere except Alaska, Porto Rico, and Hawaii. The movement of aliens between United States and Alaska, Porto Rico, and Hawaii is small in comparison with the foregoing. It can be classified by immigrant and nonimmigrant during 1918 to 1924 only.

[d] From 1919 to 1932 includes movement between United States and elsewhere; hence differs slightly from Column 1 minus Column 2 plus Column 3 minus Column 4. See Table 109 of *Annual Report of the Commissioner General of Immigration, 1929* and corresponding table in reports for subsequent years.

[e] Includes movement between the United States and elsewhere, except Alaska in all years, and except Porto Rico and Hawaii from 1910 to 1932, inclusive. See Table 110 of *Annual Report of the Commissioner General of Immigration, 1929* and corresponding table in reports for subsequent years.

recent "public charge" restrictions and the depression reduced arrivals below departures in 1931 and 1932.

The trend of the net addition to the population from the excess of alien arrivals over departures has been much the same as that of immigrant aliens arriving, the chief difference being the smaller numbers of the net movement and the reaching of highs or lows in slightly different years (Figure 33). The largest addition on record was 817,000 in 1910, whereas the largest number of immigrant arrivals was 1,337,000 in 1907. After the United States entered the World War, net arrivals fell off, reaching the low mark of 20,000 in 1918, or less than one-fortieth of the 1910 figure (Figure 27). A rapid recovery took place after the close of the war, the excess of arrivals reaching 554,000 in 1921 and 662,000 in 1924, following which the revised quotas reduced net additions to 234,000 in 1925. This level was maintained with comparatively little change through 1930, but in 1931 and 1932 the "public charge" restriction so reduced arrivals while the depression so speeded up departures that net losses of 10,000 and 112,000 occurred.

The effect on the size of the population of the difference between the inward and outward movement of citizens has not been of great importance. In most years from 1910 to 1922 departures exceeded arrivals, averaging 60,000 per year with a maximum difference of 200,000 in 1918. During 1923–1930, the balance was on the other side, net arrivals of citizens averaging almost 28,000 per year, but in 1931 and 1932 the net movement was outward. It should be remembered, however, that citizens include naturalized persons as well as those native born; hence an excess of citizens departing over those arriving may decrease the foreign-born population as well as the native population, while an excess of citizens arriving over those departing may add to both the native and the foreign-born groups.

Prior to the opening of the World War almost all of the additions to population through immigration accrued to the white race, over 95 per cent of net arrivals of aliens during 1909–1914 consisting of white persons (Table 83). The excess of Mexicans arriving over those departing averaged less than 18,000 annually during this period and of Negroes about 5,500. During certain earlier years a rather large number of Chinese and Japanese had entered, but these movements were small in comparison with that of whites and were soon ended by laws and regulations. From 1915 to 1919 immigration from Europe was so curtailed by the World War that Mexicans made up almost one-fifth of the net arrivals even though the actual number entering did not change greatly. After the close of the war the large influx of immigrants from Europe raised the proportion of whites to about 85 per cent during 1921–1924 in spite of a considerable increase in Mexican arrivals. The reduction of quota limits in 1925 affected the Eastern Hemisphere but not the Western, the proportion of Mexicans rising to over 20 per cent during 1925–1929. During these years net admissions of Negroes barely averaged 1,000 per year, while net departures of Chinese averaged almost 1,000, and of Japanese 3,700. In 1932 the Negro movement balanced, net departures of Chinese reached a new high, and the net arrival of Mexicans prior to 1931 was

POPULATION TRENDS IN THE UNITED STATES

TABLE 83.—EXCESS OF ARRIVALS OVER DEPARTURES, BY RACE OR PEOPLE, 1909–1932[a]
(Thousands)

Fiscal year[b]	All aliens[c]	White aliens[d]	Negro aliens	Japanese aliens	Chinese aliens	Mexican aliens
1909	543.8	528.1	3.6	−3.1	−2.6	17.5
1910	817.6	796.5	4.2	−3.4	−1.1	19.8
1911	512.1	488.0	6.5	−1.8	−1.4	20.6
1912	401.9	372.7	6.2	0.5	−1.0	23.6
1913	815.3	795.1	5.7	3.2	−1.4	12.7
1914	769.3	746.9	7.5	4.1	−2.1	12.9
1915	50.1	26.9	4.4	3.8	−0.8	16.0
1916	125.9	97.4	3.8	3.3	−0.9	22.3
1917	216.5	183.1	7.8	4.1	−1.8	23.2
1918	18.6	5.5	5.5	4.2	−0.2	3.0
1919	20.8	− 9.3	8.3	3.7	−0.5	18.2
1920	193.5	125.7	10.2	0.5	−0.4	57.2
1921	552.1	505.9	10.1	−1.3	−1.7	38.9
1922	87.1	63.4	4.1	−2.4	−0.8	22.8
1923	472.8	390.5	8.8	0.4	1.0	72.1
1924	662.6	540.2	14.5	4.0	1.6	102.2
1925	232.9	193.6	− 0.2	−5.1	−0.3	45.0
1926	268.4	218.1	0.6	−4.6	−0.4	54.4
1927	284.5	219.5	1.2	−4.3	−1.6	69.7
1928	226.3	180.8	1.3	−3.0	−1.4	48.6
1929	226.8	194.7	2.4	−1.5	−0.9	31.9
1930	173.8	170.0	2.0	−2.1	−1.4	5.4
1931	− 10.2	4.4	0.8	−1.6	−2.0	− 11.8
1932	−112.8	− 70.3	(e)	−2.8	−4.0	− 35.5

[a] From *Annual Report of the Commissioner General of Immigration: 1909*, Table 4, and corresponding table in reports for subsequent years. Includes movement between United States (including Alaska, Porto Rico, and Hawaii) and elsewhere.

[b] For the 12 months ending June 30 of year indicated.

[c] Data for certain years differ from Table 82 because here Alaska, Porto Rico, and Hawaii are included with the United States.

[d] Does not include Mexicans.

[e] Net departure of 11 Negroes.

changed to the net departure of 35,500, the "public charge" regulation affecting the latter particularly. There was thus a net decrease of 42,500 colored aliens and 70,300 white aliens, a much greater loss relatively in the former case.[1]

3. FUTURE IMMIGRATION

In view of the extreme fluctuations of immigration in the past, and the extent to which it is affected by economic conditions, legislative action, and administrative regulation, there is all too little basis for estimating future trends. The lower limit of the increase of population from an excess of arrivals over departures seems fairly obvious, for in spite of a net loss of 154,000 aliens and citizens during the fiscal year

[1] Mexicans are classified as colored in this comparison.

1932, it is unlikely that departures will do much more than offset arrivals on the whole during coming decades. An upper limit is not so apparent, however. If immigration restrictions should be removed, it is quite probable that net arrivals of aliens would rise to a figure well above the record of 817,000 during the fiscal year 1910. Judging from the present temper of the nation, however, it is unlikely that this will occur. With the end of the depression the "public charge" regulation may be dropped, but there would seem to be more likelihood of the quota system being extended to countries in the Western Hemisphere than of its being abolished.

Because of the wide range of possibilities, the estimates of future population growth in Table 88, p. 316, contain several assumptions regarding immigration. The "low" is that arrivals will be balanced by departures (Columns A, B, and C). Intermediate estimates are given in Columns D to H, while in Column I it is assumed that net arrivals of whites will average 20,000 annually during 1930–1934, 100,000 annually during 1935–1939, and 200,000 annually thereafter, and of Negroes 800 annually during 1930–1934, and 1,600 thereafter. This is approximately what might occur if the present quotas permitting 153,714 immigrants from countries in the Eastern Hemisphere were filled, and quotas for other countries established on a similar basis. Comparing Columns C, D, and E, or Columns I and J, shows the effect of more or less immigration on population growth under the stated conditions of birth and death rates and permits the making of a variety of combinations.

4. ANNUAL NATURAL INCREASE AND NET IMMIGRATION, 1910–1931

Although births and deaths were not registered with sufficient completeness in South Dakota and Texas to meet the requirements of the United States registration area as late as 1931, the state and federal reports on vital statistics provide a basis for estimating the annual natural increase of the United States since 1910. These estimates should be fairly accurate since 1920, although only rough approximations previously. By combining figures for immigration with these data, the annual population growth from all sources may be indicated. From 1910–1915 deaths were declining faster than births; hence there was a gain in natural increase, the amount rising from about 1,055,000 in 1910 to 1,344,000 in 1915 (Figure 34 and Table 84). The influenza epidemic increased deaths to such an extent as to lower natural increase to 824,000 during 1918, but the unusually large number of births following demobilization raised it to 1,625,000 in 1921, the highest mark for all time. Since 1921, births have been decreasing in numbers more rapidly than deaths; hence natural increase has been declining with minor interruptions in trend. It was just under 1,000,000 in 1931 and probably fell still lower in 1932.

Because natural increase was more important than net immigration in contributing to population growth during this period, the general trend of growth has been like that of natural increase. The immediate effect of the large variations in immigration has usually been to exaggerate the

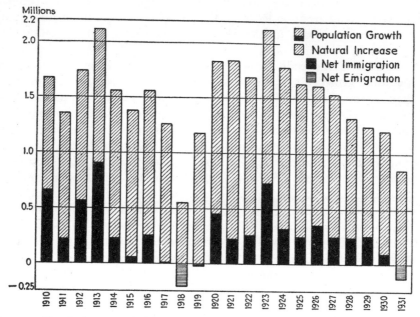

Fig. 34.—Population growth from natural increase and net immigration, 1930–1931. (Based on Table 84.)

upward and downward movements. Total gain in population rose more rapidly than natural increase from 1910 to 1913, declined more rapidly from 1914 to 1918, again rose more rapidly from 1919 to 1923, and again declined more rapidly from 1924 to 1931. Fluctuations in the natural increase and total gain of the white population from 1910 to 1931 have been much the same as those of the total population because whites are nine times as numerous as colored persons.

Annual figures for native whites, foreign-born whites, and Negroes are first available in 1920. Because emigration is small, natural increase and total growth have been almost identical for native whites. The largest native white gain (1,651,000) was made in 1921, but this level was held fairly well up to 1924, after which there was a decline of almost one-third to 1931, when growth was 1,129,000. Quite different from this has been the situation among the foreign-born whites. Net immigration exceeded deaths from 1920 to 1924, the excess reaching a maximum of 391,000 in

GROWTH FROM IMMIGRATION

TABLE 84.—POPULATION GROWTH FROM NATURAL INCREASE AND NET IMMIGRATION, BY RACE AND NATIVITY, 1910–1931

(Thousands)

Calendar Year	Population growth[a]	Natural increase[b]	Net immigration[c]	Calendar Year	Population growth[a]	Natural increase[b]	Net immigration[c]
TOTAL POPULATION				TOTAL WHITE[d]			
1910............	1,691	1,055	636	1910............	1,616	988	628
1911............	1,369	1,156	213	1911............	1,276	1,083	193
1912............	1,743	1,208	535	1912............	1,656	1,130	526
1913............	2,099	1,207	892	1913............	2,023	1,132	891
1914............	1,565	1,337	228	1914............	1,470	1,252	218
1915............	1,399	1,344	55	1915............	1,306	1,272	34
1916............	1,550	1,289	260	1916............	1,430	1,201	229
1917............	1,254	1,250	4	1917............	1,173	1,183	− 10
1918............	607	824	−217	1918............	615	843	−228
1919............	1,167	1,178	− 11	1919............	1,035	1,095	− 60
1920............	1,834	1,389	445	1920............	1,689	1,253	436
1921............	1,854	1,625	229	1921............	1,680	1,451	229
1922............	1,698	1,423	274	1922............	1,536	1,268	268
1923............	2,119	1,380	739	1923............	1,958	1,236	722
1924............	1,794	1,481	313	1924............	1,628	1,323	305
1925............	1,625	1,380	245	1925............	1,480	1,229	251
1926............	1,602	1,250	352	1926............	1,459	1,107	352
1927............	1,536	1,293	243	1927............	1,403	1,155	248
1928............	1,326	1,080	246	1928............	1,223	978	245
1929............	1,245	993	252	1929............	1,147	898	249
1930............	1,204	1,108	96	1930............	1,087	988	99
1931............	872	999	−127	1931............	780	901	−121
1932............	828	998	−170				
NATIVE WHITE[d]				FOREIGN-BORN WHITE[d]			
1920............	1,488	1,497	− 9	1920............	204	−250	454
1921............	1,651	1,675	− 24	1921............	29	−230	258
1922............	1,530	1,508	21	1922............	5	−246	251
1923............	1,574	1,490	84	1923............	391	−260	651
1924............	1,613	1,571	42	1924............	14	−254	268
1925............	1,499	1,485	14	1925............	− 20	−262	242
1926............	1,443	1,375	68	1926............	16	−274	290
1927............	1,424	1,413	11	1927............	− 22	−263	241
1928............	1,301	1,256	44	1928............	− 80	−285	205
1929............	1,219	1,174	44	1929............	− 74	−283	209
1930............	1,267	1,254	13	1930............	−184	−272	88
1931............	1,129	1,164	− 35	1931............	−356	−269	− 87
NEGRO				NEGRO			
1920............	128	118	10	1926............	127	126	1
1921............	156	151	5	1927............	122	121	1
1922............	139	134	5	1928............	93	91	2
1923............	135	123	12	1929............	86	84	2
1924............	141	135	6	1930............	99	97	2
1925............	131	131	....	1931............	87	87	....

[a] "Natural increase" plus "Net immigration." The sum of the increases for the calendar years 1910 to 1919, inclusive, or 1920 to 1929 is not equal to the intercensal increase shown in Table 1 since the 1910 census was taken on April 15 and the 1930 census on April 1.

[b] Births (Table 75) minus deaths (Table 64) adjusted so that natural increase plus net immigration between census dates equals the population growth shown by the census. For this purpose, the 1920 census is increased by 150,000 to allow for the probable deficiency in the enumeration of Negroes (see *Fifteenth Census of the United States: 1930*, Vol. III, Pt. 1, p. 7). The adjustments for births, deaths, and immigration are as follows: total population 1910–1919, 1.6 per cent; 1920–1929, 0.6 per cent; total white 1910–1919, 1.5 per cent; 1920–1929, 0.7 per cent; native white 0.9 per cent; foreign-born white 1.5 per cent; Negro 2.2 per cent.

[c] Excess of arrivals over departures for citizens and aliens for calendar years similar to data for fiscal years in Tables 82 and 83. Arrivals and departures are adjusted to the same extent and for the same reason as births and deaths (see Note b).

[d] Mexicans are classified as white since their births and deaths are so classified by the Division of Vital Statistics.

1923. But from 1927 to 1931 the reverse was true and deaths exceeded net immigration, the number of foreign-born whites declining over 350,000 in 1931 for this reason.

Practically all of the Negro growth has come from natural increase, immigration having been an insignificant factor (Tables 65 and 84). The largest gain was 156,000 in 1921, the next five years being fairly stable around 135,000. Growth since 1928 has averaged well under 100,000, the 1931 figure of 87,000 being nearly 45 per cent below the high point of 1921.

5. ESTIMATED NATURAL INCREASE AND NET IMMIGRATION, 1800–1930

Although there is no adequate basis for annual estimates of natural increase and total growth of population prior to 1910, the data presented in Tables 62, 63, 74, and 81 enable a rough approximation by decades for the white population back to 1800. The sum of the estimated natural increase and immigration is above the gain shown between censuses for every decade, the adjustment required in births, deaths, and immigration in order to eliminate this difference varying from as little as 0.7 per cent during 1920–1930 to 5.3 per cent during 1830–1840 and 1860–1870 (Table 85). But considering the fragmentary information regarding deaths, the incompleteness of birth registration and of the census enumeration of children, and the absolute lack of information prior to 1907 regarding the departures of aliens who entered as immigrants and the arrivals and departures of citizens and nonimmigrant aliens, the wonder is that the difference between the estimates and the census figures is not larger before 1920.

Ignorance of the movement of aliens other than immigrant arrivals is especially serious, for during the fiscal years 1908–1932, inclusive, immigrant aliens arriving totaled 12,463,000, over half again as much as the excess of all aliens arriving over all aliens departing, which only amounted to 7,769,000. The ratio of net arrivals to immigrants probably was smaller in earlier years. Nevertheless the nonexistence of data regarding other alien movements than immigrant arrivals prior to 1908 undoubtedly contributes much to the size of the adjustment needed in Table 85. The number of aliens departing probably rose in proportion to arrivals during 1860–1870 because of the Civil War, during 1890–1900 because of the hard times, and during 1900–1907 because of the change in the type of immigrants.

The estimates of natural increase may need as much adjustment as those of immigration or even more. It is possible that the allowance made for an underenumeration of children is too high and hence the estimated number of births in Table 74 is too high, although a large discrepancy is unlikely in view of the undernumeration in recent censuses. It is quite probable that deaths are underestimated because the crude death rates shown in Table 62 are too low for the entire United States. This is particularly true for 1860–1870, since no allowance was made for the unusual losses due to the Civil War.

The estimates in Table 85 are of value as a check on the preceding discussion of births, deaths, and immigration, but much more important

TABLE 85.—ESTIMATED GROWTH OF THE WHITE POPULATION FROM NATURAL INCREASE AND NET IMMIGRATION, BY DECADES, 1800–1930

Decade	White population growth[a] (thousands)	Natural increase[b]		Immigration[c]		Adjustment,[b] per cent
		Thousands	Per cent of population growth	Thousands	Per cent of population growth	
	A	B	C	D	E	F
1800–10.................	1,556	1,494	96.0	62	4.0	4.4
1810–20.................	2,005	1,934	96.5	71	3.5	5.2
1820–30.................	2,671	2,548	95.4	123	4.6	4.7
1830–40.................	3,658	3,165	86.5	493	13.5	5.3
1840–50.................	5,357	3,937	73.5	1,420	26.5	3.4
1850–60.................	7,369	4,811	65.3	2,558	34.7	3.6
1860–70.................	7,415	5,341	72.0	2,074	28.0	5.3
1870–80.................	9,066	6,486	71.5	2,580	28.5	2.7
1880–90.................	11,581	6,617	57.1	4,964	42.9	4.0
1890–1900..............	11,708	8,019	68.5	3,689	31.5	2.4
1900–10.................	14,923	8,680	58.2	6,243	41.8	2.8
1910–20.................	13,089	10,864	83.0	2,225	17.0	1.6
1920–30.................	15,466	12,131	78.4	3,335	21.6	0.7

a *Fourteenth Census of the United States: 1920*, Vol. II, p 29, and *Fifteenth Census of the United States: 1930*, Vol. III, Pt. 1, pp. 24, 27.

Births, deaths. and immigration have been adjusted as explained below so that in each decade natural increase plus immigration equals the intercensal growth. Mexicans are included with whites in 1930 in accordance with prior census practice.

b The excess of births over deaths. Births for 1800 to 1909 are estimated from Table 74, Column E, by straight-line interpolation; for 1910 to 1929, see Table 75. Deaths for 1800 to 1909 are estimated by applying crude rates in Tables 62 and 63 to the current population and interpolating for intervening years; for 1910 to 1929, see Table 64. These estimates for births are decreased and for deaths increased by the percentages shown in Column F so that in each decade natural increase plus immigration equals the intercensal growth.

c For 1800 to 1819 arbitrary assumptions based on the estimated arrival of 250,000 immigrants from the close of the Revolutionary War to 1819 (see *Annual Report of the Commissioner General of Immigration: 1931*); for 1820 to 1908 immigrant arrivals adjusted from Table 81 with deductions for colored immigrants and with an increasing deduction from 1900 to 1908 to allow for departing aliens (in the fiscal year 1909 net arrivals of white aliens were 71.2 per cent of white immigrants arriving); for 1909 to 1929 net arrival of whites based on Table 83. These figures for immigrant arrivals are decreased and for returning immigrants are increased by the percentages shown in Column F so that in each decade natural increase plus immigration equals the intercensal growth.

is their showing the small part that immigration played directly as compared with natural increase in contributing to the population growth of most decades. From 1800 to 1830 less than 5 per cent of population growth came from immigrant arrivals, and from 1830 to 1840 less than 15 per cent. In the decades from 1840 to 1910 immigration varied between 27 and 43 per cent of the population growth, averaging about 33 per cent.

Since 1910 almost four-fifths of the population growth has come from natural increase, nearly as much as was the case more than a century ago.

6. HAS IMMIGRATION INCREASED POPULATION?

The fact that the population growth during each decade has come so largely from natural increase rather than from immigration does not contradict the Walker theory that immigration "instead of constituting a new reënforcement to the population, simply resulted in a replacement of native by foreign elements,"[1] for there is nothing in Table 85 to prove that natural increase would not have been still larger if no immigration had taken place. A strict interpretation of the Walker theory is that births in past intervals have been reduced by an amount equal to or larger than the net arrivals of immigrants in that period.[2] But unless the reduction in births was considerably larger than the net immigration, it would seem that immigration increased the population almost at once. Most of the foreigners arriving were young adults among whom death rates were low. Although there was an excess of males, there was nevertheless a large number of females, most of whom were in the childbearing ages. Specific birth rates were high among foreign-born women; hence the immigrants not only contributed themselves to population growth on their arrival but also contributed their children born subsequently. If immigration prevented a number of births equal to net arrivals of immigrants, it prevented the addition to the population of infants subject to high death rates. Survivors from such a group would not reach the childbearing period and contribute in their turn to population growth for at least 15 years. Hence it would seem that if immigration did not add to current population growth, births to native persons must have been reduced by an amount equal to the net arrival of foreigners plus the children born to them within a few years of their arrival plus an allowance for higher death rates among native infants than young foreign adults.[3] Advocates of the Walker theory may contend that immigrants arriving

[1] Francis A. Walker, "Restriction of Immigration," *Atlantic Monthly*, Vol. 77, No. 464 (June, 1896), p. 824.

Perhaps this should be referred to as the Franklin theory rather than the Walker theory, for in 1751 Benjamin Franklin wrote "The Importation of Foreigners into a Country, that has as many Inhabitants as the present Employments and the Provisions for Subsistence will bear, will be in the End no Increase of People; unless the New Comers have more Industry and Frugality than the Natives, and then they will provide more Subsistence, and increase in the Country; but they will gradually eat the natives out." See *The Writings of Benjamin Franklin*, collected and edited by Albert Henry Smyth, New York, The Macmillan Company, 1907, Vol. III, "1750–1759." *Cf.* p. 70.

[2] Walker mentioned the period 1830–1860 in particular. *Loc. cit.*

[3] See Table 88, Columns *D*, *E*, and *F*, for the effect on population growth of a given annual increase in net immigration and of an equal increase in births.

in a given period would feel the competition of later arrivals; hence births among them would be reduced the same as among the native groups. This may be true to some extent, but because there is so much evidence of high birth rates to foreign-born women the additions to the population from these births would be large nevertheless.

7. SHORT-TIME EFFECT OF IMMIGRATION

According to Walker and his supporters, immigration was a process of substitution in the population not because it prevented the birth rate from rising, but because it caused the rate to fall.[1] As far as the authors are aware, however, no attempt has been made to measure what would have been the probable effect on population growth of no immigration combined with a smaller decline in the birth rate than has actually taken place. It is admitted that such measurements cannot be made with absolute accuracy, but it is believed that available data permit approximations.[2] The indications are that the birth rate to white women aged 15 to 44 decreased from 1800 to 1810 and during every subsequent decade; hence maintaining the rate as it was at the beginning of any decade would have resulted in more births. Such a stabilizing of the birth rate would have added only 20,000 births during 1800–1810, but over 1,000,000 during 1880–1890, 1900–1910, and over 3,000,000 during 1920–1930 (Table 86). These amounts are large, but the number of immigrant arrivals in each decade was much larger, especially from 1840 to 1920. In making this comparison, births to mothers who entered as immigrants during the decade have not been deducted from white births, but neither have emigrant aliens been deducted from immigrants prior to 1900. The former should be the more important factor; hence the excess of immigrants over the number of births lost because of the declining birth rate is even larger than these figures indicate. Clearly there has been no decade since 1830, taken by itself, in which current immigration has not added to population growth.

[1] For a discussion of the theory and for supporting arguments, see Francis A. Walker, "Restriction of Immigration," *Atlantic Monthly*, Vol. 77, No. 464 (June, 1896), pp. 822–829; "Immigration and Degradation," *Forum*, Vol. 11 (August, 1891), pp. 634–644. Henry Pratt Fairchild, *Immigration*, New York, The Macmillan Company, 1913, pp. 215–225. Prescott F. Hall, *Immigration*, 2d ed., New York, Henry Holt & Company, 1908, pp. 107–120. Sydney C. Fisher, "Has Immigration Increased Population?" *Popular Science Monthly*, Vol. 48 (December, 1895), pp. 244–255. Fisher states "immigration has not materially increased, but on the contrary, has somewhat decreased the American population."

For dissenting arguments, see the following: Frederick A. Bushee, *Principles of Sociology*, New York, Henry Holt & Company, ᶜ 1923, 577 pp. J. M. Gillette, "Immigration and the Increase of Population in the United States," *Social Forces*, Vol. 5, No. 1 (September, 1926), pp. 37–51. E. A. Goldenweiser, "Walker's Theory of Immigration," *American Journal of Sociology*, Vol. 18, No. 3 (November, 1912), pp. 342–351.

[2] A more detailed analysis supporting the summary here presented is planned for later publication.

TABLE 86.—IMMIGRATION OF WHITES AND ESTIMATED DECREASE IN WHITE BIRTHS DUE TO DECLINING BIRTH RATE, BY 10-, 20-, AND 30-YEAR PERIODS, 1800–1930

Period	Birth rate per 1,000 women 15–44		Number of births in period at birth rate of		Decrease in births due to decrease in birth rate[e] (thousands)	Immigration[f] (thousands)	Excess of immigration over decrease in births[g] (thousands)
	First year of period[a]	Average of period[b]	First year[c] (thousands)	Average of period[d] (thousands)			
	A	B	C	D	E	F	G
TEN-YEAR PERIOD							
1800–10	278	276	2,820	2,800	20	70	50
1810–20	274	267	3,790	3,690	100	80	−20
1820–30	260	250	5,010	4,820	190	130	−60
1830–40	240	231	6,420	6,180	240	520	280
1840–50	222	208	8,230	7,710	520	1,470	950
1850–60	194	189	10,350	10,080	270	2,650	2,380
1860–70	184	176	12,480	11,940	540	2,190	1,650
1870–80	167	161	14,790	14,260	530	2,650	2,120
1880–90	155	146	17,280	16,260	1,000	5,170	4,170
1890–1900	137	134	19,250	18,830	420	3,780	3,360
1900–10	130	124	22,630	21,580	1,040	6,620	5,580
1910–20	117	115	24,590	24,170	420	2,790	2,370
1920–30	113	100	27,210	24,080	3,130	3,370	240
1930–40	87	...	......	......	.....	.....	.....
TWENTY-YEAR PERIOD							
1800–20	278	272	6,630	6,490	140	150	10
1810–30	274	258	9,040	8,510	530	210	−320
1820–40	260	240	11,920	10,990	920	650	−270
1830–50	240	220	15,150	13,890	1,260	1,990	730
1840–60	222	198	19,950	17,800	2,160	4,120	1,960
1850–70	194	182	23,470	22,020	1,450	4,840	3,390
1860–80	184	168	28,700	26,190	2,500	4,840	2,340
1870–90	167	154	33,100	30,510	2,580	7,820	5,240
1880–1900	155	140	38,850	35,080	3,760	8,950	5,190
1890–1910	137	129	42,920	40,410	2,510	10,400	7,890
1900–20	130	120	49,560	45,750	3,810	9,410	5,600
1910–30	117	108	52,270	48,250	4,020	6,160	2,140
THIRTY-YEAR PERIOD							
1800–30	278	264	11,900	11,300	600	280	−320
1810–40	274	249	16,150	14,680	1,470	730	−740
1820–50	260	230	21,140	18,700	2,440	2,120	−320
1830–60	240	209	27,530	23,970	3,560	4,640	1,080
1840–70	222	191	34,550	29,730	4,820	6,320	1,500
1850–80	194	175	40,220	36,280	3,940	7,500	3,560
1860–90	184	161	48,520	42,450	6,070	10,020	3,950
1870–1900	167	147	56,060	49,340	6,720	11,600	4,880
1880–1910	155	135	65,060	56,670	8,390	15,570	7,180
1890–1920	137	124	71,350	64,580	6,770	13,190	6,420
1900–30	130	113	80,330	69,830	10,500	12,780	2,280

[a] From Table 74, Column G, p. 263. Estimates for some decades may be as much as 5.3 per cent too high (see Table 85).

[b] Average of rates in Column A, e.g., the average of 264 for the 30-year period 1800–1830 is obtained from the figures for 1800 to 1830, inclusive, the first and last having a weight of 1 and the others of 2.

[c] Column C bears the same ratio to D as A does to B.

[d] From Table 74.

[e] Column C minus Column D.

[f] From Table 85, Column D, but without adjustment described in Note c of that table.

[g] Column F minus Column E.

NOTE: Certain apparent discrepancies in arithmetic in this table are due to the fact that it its preparation, numbers were carried out to the nearest 100 although shown here only to the nearest 10,000. Because of the estimates required by inadequate data, the results are only rough approximations.

Even if a 20-year period is considered, the results are similar. Thus, if the birth rate during 1830–1850 (a period of rapid fall) had remained as it was in 1830, there would have been about 1,260,000 more births in these 20 years (Table 86). But during this period 1,990,000 immigrants entered, exceeding these births by 730,000. The margin is much greater during 1870–1890, also a period of rapid decline in birth rate, but one of much larger immigration relative to population. Stabilizing the birth rate at the 1870 figure would have resulted in nearly 2,600,000 more births in the following 20 years, but this is only one-third of the 7,800,000 immigrants who arrived. During most years from 1910 to 1930 immigration was restricted by the World War and by quota laws, the excess of alien arrivals over departures amounting to 6,160,000. Although this period witnessed the largest percentage decline in birth rate, stabilizing the rate at the 1910 figure would have increased births by only 4,000,000, which is one-third below *net* immigration.

If the additional births that would have occurred by stabilizing the birth rate over a 30-year period are compared with immigrant arrivals during this period, the differences are smaller but still indicate that immigration has added to current population growth on the whole. For 30-year periods commencing in 1800, 1810, or 1820, stabilization of the birth rate at the initial figure would have added a number of births in excess of the number of immigrants entering and hence have resulted in a larger population at the end of 30 years than the actual population with immigration (Table 86). This is to be expected because of the small amount of immigration in proportion to the population during decades before 1830. For 30-year periods starting in 1830 and later the opposite is true; the number of births which would have been added by stabilizing the birth rate at the initial figure was less than the large number of foreigners that would have been kept out by the stoppage of immigration. During the particular period which Walker mentioned, 1830–1860, maintenance of the 1830 birth rate to women 15 to 44 would have added about 3,560,000 births. From the 4,640,000 foreigners who entered in these years should be subtracted those who departed; similarly, the number of births to immigrant women should be deducted from white births. Allowing for both these factors would still leave an excess of immigrants over births lost because of the decline in the birth rate. This excess increased rapidly in later 30-year periods up to 1880–1910 but was sharply reduced in 1900–1930. These data bear only on the immediate effect of immigration, but they do prove that in any 10-, 20-, or 30-year period commencing later than 1830 the population has grown faster with current immigration than it would have grown without this movement.

Much circumstantial evidence in favor of his theory was advanced by Walker, and more has been added by his supporters. That most of it is valid up to a certain point few students of population would deny. But the statistical argument is weak, as the Walker group themselves have admitted; either none is attempted, or else the falling off of the intercensal rate of growth is cited as proof. It is believed that the quantitative conclusions of Walker and his followers would have been modified considerably by a careful study of the birth rate to women 15 to 44, which can be estimated from the ratio of children to women of this age and from available facts regarding infant and child mortality.[1]

8. CUMULATIVE EFFECT OF IMMIGRATION

Although it seems certain that immigration was not entirely a process of substitution rather than of addition throughout past decades, it seems equally certain that population growth was not increased by the full amount of net immigration. The birth rate was declining steadily while this movement went on, and although many causes were at work there are several reasons for believing that immigration was one of them. Foreigners shortened the period of pioneering by undertaking tasks which otherwise would have later been the lot of natives, and at the same time hastened industrialization by supplying an abundance of cheap labor. In these ways they probably accelerated the decline of the birth rate generally, for it is in urbanized and industrialized populations that falling birth rates first appeared as a rule. Likewise it seems probable that the presence of large numbers of immigrants tended to arouse the desire of the older natives, particularly in the cities, to distinguish themselves occupationally from the newcomers. As a consequence many types of unskilled hand work have come to be regarded as "immigrant jobs"; natives have more and more entered the white-collar class. The birth rate of the white-collar class is usually well below that of the laboring class; hence it seems likely that in this way the immigrants have also speeded up the decline in the native birth rate. To the extent that the native birth rate has fallen for such reasons, immigration undoubtedly has been a process of substitution.[2] In a large and richly endowed country like the United States, however, such changes are usually brought about slowly and with considerable lag.

It has been shown that in almost every 10-, 20-, or 30-year period up to the present time births have not been reduced because of immigration and other factors combined by an amount as large as the net arrival of aliens. Data will now be presented on which to base a cumulative com-

---

[1] In *International Migrations*, Vol. II, p. 103, Willcox writes that the Walker theory "had its value as a challenge of the current belief that immigration regularly increased the population by an amount equal to its number. But it is almost equally incorrect to maintain that it did not increase the population at all."

[2] For additional arguments that immigration has been a process of substitution, see the works cited on pp. 304, 305.

parison for the entire period since 1800. To illustrate, it will be assumed that one-fifth of the decline in the birth rate has been due to the arrival of immigrants; that without immigration the birth rate to white women 15 to 44 would have declined from 278 in 1800 to 125 in 1930 instead of to 87, with correspondingly smaller decreases at earlier years. This slower downward trend would have resulted in about 4,000 more births during 1800–1810, gradually increasing to over 8,600,000 during 1920–1930 (see Table 87). Immigration was larger, however, in every decade up to 1890 and in the 1800 to 1920 period as a whole; hence a reduction of one-fifth in the decline in the birth rate would not have increased births by an amount equal to immigrant arrivals. Prior to 1910 it appears certain that immigration would have had to be responsible for more than one-fifth of the decrease in the birth rate in order for the stoppage of immigration to have resulted in a larger population. But if the decline in the birth rate from 1800 to 1930 had been smaller by one-fifth and there had been no immigration, the 1930 population might have exceeded the actual figure. After 1940 the difference in favor of no immigration would become marked.

The effect on population growth may be ascertained for other assumptions regarding the portion of the birth-rate decline due to immigration. If immigration has caused less than one-sixth of the decline, it has added to population growth during 1800–1930, though perhaps it will not have done so by 1940 or 1950. If the decline in birth rate had been reduced one-third by prohibiting the entrance of foreigners, the population would have been smaller than it actually was up to the 1890's, but larger in subsequent years.

In considering a relation between immigration and a decline in the birth rate, however, it should be remembered that in the white population the ratio of children to women 15 to 44 and the estimated birth rate of these women were both declining rapidly early in the nineteenth century when immigration was much smaller relative to population than later on. Thus there were about 240 births per 1,000 women 15 to 44 in 1830 compared with 260 in 1820 and 274 in 1810; yet immigration averaged less than 13,000 annually from 1820 to 1830 and appears to have been considerably smaller previously (Table 85). Furthermore, in later decades there was little relation between the drop in the birth rate and the number of immigrant arrivals. During 1840–1850 immigration was over eleven times as large as during 1820–1830; yet the birth rate declined only 28 points compared with 20 in the earlier decade. The decade 1900–1910 saw by far the largest number of immigrants arrive and stood second in ratio of immigrant arrivals to population; yet the birth rate to women 15 to 44 declined only 13 points (from 130 to 117). On the other hand, immigrant arrivals were barely half as large during 1920–1930 and the ratio of

TABLE 87.—IMMIGRATION OF WHITES, AND ESTIMATED DECREASE IN WHITE BIRTHS IF ONE-FIFTH OF THE DECLINE IN BIRTH RATE FROM 1800 TO 1930 WAS DUE TO IMMIGRATION

(Numbers in thousands)

Decade	Birth rate per 1,000 women 15–44		Number of births in decade at birth rate indicated		Decrease in births caused by one-fifth of decline in birth rate		Immigration		Excess of immigration over one-fifth of decrease in births	
	Actual[a]	One-fifth less decline since 1800[b]	Actual[c]	One-fifth less decline since 1800[d]	Single decades[e]	Cumulative[f]	Single decades[g]	Cumulative[f]	Single decades[h]	Cumulative[f]
	A	B	C	D	E	F	G	H	I	J
1800–10......	276	276	2,800	2,800	.....	......	70	70	70	70
1810–20......	267	269	3,690	3,720	30	30	80	150	50	120
1820–30......	250	256	4,820	4,940	120	150	130	280	10	130
1830–40......	231	240	6,180	6,420	240	390	520	800	280	410
1840–50......	208	222	7,710	8,230	520	910	1,470	2,270	950	1,360
1850–60......	189	207	10,080	11,040	960	1,870	2,650	4,920	1,690	3,050
1860–70......	176	196	11,940	13,300	1,360	3,230	2,190	7,110	830	3,830
1870–80......	161	184	14,260	16,300	2,040	5,270	2,650	9,760	610	4 490
1880–90......	146	172	16,260	19,160	2,900	8.170	5,170	14,930	2,270	6,760
1890–1900....	134	163	18,830	22,900	4,070	12,240	3,780	18,710	− 290	6,470
1900–10......	124	155	21,580	26,980	5,400	17,640	6,620	25,330	1,220	7,690
1910–20..:...	115	148	24,170	31,110	6,940	24,580	2,790	28,120	−4,150	3,540
1920–30......	100	136	24,080	32,750	8,670	33,250	3,370	31,490	−5,300	−1,760

[a] From Table 86, Column B, 10-year periods.

[b] Calculated from Column A, this table, and Table 86; e.g., the value 148 for 1910–1920 is obtained by adding to 115 one-fifth of the difference between 115 and 278, the latter being the value for 1800 in Table 86. Column A.

[c] From Table 86, Column D.

[d] Column D bears the same ratio to C as B does to A.

[e] Column D minus Column C.

[f] The total of the current and all preceding decades in column to left.

[g] From Table 86, Column F.

[h] Column G minus Column E.

NOTE: This table yields results that are only rough approximations. In the first place, the birth rate in Column A and the number of births in Column C may be as much as 5.3 per cent too high in some decades prior to 1900 (see Tables 74 and 85 and discussion on p. 302). This exaggerates proportionally the decrease in births due to one-fifth of the decline in the birth rate. Secondly the number of births in Column D are obtained by applying rates in Column B to the actual population. No additions are made to the population to allow at first for survivors from the higher number of births, and later for births to these survivors and their descendants. But neither are deductions made from the population to allow for the following losses which would have resulted from the stopping of immigration: first the immigrants themselves; second and immediately following, the births to this group; and finally for the descendants of the survivors from these births. Up to 1900 the cumulative number of births lost by one-fifth of the decline in the birth rate was considerably smaller than the immigration which occurred. In this period, therefore, the deductions from the population would have exceeded the additions, and a more rigorous method would show a smaller number of births lost by one-fifth of the decline in the birth rate. But considering the 1800–1930 period as a whole, the two corrections would more nearly offset each other. Hence, it is believed that the conclusions in the text may be properly drawn from these data. A more exact and detailed analysis is planned for later publication.

immigration to population still lower; nevertheless the second largest absolute decline and by far the largest relative decline in this birth rate was from 113 in 1920 to 87 in 1930. All this would seem to indicate that, although immigration may have helped the downward movement of the birth rate, it was not the predominant factor.

Just how important a part immigration has played in lowering the birth rate in the past must remain largely a matter of opinion. At the present time there are no facts to prove definitely how much of the rapid decline in the birth rate during even the last decade is the result of changes in biological structure, in diet, in type of work or activity, in the practice of abortion, or in the use of contraceptives. Still less is known of the relative importance of the motives that lead to abortion or birth control. With this blank situation regarding the recent past it seems hopeless to expect an accurate analysis of the more distant past.

The evidence available indicates that the Walker theory is partially correct in explaining the past growth of population; immigration has not been entirely a process of addition throughout the past, but in part a process of substitution. How correct it will be in years to come may be another question. The maximum population that will be reached at some future date may or may not be smaller because of immigration then it would be if immigration had been prohibited after 1800. Maximum population may be highly correlated with social and economic standards of living as well as with available resources. Living standards in turn may be greatly influenced by the sources of origin of the population. Hence the maximum population that will result from growth under conditions that have existed may be quite different from the maximum that would result if there had been no immigration. But this cannot be discussed further here.

CHAPTER X

PROBABLE TRENDS AND CONSEQUENCES OF FUTURE GROWTH

1. POPULATION GROWTH IN FUTURE YEARS

AT VARIOUS places in this monograph, references have been made to the probable size and make-up of the population in future years. Extrapolation of the figures on natural increase and net immigration in Table 84, p. 301, indicates that population growth may average about 1,000,000 a year during 1930–1934 and the population amount to 128,-000,000 by 1935 and perhaps to 133,000,000 by 1940. But if it is desired to have more accurate estimates and to project them forward to more distant years, some other method needs to be followed. There is no way of knowing definitely just what the future has in store regarding population growth; nevertheless it should be a matter of interest and practical value to estimate what seems likely to occur judging from a study of past trends and their causes.

No one knows when the first estimates of the future course of population were prepared, but the occupation seems to have become especially popular in the last decade or two among sales managers, advertising agents, editors, college presidents, and research workers. The unfortunate way in which actual population growth usually has departed from the predictions of most earlier forecasters has not stopped the issue of new sets of estimates, perhaps because there is always the chance of being right. For example, in about 1815 Elkanah Watson constructed a table of the probable future population of the United States up to 1900 which proved to be remarkably accurate for several decades.[1] His estimates differed from the actual census counts of 1820, 1830, 1840, 1850, and 1860 by less than 1 per cent, although subsequently the error rose until in 1900 his figure was 31 per cent too high. Francis Bonynge did almost as well, for the estimates he published in 1852 differed from the census by less than 1.5 per cent up to 1890 and by only 2.2 per cent in 1900.[2] The error in his estimates for later years is much greater, as he predicted the population would amount to 186,790,000 in 1940 and would reach the fantastic height of 703,000,000 in 2000 A.D.

[1] Referred to by Francis A. Walker, "The Great Count of 1890," *Forum*, Vol. 11 (June, 1891), pp. 406–418.
[2] Francis Bonynge, *The Future Wealth of America*, New York, Author, 1852, 242 pp.

Methods of preparing estimates in the past usually have dealt only with figures for the total population. One method, the arithmetic, has been to assume that the numerical growth of past years would be continued in the future. This has been followed until recently and with fair results by the Bureau of the Census in estimating the population for years since the last census, but it would not hold nearly so well in extrapolating for intervals of two decades or more. A second method, the geometric, has been to assume that the rate of increase followed in the past would be continued in the future. Watson used the geometric plan with high accuracy in 1815, because the rate of increase was 36.4 per cent in the preceding decade and between 32.7 and 35.9 per cent in the four following decades. Bonynge modified the geometric plan by assuming the white rate of increase would be 35 per cent for 1850–1860 (approximately the rate of preceding decades), 30 per cent for 1860–1870, and 25 per cent for later decades, and that the Negro rate of increase per decade would remain stationary at 23 per cent for slaves and 15 per cent for free colored, slightly under the rates of 1830–1840 and considerably under those of other decades prior to 1850. Bonynge's failure to make larger decreases in the Negro rate after 1880 and in the white rate after 1910 explains his large overestimate of Negroes at an early date, and of whites and the total population after 1910. By that time the Negro rate of increase had dropped below 7 per cent and the white rate to 16 per cent.

Because the arithmetic method in the past tended to underestimate growth and the geometric method to overestimate it, many people have tried to fit parabolas, logistic curves, or other formulas to the actual population on census dates and to calculate the population on any future date from them. Probably the best known estimates of the curve type are those of Pearl and Reed, whose logistic curves fit past populations well and may prove to do so for the future.[1] It should be pointed out, however, that there is no certainty that a given mathematical formula will forecast population growth accurately even though it may describe past growth almost exactly. The authors believe the estimates of Pearl and Reed for the United States population after 1950 are too high, because of the rapid fall in the birth rate that has occurred and the restrictions of immigration that have been put into effect. Pearl and Reed have shown that it may be necessary to join together two S-shaped curves to fit the population in past years when conditions of growth have changed sufficiently in a country. But the difficulty is to tell in any current year whether a new curve needs to be joined to the past curve and to compute what particular course the new curve should follow. It is much easier to look back after several years have passed and make the proper computations.

[1] Raymond S. Pearl, *Studies in Human Biology*, Baltimore, Williams & Wilkins Company, 1924, 653 pp. See Chaps. XXIV, XXV.

A more promising method for the United States, although no less arbitrary, seems to be to make separate assumptions for the future trend of birth rates, death rates, and net immigration and to calculate what the resulting growth and population will be. The expectation of life has fluctuated within narrow limits along an upward trend in the past and may be expected to do so in the future. Birth rates have fallen about two-thirds since 1800, but are more subject to human control; hence their future course is correspondingly more difficult to judge. The erratic fluctuations in immigration arising from economic conditions and governmental control make the size of future movements a matter of opinion. Not claiming the infallability of the seventh son of a seventh son, the authors believe it will be of most service to outline several possibilities regarding each of these factors, to show the population that will result from different combinations of them, and to give reasons why certain combinations seem more probable. Each reader may thus judge what seems to him the most likely set of conditions for the future, and compare the corresponding population with the figures based on other assumptions.

In all cases the 1930 census population of native whites, foreign-born whites, and Negroes by five-year age periods is taken as a starting point. Deaths by age in each group during five years are calculated by means of assumed specific death rates, and births to women of each age period by means of assumed specific birth rates. Subtracting the calculated number of deaths and adding those of births and net immigration give the population by five-year age periods five years later. By repeating the process, it is possible to calculate by five-year age periods the white and Negro population that will result in future years according to the trends assumed for birth rates, death rates, and immigration. By varying these assumptions, different population trends may be obtained. Because of the relatively small number of other colored in the population, the size of this group is calculated as a certain percentage of the white and Negro. The total population is then obtained by adding the native white, foreign-born white, Negro, and "other colored" groups.

In the preceding discussion of births, deaths, and immigration, several trends for the future have been described, all of which are believed to be well within the range of possibility[1] (Figure 35). If birth rates, expectation of life, and immigration follow the "low" trends described and the percentage of other colored remains as it was in 1930, the population will increase slowly to about 138,000,000 between 1955 and 1960 and then gradually decline, amounting to about 129,000,000 in 1980 (Figure 36 and Table 88, Column A). The effect of 100,000 fewer births per year during 1930–1934 and birth rates declining to the same level in 1980 may be seen by comparing Columns A and B. In the latter the population will

[1] For deaths, pp. 260, 261; for births, pp. 288–291; for immigration, pp. 298, 299.

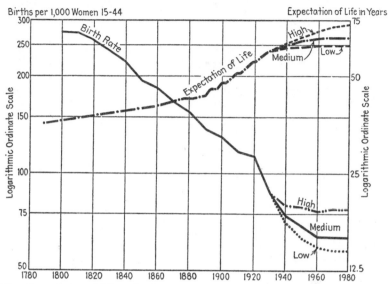

Fig. 35.—Expectation of life at birth, 1789–1980, and births per 1,000 women 15 to 44, 1800–1980, white population. (Based on Tables 66 and 74.)

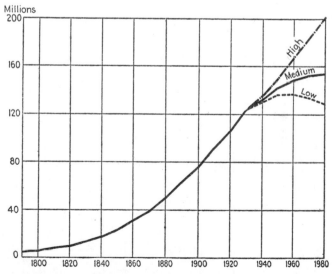

Fig. 36.—Population of the United States, 1790–1980; future estimates on three assumptions. (Based on Table 3.)

TABLE 88.—FUTURE POPULATION OF THE UNITED STATES ACCORDING TO CERTAIN ASSUMED TRENDS OF NET IMMIGRATION, SPECIFIC BIRTH RATES, AND EXPECTATION OF LIFE[a]

Year	A "Low" birth rates and expectation of life, no immigration	B Same as A except fewer births	C Same as A except "medium" expectation of life	D Same as C except some immigration	E Same as D except more immigration	F Same as D except more births	G Same as D except "high" expectation of life	H "Medium" birth rates, expectation of life, and immigration	I Same as J except less immigration	J "High" birth rates, expectation of life, and immigration
FUTURE POPULATION (MILLIONS)										
1930	122.8	122.8	122.8	122.8	122.8	122.8	122.8	122.8	122.8	122.8
1935	127.3	127.3	127.8	127.8	127.8	127.8	127.8	128.0	128.4	128.4
1940	131.9	130.9	132.2	132.5	133.0	132.9	132.5	133.1	134.5	135.1
1945	135.0	133.7	135.9	136.8	138.0	137.7	137.1	138.3	141.5	142.8
1950	137.1	135.5	138.8	140.4	142.3	141.8	141.1	142.8	148.7	150.8
1955	138.0	136.4	140.9	143.2	145.8	145.0	144.6	146.8	156.0	159.0
1960	137.9	136.0	141.9	145.0	148.4	147.4	147.7	149.8	163.3	167.3
1965	136.8	134.6	142.1	145.9	150.2	149.0	150.3	152.2	170.7	175.6
1970	134.9	132.5	141.4	146.1	151.2	149.9	152.3	153.8	178.1	184.2
1975	132.3	129.7	139.9	145.5	151.4	150.0	153.9	154.8	185.8	193.0
1980	129.2	126.5	137.8	144.2	151.0	149.6	155.1	155.2	193.5	202.0
DECENNIAL INCREASE (MILLIONS)										
1930–40	9.1	8.1	9.4	9.7	10.3	10.2	9.8	10.3	11.7	12.3
1940–50	5.2	4.7	6.7	7.9	9.3	8.9	8.5	9.8	14.2	15.7
1950–60	0.8	0.5	3.1	4.5	6.1	5.6	6.7	7.0	14.7	16.5
1960–70	-3.0	-3.5	-0.5	-1.1	2.7	2.5	4.6	3.9	14.8	16.9
1970–80	-5.7	-6.0	-3.6	-1.9	-0.2	-0.3	2.7	1.5	15.3	17.8
PERCENTAGE INCREASE										
1930–40	7.4	6.6	7.7	7.9	8.4	8.3	8.0	8.4	9.5	10.0
1940–50	3.9	3.6	5.0	6.0	7.0	6.7	6.4	7.3	10.6	11.7
1950–60	0.5	0.2	2.2	3.3	4.3	4.0	4.7	4.9	9.9	10.9
1960–70	-2.2	-2.6	-0.4	0.8	1.8	1.7	3.1	2.6	9.1	10.1
1970–80	-4.2	-4.5	-2.5	-1.3	-0.1	-0.2	1.8	0.9	8.6	9.7

	A	B	C	D	E	F	G	H	I	J
SPECIFIC BIRTH RATES ASSUMED (IN PERCENTAGE OF 1925–1929)[b]										
Native white 1930–34	90.4	86.0	Same as A	Same as A	Same as A	Rates in A increased by 100,000 births annually starting in 1935	Same as A	91.2	Same as J	92.4
Native white 1935–39	82.8	79.5						85.3		89.2
Native white 1950–54	69.8	69.4						77.8		88.3
Native white 1975–79	67.0	67.0						72.8		88.3
Foreign-born white 1930–34	83.8	81.2						84.4		85.5
Foreign-born white 1935–39	75.4	74.5						77.6		82.5
Foreign-born white 1950–54	67.0	67.0						71.9		81.7
Foreign-born white 1975–79	65.0	65.0						69.4		81.7
Negro 1930–34	92.0	84.3						91.9		92.0
Negro 1935–39	85.9	79.0						85.9		88.3
Negro 1950–54	73.8	70.0						69.7		85.6
Negro 1975–79	64.0	64.0						69.4		85.6
EXPECTATION OF LIFE AT BIRTH ASSUMED[c]										
White 1930–34	60.6	Same as A	60.6	Same as C	Same as C	Same as C	Same as J	Same as C	Same as J	60.6
White 1950–54	62.3		65.0							67.0
White 1970–74	62.3		66.0							72.0
Negro 1930–34	48.4		48.4							49.2
Negro 1950–54	51.4		53.0							55.7
Negro 1970–74	51.4		54.0							61.0
ANNUAL IMMIGRATION ASSUMED (THOUSANDS)[d]										
White 1930–34	None	None	None	None	None	Same as D	Same as D	10	20	20
White 1935–39	None	None	None	50	150			75	100	200
White 1940–79	None	None	None	100	200			150	200	300
Negro 1930–34	None	None	None	None	None	Same as D	Same as D	(e)	1	1
Negro 1935–39	None	None	None	1	2			1	2	3
Negro 1940–79	None	None	None	1	2			1	2	3

[a] Prepared by the Scripps Foundation for Research in Population Problems. Calculations have been made for native whites, foreign-born whites, and Negroes according to the method explained in text. To obtain the total population, it has been assumed in Columns A to H that the "other colored" will continue to constitute 1.67 per cent of the total population as in 1930, but in Columns I and J that the percentage of "other colored" will gradually rise to 4 in 1980.

[b] See discussion on pp. 288–291.

[c] See Table 63, p. 240, and discussion on pp. 260, 261.

[d] See discussion on pp. 298, 299.

[e] Annual Negro immigration 400.

NOTE: The terms "high" and "low" in column headings are used to indicate limits that the authors believe are unlikely to be exceeded rather than absolute limits. The absolute "low" for the birth rate would be zero, but the authors do not believe a larger decline than that shown in Column A is likely to occur by 1980. Similarly, the absolute "high" for the birth rate would be more than one birth per year for every woman in the childbearing ages, but the authors do not believe a smaller decline than that shown in Column H is likely to occur by 1980.

barely reach 136,000,000 between 1955 and 1960 and then will decline almost to 126,000,000 by 1980. In other words, it will be back practically to the same size as in 1933.

Under the "low" assumptions for birth rates and immigration but with a "medium" increase in expectation of life, the population will be largest in 1965, at about 142,000,000, and will amount to almost 138,-000,000 in 1980 (Column C). If net immigration amounts to about 50,000 annually during 1935–1939 and 100,000 annually thereafter but other conditions remain as in Column C, the largest population will be about 146,000,000 in 1970, and the 1980 figure will be over 144,000,000 (Column D). The effect of further increases in immigration may be seen by comparing Columns D and E, an additional net immigration of about 100,000 annually prolonging growth by about five years and increasing the 1980 population nearly 7,000,000, or to 151,000,000. If net arrivals are increased by still another 100,000 (that is, to a total of over 300,000 annually beginning in 1940), the resulting population will be larger by nearly another 7,000,000 in 1980, amounting to almost 158,000,000.

The effect of 100,000 additional births annually, beginning in 1935, may be seen by comparing Columns D and F. The annual addition of 100,000 births does not speed up population growth quite so much as that of 100,000 net immigrants, the 1980 population of Column F being about 5,400,000 larger than that of Column D, but that of Column E being 6,800,000 larger. The reason for this is that adding immigrants increases the population in the childbearing ages almost at once, while adding births does not do so for several years, by which time there have been losses due to death. Adding 200,000 births a year doubles the increase of Column F over Column D, raising the 1980 population to about 155,000,000, and adding 300,000 births raises the 1980 population to over 160,000,000.

According to the "high" assumptions—a small decline in birth rates, a large increase in expectation of life, and net immigration after 1940 at 300,000 annually—the population will increase at a considerably more rapid rate and will exceed 200,000,000 in 1980 with no indication of growth ceasing for several decades thereafter (see Column J). If annual net immigration is reduced by 100,000 after 1940, the 1980 population will be smaller by about 8,500,000 (see Column I). Similarly, increasing annual net immigration by 100,000 would increase population growth by the same amount, making the 1980 population exceed 210,000,000. Varying the immigration assumption by 100,000 annually makes a difference of 8,500,000 when applied to Column J and of only 6,800,000 when applied to Column D. The reason for this situation is that the death rates are higher in Column D than in Column J, and the birth rates lower.

Immigrants added to Column *D* would die off faster and would contribute fewer children to the next generation.

If birth rates follow the "high" trend assumed instead of the "low," the effect on population growth will be somewhat greater than a similar change in the course of death rates. The 1980 population in Column *G* is about 26,000,000 larger than that in Column *A*. Approximately 7,000,000 is accounted for by more immigration (Column *D* minus Column *C*), leaving 19,000,000 attributable to the "high" expectation of life instead of the "low." The effect of shifting from the "low" assumptions for birth rates to the "high" may be judged from Columns *G* and *I*. The difference of 38,000,000 in 1980 may be apportioned roughly 7,000,000 to immigration (Column *E* minus Column *D*), 3,500,000 to a larger allowance for other colored, and 27,500,000 to the "high" instead the "low" birth rates. Comparing Column *A* with Column *I*, therefore, indicates that the difference of 64,000,000 in 1980 is caused somewhat as follows: 14,000,000 by more immigration, 4,000,000 by more other colored, 20,000,000 by the "high" expectation of life instead of the "low," and 26,000,000 by the "high" birth rates instead of the "low."[1]

To the authors it seems almost certain that the population of the future will be smaller than the figures given in Columns *I* or *J*, and quite probable that it will be larger than those in Columns *A* or *B*. The course followed may be more like that of Column *H* than any other; that is, growth slowing up gradually so that in 1980 the population will be almost at its maximum size with about 155,000,000 persons. The "medium" assumptions here regarding birth and death rates are more like the "low" in Column *A* than the "high" in Column *J*; nevertheless the authors believe them more apt to overstate probable future growth than to understate it. Considering how birth rates have fallen in the past, it seems more probable that a fair-sized decline will occur in the future than the small decline which is assumed in Column *J*.[2] According to the latter assumption, the stationary level which will be reached by 1945 represents less fall after 1930–1934 than occurred from 1920–1924 to 1925–1929. Similarly, the slight lengthening of the expectation of life at ages 7 and above which has been achieved since 1921 seems to indicate that in 1980 the expectation of life at birth will be nearer 62 years as assumed in Column *A* than 73 years as assumed in Column *J*.[3] Immigration is anyone's guess, but the present temper of the nation, plus the possibility that the problems of technological unemployment may not be solved for several years, seem to favor

[1] The figures are not exactly the same as in preceding sentences because there the effect of changes in birth rate was based on a population with the "high" expectation of life, while the effect of changes in expectation of life was based on a population with the "low" birth rates.

[2] See p. 289.

[3] See pp. 260, 261.

low estimates for net arrivals. The "medium" assumption after 1935 is a figure slightly above the present quotas.[1]

It will be readily appreciated that the difference between the population as calculated and its actual size on some future date is likely to increase as the date is projected farther into the future. But it may not be realized that there should be comparatively little chance for error in calculating the size of an important part of the population 20 years ahead. For example, the United States in 1950 should contain between 96,000,000 and 97,000,000 survivors from the population of 122,775,000 in 1930, these numbers being calculated by applying death rates to the 1930 population and allowing for emigration. The margin of 1,000,000 should be sufficient to care for errors of estimating, since death rates at ages over one have changed but little in the last 20 years, and emigration has been comparatively unimportant under the quota system of immigration control. The remainder of the 1950 population will be composed of persons born in the United States or entering it after 1930. Both of these movements are much more difficult to evaluate than the loss by death; hence the calculated size of the total population in 1950 varies from 135,600,000 in Column B to 150,800,000 in Column J. But even with this numerical difference of 15,200,000, the 1950 population of Column J is less than 12 per cent above that of Column B because of the stability of the large proportion of the 1950 population which will be made up of survivors from present inhabitants.

2. CONSEQUENCES OF SLOWER FUTURE GROWTH

The consequences upon social and economic life of the slower future growth of population that seems assured are likely to be many and varied. In the past there has been widespread belief that a rapidly growing population was one of the essential conditions of general progress. Although rapid growth of population undoubtedly has contributed to past progress in certain respects, the slowing up of growth in the future need not be accompanied by gradual stagnation. Social progress consists in the organization of the community to secure the greatest good of the greatest number rather than mere increase in size. It is quite natural that, in a community which has been growing rapidly in numbers at the same time that the welfare of the masses of the people has been improving,[2] growth in numbers should be regarded as an essential element in social

---

[1] See p. 299.

[2] Perhaps the best simple measure of improvement in welfare is the decline of the death rate, since it is in a real sense the algebraic sum of many factors affecting the life of the people. It would not be maintained for an instant, however, that the level of the death rate is a satisfactory measure of welfare, or that at times it may not be actually misleading, but only that as a rule a decline in the death rate is fairly good proof that the masses of the people are living better than they have been.

progress. The fact that growth and progress have been associated in the minds of people for some decades makes it difficult to dissociate them at once, even if there is no causal connection between them. It is likely, therefore, that many people will be disposed to look with misgiving upon a population which is ceasing to grow; some will even feel that to believe such a thing possible is a sign of a subversive mental bias. Because of such attitudes, the practical certainty that the population will grow more slowly in the future, and the possibility that a decrease in numbers may set in, it is essential that a reappraisal of the importance of growth in the national life be undertaken.

Changes in the life of the community should come to be appraised in other than quantitative terms. This has already occurred in many cases where the need for something to feel proud of in the absence of rapid increase in numbers has led a community to set up other ideals of attainment. As an example of what is meant, attention is directed to the change in civic attitudes in Cincinnati during the last few years.

Cincinnati was long one of the most boss-ridden cities of the country. It was looked upon by many people as unfortunate in having grown slowly for some decades. On the whole, it was given a rather lowly place in the average person's estimation of American cities. Within a decade, however, Cincinnati has shaken off boss rule and organized under a new charter which enables public-spirited citizens to exercise a largely increased influence in municipal affairs. The result has been a great improvement in the business organization of the city and the morale of its officials. To the outsider looking on, this change is vastly interesting as showing how the community has found something to be proud of which has nothing to do with size and rate of growth. Today the Cincinnati newspapers feature the low cost of city government, the excellent condition of city finances and the resulting high credit rating, and the efficiency of administration of city affairs. An admirable spirit of civic pride is developing which has nothing to do with size but is based on the improvement in the operation of the governmental agencies affecting the welfare of the community. It has not yet extended itself to many important aspects of general welfare; for example, to creating standards of housing and to providing public health service better than in other cities. But an excellent beginning in civic improvement has been made and there is genuine pride in the achievements already secured. The basis of a new attitude toward the function of the organized community is being laid; it is not based on numbers, bank clearings, or other indices of quantitative growth.

Many other examples might be cited to show how communities are abandoning rapid growth as an ideal and are turning to other achievements—such as parks, better housing, a good school system, wholesome recreation, and adequate public health facilities—to find a basis for pride in their localities. All this implies an extensive recasting of values or standards of judgment. It is believed that this process may be much hastened by the slowing up of population growth. By this very fact of slower growth communities will be forced to find something else than mere size to be proud of, and they will probably not be long in doing so.

It is impossible to foretell the direction or the extent of the changes in mental outlook which will ensue, but there is probably little hazard in predicting that the quality of living will secure greater attention than heretofore. There is the more reason to believe in the probability of such a shift in outlook because it appears that in the past much of the preoccupation with mere size was unavoidable in a country where population was growing as rapidly as here. Such a growth coupled with the vastly increased complexity of modern life has taxed the ability of men in every line of endeavor to meet the demands of their particular jobs. Few of the people in strategic positions have been able to take time to measure their achievements by any standard other than that supplied by quantitative growth. But once quantitative growth is slow or nonexistent, men's minds will probably turn to other matters. More and more it will be asked: What constitutes the good life? How may the community organize to secure it?

To turn attention to the more immediately practical consequences of slower population growth, it seems probable that one of the first efforts at adjustment will be made in business activity. In all likelihood this adjustment will not be particularly difficult in most lines, once business men are fully convinced that population growth will slacken, and are able to estimate with fair accuracy the population for 5 or 10 years in advance. But that business men are rather loath to believe in slower growth is indicated by the fact that a population of from 200,000,000 to 300,000,000 by the year 2000 is frequently predicted in sales managers' talks and is taken for granted in executives' programs. Just because the population in 1860 was eight times as large as in 1790 (70 years earlier), and in 1930 was four times as large as in 1860 (also 70 years earlier), does not justify saying that in 2000 it will be 245,000,000, or twice as large as in 1930.

Certain industries will face difficult and extensive problems in adjusting to a slower population growth. They include industries in which technical improvements are increasing human efficiency at a rapid rate, whose products have a relatively inelastic per capita consumption, whose productive capacity is already largely in excess of the effective demand, and those in which capital (including land) is relatively durable and nontransferable and has a high value per unit of product.

Such industries, of which agriculture unfortunately is an example, will be particularly handicapped by the operation of several of these factors. Farm production has been overexpanded since the World War, efficiency has increased rapidly, foods in general face an inelastic demand, and the proportion of capital in land is high, as is also land value per unit of product. Certainly it will be a formidable task to work out policies for the utilization of farm land in the future which will provide for adjusting agriculture to slower population growth and at the same time prevent its sinking to a low economic level.

It also seems likely that the slower growth of population will affect the utilization of land for building sites and hence land values in and around cities, but in lesser degree than the utilization of land for farms. What may happen in any given community cannot be foretold with assurance, but it seems probable that the boom land prices of 1929 will not again be attained in most cities for many years. Indeed, if decentralization of population should set in, as many people think likely, the high values of the past may never be reached again in the central cities. The building industry in particular seems likely to be affected by slower population growth in marked degree. Clearly an increase of 10,000,000 persons from 1930 to 1940 will demand less new housing than did the increase of 17,000,000 from 1920 to 1930. Also the smaller increase will require fewer new schools, factories, stores, and offices. Slower growth of population can be offset in part by improving the housing of the lower economic classes—by tearing down slum districts and rebuilding on modern lines. But this may require public rather than private action.

Many other industries are more or less directly dependent upon population increase for their growth. These industries will feel the effects of an approaching stationary population in proportion to the degree that they have a stable product or have already reached the saturation point. It is hard to conceive that the average family would use two radios or two kitchen stoves, for example; but the present radio may be replaced by an improved model at any time, while the kitchen stove is likely to be kept until worn out. The point is that some industries can expect to expand only as population grows, even if per capita purchasing power increases considerably. There is, of course, no industry which has reached the absolute saturation point even with a stable product, but certainly the demand for the necessities of life such as food, clothing, and shelter will expand less rapidly with rising incomes than the demand for conveniences and luxuries. The industries producing necessities may expect a relatively stable demand as population growth lessens, but they can scarcely hope for the expansion they have experienced in the past when population increased by leaps and bounds.

On the other hand, there are many industries, probably producing the majority of all industrial goods, whose growth is largely independent of population increase. They could sell their product in much greater quantity and improved quality if the public had the money to buy it. To such industries the raising of the per capita purchasing power of the public will be of vastly greater concern as population growth is retarded. Making better customers of the population at large may mean relatively lower selling prices and higher wages, which may temporarily reduce profits to some extent. But there will be small need for profits to finance additions to plant capacity of most industries until the increased purchasing power of the bulk of the consumers has offset slower population growth. In the future, plant expansion in these non-necessity producing industries should be based upon probable increases in the purchasing power of the population rather than upon the belief that population growth will soon overtake any expansion which available capital makes possible. It would seem, therefore, that even in industries where population growth is a minor factor in expansion, consumption must be studied more carefully than in the past, since growth in numbers can no longer be relied upon, as in former years, to make up for lack of expansion in purchasing power.

It may be argued that, even though the population of the United States will grow less rapidly and may cease to grow in a few decades, industry can continue to expand at much the same rate as in the past by increasing foreign trade. In the long run, however, it seems debatable whether much expansion can be achieved in this direction. In the first place, population growth is slowing up in practically all of the countries with which the United States trades on a large scale, and will soon be stationary in many of them. Moreover, there are no signs in any of these countries of an improvement in standards of living sufficiently great to demand largely increased imports of the goods the United States is in position to export. Secondly, certain nations which formerly imported most of their manufactured products are industrializing as rapidly as possible in the endeavor to become self-sufficient economically. At the same time other nations which heretofore have been content merely to supply their own needs in certain industrial lines are beginning to look about for foreign markets. These changes together with the fact that foreign trade is a life and death matter for such countries as England and Germany are making the competition for foreign trade more and more intense and are rendering such trade both less stable and less profitable than it has been in the past. Finally, the tendency to raise high tariff barriers, like those of the United States, shows no sign of abatement and greatly handicaps international trade. Indeed, at the present time the movement toward national self-sufficiency is stronger than during any peace-time period since the Industrial Revolution. It is perhaps impossible for any nation to become entirely self-sufficient on a high industrial level, but it may well be that the present tariff madness will result in foreign trade being reduced to a very low level and being held there for some time. It seems unduly optimistic, therefore, to expect that foreign trade will compensate for a slower increase in productive capacity arising from slower population growth. Foreign countries are more likely to buy a smaller than a larger proportion of the national production in the future. This will add to the difficulties of adjusting production to markets rather than alleviate them.

In so far as the present depression (1929 to 1933) is a consequence of a too rapid accumulation of capital goods, it has been both hastened and accentuated by the decline in the average size of the family. There can be no doubt that among families having the same income, those with two children will make considerably larger savings on the average than those with five. If, therefore, only as many as 10 per cent of the 30,000,000 American families have reduced their numbers of children by two or three, it seems quite reasonable to suppose that savings have been greatly increased thereby within the last two or three decades. The decrease in young dependents which makes for larger savings by persons in the prime of life has been accompanied by an increase in older people who must draw on their savings or on the current production of the community for their needs. The latter, however, has offset the former only partially. Since savings, on the whole, are invested in some form of business enterprise, the capital available for investment may have been increasing most rapidly at just the time when the number of persons for whom necessities must be provided has been increasing most slowly. In this manner the decline in the birth rate has contributed directly to the lack of balance in the industrial system which is in part responsible for the present troubles.

It is not the intention of the authors to suggest that slower population growth has brought on the present depression; although the decline in annual growth since 1923 may have been a contributory factor. But because "business as usual" has been predicated to such a large extent on a rapidly growing population in the past, it is reasonable to urge that the change in the rate of population growth now going on, and to be expected in the future, be given careful consideration in planning for the rationalization of social and economic life.

CHAPTER XI

POPULATION POLICY

1. THE POLICY OF THE UNITED STATES

THOUGH perhaps it is not generally realized, it is nevertheless a fact that the United States has had a definite and effective policy regarding the increase of population practically from the commencement of white settlement. From the very moment of their founding, most communities wanted more and more people, at first to increase the safety of life and property, and later to raise land values. Most of the individuals and companies that received large grants of land, or that were able to purchase it cheaply from public authorities, made more or less effective efforts to have their lands occupied quickly. It is well known, for example, that William Penn made strenuous efforts to attract settlers to his grant and that at times his success was sufficient to incur the dislike of men in other communities who were less successful in filling up their territories.

Because of the advantages to be derived from the increase of numbers, the settlement of the land was encouraged in a variety of ways. The land policy pursued by the various governmental bodies provided free or cheap land in farm units to foreigners as well as natives if they would settle and work it. Furthermore, for over two centuries immigration policies not only made entry easy and offered political asylum to the oppressed, but for a time allowed the importation of slaves, and until rather recently actively encouraged European immigration. Moreover, political leaders broadcast the idea that here the common man had opportunities never before open to him. All these efforts to people the land were richly rewarded; immigrants came in great numbers, and the surplus youth of eastern states moved westward in a steady stream. By about 1890 the actual settlement of farm land was almost completed; but since the industrial development of the country was also well under way by this time, there was still need of immigrants to help man the factories and to assist in the great construction works being undertaken. The steamship companies and other interests that profited by immigration saw to it that the advantages of coming to the United States were well advertised in those parts of Europe where the prospects of receiving passengers were best. The land policy and the "open door" were very successful in attracting Europeans.

2. GRADUAL RESTRICTION OF IMMIGRATION

Notwithstanding this public encouragement of immigration, there have always been those who felt that the "new" immigrants at any period were inferior and that something should be done to reserve the economic advantages of the country for the children of those who were early on the ground and to maintain a high degree of cultural homogeneity.[1] Nevertheless, it was not until about 50 years ago that effective steps were taken by the federal government to close the open door to "undesirable" groups.[2] In 1882, partly as a consequence of some racial troubles in the West, the first Chinese Exclusion Act was passed. In 1885, under pressure of organized labor, the Alien Contract Labor Law was passed. This forbade the entrance of foreigners under contract to individuals or firms and was intended to prevent employers from breaking strikes and undercutting wages by using cheap labor recruited by their agents in foreign countries. These acts clearly indicate that under certain circumstances an increase of numbers was not considered the highest good by all groups. The open-door policy which had prevailed hitherto was being changed. Since these early attempts at regulation, the laws controlling immigration have steadily increased in number and effectiveness. Their chief purpose until recently was to reduce the number of criminals, paupers, and defectives among the immigrants. With the passage of the quota laws immigration policy has entered a new phase. The purpose of this law was not only to reduce the number of immigrants, but also to select those who were believed to be most readily assimilable.

The present quota law assigns to each country in the Eastern Hemisphere a maximum number of persons who may move to the United States each year.[3] As just noted, the various quota laws in effect since June 3, 1921, are also intended to influence the make-up of the population, to preserve as far as possible the national origins of the population as they were before the children of the eastern and southern Europeans who came during the present century became numerous.[4] The quotas in effect since July 1, 1929, are based upon the proportion of the 1920 population springing from different national stocks; hence most of the immigrants now allowed to enter come from northern and western Europe. Quotas have not yet been applied to Canada and Latin America but may be

[1] *The Writings of Benjamin Franklin,* collected and edited by Albert Henry Smyth, New York, The Macmillan Company, 1907, Vol. III, "1750–1759," see p. 72.

[2] From the founding of the nation until 1882 the regulation of immigration was in the hands of the local authorities and such control as was exercised was both desultory and ineffective.

[3] No immigration of Orientals ineligible to citizenship is allowed.

[4] *Supra,* p. 92.

at any time. The open-door policy of the past has been completely abandoned.

Supplementing the quota laws are various administrative regulations. Those providing for the deportation of aliens who have entered illegally have been vigorously enforced of late years, resulting in thousands of expulsions plus a large but unknown number of departures caused by fear of deportation. A more drastic influence in restricting immigration, however, has been the regulation in force since the summer of 1930 under which visas are denied to prospective immigrants if it is believed they may become public charges in the United States. This practically excludes aliens without jobs (unless wealthy), while the Alien Contract Labor Law excludes aliens with jobs. As a result, the stream of immigration has been reversed, and since November, 1930, more aliens have been leaving the United States than entering.[1]

3. CHANGING ATTITUDE TOWARD LARGE FAMILIES

The same attitudes of mind which counted unrestricted immigration as a good also encouraged the raising of large families. Furthermore, large families were of direct advantage to much of the population. Farmers with several sons were assured of a steady labor supply with little or no wage payment, while other working men had family incomes augmented if several minor children were at work. Besides, numerous children were probably the most certain form of old-age insurance in a pioneering agricultural community.

The general attitude of the community toward a high birth rate prior to about 1870 might be shown in numerous ways, but only one incident will be mentioned here. In 1832, Dr. Charles Knowlton wrote a little pamphlet (published in New York City) entitled "Fruits of Philosophy; or, the Private Companion of Young Married People" in which he advocated contraception and described some of the methods by which it might be accomplished.[2] This was considered an offense against public morality and was punished in his case by fine and later by imprisonment. But in spite of Dr. Knowlton's unpleasant experiences, it appears that his book circulated widely in certain localities, particularly in Massachusetts, and exercised a considerable influence among certain groups of the population. It is impossible, however, to trace any close relation between the appearance and spread of the "Fruits of Philosophy" and the decline of the birth rate as shown in Chapter VIII.

There do not appear to have been any dramatic incidents in the spread of the birth control information between Knowlton's time and

[1] *Supra*, p. 296.
[2] Norman E. Himes, "Charles Knowlton's Revolutionary Influence on the English Birth Rate," *New England Journal of Medicine*, Vol. 199, No. 10 (September 6, 1928).

1873, when Congress passed the so-called Comstock Laws "for the suppression of trade in, and circulation of obscene literature and articles of immoral use," which covered devices and information about practices for preventing conception. But the passage of these laws would seem to be clear evidence that birth control was becoming sufficiently common to attract the attention of those who were opposed to it on any grounds. In more recent years, particularly since 1916, when Margaret Sanger opened the first birth control clinic in America,[1] there has been considerable legal conflict between those who believe that man has the right to control his family numbers as he sees fit and those who believe that such control of births is harmful from a religious, moral, national, or personal point of view. Slowly but surely this conflict is being resolved in favor of those opposing all measures that interfere with the individual control of the size of the family. Between mild enforcement of restrictive laws by public authorities and the breaking of them by individuals their influence in maintaining the birth rate has steadily dwindled.

It seems probable, however, that birth control legislation not only retarded the decline of the birth rate in the past but had some effect upon the sources of growth of the population. Had no restrictions been placed on the spread of birth control information and had clinics been permitted to function freely at all times, it is probable that birth control would have spread more evenly through all economic and social classes, with the result that the decline in the birth rate among poorer and less educated people would have been more comparable with the decline among the more educated and well-to-do. Under these circumstances the former would have contributed a smaller amount to the total population increase, thus raising the proportion from the latter. That such restrictive legislation would increase class differentials in the birth rate undoubtedly was not foreseen by Comstock and his followers.

Laws against the willful inducing of abortion have long been on the statute books and have undoubtedly been fairly successful in keeping down the number of abortions. Nevertheless, it is the opinion of many persons in a position to judge the matter that countless thousands of abortions are brought about in the United States each year, with a restricting effect on population growth.

There are certain other laws which also exert a considerable influence upon population growth, although they were passed with little if any thought of doing so. Child labor and compulsory school attendance laws have gradually reduced the economic value of children to their parents, thus making more effective the economic motives in family limitation. Working in the opposite direction, but of far less potency, are free child

[1] Margaret Sanger, *My Fight for Birth Control*, New York, Farrar & Rinehart, Inc., 1931, 360 pp. See p. 157.

health clinics, free lunches in schools, and income tax exemption on account of children.

4. REGULATION OF NUMBERS

At the present time, then, it may be said that the effective population policy being pursued in this country is one of restriction by individuals as regards increase from within (births), and by the government as regards increase from without (immigration). Judging from the conduct of individuals, there is a growing belief that family life will be more satisfactory if children are limited to make possible the maintenance of a desired standard of living. This does not mean that there is general conscious agreement upon such a policy or that family limitation is being practiced by all. As a matter of fact, restriction from within is haphazard in operation from a national standpoint, neither the objectives of such a policy nor the means of attaining them being clearly defined. Granting, then, that the nation is going to follow some restrictive policy as regards growth from within (births), it would seem highly desirable that at least as much thought should be bestowed upon it as has been bestowed upon restricting growth from without (immigration). The policy to be followed in both cases should be the result of deliberate choice arrived at after a careful consideration of all aspects of the problem; otherwise the restriction may not result either in the most desirable size of population or in the best possible quality.

Just what constitutes the optimum population for a country is a highly controversial topic. Militarists have always insisted that a large and rapidly growing population was desirable. Many religious groups and ethical teachers have held the same view, though for quite different reasons. On the other hand, there have ever been individuals believing that personal development and the service of God and man are better performed by those having few or no children. Today there is a rapidly growing body of people who are convinced that man's numbers should be adjusted to the economic resources available for their support. Since these various views of the best size of population are based upon fundamental differences in belief as to what constitutes the meaning and purpose of life, there does not appear to be any immediate prospect of securing general agreement upon a policy of numbers.

It is not hard to understand that one who believes the military power of the state is the prime good in this world may easily convince himself that the restriction of numbers is a grave danger to the maintenance and increase of such power. Certainly "cannon fodder" is of great value to the military state, even though mere numbers are not so important a consideration in a machine age as they were in the past. Today, as never before, the militarist needs to consider carefully the relation of military power to standards of living and how these in turn depend upon whether a nation has a population of 150,000,000 or 300,000,000.

It is also easy to understand that those who believe man exists to worship and glorify God according to certain formulas may convince themselves that the more people there are to accomplish this the better pleased will be the God who demands such worship. Clearly, a population policy based on such beliefs will disregard all social and economic considerations. It relies on the "will of God" as interpreted by "His priests" for the final authority in such matters.

The large decline in the birth rate during the last century shows beyond doubt that such beliefs as those of the militarist and the religious zealot are becoming less and less effective in the United States today. A growing proportion of the people clearly believe that man can and should control his numbers to the end that his life may be more complete, the first requisite being to adjust numbers to the means available for their support. The manifestation of such an attitude is very naturally the restriction of the size of the family by married couples in order to give their children the opportunities they want them to have, or at least not to be driven into poverty because of too many mouths to feed and backs to clothe. The current drift is in this direction. But even among those who hold restriction of numbers desirable, there are many points of difference regarding the criteria by which the optimum population should be determined.

It is no doubt theoretically possible to state the economic optimum for any given area under any given state of the productive arts. But practically even such an optimum population can be ascertained only within wide limits because of the rapidly changing state of the productive arts, because of the differing notions as to proper consumption requirements, and because of the fact that every change in numbers in itself issues in new relations between numbers, resources, the productive arts, and the prevailing forms of social and economic organization.

To define the optimum population in any nation as that population which would ensure the largest economic return per capita under the given state of the productive arts with a given quantity of natural resources, as is frequently done, does not help a great deal in the practical solution of the problem of numbers in any nation. Furthermore, the assumption implicit in such a statement—namely, that man can live fully or even satisfactorily when he attains the largest possible consumption of the goods he is equipped to produce—will not be accepted by many who believe in the quest for the optimum population. But even though the exact number of persons best suited to live well in any nation is not susceptible of precise determination, it may be worth while to give attention briefly to the means that might be used in the further-ance of any policy that might be agreed upon.

a. Means for Regulating Numbers.—It seems highly probable that numbers can now be kept as low as the community may decide expedient, because the control of immigration is proving a fairly simple matter, and because it will require but little improvement in present methods of contraception to enable man to exercise almost complete control over births. It is true, however, that many people have political, religious, moral, or personal scruples against limiting their families, and that there are mentally inferior and diseased people who cannot be expected to practice birth control because they have no interest either in their ability to provide for their children or in the quality of their descendants. But assuming that the responsible part of the community would agree upon a policy of restriction and the irresponsible part would be made to conform by means of sterilization, there should be little difficulty in keeping numbers down to the limits determined upon. The technical difficulties of restricting births are well on the way to being surmounted.

If the mere continuance of the decline in the birth rate, with the decline in numbers which will inevitably follow within two or three decades, is the desired end, it seems to the authors that the present manner of life can be little improved upon to bring it about, in practically all classes of the population. In present-day society parenthood is penal-ized in a variety of ways, or to express it in positive terms, childlessness or near-childlessness is encouraged by the personal advantages it offers.[1] In the first place, modern industry makes no distinction in wages between those who raise children and those who do not, even though the children themselves contribute little to the family income. In an agricultural society, on the other hand, and to a certain extent in an industrial society permitting child labor, children supplement the family income to a considerable extent. Because of the increasing burden of rearing children in modern industrial society, it is natural that a rising proportion of married couples limit their families. A larger number of children in most families would mean a lower standard of living. This is a serious matter not only from the standpoint of personal opportunity and comfort, but also because position in the community, particularly in a young community where there is much migration, is very largely determined by the family standard of living. For all but a small fraction of the population, even three or four children seriously interfere with the maintenance of the standard that the family desires.

[1] For a statement of some of the advantages of childlessness in the comfortable white-collar class, see Anonymous, "Must I Have Children?" *Forum*, Vol. 89, No. 1 (January, 1933), pp. 52–54.

It should further be noted that men who devote much time and effort to their children are often made to feel that they are not in line to succeed. They must economically yield place to those whose energies are not turned from the customary paths of success by the care of families. This is particularly true in the professional and managerial classes where the bachelor, or the childless man, who devotes himself entirely to business often gains promotion in preference to the family man who cannot give himself so completely to his work. On the other hand, in the laboring class the family man is frequently given the preference when hands are laid off and minor supervisory jobs are being filled. Among women, too, the childless wife frequently derives considerable advantage from her childlessness. If she, too, works, the family income thus secured enables the couple to do many things that they could not otherwise do. If she does not work outside the home, she yet enjoys a measure of freedom which is quite impossible to the woman raising a family of children. Furthermore, women who raise several children are quite frequently made to feel the pity of their more "emancipated" sisters who prefer to devote their energies to business, travel, lectures, or bridge. Thus many women come to feel that the raising of children is a thankless task and that in devoting their best years to it they are being deprived of many of the worth-while things in life. Then, too, in spite of all that is said about "child welfare" and this being "the age of the child," the entire urban-industrial organization of today has almost no place for the child in its scheme of operation. Families with young children are not allowed to rent many of the better apartments; and, city rents being on the room basis, the large family necessarily incurs much heavier costs for adequate living quarters than the small family. Then, too, the family as a unit is not provided for in the present social and recreational life of cities. The modern city is almost exclusively organized around the work and recreation of the adult at or near the prime of life. Hence, in spite of all the vast expenditure on children in the cities, they are essentially a misfit in the urban scheme of life.

It may be that the sum of these and other attitudes affecting people's willingness to raise children do not deserve to be called a population policy—certainly they have not been consciously developed—but they actually constitute a social *milieu* in which married couples find little encouragement to raise the families of even three children which are necessary to maintain population with the present death rates. It is essentially correct, therefore, to say that the attitudes determining reproduction constitute in effect a policy of restriction. But since restriction is based upon the judgment of individuals regarding the advantages they personally will obtain, it can scarcely be called a well-rounded public policy. It does not take into account the interests of the community in population growth and it also ignores some of the basic elements in personal life. Such a haphazard sort of policy might possibly issue in the optimum numbers, but there is no reasonable assurance that it will do so, nor is there any assurance that the quality of the population produced under such conditions will be the best possible. It should be added, however, that neither is there any clear evidence that the average quality of people now being produced is deteriorating.

If, on the other hand, a larger and a more native population is wanted, the most helpful measures probably would be to continue present immigration restrictions and at the same time make it economically easier for the more responsible members of the community to raise larger families. Maternity allowances and tax exemptions graduated to the size of the family, not too stringent regulation of school attendance and child labor, and preference in employment for fathers of families of the size deemed desirable, are the types of economic benefits which might be set up. The assumption here is that if the community shows that it really places a high value on children and is willing to subsidize them, this very fact will not only remove some of the economic obstacles now put in the path of those who want families, but will also make women feel that they are performing a worth-while service in raising several children. Under these conditions a considerable number of couples may raise one or two more children than they are now willing to do. The community might counteract the unfavorable attitudes toward the rearing of children now developing in urban-industrial society by removing the economic handicaps of the parents of several children, handicaps which now exert a very depressing effect upon the size of families. If by such measures as those just mentioned and by others which may seem wise as conditions change, the community shows that it approves families of four or five children, let us say, there is some reason to believe enough people will respond to such encouragement to keep the population growing at the desired rate.

It is true that the experience of France in encouraging larger families has not yet had any significant results. On the economic side such assistance as is given is far from adequate, and on the social side there has apparently been no appreciable change in the attitudes toward the family which are effective in determining its size; for example, there has been no change in the laws of inheritance which require equal division of the estate among children and which are generally supposed to be an important factor in "the two-child system."

If the community wants more children, it must make parents feel that the effort they expend in raising several children is appreciated. Besides, the mother, in particular, must be made to feel that not only is a mother's task highly valued, but that the community guarantees her reasonable economic security in performing it. As pointed out above, an urban-industrial society removes much of the economic security of the family which it possessed under a simpler agricultural economy. This must be restored by guarantee of the community before people will be willing to undertake the responsibilities of larger families. Mothers' wages would be one means of restoring security to the family. Such a wage would also do much to equalize economic opportunity as between the couple raising several children and that raising none or only one or two. In a society operating on a money economy, mothers' wages would also do much to increase the self-reliance and dignity of women with several children. They would not be driven to seek the approval of the Joneses because they would be relatively free to choose between different manners of life and to adopt that which they thought most worth while. Once this change in attitude toward the rearing of children has been effected, it seems quite reasonable to believe that the nation can have as large a population as it is prepared to support at the accepted standards.

In this connection it should be pointed out that the payment of mothers' wages would necessarily have to be made contingent upon certain conditions. The distinctly unfit should be excluded from its benefits. The amount of the wage should be graded to the number of children desired by the community, so that too large a population would not be produced. No doubt it would also be necessary to adjust the wage within certain limits to the social status of the family. But details of any scheme for mothers' wages can be worked out only after the general policy is decided upon; for manifestly they must be adjusted to secure the ends of such a policy and these ends cannot be confined to numbers only. They must also be shaped to secure the highest possible quality of people the community can secure.

b. Improvement of Quality.—Many students of population, as well as the eugenists, are convinced that differentials in birth rates, in addition to causing undesirable social effects, have already resulted in some deterioration in the biological soundness of the national stock. There is reason to think that the biological consequences of these differentials are much exaggerated; nevertheless, it seems clear that no population policy can be considered comprehensive which does not take into account the fact that there are native differences between people, and that as soon as any agreement can be reached regarding the methods by which "undesirables" can be selected from the population, they should be prevented from propagating, while the "desirables" should be encouraged to raise families of the size wanted. In the present state of knowledge there is bound to be violent disagreement as to who are "desirable" and "undesirable" biologically, for it is by no means possible to say positively whether many types of behavior result from hereditary or environmental

[335]

causes. Indeed, there is a vast deal of confusion in the minds of many people on this matter; hence the methods of determining the "fit" and the "unfit" are often sadly unscientific. It is extremely easy, for example, to impute certain types of antisocial behavior to defects in heredity when they may be due to defects in upbringing, arising from the inadequacy of the social agencies of the community. Also "intelligence" as measured by tests is the resultant of the action of environmental forces upon a given hereditary endowment. There is as yet no means of accurately measuring each of these factors separately; hence there must be a wide margin of probable error in attributing the end result to either factor, proportionally, or *in toto*.

This is not to say, however, that there are not many cases in which there is reasonable assurance that one or the other of these two factors is defective. Workers trained in dealing with incompetents have comparatively little difficulty in agreeing that certain types of feeble-mindedness and of other mental defects are hereditary. About the disposition of these cases, there is comparatively little dispute, as will be shown presently. But it will probably be a long time before even highly trained men will be able to agree upon an interpretation of behavior that can be applied to cases on the border between normality and abnormality. Hence progress in their elimination will be slow. But eugenic sterilization laws and the sterilization of certain groups of the mentally incompetent through segregation are making headway.

The desirability of both of these methods of sterilization of the unfit as a means of improving the quality of the population is no longer in dispute between the social and the biological students of population. They are agreed that those who are hereditarily defective should not be allowed to reproduce. The real question in dispute between them is whether poverty, or crime, or unemployability, or general irresponsibility, or any other form of behavior quite generally condemned by the community arises from hereditary taint or from environmental conditions that the community could correct. If the evidence clearly indicates that heredity is at fault, then almost all realists would agree that reproduction should be forbidden. If the cause is environmental but the person is hopelessly handicapped—an imbecile by accident, for example—then again it would be generally agreed that sterilization would be the best way to deal with the situation because such persons, even if they had hereditarily normal children, would seldom be able to give them an upbringing which would render them good citizens. But in many borderline cases it is quite impossible to be sure that there is hereditary taint or that the parents will not be able to rear their children to become useful citizens. It is in dealing with these cases that care is needed. Social inadequacy is no proof of hereditary taint; it is often the result of a bad social system. Under a better social system many persons who are now regarded as inferior might actually prove useful citizens; until they have had a chance under such an improved system, they should not be deprived of their right to have a family. Social inadequacy is probably more often the consequence of lack of opportunity than of a defective heredity.

Sterilization, however accomplished, will prevent the birth of children to those sterilized, but it will not prevent the birth of many unfit whose deficiencies arise from the accidents of environment or from the joining of hereditary strains in which defects are recessive and crop out only sporadically when the proper combinations occur. This group, which is by no means small, will always be present. It will be lessened no doubt by sterilization as time goes on, but it cannot be eliminated. It will constitute a relatively heavy burden on the community, even under the best of conditions, if it is to be cared for by the type of segregation now approved. This fact naturally raises the question whether segregation is the best method of caring for that portion of the subnormal individuals which is permanently unable to look after itself. The alternative would seem to be euthanasia, some painless method of inducing death. Most of those who are permanently unable to look after themselves live only a vegetative existence at best and to hasten their end, once competent authorities pronounce their condition hopeless, has much to recommend it from the standpoint of the community. From the standpoint of the individual who is thus hopelessly handicapped, it would seem that he is not being deprived of any essentially human right in thus being eased out of an existence which is distinctly below the human level. It is hard to see how the hopeless idiot has any claim to life which the community need hesitate to abrogate.

It will no doubt be thought by many that the taking of human life in this manner is a reversion to barbarism. The answer to this is that the idiot is not human in any real sense; he does not share in those activities and attitudes of mind which distinguish man from the lower animals. He is not a true member of the community and no amount of effort expended in his training will make him other than he is. Furthermore, the community has never hesitated to take life (capital punishment and war) when it appeared to its advantage to do so. Why, then, should hopeless idiots be nursed along in an existence which is burdensome to all about them? Certainly, with the improvement of living conditions and the extension of medical knowledge, many of these creatures can be kept alive for many years, but it is time to ask whether a rational and humane population policy would not provide an easy way out for those who can never find a place for themselves in the life of the community.

However, those interested in improving the quality of the population are by no means satisfied with eliminating the unfit. They hold that it is also essential to encourage the increase of the "desirable." Important as this may be, it appears that little can be done about it at present. There is now the widest possible divergence of views regarding who are desirable, how they are to be mated, and how encouraged to raise families larger than the average once they are mated. As a beginning, any general population policy should make provision for sufficient biological education in the secondary schools to insure appreciation of the biological problems involved in mating, and sufficient civic education to make people appreciate the importance of participating in the continuing life of the community through their children. Any positive encouragement of *good* stock beyond such education, and the equalization of economic conditions between those who do and those who do not raise families, such as that suggested above, seem inadvisable until more is known about the inheritance of human traits.

The population policy of the future will have to be woven out of these factors and others now unforeseen and will have to be determined in the give-and-take of everyday life, as is the case with other important national policies. It is not likely that the best possible policy will be hit upon at once. But this should not deter the nation from making a conscious effort to control population growth both quantitatively and qualitatively. The quantitative goal may well be to adjust numbers to national means so that a high standard of living can be maintained and reasonable economic security can be guaranteed, and the qualitative goal to forestall the increase of undesirable stock and stimulate that of desirable stock within the quantitative limits. The achieving of these goals should issue in a finer quality of living.

APPENDIX TABLES

TABLE 1.—POPULATION AND PERCENTAGE DISTRIBUTION, BY SIZE OF COMMUNITY, BY REGIONS, 1820–1930[a]

Size of community	1820	1840	1850	1870	1890	1910	1920	1930
POPULATION (THOUSANDS)								
Northeast:[b]								
Total	4,356	6,761	8,627	12,299	17,407	25,869	29,662	34,427
1,000,000+	.....	.....	.....	.....	2,562	6,316	7,444	8,881
500,000–1,000,000	.....	.....	516	1,616	806	1,204	1,843	2,024
250,000– 500,000	.....	313	.....	647	704	1,039	1,008	1,340
100,000– 250,000	124	.....	258	223	955	1,648	2,458	2,905
25,000– 100,000	106	347	665	1,023	2,111	3,712	4,053	4,806
10,000– 25,000	70	289	401	908	1,438	2,269	2,914	3,740
2,500– 10,000	163	450	831	1,263	1,812	2,461	2,865	3,009
Rural	3,893	5,363	5,957	6,619	7,018	7,220	7,077	7,720
Farm	.....	.....	.....	.....	.....	.....	2,397	2,173
Nonfarm	.....	.....	.....	.....	.....	.....	4,680	5,548
PERCENTAGE DISTRIBUTION								
Total	100.0	100.0	100.0	100.0	100.0	100.0	100.0	100.0
1,000,000+	.....	.....	.....	.....	14.7	24.4	25.1	25.8
500,000–1,000,000	.....	.....	6.0	13.1	4.0	4.7	6.2	5.0
250,000– 500,000	.....	4.6	.....	5.3	4.0	4.0	3.4	3.9
100,000– 250,000	2.8	.....	3.0	1.8	5.5	6.4	8.3	8.4
25,000– 100,000	2.4	5.1	7.7	8.3	12.1	14.3	13.7	14.0
10,000– 25,000	1.6	4.3	4.6	7.4	8.3	8.8	9.8	10.9
2,500– 10,000	3.7	6.7	9.6	10.3	10.4	9.5	9.7	8.7
Rural	89.4	79.3	69.1	53.8	40.3	27.9	23.9	22.4
Farm	.....	.....	.....	.....	.....	.....	8.1	6.3
Nonfarm	.....	.....	.....	.....	.....	.....	15.8	16.1
POPULATION (THOUSANDS)								
North Center:[b]								
Total	859	3,352	5,404	12,981	22,410	29,889	34,020	38,594
1,000,000+	...	.....	.....	.....	1,100	2,185	2,702	4,945
500,000–1,000,000	...	.....	.....	.....	.....	1,248	2,563	2,301
250,000– 500,000	...	.....	.....	311	1,010	1,505	1,878	2,787
100,000– 250,000	...	.....	115	515	1,087	1,400	1,765	2,019
25,000– 100,000	...	46	78	418	1,053	2,356	3,415	4,241
10,000– 25,000	...	16	117	524	1,250	1,852	2,249	2,679
2,500– 10,000	12	68	181	917	1,914	2,946	3,204	3,379
Rural	847	3,221	4,912	10,296	14,997	16,398	16,244	16,243
Farm	...	.....	.....	.....	.....	.....	10,040	9,489
Nonfarm	...	.....	.....	.....	.....	.....	6,204	6,754
PERCENTAGE DISTRIBUTION								
Total	100.0	100.0	100.0	100.0	100.0	100.0	100.0	100.0
1,000,000+	.....	.....	.....	.....	4.9	7.3	7.9	12.8
500,000–1,000,000	.....	.....	.....	.....	.....	4.2	7.5	6.0
250,000– 500,000	.....	.....	.....	2.4	4.5	5.0	5.5	7.2
100,000– 250,000	.....	.....	2.1	4.0	4.9	4.7	5.2	5.2
25,000– 100,000	.....	1.3	1.4	3.2	4.7	7.9	10.0	11.0
10,000– 25,000	.....	0.5	2.2	4.0	5.6	6.2	6.6	6.9
2,500– 10,000	1.4	2.0	3.4	7.1	8.5	9.9	9.4	8.8
Rural	98.6	96.1	90.9	79.3	66.9	54.9	47.7	42.1
Farm	.....	.....	.....	.....	.....	.....	29.5	24.6
Nonfarm	.....	.....	.....	.....	.....	.....	18.2	17.5

TABLE 1.—POPULATION AND PERCENTAGE DISTRIBUTION, BY SIZE OF COMMUNITY, BY REGIONS, 1820–1930.[a]—(Continued)

Size of community	1820	1840	1850	1870	1890	1910	1920	1930
POPULATION (THOUSANDS)								
South:[b]								
Total	4,418	6,950	8,983	12,288	20,028	29,389	33,126	37,858
500,000–1,000,000	.....	.....	.....	.....	.....	558	734	805
250,000– 500,000	.....	.....	.....	267	434	670	825	2,589
100,000– 250,000	.....	205	285	401	634	881	1,858	1,964
25,000– 100,000	90	29	154	257	832	1,639	2,095	2,719
10,000– 25,000	50	111	124	270	553	1,020	1,397	1,829
2,500– 10,000	60	100	170	302	817	1,862	2,394	2,998
Rural	4,219	6,506	8,249	10,790	16,758	22,759	23,824	24,953
Farm	.....	.....	.....	.....	.....	.....	16,783	16,271
Nonfarm	.....	.....	.....	.....	.....	.....	7,041	8,682
PERCENTAGE DISTRIBUTION								
Total	100.0	100.0	100.0	100.0	100.0	100.0	100.0	100.0
500,000–1,000,000	.....	.....	.....	.....	.....	1.9	2.2	2.1
250,000– 500,000	.....	.....	.....	2.2	2.2	2.3	2.5	6.8
100,000– 250,000	.....	2.9	3.2	3.2	3.2	3.0	5.6	5.2
25,000– 100,000	2.0	0.4	1.7	2.1	4.2	5.6	6.3	7.2
10,000– 25,000	1.1	1.6	1.4	2.2	2.8	3.5	4.2	4.8
2,500– 10,000	1.3	1.4	1.9	2.4	4.1	6.3	7.2	7.9
Rural	95.5	93.6	91.8	87.9	83.7	77.4	71.9	65.9
Farm	.....	.....	.....	.....	.....	.....	50.7	43.0
Nonfarm	.....	.....	.....	.....	.....	.....	21.3	32.9
POPULATION (THOUSANDS)								
West:[b]								
Total	.....	.....	179	991	3,102	6,826	8,903	11,896
1,000,000+	.....	.....	.....	.....	.....	.....	.....	1,238
500,000–1,000,000	.....	.....	.....	.....	.....	.....	1,083	634
250,000– 500,000	.....	.....	.....	.....	299	736	830	1,239
100,000– 250,000	.....	.....	.....	149	107	912	439	653
25,000– 100,000	.....	.....	.....	.....	296	498	778	1,151
10,000– 25,000	.....	.....	.....	39	198	452	532	848
2,500– 10,000	.....	.....	7	43	258	731	1,032	1,229
Rural	.....	.....	172[c]	759	1,945	3,496	4,209	4,903
Farm	.....	.....	.....	.....	.....	.....	2,138	2,225
Nonfarm	.....	.....	.....	.....	.....	.....	2,071	2,679
PERCENTAGE DISTRIBUTION								
Total	.....	.....	100.0	100.0	100.0	100.0	100.0	100.0
1,000,000+	.....	.....	.....	.....	.....	.....	.....	10.4
500,000–1,000,000	.....	.....	.....	.....	.....	.....	12.2	5.3
250,000– 500,000	.....	.....	.....	.....	9.6	10.8	9.3	10.4
100,000– 250,000	.....	.....	.....	15.1	3.4	13.4	4.9	5.5
25,000– 100,000	.....	.....	.....	.....	9.5	7.3	8.7	9.7
10,000– 25,000	.....	.....	.....	4.0	6.4	6.6	6.0	7.1
2,500– 10,000	.....	.....	3.8	4.3	8.3	10.7	11.6	10.3
Rural	.....	.....	96.2	76.6	62.7	51.2	47.3	41.2
Farm	.....	.....	.....	.....	.....	.....	24.0	18.7
Nonfarm	.....	.....	.....	.....	.....	.....	23.3	22.5

[a] See Note a to Table 8, p. 24.

[b] Northeast includes the New England and Middle Atlantic divisions; North Center includes the East North Central and West North Central divisions; South includes the South Atlantic, East South Central; and West South Central divisions; West includes the Mountain and Pacific divisions.

[c] Census reports for San Francisco were destroyed by fire in 1850. Since the rural population is obtained by subtraction, San Francisco is included here. A special state census in 1850 reported a population of 34,776 in San Francisco.

APPENDIX TABLES

TABLE 2.—POPULATION AND RATE OF INCREASE BY SIZE OF COMMUNITY, BY REGIONS, 1820–1930[a]

Year	1,000,000 or over	500,000– 1,000,000	250,000– 500,000	100,000– 250,000	25,000– 100,000	10,000– 25,000	2,500– 10,000	Rural	Total

NUMBER OF CITIES

Northeast:[b]									
1820.............	..	..	..	1	2	5	32	..	..
1830.............	..	..	..	1	3	12	41	..	..
1840.............	..	..	1	..	7	19	89	..	..
1850.............	..	1	1	2	8	28	159	..	..
1860.............	..	2	1	1	16	39	194	..	..
1870.............	..	2	2	3	21	60	257	..	..
1880.............	1	2	1	5	30	70	301	..	..
1890.............	2	..	2	6	46	93	350	..	..
1900.............	2	1	2	10	54	121	404	..	..
1910.............	2	2	3	12	78	155	474	..	..
1920.............	2	3	3	18	83	190	542	..	..

POPULATION (THOUSANDS)

1820.............	.....	.....	.....	124	108	70	163	3,895	4,360
1830.............	.....	.....	.....	203	171	174	219	4,776	5,542
1840.............	.....	.....	313	.....	347	300	434	5,367	6,761
1850.............	.....	516	409	268	326	425	761	5,922	8,627
1860.............	.....	1,371	267	213	694	594	972	6,483	10,594
1870.............	.....	1,645	689	342	916	926	1,231	6,550	12,299
1880.............	1,206	1,427	363	674	1,354	1,076	1,451	6,956	14,507
1890.............	3,581	.....	704	957	2,147	1,414	1,777	6,827	17,407
1900.............	4,731	561	815	1,440	2,585	1,884	2,063	6,967	21,047
1910.............	6,316	1,220	1,039	1,649	3,745	2,293	2,413	7,193	25,869
1920.............	7,444	1,880	1,008	2,460	4,106	2,938	2,795	7,032	29,662

PERCENTAGE INCREASE[c]

1820–30..........	....	....	....	63.8	31.7	48.8	45.3	24.7	27.1
1830–40..........	....	....	....	54.4	29.8	57.2	48.6	17.8	22.0
1840–50..........	....	....	64.9	....	121.8	75.1	49.3	14.9	27.6
1850–60..........	....	56.3	38.4	65.7	34.8	44.3	31.6	13.5	22.8
1860–70..........	....	17.9	48.5	17.8	38.7	37.7	29.6	7.9	16.1
1870–80..........	....	24.8	35.0	31.1	32.9	27.3	22.9	9.4	18.0
1880–90..........	25.6	29.8	23.6	44.2	35.6	37.2	34.1	5.8	20.0
1890–1900........	32.1	....	29.7	29.8	30.0	28.3	22.8	8.0	20.9
1900–10..........	33.5	19.6	17.5	28.4	29.2	25.4	28.2	10.9	22.9
1910–20..........	17.9	9.5	17.4	16.5	21.2	18.9	18.2	6.0	14.7
1920–30..........	19.3	7.7	7.8	6.5	13.8	17.0	27.6	15.7	16.1

NUMBER OF CITIES

North Center:[b]									
1820.............	..	..	..	..	..	...	2	..	..
1830.............	..	..	..	..	..	1	4	..	..
1840.............	..	..	..	..	1	1	15	..	..
1850.............	..	..	..	1	3	4	45	..	..
1860.............	..	..	..	3	3	12	109	..	..
1870.............	..	..	2	1	8	36	204	..	..
1880.............	..	1	2	3	16	47	309	..	..
1890.............	1	..	3	7	25	85	403	..	..
1900.............	1	1	4	8	35	100	528	..	..
1910.............	1	2	4	8	55	120	604	..	..
1920.............	2	2	5	10	75	150	657	..	..

[341]

TABLE 2.—POPULATION AND RATE OF INCREASE BY SIZE OF COMMUNITY, BY REGIONS, 1820–1930.ᵃ—(Continued)

Year	1,000,000 or over	500,000–1,000,000	250,000–500,000	100,000–250,000	25,000–100,000	10,000–25,000	2,500–10,000	Rural	Total

POPULATION (THOUSANDS)

Year	1,000,000 or over	500,000–1,000,000	250,000–500,000	100,000–250,000	25,000–100,000	10,000–25,000	2,500–10,000	Rural	Total
North Center:ᵇ(Cont'd)									
1820	.....	.....	.....	.....	.....	.....	12	847	859
1830	.....	.....	.....	.....	.....	25	12	1,574	1,610
1840	.....	.....	.....	.....	46	16	68	3,221	3,352
1850	.....	.....	.....	115	108	87	189	4,904	5,404
1860	.....	.....	.....	438	134	169	527	7,828	9,097
1870	.....	.....	610	216	420	531	930	10,274	12,981
1880	.....	549	606	395	626	685	1,389	13,115	17,364
1890	1,100	.....	1,024	1,106	1,060	1,283	1,854	14,984	22,410
1900	1,699	575	1,287	1,162	1,405	1,583	2,457	16,165	26,333
1910	2,190	1,256	1,527	1,432	2,355	1,831	2,908	16,389	29,889
1920	3,704	1,578	1,883	1,788	3,432	2,267	3,158	16,211	34,020

PERCENTAGE INCREASEᶜ

Year	1,000,000 or over	500,000–1,000,000	250,000–500,000	100,000–250,000	25,000–100,000	10,000–25,000	2,500–10,000	Rural	Total
1820–30	....	.....	....	....	.....	.....	128.0	86.8	87.4
1830–40	....	.....	....	....	.....	86.6	69.2	106.0	105.4ᵈ
1840–50	....	.....	....	....	149.1	372.8	132.0	56.9	61.2
1850–60	....	.....	....	39.5	153.1	98.8	69.3	63.7	65.7ᵉ
1860–70	....	.....	....	88.6	81.6	79.9	62.1	37.7	43.0ᶠ
1870–80	....	.....	40.0	18.0	58.4	39.0	31.5	32.7	33.8
1880–90	....	100.4	23.6	70.1	98.4	47.0	46.3	19.0	29.1
1890–1900	54.4	.....	25.3	24.1	29.0	22.2	25.2	11.6	17.5
1900–10	28.7	19.4	37.0	33.4	32.9	23.1	21.8	4.5	13.5
1910–20	23.4	25.0	46.2	28.1	33.1	29.0	21.7	1.6	13.8
1920–30	33.5	9.1	19.9	18.9	26.3	21.2	18.9	3.0	13.4

NUMBER OF CITIES

Year	1,000,000 or over	500,000–1,000,000	250,000–500,000	100,000–250,000	25,000–100,000	10,000–25,000	2,500–10,000	Rural	Total
South:ᵇ									
1820	...	..	..	..	2	3	7	...	...
1830	...	..	..	..	3	3	13	...	...
1840	...	..	..	2	1	7	19	...	...
1850	...	..	..	2	4	8	33	...	...
1860	...	..	..	2	5	11	47	...	...
1870	...	..	1	3	7	17	62	...	...
1880	...	..	1	3	10	22	103	...	...
1890	...	..	1	3	20	36	188	...	...
1900	...	1	2	2	24	48	271	...	...
1910	...	1	2	6	35	69	408	...	...
1920	...	1	2	12	44	96	533	...	...

POPULATION (THOUSANDS)

Year	1,000,000 or over	500,000–1,000,000	250,000–500,000	100,000–250,000	25,000–100,000	10,000–25,000	2,500–10,000	Rural	Total
1820	...	...	.....	.....	90	50	44	4,236	4,419
1830	...	...	.....	.....	161	45	70	5,432	5,708
1840	...	...	.....	205	29	111	100	6,507	6,951
1850	...	...	.....	300	154	111	179	8,239	8,983
1860	...	...	.....	392	251	182	241	10,068	11,133
1870	...	...	267	424	262	263	295	10,777	12,288
1880	...	...	332	517	392	340	458	14,477	16,517
1890	...	...	434	636	859	534	805	16,760	20,028
1900	...	509	566	308	1,147	717	1,196	20,081	24,524
1910	...	616	670	882	1,673	1,038	1,826	22,684	29,389
1920	...	734	825	1,881	2,127	1,420	2,337	23,802	33,126

APPENDIX TABLES

TABLE 2.—POPULATION AND RATE OF INCREASE BY SIZE OF COMMUNITY, BY REGIONS, 1820–1930.ᵃ—(*Continued*)

Year	1,000,000 or over	500,000– 1,000,000	250,000– 500,000	100,000– 250,000	25,000– 100,000	10,000– 25,000	2,500– 10,000	Rural	Total

PERCENTAGE INCREASEᶜ

South:ᵇ (*Continued*)									
1820–30...........	....	....	....	....	22.7	30.1	27.3	28.5	28.4ᵍ
1830–40...........	....	....	....	....	45.4	43.1	26.8	20.8	21.8
1840–50...........	....	....	....	39.6	46.9	58.1	44.4	24.8	26.2ʰ
1850–60...........	....	....	....	27.2	35.0	34.1	37.1	23.2	23.9
1860–70...........	....	....	....	17.0	45.3	38.2	33.4	8.2	10.4
1870–80...........	....	....	24.3	22.1	11.9	29.3	31.3	35.9	34.4
1880–90..........	....	....	30.7	22.4	40.3	50.1	60.4	17.3	20.2ⁱ
1890–1900........	....	....	17.2	21.1	24.5	22.8	30.7	22.1	22.4
1900–10..........	....	9.7	18.4	15.3	44.5	50.4	37.3	16.7	19.8
1910–20..........	....	19.1	23.1	20.9	40.1	32.7	26.3	7.9	12.7
1920–30..........	....	9.7	14.7	38.8	36.0	40.2	26.9	7.7	14.3

NUMBER OF CITIES

West:ᵇ									
1850..............	..	..	..	..	1	..	2	...	...
1860..............	..	..	..	..	1	1	7	...	...
1870..............	..	..	..	1	..	4	9	...	...
1880..............	..	..	..	1	2	8	34	...	...
1890..............	..	..	1	1	8	12	63	...	...
1900..............	..	..	1	2	9	15	97	...	...
1910..............	..	..	2	5	11	31	161	...	...
1920..............	..	2	3	3	17	37	216	...	...

POPULATION (THOUSANDS)

1850..............	.....	.....	.....	...	35	...	12	132	179
1860..............	.....	.....	.....	...	57	14	29	520	619
1870..............	.....	.....	.....	149	.....	50	50	741	991
1880..............	.....	.....	.....	234	70	124	132	1,207	1,768
1890..............	.....	.....	299	112	339	163	244	1,945	3,102
1900..............	.....	.....	343	238	460	220	406	2,425	4,091
1910..............	.....	.....	736	919	504	452	724	3,491	6,826
1920..............	.....	1,083	830	443	783	534	1,010	4,220	8,903

PERCENTAGE INCREASEᶜ

1850–60...........	....	....	....	.....	63.3	....	57.9	310.8	246.1
1860–70...........	....	....	....	.....	163.1	18.1	62.7	44.0	55.2ʲ
1870–80...........	....	....	....	56.5	.....	75.1	117.1	80.5	78.5
1880–90...........	....	....	....	27.8	204.1	76.3	102.9	74.2	75.5
1890–1900........	....	....	14.6	19.7	44.3	39.5	29.5	32.7	31.9
1900–10..........	....	....	21.6	123.7	118.4	50.3	66.7	59.4	66.8
1910–20..........	....	....	47.2	25.2	27.7	40.0	26.1	28.3	30.4
1920–30..........	....	72.8	15.0	21.9	42.4	42.8	41.3	23.8	33.6

ᵃ From special compilation made for this study. See Notes *a* and *b*, Table 9, p. 26.
ᵇ See Note *b*, Appendix Table 1.
ᶜ See Note *c*, Table 9.
ᵈ Excludes Iowa Territory (43,112) in 1840, as data are not given in 1830.
ᵉ Excludes Kansas, Nebraska, and the Dakotas (140,844) in 1860 since these areas were not enumerated in 1850.
ᶠ Includes Montana (20,595) and Wyoming (9,118) in 1870 since nearly all of Montana and nearly all of Idaho were part of the Dakota Territory and part of Nebraska Territory in 1860. See West.
ᵍ Florida (34,730) excluded in 1830 because it was not enumerated in 1820.
ʰ Excludes Texas (212,592) in 1850 since it belonged to Mexico in 1840.
ⁱ Excludes Indian Territory (180,182) in 1890 since it was not enumerated in 1880.
ʲ Excludes Montana and Wyoming (29,713) in 1870. See Note *f* above.

TABLE 3.—NUMBER AND PROPORTION OF CITIES DECREASING IN POPULATION, BY SIZE GROUPS, 1910–1920 AND 1920–1930[a]

Size of community	1910–20			1920–30		
	Number of cities	Cities decreasing in population		Number of cities	Cities decreasing in population	
		Number	Percentage of all cities		Number	Percentage of all cities
All cities......................	2,254	393	17.4	2,708	532	19.6
Over 1,000,000....................	3	...	...,.	4	...	....
500,000–1,000,000................	5	...	....	8	...	...•
250,000– 500,000................	11	...	....	13	...	....
100,000– 250,000................	31	...	....	43	4	9.3
50,000– 100,000................	59	2	3.4	77	12	15.6
25,000– 50,000................	120	8	6.7	142	9	6.3
15,000– 25,000................	155	15	9.7	209	31	14.8
10,000– 15,000................	220	32	14.5	264	44	16.7
5,000– 10,000................	600	90	15.0	712	145	20.4
2,500– 5,000................	1,047	246	23.5	1,236	287	23.2

[a] For Basis of compilation, see notes to Table 9, p. 26.

TABLE 4.—NATIVE WHITE POPULATION OF NATIVE PARENTAGE AND PERCENTAGE DISTRIBUTION, BY SIZE OF COMMUNITY, BY REGIONS, 1820–1930[a]

Size of community	Total white			Native white		Native white of native parentage			
	1820	1840	1870	1870	1890	1890	1910	1920	1930
POPULATION (THOUSANDS)									
Northeast:									
Total....................	4,246	6,619	12,117	9,600	13,247	8,891	11,076	12,434	14,617
1,000,000+................	.....	.....	.....	.....	1,591	685	1,505	1,864	2,246
500,000–1,000,000........	.....	.....	1,581	979	535	223	334	563	685
250,000– 500,000........	.....	296	638	406	449	192	289	312	407
100,000– 250,000........	113	.....	220	138	645	292	473	806	1,017
25,000– 100,000........	97	328	1,008	687	1,475	842	1,450	1,569	1,941
10,000– 25,000........	66	277	891	653	1,053	660	975	1,201	1,722
2,500– 10,000........	156	439	1,243	969	1,421	986	1,311	1,528	1,633
Rural....................	3,814	5,279	6,536	5,769	6,079	5,011	4,739	4,590	4,967
PERCENTAGE DISTRIBUTION									
Total....................	100.0	100.0	100.0	100.0	100.0	100.0	100.0	100.0	100.0
1,000,000+................	.....	.....	.....	.....	12.0	7.7	13.6	15.0	15.4
500,000–1,000,000........	.....	.....	13.0	10.2	4.0	2.5	3.0	4.5	4.7
250,000– 500,000........	.....	4.5	5.3	4.2	3.4	2.2	2.6	2.5	2.8
100,000– 250,000........	2.7	.....	1.8	1.4	4.9	3.3	4.3	6.5	7.0
25,000– 100,000........	2.3	5.0	8.3	7.2	11.1	9.5	13.1	12.6	13.3
10,000– 25,000........	1.6	4.2	7.4	6.8	7.9	7.4	8.8	9.7	11.8
2,500– 10,000........	3.7	6.6	10.3	10.1	10.7	11.1	11.8	12.3	11.2
Rural....................	89.8	79.8	53.9	60.1	45.9	56.4	42.8	36.9	34.0
POPULATION (THOUSANDS)									
North Center:									
Total....................	841	3,262	12,699	10,368	17,860	12,252	16,276	19,266	23,048
1,000,000+................	...	.....	.....	.....	635	223	445	643	1,481
500,000–1,000,000........	...	.....	.....	.....	.....	.....	402	886	899
250,000– 500,000........	...	.....	289	177	685	261	445	899	1,636
100,000– 250,000........	...	.....	506	282	708	354	724	917	1,175
25,000– 100,000........	...	44	404	252	785	476	1,218	1,874	2,518
10,000– 25,000........	...	14	504	352	932	565	978	1,339	1,708
2,500– 10,000........	12	65	880	662	1,517	1,054	1,786	2,041	2,297
Rural....................	829	3,139	10,115	8,644	12,597	9,320	10,277	10,667	11,333
PERCENTAGE DISTRIBUTION									
Total....................	100.0	100.0	100.0	100.0	100.0	100.0	100.0	100.0	100.0
1,000,000+................	.....	.....	.....	.....	3.6	1.8	2.7	3.3	6.4
500,000–1,000,000........	.....	.....	.....	.....	.....	.....	2.5	4.6	3.9
250,000– 500,000........	.....	.....	2.3	1.7	3.8	2.1	2.7	4.7	7.1
100,000– 250,000........	.....	.....	4.0	2.7	4.0	2.9	4.4	4.8	5.1
25,000– 100,000........	.....	1.4	3.2	2.4	4.4	3.9	7.5	9.7	10.9
10,000– 25,000........	.....	0.4	4.0	3.4	5.2	4.6	6.0	7.0	7.4
2,500– 10,000........	1.4	2.0	6.9	6.4	8.5	8.6	11.0	10.6	10.0
Rural....................	98.6	96.2	79.7	83.4	70.5	76.1	63.1	55.4	49.2
POPULATION (THOUSANDS)									
South:									
Total....................	2,776	4,308	7,863	7,468	12,673	11,843	18,561	21,832	25,738
500,000–1,000,000........	.....	.....	.....	.....	.....	.....	261	378	427
250,000– 500,000........	.....	.....	228	171	299	187	314	430	1,528
100,000– 250,000........	.....	141	300	213	389	241	465	1,068	1,216
25,000– 100,000........	62	13	152	121	465	352	863	1,253	1,751
10,000– 25,000........	27	70	179	143	305	249	600	896	1,238
2,500– 10,000........	39	67	179	156	480	427	1,172	1,670	2,165
Rural....................	2,649	4,017	6,825	6,664	10,735	10,387	14,886	16,137	17,411

TABLE 4.—NATIVE WHITE POPULATION OF NATIVE PARENTAGE AND PERCENTAGE DISTRIBUTION, BY SIZE OF COMMUNITY, BY REGIONS, 1820–1930.ᵃ—(*Continued*)

Size of community	Total white			Native white		Native white of native parentage			
	1820	1840	1870	1870	1890	1890	1910	1920	1930

PERCENTAGE DISTRIBUTION

	1820	1840	1870	1870	1890	1890	1910	1920	1930
South: (*Continued*)									
Total....................	100.0	100.0	100.0	100.0	100.0	100.0	100.0	100.0	100.0
500,000–1,000,000.........	.....	.....	...	...	.....	.....	1.4	1.7	1.7
250,000– 500,000.........	.....	.....	2.9	2.3	2.4	1.6	1.7	2.0	5.9
100,000– 250,000.........	.....	3.3	3.8	2.8	3.1	2.0	2.5	4.9	4.7
25,000– 100,000.........	2.2	0.3	1.9	1.6	3.7	3.0	4.6	5.7	6.8
10,000– 25,000.........	1.0	1.6	2.3	1.9	2.4	2.1	3.2	4.1	4.8
2,500– 10,000.........	1.4	1.6	2.3	2.1	3.8	3.6	6.3	7.6	8.4
Rural...................	95.4	93.2	86.8	89.2	84.7	87.7	80.2	73.9	67.6

POPULATION (THOUSANDS)

	1820	1840	1870	1870	1890	1890	1910	1920	1930
West:									
Total...................	.....	.....	910	661	2,199	1,490	3,575	4,890	6,734
1,000,000+...............	.....	.....	...	...	.....	.....	.....	.....	618
500,000–1,000,000.........	.....	.....	...	...	.....	.....	.....	462	235
250,000– 500,000.........	.....	.....	...	...	169	62	285	421	642
100,000– 250,000.........	.....	.....	136	69	78	55	427	204	386
25,000– 100,000.........	.....	.....	...	...	200	122	236	407	638
10,000– 25,000.........	.....	.....	36	23	145	100	240	320	537
2,500– 10,000.........	.....	.....	39	28	187	126	422	607	750
Rural...................	.....	.....	699	541	1,420	1,025	1,966	2,471	2,928

PERCENTAGE DISTRIBUTION

	1820	1840	1870	1870	1890	1890	1910	1920	1930
Total...................	.....	.....	100.0	100.0	100.0	100.0	100.0	100.0	100.0
1,000,000+...............	.....	.....	...	...	.....	.....	.....	.....	9.2
500,000–1,000,000.........	.....	.....	.....	.....	.....	.....	.....	9.4	3.5
250,000– 500,000.........	.....	.....	...	...	7.7	4.2	8.0	8.6	9.5
100,000– 250,000.........	.....	.....	14.9	10.4	3.6	3.7	11.9	4.2	5.7
25,000– 100,000.........	.....	.....	.....	.....	9.1	8.2	6.6	8.3	9.5
10,000– 25,000.........	.....	.....	4.0	3.4	6.6	6.7	6.7	6.5	8.0
2,500– 10,000.........	.....	.....	4.3	4.3	8.5	8.5	11.8	12.4	11.1
Rural...................	.....	.....	76.8	81.8	64.6	68.8	55.0	50.5	43.5

ᵃ For sources of data and method of compilation, see Table 13, p. 47.

TABLE 5.—PERCENTAGE DISTRIBUTION OF THE POPULATION IN COMMUNITIES OF DIFFERENT SIZES, BY RACE AND NATIVITY, BY REGIONS, 1870–1930[a]

Size of community	Year	Native whites of native parentage	Native whites of foreign or mixed parentage	Foreign-born whites	Negroes
Northeast:					
1,000,000+	1890	26.7	35.4	35.3	2.5
	1910	23.8	36.7	36.6	2.8
	1920	25.0	38.9	32.1	3.9
	1930	25.3	38.2	30.0	6.2
	1870	60.5		37.3	2.2
	1890	27.6	38.7	32.3	1.3
500,000–1,000,000	1910	27.7	37.2	31.6	3.3
	1920	30.6	40.0	26.1	3.2
	1930	33.8	39.0	22.6	4.4
	1870	62.7		36.0	1.3
	1890	27.3	36.4	34.9	1.3
250,000– 500,000	1910	27.8	40.9	29.5	1.7
	1920	31.0	40.1	26.2	2.6
	1930	30.4	40.8	24.2	4.4
	1870	62.0		36.9	1.1
	1890	30.6	37.0	30.1	2.2
100,000– 250,000	1910	28.7	38.2	31.6	1.3
	1920	32.8	38.3	26.7	2.1
	1930	35.0	39.4	23.1	2.4
	1870	67.1		31.4	1.5
	1890	39.9	30.0	28.5	1.6
25,000– 100,000	1910	39.1	31.4	27.6	1.8
	1920	38.7	35.1	24.3	1.9
	1930	40.4	35.8	21.3	2.4
	1870	71.9		26.2	1.9
	1890	45.9	27.3	25.3	1.4
10,000– 25,000	1910	44.3	29.9	24.1	1.7
	1920	43.6	33.5	21.1	1.7
	1930	46.1	33.9	17.5	2.4
	1870	76.7		21.7	1.6
	1890	54.4	24.0	19.8	1.8
2,500– 10,000	1910	50.4	27.2	21.1	1.3
	1920	51.3	29.5	17.7	1.5
	1930	54.2	29.6	14.5	1.6
	1870	87.1		11.6	1.2
	1890	71.4	15.2	12.2	1.1
Rural	1910	66.3	18.1	14.2	1.2
	1920	64.4	21.5	12.7	1.3
	1930	64.3	22.6	11.3	1.6
North Center:					
1,000,000+	1890	20.3	37.5	40.9	1.3
	1910	20.4	41.8	35.7	2.0
	1920	23.8	42.2	29.8	4.1
	1930	30.0	37.1	25.1	7.2

TABLE 5.—PERCENTAGE DISTRIBUTION OF THE POPULATION IN COMMUNITIES OF DIFFERENT SIZES, BY RACE AND NATIVITY, BY REGIONS, 1870–1930.ª—(*Continued*)

Size of community	Year	Native whites of native parentage	Native whites of foreign or mixed parentage	Foreign-born whites	Negroes
North Center: (*Continued*)					
500,000–1,000,000	1910	32.2	37.7	25.8	4.2
	1920	34.6	35.0	24.7	5.7
	1930	39.1	35.0	18.2	7.5
	1870	56.8		36.1	7.1
	1890	25.8	42.0	28.0	4.1
250,000– 500,000	1910	29.6	41.2	27.3	1.9
	1920	47.9	31.5	15.2	5.4
	1930	58.7	24.0	10.0	7.0
	1870	54.6		43.5	1.9
	1890	32.5	32.6	31.7	3.1
100,000– 250,000	1910	51.7	27.4	15.7	5.2
	1920	51.9	27.5	15.7	4.7
	1930	58.2	24.0	11.3	5.9
	1870	60.3		36.5	3.2
	1890	45.2	29.4	21.5	3.9
25,000– 100,000	1910	51.7	28.2	17.0	3.0
	1920	54.9	27.3	15.0	2.8
	1930	59.4	25.7	11.4	3.0
	1870	67.1		29.2	3.7
	1890	45.2	29.3	21.9	3.5
10,000– 25,000	1910	52.8	28.0	16.2	2.8
	1920	59.6	25.6	11.9	2.8
	1930	63.8	23.8	9.2	2.8
	1870	72.2		23.8	4.0
	1890	55.1	24.2	17.2	3.4
2,500– 10,000	1910	60.6	23.7	13.2	2.5
	1920	63.7	23.6	10.6	1.9
	1930	68.0	21.9	8.0	1.9
	1870	83.9		14.3	1.7
	1890	62.1	21.9	14.3	1.3
Rural..........................	1910	62.7	24.7	11.3	0.9
	1920	65.7	24.1	9.1	0.8
	1930	69.8	21.9	6.9	1.0
South:					
500,000–1,000,000	1910	46.8	24.1	13.8	15.2
	1920	51.6	22.2	11.4	14.8
	1930	53.1	19.9	9.2	17.7
	1870	64.1		21.1	14.8
	1890	43.0	25.8	15.8	15.4
250,000– 500,000	1910	46.9	17.8	7.8	27.4
	1920	52.2	15.5	6.6	25.6
	1930	59.0	9.6	3.6	25.4

TABLE 5.—PERCENTAGE DISTRIBUTION OF THE POPULATION IN COMMUNITIES OF DIFFERENT SIZES, BY RACE AND NATIVITY, BY REGIONS, 1870–1930.ᵃ—(*Continued*)

Size of community	Year	Native whites of native parentage	Native whites of foreign or mixed parentage	Foreign-born whites	Negroes
South: (*Continued*)					
	1870	53.0		21.9	25.1
	1890	38.0	23.4	12.0	26.6
100,000– 250,000	1910	52.8	10.7	4.7	31.8
	1920	57.5	10.8	6.6	25.1
	1930	61.9	8.0	3.6	20.7
	1870	47.1		12.2	40.7
	1890	42.3	13.6	8.9	35.1
25,000– 100,000	1910	52.7	12.0	7.6	27.8
	1920	59.8	8.6	5.4	26.1
	1930	64.4	5.9	2.2	25.6
	1870	52.9		13.2	33.9
	1890	45.1	10.1	7.7	37.0
10,000– 25,000	1910	58.8	6.6	4.0	30.5
	1920	64.3	5.7	3.8	26.2
	1930	67.7	3.8	1.5	24.9
	1870	51.5		7.9	40.6
	1890	52.3	6.5	4.1	37.1
2,500– 10,000	1910	63.1	4.8	2.8	29.1
	1920	69.6	4.5	2.6	23.1
	1930	72.2	3.6	1.3	20.3
	1870	61.8		1.5	36.7
	1890	62.0	2.1	1.4	34.2
Rural	1910	65.4	2.4	1.5	30.3
	1920	67.7	2.5	1.5	28.0
	1930	69.8	2.0	0.7	25.6
West:					
1,000,000 +	1930	49.9	22.1	14.7	0.3
500,000–1,000,000	1920	42.6	29.8	23.3	1.7
	1930	37.1	32.6	24.2	0.6
	1890	20.8	35.8	33.9	0.6
250,000– 500,000	1910	38.7	31.1	26.0	1.3
	1920	50.7	27.2	19.1	1.3
	1930	51.8	27.6	16.3	1.6
	1870	46.1		44.9	0.9
	1890	51.1	22.2	22.9	2.9
100,000– 250,000	1910	46.8	27.4	22.1	1.4
	1920	46.5	31.7	18.6	1.6
	1930	59.1	24.8	12.7	0.8
	1890	41.2	26.6	27.5	1.2
25,000– 100,000	1910	47.2	29.1	20.7	1.4
	1920	52.2	26.8	17.8	1.2
	1930	55.4	22.3	12.0	1.6

TABLE 5.—PERCENTAGE DISTRIBUTION OF THE POPULATION IN COMMUNITIES OF DIFFERENT SIZES, BY RACE AND NATIVITY, BY REGIONS, 1870–1930.[a]—(Continued)

Size of community	Year	Native whites of natives parentage	Native whites of foreign or mixed parentage	Foreign-born whites	Negroes
West: (Continued)					
10,000– 25,000	1870	58.0		34.2	1.6
	1890	50.3	22.7	22.3	1.8
	1910	53.0	24.5	18.9	1.2
	1920	58.3	23.9	15.6	1.0
	1930	63.3	21.3	10.8	0.7
2,500–100,000	1870	65.5		25.8	1.7
	1890	48.9	23.7	22.7	1.0
	1910	57.8	23.7	16.5	0.8
	1920	60.2	22.9	14.8	0.8
	1930	61.0	20.1	9.5	0.6
Rural	1870	71.2		20.9	0.5
	1890	52.7	20.3	18.6	0.6
	1910	56.2	21.8	17.1	0.3
	1920	58.6	22.1	14.7	0.5
	1930	59.7	19.4	9.8	0.4

[a] From a special compilation made for this study and from *Fourteenth Census of the United States: 1920*, Vol. II, p. 90. All Mexicans were classified as whites prior to 1930. The percentages do not add to 100 because "other colored" are not included.

APPENDIX TABLES

TABLE 6.—FOREIGN-BORN WHITE POPULATION AND PERCENTAGE DISTRIBUTION BY SIZE OF COMMUNITY, BY REGIONS, 1870–1930[a]

Size of community	1870	1890	1910	1920	1930
POPULATION (THOUSAND)					
Northeast:					
Total	2,517	3,875	6,641	6,783	7,103
1,000,000+	.....	905	2,310	2,389	2,662
500,000–1,000,000	602	261	381	481	457
250,000– 500,000	233	246	307	264	325
100,000– 250,000	82	288	521	657	671
25,000– 100,000	322	602	1,026	983	1,023
10,000– 25,000	238	364	530	580	656
2,500– 10,000	274	359	549	527	485
Rural	767	850	1,017	902	874
PERCENTAGE DISTRIBUTION					
Total	100.0	100.0	100.0	100.0	100.0
1,000,000+	....	23.4	34.8	35.2	37.5
500,000–1,000,000	23.9	6.7	5.7	7.1	6.4
250,000– 500,000	9.2	6.3	4.6	3.9	4.6
100,000– 250,000	3.3	7.4	7.8	9.7	9.4
25,000– 100,000	12.8	15.5	15.4	14.5	14.4
10,000– 25,000	9.5	9.4	8.0	8.6	9.2
2,500– 10,000	10.9	9.3	8.3	7.8	6.1
Rural	30.5	21.9	15.3	13.3	12.3
POPULATION (THOUSANDS)					
North Center:					
Total	2,331	4,053	4,680	4,595	4,283
1,000,000+	.....	450	781	805	1,241
500,000–1,000,000	.....	.....	321	632	419
250,000– 500,000	112	283	411	285	278
100,000– 250,000	224	344	219	277	227
25,000– 100,000	152	226	401	511	485
10,000– 25,000	153	274	300	267	247
2,500– 10,000	218	330	388	341	270
Rural	1,472	2,147	1,859	1,476	1,115
PERCENTAGE DISTRIBUTION					
Total	100.0	100.0	100.0	100.0	100.0
1,000,000,+	.....	11.1	16.7	17.5	29.0
500,000–1,000,000	.....	.....	6.9	13.8	9.8
250,000– 500,000	4.8	7.0	8.8	6.2	6.5
100,000– 250,000	9.6	8.5	4.7	6.0	5.3
25,000– 100,000	6.5	5.6	8.6	11.1	11.3
10,000– 25,000	6.5	6.7	6.4	5.8	5.8
2,500– 10,000	9.3	8.1	8.3	7.4	6.3
Rural	63.2	53.0	39.7	32.1	26.0

TABLE 6.—FOREIGN-BORN WHITE POPULATION AND PERCENTAGE DISTRIBUTION BY SIZE OF COMMUNITY, BY REGIONS, 1870–1930.ᵃ—(*Continued*)

Size of community	1870	1890	1910	1920	1930
		POPULATION (THOUSANDS)			
South:					
Total..............................	396	521	726	847	532
500,000–1,000,000.....................	...	...	77	84	74
250,000– 500,000.....................	56	69	52	55	92
100,000– 250,000.....................	88	76	41	123	72
25,000– 100,000.....................	31	74	124	114	59
10,000– 25,000.....................	36	43	41	53	27
2,500– 10,000.....................	24	33	52	63	39
Rural..............................	161	226	340	356	169
		PERCENTAGE DISTRIBUTION			
Total..............................	100.0	100.0	100.0	100.0	100.0
500,000–1,000,000.....................	....	....	10.6	9.9	14.0
250,000– 500,000.....................	14.3	13.2	7.2	6.4	17.3
100,000– 250,000.....................	22.2	14.6	5.7	14.5	13.5
25,000– 100,000.....................	7.9	14.2	17.0	13.5	11.0
10,000– 25,000.....................	9.0	8.2	5.6	6.2	5.0
2,500– 10,000.....................	6.0	6.4	7.1	7.5	7.3
Rural..............................	40.7	43.4	46.8	42.0	31.8
		POPULATION (THOUSANDS)			
West:					
Total..............................	250	673	1,298	1,487	1,448
1,000,000+...........................	...	...	.....	.....	182
500,000–1,000,000.....................	...	...	.....	252	153
250,000– 500,000.....................	...	101	191	159	202
100,000– 250,000.....................	67	24	202	81	83
25,000– 100,000.....................	...	81	103	138	138
10,000– 25,000.....................	13	44	85	85	92
2,500– 10,000.....................	11	59	120	149	117
Rural..............................	158	363	597	622	481
		PERCENTAGE DISTRIBUTION			
Total..............................	100.0	100.0	100.0	100.0	100.0
1,000,000+...........................	.....	.....	.....	.....	12.6
500,000–1,000,000.....................	.....	.....	.....	17.0	10.6
250,000– 500,000.....................	.....	15.1	14.7	10.7	14.0
100,000– 250,000.....................	26.9	3.6	15.5	5.5	5.7
25,000– 100,000.....................	.....	12.1	7.9	9.3	9.5
10,000– 25,000.....................	5.4	6.6	6.6	5.7	6.3
2,500– 10,000.....................	4.4	8.7	9.3	10.0	8.1
Rural..............................	63.3	53.9	45.9	41.8	33.2

ᵃ From special compilation made for this study and from *Fourteenth Census of the United States: 1920*, Vol. II, p. 90. All Mexicans were classified as whites prior to 1930.

TABLE 7.—NATIVE WHITE POPULATION OF FOREIGN OR MIXED PARENTAGE AND PERCENTAGE DISTRIBUTION BY SIZE OF COMMUNITY, BY REGIONS, 1890-1930[a]

Size of community	1890	1910	1920	1930
POPULATION (THOUSANDS)				
Northeast:				
Total	4,356	7,644	9,741	11,517
1,000,000+	906	2,317	2,895	3,408
500,000–1,000,000	312	449	739	790
250,000– 500,000	256	425	405	547
100,000– 250,000	353	630	941	1,146
25,000– 100,000	633	1,166	1,423	1,720
10,000– 25,000	393	657	922	1,269
2,500– 10,000	434	706	881	892
Rural	1,068	1,294	1,535	1,744
PERCENTAGE DISTRIBUTION				
Total	100.0	100.0	100.0	100.0
1,000,000+	20.8	30.3	29.7	29.6
500,000–1,000,000	7.2	5.9	7.6	6.9
250,000– 500,000	5.9	5.6	4.2	4.8
100,000– 250,000	8.1	8.2	9.7	10.0
25,000– 100,000	14.5	15.3	14.6	14.9
10,000– 25,000	9.0	8.6	9.5	11.0
2,500– 10,000	10.0	9.2	9.0	7.7
Rural	24.5	16.9	15.8	15.1
POPULATION (THOUSANDS)				
North Center:				
Total	5,608	8,323	9,303	9,820
1,000,000+	412	913	1,141	1,835
500,000–1,000,000	...	471	899	804
250,000– 500,000	425	620	591	671
100,000– 250,000	355	383	486	486
25,000– 100,000	309	664	933	1,090
10,000– 25,000	367	519	577	638
2,500– 10,000	463	699	758	740
Rural	3,278	4,055	3,918	3,555
PERCENTAGE DISTRIBUTION				
Total	100.0	100.0	100.0	100.0
1,000,000+	7.3	11.0	12.3	18.7
500,000–1,000,000	....	5.7	9.7	8.2
250,000– 500,000	7.6	7.4	6.4	6.8
100,000– 250,000	6.3	4.6	5.2	5.0
25,000– 100,000	5.5	8.0	10.0	11.1
10,000– 25,000	6.5	6.2	6.2	6.5
2,500– 10,000	8.3	8.4	8.1	7.5
Rural	58.4	48.7	42.1	36.2

TABLE 7.—NATIVE WHITE POPULATION OF FOREIGN OR MIXED PARENTAGE AND PERCENTAGE DISTRIBUTION OF SIZE OF COMMUNITY, BY REGIONS, 1890–1930.[a]—
(*Continued*)

Size of community	1890	1910	1920	1930
POPULATION (THOUSANDS)				
South:				
Total.....................................	830	1,260	1,453	1,404
500,000–1,000,000........................	...	135	163	160
250,000– 500,000........................	112	119	128	249
100,000– 250,000........................	148	94	200	158
25,000– 100,000........................	113	195	180	160
10,000– 25,000........................	56	67	78	70
2,500– 10,000	53	89	107	108
Rural.....................................	348	560	596	499
PERCENTAGE DISTRIBUTION				
Total.....................................	100.0	100.0	100.0	100.0
500,000–1,000,000........................	....	10.7	11.2	11.4
250,000– 500,000........................	13.5	9.5	8.8	17.8
100,000– 250,000........................	17.8	7.5	13.8	11.2
25,000– 100,000........................	13.6	15.5	12.4	11.4
10,000– 25,000........................	6.7	5.3	5.4	5.0
2,500– 10,000........................	6.4	7.1	7.4	7.7
Rural.....................................	41.9	44.5	41.0	35.5
POPULATION (THOUSANDS)				
West:				
Total.....................................	710	1,671	2,190	2,620
1,000,000+...............................	...	.....	.....	274
500,000–1,000,000........................	...	.....	323	206
250,000– 500,000........................	107	229	226	343
100,000– 250,000........................	24	251	139	162
25,000– 100,000........................	79	145	209	258
10,000– 25,000........................	45	111	131	180
2,500– 10,000........................	61	173	231	247
Rural.....................................	394	763	931	951
PERCENTAGE DISTRIBUTION				
Total.....................................	100.0	100.0	100.0	100.0
1,000,000+...............................	.....	.....	.....	10.4
500,000–1,000,000........................	.....	.....	14.8	7.9
250,000– 500,000........................	15.1	13.7	10.3	13.1
100,000– 250,000........................	3.3	15.0	6.3	6.2
25,000– 100,000........................	11.1	8.7	9.6	9.8
10,000– 25,000........................	6.3	6.6	6.0	6.9
2,500– 10,000........................	8.6	10.3	10.5	9.4
Rural.....................................	55.6	45.7	42.5	36.3

[a] From special compilation made for this study and from *Fourteenth Census of the United States: 1920*, Vol. II, p. 90.

APPENDIX TABLES

TABLE 8.—POPULATION AND PERCENTAGE DISTRIBUTION OF NATIVE WHITES OF FOREIGN PARENTAGE AND NATIVE WHITES OF MIXED PARENTAGE, BY SIZE OF COMMUNITY, BY REGIONS, 1910–1930[a]

Size of community	Native whites of foreign parentage			Native whites of mixed parentage		
	1910	1920	1930	1910	1920	1930
POPULATION (THOUSANDS)						
Northeast:						
Total	5,574	7,304	8,375	2,070	2,436	3,142
1,000,000+	1,807	2,320	2,676	510	574	732
500,000–1,000,000	334	550	575	115	188	215
250,000– 500,000	317	310	413	108	94	135
100,000– 250,000	467	717	840	163	224	306
25,000– 100,000	855	1,057	1,238	311	365	482
10,000– 25,000	464	672	884	193	251	385
2,500– 10,000	485	621	605	221	260	287
Rural	845	1,056	1,143	449	479	601
PERCENTAGE DISTRIBUTION						
Total	100.0	100.0	100.0	100.0	100.0	100.0
1,000,000+	32.4	31.8	32.0	24.6	23.6	23.3
500,000–1,000,000	6.0	7.5	6.9	5.5	7.7	6.8
250,000– 500,000	5.7	4.3	4.9	5.2	3.9	4.3
100,000– 250,000	8.4	9.8	10.0	7.9	9.2	9.7
25,000– 100,000	15.3	14.5	14.8	15.0	15.0	15.3
10,000– 25,000	8.3	9.2	10.6	9.3	10.3	12.3
2,500– 10,000	8.7	8.5	7.2	10.7	10.7	9.1
Rural	15.2	14.5	13.7	21.7	19.7	19.1
POPULATION (THOUSANDS)						
North Center:						
Total	5,553	6,170	6,317	2,770	3,133	3,503
1,000,000+	705	888	1,360	208	252	475
500,000–1,000,000	335	652	579	136	247	225
250,000– 500,000	441	404	430	178	187	240
100,000– 250,000	260	331	316	123	156	170
25,000– 100,000	441	618	699	223	315	391
10,000– 25,000	346	374	395	173	203	244
2,500– 10,000	445	481	446	254	277	295
Rural	2,580	2,422	2,092	1,475	1,496	1,463
PERCENTAGE DISTRIBUTION						
Total	100.0	100.0	100.0	100.0	100.0	100.0
1,000,000+	12.7	14.4	21.5	7.5	8.1	13.6
500,000–1,000,000	6.0	10.6	9.2	4.9	7.9	6.4
250,000– 500,000	7.9	6.5	6.8	6.4	6.0	6.9
100,000– 250,000	4.7	5.4	5.0	4.4	5.0	4.9
25,000– 100,000	7.9	10.0	11.1	8.1	10.0	11.2
10,000– 25,000	6.2	6.1	6.2	6.2	6.5	7.0
2,500– 10,000	8.0	7.8	7.1	9.2	8.8	8.4
Rural	46.5	39.3	33.1	53.2	47.7	41.8
POPULATION (THOUSANDS)						
South:						
Total	762	885	788	498	568	616
500,000–1,000,000	97	117	112	38	46	48
250,000– 500,000	72	77	143	47	51	107
100,000– 250,000	58	125	91	36	74	67
25,000– 100,000	122	109	87	73	71	73
10,000– 25,000	37	44	35	30	34	35
2,500– 10,000	49	60	56	40	47	52
Rural	326	352	265	234	244	234

TABLE 8.—POPULATION AND PERCENTAGE DISTRIBUTION OF NATIVE WHITES OF FOREIGN PARENTAGE AND NATIVE WHITES OF MIXED PARENTAGE, BY SIZE OF COMMUNITY, BY REGIONS, 1910–1930.ᵃ—(Continued)

Size of community	Native whites of foreign parentage			Native whites of mixed parentage		
	1910	1920	1930	1910	1920	1930
PERCENTAGE DISTRIBUTION						
South: (Continued)						
Total..............................	100.0	100.0	100.0	100.0	100.0	100.0
500,000–1,000,000.................	12.7	13.2	14.2	7.7	8.1	7.8
250,000– 500,000.................	9.5	8.7	18.1	9.4	9.0	17.3
100,000– 250,000.................	7.7	14.2	11.5	7.2	13.1	10.8
25,000– 100,000.................	16.0	12.3	11.0	14.7	12.5	11.9
10,000– 25,000.................	4.9	5.0	4.5	6.0	6.0	5.6
2,500– 10,000.................	6.5	6.8	7.1	8.0	8.3	8.5
Rural..............................	42.8	39.8	33.6	47.1	42.9	38.0
POPULATION (THOUSANDS)						
West:						
Total..............................	1,028	1,336	1,519	643	854	1,101
1,000,000+........................	.....	.....	165	...	...	109
500,000–1,000,000.................	.....	212	137	...	111	69
250,000– 500,000.................	153	140	205	76	86	138
100,000– 250,000.................	161	84	89	90	55	73
25,000– 100,000.................	90	128	148	55	81	110
10,000– 25,000.................	66	78	99	44	53	81
2,500– 10,000.................	102	134	137	71	96	110
Rural..............................	455	559	540	308	372	411
PERCENTAGE DISTRIBUTION						
Total..............................	100.0	100.0	100.0	100.0	100.0	100.0
1,000,000+........................	.....	.....	10.8	.....	.....	9.9
500,000–1,000,000.................	.....	15.9	9.0	.....	12.9	6.3
250,000– 500,000.................	14.9	10.5	13.5	11.7	10.1	12.5
100,000– 250,000.................	15.7	6.3	5.8	13.9	6.4	6.6
25,000– 100,000.................	8.8	9.6	9.7	8.6	9.5	10.0
10,000– 25,000.................	6.5	5.8	6.5	6.9	6.2	7.4
2,500– 10,000.................	9.9	10.1	9.0	11.0	11.3	10.0
Rural..............................	44.3	41.9	35.6	47.9	43.5	37.3

ᵃ From special compilation made for this study and from *Fourteenth Census of the United States: 1920*, Vol. II, p. 90.

TABLE 9.—NEGRO POPULATION AND PERCENTAGE DISTRIBUTION, BY SIZE OF COMMUNITY, BY REGIONS, 1820–1930[a]

Size of community	1820	1830	1840	1850	1870	1890	1910	1920	1930
POPULATION (THOUSANDS)									
Northeast:									
Total	111	125	142	150	180	270	484	679	1,147
1,000,000+	...	...	...	...	...	63	176	287	547
500,000–1,000,000	...	...	...	14	35	10	39	59	89
250,000– 500,000	...	...	16	...	8	9	17	27	60
100,000– 250,000	11	14	...	13	2	21	22	52	69
25,000– 100,000	9	13	19	18	15	34	68	75	118
10,000– 25,000	4	8	12	8	17	20	38	47	90
2,500– 10,000	7	9	11	15	20	32	35	43	47
Rural	79	82	84	83	82	80	88	90	126
PERCENTAGE DISTRIBUTION									
Total	100.0	100.0	100.0	100.0	100.0	100.0	100.0	100.0	100.0
1,000,000+	.....	.....	.....	.....	.....	23.3	36.4	42.2	47.7
500,000–1,000,000	.....	.....	.....	9.2	19.6	3.8	8.1	8.6	7.8
250,000– 500,000	.....	.....	11.5	.....	4.7	3.4	3.6	3.9	5.2
100,000– 250,000	9.8	11.2	.....	8.5	1.4	7.8	4.5	7.6	6.0
25,000– 100,000	8.4	10.1	13.5	11.8	8.5	12.5	14.1	11.1	10.3
10,000– 25,000	3.5	6.5	8.2	5.4	9.4	7.6	7.9	6.9	7.9
2,500– 10,000	6.7	6.8	8.0	10.0	11.1	11.8	7.2	6.4	4.1
Rural	71.5	65.4	58.8	55.1	45.4	29.8	18.3	13.3	11.0
POPULATION (THOUSANDS)									
North Center:									
Total	18	42	89	136	273	431	543	793	1,262
1,000,000+	..	..	..	...	...	14	44	109	354
500,000–1,000,000	..	..	..	...	...	...	52	145	173
250,000– 500,000	..	..	..	...	22	42	29	102	196
100,000– 250,000	..	..	..	3	10	34	73	84	119
25,000– 100,000	..	..	2	4	13	41	71	96	127
10,000– 25,000	..	1	2	3	19	43	52	63	76
2,500– 10,000	(b)	1	3	7	37	66	72	62	63
Rural	18	40	82	119	172	191	149	132	154
PERCENTAGE DISTRIBUTION									
Total	100.0	100.0	100.0	100.0	100.0	100.0	100.0	100.0	100.0
1,000,000+	.....	.....	.....	.....	.....	3.3	8.1	13.8	28.0
500,000–1,000,000	.....	.....	.....	.....	.....	.....	9.6	18.3	13.7
250,000– 500,000	.....	.....	.....	.....	8.1	9.6	5.3	12.8	15.5
100,000– 250,000	.....	.....	.....	2.4	3.5	7.9	13.4	10.6	9.4
25,000– 100,000	.....	.....	2.5	3.0	4.9	9.6	13.1	12.1	10.0
10,000– 25,000	.....	2.6	2.3	2.0	7.1	10.1	9.7	8.0	6.0
2,500– 10,000	2.7	1.9	3.2	4.9	13.5	15.3	13.3	7.9	5.0
Rural	97.3	95.4	92.0	87.7	62.9	44.2	27.4	16.6	12.2

POPULATION TRENDS IN THE UNITED STATES

TABLE 9.—NEGRO POPULATION AND PERCENTAGE DISTRIBUTION, BY SIZE OF COMMUNITY, BY REGIONS, 1820–1930.[a]—(Continued)

Size of community	1820	1830	1840	1850	1870	1890	1910	1920	1930
POPULATION (THOUSANDS)									
South:									
Total	1,643	2,162	2,642	3,352	4,421	6,761	8,749	8,912	9,362
500,000–1,000,000	.....	.....	.....	.....	.....	.....	85	108	142
250,000–500,000	.....	.....	.....	.....	40	67	184	211	658
100,000–250,000	.....	.....	64	55	101	169	280	466	407
25,000–100,000	28	65	16	53	105	292	455	546	695
10,000–25,000	23	16	40	39	92	204	311	365	456
2,500–10,000	21	30	33	53	123	303	540	555	608
Rural	1,570	2,050	2,489	3,153	3,962	5,725	6,895	6,661	6,395
PERCENTAGE DISTRIBUTION									
Total	100.0	100.0	100.0	100.0	100.0	100.0	100.0	100.0	100.0
500,000–1,000,000	.....	.....	.....	.....	.....	.....	1.0	1.2	1.5
250,000–500,000	.....	.....	.....	.....	0.9	1.0	2.1	2.5	7.0
100,000–250,000	.....	.....	2.4	1.6	2.3	2.5	3.2	5.2	4.4
25,000–100,000	1.7	3.0	0.6	1.6	2.4	4.3	5.2	6.1	7.4
10,000–25,000	1.4	0.8	1.5	1.2	2.1	3.0	3.6	4.1	4.9
2,500–10,000	1.3	1.4	1.2	1.6	2.8	4.5	6.2	6.2	6.5
Rural	95.6	94.8	94.2	94.1	89.6	84.7	78.8	74.7	68.3
POPULATION (THOUSANDS)									
West:									
Total	...	...	...	1	6	27	51	79	120
1,000,000+	...	...	...	..	..	..	..	..	39
500,000–1,000,000	...	...	...	..	..	..	..	18	4
250,000–500,000	...	...	...	..	..	2	9	11	20
100,000–250,000	...	...	...	..	1	3	13	7	5
25,000–100,000	...	...	...	..	..	4	7	10	18
10,000–25,000	...	...	...	..	1	4	6	5	6
2,500–10,000	...	...	...	(b)	1	3	6	8	8
Rural	...	...	...	1	4	12	11	20	21
PERCENTAGE DISTRIBUTION									
Total	.....	.....	.....	100.0	100.0	100.0	100.0	100.0	100.0
1,000,000+	.....	.....	.....	.....	.....	.....	.....	.....	32.3
500,000–1,000,000	.....	.....	.....	.....	.....	.....	.....	22.9	3.2
250,000–500,000	.....	.....	.....	.....	.....	6.8	18.2	13.4	16.3
100,000–250,000	.....	.....	.....	.....	20.8	11.2	24.8	8.8	4.2
25,000–100,000	.....	.....	.....	.....	.....	13.5	13.5	12.4	15.4
10,000–25,000	.....	.....	.....	.....	9.7	13.1	10.9	6.8	4.7
2,500–10,000	.....	.....	.....	15.4	11.6	9.4	11.2	9.8	6.5
Rural	.....	.....	.....	84.6	57.8	46.0	21.4	26.0	17.5

[a] From special compilation made for this study and from *Fourteenth Census of the United States: 1920*, Vol. II, p. 90.

[b] Less than 500 Negroes.

APPENDIX TABLES

TABLE 10.—TOTAL POPULATION BY FIVE-YEAR AGE PERIODS BY SEX, 1880, 1930, AND 1980[a]

(Thousands)

Age	1880			1930			1980		
	Total	Male	Female	Total	Male	Female	Total	Male	Female
0–4	6,915	3,508	3,407	11,444	5,806	5,638	9,967	5,057	4,910
5–9	6,480	3,275	3,205	12,608	6,381	6,227	10,389	5,258	5,131
10–14	5,715	2,907	2,808	12,005	6,069	5,936	10,446	5,281	5,165
15–19	5,011	2,476	2,535	11,552	5,758	5,794	10,613	5,290	5,323
20–24	5,088	2,555	2,533	10,870	5,337	5,534	10,868	5,342	5,526
25–29	4,081	2,110	1,971	9,834	4,860	4,973	11,100	5,471	5,629
30–34	3,369	1,744	1,625	9,120	4,562	4,559	11,226	5,566	5,660
35–39	3,000	1,527	1,473	9,209	4,680	4,529	11,100	5,548	5,552
40–44	2,469	1,244	1,225	7,990	4,136	3,854	10,776	5,383	5,393
45–49	2,089	1,079	1,011	7,042	3,672	3,370	10,484	5,335	5,149
50–54	1,840	967	873	5,976	3,132	2,844	10,299	5,241	5,058
55–59	1,271	675	597	4,646	2,426	2,220	10,278	5,265	5,013
60–64	1,104	585	519	3,751	1,942	1,810	8,917	4,562	4,355
65–69	726	379	346	2,771	1,418	1,353	7,261	3,039	3,622
70–74	495	250	245	1,950	992	958	5,356	2,681	2,675
75–79	281	139	142	1,106	548	559	3,394	1,617	1,777
80–84	146	68	78	535	251	284	1,801	864	937
85–89	50	22	28	205	91	115	750	365	385
90–94	16	6	10	52	20	31	177	86	91
95+	9	3	6	15	6	9	26	13	13

[a] For 1880 and 1930 from *Fifteenth Census of the United States: 1930*, Vol. II, p. 576; for 1980 from "medium" population (Table 88, p. 316, Column *H*).

TABLE 11.—PERCENTAGE DISTRIBUTION OF THE POPULATION BY FIVE-YEAR AGE PERIODS, BY REGIONS, 1930[a]

Age	Northeast	North Center	South	West
Under 5	8.4	8.9	11.0	8.2
5–9	9.4	9.7	12.0	9.2
10–14	9.3	9.4	11.0	8.6
15–19	8.9	9.0	10.6	8.4
20–24	8.6	8.6	9.5	8.5
25–29	8.1	8.0	7.9	8.1
30–34	7.9	7.6	6.7	7.8
35–39	8.0	7.7	6.7	8.0
40–44	7.0	6.8	5.5	7.4
45–49	6.1	5.9	5.0	6.5
50–54	5.2	5.0	4.3	5.5
55–59	4.1	4.0	3.1	4.2
60–64	3.3	3.3	2.4	3.4
65–69	2.4	2.6	1.7	2.6
70–74	1.6	1.8	1.2	1.8
75–79	0.9	1.0	0.7	1.0
80–84	0.4	0.5	0.4	0.5
85–89	0.2	0.2	0.1	0.2
90–94	(b)	(b)	(b)	(b)
95–99	(b)	(b)	(b)	(b)
100+	(b)	(b)	(b)	(b)

[a] *Fifteenth Census of the United States: 1930*, Vol. II, pp. 602–610.

[b] Less than one-tenth of 1 per cent.

[359]

TABLE 12.—PERCENTAGE DISTRIBUTION, BY AGE OF THE POPULATION OF KNOWN AGES
OF CERTAIN CITIES, 1890–1930[a]

City and year	0–4	5–19	20–29	30–44	45–64	65+	Total
Birmingham, Ala.:							
1890	9.4	29.8	29.0	21.0	9.8	1.2	100.0
1900	9.5	27.5	27.0	22.9	11.5	1.7	100.0
1910	10.7	27.8	24.7	23.0	11.7	2.1	100.0
1920	9.3	28.4	22.8	24.2	13.1	2.3	100.0
1930	8.8	27.3	22.3	24.4	14.3	2.8	100.0
Boston, Mass.:							
1890	9.0	25.2	23.4	23.4	15.2	3.8	100.0
1900	10.3	23.9	22.0	25.3	14.9	3.6	100.0
1910	9.5	25.1	20.1	25.0	16.2	4.0	100.0
1920	9.5	24.7	18.7	23.8	18.8	4.4	100.0
1930	8.0	25.3	17.7	23.4	20.1	5.5	100.0
Chicago, Ill.:							
1890	12.8	28.7	23.0	22.1	11.3	2.0	100.0
1900	11.2	29.2	20.1	24.7	12.2	2.5	100.0
1910	10.3	26.9	22.4	23.5	14.1	2.8	100.0
1920	10.1	25.3	20.0	25.2	16.2	3.2	100.0
1930	7.6	25.2	19.4	26.5	17.3	4.0	100.0
Cncinnati, Ohio:							
1890	10.6	30.5	21.1	20.8	13.6	3.4	100.0
1900	9.2	28.9	20.2	23.3	14.5	4.0	100.0
1910	8.0	25.1	20.9	24.1	17.4	4.4	100.0
1920	7.7	22.8	18.7	24.7	20.7	5.4	100.0
1930	7.3	22.6	18.4	24.5	20.6	6.5	100.0
Cleveland, Ohio:							
1890	11.9	31.1	20.7	20.8	12.4	3.0	100.0
1900	11.1	30.0	20.5	22.4	13.0	3.0	100.0
1910	11.2	26.8	22.3	23.4	13.5	3.0	100.0
1920	11.1	25.8	20.5	25.4	14.3	2.9	100.0
1930	7.8	27.8	18.4	25.5	16.9	3.6	100.0
Dallas, Tex.:							
1890	10.5	29.3	25.2	23.3	10.2	1.5	100.0
1900	9.6	29.6	22.6	23.1	12.9	2.3	100.0
1910[b]	....	....	....	....	..	..	.....
1920	8.1	24.8	24.4	25.6	14.0	3.1	100.0
1930	8.0	24.6	22.8	26.1	15.0	3.6	100.0
Detroit, Mich.:							
1890	12.5	30.6	20.6	20.6	12.7	3.1	100.0
1900	10.9	30.2	19.6	22.3	13.5	3.4	100.0
1910	10.5	26.0	23.3	22.9	14.0	3.3	100.0
1920	11.3	22.9	24.3	26.2	12.9	2.5	100.0
1930	9.4	25.8	20.5	27.8	13.8	2.7	100.0
Los Angeles, Calif.:							
1890	9.3	27.0	20.9	25.0	15.1	2.7	100.0
1900	7.6	26.2	17.9	25.9	17.9	4.4	100.0
1910	7.2	21.1	21.2	27.1	18.7	4.8	100.0
1920	6.6	20.0	18.1	27.5	21.7	6.2	100.0
1930	6.4	20.1	18.8	26.9	21.6	6.3	100.0

TABLE 12.—PERCENTAGE DISTRIBUTION, BY AGE OF THE POPULATION OF KNOWN AGES OF CERTAIN CITIES, 1890–1930.[a]—(Continued)

City and year	0–4	5–19	20–29	30–44	45–64	65	Total
New York, N. Y.:							
1890	11.0	28.3	22.3	22.1	13.6	2.7	100.0
1900	11.6	27.9	20.9	23.7	13.1	2.8	100.0
1910	10.7	27.7	21.7	23.4	13.7	2.8	100.0
1920	10.0	26.5	20.0	24.4	16.1	3.1	100.0
1930	7.7	25.3	20.0	25.8	17.3	3.8	100.0
Pittsburgh, Pa.:							
1890	11.9	31.3	21.9	20.7	11.7	2.5	100.0
1900	11.3	29.2	22.0	22.7	12.4	2.5	100.0
1910	10.8	27.4	21.6	23.6	13.7	2.9	100.0
1920	10.5	27.0	19.0	23.9	16.3	3.4	100.0
1930	8.5	27.3	17.9	23.3	18.1	4.3	100.0
Portland, Ore.:							
1890	6.6	21.0	29.1	29.6	12.1	1.6	100.0
1900	7.0	23.7	20.8	29.8	16.1	2.5	100.0
1910	6.8	20.0	25.5	27.8	16.7	3.2	100.0
1920	7.7	22.4	18.4	27.3	19.5	4.7	100.0
1930	5.6	22.5	16.8	25.9	22.5	6.6	100.0
St. Louis, Mo.:							
1890	11.2	30.9	22.0	20.2	13.0	2.7	100.0
1900	10.0	29.3	21.1	23.1	13.2	3.3	100.0
1910	8.8	25.9	21.9	24.6	15.3	3.7	100.0
1920	7.6	24.0	20.0	25.5	18.7	4.2	100.0
1930	7.1	22.8	19.6	25.1	20.0	5.3	100.0
San Diego, Calif.:[c]							
1930	7.0	21.8	16.6	23.7	21.8	9.1	100.0

[a] Taken from current census reports.
[b] Data available only by broad age groups.
[c] Data prior to 1930 available only by broad age groups.

TABLE 13.—POPULATION OF KNOWN AGES AND PERCENTAGE DISTRIBUTION BY AGE, BY SIZE OF COMMUNITY, BY REGIONS, 1820–1930[a]

Size of community	0–4	5–19	20–29	30–44	45–64	65+	Total	0–4	5–19	20–29	30–44	45–64	65+	Total
	POPULATION (THOUSANDS)							PERCENTAGE DISTRIBUTION						
Northeast:														
1820:[b]														
100,000–500,000..								15.9	34.4		38.4		11.4	100.0
25,000–100,000..								14.6	35.3		39.0		11.1	100.0
2,500– 25,000..								15.5	37.3		33.7		13.5	100.0
Rural..........								17.2	39.3		30.1		13.4	100.0
1840:[b]														
100,000–500,000..								15.5	29.2	25.9	20.2	7.6	1.6	100.0
25,000–100,000..								14.4	30.3	25.0	19.8	8.6	1.9	100.0
2,500– 25,000..								14.6	33.0	22.1	18.2	9.5	2.6	100.0
Rural..........								15.5	36.7	17.3	16.3	10.7	3.5	100.0
1890:														
500,000 and over.	359	943	743	746	467	104	3,362	10.7	28.1	22.1	22.2	13.9	3.1	100.0
100,000–500,000..	178	477	361	360	224	55	1,655	10.7	28.8	21.8	21.8	13.6	3.3	100.0
25,000–100,000..	212	614	445	446	310	80	2,106	10.1	29.1	21.1	21.2	14.7	3.8	100.0
2,500– 25,000 } Rural	1,032	3,088	1,826	1,989	1,660	643	10,238	10.1	30.2	17.8	19.4	16.2	6.3	100.0
1910:														
500,000 and over.	781	2,039	1,587	1,770	1,082	240	7,500	10.4	27.2	21.2	23.6	14.4	3.2	100.0
100,000–500,000..	272	731	545	623	410	101	2,682	10.2	27.3	20.3	23.2	15.3	3.8	100.0
25,000–100,000..	380	1,003	759	869	577	155	3,743	10.2	26.8	20.3	23.2	15.4	4.1	100.0
2,500– 25,000..	540	1,409	984	1,159	849	274	5,214	10.3	27.0	18.9	22.2	16.3	5.3	100.0
Rural..........	716	1,885	1,080	1,349	1,178	465	6,673	10.7	28.2	16.2	20.2	17.7	7.0	100.0
1920:														
500,000 and over.	924	2,421	1,819	2,229	1,546	325	9,264	10.0	26.1	19.6	24.1	16.7	3.5	100.0
100,000–500,000..	361	910	647	807	596	140	3,462	10.4	26.3	18.7	23.3	17.2	4.0	100.0
25,000–100,000..	422	1,066	737	934	707	182	4,048	10.4	26.3	18.2	23.1	17.5	4.5	100.0
2,500– 25,000..	618	1,581	959	1,249	1,015	302	5,723	10.8	27.6	16.8	21.8	17.7	5.3	100.0
Rural..........	782	2,061	1,018	1,417	1,330	504	7,111	11.0	29.0	14.3	19.9	18.7	7.1	100.0
1930:														
500,000 and over.	850	2,794	2,092	2,734	1,943	462	10,875	7.8	25.7	19.2	25.1	17.9	4.3	100.0
100,000–500,000..	341	1,162	721	994	802	220	4,240	8.0	27.4	17.0	23.5	18.9	5.2	100.0
25,000–100,000..	396	1,317	808	1,117	903	257	4,798	8.3	27.4	16.8	23.2	18.8	5.4	100.0
2,500– 25,000..	537	1,930	1,057	1,501	1,267	399	6,741	8.7	28.6	15.7	22.3	18.8	5.9	100.0
Rural..........	728	2,309	1,068	1,523	1,493	586	7,707	9.4	30.0	13.9	19.8	19.4	7.6	100.0
Farm..........	186	694	257	382	468	182	2,170	8.6	32.0	11.9	17.6	21.6	8.4	100.0
Nonfarm......	542	1,614	810	1,141	1,025	404	5,537	9.8	29.3	14.6	20.6	18.5	7.3	100.0
North Center:														
1820:[b]														
2,500–25,000....								17.2	36.4		38.4		8.0	100.0
Rural..........								21.6	40.0		29.1		9.2	100.0
1840:[b]														
25,000–100,000.ᵗ								15.4	29.3	28.5	18.7	6.9	1.2	100.0
2,500– 25,000..								15.4	31.3	27.7	18.2	6.3	1.0	100.0
Rural..........								19.5	39.0	17.8	14.5	7.6	1.6	100.0
1890:														
500,000 and over.	141	315	252	243	124	22	1,097	12.8	28.7	23.0	22.1	11.3	2.0	100.0
100,000–500,000..	242	623	474	444	251	56	2,090	11.6	29.8	22.7	21.3	12.0	2.7	100.0
25,000–100,000..	115	323	232	221	129	30	1,050	10.9	30.8	22.1	21.0	12.3	2.8	100.0
2,500– 25,000 } Rural	2,247	6,238	3,170	3,261	2,425	747	18,083	12.4	34.5	17.5	18.0	13.4	4.1	100.0
1910:														
500,000 and over.	346	912	762	811	487	102	3,420	10.1	26.7	22.3	23.7	14.2	3.0	100.0
100,000–500,000..	260	738	653	685	452	107	2,895	9.0	25.5	22.6	23.7	15.6	3.7	100.0
25.000–100,000..	220	616	509	541	366	98	2,350	9.4	26.2	21.6	23.0	15.6	4.2	100.0
2,500– 25,000..	465	1,307	937	1,032	786	255	4,782	9.7	27.3	19.6	21.6	16.4	5.3	100.0
Rural..........	1,919	5,231	2,700	3,021	2,553	897	16,320	11.8	32.1	16.5	18.5	15.6	5.5	100.0
1920:														
500,000 and over.	532	1,301	1,096	1,338	822	165	5,254	10.1	24.8	20.9	25.5	15.7	3.1	100.0
100,000–500,000..	329	864	755	901	633	154	3,635	9.0	23.8	20.8	24.8	17.4	4.2	100.0
25,000–100,000..	331	862	668	804	597	149	3,411	9.7	25.3	19.6	23.6	17.5	4.4	100.0
2,500– 25,000..	525	1,475	946	1,178	978	336	5,438	9.7	27.1	17.4	21.7	18.0	6.2	100.0
Rural..........	1,837	5,068	2,478	3,075	2,741	980	16,179	11.4	31.3	15.3	19.0	16.9	6.1	100.0

TABLE 13.—POPULATION OF KNOWN AGES AND PERCENTAGE DISTRIBUTION BY AGE, BY SIZE OF COMMUNITY, BY REGIONS, 1820–1930.[a]—(*Continued*)

Size of community	0–4	5–19	20–29	30–44	45–64	65+	Total	0–4	5–19	20–29	30–44	45–64	65+	Total
North Center: (Cont'd)														
1930:														
500,000 and over	574	1,832	1,403	1,898	1,214	280	7,201	8.0	25.4	19.5	26.4	16.9	3.9	100.0
100,000–500,000	384	1,187	891	1,187	884	251	4,783	8.0	24.8	18.6	24.8	18.5	5.2	100.0
25,000–100,000	351	1,087	762	995	780	236	4,211	8.3	25.8	18.1	23.6	18.5	5.6	100.0
2,500–25,000	516	1,650	990	1,314	1,143	432	6,045	8.5	27.3	16.4	21.7	18.9	7.1	100.0
Rural	1,564	5,023	2,283	3,095	2,997	1,186	16,149	9.7	31.1	14.1	19.2	18.6	7.3	100.0
Farm	937	3,162	1,289	1,769	1,730	563	9,449	9.9	33.5	13.6	18.7	18.3	6.0	100.0
Nonfarm	628	1,861	995	1,326	1,267	624	6,700	9.4	27.8	14.8	19.8	18.9	9.3	100.0
South:														
1820:[b]														
25,000–100,000								14.7	35.4		38.9	11.0		100.0
2,500–25,000								15.2	36.6		36.5	11.6		100.0
Rural								20.0	40.0		28.6	11.3		100.0
1840:[b]														
100,000–500,000								14.9	30.4	23.6	20.8	8.7	1.6	100.0
25,000–100,000								14.0	30.5	23.5	20.5	9.4	2.1	100.0
2,500–25,000								15.0	32.6	23.9	18.6	8.4	1.8	100.0
Rural								19.5	38.9	17.0	14.2	8.2	2.2	100.0
1890:														
100,000–500,000	108	327	216	217	156	40	1,064	10.1	30.7	20.3	20.4	14.6	3.7	100.0
25,000–100,000	84	258	182	172	106	23	824	10.1	31.4	22.0	20.9	12.9	2.7	100.0
2,500–25,000 } Rural	2,599	7,114	2,876	2,830	1,922	541	17,882	14.5	39.8	16.1	15.8	10.7	3.0	100.0
1910:														
500,000 and over	52	152	113	126	91	24	557	9.3	27.3	20.3	22.5	16.3	4.2	100.0
100,000–500,000	140	412	342	365	227	59	1,544	9.1	26.7	22.1	23.7	14.7	3.8	100.0
25,000–100,000	154	444	379	382	222	50	1,631	9.5	27.2	23.2	23.4	13.6	3.1	100.0
2,500–25,000	314	870	600	598	383	97	2,861	11.0	30.4	21.0	20.9	13.4	3.4	100.0
Rural	3,376	8,362	3,852	3,648	2,658	751	22,648	14.9	36.9	17.0	16.1	11.7	3.3	100.0
1920:														
500,000 and over	69	188	145	170	128	32	783	9.5	25.7	19.8	23.2	17.5	4.4	100.0
100,000–500,000	220	680	594	653	427	99	2,674	8.2	25.4	22.2	24.4	16.0	3.7	100.0
25,000–100,000	191	566	458	495	306	69	2,084	9.1	27.1	22.0	23.7	14.7	3.3	100.0
2,500–25,000	375	1,148	745	804	556	149	3,776	9.9	30.4	19.7	21.3	14.7	3.9	100.0
Rural	3,167	8,888	3,756	3,976	3,020	920	23,727	13.3	37.5	15.8	16.8	12.7	3.9	100.0
1930:														
500,000 and over	64	209	148	192	146	41	801	8.0	26.1	18.5	24.0	18.3	5.1	100.0
100,000–500,000	347	1,102	922	1,080	737	180	4,875	7.9	25.2	21.1	24.8	16.9	4.1	100.0
25,000–100,000	233	735	563	628	426	107	2,691	8.6	27.3	20.9	23.3	15.8	4.0	100.0
2,500–25,000	432	1,386	909	995	748	209	4,679	9.2	29.6	19.4	21.3	16.0	4.5	100.0
Rural	2,958	8,957	3,911	4,109	3,482	1,046	24,464	12.1	36.6	16.0	16.8	14.2	4.3	100.0
Farm	1,946	6,209	2,344	2,474	2,299	675	15,948	12.2	38.9	14.7	15.5	14.4	4.2	100.0
Nonfarm	1,012	2,748	1,567	1,635	1,183	371	8,516	11.9	32.3	18.4	19.2	13.9	4.4	100.0
West:														
1890:														
100,000–500,000	33	100	98	104	58	9	402	8.1	24.9	24.5	25.8	14.5	2.2	100.0
25,000–100,000	26	74	74	75	39	7	294	8.9	25.2	25.1	25.4	13.1	2.2	100.0
2,500–25,000 } Rural	260	676	476	522	317	62	2,314	11.2	29.2	20.6	22.6	13.7	2.7	100.0
1910:														
100,000–500,000	120	343	367	439	269	62	1,599	7.5	21.4	23.0	27.5	16.8	3.9	100.0
25,000–100,000	43	120	102	121	81	21	487	8.9	24.6	20.9	24.8	16.5	4.3	100.0
2,500–25,000	107	296	245	278	184	48	1,158	9.2	25.6	21.1	24.0	15.9	4.1	100.0
Rural	379	954	641	720	504	129	3,327	11.4	28.7	19.3	21.6	15.1	3.9	100.0
1920:														
500,000 and over	67	211	197	297	222	57	1,051	6.4	20.1	18.8	28.3	21.1	5.4	100.0
100,000–500,000	97	283	230	332	240	56	1,238	7.8	22.9	18.6	26.8	19.4	4.5	100.0
25,000–100,000	60	179	130	187	158	46	760	7.8	23.5	17.2	24.6	20.9	6.0	100.0
2,500–25,000	144	405	268	365	272	76	1,531	9.4	26.4	17.5	23.9	17.7	5.0	100.0
Rural	468	1,200	644	881	669	177	4,039	11.6	29.7	16.0	21.8	16.6	4.4	100.0
1930:														
500,000 and over	91	319	321	474	390	109	1,703	5.3	18.7	18.9	27.8	22.9	6.4	100.0
100,000–500,000	117	422	313	457	401	127	1,839	6.4	23.0	17.0	24.9	21.8	6.9	100.0
25,000–100,000	69	246	177	257	227	76	1,052	6.6	23.4	16.9	24.4	21.6	7.2	100.0
2,500–25,000	152	508	325	455	375	119	1,934	7.8	26.3	16.8	23.5	19.4	6.2	100.0
Rural	405	1,309	651	922	830	261	4,377	9.2	29.9	14.9	21.1	19.0	6.0	100.0
Farm	185	652	263	384	391	115	1,990	9.3	32.8	13.2	19.3	19.7	5.8	100.0
Nonfarm	220	657	388	538	439	145	2,387	9.2	27.5	16.2	22.6	18.4	6.1	100.0

[a] For sources of data and method of compilation, see Tables 34 and 35, pp. 128 and 130.
[b] White population only.

TABLE 14.—WHITE POPULATION OF KNOWN AGES AND PERCENTAGE DISTRIBUTION BY AGE, BY REGIONS, 1820–1930[a]

Region and year	0–4	5–19	20–29	30–44	45–64	65+	Total

POPULATION (THOUSANDS)

Region and year	0–4	5–19	20–29	30–44	45–64	65+	Total
Northeast:							
1820	717	1,658	1,304		567		4,246
1840	1,017	2,361	1,230	1,117	678	216	6,619
1850	1,117	2,918	1,638	1,530	980	290	8,472
1870	1,486	3,919	2,152	2,337	1,716	505	12,115
1890	1,756	5,046	3,309	3,476	2,625	871	17,083
1910	2,649	6,958	4,836	5,635	4,031	1,221	25,330
1920	3,051	7,889	5,022	6,439	5,094	1,435	28,930
1930	2,799	9,242	5,486	7,547	6,242	1,899	33,216

PERCENTAGE DISTRIBUTION

Region and year	0–4	5–19	20–29	30–44	45–64	65+	Total
1820	16.9	39.1	30.7		13.3		100.0
1840	15.4	35.7	18.6	16.9	10.2	3.3	100.0
1850	13.2	34.4	19.3	18.1	11.6	3.4	100.0
1870	12.3	32.3	17.8	19.3	14.2	4.2	100.0
1890	10.3	29.5	19.4	20.3	15.4	5.1	100.0
1910	10.5	27.5	19.1	22.2	15.9	4.8	100.0
1920	10.5	27.3	17.4	22.3	17.6	5.0	100.0
1930	8.4	27.8	16.5	22.7	18.8	5.7	100.0

POPULATION (THOUSANDS)

Region and year	0–4	5–19	20–29	30–44	45–64	65+	Total
North Center:							
1820	181	336	246		78		841
1840	631	1,262	594	479	246	51	3,262
1850	860	2,061	934	851	464	96	5,266
1870	1,918	4,635	2,210	2,211	1,417	307	12,698
1890	2,696	7,340	4,039	4,083	2,875	841	21,872
1910	3,168	8,670	5,441	5,951	4,561	1,437	29,227
1920	3,497	9,393	5,764	7,073	5,643	1,755	33,125
1930	3,285	10,486	6,064	8,131	6,817	2,347	37,129

PERCENTAGE DISTRIBUTION

Region and year	0–4	5–19	20–29	30–44	45–64	65+	Total
1820	21.6	40.0	29.2		9.2		100.0
1840	19.3	38.7	18.2	14.7	7.5	1.6	100.0
1850	16.3	39.1	17.7	16.2	8.8	1.8	100.0
1870	15.1	36.5	17.4	17.4	11.2	2.4	100.0
1890	12.3	33.6	18.5	18.7	13.1	3.8	100.0
1910	10.8	29.7	18.6	20.4	15.6	4.9	100.0
1920	10.6	28.4	17.4	21.4	17.0	5.3	100.0
1930	8.8	28.2	16.3	21.9	18.4	6.3	100.0

APPENDIX TABLES

TABLE 14.—WHITE POPULATION OF KNOWN AGES AND PERCENTAGE DISTRIBUTION BY AGE, BY REGIONS, 1820–1930.ᵃ—(*Continued*)

Region and year	0–4	5–19	20–29	30–44	45–64	65+	Total

POPULATION (THOUSANDS)

Region and year	0–4	5–19	20–29	30–44	45–64	65+	Total
South:							
1820.........................	549	1,107	806		314		2,776
1840.........................	826	1,653	752	628	356	94	4,308
1850.........................	905	2,215	992	875	510	131	5,629
1870.........................	1,189	2,976	1,384	1,241	865	207	7,863
1890.........................	1,815	4,927	2,136	2,251	1,505	415	13,050
1910.........................	2,860	7,030	3,624	3,652	2,629	724	20,519
1920.........................	2,995	8,226	4,090	4,508	3,300	983	24,102
1930.........................	3,017	9,107	4,724	5,284	4,245	1,279	27,657

PERCENTAGE DISTRIBUTION

Region and year	0–4	5–19	20–29	30–44	45–64	65+	Total
1820.........................	19.8	39.9	29.0		11.3		100.0
1840.........................	19.2	38.4	17.5	14.6	8.3	2.2	100.0
1850.........................	16.1	39.4	17.6	15.6	9.1	2.3	100.0
1870.........................	15.1	37.8	17.6	15.8	11.0	2.6	100.0
1890.........................	13.9	37.8	16.4	17.3	11.5	3.2	100.0
1910.........................	13.9	34.3	17.7	17.8	12.8	3.5	100.0
1920.........................	12.4	34.1	17.0	18.7	13.7	4.1	100.0
1930.........................	10.9	32.9	17.1	19.1	15.3	4.6	100.0

POPULATION (THOUSANDS)

Region and year	0–4	5–19	20–29	30–44	45–64	65+	Total
West:							
1850.........................	15	41	64	41	13	2	177
1870.........................	126	271	168	239	95	12	010
1890.........................	312	828	611	640	390	75	2,857
1910.........................	646	1,704	1,343	1,542	1,029	258	6,521
1920.........................	831	2,263	1,451	2,040	1,546	409	8,540
1930.........................	826	2,780	1,766	2,530	2,198	687	10,786

PERCENTAGE DISTRIBUTION

Region and year	0–4	5–19	20–29	30–44	45–64	65+	Total
1850.........................	8.4	23.1	36.4	23.3	7.5	1.3	100.0
1870.........................	13.9	29.8	18.5	26.2	10.4	1.3	100.0
1890.........................	10.9	29.0	21.4	22.4	13.6	2.6	100.0
1910.........................	9.9	26.1	20.6	23.6	15.8	4.0	100.0
1920.........................	9.7	26.5	17.0	23.9	18.1	4.8	100.0
1930.........................	7.7	25.8	16.4	23.5	20.4	6.4	100.0

ᵃ For 1820 from *Fourth Census of the United States: 1820*, p. 1; 1840 from *Sixth Census of the United States: 1840*, p. 474; 1850 and 1870 from *Ninth Census of the United States: 1870*, Vol. II, pp. 608–621; 1890 from *Eleventh Census of the United States: 1890*, Vol. I, Pt. 2, pp. 106–111; 1910 and 1920 from *Fourteenth Census of the United States: 1920*, Vol. II, pp. 170–186; 1930 from *Fifteenth Census of the United States: 1930*, Vol. III, Pt. 1, pp. 38, 39. For method of compilation, see Table 31, p. 109.

TABLE 15.—WHITE POPULATION OF KNOWN AGES AND PERCENTAGE DISTRIBUTION BY AGE, BY SIZE OF COMMUNITY, BY REGIONS, 1820–1930[a]

Size of community	0–4	5–19	20–29	30–44	45–64	65+	Total	0–4	5–19	20–29	30–44	45–64	65+	Total
			POPULATION (THOUSANDS)							PERCENTAGE DISTRIBUTION				
Northeast:														
1820:														
100,000–500,000..	18	39	43		13		113	15.9	34.4	38.4		11.4		100.0
25,000–100,000..	14	34	38		11		97	14.6	35.3	39.0		11.1		100.0
2,500–25,000..	34	83	75		30		222	15.5	37.3	33.7		13.5		100.0
Rural..........	655	1,499	1,147		513		3,814	17.2	39.3	30.1		13.4		100.0
1840:														
100,000–500,000..	46	87	77	60	23	5	296	15.5	29.2	25.9	20.2	7.6	1.6	100.0
25,000–100,000..	47	99	82	65	28	6	328	14.4	30.3	25.0	19.8	8.6	1.9	100.0
2,500–25,000..	104	236	158	131	68	19	716	14.6	33.0	22.1	18.2	9.5	2.6	100.0
Rural..........	820	1,939	913	862	559	187	5,279	15.5	36.7	17.3	16.3	10.7	3.5	100.0
1890:														
500,000 and over.	354	926	722	724	458	102	3,285	10.8	28.2	22.0	22.0	13.9	3.1	100.0
100,000–500,000..	175	470	353	352	220	54	1,624	10.8	28.9	21.7	21.7	13.6	3.3	100.0
25,000–100,000..	209	605	438	438	305	79	2,072	10.1	29.2	21.1	21.1	14.7	3.8	100.0
2,500–25,000 } Rural.........	1,019	3,046	1,797	1,962	1,642	637	10,103	10.1	30.1	17.8	19.4	16.2	6.3	100.0
1910:														
500,000 and over.	765	1,999	1,528	1,703	1,055	236	7,286	10.5	27.4	21.0	23.4	14.5	3.2	100.0
100,000–500,000..	269	722	536	611	405	100	2,643	10.2	27.3	20.3	23.1	15.3	3.8	100.0
25,000–100,000..	375	988	743	850	567	153	3,675	10.2	26.9	20.2	23.1	15.4	4.2	100.0
2,500–25,000..	533	1,389	966	1,140	838	271	5,137	10.4	27.0	18.8	22.2	16.3	5.3	100.0
Rural..........	708	1,861	1,063	1,331	1,167	461	6,589	10.7	28.2	16.1	20.2	17.7	7.0	100.0
1920:														
500,000 and over.	899	2,355	1,729	2,119	1,499	319	8,919	10.1	26.4	19.4	23.8	16.8	3.6	100.0
100,000–500,000..	354	892	631	785	584	138	3,383	10.5	26.4	18.6	23.2	17.3	4.1	100.0
25,000–100,000..	416	1,049	721	912	695	180	3,973	10.5	26.4	18.2	23.0	17.5	4.5	100.0
2,500–25,000..	610	1,558	940	1,227	1,001	299	5,633	10.8	27.7	16.7	21.8	17.8	5.3	100.0
Rural..........	773	2,035	1,001	1,396	1,316	500	7,021	11.0	29.0	14.3	19.9	18.7	7.1	100.0
1930:														
500,000 and over.	797	2,659	1,936	2,540	1,857	452	10,239	7.8	26.0	18.9	24.8	18.1	4.4	100.0
100,000–500,000..	328	1,129	693	961	783	217	4,111	8.0	27.5	16.9	23.4	19.0	5.3	100.0
25,000–100,000..	386	1,288	783	1,086	885	254	4,681	8.2	27.5	16.7	23.2	18.9	5.4	100.0
2,500–25,000..	574	1,894	1,029	1,467	1,245	395	6,604	8.7	28.7	15.6	22.2	18.9	6.0	100.0
Rural..........	715	2,272	1,045	1,494	1,473	582	7,581	9.4	30.0	13.8	19.7	19.4	7.7	100.0
Farm..........	185	691	256	380	466	182	2,158	8.6	32.0	11.8	17.6	21.6	8.4	100.0
Nonfarm......	530	1,582	790	1,114	1,007	400	5,423	9.8	29.2	14.6	20.5	18.6	7.4	100.0
North Center:														
1820:														
2,500–25,000.....	2	4	4		1		12	17.2	36.4	38.4		8.0		100.0
Rural..........	179	332	241		77		829	21.6	40.0	29.1		9.2		100.0
1840:														
25,000–100,000...	7	13	13	8	3	1	44	15.4	29.3	28.5	18.7	6.9	1.2	100.0
2,500–25,000...	12	25	22	14	5	1	79	15.4	31.3	27.7	18.2	6.3	1.0	100.0
Rural..........	612	1,224	559	456	238	50	3,139	19.5	39.0	17.8	14.5	7.6	1.6	100.0

TABLE 15.—WHITE POPULATION OF KNOWN AGES AND PERCENTAGE DISTRIBUTION BY AGE, BY SIZE OF COMMUNITY BY REGIONS, 1820–1930.ᵃ—(Continued)

Size of community	0-4	5-19	20-29	30-44	45-64	65+	Total	0-4	5-19	20-29	30-44	45-64	65+	Total
	POPULATION (THOUSANDS)							PERCENTAGE DISTRIBUTION						
North Center: (Cont'd)														
1890:														
500,000 and over.	140	312	247	238	123	22	1,082	12.9	28.9	22.8	22.0	11.3	2.1	100.0
100,000–500,000..	235	603	454	425	242	54	2,014	11.7	29.9	22.5	21.1	12.0	2.7	100.0
25,000–100,000..	111	310	223	212	124	29	1,008	11.0	30.7	22.1	21.0	12.3	2.8	100.0
2,500– 25,000 } Rural......... }	2,209	6,115	3,115	3,208	2,385	736	17,768	12.4	34.4	17.5	18.1	13.4	4.1	100.0
1910:														
500,000 and over.	341	895	737	779	473	100	3,324	10.2	26.9	22.2	23.4	14.2	3.0	100.0
100,000–500,000..	254	719	627	654	437	104	2,794	9.1	25.7	22.4	23.4	15.6	3.7	100.0
25,000–100,000..	215	599	492	522	356	95	2,279	9.4	26.3	21.6	22.9	15.6	4.2	100.0
2,500– 25,000..	455	1,273	912	1,003	766	249	4,658	9.8	27.3	19.6	21.5	16.4	5.3	100.0
Rural..........	1,904	5,184	2,674	2,993	2,530	888	16,172	11.8	32.1	16.5	18.5	15.6	5.5	100.0
1920:														
500,000 and over.	516	1,254	1,027	1,255	787	161	5,000	10.3	25.1	20.6	25.1	15.7	3.2	100.0
100,000–500,000..	316	826	711	845	603	149	3,450	9.2	23.9	20.6	24.5	17.5	4.3	100.0
25,000–100,000..	324	840	647	777	581	146	3,315	9.8	25.3	19.5	23.4	17.5	4.4	100.0
2,500– 25,000..	515	1,443	923	1,148	955	329	5,313	9.7	27.2	17.4	21.6	18.0	6.2	100.0
Rural...........	1,825	5,029	2,457	3,049	2,717	971	16,047	11.4	31.3	15.3	19.0	16.9	6.0	100.0
1930:														
500,000 and over.	532	1,723	1,275	1,731	1,142	271	6,675	8.0	25.8	19.1	25.9	17.1	4.1	100.0
100,000–500,000..	358	1,115	827	1,096	831	242	4,469	8.0	24.9	18.5	24.5	18.6	5.4	100.0
25,000–100,000..	340	1,056	737	961	759	232	4,085	8.3	25.9	18.0	23.5	18.6	5.7	100.0
2,500– 25,000..	505	1,613	966	1,281	1,116	424	5,906	8.5	27.3	16.4	21.7	18.9	7.2	100.0
Rural..........	1,551	4,979	2,259	3,062	2,968	1,177	15,995	9.7	31.1	14.1	19.1	18.6	7.4	100.0
Farm.........	931	3,145	1,281	1,759	1,720	559	9,396	9.9	33.5	13.6	18.7	18.3	6.0	100.0
Nonfarm......	619	1,834	978	1,302	1,248	617	6,599	9.4	27.8	14.8	19.7	18.9	9.4	100.0
South:														
1820:														
25,000–100,000...	9	22	24		7		62	14.7	35.4	38.9		11.0		100.0
2,500– 25,000...	10	24	24		8		65	15.2	36.6	36.5		11.6		100.0
Rural..........	531	1,060	758		299		2,649	20.0	40.0	28.6		11.3		100.0
1840:														
100,000–500,000..	21	43	33	29	12	2	141	14.9	30.4	23.6	20.8	8.7	1.6	100.0
25,000–100,000..	2	4	3	3	1	x	13	14.0	30.5	23.5	20.5	9.4	2.1	100.0
2,500– 25,000..	21	45	33	26	12	2	137	15.0	32.6	23.9	18.6	8.4	1.6	100.0
Rural..........	783	1,561	683	570	331	89	4,017	19.5	38.9	17.0	14.2	8.2	2.2	100.0
1890:														
100,000–500,000..	85	255	166	167	124	33	830	10.3	30.7	20.0	20.1	14.9	3.9	100.0
25,000–100,000..	55	165	114	112	72	15	535	10.3	30.9	21.4	21.0	13.5	2.9	100.0
2,500– 25,000 } Rural......... }	1,675	4,506	1,855	1,972	1,309	367	11,686	14.3	38.6	15.9	16.9	11.2	3.1	100.0
1910:														
500,000 and over.	45	132	92	104	78	21	473	9.6	28.0	19.5	21.9	16.5	4.5	100.0
100,000–500,000..	103	293	224	251	166	45	1,082	9.5	27.1	20.7	23.2	15.3	4.2	100.0
25,000–100,000..	117	322	261	272	167	39	1,179	9.9	27.3	22.2	23.1	14.2	3.3	100.0
2,500– 25,000..	229	603	409	424	280	71	2,016	11.3	29.9	20.3	21.0	13.9	3.5	100.0
Rural..........	2,367	5,680	2,637	2,601	1,938	547	15,770	15.0	36.0	16.7	16.5	12.3	3.5	100.0

TABLE 15.—WHITE POPULATION OF KNOWN AGES AND PERCENTAGE DISTRIBUTION BY AGE, BY SIZE OF COMMUNITY BY REGIONS, 1820–1930.ᵃ—(*Continued*)

Size of community	0–4	5–19	20–29	30–44	45–64	65+	Total	0–4	5–19	20–29	30–44	45–64	65+	Total
	POPULATION (THOUSANDS)							PERCENTAGE DISTRIBUTION						
South: (*Continued*)														
1920:														
500,000 and over.	61	164	119	141	111	29	625	9.8	26.3	19.1	22.5	17.8	4.7	100.0
100,000–500,000..	172	511	432	476	328	81	1,999	8.6	25.6	21.6	23.8	16.4	4.1	100.0
25,000–100,000..	149	421	322	359	234	56	1,541	9.7	27.3	20.9	23.3	15.2	3.6	100.0
2,500– 25,000..	299	866	548	605	425	117	2,861	10.4	30.3	19.2	21.2	14.9	4.1	100.0
Rural..........	2,314	6,263	2,669	2,927	2,202	701	17,075	13.5	36.7	15.6	17.1	12.9	4.1	100.0
1930:														
500,000 and over.	52	175	117	154	125	37	660	7.9	26.5	17.7	23.3	18.9	5.7	100.0
100,000–500,000..	264	832	677	806	579	153	3,311	8.0	25.1	20.4	24.4	17.5	4.6	100.0
25,000–100,000..	174	535	395	453	326	88	1,972	8.8	27.1	20.0	23.0	16.6	4.5	100.0
2,500– 25,000..	343	1,070	692	772	592	172	3,641	9.4	29.4	19.0	21.2	16.3	4.7	100.0
Rural..........	2,184	6,496	2,844	3,099	2,623	827	18,072	12.1	35.9	15.7	17.1	14.5	4.6	100.0
Farm..........	1,365	4,320	1,639	1,808	1,685	524	11,340	12.0	38.1	14.5	15.9	14.9	4.6	100.0
Nonfarm......	820	2,176	1,204	1,291	938	304	6,732	12.2	32.3	17.9	19.2	13.9	4.5	100.0
West:														
1890:														
100,000–500,000,.	32	97	89	90	55	9	371	8.6	26.1	24.0	24.2	14.8	2.3	100.0
25,000–100,000..	26	73	70	68	37	6	280	9.2	25.9	25.0	24.4	13.1	2.3	000.0
2,500– 25,000 }	255	659	453	482	298	60	2,206	11.5	29.9	20.5	21.8	13.5	2.7	100.0
Rural.......... }														
1910:														
100,000–500,000..	119	339	362	432	265	61	1,578	7.5	21.5	22.9	27.4	16.8	3.9	100.0
25,000–100,000..	43	119	101	118	79	21	481	9.0	24.7	20.9	24.6	16.5	4.3	100.0
2,500– 25,000..	106	294	242	275	182	48	1,147	9.2	25.7	21.1	23.9	15.9	4.2	100.0
Rural..........	378	952	638	717	502	129	3,317	11.4	28.7	19.3	21.6	15.1	3.9	100.0
1920:														
500,000 and over.	66	207	193	291	219	56	1,033	6.4	20.1	18.7	28.2	21.2	5.5	100.0
100,000–500,000..	96	281	226	326	236	56	1,221	7.9	23.0	18.5	26.7	19.4	4.5	100.0
25,000–100,000..	59	177	129	184	156	45	750	7.8	23.5	17.2	24.6	20.8	6.0	100.0
2,500– 25,000..	143	402	266	362	269	76	1,518	9.4	26.5	17.5	23.8	17.7	5.0	100.0
Rural..........	467	1,197	636	876	666	176	4,018	11.6	29.8	15.8	21.8	16.6	4.4	100.0
1930:														
500,000 and over.	88	310	313	461	382	107	1,661	5.3	18.7	18.8	27.7	23.0	6.5	100.0
100,000–500,000..	116	418	309	450	395	126	1,814	6.4	23.0	17.0	24.8	21.8	6.9	100.0
25,000–100,000..	68	242	174	252	223	75	1,034	6.6	23.4	16.9	24.3	21.6	7.3	100.0
2,500– 25,000..	151	506	323	451	372	119	1,921	7.9	26.3	16.8	23.5	19.3	6.2	100.0
Rural..........	403	1,304	647	916	826	260	4,356	9.3	29.9	14.9	21.0	19.0	6.0	100.0
Farm..........	185	650	262	382	390	115	1,984	9.3	32.8	13.2	19.3	19.7	5.8	100.0
Nonfarm......	219	654	385	534	436	145	2,372	9.2	27.6	16.2	22.5	18.4	6.1	100.0

ᵃ From special compilation made for this study. For sources of data and method of compilation, see Tables 34 and 35, pp. 128 and 130.

APPENDIX TABLES

TABLE 16.—NATIVE WHITE POPULATION OF KNOWN AGES AND PERCENTAGE DISTRIBUTION BY AGE, BY REGIONS, 1870–1930[a]

Region and year	0–4	5–19	20–29	30–44	45–64	65+	Total
POPULATION (THOUSANDS)							
Northeast:							
1870	1,450	3,617	1,531	1,436	1,164	401	9,599
1890	1,713	4,534	2,395	2,356	1,611	610	13,221
1910	2,594	6,160	3,106	3,469	2,577	792	18,699
1920	3,036	7,381	3,691	3,911	3,185	951	22,155
1930	2,783	8,902	4,480	4,935	3,776	1,240	26,117
PERCENTAGE DISTRIBUTION							
1870	15.1	37.7	15.9	15.0	12.1	4.3	100.0
1890	13.0	34.3	18.1	17.8	12.2	4.6	100.0
1910	13.9	32.9	16.6	18.5	13.8	4.2	100.0
1920	13.7	33.3	16.7	17.7	14.4	4.3	100.0
1930	10.7	34.1	17.2	18.9	14.5	4.7	100.0
POPULATION (THOUSANDS)							
North Center:							
1870	1,877	4,288	1,670	1,418	903	211	10,367
1890	2,662	6,803	3,217	2,912	1,735	498	17,826
1910	3,138	8,320	4,525	4,547	3,164	861	24,555
1920	3,488	9,112	5,092	5,557	4,147	1,139	28,536
1930	3,277	10,319	5,598	6,782	5,229	1,643	32,849
PERCENTAGE DISTRIBUTION							
1870	18.1	41.4	16.1	13.7	8.7	2.0	100.0
1890	14.9	38.2	18.0	16.3	9.7	2.8	100.0
1910	12.8	33.9	18.4	18.5	12.9	3.5	100.0
1920	12.2	31.9	17.8	19.4	14.5	4.0	100.0
1930	10.0	31.4	17.0	20.6	15.9	5.0	100.0
POPULATION (THOUSANDS)							
South:							
1870	1,185	2,939	1,298	1,091	765	191	7,468
1890	1,811	4,870	2,046	2,106	1,331	367	12,531
1910	2,852	6,945	3,478	3,440	2,435	646	19,796
1920	2,985	8,113	3,934	4,252	3,073	900	23,257
1930	3,017	9,088	4,669	5,116	4,040	1,195	27,125
PERCENTAGE DISTRIBUTION							
1870	15.9	39.4	17.4	14.6	10.2	2.6	100.0
1890	14.5	38.9	16.3	16.8	10.6	2.9	100.0
1910	14.4	35.1	17.6	17.4	12.3	3.3	100.0
1920	12.8	34.9	16.9	18.3	13.2	3.9	100.0
1930	11.1	33.5	17.2	18.9	14.9	4.4	100.0
POPULATION (THOUSANDS)							
West:							
1870	124	250	100	125	54	7	660
1890	307	767	447	404	218	44	2,187
1910	636	1,606	1,041	1,107	681	158	5,229
1920	820	2,135	1,228	1,522	1,086	265	7,057
1930	823	2,711	1,609	2,086	1,635	476	9,340
PERCENTAGE DISTRIBUTION							
1870	18.8	37.8	15.2	18.9	8.2	1.1	100.0
1890	14.0	35.1	20.4	18.5	10.0	2.0	100.0
1910	12.2	30.7	19.9	21.2	13.0	3.0	100.0
1920	11.6	30.3	17.4	21.6	15.4	3.8	100.0
1930	8.8	29.0	17.2	22.3	17.5	5.1	100.0

[a] For 1870 from *Ninth Census of the United States: 1870*, Vol. II, pp. 624–634; 1890 from *Eleventh Census of the United States: 1890*, Vol. I, Pt. 2, pp. 106–107; 1910 and 1920 from *Fourteenth Census of the United States: 1920*, Vol. II, pp. 170–186; 1930 from *Fifteenth Census of the United States: 1930*, Vol. III, Pt. 1, pp. 38, 39.

POPULATION TRENDS IN THE UNITED STATES

TABLE 17.—NATIVE WHITE POPULATION OF KNOWN AGES AND PERCENTAGE DISTRIBUTION BY AGE, BY SIZE OF COMMUNITY, UNITED STATES AND REGIONS, 1890–1930ᵃ

Size of community	0–4	5–19	20–29	30–44	45–64	65+	Total	0–4	5–19	20–29	30–44	45–64	65+	Total
	POPULATION (THOUSANDS)							PERCENTAGE DISTRIBUTION						
United States:														
1890:														
500,000 and over..	478	1,028	561	450	192	44	2,755	17.4	37.3	20.4	16.3	7.0	1.6	100.0
100,000–500,000...	514	1,255	734	595	256	56	3,411	15.1	36.8	21.5	17.4	7.5	1.7	100.0
25,000–100,000...	389	1,017	611	542	283	71	2,915	13.4	34.9	21.0	18.6	9.7	2.4	100.0
2,500– 25,000 } Rural........ }	5,111	13,674	6,199	6,190	4,163	1,348	36,685	13.9	37.3	16.9	16.9	11.3	3.7	100.0
1910:														
500,000 and over..	1,122	2,548	1,345	1,326	741	133	7,215	15.6	35.3	18.6	18.4	10.3	1.8	100.0
100,000–500,000...	730	1,897	1,299	1,314	765	151	6,156	11.9	30.8	21.1	21.3	12.4	2.5	100.0
25,000–100,000...	735	1,850	1,182	1,224	778	184	5,952	12.3	31.1	19.9	20.6	13.1	3.1	100.0
2,500– 25,000...	1,305	3,355	2,018	2,160	1,531	439	10,807	12.1	31.0	18.7	20.0	14.2	4.1	100.0
Rural............	5,329	13,382	6,307	6,539	5,043	1,549	38,149	14.0	35.1	16.5	17.1	13.2	4.1	100.0
1920:														
500,000 and over..	1,532	3,627	2,126	2,078	1,327	249	10,939	14.0	33.2	19.4	19.0	12.1	2.3	100.0
100,000–500,000...	932	2,370	1,660	1,758	1,181	253	8,155	11.4	29.1	20.4	21.6	14.5	3.1	100.0
25,000–100,000...	942	2,354	1,494	1,607	1,166	282	7,846	12.0	30.0	19.0	20.5	14.9	3.6	100.0
2,500– 25,000...	1,560	4,117	2,336	2,615	2,029	596	13,253	11.8	31.1	17.6	19.7	15.3	4.5	100.0
Rural............	5,363	14,273	6,329	7,184	5,788	1,874	40,811	13.1	35.0	15.5	17.6	14.2	4.6	100.0
1930:														
500,000 and over..	1,456	4,612	2,814	2,946	1,803	419	14,050	10.4	32.8	20.0	21.0	12.8	3.0	100.0
100,000–500,000...	1,062	3,407	2,271	2,648	1,871	502	11,760	9.0	29.0	19.3	22.5	15.9	4.3	100.0
25,000–100,000...	964	3,040	1,875	2,154	1,579	451	10,064	9.6	30.2	18.6	21.4	15.7	4.5	100.0
2,500– 25,000...	1,569	5,001	2,811	3,342	2,622	844	16,190	9.7	30.9	17.4	20.6	16.2	5.2	100.0
Rural............	4,849	14,959	6,586	7,829	6,805	2,338	43,366	11.2	34.5	15.2	18.1	15.7	5.4	100.0
Farm....:....	2,664	8,773	3,369	4,068	3,765	1,157	23,795	11.2	36.7	14.2	17.1	15.8	4.9	100.0
Nonfarm......	2,185	6,186	3,217	3,761	3,041	1,182	19,572	11.2	31.6	16.4	19.2	15.5	6.0	100.0
Northeast:														
1890:														
500,000 and over..	343	784	436	360	161	39	2,122	16.2	36.9	20.5	17.0	7.6	1.8	100.0
100,000–500,000...	169	402	221	190	87	22	1,091	15.5	36.9	20.2	17.4	8.0	2.0	100.0
25,000–100,000...	201	514	290	268	153	46	1,472	13.7	34.9	19.7	18.2	10.4	3.1	100.0
2,500– 25,000 } Rural........ }	1,000	2,834	1,449	1,539	1,210	504	8,536	11.7	33.2	17.0	18.0	14.2	5.9	100.0
1910:														
500,000 and over..	745	1,637	811	830	482	92	4,597	16.2	35.6	17.6	18.1	10.5	2.0	100.0
100,000–500,000...	262	632	333	339	207	43	1,816	14.5	34.8	18.3	18.7	11.4	2.4	100.0
25,000–100,000...	365	863	467	507	346	92	2,640	13.8	32.7	17.7	19.2	13.1	3.5	100.0
2,500– 25,000...	522	1,259	661	759	580	187	3,969	13.2	31.7	16.7	19.1	14.6	4.7	100.0
Rural............	700	1,768	835	1,033	963	379	5,677	12.3	31.1	14.7	18.2	17.0	6.7	100.0
1920:														
500,000 and over..	893	2,132	1,128	1,053	709	138	6,053	14.8	35.2	18.6	17.4	11.7	2.3	100.0
100,000–500,000...	352	823	448	446	321	73	2,463	14.3	33.4	18.2	18.1	13.0	3.0	100.0
25,000–100,000...	414	976	523	544	420	112	2,990	13.8	32.7	17.5	18.2	14.1	3.7	100.0
2,500– 25,000...	607	1,480	734	811	685	212	4,529	13.4	32.7	16.2	17.9	15.1	4.7	100.0
Rural............	770	1,969	857	1,057	1,051	416	6,120	12.6	32.2	14.0	17.3	17.2	6.8	100.0
1930:														
500,000 and over..	789	2,507	1,409	1,371	842	204	7,123	11.1	35.2	19.8	19.3	11.8	2.9	100.0
100,000–500,000...	326	1,083	563	596	428	120	3,115	10.5	34.8	18.1	19.1	13.7	3.9	100.0
25,000–100,000...	383	1,236	646	711	524	158	3,658	10.5	33.8	17.7	19.4	14.3	4.3	100.0
2,500– 25,000...	572	1,843	904	1,068	846	281	5,514	10.4	33.4	16.4	19.4	15.3	5.1	100.0
Rural............	713	2,232	959	1,189	1,137	477	6,707	10.6	33.3	14.3	17.7	17.0	7.1	100.0
Farm.........	184	681	241	322	385	156	1,969	9.3	34.6	12.3	16.3	19.6	7.9	100.0
Nonfarm......	529	1,551	718	867	752	321	4,738	11.2	32.7	15.1	18.3	15.9	6.8	100.0
North Center:														
1890:														
500,000 and over..	135	244	126	91	32	6	633	21.3	38.6	19.9	14.3	5.0	0.9	100.0
100,000–500,000...	229	521	308	231	82	16	1,389	16.5	37.6	22.2	16.7	5.9	1.1	100.0
25,000–100,000...	109	280	172	144	64	13	782	13.9	35.8	22.0	18.4	8.2	1.6	100.0
2,500– 25,000 } Rural........ }	2,189	5,757	2,610	2,446	1,556	464	15,022	14.6	38.3	17.4	16.3	10.4	3.1	100.0
1910:														
500,000 and over..	332	787	457	415	201	29	2,223	15.0	35.4	20.6	18.7	9.1	1.3	100.0
100,000–500,000...	249	667	486	456	261	46	2,165	11.5	30.8	22.5	21.0	12.1	2.1	100.0
25,000–100,000...	211	569	403	398	246	53	1,879	11.3	30.3	21.4	21.2	13.1	2.8	100.0
2,500– 25,000...	451	1,226	772	797	567	159	3,972	11.4	30.9	19.4	20.1	14.3	4.0	100.0
Rural............	1,895	5,072	2,407	2,480	1,889	575	14,317	13.2	35.4	16.8	17.3	13.2	4.0	100.0

[370]

TABLE 17.—NATIVE WHITE POPULATION OF KNOWN AGES AND PERCENTAGE DISTRIBUTION BY AGE, BY SIZE OF COMMUNITY, UNITED STATES AND REGIONS, 1890–1930.[a]—(*Continued*)

Size of community	0-4	5-19	20-29	30-44	45-64	65+	Total	0-4	5-19	20-29	30-44	45-64	65+	Total
	POPULATION (THOUSANDS)							PERCENTAGE DISTRIBUTION						
North Center: (*Cont'd*)														
1920:														
500,000 and over..	513	1,149	740	712	391	59	3,564	14.4	32.2	20.8	20.0	11.0	1.6	100.0
100,000–500,000...	315	790	622	652	424	86	2,888	10.9	27.4	21.5	22.6	14.7	3.0	100.0
25,000–100,000...	323	806	560	601	432	95	2,816	11.5	28.6	19.9	21.3	15.3	3.4	100.0
2,500– 25,000...	514	1,409	845	951	751	226	4,695	10.9	30.0	18.0	20.3	16.0	4.8	100.0
Rural	1,823	4,959	2,326	2,641	2,150	674	14,573	12.5	34.0	16.0	18.1	14.8	4.6	100.0
1930:														
500,000 and over..	527	1,639	1,030	1,098	603	118	5,015	10.5	32.7	20.5	21.9	12.0	2.3	100.0
100,000–500,000...	357	1,095	771	932	642	169	3,966	9.0	27.6	19.4	23.5	16.2	4.3	100.0
25,000–100,000...	339	1,036	681	800	584	161	3,601	9.4	28.8	18.9	22.2	16.2	4.5	100.0
2,500– 25,000...	504	1,595	921	1,135	916	314	5,385	9.4	29.6	17.1	21.1	17.0	5.8	100.0
Rural	1,550	4,953	2,195	2,818	2,484	881	14,881	10.4	33.3	14.8	18.9	16.7	5.9	100.0
Farm	931	3,132	1,249	1,631	1,434	413	8,791	10.6	35.6	14.2	18.6	16.3	4.7	100.0
Nonfarm	619	1,821	946	1,187	1,050	468	6,090	10.2	29.9	15.5	19.5	17.2	7.7	100.0
South:														
1890:														
100,000–500,000...	85	244	145	129	67	16	686	12.3	35.6	21.2	18.8	9.8	2.3	100.0
25,000–100,000...	55	159	101	90	47	10	461	11.8	34.4	21.9	19.5	10.3	2.1	100.0
2,500– 25,000 } Rural	1,672	4,468	1,800	1,887	1,216	342	11,385	14.7	39.2	15.8	16.6	10.7	3.0	100.0
1910:														
500,000 and over..	45	123	77	81	58	12	396	11.3	31.2	19.4	20.4	14.6	3.1	100.0
100,000–500,000...	102	286	208	225	138	31	989	10.3	28.9	21.0	22.7	13.9	3.1	100.0
25,000–100,000...	116	307	235	235	136	28	1,055	11.0	29.1	22.3	22.2	12.9	2.6	100.0
2,500– 25,000...	227	592	389	397	256	62	1,924	11.8	30.8	20.2	20.6	13.3	3.2	100.0
Rural	2,361	5,637	2,569	2,504	1,848	513	15,432	15.3	36.5	16.6	16.2	12.0	3.3	100.0
1920:														
500,000 and over..	61	158	104	112	85	20	541	11.2	29.2	19.3	20.8	15.7	3.7	100.0
100,000–500,000...	171	492	397	420	280	62	1,822	9.4	27.0	21.8	23.1	15.4	3.4	100.0
25,000–100,000...	148	405	301	324	204	45	1,428	10.3	28.4	21.1	22.7	14.3	3.2	100.0
2,500– 25,000...	297	849	527	571	395	106	2,745	10.8	30.9	19.2	20.8	14.4	3.9	100.0
Rural	2,309	6,209	2,605	2,824	2,108	665	16,721	13.8	37.1	15.6	16.9	12.6	4.0	100.0
1930:														
500,000 and over..	52	172	108	129	97	28	586	8.9	29.4	18.4	21.9	16.5	4.8	100.0
100,000–500,000...	263	825	657	752	519	131	3,148	8.4	26.2	20.9	23.9	16.5	4.2	100.0
25,000–100,000...	174	532	399	433	303	79	1,910	9.1	27.9	20.3	22.7	15.9	4.1	100.0
2,500– 25,000...	343	1,067	686	753	568	162	3,579	9.6	29.8	19.2	21.0	15.9	4.5	100.0
Rural	2,184	6,491	2,830	3,050	2,553	795	17,903	12.2	36.3	15.8	17.0	14.3	4.4	100.0
Farm	1,364	4,318	1,636	1,794	1,652	507	11,272	12.1	38.3	14.5	15.9	14.7	4.5	100.0
Nonfarm	819	2,172	1,194	1,256	901	288	6,631	12.4	32.8	18.0	18.9	13.6	4.3	100.0
West:														
1890:														
100,000–500,000...	31	88	60	45	19	3	245	12.7	35.8	24.3	18.2	7.9	1.3	100.0
25,000–100,000...	25	64	48	41	18	3	199	12.6	32.2	23.9	20.4	9.3	1.7	100.0
2,500– 25,000 } Rural	251	615	340	319	181	38	1,743	14.4	35.3	19.5	18.3	10.4	2.2	100.0
1910:														
100,000–500,000...	116	312	272	295	160	32	1,186	9.8	26.3	22.9	24.8	13.5	2.7	100.0
25,000–100,000...	42	111	78	84	51	12	378	11.2	29.4	20.6	22.2	13.4	3.2	100.0
2,500– 25,000...	104	278	195	206	128	31	942	11.0	29.5	20.7	21.9	13.5	3.3	100.0
Rural	373	905	496	522	343	83	2,723	13.7	33.2	18.2	19.2	12.6	3.1	100.0
1920:														
500,000 and over..	65	188	154	201	142	33	781	8.3	24.1	19.7	25.7	18.2	4.2	100.0
100,000–500,000...	95	265	193	240	156	32	982	9.7	27.0	19.7	24.4	15.9	3.3	100.0
25,000–100,000...	58	166	110	138	110	30	612	9.5	27.2	18.0	22.5	18.0	4.9	100.0
2,500– 25,000...	141	379	230	282	199	52	1,284	11.0	29.5	17.9	22.0	15.5	4.1	100.0
Rural	461	1,136	541	662	479	118	3,398	13.6	33.4	15.9	19.5	14.1	3.5	100.0
1930:														
500,000 and over..	87	293	267	348	261	69	1,326	6.6	22.1	20.1	26.3	19.7	5.2	100.0
100,000–500,000...	115	403	280	368	283	81	1,530	7.5	26.3	18.3	24.0	18.5	5.3	100.0
25,000–100,000...	68	235	160	210	168	54	896	7.6	26.3	17.9	23.5	18.8	6.0	100.0
2,500– 25,000...	150	495	300	387	292	86	1,712	8.8	28.9	17.6	22.6	17.1	5.1	100.0
Rural	402	1,284	602	772	631	185	3,876	10.4	33.1	15.5	19.9	16.3	4.8	100.0
Farm	184	642	243	320	294	80	1,763	10.5	36.4	13.8	18.2	16.7	4.5	100.0
Nonfarm	218	642	359	451	337	104	2,113	10.3	30.4	17.0	21.4	16.0	4.9	100.0

[a] From special compilation made for this study.

TABLE 18.—FOREIGN-BORN WHITE POPULATION OF KNOWN AGES AND PERCENTAGE DISTRIBUTION BY AGE, BY REGIONS, 1870–1930[a]

Region and year	0–4	5–19	20–29	30–44	45–64	65+	Total
POPULATION (THOUSANDS)							
Northeast:							
1870	36	302	621	901	552	104	2,516
1890	43	511	914	1,120	1,014	261	3,863
1910	54	798	1,730	2,166	1,454	429	6,631
1920	16	509	1,330	2,528	1,909	484	6,776
1930	16	340	1,005	2,612	2,466	659	7,099
PERCENTAGE DISTRIBUTION							
1870	1.4	12.0	24.7	35.8	21.9	4.1	100.0
1890	1.1	13.2	23.7	29.0	26.2	6.7	100.0
1910	0.8	12.0	26.1	32.7	21.9	6.5	100.0
1920	0.2	7.5	19.6	37.3	28.2	7.1	100.0
1930	0.2	4.8	14.2	36.8	34.7	9.3	100.0
POPULATION (THOUSANDS)							
North Center:							
1870	41	347	540	793	514	95	2,331
1890	34	537	822	1,171	1,140	343	4,046
1910	29	350	915	1,404	1,396	576	4,672
1920	9	280	672	1,516	1,495	617	4,589
1930	8	167	465	1,349	1,588	704	4,280
PERCENTAGE DISTRIBUTION							
1870	1.8	14.9	23.2	34.0	22.1	4.1	100.0
1890	0.8	13.3	20.3	28.9	28.1	8.5	100.0
1910	0.6	7.5	19.6	30.1	29.9	12.3	100.0
1920	0.2	6.1	14.6	33.0	32.6	13.4	100.0
1930	0.2	3.9	10.9	31.5	37.0	16.4	100.0
POPULATION (THOUSANDS)							
South:							
1870	5	37	86	150	100	17	396
1890	4	57	89	146	174	48	518
1910	9	85	146	212	194	79	724
1920	9	112	156	256	227	83	845
1930	1	19	55	168	205	83	532
PERCENTAGE DISTRIBUTION							
1870	1.2	9.5	21.8	38.0	25.3	4.2	100.0
1890	0.9	10.9	17.2	28.1	33.6	9.3	100.0
1910	1.2	11.7	20.1	29.2	26.8	10.9	100.0
1920	1.1	13.3	18.5	30.4	26.9	9.9	100.0
1930	0.2	3.5	10.4	31.6	38.6	15.7	100.0
POPULATION (THOUSANDS)							
West:							
1870	2	21	68	114	41	4	250
1890	5	61	164	236	172	31	670
1910	10	98	302	436	348	100	1,293
1920	11	128	223	517	460	144	1,483
1930	2	69	157	444	563	211	1,446
PERCENTAGE DISTRIBUTION							
1870	0.8	8.5	27.1	45.6	16.3	1.7	100.0
1890	0.8	9.2	24.5	35.2	25.6	4.6	100.0
1910	0.8	7.6	23.3	33.7	26.9	7.7	100.0
1920	0.7	8.6	15.0	34.9	31.0	9.7	100.0
1930	0.2	4.8	10.9	30.7	38.9	14.6	100.0

[a] For 1870 from *Ninth Census of the United States: 1870*, Vol. II, pp. 636–645; 1890 from *Eleventh Census of the United States: 1890*, Vol. I, Pt. 2, pp. 110–111; 1910 and 1920 from *Fourteenth Census of the United States: 1920*, Vol. II, pp. 170–187; 1930 from *Fifteenth Census of the United States: 1930*, Vol. III, Pt. 1, pp. 38, 39.

APPENDIX TABLES

Table 19.—Foreign-born White Population of Known Ages and Percentage Distribution by Age, by Size of Community, by Regions, 1890-1930[a]

Size of community	0-4	5-19	20-29	30-44	45-64	65+	Total	0-4	5-19	20-29	30-44	45-64	65+	Total
	POPULATION (THOUSANDS)							PERCENTAGE DISTRIBUTION						
Northeast:														
1890:														
500,000 and over...	10	142	286	364	297	63	1,164	0.9	12.2	24.6	31.3	25.6	5.4	100.0
100,000–500,000....	6	67	132	162	133	32	533	1.2	12.6	24.8	30.4	25.0	6.0	100.0
25,000–100,000....	8	91	147	170	151	33	600	1.3	15.1	24.6	28.4	25.2	5.5	100.0
2,500– 25,000..} Rural............}	19	211	348	423	432	133	1,567	1.2	13.5	22.2	27.0	27.6	8.5	100.0
1910:														
500,000 and over...	20	361	717	873	573	144	2,689	0.7	13.4	26.7	32.5	21.3	5.4	100.0
100,000–500,000....	7	90	204	272	198	57	827	0.8	10.9	24.6	32.9	23.9	6.9	100.0
25,000–100,000....	10	125	276	342	221	61	1,035	0.9	12.0	26.7	33.1	21.4	5.9	100.0
2,500– 25,000....	10	129	305	381	258	84	1,168	0.9	11.1	26.1	32.6	22.1	7.2	100.0
Rural............	8	92	228	297	204	83	912	0.9	10.1	25.0	32.6	22.3	9.1	100.0
1920:														
500,000 and over...	6	223	601	1,066	790	181	2,866	0.2	7.8	21.0	37.2	27.6	6.3	100.0
100,000–500,000....	2	69	182	339	263	65	920	0.2	7.5	19.8	36.8	28.6	7.1	100.0
25,000–100,000....	2	73	198	368	275	68	984	0.2	7.4	20.1	37.4	27.9	6.9	100.0
2,500– 25,000....	3	78	205	415	317	87	1,104	0.3	7.1	18.6	37.6	28.7	7.8	100.0
Rural............	3	66	144	339	265	84	901	0.3	7.3	16.0	37.6	29.4	9.3	100.0
1930:														
500,000 and over...	7	151	526	1,169	1,015	248	3,117	0.2	4.9	16.9	37.5	32.6	8.0	100.0
100,000–500,000....	2	46	131	365	355	97	996	0.2	4.6	13.1	36.6	35.7	9.7	100.0
25,000–100,000....	2	52	137	374	361	96	1,023	0.2	5.1	13.4	36.6	35.3	9.4	100.0
2,500– 25,000....	2	51	125	399	399	113	1,090	0.2	4.6	11.5	36.6	36.6	10.4	100.0
Rural............	2	40	86	305	336	105	874	0.3	4.6	9.9	34.9	38.5	12.0	100.0
Farm............	1	10	14	58	81	25	188	0.3	5.1	7.5	30.6	42.9	13.5	100.0
Nonfarm........	2	30	72	247	255	79	685	0.2	4.4	10.5	36.0	37.3	11.5	100.0
North Center:														
1890:														
500,000 and over...	5	68	121	147	91	17	449	1.1	15.1	27.1	32.8	20.2	3.7	100.0
100,000–500,000....	6	81	146	194	160	39	626	0.9	13.0	23.3	31.0	25.6	6.2	100.0
25,000–100,000....	2	30	50	68	60	16	226	0.9	13.2	22.2	30.1	26.6	7.0	100.0
2,500– 25,000..} Rural............}	21	358	505	762	829	272	2,746	0.8	13.0	18.4	27.7	30.2	9.9	100.0
1910:														
500,000 and over...	8	108	279	364	271	71	1,101	0.7	9.8	25.3	33.0	24.6	6.4	100.0
100,000–500,000....	5	52	140	198	175	59	629	0.7	8.3	22.3	31.5	27.9	9.3	100.0
25,000–100,000....	3	31	89	124	110	42	400	0.8	7.7	22.4	31.0	27.6	10.6	100.0
2,500– 25,000....	4	47	140	206	198	90	686	0.7	6.9	20.4	30.0	28.9	13.1	100.0
Rural............	0	112	267	512	641	314	1,855	0.5	6.1	14.4	27.6	34.6	16.9	100.0
1920:														
500,000 and over...	3	105	287	542	396	102	1,436	0.2	7.3	20.0	37.8	27.6	7.1	100.0
100,000–500,000....	1	36	89	193	179	63	562	0.2	6.5	15.9	34.4	31.8	11.2	100.0
25,000–100,000....	1	34	87	176	150	51	499	0.3	6.8	17.4	35.3	30.0	10.2	100.0
2,500– 25,000....	1	34	78	197	204	104	618	0.2	5.5	12.6	31.8	33.0	16.8	100.0
Rural............	2	70	130	408	567	297	1,475	0.2	4.8	8.8	27.6	38.5	20.1	100.0
1930:														
500,000 and over...	4	84	246	633	539	153	1,659	0.3	5.0	14.8	38.2	32.5	9.2	100.0
100,000–500,000....	1	19	56	164	189	73	503	0.2	3.9	11.1	32.7	37.7	14.6	100.0
25,000–100,000....	1	20	56	161	175	71	484	0.2	4.1	11.6	33.3	36.1	14.8	100.0
2,500–25,000.....	1	18	44	146	200	110	520	0.2	3.5	8.6	28.1	38.5	21.2	100.0
Rural............	1	26	64	244	484	296	1,114	0.1	2.3	5.7	21.9	43.5	26.5	100.0
Farm............	(b)	12	32	128	286	146	605	0.1	2.0	5.3	21.1	47.3	24.1	100.0
Nonfarm........	1	13	32	116	198	150	509	0.1	2.6	6.2	22.7	38.9	29.4	100.0
South:														
1890:														
100,000–500,000....	1	11	21	38	57	17	144	0.5	7.7	14.4	26.3	39.3	11.8	100.0
25,000–100,000....	(b)	7	13	22	25	6	74	0.6	9.2	17.9	30.5	33.9	7.9	100.0
2,500– 25,000..} Rural............}	3	39	55	85	93	25	301	1.1	12.9	18.4	28.4	30.9	8.4	100.0
1910:														
500,000 and over...	(b)	9	16	23	20	9	77	0.6	11.4	20.2	29.9	26.5	11.3	100.0
100,000–500,000....	(b)	7	16	26	28	15	93	0.5	7.7	17.3	28.3	30.1	16.1	100.0
25,000–100,000....	2	15	26	37	32	12	124	1.3	12.1	21.4	30.1	25.5	9.6	100.0
2,500– 25,000....	1	11	20	28	24	9	92	1.3	11.5	21.3	30.1	26.0	9.8	100.0
Rural............	5	43	68	97	90	34	338	1.5	12.8	20.0	28.8	26.6	10.2	100.0

TABLE 19.—FOREIGN-BORN WHITE POPULATION OF KNOWN AGES AND PERCENTAGE DISTRIBUTION BY AGE, BY SIZE OF COMMUNITY, BY REGIONS, 1890–1930.[a]—(Continued)

Size of community	0-4	5-19	20-29	30-44	45-64	65+	Total	0-4	5-19	20-29	30-44	45-64	65+	Total
	POPULATION (THOUSANDS)							PERCENTAGE DISTRIBUTION						
South: (Continued)														
1920:														
500,000 and over...	(b)	6	15	28	26	9	84	0.1	7.4	17.5	33.5	30.8	10.6	100.0
100,000–500,000....	1	19	35	56	48	19	177	0.8	10.7	19.6	31.4	27.0	10.5	100.0
25,000–100,000....	1	16	21	35	29	10	114	1.2	14.3	18.8	31.0	25.9	8.9	100.0
2,500– 25,000....	2	17	22	35	30	11	116	1.3	14.6	18.7	30.1	26.0	9.2	100.0
Rural............	5	54	64	103	94	35	355	1.4	15.3	18.0	28.9	26.5	9.9	100.0
1930:														
500,000 and over...	(b)	2	9	25	28	9	74	0.1	3.3	12.1	33.9	38.0	12.5	100.0
100,000–500,000....	(b)	6	20	54	60	23	164	0.2	4.0	12.1	33.1	36.8	13.8	100.0
25,000–100,000....	(b)	2	7	20	23	10	62	0.1	3.5	10.7	32.5	37.7	15.4	100.0
2,500– 25,000....	(b)	2	6	20	24	10	62	0.2	3.7	10.0	32.0	37.9	16.2	100.0
Rural............	(b)	5	14	49	70	32	169	0.1	3.1	8.1	28.7	41.1	18.9	100.0
Farm............	(b)	1	4	14	33	17	69	0.1	2.1	5.5	19.8	48.2	24.4	100.0
Nonfarm........	(b)	4	10	35	36	15	100	0.2	3.7	10.0	34.8	36.3	15.1	100.0
West:														
1890:														
100,000–500,000....	1	9	29	45	36	6	126	0.6	7.3	23.3	35.9	28.5	4.5	100.0
25,000–100,000....	1	8	22	28	18	3	81	1.0	10.4	27.7	34.3	22.6	3.9	100.0
2,500– 25,000.. } Rural............}	4	44	113	163	118	22	463	0.8	9.4	24.3	35.2	25.4	4.8	100.0
1910:														
100,000–500,000....	2	27	90	137	106	29	391	0.6	6.9	23.0	35.1	27.0	7.4	100.0
25,000–100,000....	1	8	23	35	29	9	103	0.7	7.4	22.0	33.6	28.0	8.3	100.0
2,500– 25,000....	2	16	47	68	55	17	205	0.9	7.9	22.9	33.2	26.9	8.1	100.0
Rural............	5	47	142	196	158	45	594	0.8	7.9	23.9	33.0	26.7	7.7	100.0
1920:														
500,000 and over...	1	19	40	91	77	24	251	0.5	7.5	15.8	36.2	30.5	9.5	100.0
100,000–500,000....	1	16	33	86	80	23	239	0.5	6.6	13.8	36.0	33.4	9.7	100.0
25,000–100,000....	1	10	19	47	46	15	138	0.6	7.4	13.6	33.8	33.7	10.9	100.0
2,500– 25,000....	2	23	36	79	70	24	234	0.9	9.9	15.2	33.8	30.0	10.1	100.0
Rural............	5	60	95	214	187	58	621	0.9	9.7	15.4	34.5	30.2	9.4	100.0
1930:														
500,000 and over...	1	17	46	112	121	38	334	0.2	5.0	13.8	33.6	36.1	11.4	100.0
100,000–500,000....	1	15	29	82	113	44	284	0.2	5.1	10.3	28.9	39.8	15.7	100.0
25,000–100,000.....	(b)	7	14	41	55	21	138	0.2	4.7	10.0	29.9	39.6	15.5	100.0
2,500– 25,000.....	(b)	10	22	64	80	32	209	0.2	5.0	10.7	30.6	38.1	15.4	100.0
Rural............	1	20	45	145	195	75	481	0.2	4.2	9.4	30.1	40.6	15.6	100.0
Farm............	(b)	9	20	62	96	34	221	0.1	3.9	8.9	28.0	43.5	15.6	100.0
Nonfarm........	(b)	12	26	83	99	40	259	0.2	4.5	9.9	31.8	38.1	15.6	100.0

[a] From special compilation made for this study.
[b] Less than 500.

APPENDIX TABLES

Table 20.—Negro Population of Known Ages and Percentage Distribution by Age, by Regions, 1870–1930[a]

Region and year	0–4	5–19	20–29	30–44	45–64	65+	Total
			POPULATION (THOUSANDS)				
Northeast:							
1850...............	19	49	29	29	18	5	150
1870...............	20	54	39	35	25	7	180
1890[b]...............	25	76	65	66	37	10	277
1910...............	41	109	119	135	65	14	483
1920...............	55	150	159	196	101	17	678
1930...............	102	268	259	323	166	25	1,145
			PERCENTAGE DISTRIBUTION				
1850...............	12.7	32.4	19.4	19.7	12.2	3.6	100.0
1870...............	10.9	30.0	21.9	19.5	13.8	3.9	100.0
1890[b]...............	9.0	27.4	23.3	23.6	13.2	3.5	100.0
1910...............	8.5	22.5	24.7	28.0	13.4	2.8	100.0
1920...............	8.1	22.1	23.4	29.0	14.9	2.5	100.0
1930...............	8.9	23.4	22.6	28.2	14.5	2.2	100.0
			POPULATION (THOUSANDS)				
North Center:							
1850...............	23	56	26	19	10	2	136
1870...............	40	102	54	45	26	6	273
1890[b]...............	49	155	89	86	54	15	447
1910...............	43	135	120	138	83	22	541
1920...............	57	178	179	222	128	28	791
1930...............	104	294	266	358	201	39	1,260
			PERCENTAGE DISTRIBUTION				
1850...............	17.0	41.1	18.9	13.9	7.4	1.7	100.0
1870...............	14.8	37.3	19.6	16.5	9.7	2.1	100.0
1890[b]...............	10.9	34.6	19.8	19.3	12.1	3.3	100.0
1910...............	7.9	24.9	22.0	25.6	15.4	4.1	100.0
1920...............	7.2	22.5	22.6	28.1	16.1	3.5	100.0
1930...............	8.1	23.3	21.1	28.4	15.9	3.1	100.0
			POPULATION (THOUSANDS)				
South:							
1850...............	559	1,322	595	504	289	80	3,348
1870...............	731	1,668	784	679	450	109	4,421
1890[b]...............	975	2,772	1,139	968	678	188	6,720
1910...............	1,176	3,209	1,661	1,467	952	257	8,723
1920...............	1,028	3,245	1,608	1,589	1,139	285	8,893
1930...............	1,017	3,283	1,728	1,726	1,294	304	9,352

TABLE 20.—NEGRO POPULATION OF KNOWN AGES AND PERCENTAGE DISTRIBUTION BY AGE, BY REGIONS, 1870–1930.ᵃ—(Continued)

Region and year	0-4	5-19	20-29	30-44	45-64	65+	Total
	PERCENTAGE DISTRIBUTION						
South: (Continued)							
1850........................	16.7	39.5	17.8	15.0	8.6	2.4	100.0
1870........................	16.5	37.7	17.7	15.3	10.2	2.5	100.0
1890ᵇ........................	14.5	41.2	16.9	14.4	10.1	2.8	100.0
1910........................	13.5	36.8	19.0	16.8	10.9	2.9	100.0
1920........................	11.6	36.5	18.1	17.9	12.8	3.2	100.0
1930........................	10.9	35.1	18.5	18.5	13.8	3.2	100.0
	POPULATION (THOUSANDS)						
West:							
1850........................	(c)	(c)	(c)	(c)	(c)	(c)	1
1870........................	1	2	1	2	1	(c)	6
1890ᵇ........................	6	22	37	60	24	3	152
1910........................	3	10	12	16	8	1	50
1920........................	5	14	19	24	14	2	78
1930........................	8	25	21	36	25	5	120
	PERCENTAGE DISTRIBUTION						
1850........................	4.8	17.6	38.2	31.2	7.9	0.3	100.0
1870........................	9.4	23.8	21.3	27.9	15.5	2.1	100.0
1890ᵇ........................	3.9	14.3	24.4	39.6	15.9	1.8	100.0
1910........................	6.4	19.4	23.6	31.4	16.2	2.9	100.0
1920........................	5.9	18.3	24.7	30.2	17.7	3.2	100.0
1930........................	6.6	20.8	17.9	30.1	20.8	3.9	100.0

ᵃ For 1850 and 1870 from Ninth Census of the United States: 1870, Vol. II, pp. 648–660; 1890 from Eleventh Census of the United States: 1890, Vol. I, Pt. 2, pp. 112–113; 1910 and 1920 from Fourteenth Census of the United States: 1920, Vol. II, pp. 170–186; 1930 from Fifteenth Census of the United States: 1930, Vol. III, Pt. 1, pp. 38, 39.

ᵇ All colored, but excludes 18,636 Negroes, 189,447 Indians, and 13 Chinese specially enumerated in 1890 in Indian Territory and on Indian reservations, for whom statistics of age are not available.

ᶜ Less than 500.

APPENDIX TABLES

TABLE 21.—NEGRO POPULATION OF KNOWN AGES AND PERCENTAGE DISTRIBUTION BY AGE, BY SIZE OF COMMUNITY, BY REGIONS, 1890–1930ᵃ

Size of community	0–4	5–19	20–29	30–44	45–64	65+	Total	0–4	5–19	20–29	30–44	45–64	65+	Total
	POPULATION (THOUSANDS)							PERCENTAGE DISTRIBUTION						
Northeast:ᵇ														
1890:														
500,000 and over..	6	17	21	21	9	2	76	7.6	22.7	27.0	28.1	12.2	2.5	100.0
100,000–500,000...	3	7	8	9	4	1	31	8.3	23.8	25.6	27.7	12.4	2.3	100.0
25,000–100,000...	3	9	7	9	5	1	34	9.4	26.8	21.2	24.9	14.3	3.3	100.0
2,500– 25,000 } Rural	13	42	29	27	18	6	135	9.9	31.0	21.2	19.9	13.6	4.4	100.0
1910:														
500,000 and over..	17	41	59	67	26	4	215	7.9	19.0	27.6	31.3	12.3	1.9	100.0
100,000–500,000...	3	9	9	11	6	1	39	8.5	21.9	22.7	29.2	15.0	2.7	100.0
25,000–100,000...	6	15	16	19	10	2	69	8.3	22.5	23.5	27.9	14.7	3.0	100.0
2,500– 25,000...	7	20	17	19	11	3	77	9.0	25.9	22.5	24.9	14.2	3.6	100.0
Rural............	9	24	18	19	11	4	84	10.2	28.6	21.1	22.1	13.6	4.3	100.0
1920:														
500,000 and over..	25	66	90	110	48	6	344	7.3	19.1	26.1	31.9	13.9	1.8	100.0
100,000–500,000...	7	18	17	22	12	2	78	9.1	23.2	21.6	27.9	15.6	2.6	100.0
25,000–100,000...	6	17	16	22	12	2	75	7.7	22.3	21.2	29.3	16.6	2.9	100.0
2,500– 25,000...	8	23	20	22	14	3	90	8.7	25.6	21.9	24.6	15.7	3.4	100.0
Rural............	9	26	16	21	14	4	90	9.8	29.0	18.3	22.8	15.9	4.2	100.0
1930:														
500,000 and over..	53	135	156	194	86	11	636	8.4	21.3	24.6	30.5	13.6	1.7	100.0
100,000–500,000...	13	33	27	34	19	3	129	9.9	25.5	21.2	26.2	14.7	2.4	100.0
25,000–100,000...	10	28	25	32	19	3	118	8.8	24.1	21.6	26.9	15.9	2.7	100.0
2,500– 25,000...	13	36	28	35	22	4	137	9.3	26.0	20.3	25.3	16.1	3.0	100.0
Rural............	13	36	23	29	20	5	126	10.2	28.8	17.9	23.4	16.1	3.6	100.0
Farm..........	1	4	2	2	2	1	12	9.9	31.9	16.2	20.0	17.8	4.2	100.0
Nonfarm.......	12	33	21	27	18	4	114	10.2	28.5	18.1	23.7	15.9	3.5	100.0
North Center:														
1890:ᵇ														
500,000 and over..	1	3	5	5	1	(ᶜ)	15	5.7	18.4	31.3	32.7	9.9	2.0	100.0
100,000–500,000...	6	20	20	19	8	2	75	8.3	26.7	26.8	25.0	11.2	2.1	100.0
25,000–100,000...	4	13	9	9	5	1	41	9.8	31.4	22.5	21.8	12.0	2.6	100.0
2,500– 25,000 } Rural	38	119	55	54	39	12	315	12.0	37.6	17.3	17.0	12.4	3.7	100.0
1910:														
500,000 and over..	6	17	25	32	14	2	96	5.9	17.7	26.0	33.4	14.5	2.5	100.0
100,000–500,000...	6	20	27	31	15	3	101	6.1	19.3	26.4	30.6	15.0	2.6	100.0
25,000–100,000...	5	17	17	19	11	2	71	7.6	24.1	23.3	26.6	14.9	3.5	100.0
2,500– 25,000...	10	34	26	28	20	6	124	8.1	27.2	20.6	22.9	16.3	4.9	100.0
Rural............	15	47	26	28	23	9	148	10.3	31.8	17.4	18.8	15.8	5.9	100.0
1920:														
500,000 and over..	15	47	68	83	36	5	254	6.1	18.4	27.0	32.8	14.0	1.8	100.0
100,000–500,000...	12	38	44	57	30	5	185	6.6	20.3	23.6	30.6	16.3	2.6	100.0
25,000–100,000...	7	22	22	26	15	3	95	7.5	23.0	22.7	27.3	16.1	3.4	100.0
2,500– 25,000...	10	33	23	30	23	7	125	7.8	26.0	18.6	24.1	18.3	5.2	100.0
Rural............	12	39	22	26	24	9	131	9.2	29.7	16.4	20.0	18.0	6.8	100.0
1930:														
500,000 and over..	42	109	128	167	72	9	526	7.9	20.8	24.2	31.7	13.7	1.7	100.0
100,000–500,000...	26	73	64	91	52	8	314	8.1	23.1	20.4	29.0	16.7	2.7	100.0
25,000–100,000...	11	31	25	34	21	4	126	8.7	24.7	19.9	26.7	16.6	3.4	100.0
2,500– 25,000...	12	37	24	33	27	8	139	8.3	26.2	17.3	23.8	19.0	5.4	100.0
Rural............	14	44	25	33	29	10	154	8.9	28.7	16.1	21.5	18.6	6.2	100.0
Farm..........	6	18	8	9	10	3	53	10.4	33.3	14.1	17.5	18.6	6.1	100.0
Nonfarm.......	8	26	17	24	19	6	101	8.1	26.3	17.1	23.6	18.6	6.3	100.0
South:														
1890:ᵇ														
100,000–500,000...	22	72	50	50	32	7	235	9.6	30.7	21.5	21.5	13.6	3.1	100.0
25,000–100,000...	29	93	67	59	34	7	280	9.9	32.1	23.3	20.6	11.6	2.5	100.0
2,500– 25,000 } Rural	924	2,607	1,021	858	613	174	6,197	14.9	42.1	16.5	13.8	9.9	2.8	100.0
1910:														
500,000 and over..	7	20	21	22	13	2	85	7.8	23.9	24.3	25.9	15.2	2.9	100.0
100,000–500,000...	37	119	117	114	61	13	463	8.0	25.7	25.4	24.7	13.3	2.9	100.0
25,000–100,000...	37	122	117	110	54	11	452	8.2	26.9	25.9	24.4	12.1	2.4	100.0
2,500– 25,000...	86	267	191	173	103	26	846	10.1	31.6	22.6	20.5	12.1	3.1	100.0
Rural............	1,010	2,681	1,216	1,048	720	204	6,878	14.7	39.0	17.7	15.2	10.5	3.0	100.0

TABLE 21.—NEGRO POPULATION OF KNOWN AGES AND PERCENTAGE DISTRIBUTION BY AGE, BY SIZE OF COMMUNITY BY REGIONS, 1890–1930.[a]—(Continued)

Size of community	0–4	5–19	20–29	30–44	45–64	65+	Total	0–4	5–19	20–29	30–44	45–64	65+	Total
	POPULATION (THOUSANDS)							PERCENTAGE DISTRIBUTION						
South: (Continued)														
1920:														
500,000 and over..	8	24	26	30	17	3	108	7.7	22.2	23.8	27.6	15.9	2.8	100.0
100,000–500,000...	48	169	163	177	99	18	675	7.1	25.0	24.1	26.3	14.7	2.7	100.0
25,000–100,000...	42	145	136	135	72	13	543	7.7	26.6	25.1	24.9	13.3	2.4	100.0
2,500– 25,000...	76	282	197	198	131	32	915	8.3	30.8	21.5	21.7	14.3	3.4	100.0
Rural............	854	2,625	1,087	1,049	819	219	6,652	12.8	39.5	16.3	15.8	12.3	3.3	100.0
1930:														
500,000 and over..	12	35	31	38	21	4	141	8.7	24.5	22.0	27.1	15.1	2.6	100.0
100,000–500,000...	83	271	245	279	158	27	1,063	7.8	25.5	23.1	26.3	14.9	2.5	100.0
25,000–100,000...	58	200	168	175	99	18	719	8.1	27.9	23.3	24.3	13.8	2.6	100.0
2,500– 25,000...	88	316	218	223	156	36	1,038	8.5	30.5	21.0	21.5	15.1	3.5	100.0
Rural............	774	2,461	1,067	1,010	859	219	6,391	12.1	38.5	16.7	15.8	13.4	3.4	100.0
Farm...........	581	1,889	705	666	614	152	4,607	12.6	41.0	15.3	14.5	13.3	3.3	100.0
Nonfarm......	193	572	363	344	245	67	1,784	10.8	32.1	20.3	19.3	13.8	3.8	100.0
West:														
1890:[b]														
100,000–500,000...	1	3	10	14	3	(c)	31	2.2	10.6	30.6	45.4	10.6	0.6	100.0
25,000–100,000...	(c)	1	4	6	2	(c)	14	2.5	10.1	27.7	45.1	13.6	0.9	100.0
2,500– 25,000 } Rural	5	17	24	40	19	2	107	4.6	15.9	22.1	37.2	17.7	2.3	100.0
1910:														
100,000–500,000...	1	4	5	7	3	1	22	6.3	18.2	24.3	32.6	16.0	2.5	100.0
25,000–100,000...	(c)	1	1	2	1	(c)	7	6.1	19.9	20.8	33.6	17.1	2.5	100.0
2,500– 25,000...	1	2	3	3	2	(c)	11	7.1	20.2	23.2	30.5	16.0	3.0	100.0
Rural............	1	2	3	3	2	(c)	11	6.1	20.7	24.5	28.5	16.4	3.8	100.0
1920:														
500,000 and over..	1	4	4	6	3	1	18	6.3	19.9	20.9	32.0	18.0	2.9	100.0
100,000–500,000...	1	3	4	6	3	1	17	5.2	16.7	20.7	34.7	19.6	3.2	100.0
25,000–100,000...	1	2	2	3	2	(c)	10	7.3	20.0	17.0	29.9	21.7	4.1	100.0
2,500– 25,000...	1	3	2	4	3	(c)	13	7.2	20.7	18.1	30.2	20.1	3.8	100.0
Rural............	1	3	8	5	3	1	20	4.9	16.0	39.2	25.0	12.3	2.6	100.0
1930:														
500,000 and over..	3	8	9	14	8	1	43	6.1	19.8	20.1	32.0	18.8	3.2	100.0
100,000–500,000...	1	5	4	7	6	1	25	6.0	19.2	15.9	30.3	24.1	4.5	100.0
25,000–100,000...	1	4	3	5	4	1	18	6.7	22.3	16.9	28.5	21.6	4.2	100.0
2,500– 25,000...	1	3	2	4	3	1	13	6.6	19.4	17.4	29.8	22.5	4.2	100.0
Rural............	2	5	4	6	4	1	21	8.0	24.2	17.0	27.8	19.0	4.0	100.0
Farm...........	1	2	1	1	1	(c)	6	11.0	32.0	13.6	20.5	19.2	3.7	100.0
Nonfarm......	1	3	3	5	3	1	15	6.8	20.9	18.4	30.8	19.0	4.2	100.0

[a] From special compilation made for this study.
[b] All colored, but excludes 18,636 Negroes, 189,447 Indians, and 13 Chinese specially enumerated in 1890 in Indian Territory and on Indian reservations, for whom statistics of age are not available.
[c] Less than 500.

TABLE 22.—SEX RATIO IN RURAL AREAS AND IN CITIES GROUPED BY SIZE, BY RACE AND NATIVITY, 1820–1930[a]

Region and year	Rural[b]		Cities with population of:				
	Farm	Nonfarm	2,500–25,000	25,000–100,000	100,000–250,000	250,000–500,000	500,000 and over

TOTAL POPULATION[c]

Region and year	Farm	Nonfarm	2,500–25,000	25,000–100,000	100,000–250,000	250,000–500,000	500,000 and over
Northeast:							
1820	101.9		92.3	89.0	93.2	.....	....
1840	103.1		94.5	92.2	....	91.8	....
1860	102.5		94.0	92.8	92.0	91.3	93.2
1890	.....		.....	94.8	99.5	97.0	96.3
1910	110.0		101.4	98.6	97.9	101.4	99.0
1920	110.6	104.0	99.5	97.6	97.4	100.3	99.1
1930	115.1	103.6	97.6	96.7	96.0	98.2	99.3

WHITE POPULATION

Region and year	Farm	Nonfarm	2,500–25,000	25,000–100,000	100,000–250,000	250,000–500,000	500,000 and over
1820	101.9		93.0	90.7	96.2	.....	....
1840	103.0		94.7	93.3	....	92.9	....
1860	102.5		94.1	92.9	92.1	91.6	93.9
1890	.....		.....	94.8	99.2	96.7	96.4
1910	109.5		10˙.5	98.7	98.0	101.5	99.3
1920	110.5	103.8	99.4	97.6	97.2	100.3	99.2
1930	115.0	103.4	97.5	96.7	95.9	98.2	99.6

NATIVE WHITE POPULATION

Region and year	Farm	Nonfarm	2,500–25,000	25,000–100,000	100,000–250,000	250,000–500,000	500,000 and over
1890	.....		....	95.1	97.1	98.7	96.0
1910	103.2		95.4	94.5	93.9	96.6	96.0
1920	109.9	99.7	95.5	04.4	94.4	96.5	96.4
1930	114.4	101.6	95.5	94.8	94.0	95.7	97.3

FOREIGN-BORN WHITE POPULATION

Region and year	Farm	Nonfarm	2,500–25,000	25,000–100,000	100,000–250,000	250,000–500,000	500,000 and over
1890	.....		.....	94.0	104.1	93.2	97.3
1910	159.0		125.5	110.5	107.3	113.9	105.0
1920	118.6	130.1	117.3	108.0	105.2	111.1	105.5
1930	121.0	116.5	108.7	103.9	102.5	106.1	105.0

NEGRO POPULATION[d]

Region and year	Farm	Nonfarm	2,500–25,000	25,000–100,000	100,000–250,000	250,000–500,000	500,000 and over
1820	105.0		ʳ79.8	73.1	67.1	.....	....
1840	105.6		88.6	74.9	.....	73.4	....
1860	101.4		85.4	83.5	82.3	77.6	72.5
1910	115.7		95.3	92.5	92.9	96.0	89.2
1920	121.2	109.6	106.8	98.4	103.1	101.8	97.2
1930	137.6	111.8	99.5	93.6	100.9	97.6	95.4

TABLE 22.—SEX RATIO IN RURAL AREAS AND IN CITIES GROUPED BY SIZE, BY RACE AND NATIVITY, 1820–1930.[a]—(Continued)

Region and year	Rural[b]		Cities with population of:				
	Farm	Nonfarm	2,500–25,000	25,000–100,000	100,000–250,000	250,000–500,000	500,000 and over
TOTAL POPULATION[c]							
North Center:							
1820	111.4		113.5	.....	.....	.....	.....
1840	110.1		117.7	109.9	.....	.....	.....
1860	110.0		101.4	96.1	106.7	.....	.....
1890	.....		.....	105.2	107.4	100.2	107.0
1910	110.8		101.5	105.2	102.5	103.1	104.9
1920	113.0	103.9	98.4	105.0	106.5	98.2	105.6
1930	115.7	103.9	97.7	98.3	99.9	96.1	102.9
WHITE POPULATION							
1820	111.4		114.3	.....	.....	.....	.....
1840	110.4		119.3	111.6	.....	.....	.....
1860	110.1		101.8	96.2	107.2	.....	.....
1890	.....		.....	105.2	107.3	100.4	106.6
1910	110.7		101.5	105.2	102.4	103.1	104.9
1920	113.0	103.7	98.3	104.8	106.1	98.0	105.4
1930	115.7	103.4	97.6	98.1	99.7	95.8	103.1
NATIVE WHITE POPULATION							
1890	.....		....	102.1	103.9	96.7	103.0
1910	107.2		96.3	98.9	98.1	96.1	97.2
1920	111.3	100.3	95.5	99.6	101.1	94.2	99.4
1930	114.2	101.5	95.8	95.6	96.7	93.8	98.6
FOREIGN-BORN WHITE POPULATION							
1890	.....		.....	116.9	114.5	110.0	112.0
1910	143.0		138.2	141.0	127.0	123.6	122.3
1920	133.9	137.4	123.1	140.4	135.5	120.1	122.0
1930	138.9	129.0	118.3	119.4	124.9	114.8	118.0
NEGRO POPULATION[d]							
1820	111.8		97.2	.....	.....	.....	.....
1840	101.2		94.9	81.4	.....	.....	.....
1860	102.9		88.5	92.0	84.5	.....	.....
1910	118.3		101.6	107.9	105.3	105.2	103.8
1920	119.4	122.0	103.9	111.9	116.2	102.1	110.4
1930	117.8	130.2	101.1	104.2	103.0	100.1	100.2

APPENDIX TABLES

TABLE 22.—SEX RATIO IN RURAL AREAS AND IN CITIES GROUPED BY SIZE, BY RACE AND NATIVITY, 1820–1930.[a]—(*Continued*)

Year	Rural[b]		Cities with population of:				
	Farm	Nonfarm	2,500–25,000	25,000–100,000	100,000–250,000	250,000–500,000	500,000 and over

TOTAL POPULATION[c]

South:							
1820	104.9		95.0	94.4	....	....	....
1840	103.5		97.8	88.6	96.5	....	....
1860	103.8		101.4	99.8	94.1	....	....
1890	....		....	96.7	90.9	90.3	....
1910	105.2		96.6	98.6	95.1	91.5	92.3
1920	105.0	104.8	97.1	97.6	97.0	90.5	97.0
1930	106.2	102.4	93.7	92.4	95.5	92.3	96.7

WHITE POPULATION

1820	104.5		104.6	109.3	.....	....	....
1840	104.9		107.2	110.1	110.2	....	....
1860	105.5		107.6	103.7	99.2	....	....
1890	....		.....	103.5	94.4	93.0	....
1910	106.9		100.4	103.2	98.6	94.8	93.6
1920	107.2	105.8	99.5	99.9	99.1	92.0	97.3
1930	108.2	102.7	96.3	95.7	97.4	94.3	96.6

NATIVE WHITE POPULATION

1890	.....		....	100.2	93.1	92.5	....
1910	105.9		98.6	100.7	97.0	92.9	92.3
1920	106.9	103.8	98.4	98.6	96.6	89.1	95.4
1930	108.1	102.0	95.8	94.7	96.4	93.1	95.2

FOREIGN-BORN WHITE POPULATION

1890	.....		.....	126.7	101.1	95.2	.....
1910	168.3		144.6	127.4	122.4	112.6	100.6
1920	131.8	178.5	131.3	119.3	128.5	128.0	110.4
1930	134.7	160.2	137.3	132.0	120.5	119.9	108.2

NEGRO POPULATION[d]

1820	105.4		82.3	68.3	....	....	.....
1840	101.3		82.2	74.3	71.7	....	.....
1860	101.0		86.7	88.6	67.1	....	.....
1910	101.5		88.3	87.6	88.1	83.4	85.5
1920	100.0	101.5	90.0	91.1	91.2	86.4	95.4
1930	100.9	100.5	84.9	84.1	88.2	87.1	102.9

TABLE 22.—SEX RATIO IN RURAL AREAS AND IN CITIES GROUPED BY SIZE, BY RACE AND NATIVITY, 1820–1930.[a]—(*Continued*)

Year	Rural[b] Farm	Rural[b] Nonfarm	Cities with population of: 2,500–25,000	25,000–100,000	100,000–250,000	250,000–500,000	500,000 and over
TOTAL POPULATION[c]							
West:							
1860	214.8		161.9	157.9	.....	.....	.....
1890	.....		.....	132.3	132.1	131.4	.....
1910	137.9		115.9	108.7	116.4	113.8	.....
1920	123.0	127.4	106.1	99.4	101.6	106.0	103.7
1930	124.5	119.9	103.3	97.0	97.4	98.5	100.0
WHITE POPULATION							
1860	214.7		161.8	157.1	.....	.....	.....
1890	.....		.....	126.9	130.4	114.1	.....
1910	137.8		116.0	108.8	116.4	114.0	.....
1920	122.3	125.6	106.0	99.4	101.3	105.9	103.8
1930	123.4	118.1	103.2	97.1	97.4	98.5	100.2
NATIVE WHITE POPULATION							
1890	.....		.....	119.6	127.2	104.8	....
1910	123.7		108.1	102.1	107.5	103.8	....
1920	117.4	115.3	101.5	94.4	97.0	99.3	96.5
1930	119.4	113.2	100.4	94.3	95.6	94.6	95.5
FOREIGN-BORN WHITE POPULATION							
1890	.....		.....	147.0	141.0	131.8	.....
1910	234.2		161.8	137.3	152.7	147.2	.....
1920	161.6	188.4	135.4	125.0	121.6	137.8	130.7
1930	160.6	167.5	129.4	116.9	110.5	120.1	121.3
NEGRO POPULATION[d]							
1860	243.9		170.0	201.5	.....	.....	....
1910	182.7		107.7	105.2	113.3	114.0	....
1920	138.7	326.1	110.9	97.7	121.5	111.2	94.6
1930	127.8	155.9	111.4	93.3	101.4	98.5	92.3

[a] From special compilations made for this study, based on current census reports.

[b] Data are not available for rural areas and cities of 2,500 to 25,000 separately in 1890, or for rural-farm and rural-nonfarm prior to 1920.

[c] Includes whites and Negroes only, except in 1890. See Note d.

[d] Ratios are available for the colored population but not for Negroes in 1890.

APPENDIX TABLES

TABLE 23.—SEX RATIO AT SELECTED AGES, BY SIZE OF COMMUNITY, BY RACE AND NATIVITY, 1890–1930[a]

Size of community	Ages 0–4				Ages 5–19			
	1890	1910	1920	1930	1890	1910	1920	1930

TOTAL POPULATION[b]

Size of community	1890	1910	1920	1930	1890	1910	1920	1930
500,000+	101.4	101.9	102.0	103.2	96.1	96.6	98.4	98.8
250,000–500,000	102.5	101.7	101.8	102.8	96.2	97.3	96.1	96.0
100,000–250,000	102.1	101.9	101.1	103.2	95.5	97.1	96.2	97.1
25,000–100,000	102.2	101.3	101.8	103.2	95.6	96.9	96.5	96.7
2,500–25,000	(c)	102.0	102.1	102.9	(c)	97.1	96.6	97.7
Rural { nonfarm	} (c)	} 102.9 {	102.1	103.0	} (c)	} 104.3 {	99.6	100.8
Rural { farm			103.5	103.0			106.2	108.3

NATIVE WHITE POPULATION

Size of community	1890	1910	1920	1930	1890	1910	1920	1930
500,000+	101.4	102.0	102.2	103.6	97.4	98.0	99.1	99.6
250,000–500,000	102.9	102.0	102.3	103.2	97.1	97.7	96.7	97.4
100,000–250,000	102.2	102.2	101.4	103.6	96.9	97.3	97.1	97.8
25,000–100,000	102.3	101.6	102.2	103.6	97.0	97.7	97.4	97.8
2,500–25,000	(c)	102.2	102.4	103.3	(c)	97.2	97.2	98.5
Rural { nonfarm	} (c)	} 103.6 {	102.5	103.5	} (c)	} 104.6 {	99.9	101.3
Rural { farm			104.2	103.9			107.6	109.6

FOREIGN-BORN WHITE POPULATION

Size of community	1890	1910	1920	1930	1890	1910	1920	1930
500,000+	103.5	101.3	101.1	101.9	90.8	91.7	95.5	94.7
250,000–500,000	97.5	102.0	100.3	102.2	92.4	102.3	96.9	93.4
100,000–250,000	103.4	100.7	109.1	110.4	92.2	103.6	95.4	94.8
25,000–100,000	103.1	99.8	101.0	101.6	92.2	98.8	94.0	94.1
2,500–25,000	(c)	104.3	101.2	104.1	(c)	109.7	97.1	95.1
Rural { nonfarm	} (c)	} 105.6 {	105.4	108.3	} (c)	} 137.5 {	107.8	103.4
Rural { farm			106.5	105.3			114.7	122.9

NEGRO POPULATION[d]

Size of community	1890	1910	1920	1930	1890	1910	1920	1930
500,000+	.....	96.1	96.1	99.3	.....	83.3	88.3	89.8
250,000–500,000	.....	97.0	95.4	100.0	.....	86.2	88.8	87.4
100,000–250,000	.....	98.1	96.2	98.8	.....	88.1	87.9	89.3
25,000–100,000	.....	97.1	95.7	98.0	.....	86.7	87.3	86.6
2,500–25,000	.....	98.3	98.3	97.9	.....	88.6	89.5	88.4
Rural { nonfarm	}	} 99.6 {	98.0	98.0	}	} 99.7 {	95.5	96.0
Rural { farm			100.0	99.0			100.3	102.4

TABLE 23.—SEX RATIO AT SELECTED AGES, BY SIZE OF COMMUNITY, BY RACE AND NATIVITY, 1890–1930.[a]—(Continued)

Size of community	Ages 30–44				Ages 45–64			
	1890	1910	1920	1930	1890	1910	1920	1930
TOTAL POPULATION[b]								
500,000+	109.8	107.3	109.9	106.6	99.9	102.8	106.4	104.1
250,000–500,000	112.2	109.1	104.5	98.9	102.0	104.4	105.5	99.7
100,000–250,000	113.3	108.2	106.2	100.6	103.4	105.4	106.3	100.7
25,000–100,000	108.4	107.6	106.6	99.5	101.6	103.3	107.5	99.7
2,500–25,000	(c)	107.3	103.2	98.7	(c)	105.2	105.6	101.3
Rural { nonfarm	(c)	114.4 {	113.6	109.2	(c)	124.0 {	118.5	113.0
{ farm			103.8	101.3			131.1	124.9
NATIVE WHITE POPULATION								
500,000+	102.1	95.8	97.8	99.2	98.9	94.5	96.6	94.0
250,000–500,000	99.7	98.5	95.9	95.3	97.9	94.8	97.0	93.1
100,000–250,000	106.7	101.5	99.0	96.7	102.4	100.0	99.2	94.6
25,000–100,000	104.0	99.3	97.9	95.6	98.2	97.8	100.8	93.9
2,500–25,000	(c)	99.0	97.3	96.1	(c)	99.4	98.8	96.6
Rural { nonfarm	(c)	109.4 {	105.8	106.4	(c)	118.7 {	110.4	108.0
{ farm			105.4	103.1			126.3	122.1
FOREIGN-BORN WHITE POPULATION								
500,000+	116.8	121.4	126.4	118.8	100.6	110.8	116.0	114.9
250,000–500,000	120.5	136.0	137.7	123.2	102.9	119.9	124.8	118.9
100,000–250,000	128.6	128.9	129.0	116.6	105.9	117.2	117.2	113.5
25,000–100,000	117.8	131.9	135.8	119.1	105.5	116.2	121.3	115.3
2,500–25,000	(c)	144.6	133.3	121.4	(c)	125.4	127.8	120.5
Rural { nonfarm	(c)	167.7 {	162.9	136.2	(c)	150.4 {	151.7	138.4
{ farm			127.2	121.4			147.7	143.3
NEGRO POPULATION[d]								
500,000+	.....	104.4	111.3	107.1	.....	98.8	126.9	112.9
250,000–500,000	.....	93.2	96.2	94.3	.....	92.2	112.1	106.7
100,000–250,000	.....	99.3	100.4	97.3	.....	100.0	124.7	111.9
25,000–100,000	.....	100.0	99.6	90.8	.....	99.1	123.3	103.1
2,500–25,000	.....	95.0	91.7	86.0	.....	99.2	116.2	103.3
Rural { nonfarm	.....	102.5 {	107.3	107.6	.....	125.5 {	136.2	120.3
{ farm			85.0	85.2			144.7	128.3

[a] Compiled from current census reports. For similar ratios for other age periods, see Table 56, p. 200.

[b] Includes whites and Negroes only, except in 1890. See Note d.

[c] Sex ratio by age in 1890 cannot be computed separately for cities of 2,500 to 25,000 and for rural areas, the data not having been published by the Bureau of the Census.

[d] Ratios are available for the colored population but not for Negroes in 1890.

TABLE 24.—SEX RATIO AT SELECTED AGES, BY SIZE OF COMMUNITY, BY RACE AND NATIVITY, BY REGIONS, 1890–1930[a]

Size of community	Ages 0–4				Ages 5–19				Ages 20–29			
	1890	1910	1920	1930	1890	1910	1920	1930	1890	1910	1920	1930
TOTAL POPULATION[b]												
Northeast:												
500,000+	101.0	101.8	102.2	103.3	95.8	96.5	98.5	99.4	89.4	96.2	91.2	93.2
250,000–500,000	103.1	101.7	102.8	102.7	97.0	97.3	98.4	99.0	93.5	101.9	93.6	94.4
100,000–250,000	102.4	101.6	100.8	102.9	97.4	98.3	97.0	98.4	97.6	98.5	92.3	90.2
25,000–100,000	101.8	101.5	101.5	103.0	97.0	97.8	98.0	99.2	90.8	99.1	92.1	92.1
2,500–25,000	(c)	101.6	102.2	102.9	(c)	99.3	98.5	99.6	(c)	104.7	95.8	93.4
Rural nonfarm	(c)	102.3	102.3	103.2	(c)	105.9	104.3	103.4	(c)	115.3	103.2	99.6
Rural farm				103.8				112.3				129.4
NATIVE WHITE POPULATION												
500,000+	101.1	102.0	102.1	103.6	97.4	98.5	99.3	100.3	90.2	91.6	92.3	94.6
250,000–500,000	103.5	101.8	102.9	103.1	98.5	97.8	98.8	99.8	98.1	92.8	92.3	94.3
100,000–250,000	102.4	101.6	100.9	102.9	98.2	98.2	97.5	98.8	94.2	89.8	91.0	90.2
25,000–100,000	101.9	101.8	101.6	103.2	98.2	98.6	98.4	99.7	92.4	91.3	91.3	93.0
2,500–25,000	(c)	101.6	102.2	103.0	(c)	98.8	98.7	100.0	(c)	91.7	92.6	93.7
Rural nonfarm	(c)	102.3	102.4	103.2	(c)	104.5	104.3	103.6	(c)	100.8	101.8	100.0
Rural farm				103.8				112.1				129.1
FOREIGN-BORN WHITE POPULATION												
500,000+	102.0	101.5	101.2	101.8	88.8	89.9	94.6	93.1	88.3	103.4	90.1	92.1
250,000–500,000	96.8	103.2	102.0	104.5	89.6	94.8	95.7	92.7	86.4	121.8	98.2	96.9
100,000–250,000	104.3	100.6	109.8	111.1	92.8	100.6	92.7	92.5	102.9	114.4	94.6	90.1
25,000–100,000	101.7	98.4	100.7	99.0	91.3	94.1	93.7	93.2	87.1	115.0	94.0	89.3
2,500–25,000	(c)	105.0	100.3	105.7	(c)	106.0	97.3	93.3	(c)	141.4	107.2	91.3
Rural nonfarm	(c)	103.8	100.9	111.5	(c)	137.0	107.1	101.7	(c)	192.9	111.1	94.5
Rural farm				105.1				118.3				131.4
NEGRO POPULATION[d]												
500,000+	......	96.0	96.0	99.3	......	82.2	87.6	89.3	......	78.3	86.3	84.6
250,000–500,000	......	95.6	96.3	95.9	......	87.1	95.2	89.0	......	83.9	83.9	88.6
100,000–250,000	......	101.9	94.2	100.5	......	87.7	92.9	94.3	......	83.9	103.1	92.2
25,000–100,000	......	94.3	94.2	99.1	......	86.8	90.5	90.8	......	83.0	97.8	84.0
2,500–25,000	......	96.6	97.9	97.7	......	87.3	93.7	90.4	......	89.2	107.1	94.2
Rural nonfarm	.....	99.7	95.3	99.7	.....	106.3	102.4	99.7	.....	118.9	108.4	104.3
Rural farm				102.7				121.7				160.2

TABLE 24.—SEX RATIO AT SELECTED AGES, BY SIZE OF COMMUNITY, BY RACE AND NATIVITY, BY REGIONS, 1890–1930.[a]—(Continued)

Size of community	Ages 30–44 1890	1910	1920	1930	Ages 45–64 1890	1910	1920	1930	Ages 65 and over 1890	1910	1920	1930
TOTAL POPULATION[b]												
Northeast: (Continued)												
500,000+	105.0	105.2	105.7	104.5	96.3	100.6	103.4	101.6	78.2	79.0	80.6	83.5
250,000–500,000	103.1	108.3	108.9	101.8	93.7	103.6	103.7	99.2	75.9	78.9	77.0	80.8
100,000–250,000	106.9	101.9	102.8	99.4	98.0	94.7	99.9	96.6	80.0	76.7	76.9	78.7
25,000–100,000	97.3	103.5	102.7	98.7	92.9	96.8	99.8	97.7	77.0	76.8	78.1	78.3
2,500–25,000	(c)	106.5	104.5	99.5	(c)	100.5	102.9	98.9	(c)	84.0	81.9	81.3
Rural { nonfarm	(c)	115.3	107.8	105.6	(c)	112.2	113.6	108.0	(c)	100.6	101.6	95.7
Rural { farm				103.6				120.9				131.2
NATIVE WHITE POPULATION												
500,000+	98.3	94.8	95.2	98.0	95.9	93.6	94.3	92.4	71.8	74.1	74.1	75.0
250,000–500,000	99.7	97.4	97.1	94.4	95.1	94.4	93.8	89.8	74.3	74.6	73.2	73.3
100,000–250,000	97.4	92.2	93.1	93.5	94.3	89.3	92.7	88.7	72.8	69.7	72.0	73.0
25,000–100,000	94.2	92.5	92.0	92.9	90.3	91.0	91.7	90.2	72.6	72.1	73.7	72.9
2,500–25,000	(c)	94.1	93.5	94.0	(c)	94.0	94.4	91.6	(c)	80.3	78.3	76.8
Rural { nonfarm	(c)	102.7	100.2	102.0	(c)	106.5	107.7	102.0	(c)	97.9	99.2	91.5
Rural { farm				104.3				118.6				129.2
FOREIGN-BORN WHITE POPULATION												
500,000+	112.1	116.6	117.4	112.6	96.8	107.1	111.2	109.2	83.4	82.6	86.3	91.7
250,000–500,000	105.8	124.1	127.1	113.0	92.3	113.4	115.1	109.8	77.4	81.4	80.6	89.4
100,000–250,000	118.6	115.2	116.5	109.4	99.8	100.9	108.6	106.6	85.7	83.5	83.3	86.5
25,000–100,000	102.0	122.4	121.2	111.0	95.4	106.7	112.6	109.1	83.9	83.9	85.4	87.9
2,500–25,000	(c)	136.6	129.2	115.0	(c)	117.0	123.2	115.7	(c)	92.5	90.8	93.2
Rural { nonfarm	(c)	173.3	135.3	117.4	(c)	143.2	138.8	125.8	(c)	112.9	113.5	113.1
Rural { farm				98.7				131.6				142.8
NEGRO POPULATION[d]												
500,000+	......	101.8	105.4	104.2	......	97.0	122.2	108.9	......	65.9	69.8	71.4
250,000–500,000	......	110.4	111.1	109.3	......	107.5	137.9	112.8	......	73.0	75.2	84.3
100,000–250,000	......	101.6	109.2	109.8	......	97.1	120.6	113.9	......	79.9	79.8	84.1
25,000–100,000	......	103.7	97.7	97.3	......	97.0	117.6	104.8	......	89.1	84.9	83.0
2,500–25,000	......	106.6	117.5	108.7	......	101.2	122.4	111.0	......	93.1	92.8	90.3
Rural { nonfarm	......	127.4	112.9	125.2	......	125.3	142.1	133.0	......	120.9	117.8	118.9
Rural { farm				137.0				167.6				181.2

APPENDIX TABLES

TABLE 24.—SEX RATIO AT SELECTED AGES, BY SIZE OF COMMUNITY, BY RACE AND NATIVITY, BY REGIONS, 1890–1930.ᵃ—(Continued)

Size of community	Ages 0–4				Ages 5–19				Ages 20–29			
	1890	1910	1920	1930	1890	1910	1920	1930	1890	1910	1920	1930
TOTAL POPULATIONᵇ												
North Center:												
500,000+	102.3	102.0	102.2	103.1	96.8	97.5	98.4	98.2	103.2	105.3	99.6	96.0
250,000–500,000..	102.3	102.2	101.9	102.2	96.5	98.1	95.6	96.5	95.6	106.1	90.9	87.6
100,000–250,000..	102.4	102.3	101.6	104.3	95.8	96.9	98.6	96.7	104.2	101.3	107.9	92.0
25,000–100,000..	102.4	100.9	102.6	104.0	95.8	97.8	97.4	96.4	104.3	108.3	101.1	92.6
2,500–ʲ 25,000..	(ᶜ)	102.1	102.5	103.3	(ᶜ)	96.8	96.7	98.4	(ᶜ)	101.7	93.9	91.0
Rural{ nonfarm.. / farm....	} (ᶜ)	103.3	103.6{	103.9 / 104.2 }	(ᶜ)	105.3	105.2{	101.1 / 110.8 }	(ᶜ)	110.8	106.1{	96.5 / 123.4
NATIVE WHITE POPULATION												
500,000+	102.1	102.2	102.4	103.4	97.4	97.5	98.9	98.7	100.9	92.6	95.8	95.5
250,000–500,000..	102.6	102.1	102.1	102.5	97.0	97.5	95.9	96.9	90.4	93.7	88.2	86.9
100,000–250,000..	102.2	102.4	101.8	104.1	96.8	96.8	98.8	96.8	101.7	95.1	102.9	91.0
25,000–100,000..	102.1	101.0	102.8	104.1	96.2	96.9	97.5	96.5	101.4	97.1	95.3	91.5
2,500– 25,000..	(ᶜ)	102.3	102.5	103.4	(ᶜ)	96.1	96.7	98.5	(ᶜ)	91.9	91.2	90.6
Rural{ nonfarm.. / farm....	} (ᶜ)	103.3	103.6{	104.0 / 104.2 }	(ᶜ)	104.7	105.1{	101.0 / 110.8 }	(ᶜ)	104.8	104.2{	95.5 / 122.7
FOREIGN-BORN WHITE POPULATION												
500,000+	106.9	99.7	100.2	102.5	95.0	98.4	96.4	97.6	104.6	131.3	109.9	103.5
250,000–500,000..	96.9	101.7	105.2	90.9	94.6	106.4	97.0	94.3	112.8	146.6	118.1	99.9
100,000–250,000..	102.5	97.2	117.2	111.4	91.8	108.3	99.1	101.3	108.1	146.4	144.4	107.0
25,000–100,000..	115.2	101.7	100.2	116.3	92.9	117.9	95.9	94.3	114.5	180.9	147.8	104.9
2,500– 25,000..	(ᶜ)	102.5	93.5	102.1	(ᶜ)	119.1	96.9	97.5	(ᶜ)	181.2	126.4	96.5
Rural{ nonfarm.. / farm....	} (ᶜ)	106.0	106.2{	99.0 / 110.9 }	(ᶜ)	132.6	111.3{	103.3 / 130.2 }	(ᶜ)	183.7	141.8{	106.9 / 159.0
NEGRO POPULATIONᵈ												
500,000+	......	95.9	96.5	99.3	......	91.4	92.3	91.3	......	97.5	100.5	86.9
250,000–500,000..	......	106.4	95.6	98.7	......	91.2	89.9	91.1	......	94.6	86.8	87.2
100,000–250,000..	......	102.5	96.1	98.6	......	87.7	94.5	93.1	......	98.1	108.8	89.8
25,000–100,000..	......	96.2	96.0	100.6	......	94.4	97.2	94.2	......	104.3	104.3	94.9
2,500– 25,000..	......	93.1	99.9	96.9	......	92.1	94.1	96.1	......	100.9	99.9	95.8
Rural{ nonfarm.. / farm.:..	}	99.2	99.9{	98.6 / 104.0 }	.....	104.3	105.2{	106.9 / 106.7 }	.....	120.5	123.1{	147.3 / 108.5

[387]

TABLE 24.—SEX RATIO AT SELECTED AGES, BY SIZE OF COMMUNITY, BY RACE AND NATIVITY, BY REGIONS, 1890–1930.[a]—(Continued)

Size of community	Ages 30–44				Ages 45–64				Ages 65 and over			
	1890	1910	1920	1930	1890	1910	1920	1930	1890	1910	1920	1930
TOTAL POPULATION[b]												
North Center:												
(Continued)												
500,000+	126.0	114.3	118.7	111.0	114.5	110.1	112.8	110.2	88.8	85.5	85.4	87.3
250,000–500,000	110.6	109.2	103.6	100.6	101.9	104.6	104.7	100.4	86.0	82.4	84.4	83.5
100,000–250,000	128.0	107.2	115.6	105.4	114.8	109.5	111.2	106.2	93.7	90.4	90.0	92.3
25,000–100,000	117.8	112.4	113.8	102.8	113.7	110.2	115.3	102.1	97.1	92.7	90.2	87.4
2,500–25,000	(c)	106.3	101.6	99.3	(c)	104.8	101.6	100.3	(c)	95.4	93.5	92.5
Rural { nonfarm	(c)	114.0	109.6	107.8	(c)	122.3	122.0	108.7	(c)	119.2	118.6	104.7
Rural { farm				108.1				125.9				144.7
NATIVE WHITE POPULATION												
500,000+	118.6	98.8	102.6	101.8	115.4	98.9	101.8	98.2	85.2	78.1	78.2	78.6
250,000–500,000	99.4	95.9	95.2	95.9	97.4	93.2	96.1	94.0	77.6	77.6	81.0	80.3
100,000–250,000	119.9	100.1	103.5	99.3	113.3	102.3	102.4	97.9	90.0	85.5	85.1	86.4
25,000–100,000	110.8	101.6	100.4	97.0	109.4	102.8	108.9	95.8	90.6	87.8	87.7	82.7
2,500–25,000	(c)	97.2	95.7	95.9	(c)	98.1	95.1	95.7	(c)	91.2	89.0	86.6
Rural { nonfarm	(c)	108.4	105.6	104.2	(c)	117.3	117.4	104.1	(c)	114.7	115.3	99.5
Rural { farm				107.0				122.9				143.7
FOREIGN-BORN WHITE POPULATION												
500,000+	129.4	134.7	143.0	128.8	114.2	119.4	122.5	124.1	89.5	89.0	90.2	95.5
250,000–500,000	126.8	134.2	139.0	132.4	104.0	116.5	122.4	119.9	90.3	84.7	88.3	90.3
100,000–250,000	137.4	133.3	159.5	136.5	115.6	126.0	129.2	130.8	95.7	96.8	97.7	106.5
25,000–100,000	134.1	155.0	174.9	134.5	117.4	127.4	133.3	124.2	103.3	98.4	94.2	98.5
2,500–25,000	(c)	150.7	134.9	129.6	(c)	125.9	127.2	122.2	(c)	102.5	103.6	111.3
Rural { nonfarm	(c)	144.9	138.6	143.1	(c)	137.8	140.5	133.3	(c)	127.4	125.6	121.2
Rural { farm				122.9				141.0				146.9
NEGRO POPULATION[d]												
500,000+	......	118.5	124.3	111.8	......	107.9	141.4	120.0	......	78.7	76.1	74.1
250,000–500,000	......	116.1	109.9	106.4	......	128.3	135.2	122.5	......	81.8	91.6	92.0
100,000–250,000	......	118.8	131.0	112.2	......	121.9	151.9	127.6	......	95.9	96.5	100.1
25,000–100,000	......	119.6	122.7	114.4	......	125.1	141.5	121.2	......	106.7	105.4	95.8
2,500–25,000	......	111.0	108.0	102.2	......	111.1	122.0	115.1	......	102.9	99.7	98.9
Rural { nonfarm	.....	128.7	125.6	149.2	.....	140.1	148.3	143.9	.....	148.8	147.6	137.2
Rural { farm				108.1				152.7				182.6

APPENDIX TABLES

TABLE 24.—SEX RATIO AT SELECTED AGES, BY SIZE OF COMMUNITY, BY RACE AND NATIVITY, BY REGIONS, 1890–1930.ª—(Continued)

Size of community	Ages 0–4				Ages 5–19				Ages 20–29			
	1890	1910	1920	1930	1890	1910	1920	1930	1890	1910	1920	1930

TOTAL POPULATIONᵇ

Size of community	1890	1910	1920	1930	1890	1910	1920	1930	1890	1910	1920	1930
South:												
500,000+............	......	101.5	100.8	103.3	......	93.0	96.3	97.3	......	89.8	95.9	94.9
250,000–500,000..	101.4	99.8	100.2	103.3	92.1	94.1	94.4	93.8	82.8	87.9	84.9	84.6
100,000–250,000..	101.0	101.5	100.6	102.7	92.7	94.6	93.0	94.9	83.7	91.0	90.1	86.6
25,000– 10,000..	102.1	100.7	100.7	101.9	91.8	93.8	92.5	92.8	92.8	94.0	89.3	81.7
2,500– 25,000..	(c)	102.0	101.4	102.0	(c)	93.6	93.7	93.9	(c)	89.6	89.8	84.3
Rural { nonfarm..	} (c)	102.8	102.7 {	102.3	} (c)	102.8	102.8 {	98.5	} (c)	98.8	96.0 {	96.5
Rural { farm.....				102.3				106.4				101.1

NATIVE WHITE POPULATION

Size of community	1890	1910	1920	1930	1890	1910	1920	1930	1890	1910	1920	1930
500,000+............	......	102.1	101.7	104.4	......	95.8	98.4	99.8	......	90.5	96.2	95.6
250,000–500,000..	102.8	101.1	102.0	104.3	95.6	97.6	96.7	96.8	87.1	91.6	88.3	88.7
100,000–250,000..	102.0	103.3	101.7	103.7	95.1	97.3	95.0	96.9	87.4	94.9	91.1	90.0
25,000–100,000..	103.2	101.6	102.2	103.5	94.9	97.0	95.3	95.9	101.1	99.3	92.5	86.4
2,500– 25,000..	(c)	103.1	102.2	103.1	(c)	95.8	95.5	96.0	(c)	93.0	92.5	88.2
Rural { nonfarm..	} (c)	104.2	103.9 {	103.4	} (c)	104.2	104.2 {	99.3	} (c)	100.0	99.4 {	95.8
Rural { farm.....				103.8				108.2				106.1

FOREIGN-BORN WHITE POPULATION

Size of community	1890	1910	1920	1930	1890	1910	1920	1930	1890	1910	1920	1930
500,000+............	......	119.4	94.6	68.1	......	89.4	96.5	98.6	......	104.3	107.0	93.9
250,000–500,000..	96.1	93.3	81.9	110.7	91.1	93.6	109.7	89.7	86.3	122.6	151.4	97.4
100,000–250,000..	111.7	99.0	104.2	103.5	97.1	112.5	99.6	98.3	103.8	143.0	140.4	99.5
25,000–100,000..	102.4	104.2	100.4	89.4	100.5	98.4	89.5	101.8	130.2	135.3	112.4	97.3
2,500– 25,000..	(c)	99.1	109.9	144.2	(c)	110.4	96.7	103.6	(c)	158.2	130.2	93.0
Rural { nonfarm..	} (c)	105.9	112.1 {	107.1	} (c)	130.4	113.7 {	114.3	} (c)	195.5	166.0 {	129.0
Rural { farm.....				90.2				112.3				121.1

NEGRO POPULATIONᵈ

Size of community	1890	1910	1920	1930	1890	1910	1920	1930	1890	1910	1920	1930
500,000+............	......	96.4	94.4	98.8	......	79.0	83.4	85.9	......	77.7	89.0	92.7
250,000–500,000..	......	96.3	95.2	100.8	......	85.5	87.6	86.4	......	75.4	79.0	75.1
100,000–250,000..	......	97.0	96.5	98.3	......	88.1	86.4	87.3	......	81.4	79.7	74.8
25,000–100,000..	......	97.8	95.8	97.2	......	85.7	85.5	84.8	......	77.6	79.8	71.0
2,500– 25,000..	......	99.1	98.0	98.1	......	88.3	88.6	87.2	......	78.2	79.4	72.6
Rural { nonfarm..	}	99.6	99.6 {	97.9	}	99.6	99.1 {	95.3	}	93.0	85.5 {	98.0
Rural { farm.....				99.0				102.3				90.4

TABLE 24.—SEX RATIO AT SELECTED AGES, BY SIZE OF COMMUNITY, BY RACE AND NATIVITY, BY REGIONS, 1890-1930.[a]—(Continued)

Size of community	Ages 30-44				Ages 45-64				Ages 65 and over			
	1890	1910	1920	1930	1890	1910	1920	1930	1890	1910	1920	1930
TOTAL POPULATION[b]												
South: (Continued)												
500,000+........	......	94.3	100.1	100.7	......	92.2	98.9	95.6	......	73.0	77.7	77.9
250,000–500,000..	93.9	92.9	90.8	95.2	89.7	89.6	94.2	95.7	72.6	78.5	69.3	75.2
100,000–250,000..	91.1	99.0	101.7	98.2	93.9	97.0	109.6	103.0	77.7	77.9	81.7	87.6
25,000–100,000..	104.2	107.1	104.0	96.0	100.3	105.6	112.7	100.0	75.9	81.2	83.2	81.9
2,500–25,000..	(c)	101.9	99.1	94.1	(c)	105.8	111.1	101.6	(c)	87.4	92.2	89.6
Rural { nonfarm.. / farm...... }	(c)	107.3	101.2	{ 108.0 / 94.2 }	(c)	123.0	128.6	{ 112.4 / 121.9 }	(c)	110.0	118.1	{ 100.2 / 129.7 }
NATIVE WHITE POPULATION												
500,000+........	......	90.4	94.4	95.5	......	87.9	91.9	89.2	......	70.3	74.1	73.0
250,000–500,000..	92.4	91.4	87.5	95.6	88.6	86.4	87.9	91.0	65.4	77.4	65.6	71.1
100,000–250,000..	91.3	100.2	101.1	98.6	95.6	95.0	102.2	99.9	77.4	74.6	78.5	85.5
25,000–100,000..	106.8	108.0	104.7	98.4	97.6	103.8	106.7	97.7	73.3	78.6	81.9	80.0
2,500–25,000..	(c)	104.2	101.7	97.3	(c)	105.9	107.8	100.6	(c)	84.6	90.9	88.9
Rural { nonfarm.. / farm...... }	(c)	108.0	104.0	{ 107.9 / 97.9 }	(c)	120.2	122.3	{ 109.4 / 119.5 }	(c)	104.6	114.9	{ 99.0 / 129.0 }
FOREIGN-BORN WHITE POPULATION												
500,000+........	......	109.6	123.0	122.3	......	104.5	113.2	107.7	......	77.0	84.7	93.2
250,000–500,000..	110.2	129.2	139.3	132.9	93.5	115.3	131.0	126.9	86.9	86.1	86.5	106.4
100,000–250,000..	113.7	135.9	139.7	129.3	97.1	122.4	134.9	123.8	89.7	89.4	101.8	114.0
25,000–100,000..	149.9	141.8	131.7	150.1	121.4	137.0	140.1	139.2	99.0	94.5	98.2	117.1
2,500–25,000..	(c)	152.1	140.5	151.7	(c)	158.3	149.3	146.5	(c)	117.7	124.9	132.4
Rural { nonfarm.. / farm...... }	(c)	170.9	159.1	{ 175.5 / 109.7 }	(c)	175.0	172.1	{ 168.7 / 137.2 }	(c)	162.8	159.3	{ 145.2 / 160.8 }
NEGRO POPULATION[d]												
500,000+........	......	93.8	102.6	105.9	......	93.2	116.2	111.4	......	72.9	82.3	80.8
250,000–500,000..	......	86.6	86.2	89.4	......	84.4	97.7	100.9	......	75.2	64.3	72.7
100,000–250,000..	......	91.9	93.5	90.5	......	93.3	120.5	106.3	......	75.8	76.2	78.6
25,000–100,000..	......	95.9	96.0	85.7	......	94.6	120.6	99.2	......	74.8	76.9	75.3
2,500–25,000..	......	91.0	86.6	80.4	......	96.2	114.1	99.9	......	85.1	87.3	83.2
Rural { nonfarm.. / farm...... }	.....	101.2	90.0	{ 103.3 / 84.7 }	......	124.9	141.9	{ 117.2 / 127.7 }	.....	117.2	122.6	{ 96.9 / 129.2 }

TABLE 24.—SEX RATIO AT SELECTED AGES, BY SIZE OF COMMUNITY, BY RACE AND NATIVITY, BY REGIONS, 1890-1930.ᵃ—(Continued)

Size of community	Ages 0-4				Ages 5-19				Ages 20-29			
	1890	1910	1920	1930	1890	1910	1920	1930	1890	1910	1920	1930
TOTAL POPULATIONᵇ												
West:												
500,000+			101.9	104.1			99.3	98.0			96.9	97.7
250,000-500,000	103.5	102.8	101.9	103.1	99.9	99.2	95.5	96.2	129.3	117.1	94.4	90.1
100,000-250,000	101.7	102.2	102.1	102.5	93.1	97.4	96.1	98.7	144.7	119.7	92.3	91.6
25,000-100,000	104.2	103.6	103.6	104.2	96.0	97.3	96.0	97.4	146.6	111.5	91.0	93.5
2,500-25,000	(c)	103.0	102.8	104.3	(c)	98.5	97.6	98.7	(c)	122.1	98.0	96.7
Rural {nonfarm/farm}	(c)	103.3	103.8	103.6/103.2	(c)	108.9	106.5	103.4/111.1	(c)	159.0	121.0	110.8/132.7
NATIVE WHITE POPULATION												
500,000+			101.8	104.1			99.5	98.3			91.8	96.6
250,000-500,000	103.3	102.9	101.9	103.1	96.6	98.1	95.6	96.4	98.0	104.2	89.8	89.1
100,000-250,000	101.8	102.2	102.0	102.4	94.2	96.6	96.2	98.8	145.6	107.4	87.8	93.4
25,000-100,000	104.6	103.8	103.6	104.3	95.3	96.6	95.9	97.5	131.8	100.9	86.8	93.1
2,500-25,000	(c)	103.1	102.8	104.3	(c)	97.8	97.6	98.7	(c)	109.5	93.5	95.4
Rural {nonfarm/farm}	(c)	103.2	103.8	103.6/103.2	(c)	106.8	106.2	103.4/110.9	(c)	131.3	110.5	108.8/130.6
FOREIGN-BORN WHITE POPULATION												
500,000+			103.9	104.1			99.5	94.9			121.0	107.7
250,000-500,000	105.8	102.8	99.8	105.1	98.3	113.5	95.3	94.7	124.7	164.3	125.1	100.1
100,000-250,000	100.0	104.8	112.9	109.2	85.6	109.2	95.1	94.3	135.2	173.3	120.4	71.4
25,000-100,000	88.0	101.4	104.1	77.3	92.6	109.2	97.8	98.8	154.2	161.1	122.8	102.0
2,500-25,000	(c)	107.8	101.6	90.6	(c)	113.2	97.3	98.3	(c)	199.5	133.4	116.3
Rural {nonfarm/farm}	(c)	107.8	102.8	110.1/100.0	(c)	159.0	111.0	104.7/119.9	(c)	342.3	185.6	135.9/163.3
NEGRO POPULATIONᵈ												
500,000+			105.7	101.0			86.8	93.7			84.1	81.2
250,000-500,000		93.2	96.6	98.9		87.6	90.6	86.7		100.0	100.9	80.3
100,000-250,000		94.5	97.4	106.3		90.0	95.1	92.7		104.4	123.0	75.6
25,000-100,000		88.5	102.9	103.4		85.1	91.3	92.4		85.8	75.2	79.7
2,500-25,000		86.6	101.3	98.4		87.0	89.9	100.9		93.7	93.2	92.6
Rural {nonfarm/farm}		97.3	110.8	96.9/100.0		115.0	122.0	106.3/113.8		234.5	599.4	178.2/106.4

TABLE 24.—SEX RATIO AT SELECTED AGES, BY SIZE OF COMMUNITY, BY RACE AND NATIVITY, BY REGIONS, 1890–1930.ᵃ—(*Continued*)

Size of community	Ages 30–44				Ages 45–64				Ages 65 and over			
	1890	1910	1920	1930	1890	1910	1920	1930	1890	1910	1920	1930
TOTAL POPULATIONᵇ												
West: (*Continued*)												
500,000+	. . . . . .	. . . . .	109.9	104.6	. . . . . .	. . . . .	109.3	101.4	. . . . . .	. . . . .	93.6	85.8
250,000–500,000 . .	174.9	125.3	115.4	100.1	145.1	119.2	121.0	105.8	136.0	101.4	102.2	95.1
100,000–250,000 . .	165.2	130.2	107.6	98.5	140.0	129.7	113.5	99.2	94.7	100.5	90.6	93.8
25,000–100,000 . .	178.5	118.2	103.5	98.5	149.9	115.4	104.6	98.9	112.4	98.7	98.3	87.7
2,500– 25,000 . .	(ᶜ)	127.6	113.4	105.5	(ᶜ)	131.0	120.2	112.5	(ᶜ)	114.8	108.6	104.4
Rural { nonfarm . . / farm	} (ᶜ)	158.6	136.3 {	125.7 / 116.9	} (ᶜ)	176.3	158.5 {	143.1 / 144.3	} (ᶜ)	173.8	163.8 {	143.8 / 181.4
NATIVE WHITE POPULATION												
500,000+	. . . . . .	. . . . .	97.0	97.5	. . . . . .	. . . . .	97.0	91.4	. . . . . .	. . . . .	85.6	76.6
250,000–500,000 . .	119.8	110.2	103.7	94.2	138.0	105.9	111.2	97.1	148.4	91.9	94.2	86.4
100,000–250,000 . .	158.0	118.5	98.7	95.1	137.5	118.8	107.1	93.6	97.3	94.5	86.6	86.9
25,000–100,000 . .	152.0	108.2	94.9	93.9	137.9	106.6	96.1	92.6	118.9	96.9	91.0	80.9
2,500– 25,000 . .	(ᶜ)	115.9	105.2	100.9	(ᶜ)	121.5	76.5	106.8	(ᶜ)	112.2	102.6	98.5
Rural { nonfarm . . / farm	} (ᶜ)	137.9	122.6 {	117.5 / 111.9	} (ᶜ)	161.8	96.1 {	133.7 / 138.2	} (ᶜ)	171.1	160.1 {	137.8 / 177.8
FOREIGN-BORN WHITE POPULATION												
500,000+	. . . . . .	. . . . .	146.3	131.8	. . . . . .	. . . . .	136.8	127.2	. . . . . .	. . . . .	105.9	105.9
250,000–500,000 . .	146.0	163.2	154.8	127.5	130.8	139.9	143.2	128.0	128.8	110.4	116.6	111.7
100,000–250,000 . .	173.4	162.5	135.4	120.7	142.3	150.8	125.6	117.1	85.6	109.5	95.0	110.4
25,000–100,000 . .	174.0	146.1	134.6	126.9	142.9	132.4	127.2	120.4	105.2	101.5	115.0	106.9
2,500– 25,000 . .	(ᶜ)	172.6	148.7	137.7	(ᶜ)	156.1	143.3	135.2	(ᶜ)	119.7	122.5	121.8
Rural { nonfarm . . / farm	} (ᶜ)	236.8	188.9 {	180.5 / 147.2	} (ᶜ)	213.6	190.2 {	179.8 / 164.2	} (ᶜ)	178.8	171.0 {	160.0 / 189.7
NEGRO POPULATIONᵈ												
500,000+	. . . . . .	. . . . .	98.1	95.5	. . . . . .	. . . . .	108.8	99.4	. . . . . .	. . . . .	86.7	72.9
250,000–500,000 . .	. . . . . .	113.9	117.4	101.7	. . . . . .	119.8	136.0	121.6	. . . . . .	117.5	112.9	89.9
100,000–250,000 . .	. . . . . .	131.9	139.4	101.1	. . . . . .	129.6	130.8	129.4	. . . . . .	67.0	92.3	110.1
25,000–100,000 . .	. . . . . .	129.4	98.6	91.3	. . . . . .	125.4	125.1	105.9	. . . . . .	89.9	92.6	95.7
2,500– 25,000 . .	. . . . . .	123.4	116.7	113.2	. . . . . .	143.6	147.7	137.7	. . . . . .	124.5	142.2	132.9
Rural { nonfarm . . / farm	}	221.2	247.0 {	176.3 / 115.1	}	219.9	236.4 {	199.5 / 207.0	}	186.0	211.9 {	198.6 / 252.3

ᵃ Compiled from current census reports.

ᵇ Includes whites and Negroes only, except in 1890. See Note d.

ᶜ Sex ratios for age in 1890 cannot be computed separately for cities of 2,500 to 25,000 and for rural areas, the required data not having been published by the Bureau of the Census.

ᵈ Ratios are available for the colored population but not for Negroes in 1890.

TABLE 25.—PERCENTAGE DISTRIBUTION OF THE POPULATION 15 YEARS OF AGE AND OVER
BY MARITAL CONDITION, BY SEX, BY RACE AND NATIVITY, AND BY AGE,
1890–1930[a]

Nativity, age, and year	Male					Female				
	Total	Single	Married	Widowed	Divorced	Total	Single	Married	Widowed	Divorced
Native white of native parentage:										
15–19:										
1890	100.0	99.4	0.6	(b)	(b)	100.0	89.0	10.8	0.1	(b)
1900	100.0	98.7	1.2	(b)	(b)	100.0	87.4	12.2	0.2	0.1
1910	100.0	98.1	1.3	(b)	(b)	100.0	86.7	12.5	0.2	0.1
1920	100.0	97.5	2.3	(b)	(b)	100.0	86.3	13.3	0.2	0.1
1930	100.0	97.9	2.0	(b)	(b)	100.0	85.6	14.0	0.2	0.2
20–24:										
1890	100.0	79.4	20.2	0.2	0.1	100.0	48.4	50.3	0.9	0.2
1900	100.0	76.2	23.1	0.4	0.1	100.0	48.7	49.8	1.1	0.4
1910	100.0	72.5	26.5	0.4	0.2	100.0	46.6	51.8	0.9	0.5
1920	100.0	68.6	30.4	0.4	0.2	100.0	44.7	53.4	1.1	0.6
1930	100.0	68.1	30.9	0.3	0.4	100.0	43.6	54.4	0.7	1.1
25–29:										
1890	100.0	42.3	56.2	1.1	0.2	100.0	23.2	74.0	2.3	0.5
1900	100.0	42.4	55.8	1.2	0.3	100.0	25.2	71.8	2.3	0.6
1910	100.0	38.5	59.8	1.1	0.4	100.0	23.3	73.9	1.9	0.8
1920	100.0	35.7	62.4	1.1	0.6	100.0	22.7	74.0	2.2	1.0
1930	100.0	32.5	65.5	0.7	1.2	100.0	20.3	76.3	1.5	1.9
30–34:										
1890	100.0	23.7	74.0	1.9	0.3	100.0	14.7	80.8	3.8	0.6
1900	100.0	24.7	72.6	2.1	0.4	100.0	15.7	79.7	3.9	0.7
1910	100.0	22.7	74.7	1.8	0.6	100.0	14.9	80.9	3.2	0.9
1920	100.0	20.8	76.4	1.8	0.8	100.0	14.7	80.7	3.4	1.1
1930	100.0	17.9	79.3	1.2	1.5	100.0	12.8	82.5	2.6	2.0
35–44:										
1890	100.0	13.3	82.9	3.3	0.4	100.0	10.4	81.5	7.4	0.6
1900	100.0	14.8	80.8	3.6	0.6	100.0	10.9	80.8	7.4	0.7
1910	100.0	14.5	81.3	3.2	0.8	100.0	10.8	81.9	6.3	1.0
1920	100.0	13.9	82.0	2.9	1.0	100.0	10.9	81.6	6.2	1.2
1930	100.0	12.0	83.9	2.3	1.7	100.0	10.0	82.3	5.5	2.1
45–54:										
1890	100.0	8.0	85.6	5.7	0.5	100.0	8.1	75.0	16.2	0.6
1900	100.0	9.0	83.7	6.4	0.6	100.0	8.5	75.6	15.1	0.7
1910	100.0	9.8	82.8	6.2	0.9	100.0	8.5	76.7	13.8	0.9
1920	100.0	10.6	82.4	5.7	1.2	100.0	9.2	76.1	13.5	1.1
1930	100.0	9.9	83.3	4.8	1.9	100.0	8.8	76.9	12.4	1.8
55–64:										
1890	100.0	6.1	83.7	9.5	0.6	100.0	6.8	61.6	31.0	0.5
1900	100.0	6.7	81.4	11.1	0.6	100.0	7.8	62.1	29.5	0.5
1910	100.0	7.5	80.4	11.1	0.9	100.0	7.7	64.5	27.0	0.7
1920	100.0	8.8	79.1	10.9	1.1	100.0	8.4	63.1	27.4	0.9
1930	100.0	8.9	79.6	9.6	1.7	100.0	8.6	64.2	25.8	1.3

TABLE 25.—PERCENTAGE DISTRIBUTION OF THE POPULATION 15 YEARS OF AGE AND OVER BY MARITAL CONDITION, BY SEX, BY RACE AND NATIVITY, AND BY AGE, 1890–1930.ª—(Continued)

Nativity, age, and year	Male					Female				
	Total	Single	Married	Widowed	Divorced	Total	Single	Married	Widowed	Divorced
Native white of native parentage: (Continued)										
65+:										
1890	100.0	5.0	71.8	22.7	0.4	100.0	6.6	35.7	57.3	0.3
1900	100.0	5.1	68.8	25.3	0.5	100.0	7.0	34.2	58.3	0.3
1910	100.0	5.6	67.3	26.0	0.7	100.0	7.4	35.8	56.2	0.4
1920	100.0	6.7	66.1	26.1	0.8	100.0	7.9	35.0	56.4	0.4
1930	100.0	7.6	64.5	26.4	1.2	100.0	8.3	35.0	55.9	0.6
Native white of foreign or mixed parentage:										
15–19:										
1890	100.0	99.8	0.1	(b)	(b)	100.0	95.8	4.2	(b)	(b)
1900	100.0	99.6	0.3	(b)	(b)	100.0	94.9	5.0	0.1	(b)
1910	100.0	99.1	0.3	(b)	(b)	100.0	94.4	5.0	(b)	(b)
1920	100.0	99.1	0.8	(b)	(b)	100.0	93.6	6.2	0.1	(b)
1930	100.0	99.3	0.5	(b)	(b)	100.0	94.0	5.7	(b)	(b)
20–24:										
1890	100.0	89.0	10.8	0.1	(b)	100.0	65.4	33.9	0.5	0.1
1900	100.0	86.8	12.7	0.2	(b)	100.0	64.8	34.3	0.6	0.2
1910	100.0	84.2	15.2	0.2	0.1	100.0	62.8	36.2	0.4	0.3
1920	100.0	81.3	18.1	0.2	0.1	100.0	59.2	39.6	0.7	0.4
1930	100.0	82.1	17.2	(b)	0.2	100.0	58.5	40.3	0.3	0.6
25–29:										
1890	100.0	55.2	43.9	0.7	0.1	100.0	34.9	62.7	2.0	0.3
1900	100.0	57.2	41.7	0.8	0.2	100.0	37.7	60.0	1.8	0.4
1910	100.0	52.7	46.1	0.7	0.3	100.0	36.0	61.8	1.4	0.6
1920	100.0	48.4	50.2	0.8	0.4	100.0	32.4	65.0	1.8	0.7
1930	100.0	46.0	52.7	0.4	0.7	100.0	29.1	68.5	1.0	1.3
30–34:										
1890	100.0	31.9	66.2	1.6	0.2	100.0	20.3	75.2	4.0	0.4
1900	100.0	35.9	62.0	1.7	0.3	100.0	23.6	72.1	3.7	0.5
1910	100.0	34.0	64.0	1.4	0.5	100.0	24.4	71.8	3.0	0.7
1920	100.0	30.1	67.6	1.6	0.7	100.0	22.0	74.0	3.0	0.9
1930	100.0	26.3	71.6	0.9	1.2	100.0	18.2	78.0	2.1	1.7
35–44:										
1890	100.0	19.3	77.2	3.0	0.4	100.0	12.9	78.3	8.3	0.5
1900	100.0	21.9	74.3	3.2	0.4	100.0	16.0	75.4	7.9	0.6
1910	100.0	22.7	73.6	2.8	0.7	100.0	17.8	74.7	6.5	0.8
1920	100.0	21.6	74.8	2.6	0.9	100.0	18.0	74.7	6.2	1.0
1930	100.0	18.1	78.4	1.9	1.5	100.0	14.9	78.4	4.9	1.8
45–54:										
1890	100.0	11.8	81.5	6.1	0.5	100.0	8.7	72.3	18.4	0.6
1900	100.0	14.0	79.0	6.3	0.6	100.0	10.7	71.5	17.1	0.6
1910	100.0	15.1	78.0	6.0	0.8	100.0	13.2	70.9	15.1	0.8
1920	100.0	17.1	76.5	5.3	1.0	100.0	15.3	69.6	14.1	0.9
1930	100.0	16.1	77.6	4.5	1.7	100.0	14.8	71.5	12.1	1.5

APPENDIX TABLES

Table 25.—Percentage Distribution of the Population 15 Years of Age and over by Marital Condition, by Sex, by Race and Nativity, and by Age, 1890–1930.ᵃ—(Continued)

Nativity, age, and year	Male					Female				
	Total	Single	Married	Widowed	Divorced	Total	Single	Married	Widowed	Divorced

Native white of foreign or mixed parentage: (Continued)

55–64:
1890	100.0	9.0	80.0	10.4	0.5	100.0	8.0	58.2	33.3	0.5
1900	100.0	10.6	76.6	11.9	0.8	100.0	8.5	58.9	32.0	0.6
1910	100.0	11.8	76.1	11.1	0.9	100.0	10.1	59.9	29.3	0.7
1920	100.0	13.5	74.8	10.7	1.0	100.0	12.9	57.5	28.7	0.7
1930	100.0	14.7	74.3	9.4	1.5	100.0	14.4	58.8	25.7	1.1

65+:
1890	100.0	6.3	69.1	24.0	0.5	100.0	7.6	31.9	60.1	0.3
1900	100.0	7.7	65.4	26.1	0.7	100.0	7.9	32.3	59.4	0.3
1910	100.0	8.9	64.8	25.3	0.8	100.0	8.6	35.0	55.9	0.4
1920	100.0	10.6	64.2	24.2	0.9	100.0	10.1	34.2	55.1	0.4
1930	100.0	12.1	62.9	23.7	1.2	100.0	12.9	34.5	51.9	0.5

Foreign-born white:

15–19:
1890	100.0	99.7	0.3	(ᵇ)	(ᵇ)	100.0	91.6	8.3	0.1	(ᵇ)
1900	100.0	99.1	0.7	(ᵇ)	(ᵇ)	100.0	88.8	11.0	0.1	(ᵇ)
1910	100.0	98.6	0.8	(ᵇ)	(ᵇ)	100.0	86.3	13.1	0.1	(ᵇ)
1920	100.0	98.5	1.3	(ᵇ)	(ᵇ)	100.0	85.3	14.3	0.2	0.1
1930	100.0	99.0	0.7	(ᵇ)	(ᵇ)	100.0	90.1	9.5	0.1	0.1

20–24:
1890	100.0	84.7	14.9	0.1	(ᵇ)	100.0	54.7	44.6	0.6	0.1
1900	100.0	82.4	17.0	0.2	(ᵇ)	100.0	53.3	45.8	0.6	0.1
1910	100.0	80.3	19.0	0.2	(ᵇ)	100.0	44.9	54.3	0.5	0.1
1920	100.0	75.5	23.7	0.3	0.1	100.0	37.1	61.6	1.0	0.2
1930	100.0	81.2	18.1	0.1	0.2	100.0	51.4	47.5	0.3	0.5

25–29:
1890	100.0	52.3	46.9	0.6	0.1	100.0	25.5	72.5	1.7	0.2
1900	100.0	50.2	48.8	0.6	0.1	100.0	25.4	72.6	1.7	0.2
1910	100.0	49.1	49.9	0.5	0.1	100.0	22.3	75.9	1.4	0.3
1920	100.0	45.3	53.3	0.8	0.2	100.0	16.0	81.6	1.9	0.4
1930	100.0	47.4	51.5	0.4	0.5	100.0	22.1	75.9	1.0	0.9

30–34:
1890	100.0	30.0	68.5	1.2	0.1	100.0	13.1	83.1	3.5	0.2
1900	100.0	29.4	68.9	1.3	0.2	100.0	13.1	83.2	3.4	0.3
1910	100.0	28.5	69.9	1.1	0.2	100.0	13.2	83.5	2.8	0.4
1920	100.0	27.5	70.5	1.4	0.3	100.0	9.8	86.6	3.1	0.5
1930	100.0	26.0	72.3	0.8	0.7	100.0	10.0	86.9	2.0	1.0

35–44:
1890	100.0	17.6	79.3	2.7	0.2	100.0	8.2	82.8	8.6	0.3
1900	100.0	18.0	78.8	2.7	0.2	100.0	8.3	83.8	7.4	0.3
1910	100.0	17.3	79.7	2.4	0.4	100.0	8.6	84.1	6.8	0.5
1920	100.0	17.5	79.3	2.5	0.5	100.0	8.2	84.8	6.3	0.6
1930	100.0	16.3	80.7	1.9	1.0	100.0	6.4	87.2	5.3	1.1

[395]

TABLE 25.—PERCENTAGE DISTRIBUTION OF THE POPULATION 15 YEARS OF AGE AND OVER
BY MARITAL CONDITION, BY SEX, BY RACE AND NATIVITY, AND BY AGE,
1890–1930.ᵃ—(*Continued*)

Nativity, age, and year	Male					Female				
	Total	Single	Married	Widowed	Divorced	Total	Single	Married	Widowed	Divorced
Foreign born white: (*Continued*)										
45–54:										
1890	100.0	10.7	83.0	5.9	0.3	100.0	5.3	75.0	19.3	0.3
1900	100.0	11.5	81.6	6.4	0.4	100.0	6.0	74.7	18.9	0.4
1910	100.0	11.6	82.1	5.6	0.5	100.0	6.1	77.4	15.9	0.5
1920	100.0	12.2	81.5	5.4	0.6	100.0	6.8	76.8	15.7	0.6
1930	100.0	12.1	82.0	4.7	1.1	100.0	6.3	79.3	13.3	1.0
55–64:										
1890	100.0	7.8	80.4	11.2	0.4	100.0	4.1	60.8	34.7	0.3
1900	100.0	8.7	78.1	12.5	0.5	100.0	4.7	60.1	34.7	0.4
1910	100.0	9.1	78.2	11.9	0.6	100.0	5.2	61.1	33.1	0.5
1920	100.0	10.0	78.2	10.9	0.7	100.0	5.6	62.8	30.9	0.5
1930	100.0	10.2	78.3	10.3	1.1	100.0	6.0	63.9	29.2	0.8
65+:										
1890	100.0	6.6	67.2	25.6	0.4	100.0	3.7	37.1	58.7	0.2
1900	100.0	6.7	63.8	28.8	0.4	100.0	4.1	36.0	59.5	0.2
1910	100.0	7.1	62.5	29.6	0.5	100.0	4.5	34.7	60.4	0.3
1920	100.0	7.8	62.2	29.2	0.6	100.0	4.9	32.9	61.6	0.3
1930	100.0	8.5	62.8	27.6	0.9	100.0	5.2	36.1	58.1	0.4
Negro:										
15–19:										
1890	100.0	99.0	0.9	(ᵇ)	(ᵇ)	100.0	84.9	14.4	0.5	0.1
1900	100.0	97.9	1.7	0.1	(ᵇ)	100.0	83.2	15.6	0.9	0.1
1910	100.0	96.9	2.2	0.1	(ᵇ)	100.0	81.2	17.0	0.9	0.2
1920	100.0	95.8	3.9	0.1	(ᵇ)	100.0	78.7	20.0	0.9	0.3
1930	100.0	96.0	3.7	0.1	0.1	100.0	77.9	20.5	0.9	0.6
20–24:										
1890	100.0	65.7	33.4	0.7	0.1	100.0	38.0	57.3	4.0	0.4
1900	100.0	64.5	33.6	1.1	0.2	100.0	39.8	54.6	4.7	0.8
1910	100.0	59.7	37.8	1.5	0.4	100.0	34.9	59.0	4.7	1.1
1920	100.0	54.9	43.0	1.2	0.5	100.0	31.6	62.8	4.1	1.3
1930	100.0	54.7	42.8	1.3	0.9	100.0	33.1	60.4	4.1	2.3
25–29:										
1890	100.0	30.1	67.3	2.1	0.3	100.0	17.5	73.7	7.8	0.8
1900	100.0	33.2	63.1	2.8	0.5	100.0	20.6	69.4	8.6	1.2
1910	100.0	29.7	65.9	3.2	0.8	100.0	17.1	73.2	7.9	1.5
1920	100.0	29.1	67.3	2.4	0.9	100.0	15.7	75.4	7.0	1.7
1930	100.0	27.7	67.9	2.5	1.6	100.0	15.9	73.5	7.5	3.1
30–34:										
1890	100.0	18.5	77.7	3.3	0.4	100.0	11.6	76.4	11.0	0.9
1900	100.0	21.1	73.6	4.3	0.6	100.0	12.9	73.2	12.4	1.4
1910	100.0	19.2	75.1	4.5	0.9	100.0	11.0	76.3	11.0	1.6
1920	100.0	20.0	75.2	3.5	1.1	100.0	10.5	77.6	9.9	1.8
1930	100.0	19.0	75.1	3.7	2.0	100.0	9.9	76.0	10.8	3.2

APPENDIX TABLES

TABLE 25.—PERCENTAGE DISTRIBUTION OF THE POPULATION 15 YEARS OF AGE AND OVER BY MARITAL CONDITION, BY SEX, BY RACE AND NATIVITY, AND BY AGE, 1890–1930.ᵃ—(Continued)

Nativity, age, and year	Male					Female				
	Total	Single	Married	Widowed	Divorced	Total	Single	Married	Widowed	Divorced
Negro: (Continued)										
35–44:										
1890	100.0	11.3	82.9	5.2	0.4	100.0	7.3	74.6	17.0	0.8
1900	100.0	13.2	79.0	6.8	0.7	100.0	8.0	72.3	18.3	1.2
1910	100.0	12.2	80.0	6.6	1.0	100.0	7.1	74.4	16.9	1.5
1920	100.0	13.2	80.1	5.4	1.1	100.0	7.0	75.4	15.8	1.7
1930	100.0	13.0	78.8	5.9	2.1	100.0	6.4	73.5	17.2	2.8
45–54:										
1890	100.0	6.4	85.1	8.0	0.4	100.0	4.8	66.3	28.2	0.5
1900	100.0	7.2	81.4	10.5	0.7	100.0	5.1	65.3	28.6	0.8
1910	100.0	6.8	81.4	10.6	0.9	100.0	4.7	66.4	27.7	1.1
1920	100.0	7.8	82.0	8.9	1.1	100.0	4.9	66.2	27.4	1.4
1930	100.0	8.1	79.9	10.0	1.8	100.0	4.6	64.7	28.7	2.0
55–64:										
1890	100.0	5.1	83.2	11.3	0.3	100.0	4.1	51.6	43.7	0.3
1900	100.0	5.3	78.6	15.3	0.6	100.0	4.1	51.9	43.2	0.5
1910	100.0	5.0	78.1	15.9	0.8	100.0	3.9	52.8	42.4	0.7
1920	100.0	5.8	77.7	15.4	1.0	100.0	4.2	50.7	43.9	1.0
1930	100.0	6.0	76.9	15.4	1.5	100.0	4.0	50.0	44.5	1.3
65+:										
1890	100.0	5.4	74.4	19.6	0.3	100.0	4.3	29.0	66.1	0.2
1900	100.0	4.6	69.6	25.1	0.4	100.0	4.3	28.9	66.0	0.3
1910	100.0	4.1	67.3	27.5	0.7	100.0	3.7	29.9	65.6	0.4
1920	100.0	4.9	65.5	28.6	0.7	100.0	4.1	27.2	67.7	0.5
1930	100.0	5.0	62.7	30.9	1.1	100.0	3.8	26.1	69.3	0.6

ᵃ For 1890 from *Eleventh Census of the United States: 1890*, Vol. I, Pt. 1, pp. 830–831; 1900 from *Twelfth Census of the United States: 1900*, Vol. II, Pt. 2, pp. 254–255; 1910 from *Thirteenth Census of the United States: 1910*, Vol. I, pp. 517–519; 1920 from *Fourteenth Census of the United States: 1920*, Vol. II, pp. 388–390; 1930 from *Fifteenth Census of the United States: 1930*, Vol. II, p. 844.

ᵇ Less than one-tenth of 1 per cent.

TABLE 26.—PERCENTAGE DISTRIBUTION OF THE POPULATION 15 YEARS OF AGE AND OVER BY MARITAL CONDITION, BY SEX, BY AGE, AND BY REGIONS, 1890–1930[a]

Age and year	Male					Female				
	Total	Single	Married	Widowed	Divorced	Total	Single	Married	Widowed	Divorced
Northeast:										
All ages:										
1890	100.0	40.5	54.8	4.3	0.2	100.0	34.4	53.5	11.8	0.2
1900	100.0	39.5	55.1	4.8	0.2	100.0	33.7	54.0	11.8	0.3
1910	100.0	38.9	55.9	4.5	0.3	100.0	33.0	55.5	11.0	0.4
1920	100.0	35.5	59.0	4.8	0.4	100.0	30.4	57.5	11.5	0.4
1930	100.0	35.6	59.1	4.5	0.6	100.0	30.0	58.1	11.0	0.8
15–19:										
1890	100.0	99.7	0.3	(b)	(b)	100.0	94.5	5.4	(b)	(b)
1900	100.0	99.2	0.6	(b)	(b)	100.0	93.0	6.8	0.1	(b)
1910	100.0	99.0	0.7	(b)	(b)	100.0	92.9	6.7	0.1	(b)
1920	100.0	98.7	1.2	(b)	(b)	100.0	92.3	7.5	0.1	(b)
1930	100.0	98.9	0.8	(b)	(b)	100.0	92.7	7.0	(b)	(b)
20–24:										
1890	100.0	83.1	16.6	0.2	(b)	100.0	61.9	37.4	0.6	0.1
1900	100.0	81.4	18.1	0.2	(b)	100.0	61.4	37.7	0.6	0.1
1910	100.0	79.1	20.3	0.2	0.1	100.0	57.5	41.6	0.5	0.2
1920	100.0	76.3	23.1	0.3	0.1	100.0	54.4	44.4	0.8	0.2
1930	100.0	78.7	20.6	0.1	0.1	100.0	56.9	42.0	0.4	0.4
25–29:										
1890	100.0	47.9	51.1	0.8	0.1	100.0	33.5	64.2	2.0	0.2
1900	100.0	49.1	49.7	0.8	0.1	100.0	34.8	62.9	1.9	0.3
1910	100.0	45.8	53.1	0.7	0.2	100.0	32.0	66.0	1.5	0.4
1920[c]	100.0	34.5	63.6	1.3	0.3	100.0	24.2	72.6	2.6	0.5
1930	100.0	43.5	55.4	0.5	0.4	100.0	28.5	69.3	1.2	0.9
30–34:										
1890	100.0	27.5	70.6	1.6	0.3	100.0	20.7	75.0	3.9	0.3
1900	100.0	29.1	68.8	1.6	0.2	100.0	21.5	74.2	3.8	0.4
1910	100.0	27.5	70.7	1.4	0.3	100.0	21.4	74.9	3.2	0.5
1920[d]										
1930	100.0	24.3	73.9	1.0	0.7	100.0	17.0	79.3	2.4	1.1
35–44:										
1890	100.0	16.1	80.4	3.1	0.3	100.0	13.7	77.2	8.5	0.4
1900	100.0	18.0	78.3	3.2	0.3	100.0	15.2	76.2	8.0	0.5
1910	100.0	17.5	79.1	2.8	0.4	100.0	15.5	76.8	7.0	0.6
1920	100.0	17.2	79.3	2.7	0.5	100.0	15.2	77.3	6.7	0.7
1930	100.0	15.6	81.3	2.1	0.9	100.0	13.0	80.0	5.7	1.2
45–54:										
1890	100.0	9.4	84.1	6.0	0.3	100.0	9.9	71.6	18.0	0.4
1900	100.0	11.2	81.7	6.6	0.4	100.0	11.1	70.6	17.7	0.5
1910	100.0	11.7	81.4	6.2	0.5	100.0	12.1	71.5	15.8	0.6
1920	100.0	12.9	80.6	5.7	0.6	100.0	13.1	70.9	15.3	0.6
1930	100.0	12.3	81.7	5.0	0.9	100.0	12.3	73.0	13.6	1.0
55–64:										
1890	100.0	6.8	82.2	10.5	0.3	100.0	8.1	59.0	32.5	0.3
1900	100.0	8.0	79.0	12.5	0.4	100.0	9.3	57.7	32.5	0.3
1910	100.0	9.0	78.1	12.2	0.6	100.0	10.1	58.5	30.9	0.4
1920	100.0	10.3	77.3	11.6	0.6	100.0	11.7	57.8	29.9	0.5
1930	100.0	10.7	77.6	10.6	0.9	100.0	12.2	59.4	27.6	0.7

TABLE 26.—PERCENTAGE DISTRIBUTION OF THE POPULATION 15 YEARS OF AGE AND OVER BY MARITAL CONDITION, BY SEX, BY AGE AND BY REGIONS, 1890–1930.[a]—(*Continued*)

Age and year	Male					Female				
	Total	Single	Married	Widowed	Divorced	Total	Single	Married	Widowed	Divorced
Northeast: (*Continued*)										
65+:										
1890	100.0	5.8	69.0	24.7	0.2	100.0	7.7	34.2	57.8	0.2
1900	100.0	5.8	64.9	28.7	0.3	100.0	8.4	32.1	59.1	0.2
1910	100.0	6.6	63.2	29.7	0.4	100.0	9.0	32.0	58.6	0.2
1920	100.0	8.0	62.0	29.4	0.4	100.0	10.2	30.8	58.5	0.2
1930	100.0	8.9	62.0	28.3	0.6	100.0	11.6	32.6	55.3	0.3
Age unknown:										
1890	100.0	48.2	28.3	5.1	0.3	100.0	41.2	37.2	15.9	0.3
1900	100.0	26.4	23.6	3.3	0.2	100.0	28.7	31.7	13.2	0.4
1910	100.0	28.1	24.2	4.3	0.4	100.0	34.6	34.0	15.0	0.6
1920	100.0	32.5	30.7	4.7	0.5	100.0	33.0	39.9	13.4	0.5
1930	100.0	34.8	33.4	5.2	0.7	100.0	35.3	35.6	12.6	0.9
North Center:										
All ages:										
1890	100.0	41.5	54.3	3.8	0.3	100.0	30.6	59.7	9.3	0.5
1900	100.0	40.0	54.8	4.4	0.4	100.0	30.2	59.2	9.9	0.6
1910	100.0	38.6	55.8	4.4	0.6	100.0	29.3	60.0	9.7	0.7
1920	100.0	35.2	59.1	4.7	0.8	100.0	26.7	61.8	10.4	0.9
1930	100.0	33.6	60.3	4.7	1.3	100.0	25.5	62.6	10.4	1.4
15–19:										
1890	100.0	99.7	0.2	(b)	(b)	100.0	92.0	7.9	0.1	(b)
1900	100.0	99.3	0.6	(b)	(b)	100.0	90.9	8.9	0.1	0.1
1910	100.0	98.6	0.7	(b)	(b)	100.0	90.5	8.7	0.1	0.1
1920	100.0	98.3	1.5	(b)	(b)	100.0	89.7	9.9	0.1	0.1
1930	100.0	98.7	1.2	(b)	(b)	100.0	89.3	10.4	0.1	0.2
20–24:										
1890	100.0	84.6	15.0	0.2	0.1	100.0	52.4	46.6	0.7	0.3
1900	100.0	81.6	17.9	0.2	0.1	100.0	53.3	45.4	0.8	0.4
1910	100.0	78.4	20.7	0.2	0.1	100.0	51.6	47.0	0.6	0.5
1920	100.0	73.9	25.3	0.3	0.2	100.0	48.1	50.2	0.9	0.6
1930	100.0	73.3	25.9	0.2	0.4	100.0	47.4	50.8	0.6	1.1
25–29:										
1890	100.0	47.6	51.2	0.9	0.2	100.0	23.0	74.5	1.9	0.5
1900	100.0	48.5	50.1	0.9	0.3	100.0	26.7	70.7	1.9	0.6
1910	100.0	44.7	53.8	0.8	0.4	100.0	25.3	72.2	1.6	0.8
1920[c]	100.0	33.4	64.5	1.2	0.7	100.0	19.3	77.2	2.4	1.0
1930	100.0	37.4	60.7	0.6	1.1	100.0	21.3	75.4	1.3	1.9
30–34:										
1890	100.0	25.3	72.6	1.7	0.3	100.0	12.3	83.7	3.3	0.6
1900	100.0	28.1	69.6	1.8	0.4	100.0	15.1	80.7	3.4	0.7
1910	100.0	26.4	71.2	1.5	0.6	100.0	15.6	80.6	2.8	1.0
1920[d]										
1930	100.0	21.4	75.8	1.1	1.6	100.0	12.9	82.6	2.4	2.1
35–44:										
1890	100.0	13.5	82.9	3.0	0.4	100.0	7.1	85.4	6.7	0.7
1900	100.0	16.1	80.0	3.2	0.6	100.0	9.3	83.2	6.7	0.7
1910	100.0	16.8	79.4	2.8	0.8	100.0	10.5	82.6	5.8	1.0
1920	100.0	16.8	79.3	2.7	1.0	100.0	10.9	82.2	5.6	1.3
1930	100.0	14.9	81.0	2.2	1.8	100.0	9.8	83.1	5.0	2.0

TABLE 26.—PERCENTAGE DISTRIBUTION OF THE POPULATION 15 YEARS OF AGE AND OVER BY MARITAL CONDITION, BY SEX, BY AGE AND BY REGIONS, 1890–1930.[a]—(*Continued*)

Age and year	Male					Female				
	Total	Single	Married	Widowed	Divorced	Total	Single	Married	Widowed	Divorced
North Center: (*Continued*)										
45–54:										
1890	100.0	7.6	86.2	5.6	0.6	100.0	4.5	79.8	14.9	0.8
1900	100.0	9.3	83.7	6.1	0.7	100.0	5.7	78.9	14.6	0.8
1910	100.0	10.8	82.3	5.7	1.0	100.0	7.2	78.7	13.1	1.0
1920	100.0	12.6	80.7	5.3	1.2	100.0	8.7	77.3	12.8	1.2
1930	100.0	12.2	80.9	4.8	2.0	100.0	8.7	78.1	11.4	1.8
55–64:										
1890	100.0	5.2	84.3	9.8	0.6	100.0	3.3	66.6	29.4	0.7
1900	100.0	6.4	81.8	10.9	0.8	100.0	4.2	66.3	28.7	0.7
1910	100.0	7.6	80.5	10.7	1.0	100.0	5.1	67.1	26.8	0.8
1920	100.0	9.6	78.7	10.3	1.2	100.0	6.9	65.5	26.5	0.9
1930	100.0	10.7	77.8	9.6	1.8	100.0	8.0	65.8	24.8	1.3
65+:										
1890	100.0	4.3	71.6	23.3	0.6	100.0	3.0	40.2	56.2	0.4
1900	100.0	4.5	68.7	25.9	0.6	100.0	3.4	38.9	57.1	0.4
1910	100.0	5.3	67.1	26.4	0.8	100.0	4.0	39.0	56.3	0.4
1920	100.0	6.7	65.8	26.4	0.9	100.0	5.0	37.1	57.2	0.5
1930	100.0	8.2	64.1	26.3	1.2	100.0	6.5	37.6	55.1	0.6
Age unknown:										
1890	100.0	50.0	24.8	4.8	0.6	100.0	38.2	41.6	14.9	0.8
1900	100.0	27.7	24.4	3.6	0.4	100.0	23.1	37.1	14.0	0.7
1910	100.0	25.2	17.8	3.6	0.6	100.0	26.9	35.1	13.1	0.9
1920	100.0	34.0	32.1	5.3	1.1	100.0	29.7	41.4	13.1	1.2
1930	100.0	34.5	28.4	5.6	2.3	100.0	32.6	35.7	13.7	1.7
South:										
All ages:										
1890	100.0	40.2	55.5	3.9	0.2	100.0	31.0	56.2	12.4	0.3
1900	100.0	39.2	55.5	4.7	0.3	100.0	30.3	56.8	12.3	0.5
1910	100.0	36.2	58.1	4.8	0.4	100.0	27.6	60.3	11.3	0.6
1920	100.0	33.7	60.7	4.8	0.5	100.0	26.0	61.5	11.5	0.8
1930	100.0	32.6	61.6	4.7	1.0	100.0	25.0	61.8	11.7	1.4
15–19:										
1890	100.0	99.0	1.0	(b)	(b)	100.0	85.6	14.0	0.3	(b)
1900	100.0	98.0	1.8	(b)	(b)	100.0	83.5	15.8	0.5	0.1
1910	100.0	97.2	2.1	(b)	(b)	100.0	81.6	17.3	0.5	0.1
1920	100.0	96.4	3.3	0.1	(b)	100.0	80.9	18.3	0.5	0.2
1930	100.0	96.7	3.1	0.1	(b)	100.0	80.2	18.9	0.5	0.4
20–24:										
1890	100.0	71.7	27.7	0.4	0.1	100.0	42.0	55.3	2.3	0.3
1900	100.0	69.0	29.7	0.7	0.1	100.0	42.0	54.7	2.7	0.5
1910	100.0	65.1	33.2	0.9	0.2	100.0	37.7	58.8	2.5	0.6
1920	100.0	61.6	36.9	0.8	0.3	100.0	36.5	60.2	2.4	0.8
1930	100.0	60.9	37.6	0.7	0.6	100.0	37.0	59.3	2.0	1.6
25–29:										
1890	100.0	34.9	63.2	1.5	0.2	100.0	20.0	74.7	4.8	0.5
1900	100.0	35.7	61.8	1.9	0.3	100.0	21.5	72.7	5.0	0.7
1910	100.0	32.2	65.1	1.9	0.5	100.0	18.3	76.3	4.3	0.9
1920[c]	100.0	25.8	71.4	2.0	0.6	100.0	15.1	79.0	4.7	1.0
1930	100.0	28.2	69.1	1.4	1.2	100.0	17.0	77.2	3.7	2.1

TABLE 26.—PERCENTAGE DISTRIBUTION OF THE POPULATION 15 YEARS OF AGE AND OVER BY MARITAL CONDITION, BY SEX, BY AGE AND BY REGIONS, 1890–1930.[a]—(Continued)

Age and year	Male					Female				
	Total	Single	Married	Widowed	Divorced	Total	Single	Married	Widowed	Divorced
South: (Continued)										
30–34										
1890	100.0	20.0	77.3	2.4	0.2	100.0	13.3	79.4	6.6	0.5
1900	100.0	20.7	75.8	2.9	0.3	100.0	13.5	78.5	7.1	0.7
1910	100.0	18.8	77.7	2.7	0.5	100.0	11.9	81.2	6.0	0.9
1920[d]										
1930	100.0	15.9	80.6	2.0	1.4	100.0	10.4	82.2	5.3	2.0
35–44:										
1890	100.0	11.3	84.4	3.9	0.2	100.0	9.4	78.3	11.7	0.5
1900	100.0	12.3	82.5	4.6	0.4	100.0	9.3	78.1	11.8	0.7
1910	100.0	11.6	83.4	4.3	0.6	100.0	8.4	80.5	10.1	0.8
1920	100.0	11.5	83.9	3.7	0.7	100.0	8.5	80.9	9.5	1.0
1930	100.0	10.3	84.9	3.3	1.4	100.0	7.7	81.0	9.4	1.8
45–54:										
1890	100.0	7.0	86.0	6.6	0.3	100.0	7.3	69.1	23.1	0.4
1900	100.0	7.2	84.4	7.8	0.4	100.0	7.3	71.2	20.8	0.5
1910	100.0	7.4	84.3	7.6	0.6	100.0	6.7	73.4	19.0	0.7
1920	100.0	7.8	84.6	6.6	0.7	100.0	7.1	73.6	18.3	0.8
1930	100.0	7.4	85.0	6.2	1.3	100.0	6.6	74.2	17.7	1.4
55–64:										
1890	100.0	5.6	83.7	10.3	0.3	100.0	6.3	53.5	39.7	0.3
1900	100.0	5.7	81.1	12.6	0.4	100.0	7.0	55.9	36.5	0.4
1910	100.0	5.7	81.2	12.4	0.5	100.0	6.5	60.1	32.7	0.5
1920	100.0	6.5	80.7	12.0	0.7	100.0	6.9	59.5	32.9	0.6
1930	100.0	6.4	81.7	10.6	1.1	100.0	6.7	60.6	31.7	0.9
65+										
1890	100.0	5.3	72.8	21.4	0.2	100.0	6.3	30.4	62.9	0.2
1900	100.0	4.8	69.8	24.8	0.3	100.0	6.6	29.9	62.9	0.2
1910	100.0	4.8	68.6	25.9	0.5	100.0	6.7	33.0	59.6	0.3
1920	100.0	5.3	68.0	25.9	0.5	100.0	6.9	33.2	59.1	0.3
1930	100.0	5.7	66.9	26.4	0.8	100.0	6.8	33.0	59.5	0.4
Age unknown:										
1890	100.0	39.0	37.7	4.2	0.3	100.0	31.0	44.4	20.2	0.5
1900	100.0	29.8	40.8	4.5	0.3	100.0	23.8	44.9	18.7	0.8
1910	100.0	27.3	39.0	6.1	0.5	100.0	23.7	43.2	20.9	1.0
1920	100.0	28.6	38.7	4.9	0.8	100.0	25.8	42.7	18.2	1.1
1930	100.0	26.2	39.3	5.4	1.1	100.0	25.5	36.9	16.9	1.6
West:										
All ages:										
1890	100.0	54.4	40.8	3.4	0.5	100.0	28.5	61.3	9.4	0.7
1900	100.0	48.3	45.6	4.4	0.6	100.0	28.0	60.4	10.5	0.9
1910	100.0	46.2	47.7	4.0	0.9	100.0	26.6	62.0	10.0	1.2
1920	100.0	38.1	55.2	4.7	1.4	100.0	23.5	63.4	11.3	1.6
1930	100.0	35.6	57.3	4.5	2.3	100.0	22.6	63.0	11.5	2.7
15–19:										
1890	100.0	99.6	0.3	(b)	(b)	100.0	88.1	11.6	0.1	(b)
1900	100.0	99.2	0.6	(b)	(b)	100.0	88.4	11.3	0.1	0.1
1910	100.0	98.7	0.7	(b)	(b)	100.0	88.1	11.1	0.1	0.1
1920	100.0	98.5	1.3	(b)	(b)	100.0	86.9	12.7	0.2	0.2
1930	100.0	98.6	1.1	(b)	(b)	100.0	86.9	12.6	0.1	0.3

TABLE 26.—PERCENTAGE DISTRIBUTION OF THE POPULATION 15 YEARS OF AGE AND OVER BY MARITAL CONDITION, BY SEX, BY AGE AND BY REGIONS, 1890–1930.ᵃ—(*Continued*)

Age and year	Male					Female				
	Total	Single	Married	Widowed	Divorced	Total	Single	Married	Widowed	Divorced
West: (*Continued*)										
20–24:										
1890.....................	100.0	89.3	10.0	0.2	(ᵇ)	100.0	46.9	51.5	1.0	0.4
1900.....................	100.0	86.1	13.0	0.2	0.1	100.0	49.9	48.2	1.1	0.6
1910.....................	100.0	82.9	16.0	0.2	0.2	100.0	45.8	52.3	0.8	0.7
1920.....................	100.0	75.9	23.0	0.3	0.3	100.0	42.1	55.4	1.2	1.1
1930.....................	100.0	74.6	24.2	0.2	0.6	100.0	41.9	55.2	0.7	2.0
25–29:										
1890.....................	100.0	68.0	30.6	0.6	0.2	100.0	21.2	75.3	2.6	0.7
1900.....................	100.0	62.1	36.2	0.8	0.3	100.0	24.9	71.4	2.6	1.0
1910.....................	100.0	57.9	40.2	0.7	0.5	100.0	23.0	73.7	1.9	1.3
1920ᶜ....................	100.0	38.6	58.5	1.3	1.1	100.0	16.5	78.6	3.0	1.9
1930.....................	100.0	40.9	56.4	0.6	1.9	100.0	18.1	76.9	1.6	3.3
30–34:										
1890.....................	100.0	50.4	47.2	1.4	0.3	100.0	11.0	83.5	4.5	0.9
1900.....................	100.0	43.9	53.4	1.6	0.5	100.0	13.3	81.0	4.3	.1.2
1910.....................	100.0	40.3	56.7	1.4	0.8	100.0	14.0	81.1	3.4	1.5
1920ᵈ....................										
1930.....................	100.0	25.2	70.7	1.1	2.7	100.0	10.9	82.7	2.7	3.6
35–44:										
1890.....................	100.0	36.3	59.4	2.9	0.6	100.0	6.3	83.5	9.1	1.0
1900.....................	100.0	32.3	63.3	3.3	0.8	100.0	7.8	82.3	8.5	1.3
1910.....................	100.0	27.9	67.2	3.0	1.3	100.0	9.1	82.0	7.1	1.7
1920.....................	100.0	23.1	72.0	2.8	1.8	100.0	9.4	81.5	6.8	2.2
1930.....................	100.0	18.7	75.8	2.3	3.1	100.0	8.2	82.0	6.0	3.7
45–54:										
1890.....................	100.0	25.5	66.6	6.3	0.9	100.0	4.1	75.9	18.9	1.0
1900.....................	100.0	24.2	67.7	6.7	1.1	100.0	4.7	75.7	18.3	1.2
1910.....................	100.0	20.7	71.1	6.1	1.7	100.0	6.0	76.4	16.0	1.6
1920.....................	100.0	18.8	73.0	5.7	2.2	100.0	7.7	74.6	15.4	2.2
1930.....................	100.0	16.3	75.3	4.9	3.4	100.0	7.4	75.3	13.9	3.4
55–64:										
1890.....................	100.0	21.7	65.8	10.8	1.2	100.0	3.3	61.7	34.0	0.9
1900.....................	100.0	20.3	66.0	12.1	1.3	100.0	3.6	61.6	33.8	0.9
1910.....................	100.0	17.7	68.8	11.3	1.7	100.0	4.3	62.5	31.9	1.2
1920.....................	100.0	16.8	69.9	10.8	2.2	100.0	6.0	61.1	31.1	1.7
1930.....................	100.0	15.4	71.3	9.8	3.3	100.0	7.1	61.2	29.0	2.6
65+:										
1890.....................	100.0	17.1	58.3	23.0	1.1	100.0	3.0	37.2	58.9	0.6
1900.....................	100.0	16.7	57.5	24.2	1.2	100.0	3.2	37.0	59.0	0.6
1910.....................	100.0	13.8	58.3	25.5	1.5	100.0	3.4	36.0	59.8	0.6
1920.....................	100.0	13.7	59.1	24.9	1.8	100.0	4.3	33.7	60.9	0.8
1930.....................	100.0	14.0	59.2	24.0	2.6	100.0	5.8	34.6	58.2	1.2
Age unknown:										
1890.....................	100.0	47.4	12.0	1.4	0.2	100.0	34.6	45.8	10.2	0.6
1900.....................	100.0	30.4	16.2	1.7	0.2	100.0	24.0	41.3	10.6	0.5
1910.....................	100.0	21.9	11.4	1.6	0.4	100.0	24.0	39.2	11.1	1.0
1920.....................	100.0	24.7	20.0	2.4	1.1	100.0	22.0	45.1	11.0	1.9
1930.....................	100.0	26.6	22.6	2.6	2.1	100.0	20.8	35.8	9.8	2.5

ᵃ For 1890 from *Eleventh Census of the United States: 1890*, Vol. I, Pt. 1, pp. 832–880; 1900 from *Twelfth Census of the United States: 1900*, Vol. II, Pt. 2, pp. 256–307; 1910 from *Thirteenth Census of the United States: 1910*, Vol. I, pp. 538–546 and 573–574; 1920 from *Fourteenth Census of the United States: 1920*, Vol. II, pp. 397 and 401–409; 1930 from *Fifteenth Census of the United States: 1930*, Vol. II, pp. 855–863.

ᵇ Less than one-tenth of 1 per cent.

ᶜ Age group 25 to 34.

ᵈ See Note c.

APPENDIX TABLES

TABLE 27.—PERCENTAGE DISTRIBUTION OF THE URBAN AND RURAL POPULATIONS 15 YEARS OF AGE AND OVER BY MARITAL CONDITION, BY SEX, BY AGE, AND BY RACE AND NATIVITY, 1910–1930[a]

Nativity, age, and year	Male					Female				
	Total	Single	Married	Widowed	Divorced	Total	Single	Married	Widowed	Divorced
Native whites of native parentage:										
15–19:										
Urban:										
1910	100.0	98.5	0.9	(b)	(a)	100.0	90.9	8.4	0.1	0.1
1920	100.0	97.7	2.1	(b)	(b)	100.0	88.1	11.5	0.2	0.2
1930	100.0	98.2	1.7	(b)	(b)	100.0	87.7	11.8	0.1	0.2
Rural:										
1910	100.0	97.9	1.5	(b)	(b)	100.0	84.3	14.9	0.2	0.1
1920	100.0	97.4	2.4	(b)	(b)	100.0	85.0	14.6	0.2	0.1
1930	100.0	97.6	2.2	(b)	(b)	100.0	83.8	15.8	0.2	0.2
Farm	100.0	97.7	2.2	(b)	(b)	100.0	85.0	14.6	0.2	0.1
Nonfarm	100.0	97.5	2.3	(b)	(b)	100.0	82.1	17.5	0.2	0.2
20–24:										
Urban:										
1910	100.0	76.4	22.6	0.3	0.1	100.0	55.5	42.7	0.9	0.6
1920	100.0	70.4	28.7	0.4	0.3	100.0	50.2	47.7	1.1	0.8
1930	100.0	69.0	30.0	0.2	0.5	100.0	48.0	49.7	0.6	1.5
Rural:										
1910	100.0	70.0	29.0	0.4	0.2	100.0	40.3	58.1	1.0	0.4
1920	100.0	67.1	31.9	0.5	0.2	100.0	39.6	58.6	1.2	0.4
1930	100.0	67.3	31.8	0.3	0.4	100.0	38.5	59.8	0.8	0.8
Farm	100.0	70.6	28.5	0.4	0.3	100.0	41.1	57.3	0.9	0.7
Nonfarm	100.0	63.0	36.0	0.3	0.4	100.0	35.7	62.5	0.8	0.9
25–34:										
Urban:										
1910	100.0	36.3	61.5	1.3	0.6	100.0	25.7	69.9	3.0	1.2
1920	100.0	31.3	66.2	1.4	0.9	100.0	23.8	71.4	3.2	1.5
1930	100.0	26.7	70.7	0.8	1.7	100.0	20.1	75.0	2.2	2.7
Rural:										
1910	100.0	27.6	70.3	1.5	0.4	100.0	14.9	82.3	2.2	0.5
1920	100.0	26.4	71.5	1.5	0.5	100.0	14.4	82.6	2.4	0.6
1930	100.0	24.3	73.6	1.0	0.9	100.0	12.6	84.5	1.8	1.0
Farm	100.0	27.3	70.7	1.1	0.8	100.0	12.9	84.7	1.7	0.7
Nonfarm	100.0	21.4	76.4	0.9	1.2	100.0	12.4	84.3	2.0	1.3
35–44:										
Urban:										
1910	100.0	17.2	78.2	3.2	1.1	100.0	14.8	75.4	8.2	1.5
1920	100.0	15.8	79.6	3.0	1.4	100.0	14.3	76.0	7.8	1.8
1930	100.0	12.8	82.7	2.2	2.3	100.0	12.8	77.6	6.6	3.0
Rural:										
1910	100.0	12.8	83.3	3.2	0.6	100.0	8.0	86.4	5.0	0.6
1920	100.0	12.2	84.1	2.9	0.7	100.0	7.9	86.5	4.8	0.7
1930	100.0	11.2	85.2	2.3	1.2	100.0	6.9	87.8	4.3	1.0
Farm	100.0	11.4	85.3	2.3	0.9	100.0	6.0	90.1	3.3	0.6
Nonfarm	100.0	11.0	85.0	2.3	1.5	100.0	8.0	85.0	5.5	1.5

TABLE 27.—PERCENTAGE DISTRIBUTION OF THE URBAN AND RURAL POPULATIONS 15 YEARS OF AGE AND OVER BY MARITAL CONDITION, BY SEX, BY AGE, AND BY RACE AND NATIVITY, 1910–1930.ᵃ—(Continued)

Nativity, age, and year	Male					Female				
	Total	Single	Married	Widowed	Divorced	Total	Single	Married	Widowed	Divorced
Native white of native parentage: (Continued)										
45-64:										
Urban:										
1910	100.0	9.9	80.4	8.4	1.1	100.0	10.7	64.5	23.6	1.1
1920	100.0	10.8	79.6	8.0	1.5	100.0	11.4	64.0	23.1	1.4
1930	100.0	9.7	81.3	6.7	2.2	100.0	11.0	65.8	20.9	2.2
Rural:										
1910	100.0	8.3	82.6	8.1	0.8	100.0	6.6	76.3	16.3	0.6
1920	100.0	9.2	82.2	7.5	0.9	100.0	6.9	76.6	15.7	0.7
1930	100.0	9.4	81.6	7.2	1.7	100.0	8.0	71.4	19.1	1.3
Farm	100.0	8.9	82.2	7.2	1.5	100.0	8.0	71.0	19.7	1.2
Nonfarm	100.0	10.2	80.5	7.2	1.9	100.0	8.0	72.1	18.3	1.4
65+:										
Urban:										
1910	100.0	5.8	66.5	26.9	0.7	100.0	8.6	29.9	61.0	0.4
1920	100.0	6.9	64.6	27.5	0.9	100.0	9.0	28.7	61.6	0.5
1930	100.0	7.3	63.9	27.1	1.3	100.0	9.9	29.2	60.0	0.7
Rural:										
1910	100.0	5.5	67.7	25.5	0.7	100.0	6.6	39.5	53.2	0.4
1920	100.0	6.6	66.9	25.4	0.8	100.0	7.0	39.7	52.5	0.4
1930	100.0	7.7	64.9	26.0	1.2	100.0	6.9	40.4	52.1	0.5
Farm	100.0	6.8	67.1	25.0	1.0	100.0	6.0	45.7	47.7	0.4
Nonfarm	100.0	8.8	62.4	27.1	1.4	100.0	7.6	35.7	55.9	0.6
Native whites of foreign or mixed parentage:										
15–19:										
Urban:										
1910	100.0	99.2	0.3	(ᵇ)	(ᵇ)	100.0	95.1	4.4	(ᵇ)	(ᵇ)
1920	100.0	99.1	0.8	(ᵇ)	(ᵇ)	100.0	93.9	5.9	0.1	(ᵇ)
1930	100.0	99.3	0.5	(ᵇ)	(ᵇ)	100.0	94.3	5.4	(ᵇ)	0.1
Rural:										
1910	100.0	99.0	0.3	(ᵇ)	(ᵇ)	100.0	93.0	6.3	(ᵇ)	(ᵇ)
1920	100.0	99.1	0.7	(ᵇ)	(ᵇ)	100.0	92.9	6.9	0.1	(ᵇ)
1930	100.0	99.3	0.5	(ᵇ)	(ᵇ)	100.0	93.0	6.9	(ᵇ)	0.1
Farm	100.0	99.4	0.4	(ᵇ)	(ᵇ)	100.0	94.2	5.7	(ᵇ)	(ᵇ)
Nonfarm	100.0	99.2	0.6	(ᵇ)	(ᵇ)	100.0	91.8	8.0	(ᵇ)	0.1
20–24:										
Urban:										
1910	100.0	84.1	15.3	0.2	0.1	100.0	66.3	32.7	0.5	0.3
1920	100.0	80.9	18.5	0.2	0.1	100.0	61.4	37.3	0.7	0.4
1930	100.0	81.9	17.4	0.1	0.2	100.0	60.1	38.7	0.3	0.6
Rural:										
1910	100.0	84.4	14.8	0.1	0.1	100.0	55.2	43.9	0.4	0.2
1920	100.0	82.2	17.1	0.2	0.1	100.0	52.9	45.9	0.7	0.3
1930	100.0	82.8	16.6	0.1	0.2	100.0	52.1	46.9	0.3	0.5
Farm	100.0	86.5	13.0	0.1	0.1	100.0	55.3	43.8	0.3	0.3
Nonfarm	100.0	78.8	20.5	0.1	0.2	100.0	49.6	49.2	0.4	0.6

TABLE 27.—PERCENTAGE DISTRIBUTION OF THE URBAN AND RURAL POPULATIONS 15 YEARS OF AGE AND OVER BY MARITAL CONDITION, BY SEX, BY AGE, AND BY RACE AND NATIVITY, 1910–1930.[a]—(Continued)

Nativity, age, and year	Male					Female				
	Total	Single	Married	Widowed	Divorced	Total	Single	Married	Widowed	Divorced
Native whites of foreign or mixed parentage: (Continued)										
25–34:										
Urban:										
1910	100.0	45.1	53.2	1.1	0.4	100.0	34.8	61.9	2.4	0.8
1920	100.0	40.5	57.5	1.2	0.6	100.0	30.9	65.5	2.5	1.0
1930	100.0	36.1	62.1	0.7	1.1	100.0	25.7	70.9	1.6	1.7
Rural:										
1910	100.0	41.9	56.7	0.9	0.3	100.0	21.8	76.1	1.5	0.5
1920	100.0	39.1	59.2	1.1	0.4	100.0	19.8	77.8	1.8	0.5
1930	100.0	37.2	61.2	0.7	0.7	100.0	17.5	80.4	1.2	0.8
Farm	100.0	42.4	56.4	0.6	0.5	100.0	16.8	81.7	0.9	0.5
Nonfarm	100.0	31.9	66.3	0.7	0.9	100.0	18.0	79.3	1.5	1.1
35–44:										
Urban:										
1910	100.0	23.5	72.6	3.0	0.8	100.0	20.8	70.5	7.7	0.9
1920	100.0	22.3	73.8	2.8	1.1	100.0	21.0	70.5	7.1	1.2
1930	100.0	17.7	78.6	2.0	1.7	100.0	17.0	75.4	5.5	2.1
Rural:										
1910	100.0	21.4	75.4	2.5	0.6	100.0	11.5	83.8	4.1	0.6
1920	100.0	20.3	76.6	2.4	0.6	100.0	11.3	84.0	4.0	0.6
1930	100.0	18.9	78.1	1.9	1.1	100.0	9.6	85.8	3.4	0.9
Farm	100.0	20.4	77.1	1.7	0.7	100.0	7.6	89.7	2.2	0.5
Nonfarm	100.0	17.1	79.3	2.0	1.5	100.0	11.7	82.2	4.6	1.3
45–64:										
Urban:										
1910	100.0	14.3	76.9	7.8	0.8	100.0	14.4	62.7	22.0	0.8
1920	100.0	15.9	75.3	7.7	1.1	100.0	16.6	60.3	22.2	0.9
1930	100.0	15.1	76.5	6.6	1.7	100.0	16.7	61.9	19.8	1.5
Rural:										
1910	100.0	14.0	78.2	6.8	0.9	100.0	8.4	77.6	13.3	0.6
1920	100.0	15.5	76.8	6.6	1.0	100.0	9.7	75.8	13.7	0.7
1930	100.0	16.3	76.0	6.3	1.4	100.0	9.8	76.5	12.8	0.9
Farm	100.0	15.8	77.4	5.7	1.0	100.0	7.3	82.9	9.3	0.5
Nonfarm	100.0	16.8	74.3	6.9	1.9	100.0	12.2	70.3	16.2	1.2
65+:										
Urban:										
1910	100.0	8.6	64.8	25.8	0.7	100.0	10.0	30.0	59.5	0.4
1920	100.0	10.7	63.5	24.9	0.8	100.0	11.4	29.7	58.3	0.4
1930	100.0	11.7	62.9	24.2	1.1	100.0	14.4	30.5	54.3	0.5
Rural:										
1910	100.0	9.2	64.8	24.9	1.0	100.0	6.7	42.0	50.8	0.4
1920	100.0	10.5	64.9	23.3	1.0	100.0	7.7	42.7	49.0	0.4
1930	100.0	12.6	63.0	22.9	1.3	100.0	9.5	43.4	46.5	0.5
Farm	100.0	12.1	64.4	22.3	1.1	100.0	7.9	49.8	41.8	0.4
Nonfarm	100.0	13.1	61.8	23.5	1.5	100.0	10.5	39.4	49.4	0.5

TABLE 27.—PERCENTAGE DISTRIBUTION OF THE URBAN AND RURAL POPULATIONS 15 YEARS OF AGE AND OVER BY MARITAL CONDITION, BY SEX, BY AGE, AND BY RACE AND NATIVITY, 1910–1930.ᵃ—(*Continued*)

Nativity, age, and year	Male					Female				
	Total	Single	Married	Widowed	Divorced	Total	Single	Married	Widowed	Divorced
Foreign-born whites:										
15–19:										
Urban:										
1910	100.0	98.6	0.8	(ᵇ)	(ᵇ)	100.0	87.9	11.5	0.1	(ᵇ)
1920	100.0	98.6	1.1	(ᵇ)	(ᵇ)	100.0	86.9	12.8	0.2	0.1
1930	100.0	99.0	0.6	(ᵇ)	(ᵇ)	100.0	90.5	9.1	0.1	0.1
Rural:										
1910	100.0	98.3	0.9	(ᵇ)	(ᵇ)	100.0	77.6	21.6	0.2	0.1
1920	100.0	98.1	1.6	0.1	(ᵇ)	100.0	78.9	20.7	0.3	0.1
1930	100.0	98.9	0.8	(ᵇ)	(ᵇ)	100.0	87.0	12.7	0.1	0.1
Farm	100.0	99.0	0.7	(ᵇ)	(ᵇ)	100.0	88.0	.11.7	0.1	0.1
Nonfarm	100.0	98.8	0.9	(ᵇ)	(ᵇ)	100.0	86.5	13.2	0.1	0.1
20–24:										
Urban:										
1910	100.0	79.1	20.2	0.1	(ᵇ)	100.0	47.7	51.4	0.5	0.1
1920	100.0	75.0	24.2	0.3	0.1	100.0	39.1	59.6	0.9	0.2
1930	100.0	81.0	18.2	0.1	0.2	100.0	52.7	46.2	0.3	0.5
Rural:										
1910	100.0	83.4	15.7	0.2	(ᵇ)	100.0	30.2	68.8	0.6	0.1
1920	100.0	77.1	22.0	0.3	0.1	100.0	25.6	72.9	1.2	0.2
1930	100.0	82.1	17.3	0.1	0.1	100.0	41.1	57.8	0.5	0.4
Farm	100.0	86.9	12.5	0.1	0.1	100.0	38.7	60.5	0.4	0.4
Nonfarm	100.0	78.8	20.6	0.1	0.2	100.0	42.1	56.6	0.5	0.5
25–34:										
Urban:										
1910	100.0	37.4	61.3	0.8	0.2	100.0	19.9	77.4	2.2	0.4
1920	100.0	34.2	64.1	1.1	0.2	100.0	14.0	82.9	2.6	0.4
1930	100.0	34.9	63.7	0.6	0.5	100.0	16.2	81.1	1.6	1.0
Rural:										
1910	100.0	44.6	54.0	0.8	0.1	100.0	10.6	87.5	1.6	0.3
1920	100.0	41.1	57.2	1.2	0.2	100.0	7.6	89.8	2.2	0.3
1930	100.0	39.1	59.4	0.7	0.6	100.0	10.6	87.3	1.4	0.6
Farm	100.0	45.8	52.9	0.7	0.5	100.0	7.3	91.3	0.9	0.4
Nonfarm	100.0	36.0	62.4	0.7	0.7	100.0	12.1	85.6	1.5	0.7
35–44:										
Urban:										
1910	100.0	15.7	81.2	2.5	0.4	100.0	9.6	82.2	7.5	0.5
1920	100.0	16.2	80.6	2.5	0.5	100.0	9.0	83.4	6.8	0.7
1930	100.0	15.3	81.8	1.9	1.0	100.0	6.7	86.5	5.6	1.1
Rural:										
1910	100.0	21.0	76.0	2.3	0.4	100.0	5.2	90.1	4.3	0.4
1920	100.0	21.7	75.0	2.6	0.4	100.0	5.1	89.9	4.5	0.4
1930	100.0	21.3	75.5	2.2	0.9	100.0	4.7	90.7	3.8	0.6
Farm	100.0	19.6	77.7	1.9	0.7	100.0	2.4	94.3	2.6	0.4
Nonfarm	100.0	22.2	74.3	2.3	1.1	100.0	6.2	88.4	4.6	0 8

APPENDIX TABLES

TABLE 27.—PERCENTAGE DISTRIBUTION OF THE URBAN AND RURAL POPULATIONS 15 YEARS OF AGE AND OVER BY MARITAL CONDITION, BY SEX, BY AGE, AND BY RACE AND NATIVITY, 1910–1930.[a]—(Continued)

Nativity, age, and year	Male					Female				
	Total	Single	Married	Widowed	Divorced	Total	Single	Married	Widowed	Divorced
Foreign-born whites: (Continued)										
45–64:										
Urban:										
1910	100.0	9.3	81.9	8.2	0.5	100.0	6.6	67.1	25.7	0.5
1920	100.0	10.1	81.4	7.7	0.6	100.0	7.0	68.5	23.8	0.6
1930	100.0	10.0	82.0	6.8	1.1	100.0	6.6	71.1	21.2	1.0
Rural:										
1910	100.0	13.4	78.2	7.5	0.7	100.0	3.6	79.7	16.1	0.5
1920	100.0	14.4	77.2	7.4	0.7	100.0	4.3	79.2	15.9	0.5
1930	100.0	15.7	75.8	7.1	1.2	100.0	4.7	79.8	14.7	0.7
Farm	100.0	13.6	78.8	6.6	1.0	100.0	2.6	85.5	11.4	0.5
Nonfarm	100.0	17.6	73.3	7.6	1.4	100.0	6.4	75.0	17.5	0.9
65+:										
Urban:										
1910	100.0	6.2	62.1	31.1	0.4	100.0	5.3	30.2	64.1	0.3
1920	100.0	6.8	62.4	30.0	0.5	100.0	5.5	29.5	64.5	0.3
1930	100.0	7.1	64.0	27.9	0.8	100.0	5.7	33.6	60.0	0.4
Rural:										
1910	100.0	8.3	62.9	27.9	0.7	100.0	3.0	42.7	53.8	0.3
1920	100.0	9.3	61.7	27.9	0.7	100.0	3.5	40.4	55.4	0.3
1930	100.0	11.3	60.3	27.2	1.0	100.0	3.9	42.9	52.7	0.4
Farm	100.0	9.5	62.1	27.3	1.0	100.0	2.5	45.8	51.1	0.3
Nonfarm	100.0	12.8	58.7	27.1	1.1	100.0	4.8	40.8	53.7	0.5
Negroes:										
15–19:										
Urban:										
1910	100.0	97.3	1.8	0.1	(b)	100.0	84.2	14.0	0.9	0.3
1920	100.0	95.7	4.0	0.1	0.1	100.0	77.6	20.9	0.9	0.4
1930	100.0	96.2	3.5	0.1	0.1	100.0	78.5	19.7	0.9	0.7
Rural:										
1910	100.0	96.8	2.3	0.1	(b)	100.0	80.1	18.1	0.9	0.2
1920	100.0	95.8	3.9	0.1	(b)	100.0	79.1	19.7	0.9	0.3
1930	100.0	95.9	3.8	0.1	0.1	100.0	77.5	21.0	0.9	0.5
Farm	100.0	96.0	3.8	0.1	0.1	100.0	78.9	19.7	0.9	0.5
Nonfarm	100.0	95.7	3.9	0.1	0.1	100.0	73.7	24.4	1.1	0.7
20–24:										
Urban:										
1910	100.0	66.1	31.6	1.2	0.4	100.0	42.8	50.5	5.0	1.3
1920	100.0	58.9	39.3	1.0	0.6	100.0	33.4	60.8	4.1	1.5
1930	100.0	57.6	40.1	1.1	0.8	100.0	34.8	58.2	4.3	2.6
Rural:										
1910	100.0	57.1	40.4	1.6	0.4	100.0	30.9	63.2	4.5	0.9
1920	100.0	52.4	45.3	1.4	0.4	100.0	30.4	64.2	4.0	1.1
1930	100.0	52.4	44.9	1.4	0.9	100.0	31.4	62.5	3.9	2.1
Farm	100.0	50.8	46.5	1.5	0.9	100.0	32.5	61.8	3.7	1.9
Nonfarm	100.0	55.2	41.9	1.3	0.9	100.0	29.3	63.9	4.2	2.4

TABLE 27.—PERCENTAGE DISTRIBUTION OF THE URBAN AND RURAL POPULATIONS 15 YEARS OF AGE AND OVER BY MARITAL CONDITION, BY SEX, BY AGE, AND BY RACE AND NATIVITY, 1910–1930.[a]—(Continued)

Nativity, age, and year	Male					Female				
	Total	Single	Married	Widowed	Divorced	Total	Single	Married	Widowed	Divorced
Negroes: (Continued)										
25–34:										
Urban:										
1910	100.0	33.0	62.2	3.4	0.9	100.0	20.1	66.4	11.4	2.0
1920	100.0	30.1	65.8	2.7	1.1	100.0	16.0	72.2	9.4	2.2
1930	100.0	26.7	68.5	2.9	1.8	100.0	14.9	71.2	10.1	3.7
Rural:										
1910	100.0	20.6	74.3	3.9	0.8	100.0	11.1	79.5	7.9	1.3
1920	100.0	20.7	75.1	3.1	0.8	100.0	11.3	79.9	7.3	1.4
1930	100.0	20.1	74.6	3.3	1.7	100.0	11.0	79.1	7.3	2.5
Farm	100.0	16.0	79.0	3.3	1.6	100.0	10.5	80.8	6.5	2.1
Nonfarm	100.0	25.9	68.3	3.2	1.9	100.0	11.8	76.1	8.8	3.0
35–44:										
Urban:										
1910	100.0	18.0	73.4	7.0	1.2	100.0	10.0	65.1	22.8	2.0
1920	100.0	17.7	74.9	5.7	1.4	100.0	9.0	68.7	20.0	2.2
1930	100.0	15.7	75.7	6.1	2.4	100.0	7.8	68.1	20.5	3.4
Rural:										
1910	100.0	8.8	83.8	6.3	0.9	100.0	5.3	80.1	13.3	1.2
1920	100.0	9.3	84.5	5.1	0.9	100.0	5.4	80.7	12.4	1.3
1930	100.0	9.7	82.7	5.6	1.8	100.0	4.7	79.8	13.3	2.1
Farm	100.0	6.5	86.9	5.2	1.4	100.0	4.0	83.0	11.3	1.7
Nonfarm	100.0	14.8	76.0	6.3	2.4	100.0	6.2	73.3	17.4	2.9
45–64:										
Urban:										
1910	100.0	10.2	73.7	14.8	1.1	100.0	6.0	48.8	43.8	1.2
1920	100.0	11.1	74.2	13.0	1.4	100.0	6.0	49.8	42.4	1.6
1930	100.0	10.1	74.6	13.1	2.0	100.0	5.5	51.5	40.7	2.1
Rural:										
1910	100.0	4.5	82.9	11.7	0.8	100.0	3.5	68.4	27.1	0.8
1920	100.0	5.0	84.4	9.7	0.8	100.0	3.8	68.8	26.2	1.0
1930	100.0	5.3	82.3	10.8	1.5	100.0	3.3	68.0	27.0	1.5
Farm	100.0	3.4	85.7	9.7	1.2	100.0	2.7	73.0	23.1	1.2
Nonfarm	100.0	9.5	74.7	13.3	2.1	100.0	4.8	57.4	35.5	2.0
65+:										
Urban:										
1910	100.0	5.9	60.5	32.6	0.7	100.0	4.2	20.9	74.1	0.4
1920	100.0	6.9	57.0	34.8	1.0	100.0	4.3	18.5	76.4	0.5
1930	100.0	6.5	56.7	35.3	1.3	100.0	4.3	19.1	75.7	0.6
Rural:										
1910	100.0	3.6	69.4	26.0	0.7	100.0	3.5	33.8	61.9	0.4
1920	100.0	4.1	68.5	26.4	0.7	100.0	4.0	31.9	63.2	0.5
1930	100.0	4.3	65.7	28.8	1.0	100.0	3.4	31.1	64.6	0.6
Farm	100.0	3.0	69.8	26.1	0.9	100.0	3.0	34.6	61.7	0.5
Nonfarm	100.0	7.1	56.4	34.7	1.3	100.0	4.2	25.0	69.7	0.7

[a] For 1910 from *Thirteenth Census of the United States: 1910*, Vol. I, p. 585; 1920 from *Fourteenth Census of the United States: 1920*, Vol. II, p. 577; 1930 from *Fifteenth Census of the United States: 1930*, Vol. II, pp. 848–850.

[b] Less than one-tenth of 1 per cent.

INDEX

A

Abbott, Grace, prevention of infant deaths, 257n
Abortion, 329
Adult education, need for, 165–166
Age, understatement of, effect on specific death rates, 198–199
  and sex ratios, 197–198
Age composition, 106–171, 359–378
  and birth rates, 263, 267–278
  causes of changes in, 106–107
  consequences, 163–171
  and death rates, 232, 235–238, 243–247, 250–253
  and decline in births, 283
  effect on ratio of producing and consuming units, 168–171
  future, 107–118 *passim*, 141–142, 145–146, 152
  immigrants, 115
  and marital condition (*see* Marital condition).
  Negroes, 151–159, 375–378
    future, 152
  other colored, 160–163
  population, total, 107–140, 359
    future, 107–118 *passim*
  by regions, 118–126, 148, 154–155, 359
    effects of migration on, 125–126
  in selected cities, 360–361
  and sex ratios, 181, 193–202, 383–392
  by size of community, cities, 126–140, 148–151, 155–159
    future, probable trend, 138
    ratio of children 0–19 to persons 20–44, 134–135, 165
    ratio of elders to persons 20–44, 134–135, 138, 166
    rural population (farm and nonfarm), 126–140, 148–151, 155–159 *passim*
  by regions, 138–140, 362–363
  variations between cities, causes of, 137–138
  whites by nativity, 140–151, 362–374
    future, 141–142, 145–146
    (*See also* Foreign-born whites, and Native whites.)
Agriculture, future of, 322–323
  and population growth, 15–16, 18, 32
Alien Contract Labor Law, 295, 327

B

Benjamin, Julien E., mortality in middle-age, 237n
Billings, J. S., causes of decline in birth rates, 285n
Birth control, causes of, 332–334
  and decline in births, 284–288
  and early marriage, 226
  reasons for increase of, 288
  suppression of information, 328–329
Birth control clinic, 329

Birth rates, 262–291 *passim*
  by age of mother, 263, 267–278
    decline in, 268
  and decline in births, 283
  future, 263, 290, 317
  by race and nativity, 269–278
    by regions, 272–278
  urban and rural, 272–280 *passim*
  annual trend, 266, 267
    by race, 266, 267
  decline in, 267–269
    causes, 272, 282–288, 332–333
  and future population, 314–319
  future trend, 263, 288–291, 317
  and immigration, 304–311
  and natural increase, 280–282
  by race and nativity, 263, 266, 267–280
  by regions, 272–278
  by size of community, cities, 272–280
    by race and nativity, 278–280
    rural, 272–280
  sources of data, 262
  specific (*see* Birth rates, by age).
  standardized (*see* Birth rates, by age).
  urban and rural, and early marriage, 227
  whites, 263, 265–266, 267
    future, 263, 290, 317
Birth-registration area, growth of, 262
Births, decline in, causes, 282–288, 332–333
  by nationality of mother, 92
  nonregistration of, 272
  number of, 262–267
    future trend, 263, 289–291
    by race and nativity, 265–267
  (*See also* Birth rates.)
Bonynge, Francis, population estimates of, 312, 313
Broda, R., mortality in middle-age, 237n
Brunner, Edmund de S. and J. H. Kolb, *Rural Social Trends*, 47n
Bushee, Frederick A., immigration and population growth, 305n
Business efficiency, and age changes, 167
Business outlook, 322–325

C

Carpenter, Niles, *Immigrants and Their Children*, 56n, 68n, 83n
Children under 5, 108–113, 165, 169, 359
  future trend, 108–113 *passim*, 263
  by race and nativity, 140–146, 150–152, 154–157, 160–163, 263–264, 362–378
  by regions, 118–123, 359
  in selected cities, 360–361
  by size of community, 126–131 *passim*, 133
  (*See also* Ratio of children to women.)

INDEX

INDEX

Printed in east Germany